TAKING SIDES

Clashing Views in

Drugs and Society

NINTH EDITION

Selected, Edited, and with Introductions by

Raymond Goldberg
Vance-Granville Community College

Connect
Learn
Succeed™

TAKING SIDES: CLASHING VIEWS IN DRUGS AND SOCIETY, NINTH EDITION

Published by McGraw-Hill, a business unit of The McGraw-Hill Companies, Inc., 1221 Avenue of the Americas, New York, NY 10020. Copyright © 2010 by The McGraw-Hill Companies, Inc. All rights reserved. Previous edition(s) 2008, 2006, 2004. No part of this publication may be reproduced or distributed in any form or by any means, or stored in a database or retrieval system, without the prior written consent of The McGraw-Hill Companies, Inc., including, but not limited to, in any network or other electronic storage or transmission, or broadcast for distance learning.

Some ancillaries, including electronic and print components, may not be available to customers outside the United States.

Taking Sides® is a registered trademark of the McGraw-Hill Companies, Inc.
Taking Sides is published by the **Contemporary Learning Series** group within the McGraw-Hill Higher Education division.

1 2 3 4 5 6 7 8 9 0 DOC/DOC 0 9

MHID: 0-07-812756-4
ISBN: 978-0-07-812756-4
ISSN: 1094-7566

Managing Editor: *Larry Loeppke*
Senior Managing Editor: *Faye Schilling*
Senior Developmental Editor: *Jill Meloy*
Editorial Coordinator: *Mary Foust*
Production Service Assistant: *Rita Hingtgen*
Permissions Coordinator: *Shirley Lanners*
Editorial Assistant: *Cindy Hedley*
Senior Marketing Manager: *Julie Keck*
Marketing Communications Specialist: *Mary Klein*
Marketing Coordinator: *Alice Link*
Senior Project Manager: *Jane Mohr*
Design Specialist: *Tara McDermott*
Cover Graphics: *Rick D. Noel*

Compositor: MPS Limited
Cover Image: © National Cancer Institute/Getty Images/RF

Library of Congress Cataloging-in-Publication Data

Main entry under title:
   Taking sides: clashing views in drugs and society/selected, edited, and with introductions by Raymond Goldberg.—9th ed.

   Includes bibliographical references.
   1. Drug abuse—Social aspects. I. Goldberg, Raymond, *comp.*
                                                            362.29

www.mhhe.com

Preface

One of the hallmarks of a democratic society is the freedom of its citizens to disagree. This is no more evident than on the topic of drugs. The purpose of this ninth edition of *Taking Sides: Clashing Views in Drugs and Society* is to introduce drug-related issues that (1) are pertinent to the reader and (2) have no clear resolution. In the area of drug abuse, there is much difference of opinion regarding drug prevention, causation, and treatment. For example, should drug abuse be prevented by increasing enforcement of drug laws or by making young people more aware of the potential dangers of drugs? Is drug abuse caused by heredity, personality characteristics, or environment? Is drug abuse a medical, legal, or social problem? Are the dangers of some drugs such as Ecstasy, caffeine, and steroids overexaggerated? Should there be more stringent enforcement of marijuana use and underage drinking?

There are many implications to how the preceding questions are answered. If addiction to drugs is viewed as hereditary rather than as the result of flaws in one's character or personality, then a biological rather than a psychosocial approach to treatment may be pursued. If the consensus is that the prevention of drug abuse can be achieved by eliminating the availability of drugs, then more money and effort will be allocated for interdiction and law enforcement than education. If drug abuse is viewed as a legal problem, then prosecution and incarceration will be the goal. If drug abuse is identified as a medical problem, then abusers will be given treatment. However, if drug abuse is deemed a social problem, then energy will be directed at underlying social factors, such as poverty, unemployment, health care, and education. Not all of the issues have clear answers. One may favor increasing penalties for drug violations *and* improving treatment services. And it is possible to view drug abuse as a medical *and* social *and* legal problem.

The issues debated in this volume deal with both legal and illegal drugs. Although society seems most interested in illegal drugs, it is quite pertinent to address issues related to legal drugs because they cause more deaths and disabilities. No one is untouched by drugs, and everybody is affected by drug use and abuse. Billions of tax dollars are channeled into the war on drugs. Thousands of people are treated for drug abuse, often at public expense. The drug trade spawns crime and violence. Medical treatment for illnesses and injuries resulting from drug use and abuse creates additional burdens to an already extended health care system. Babies born to mothers who used drugs while pregnant are entering schools, and teachers are expected to meet the educational needs of these children. Ritalin and other stimulants are prescribed to several million students to deal with their lack of attention in the classroom. Drug use by secondary students is rampant. The issues debated here are not whether drug abuse is a problem, but what should be done to rectify this problem.

Many of these issues have an immediate impact on the reader. For example, Issue 3, "Should the United States Drinking Age Remain at 21?" has an impact on anyone under age 21 who imbibes alcohol. Issue 14, "Should Smokeless Tobacco be Promoted as an Alternative to Cigarette Smoking?" is relevant to individuals considering alternatives to cigarette smoking. Issue 10, "Are Psychotherapeutic Drugs Overprescribed for Treating Mental Illness?" is important because millions of people have been diagnosed with depression or some other type of mental illness. And the question "Should Marijuana Be Legal?" (Issue 9) is relevant to the millions of people who smoke marijuana.

Plan of the book   In this ninth edition of *Taking Sides: Clashing Views in Drugs and Society,* there are 38 selections dealing with 19 issues. Each issue is preceded by an introduction and followed by a postscript. The purpose of the introduction is to provide some background information and to set the stage for the debate as it is argued in the "yes" and "no" selections. The postscript summarizes the debate and challenges some of the ideas brought out in the two selections, which can enable the reader to see the issue in other ways. Included in the postscripts are additional suggested readings on the issue. Also, Internet site addresses (URLs) have been provided at the beginning of each unit, which should prove useful as starting points for further research. The issues, introductions, and postscripts are designed to stimulate readers to think about and achieve an informed view of some of the critical issues facing society today. At the back of the book is a list of all the contributors to this volume, which gives information on the physicians, lawyers, professors, authors, and policymakers whose views are debated here.

Taking Sides: Clashing Views in Drugs and Society is a tool to encourage critical thinking. In reading an issue and forming your own opinion, you should not feel confined to adopt one or the other of the positions presented. Some readers may see important points on both sides of an issue and may construct for themselves a new and creative approach. Such an approach might incorporate the best of both sides, or it might provide an entirely new vantage point for understanding.

Changes to this edition   This ninth edition represents a significant revision. Seven of the 19 issues are new: Should the United States Drinking Age Remain at 21? (Issue 3); Is Drug Addiction a Brain Disease? (Issue 6); Should Employers Limit Secondhand Smoke? (Issue 8); Should Marijuana be Legalized? (Issue 9); Is Caffeine a Health Risk? (Issue 11); Should Smokeless Tobacco be Promoted as an Alternative to Cigarette Smoking? (Issue 14); and Is Abstinence an Effective Strategy for Drug Education? (Issue 19). For seven of the remaining eleven issues from the previous edition, one or both selections were replaced to reflect more current points of view.

A word to the instructor   To facilitate the use of *Taking Sides,* an *Instructor's Resource Guide with Test Questions* (multiple choice and essay) and a general guidebook called *Using Taking Sides in the Classroom,* which discusses methods and techniques for implementing the pro-con approach into any classroom setting, can be obtained from the publisher. An online version of *Using Taking Sides in the Classroom* and a correspondence service for *Taking Sides* adopters can be found at http://www.mhcls.com/usingts/. For students, we offer a field guide to analyzing argumentative essays called *Analyzing Controversy: An Introductory Guide,* with exercises and techniques to help them to decipher genuine controversies.

Taking Sides: Clashing Views in Drugs and Society is only one title in the *Taking Sides* series. If you are interested in seeing the table of contents for any of the other titles, please visit the *Taking Sides* Web site at http://www.mhcls.com/takingsides/.

Acknowledgments   A number of people have been most helpful in putting together this ninth edition. I would like to thank those professors who adopted the eighth edition of this book and took the time to make suggestions for this subsequent edition:

Victor O. Anyanwu
American InterContinental University—Buckhead Campus

Donald Brodeur
Sacred Heart University

Owen Cater
California State University, Sacramento

Mark Kaelin
Montclair State University

I am also grateful to my students and colleagues, who did not hesitate to share their perceptions and to let me know what they liked and disliked about the eighth edition. Without the editorial staff at McGraw-Hill Contemporary Learning Series, this book would not exist. Their insight and professional contributions have been most valuable. Their thoughtful perceptions and encouragement were most appreciated. In no small way can my family be thanked. I am grateful for their patience and support.

Raymond Goldberg
Dean
Health Sciences
Vance-Granville Community College
Henderson, NC

Contents In Brief

Contents

Herbert Kleber, the executive vice president of the Center on Addiction and Substance Abuse (CASA), and Joseph Califano, founder of CASA, maintain that drug laws should remain restrictive because legalization would result in increased use, especially by children. Kleber and Califano contend that drug legalization would not eliminate drug-related violence and harm caused by drugs. Author Peter Gorman states that restrictive drug laws have been ineffective. He notes that drug use and drug addiction have increased since drug laws became more stringent. Despite the crackdown on drug use, the availability of drugs has increased while the cost of drugs has decreased. In addition, restrictive drug laws, says Gorman, are racist and endanger civil liberties.

Because the trafficking of drugs represents a direct threat to national security, the U.S. State Department maintains that more effort is needed to interdict drugs coming into the United States. Better cooperation with countries in Latin America, the Caribbean, Africa, and Asia, where drugs are grown and exported, is essential. Ethan Nadelmann, the executive director of the Drug Policy Alliance, contends that attempts to stem the flow of drugs are futile and that it is unrealistic to believe that the world can be made free of drugs. Nadelmann points out that global production is about the same as it was ten years earlier and that cocaine and heroin are purer and cheaper because producers have become more efficient.

Kenneth Moritsugu, the previous United States Surgeon General, maintains that underage drinking is fraught with numerous problems ranging from motor vehicle crashes to homicide and suicide. Underage drinking is also related to unhealthy risk-taking behaviors and poor academic performance. Rather than tolerate underage drinking, more effort should be placed on enforcing underage drinking laws. Judith McMullen, a law professor at Marquette University, argues that laws prohibiting underage drinking have been ineffective. Young adults between the ages of 18 and 21 who do not live at home have opportunities to drink alcohol without parental interference. In addition, this same age group has other legal rights, such as the right to marry, drive a car, or join the military. Enforcement of underage drinking laws, says McMullen, is destined for failure.

Issue 4. Are the Dangers of Ecstasy (MDMA) Overstated? 85

Author Leslie Iversen contends that ecstasy can result in adverse effects but that the drug has been unfairly demonized. Moreover, Iversen states that its negative consequences on the brain have not been proven conclusively. Iversen acknowledges that ecstasy may produce profound effects, although those effects are subject to an individual's perception. Club drugs such as ecstasy allow partygoers to dance and remain active for long periods of time according to the National Institute on Drug Abuse (NIDA). However, ecstasy may produce a number of adverse effects such as high blood pressure, panic attacks, loss of consciousness, seizures, and death. Moreover, ecstasy can produce negative effects on the brain, resulting in confusion, depression, memory impairment, and attention difficulties.

Issue 5. Should Pregnant Drug Users Be Prosecuted? 104

Paul A. Logli, an Illinois prosecuting attorney, argues that it is the government's duty to enforce every child's right to begin life with a healthy, drug-free mind and body. Logli maintains that pregnant women who use drugs should be prosecuted because they harm the life of their unborn children. He feels that it is the state's responsibility to ensure that every baby is born as healthy as possible. Carolyn Carter, a social work professor at Howard University, argues that the stigma of drug use during pregnancy has resulted in the avoidance of treatment. Carter asserts that the prosecution of pregnant drug users is unfair because poor women are more likely to be the targets of such prosecution. To enable pregnant women who use drugs to receive perinatal care, it is necessary to define their drug use as a health problem rather than as a legal problem.

Because there are biological and chemical changes in the brain following drug abuse, the National Institute on Drug Abuse (NIDA) claims that drug addiction is a disease of the brain. One may initially use drugs voluntarily, but addiction occurs after repeated drug use. NIDA acknowledges that environment plays a role in the development of drug addiction, but one's genes plays a major role as well. Psychiatrist Sally Satel maintains that drug addiction is not a disease of the brain. Satel asserts that there are individuals who are capable of stopping their drug addiction without medical intervention. Moreover, diseases have distinct characteristics, and drug addiction does not share these characteristics. Satel feels that addicts are done a disservice by calling addiction a brain disease.

The National Institute on Drug Abuse (NIDA) warns that anabolic steroids produce numerous harmful side effects which can lead to stunted growth, breast development in males, excessive hair growth on women, acne, complications of the liver, and infections from nonsterile needles. Behaviorally, anabolic steroids have been associated with rage and aggression. According to NIDA, simply teaching about steroids does not deter their use. In her book, author Laura Egendorf cites individuals who feel that athletes are aware of the risks of taking steroids and other performance-enhancing drugs. Competition and the desire to succeed drive individuals to improve their athletic performance. Allowing steroid use would essentially level the playing field for all athletes. In addition, some experts believe that the negative consequences are exaggerated.

Merrill Matthews, a health policy advisor with the American Legislative Exchange Council, argues that the advertising of prescription drugs directly to consumers will result in better-informed consumers. Additionally, communication between doctors and patients may improve because patients will be more knowledgeable about drugs. Dominic Frosch of the UCLA School of Medicine and his colleagues maintain that direct-to-consumer drug advertisements provide limited educational value to consumers. Moreover, the benefits of some prescription drugs are exaggerated. Frosch and associates feel that the drug advertisements dissuade individuals from engaging in health-promoting activities.

Professors John Britton and Richard Adwards advocate the use of smokeless tobacco as an alternative to tobacco smoking because the harm from tobacco is rooted more in the act of smoking than from nicotine. They recognize that smokeless tobacco carries certain risks, although they note that nicotine is not a known carcinogen nor does it reduce birthweight as much as tobacco smoking. David Savitz of the Mount Sinai School of Medicine and his colleagues raise concerns about the promotion of smokeless tobacco in lieu of tobacco smoking because there are numerous health concerns associated with smokeless tobacco. They are concerned about the products used in smokeless tobacco as well as the effects of smokeless tobacco on oral health, cardiovascular disease, and reproductive health.

Markus Heilig, Clinical Director of the National Institute on Alcohol Abuse and Alcoholism, argues that molecular changes in the brain result in positive reinforcement from alcohol. Heilig notes that alcoholism has a behavioral component, but certain genes may be responsible for individuals who abuse alcohol despite its adverse consequences. Grazyna Zajdow, a lecturer in sociology at Deakin University, maintains that the concept of alcoholism results from a social construct of what it means to be alcoholic. Because alcoholism is a social stigma, it is viewed as a disease rather than as a condition caused by personal and existential pain. Environmental conditions, especially consumerism, says Zajdow, are the root cause of alcoholism.

Peter J. Cohen, an adjunct law professor at Georgetown University and a medical doctor, notes that marijuana has a long history of medicinal use. Cohen supports research to verify whether marijuana is a safe and effective therapeutic agent for various maladies. However, the federal government has presented barriers to conducting the necessary research. The Drug Enforcement Administration (DEA) states that marijuana has not been proven to have medical utility. The DEA cites the positions of the American Medical Association, the American Cancer Society, the American Academy of Pediatrics, and the National Multiple Sclerosis Society to support its position. The DEA feels that any benefits of medicinal marijuana are outweighed by its drawbacks.

The Office of National Drug Control Policy (ONDCP), an agency of the federal government, maintains that it is important to test students for illicit drugs because testing reduces drug use and improves the learning environment in schools. The ONDCP purports that the majority of students support drug testing. In addition, drug testing does not decrease participation in extracurricular activities. Jennifer Kern and associates maintain that drug testing is ineffective and that the threat of drug testing may dissuade students from participating in extracurricular activities. Moreover, drug testing is costly, it may make schools susceptible to litigation, and it undermines relationships of trust between students and teachers. Drug testing, according to Kern, does not effectively identify students who may have serious drug problems.

Author Susan L. Ettner and associates maintain that not only do people in substance abuse treatment benefit, but that taxpayers also benefit. They estimate that about seven dollars are saved for every dollar spent on treatment. Individuals in treatment are less likely to engage in criminal activity and they are more likely to be employed. The report from the United Nations Office on Drugs and Crime argues that drug abuse treatment does not cure drug abuse. Most people who go through drug treatment relapse. Drug abuse treatment does not get at the root causes of drug abuse: crime, family disruption, loss of economic productivity, and social decay. At best, treatment may minimize drug abuse.

Tracy J. Evans-Whipp, of the Murdoch Children's Research Institute in Melbourne, Australia, and her colleagues maintain that an abstinence message coupled with harsh penalties is more effective at reducing drug use than a message aimed at minimizing the harms of drugs. They contend that an abstinence message is clear and that a harm reduction message may give a mixed message. Rodney Skager, formerly a professor at UCLA, argues that a zero tolerance drug policy does not change drug-taking behavior among young people. Instead of merely punishing drug offenders, Skager suggests that effective drug education is needed. Instances in which drug use presents a significant problem for the user may require intervention and treatment. Again, zero tolerance does very little to rectify behavior.

Correlation Guide

The *Taking Sides* series presents current issues in a debate-style format designed to stimulate student interest and develop critical thinking skills. Each issue is thoughtfully framed with an issue summary, an issue introduction, and a postscript. The pro and con essays—selected for their liveliness and substance—represent the arguments of leading scholars and commentators in their fields.

Taking Sides: Clashing Views in Drugs and Society, 9/e is an easy-to-use reader that presents issues on important topics such as *drinking age, drug addiction, secondhand smoke in the workplace,* and *caffeine and health.* For more information on *Taking Sides* and other *McGraw-Hill Contemporary Learning Series* titles, visit www.mhhe.com/cls.

This convenient guide matches the issues in **Taking Sides: Clashing Views in Drugs and Society, 9/e** with the corresponding chapters in two of our best-selling McGraw-Hill Health textbooks by Fields and Hart et al.

Taking Sides: Drugs and Society, 9/e	Drugs in Perspective, 7/e by Fields	Drugs, Society & Human Behavior, 13/e by Hart et al.
Issue 1: Should Laws Against Drug Use Remain Restrictive?	**Chapter 1:** Putting Drugs in Perspective **Chapter 8:** Prevention of Substance-Abuse Problems **Chapter 11:** Alcohol/Drug Recovery Treatment and Relapse Prevention	**Chapter 2:** Drug Use as a Social Problem **Chapter 17:** Preventing Substance Abuse
Issue 2: Should the United States Put More Emphasis on Stopping the Importation of Drugs?	**Chapter 1:** Putting Drugs in Perspective	**Chapter 3:** Drug Products and Their Regulations
Issue 3: Should the United States Drinking Age Remain at 21?	**Chapter 1:** Putting Drugs in Perspective **Chapter 8:** Prevention of Substance-Abuse Problems **Chapter 11:** Alcohol/Drug Recovery Treatment and Relapse Prevention	**Chapter 9:** Alcohol **Chapter 17:** Preventing Substance Abuse
Issue 4: Are the Dangers of Ecstasy (MDMA) Overstated?	**Chapter 3:** Drug-Specific Information	**Chapter 5:** The Actions of Drugs **Chapter 14:** Hallucinogens
Issue 5: Should Pregnant Drug Users Be Prosecuted?	**Chapter 3:** Drug-Specific Information **Chapter 9:** Change, Motivation, and Intervention for Substance-Abuse Problems	**Chapter 2:** Drug Use as a Social Problem **Chapter 9:** Alcohol **Chapter 10:** Tobacco **Chapter 17:** Preventing Substance Abuse
Issue 6: Is Drug Addiction a Brain Disease?	**Chapter 2:** Why Do People Abuse Drugs? **Chapter 7:** Growing Up in an Alcoholic Family System	**Chapter 2:** Drug Use as a Social Problem **Chapter 4:** The Nervous System **Chapter 5:** The Actions of Drugs **Chapter 18:** Treating Substance Abuse and Dependence

(Continued)

Taking Sides: Drugs and Society, 9/e	Drugs in Perspective, 7/e by Fields	Drugs, Society & Human Behavior, 13/e by Hart et al.
Issue 7: Should the Federal Government Play a Larger Role in Regulating Steroid Use?	**Chapter 3:** Drug-Specific Information **Chapter 9:** Change, Motivation, and Intervention for Substance-Abuse Problems **Chapter 11:** Alcohol/Drug Recovery Treatment and Relapse Prevention	**Chapter 3:** Drug Products and Their Regulations **Chapter 16:** Performance-Enhancing Drugs
Issue 8: Should Employers Limit Secondhand Smoke?	**Chapter 3:** Drug-Specific Information	**Chapter 3:** Drug Products and Their Regulations **Chapter 10:** Tobacco
Issue 9: Should Marijuana be Legalized?	**Chapter 1:** Putting Drugs in Perspective **Chapter 3:** Drug-Specific Information **Chapter 11:** Alcohol/Drug Recovery Treatment and Relapse Prevention	**Chapter 3:** Drug Products and Their Regulations **Chapter 5:** The Actions of Drugs **Chapter 15:** Marijuana
Issue 10: Are Psychotherapeutic Drugs Overprescribed for Treating Mental Illness?	**Chapter 3:** Drug-Specific Information **Chapter 10:** Disorders Co-Occurring with Substance Abuse	**Chapter 4:** The Nervous System **Chapter 5:** The Actions of Drugs **Chapter 8:** Medication for Mental Disorders **Chapter 14:** Hallucinogens
Issue 11: Is Caffeine a Health Risk?		**Chapter 11:** Caffeine
Issue 12: Should School-Age Children With Attention Deficit/Hyperactivity Disorder (ADHD) Be Treated with Ritalin and Other Stimulants?	**Chapter 4:** Definitions of Substance Abuse, Dependence, and Addition **Chapter 10:** Disorders Co-Occurring with Substance Abuse	**Chapter 5:** The Actions of Drugs **Chapter 6:** Stimulants **Chapter 8:** Medication for Mental Disorders
Issue 13: Do Consumers Benefit When Prescription Drugs are Advertised?		**Chapter 3:** Drug Products and Their Regulation **Chapter 7:** Depressants and Inhalants
Issue 14: Should Smokeless Tobacco Be Promoted as an Alternative to Cigarette Smoking?	**Chapter 3:** Drug-Specific Information	**Chapter 5:** The Actions of Drugs **Chapter 10:** Tobacco
Issue 15: Is Alcoholism Hereditary?	**Chapter 5:** Substance Abuse and Family Systems **Chapter 7:** Growing Up in an Alcoholic Family System	**Chapter 2:** Drug Use as a Social Problem **Chapter 9:** Alcohol
Issue 16: Should Marijuana Be Approved for Medical Use?	**Chapter 1:** Putting Drugs in Perspective **Chapter 3:** Drug-Specific Information **Chapter 11:** Alcohol/Drug Recovery Treatment and Relapse Prevention	**Chapter 5:** The Actions of Drugs **Chapter 8:** Medication for Mental Disorders **Chapter 15:** Marijuana
Issue 17: Should Schools Drug Test Students?	**Chapter 8:** Prevention of Substance-Abuse Problems	**Chapter 17:** Preventing Substance Abuse
IIssue 18: Does Drug Abuse Treatment Work?	**Chapter 8:** Prevention of Substance-Abuse Problems	**Chapter 17:** Preventing Substance Abuse
Issue 19: Is Abstinence an Effective Strategy for Drug Education?	**Chapter 8:** Prevention of Substance-Abuse Problems	**Chapter 17:** Preventing Substance Abuse

Introduction

Drugs: Divergent Views

An Overview of the Problem

The topic of drugs remains controversial in today's society. Very few topics generate as much debate and concern as drugs. Drug use, either directly or indirectly, affects everyone. Drugs and issues related to drugs are evident in every aspect of life. There is much dismay that drug use and abuse cause many of the problems that plague society. Individuals, families, and communities are adversely affected by drug abuse, and many people wonder if the very fabric of society will continue to experience decay because of the abuse of drugs. The news media are replete with horrific stories about people under the influence of drugs committing crimes or perpetrating violence against others; of people who die senselessly; of men, women, and children who compromise themselves for drugs; and of women who deliver babies that are addicted or impaired by drugs. In some countries drug cartels have a major impact on government. Clearly, one does not need to be a drug user to experience their deleterious effects.

From conception until death, almost everyone is touched by drug use. For example, stimulants such as Ritalin are prescribed for children so that they can learn or behave better in school. Some college students take stimulants so that they can stay up late to write a term paper or lose a few pounds. Moreover, college students who use Ritalin and other stimulants are more likely to use illegal drugs (Teter, Esteban, Boyd, and Guthrie, 2003). Many teenagers take drugs to cope with daily stresses and increasing responsibilities or because they want to be accepted by their friends. For many people, young and old, the elixir for relaxation may be sipped, swallowed, smoked, or sniffed. Some people who live under poverty-stricken conditions anesthetize themselves with drugs as a way to escape consciously from their unpleasant environment. On the other hand, some individuals who seem to have everything immerse themselves in drugs, possibly out of boredom, emptiness in their lives, or simply to find the next thrill. To contend with the ailments that accompany getting older, the elderly often rely on drugs. Many people use drugs to confront their pains, problems, frustrations, and disappointments. Others take drugs simply because they like their effects or they take drugs due to curiosity. Some people just want to experience more happiness in their lives. Others use drugs to deal with issues of mental health. This last concern is debated in Issue 10, which examines whether or not psychotherapeutic drugs are overprescribed for treating mental illness.

Background on Drugs

Despite one's feelings about drug use, legal and illegal drugs are an integral part of society. The popularity of various drugs rises and falls with the times. For example, according to annual surveys of eighth-, tenth-, and twelfth-grade students in the United States, the use of marijuana and cocaine increased from the early 1990s to the late 1990s and then decreased from 2000 to the present (Johnston, O'Malley, Bachman, and Schulenberg, 2005). Especially alarming is the fact that approximately one of every six eighth-grade students has tried marijuana. One particular drug that increased significantly in the latter 1990s was MDMA (Ecstasy). MDMA spiked in 2001 and decreased since then. Nevertheless, Ecstasy and other club drugs remain popular with many young people. However, in 2002 many types of drugs declined in use. Nevertheless, Ecstasy and other "club drugs" such as ketamine (Special K) and GHB remain popular with many young people. Issue 4 looks at whether or not the dangers of Ecstasy are overstated.

Understanding the history and role of drugs in society is critical to our ability to address drug-related problems. Drugs have been used throughout human history. Alcohol played a significant role in the early history of the United States. According to Lee (1963), for example, the Pilgrims landed at Plymouth Rock because they ran out of beer. Marijuana use dates back nearly 5,000 years, when the Chinese Emperor Shen Nung prescribed it for medical ailments like malaria, gout, rheumatism, and gas pains. Ironically, 5,000 years after marijuana was first used medicinally, its medical benefits remain a matter of contention. Some issues simply refuse to go away. Hallucinogens have existed since the beginning of humankind and have been used for a variety of reasons. For example, hallucinogens were used to enhance beauty or to cast spells on enemies. About 150 of the estimated 500,000 different plant species have been used for hallucinogenic purposes (Schultes and Hofmann, 1979).

Opium, from which narcotics are derived, was written about extensively by the ancient Greeks and Romans; opium is even referred to in Homer's *Odyssey* (circa 1000 B.C.). In the Arab world opium and hashish were widely used (primarily because alcohol was forbidden). The Arabs were introduced to opium through their trading in India and China. Arab physician Avicenna (A.D. 1000) wrote an extremely complete medical textbook in which he describes the benefits of opium. Ironically, Avicenna died from an overdose of opium and wine. Eventually, opium played a central role in a war between China and the British government.

Caffeine remains the most commonly consumed drug throughout the world. It is estimated that more than 9 out of every 10 Americans drink beverages that include caffeine. Coffee dates back to A.D. 900, when, to stay awake during lengthy religious vigils, Muslims in Arabia consumed coffee. However, coffee was later condemned because the Koran, the holy book of Islam, described coffee as an intoxicant (Brecher, 1972). Drinking coffee became a popular activity in Europe, although it was banned for a short time. In the mid-1600s, coffeehouses were prime locations for men to converse, relax, and conduct business. Medical benefits were associated with coffee, although England's King Charles II and English physicians tried to prohibit its use. Many claims have been made regarding the safety of caffeine. A study involving 15,000 people found no relationship between caffeine and cancer (*Men's Health*, 2004). Issue 11 discusses whether or not the consequences of caffeine outweigh its benefits.

Coffeehouses served as places of learning. For a one-cent cup of coffee, one could listen to well-known literary and political leaders (Meyer, 1954). Lloyd's of London, the famous insurance company, started around 1700 from Edward Lloyd's coffeehouse. However, not everyone was pleased with these "penny universities," as they were called. In 1674, in response to the countless hours men spent at the coffeehouses, a group of women published a pamphlet titled *The Women's Petition Against Coffee,* which criticized coffee use. Despite the protestations against coffee, its use proliferated. Today, more than 300 years later, coffeehouses are still flourishing as centers for relaxation and conversation.

Coca leaves, from which cocaine is derived, have been chewed since before recorded history. Drawings found on South American pottery illustrate that coca chewing was practiced before the rise of the Incan Empire. The coca plant was held in high regard: Considered a present from the gods, it was used in religious rituals and burial ceremonies. When the Spaniards arrived in South America, they tried to regulate coca chewing by the natives but were unsuccessful. Cocaine was later included in the popular soft drink Coca-Cola. Another stimulant, amphetamine, was developed in the 1920s and was originally used to treat narcolepsy. It was later prescribed for treating asthma and for weight loss. Today, the stimulant Ritalin, and similar variations are given to approximately six million school-age children annually in the United States to address attention deficit disorders. Some people claim that too many children are receiving Ritalin, while others assert that not enough students are receiving the drug. The question of whether or not Ritalin and other stimulants should be used for treating attention deficit disorder is debated in Issue 12.

Minor tranquilizers, also called "antianxiety drugs," were first marketed in the early 1950s. The sales of these drugs were astronomical. Drugs to reduce anxiety were in high demand. Another group of antianxiety drugs are benzodiazepines. Two well-known benzodiazepines are Librium and Valium; the latter ranks as the most widely prescribed drug in the history of American medicine. Xanax, which has replaced Valium as the minor tranquilizer of choice, is one of the five most prescribed drugs in the United States today. Minor tranquilizers are noteworthy because they are legally prescribed to alter one's consciousness. Mind-altering drugs existed prior to minor tranquilizers, but they were not prescribed for that purpose. In many instances, consumers request prescribed drugs from their physicians after seeing them advertised in the media. It is estimated that one-third of all prescriptions are written at the request of the patient. Pharmaceutical companies spend more than $2.5 billion on advertising drugs to consumers (Roth, 2003). Is it a good practice for patients to encourage their physicians to prescribe drugs that they saw advertised? Whether or not there should be more regulation on advertising prescription drugs directly to consumers is examined in Issue 13.

Combating Drug Problems

The debates in *Taking Sides: Clashing Views in Drugs and Society* confront many important drug-related issues. For example, what is the most effective way to reduce drug abuse? Should laws preventing drug use and abuse be more strongly enforced, or should drug laws be less punitive? How can the needs of individuals be met while serving the greater good of society? Should drug abuse be seen as a public health problem or a legal problem? Are drugs an American problem or an international problem? The debate whether the drug problem should be fought nationally or internationally is addressed in Issue 2. Many people argue that America would benefit most by focusing its attention on stopping the proliferation of drugs in other countries. Others feel that reducing the demand for drugs should be the primary focus. If federal funding is limited, should those funds focus on reducing the demand for drugs or stopping their importation?

One of the oldest debates concerns whether or not drug use should be decriminalized. In recent years this debate has become more intense because well-known individuals such as political analyst William F. Buckley, Jr., and economist Milton Friedman have come out in support of changing drug laws. For many people the issue is not whether drug use is good or bad, but whether people should be punished for taking drugs. Is it worth the time and expense for law enforcement officials to arrest nonviolent drug offenders? One question that is basic to this debate is whether drug decriminalization causes more or less damage than keeping drugs illegal. Issue 1 addresses the question of whether restrictive drug laws are effective at reducing drug use and abuse.

In a related matter, should potentially harmful drugs be restricted even if they may be of medical benefit? Some people are concerned that drugs used for medical reasons may be illegally diverted. Yet most people agree that patients should have access to the best medicine available. In referenda in numerous states, U.S. voters have approved the medical use of marijuana. Is the federal government consistent in allowing potentially harmful drugs to be used for medical purposes? For example, narcotics are often prescribed for pain relief. Is there a chance that patients who are given narcotics will become addicted? Issue 9 debates whether or not laws prohibiting marijuana should be relaxed. Regardless whether one feels that marijuana laws should be relaxed, the fact remains that over 25 million people have used marijuana in the previous year (Pacula, 2004/2005).

Addiction to drugs is a major problem in society. Yet, most people who stop their addiction to drugs do so on their own (Parmar, Salagubang, and Smith, 2004). Issue 6 looks at the issue of drug addiction and whether addiction is based on heredity or whether it is a choice that people make. In other words, is drug abuse a disease or is it a matter of poor decisions?

A major emphasis in society today is on competition, especially athletic competition. With a win-at-all-costs mentality, many athletes try to get the upper edge. One way to achieve this is through the use of performance-enhancing drugs. A particularly alarming point is that many athletes use anabolic steroids at extremely high dosage levels (*BusinessWeek*, 2004). The issue of whether or not the federal government should play a larger role in regulating steroid use is discussed in Issue 7.

Many of the issues discussed in this book deal with drug prevention. As with most controversial issues, there is a lack of consensus on how to prevent drug-related problems. For example, Issue 5 debates whether or not prosecuting women who use drugs during pregnancy will affect drug use by other women who become pregnant. On the other hand, will pregnant women avoid prenatal care because they fear prosecution? Will newborns be better served if pregnant women who use drugs are charged with child abuse? Are these laws discriminatory, because most cases that are prosecuted involve poor women?

Some people contend that drug laws discriminate not only according to social class, but also according to age and ethnicity. Many drug laws in the United States were initiated because of their association with different ethnic groups: Opium smoking, for example, was made illegal after it was associated with Chinese immigrants. Cocaine became illegal after it was linked with blacks. And marijuana was outlawed after it was linked with Hispanics.

Drug-related issues are not limited to illegal drugs. Tobacco and alcohol are two pervasive legal drugs that generate much debate. For example, are the adverse effects of smoking exaggerated (Issue 8)? At a congressional hearing, executives from at the largest tobacco companies swore tobacco is not addictive (Godrej, 2004). Should nonsmokers be concerned about the effects of second-hand smoke on their health (Issue 14)? With regard to alcoholism, a debate is whether alcoholism is caused by one's heredity or whether it is caused by environmental factors (Issue 15). A fourth issue relating to legal drugs deals with whether or not underage drinkers should be taught how to drink responsibly (Issue 3).

Gateway Drugs

Drugs like inhalants, tobacco, and alcohol are considered "gateway" drugs. These are drugs that are often used as a prelude to other, usually illegal, drugs. Inhalants are composed of numerous products, ranging from paints and solvents to glues, aerosol sprays, petroleum products, cleaning supplies, and nitrous oxide (laughing gas). Inhalant abuse, also known as "huffing," is a relatively new phenomenon in the United States. It seems that until the media started reporting on the dangers of inhalant abuse, its use was not particularly common (Brecher, 1972). Increasingly, movies depict smoking behavior. Celebrities are shown smoking cigarettes in movies (Dalton et al., 2003).

Advertisements are an integral part of the media, and their influence can be seen in the growing popularity of cigarette smoking among adolescents. In the 1880s cigarette smoking escalated in the United States. One of the most important factors contributing to cigarettes' popularity at that time was the development of the cigarette-rolling machine (previously, cigarettes could be rolled at a rate of only four per minute). Also, cigarette smoking, which was considered an activity reserved for men, began to be seen as an option for women. As cigarettes began to be marketed toward women, cigarette smoking became more widespread. As is evident from this introduction, numerous factors affect drug use. One argument is that if young people were better educated about the hazards of drugs and were taught how to understand the role of the media, then limits on advertising would not be necessary.

Drug Prevention and Treatment

Some people maintain that educating young people about drugs is one way to prevent drug use and abuse. Studies show that by delaying the onset of drug use, the likelihood of drug abuse is reduced. In the past, however, drug education had little impact on drug-taking behavior (Goldberg, 2005). Another strategy being adopted in many schools is to drug test students. The belief is that the threat of drug testing will reduce drug use. However, one needs to balance the possible benefits against the costs. The expense of drug testing ranges from $14 to $30 per test, except in the case of anabolic steroids, which costs $100 per test (Yamaguchi, Johnston, and O'Malley, 2003). Issue 17 examines whether or not drug testing of students serves as an effective deterrent to drug use.

Another way to reduce drug abuse that has been heavily promoted is drug abuse treatment. However, is drug abuse treatment effective? Does it prevent recurring drug abuse, reduce criminal activity and violence, and halt the spread of drug-related disease? Issue 18 examines whether or not drug abuse treatment affects these outcomes. The results of drug treatment are contradictory. A European study found that the majority of people in drug treatment drop out (*The Economist,* 2004). Other studies show that drug abuse treatment may have some benefits. But do the benefits outweigh the costs of the treatment? If society feels that treatment is a better alternative to other solutions, such as incarceration, it is imperative to know if treatment works.

Some illegal drugs may produce beneficial effects. For example, marijuana is claimed to help individuals deal with the side effects of chemotherapy. Others believe that marijuana helps people with glaucoma, multiple sclerosis, and many other ailments. However, because marijuana is illegal, should it be considered for medicinal use? Can medicinal use of marijuana turn into excessive, unhealthy use? Should marijuana use be encouraged for individuals who have a history of drug abuse in their families? Issue 16 discusses whether or not marijuana should be approved for medical use.

A logical place to address drug use is in schools because schools are able to reach the greatest number of potential drug users. Schools have employed various strategies to reduce drug use by students. One strategy that has been adopted is that of abstinence. Yet, is the abstinence approach the best vehicle for reducing or stopping young people from using drugs? Issue 19 focuses on whether or not the abstinence approach is an effective strategy for drug education.

Distinguishing Between Drug Use, Misuse, and Abuse

Although the terms *drug, drug misuse,* and *drug abuse* are commonly used, they have different meanings to different people. Defining these terms may seem simple at first, but many factors affect how they are defined. Should a definition for a drug be based on its behavioral effects, its effects on society, its pharmacological properties, or its chemical composition? One simple, concise definition of a drug is "any substance that produces an effect on the mind, body, or both." One could also define a drug by how it is used. For example, if watching television and listening to music are forms of escape from daily problems, then they may be considered drugs.

Legal drugs cause far more death and disability than illegal drugs, but society appears to be most concerned with the use of illegal drugs. The potential harms of legal drugs tend to be minimized. By viewing drugs as illicit substances only, people can fail to recognize that commonly used substances such as caffeine, tobacco, alcohol, and over-the-counter preparations are drugs. If these substances are not perceived as drugs, then people might not acknowledge that they can be misused or abused.

Definitions for misuse and abuse are not affected by a drug's legal status. Drug misuse refers to the inappropriate or unintentional use of drugs. Someone who smokes marijuana to improve his or her study skills is misusing marijuana because the drug impairs short-term memory. Drug abuse alludes to physical, emotional, financial, intellectual, or social consequences arising from chronic drug use. Under this definition, can a person abuse food, aspirin, soft drinks, or chocolate? Also, should people be free to make potentially unhealthy choices?

The Cost of the War on Drugs

The United States government spends billions of dollars each year to curb the rise in drug use. A major portion of that money goes toward law enforcement. Vast sums of money are used by the military to intercept drug shipments, while foreign governments are given money to help them with their own wars on drugs. A smaller portion of the funds is used for treating and preventing drug abuse.

The expense of drug abuse to industries is staggering: Experts estimate that about 14 percent of full-time construction workers in the United States between the ages of 18 and 49 use illicit drugs while at work (Gerber and Yacoubian, 2002). The cost of drug abuse to employers is approximately $171 billion each year (Kesselring and Pittman, 2002). Compared to nonaddicted employees, drug-dependent employees are absent from their jobs more often, and drug users are less likely to maintain stable job histories than nonusers. In its report *America's Habit: Drug Abuse, Drug Trafficking and Organized Crime,* the President's Commission on Organized Crime supported testing all federal workers for drugs. It further recommended that federal contracts be withheld from private employers who do not implement drug-testing procedures. Students who use drugs on a regular basis perform more poorly academically than students who do not use drugs.

A prerequisite to being hired by many companies is passing a drug test. Drug testing may be having a positive effect. From 1987 to 1994 the number of workers testing positive declined 57 percent (Center for Substance Abuse Prevention, 1995). Many companies have reported a decrease in accidents and injuries after the initiation of drug testing. However, most Americans consider drug testing degrading and dehumanizing. An important question is, What is the purpose of drug testing? Drug testing raises three other important questions: (1) Does drug testing prevent drug use? (2) Is the point of drug testing to help employees with drug problems or to get rid of employees who use drugs? and (3) How can the civil rights of employees be balanced against the rights of companies?

How serious is the drug problem? Is it real, or is there simply an unreasonable hysteria regarding drugs? In the United States there has been a growing intolerance toward drug use. Drugs are a problem for many people. Drugs can affect one's physical, social, intellectual, and emotional health. Ironically, some people take drugs because they produce these effects. Individuals who take drugs receive some kind of reward from the drug; the reward may come from being associated with others who use drugs or from the feelings derived from the drug. Many people use illegal drugs or legal drugs like tobacco and alcohol as forms of self-medication. If people did not receive rewards from their use of drugs, then people would likely cease using drugs.

The disadvantages of drugs are numerous: They interfere with career aspirations, educational achievement, athletic performance, and individual maturation. Drugs have also been associated with violent behavior; addiction; discord among siblings, children, parents, spouses, and friends; work-related problems; financial troubles; problems in school; legal predicaments; accidents; injuries; and death. Yet are drugs the cause or the symptom of the problems that people have? Perhaps drugs are one aspect of a larger scenario in which society is experiencing much change and in which drug use is merely another thread in the social fabric.

References

E. M. Brecher, *Licit and Illicit Drugs.* Little, Brown, 1972.

BusinessWeek, "Can Drug-Busters Beat New Steroids? It's Scientist vs. Scientist as the Athens Olympics Approach," June 14, 2004, p. 82.

Center for Substance Abuse Prevention, Substance Abuse and Mental Health Services Administration, *Drug-Free for a New Century,* 1995.

M. A. Dalton, J. D. Sragent, M. L. Beach, L. Titus-Ernstoff, J. J. Gibson, M. B. Ahrens, J. J. Tickle, and T. F. Heatherton, "Effects of Viewing Smoking in Movies on Adolescent Smoking Initiation: A Cohort Study," *The Lancet,* July 26, 2003, pp. 281–290.

The Economist, "Coming Clean; Drug Treatment," October 16, 2004, p. 34.

J. K. Gerber and G. S. Yacoubian, "An Assessment of Drug Testing Within the Construction Industry," *Journal of Drug Education,* vol. 32, no. 1, 2002, pp. 53–68.

D. Godrej, "Smoke Gets In Your Eyes," *New International,* July 2004, pp. 9–12.

R. Goldberg, *Drugs Across the Spectrum.* Wadsworth Publishing, 2005.

L. D. Johnston, P. O. O'Malley, J. G. Bachman, and J. Schulenberg, *Monitoring the Future.* National Institute on Drug Abuse, 2005.

R. G. Kesselring and J. P. Pittman, "Drug Testing Laws and Employment Injuries," *Journal of Labor Research,* vol. 32, no. 2, 2002, pp. 293–302.

H. Lee, *How Dry We Were: Prohibition Revisited.* Prentice Hall, 1963.

Men's Health, "Start Me Up," October 2004, pp. 172–175.

H. Meyer, *Old English Coffee Houses*. Rodale Press, 1954.

R. L. Pacula, "Marijuana Use and Policy: What We Know and Have Yet to Learn," *NBER Reporter* Winter, 2004/2005, pp. 22–24.

N. Parmar, J. Salagubang, and S. A. Smith, "The Surprising Truth About Addiction," *Psychology Today,* May/June, 2004, pp. 43–46.

M. S. Roth, "Media and Message Effects on DTC Prescription Drug Print Advertising Awareness," *Journal of Advertising Research,* June, 2003, pp. 180–193.

R. E. Schultes and A. Hofmann, *Plants of the Gods: Origins of Hallucinogenic Use.* McGraw-Hill, 1979.

C. Teter, S. Esteban, C. Boyd, and S. Guthrie, "Illicit Methylphenidate Use in an Undergraduate Student Sample: Prevalence and Risk Factors," *Pharmacotherapy,* 2003, pp. 609–617.

R. Yamaguchi, L. D. Johnston, and P. M. O'Malley, "Relationship Between Student Illicit Drug Use and School Drug-testing Policies," *Journal of School Health,* April 2003, pp. 159–165.

Internet References . . .

Drug Policy Alliance

Formerly the Drug Policy Foundation, this site is an excellent source of information dealing with legal issues as they relate to drugs.

http://www.drugpolicyfoundation.org

Office of National Drug Control Policy (ONDCP)

This site provides information regarding the government's position on many drug-related topics. Funding allocations by the federal government to deal with drug problems is included also.

http://www.whitehousedrugpolicy.gov

National Institute on Drug Abuse—Club Drugs

Current information regarding club drugs such as Ecstasy, Rohypnol, ketamine, methamphetamines, and LSD can be accessed through this site.

http://www.clubdrugs.org

National Institute on Drug Abuse (NIDA)

Health risks associated with anabolic steroids and strategies for preventing steroid abuse can be obtained at this location.

http://www.steroidabuse.org

Drugs and Public Policy

*D*rug abuse causes a myriad of problems for society: The psycholog-ical and physical effects of drug abuse can be devastating; many drugs are addictive; wreak havoc on families; disability and death result from drug overdoses; and drugs frequently are implicated in crimes, especially violent crimes. Identifying drug-related problems is not difficult. What is unclear is the best course of action to take when dealing with these problems.

Three scenarios exist for dealing with drugs: policies can be made more restrictive, they can be made less restrictive, or they can remain the same. The position one takes depends on whether drug use and abuse are seen as legal, social, or medical problems. Perhaps the issue is not whether drugs are good or bad, but how to minimize the harm of drugs. The debates in this section explore these issues.

- Should Laws Against Drug Use Remain Restrictive?
- Should the United States Put More Emphasis on Stopping the Importation of Drugs?
- Should the United States Drinking Age Remain at 21?
- Are the Dangers of Ecstasy (MDMA) Overstated?
- Should Pregnant Drug Users Be Prosecuted?
- Is Drug Addiction a Brain Disease?
- Should the Federal Government Play a Larger Role in Regulating Steroid Use?

1

ISSUE 1

Should Laws Against Drug Use Remain Restrictive?

YES: Herbert Kleber and Joseph A. Califano Jr., from "Legalization: Panacea or Pandora's Box?" *The World & I Online* (January 2006)

NO: Peter Gorman, from "Veteran Cops Against the Drug War," *The World and I Online* (January 2006)

ISSUE SUMMARY

YES: Herbert Kleber, the executive vice president of the Center on Addiction and Substance Abuse (CASA), and Joseph Califano, founder of CASA, maintain that drug laws should remain restrictive because legalization would result in increased use, especially by children. Kleber and Califano contend that drug legalization would not eliminate drug-related violence and harm caused by drugs.

NO: Author Peter Gorman states that restrictive drug laws have been ineffective. He notes that drug use and drug addiction have increased since drug laws became more stringent. Despite the crackdown on drug use, the availability of drugs has increased while the cost of drugs has decreased. In addition, restrictive drug laws, says Gorman, are racist and endanger civil liberties.

In 2008 the federal government allocated nearly $13 billion to control drug use and to enforce laws that are designed to protect society from the perils created by drug use. Some people believe that the government's war on drugs could be more effective but that governmental agencies and communities are not fighting hard enough to stop drug use. They also hold that laws to halt drug use are too few and too lenient. Others contend that the war against drugs is unnecessary; that, in fact, society has already lost the war on drugs. These individuals feel that the best way to remedy drug problems is to end the fight altogether by ending the current restrictive policies regarding drug use.

There are conflicting views among both liberals and conservatives on whether legislation has had the intended result of curtailing the problems of drug use. Many argue that legislation and the criminalization of drugs have been counterproductive in controlling drug problems. Some suggest that the criminalization of drugs has actually contributed to and worsened the social ills associated with drugs. Proponents of drug legalization maintain that the war on drugs, not drugs themselves, is damaging to American society. They do not advocate drug use; they argue only that laws against drugs exacerbate problems related to drugs.

Proponents of drug decriminalization argue that the strict enforcement of drug laws damages American society because it drives people to violence and crime and that the drug laws have a racist element associated with them. People arrested for drug offenses overburden the court system, thus rendering it ineffective. Moreover, proponents contend that the criminalization of drugs fuels organized crime, allows children to be pulled into the drug business, and makes illegal drugs more dangerous because they are manufactured without government standards or regulations. Hence, drugs may be adulterated or of unidentified potency. Decriminalization advocates also argue that decriminalization would take the profits out of drug sales, thereby decreasing the value of and demand for drugs. In addition, the costs resulting from law enforcement are far greater to society than the benefits of criminalization.

Some decriminalization advocates argue that the federal government's prohibition stance on drugs is an immoral and impossible objective. To achieve a "drug-free society" is self-defeating and a misnomer because drugs have always been a part of human culture. Furthermore, prohibition efforts indicate a disregard for the private freedom of individuals because they assume that individuals are incapable of making their own choices. Drug proponents assert that their personal sovereignty should be respected over any government agenda, including the war on drugs. Less restrictive laws, they argue, would take the emphasis off of law enforcement policies and allow more effort to be put toward education, prevention, and treatment. Also, it is felt that most of the negative implications of drug prohibition would disappear.

Opponents of this view maintain that less restrictive drug laws are not the solution to drug problems and that it is a very dangerous idea. Less restrictive laws, they assert, will drastically increase drug use. This upsurge in drug use will come at an incredibly high price: American society will be overrun with drug-related accidents, lost worker productivity, and hospital emergency rooms filled with drug-related emergencies. Drug treatment efforts would be futile because users would have no legal incentive to stop taking drugs. Also, users may prefer drugs rather than rehabilitation, and education programs may be ineffective in dissuading children from using drugs.

Advocates of less restrictive laws maintain that drug abuse is a "victimless crime" in which the only person being hurt is the drug user. Opponents argue that this notion is ludicrous and dangerous because drug use has dire repercussions for all of society. Drugs can destroy the minds and bodies of many people. Also, regulations to control drug use have a legitimate social aim to protect society and its citizens from the harm of drugs.

In the following selections, Henry Kleber and Joseph Califano explain why they feel drugs should remain illegal, whereas Peter Gorman describes the detrimental effects that he believes occur as a result of the restrictive laws associated with drugs.

YES

Herbert Kleber and
Joseph A. Califano Jr.

Legalization:
Panacea or Pandora's Box

Introduction

Legalization of drugs has recently received some attention as a policy option for the United States. Proponents of such a radical change in policy argue that the "war on drugs" has been lost; drug prohibition, as opposed to illegal drugs themselves, spawns increasing violence and crime; drugs are available to anyone who wants them, even under present restrictions; drug abuse and addiction would not increase after legalization; individuals have a right to use whatever drugs they wish; and foreign experiments with legalization work and should be adopted in the United States.

In this, its first White Paper, the Center on Addiction and Substance Abuse at Columbia University (CASA) examines these propositions; recent trends in drug use; the probable consequences of legalization for children and drug-related violence; lessons to be learned from America's legal drugs, alcohol and tobacco; the question of civil liberties; and the experiences of foreign countries. On the basis of its review, CASA concludes that while legalization might temporarily take some burden off the criminal justice system, such a policy would impose heavy additional costs on the health care system, schools, and workplace, severely impair the ability of millions of young Americans to develop their talents, and in the long term overburden the criminal justice system.

Drugs like heroin and cocaine are not dangerous because they are illegal; they are illegal because they are dangerous. Such drugs are not a threat to American society because they are illegal; they are illegal because they are a threat to American society.

Any relaxation in standards of illegality poses a clear and present danger to the nation's children and their ability to learn and grow into productive citizens. Individuals who reach age 21 without using illegal drugs are virtually certain never to do so. Viewed from this perspective, substance abuse and addiction is a disease acquired during childhood and adolescence. Thus, legalization of drugs such as heroin, cocaine, and marijuana would threaten a pediatric pandemic in the United States.

While current prohibitions on the import, manufacture, distribution, and possession of marijuana, cocaine, heroin, and other drugs should remain,

As seen in *The World & I Online* Journal, January 2006, from a report of The National Center on Addiction and Substance Abuse at Columbia University, September 1995. Copyright © 2006 by The National Center on Addiction and Substance Abuse (CASA) at Columbia University. Reprinted by permission.

America's drug policies do need a fix. More resources and energy should be devoted to prevention and treatment, and each citizen and institution should take responsibility to combat drug abuse and addiction in America. . . .

Legalization, Decriminalization, Medicalization, Harm Reduction: What's the Difference?

The term "legalization" encompasses a wide variety of policy options from the legal use of marijuana in private to free markets for all drugs. Four terms are commonly used: legalization, decriminalization, medicalization, and harm reduction—with much variation in each.

Legalization usually implies the most radical departure from current policy. Legalization proposals vary from making marijuana cigarettes as available as tobacco cigarettes to establishing an open and free market for drugs. Variations on legalization include: making drugs legal for the adult population, but illegal for minors; having only the government produce and sell drugs; and/or allowing a private market in drugs, but with restrictions on advertising, dosage, and place of consumption. Few proponents put forth detailed visions of a legalized market.

Decriminalization proposals retain most drug laws that forbid manufacture, importation, and sale of illegal drugs, but remove criminal sanctions for possession of small amounts of drugs for personal use. Such proposals suggest that possession of drugs for personal use be legal or subject only to civil penalties such as fines. Decriminalization is most commonly advocated for marijuana.

Medicalization refers to the prescription of currently illegal drugs by physicians to addicts already dependent on such drugs. The most frequently mentioned variation is heroin maintenance. Proponents argue that providing addicts with drugs prevents them from having to commit crimes to finance their habit and insures that drugs they ingest are pure.

Harm reduction generally implies that government policies should concentrate on lowering the harm associated with drugs both for users and society, rather than on eradicating drug use and imprisoning users. Beginning with the proposition that drug use is inevitable, harm reduction proposals can include the prescription of heroin and other drugs to addicts; removal of penalties for personal use of marijuana; needle-exchange programs for injection drug users to prevent the spread of AIDS and other diseases that result from needle sharing among addicts; and making drugs available at low or no cost to eliminate the harm caused by users who commit crimes to support a drug habit.

Variations on these options are infinite. Some do not require any change in the illegal status of drugs. The government could, for instance, allow needle exchanges while maintaining current laws banning heroin, the most commonly injected drug. Others, however, represent a major shift from the current role of government and the goal of its policies with regard to drug use and availability. Some advocates use the term "harm reduction" as a politically attractive cover for legalization.

Where We Are

Most arguments for legalization in all its different forms start with the contention that the "war on drugs" has been lost and that prevailing criminal justice and social policies with respect to drug use have been a failure. To support the claim that current drug policies have failed, legalization advocates point to the 80 million Americans who have tried drugs during their lifetime. Since so many individuals have broken drug laws, these advocates argue, the laws are futile and lead to widespread disrespect for the law. A liberal democracy, they contend, should not ban what so many people do.[1]

The 80 million Americans include everyone who has ever smoked even a single joint. The majority of these individuals have used only marijuana, and for many their use was brief experimentation. In fact, the size of this number reflects the large number of young people who tried marijuana and hallucinogenic drugs during the late 1960s and the 1970s when drug use was widely tolerated. During this time, drug use was so commonly accepted that the 1972 Shafer Commission, established during the Nixon Administration, and later, President Jimmy Carter called for decriminalization of marijuana.[2]

Since then, concerned public health and government leaders have mounted energetic efforts to de-normalize drug use, including First Lady Nancy Reagan's "Just Say No" campaign. As a result, current* users of any illicit drugs, as measured by the National Household Survey on Drug Abuse, decreased from 24.8 million in 1979 to 13 million in 1994, a nearly 50 percent drop. Over the same time period, current marijuana users dropped from 23 million to 10 million and cocaine users from 4.4 million to 1.4 million.[3] The drug-using segment of the population is also aging. In 1979, 10 percent of current drug users were older than 34; today almost 30 percent are.[4]

With these results and only 6 percent of the population over age 12 currently using drugs,[5] it is difficult to say that drug reduction efforts have failed. This sharp decline in drug use occurred during a period of strict drug laws, societal disapproval, and increasing knowledge and awareness of the dangers and costs of illegal drug use.

Several factors, however, lead many to conclude that we have not made progress against drugs. This feeling of despair stems from the uneven nature of the success. While casual drug use and experimentation have declined substantially, certain neighborhoods and areas of the country remain infested with drugs and drug-related crime, and these continuing trouble spots draw media attention. At the same time, the number of drug addicts has not dropped significantly and the spread of HIV among addicts has added a deadly new dimension to the problem. The number of hardcore** cocaine users (as estimated by the Office of National Drug Control Policy based on a number of surveys including the Household Survey, Drug Use Forecasting, and Drug

---

*Throughout this paper, "current" drug users refers to individuals who have used drugs within the past month, the definition used in most drug use surveys.

**Throughout this paper, "hardcore" users refers to individuals who use drugs at least weekly.

Abuse Warning Network) has remained steady at roughly 2 million.[6] The over-all number of illicit drug addicts has hovered around 6 million, a situation that many experts attribute both to a lack of treatment facilities[7] and the large numbers of drug-using individuals already in the pipeline to addiction, even though overall casual use has dropped.

Teenage drug use has been creeping up in the past three years. In the face of the enormous decline in the number of users, however, it is difficult to con-clude that current policies have so failed that a change as radical as legaliza-tion is warranted. While strict drug laws and criminal sanctions are not likely to deter hardcore addicts, increased resources can be dedicated to treatment without legalizing drugs. Indeed, the criminal justice system can be used to place addicted offenders into treatment. In short, though substantial problems remain, we have made significant progress in our struggle against drug abuse.

Will Legalization Increase Drug Use?

Proponents of drug legalization claim that making drugs legally available would not increase the number of addicts. They argue that drugs are already available to those who want them and that a policy of legalization could be combined with education and prevention programs to discourage drug use.[8] Some contend that legalization might even reduce the number of users, arguing that there would be no pushers to lure new users and drugs would lose the "forbidden fruit" allure of illegality, which can be seductive to children.[9] Proponents of legalization also play down the consequences of drug use, saying that most drug users can func-tion normally.[10] Some legalization advocates assert that a certain level of drug addiction is inevitable and will not vary, regardless of government policies; thus, they claim, even if legalization increased the number of users, it would have little effect on the numbers of users who become addicts.[11]

The effects of legalization on the numbers of users and addicts is an impor-tant question because the answer in large part determines whether legalization will reduce crime, improve public health, and lower economic, social, and health care costs. The presumed benefits of legalization evaporate if the number of users and addicts, particularly among children, increases significantly.

Availability

An examination of this question begins with the issue of availability, which has three components:

- **Physical**, how convenient is access to drugs.
- **Psychological**, the moral and social acceptability and perceived conse-quences of drug use.
- **Economic**, the affordability of drugs.

Physical

Despite assertions to the contrary, the evidence indicates that presently drugs are not accessible to all. Fewer than 50 percent of high school seniors and young adults under 22 believed they could obtain cocaine "fairly easily" or "very easily.[12] Only 39 percent of the adult population reported they could get cocaine; and only 25 percent reported that they could obtain heroin, PCP, and LSD.[13] Thus, only one-quarter to one-half of people can easily get illegal drugs (other than marijuana). After legalization, drugs would be more widely and easily available. Currently, only 11 percent of individuals reported seeing drugs available in the area where they lived;[14] after legalization, there could be a place to purchase drugs in every neighborhood. Under such circumstances, it is logical to conclude that more individuals would use drugs.

Psychological
In arguing that legalization would not result in increased use, proponents of legalization often cite public opinion polls which indicate that the vast majority of Americans would not try drugs even if they were legally available.[15] They fail to take into account, however, that this strong public antagonism towards drugs has been formed during a period of strict prohibition when government and institutions at every level have made clear the health and criminal justice consequences of drug use. Furthermore, even if only 15 percent of population would use drugs after legalization, this would be triple the current level of 5.6 percent.

Laws define what is acceptable conduct in a society, express the will of its citizens, and represent a commitment on the part of the Congress, the President, state legislatures, and governors. Drug laws not only create a criminal sanction, they also serve as educational and normative statements that shape public attitudes.[16] Criminal laws constitute a far stronger statement than civil laws, but even the latter can discourage individual consumption. Laws regulating smoking in public and workplaces, prohibiting certain types of tobacco advertising, and mandating warning labels are in part responsible for the decline in smoking prevalence among adults.

The challenge of reducing drug abuse and addiction would be decidedly more difficult if society passed laws indicating that these substances are not sufficiently harmful to prohibit their use. Any move toward legalization would decrease the perception of risks and costs of drug use, which would lead to wider use.[17] During the late 1960s and the 1970s, as society, laws, and law enforcement became more permissive about drug use, the number of individuals smoking marijuana and using heroin, hallucinogens, and other drugs rose sharply. During the 1980s, as society's attitude became more restrictive and anti-drug laws stricter and more vigorously enforced, the perceived harmfulness of marijuana and other illicit drugs increased and use decreased.

Some legalization advocates point to the campaign against smoking as proof that reducing use is possible while substances are legally available.[18] But it has taken smoking more than 30 years to decline as much as illegal drug use did in 10.[19] Moreover, reducing use of legal drugs among the young has proven especially difficult. While use of illegal drugs by high school seniors dropped 50 percent from 1979 to 1993, tobacco use remained virtually constant.[20]

Economic
By all of the laws of economics, reducing the price of drugs will increase consumption.[21] Though interdiction and law enforcement have had limited

success in reducing supply (seizing only 25 percent to 30 percent of cocaine imports, for example)[22] the illegality of drugs has increased their price.[23] Prices of illegal drugs are roughly 10 times what they would cost to produce legally. Cocaine, for example, sells at $80 a gram today, but would cost only $10 a gram legally to produce and distribute. That would set the price of a dose at 50 cents, well within the reach of a school child's lunch money.[24]

Until the mid-1980s, cocaine was the drug of the middle and upper classes. Regular use was limited to those who had the money to purchase it or got the money through white collar crime or selling such assets as their car, house, or children's college funds. In the mid-1980s, the $5 crack cocaine vial made the drug inexpensive and available to all regardless of income. Use spread. Cocaine-exposed babies began to fill hospital neonatal wards, cocaine-related emergency room visits increased sharply, and cocaine-related crime and violence jumped.[25]

Efforts to increase the price of legal drugs by taxing them heavily in order to discourage consumption, if successful, would encourage the black market, crime, violence, and corruption associated with the illegal drug trade. Heroin addicts, who gradually build a tolerance to the drug, and cocaine addicts, who crave more of the drug as soon as its effects subside, would turn to a black market if an afford-able and rising level of drugs were not made available to them legally.

Children

Drug use among children is of particular concern since almost all individuals who use drugs begin before they are 21. Furthermore, adolescents rate drugs as the number one problem they face.[26] Since we have been unable to keep legal drugs, like tobacco and alcohol, out of the hands of children, legalization of illegal drugs could cause a pediatric pandemic of drug abuse and addiction.

Most advocates of legalization support a regulated system in which access to presently illicit drugs would be illegal for minors.[27] Such regulations would retain for children the "forbidden fruit" allure that many argue legaliza-tion would eliminate. Furthermore any such distinction between adults and minors could make drugs, like beer and cigarettes today, an attractive badge of adulthood.

The American experience with laws restricting access by children and adolescents to tobacco and alcohol makes it clear that keeping legal drugs away from minors would be a formidable, probably impossible, task. Today, 62 per-cent of high school seniors have smoked, 30 percent in the past month.[28] Three million adolescents smoke cigarettes, an average of one-half a pack per day, a $1 billion a year market.[29] Twelve million underage Americans drink beer and other alcohol, a market approaching $10 billion a year. Although alcohol use is illegal for all those under the age of 21, 87 percent of high school seniors report using alcohol, more than half in the past month.[30] These rates of use persist despite school, community, and media activities that inform youths about the dangers of smoking and drinking and despite increasing pub-lic awareness of these risks. This record indicates that efforts to ban drug use among minors while allowing it for adults would face enormous difficulty.

Moreover, in contrast to these high rates of alcohol and tobacco use, only 18 percent of seniors use illicit drugs, which are illegal for the entire society.[31] It is no accident that those substances which are mostly easily obtainable—alcohol, tobacco, and inhalants such as those found in household cleaning fluids—are those most widely used by the youngest students.[32]

Supporters and opponents of legalization generally agree that education and prevention programs are an integral part of efforts to reduce drug use by children and adolescents. School programs, media campaigns such as those of the Partnership for a Drug-Free America (PDFA), and news reports on the dangers of illegal drugs have helped reduce use by changing attitudes towards drugs. In 1992, New York City school children were surveyed on their perceptions of illegal drugs before and after a PDFA campaign of anti-drug messages on television, in newspapers, and on billboards. The second survey showed that the percentage of children who said they might want to try drugs fell 29 points and those who said drugs would make them "cool" fell 17 points.[33] Another study found that 75 percent of students who saw anti-drug advertisements reported that the ads had a deterrent effect on their own actual or intended use.[34]

Along with such educational programs, however, the stigma of illegality is especially important in preventing use among adolescents. From 1978 to 1993, current marijuana use among high school seniors dropped twice as fast as alcohol use.[35] California started a $600 million anti-smoking campaign in 1989, and by 1995, the overall smoking rate had dropped 30 percent. But among teenagers, the smoking rate remained constant—even though almost one-quarter of the campaign targeted them.[36]

In separate studies, 60 to 70 percent of New Jersey and California students reported that fear of getting in trouble with the authorities was a major reason why they did not use drugs.[37] Another study found that the greater the perceived likelihood of apprehension and swift punishment for using marijuana, the less likely adolescents are to smoke it.[38] Because a legalized system would remove much, if not all of this deterrent, drug use among teenagers could be expected to rise. Since most, teens begin using drugs because their peers do[39]—not because of pressure from pushers[40]—and most drugs users initially exhibit few ill effects, more teenagers would be likely to try drugs.[41]

As a result, legalization of marijuana, cocaine, and heroin for adults would mean that increased numbers of teenagers would smoke, snort, and inject these substances at a time when habits are formed and the social, academic, and physical skills needed for a satisfying and independent life are acquired.

Hardcore Addiction

A review of addiction in the past shows that the number of alcohol, heroin, and cocaine addicts, even when adjusted for changes in population, fluctuates widely over time, in response to changes in access, price, societal attitudes, and legal consequences. The fact that alcohol and tobacco, the most accepted and available legal drugs, are the most widely abused, demonstrates that behavior is influenced by opportunity, stigma, and price. Many soldiers who were regular heroin users in Vietnam stopped once they returned to the United States where heroin was much more difficult and dangerous to get.[42] Studies have shown that even among chronic alcoholics, alcohol taxes lower consumption.[43]

Dr. Jack Homer of the University of Southern California and a founding member of the International System Dynamics Society estimates that without retail-level drug arrests and seizures—which reduce availability, increase the danger of arrest for the drug user, and stigmatize use—the number of compulsive cocaine users would rise to between 10 and 32 million, a level 5 to 16 times the present one.[44]

Not all new users become addicts. But few individuals foresee their addiction when they start using; most think they can control their consumption.[45] Among the new users created by legalization, many, including children, would find themselves unable to live without the drug, no longer able to work, go to school, or maintain personal relationships. In fact, as University of California at Los Angeles criminologist James Q. Wilson points out with regard to cocaine,[46] the percentage of drug triers who become abusers when the drugs are illegal, socially unacceptable, and generally hard to get, may be only a fraction of the users who become addicts when drugs are legal and easily available—physically, psychologically, and economically.

Harming Thy Neighbor and Thyself: Addiction and Casual Drug Use

To offset any increased use as a result of legalization, many proponents contend that money presently spent on criminal justice and law enforcement could be used for treatment of addicts and prevention.[47] In 1995, the federal government is spending $13.2 billion to fight drug abuse, nearly two-thirds of that amount on law enforcement; state and local governments are spending at least another $16 billion on drug control efforts, largely on law enforcement.[48] Legalization proponents argue that most of this money could be used to fund treatment on demand for all addicts who want it and extensive public health campaigns to discourage new use.

With legalization, the number of prisoners would initially decrease because many are currently there for drug law violations. But to the extent that legalization increases drug use, we can expect to see more of its familiar consequences. Costs would quickly rise in health care, schools, and businesses. In the long term, wider use and addiction would increase criminal activity related to the psychological and physical effects of drug use and criminal justice costs would rise again. The higher number of casual users and addicts would reduce worker productivity and students' ability and motivation to learn, cause more highway accidents and fatalities, and fill hospital beds with individuals suffering from ailments and injuries caused or aggravated by drug abuse.

Costs

It is doubtful whether legalization would produce any cost savings, over time even in the area of law enforcement. Indeed, the legal availability of alcohol has not eliminated law enforcement costs due to alcohol-related violence. A third of state prison inmates committed their crimes while under the influence of alcohol.[49] Despite intense educational campaigns, the highest number of arrests in 1993—1.5 million—was for driving while intoxicated.[50] Even if, as some legalization proponents propose, drug sales were taxed, revenues raised would be more than offset by erosion of the general tax base as abuse and addiction limited the ability of individuals to work.

Like advocates of legalization today, opponents of alcohol prohibition claimed that taxes on the legal sale of alcohol would dramatically increase revenues and even help erase the federal deficit.[51] The real-world result has been quite different. The approximately $20 billion in state and federal revenues from alcohol taxes in 1995[52] pay for only half the $40 billion that alcohol abuse imposes in direct health care costs,[53] much less the costs laid on federal entitlement programs and the legal and criminal justice systems, to say nothing of lost economic productivity. The nearly $13 billion in federal and state cigarette tax revenue[54] is one-sixth of the $75 billion in direct health care costs attributable to tobacco,[55] to say nothing of the other costs such as the $4.6 billion in social security disability payments to individuals disabled by cancer, heart disease, and respiratory ailments caused by smoking.[56]

Health care costs directly attributable to illegal drugs exceed $30 billion,[57] an amount that would increase significantly if use spread after legalization. Experience renders it unrealistic to expect that taxes could be imposed on newly legalized drugs sufficient to cover the costs of increased use and abuse.

Public Health

Legalization proponents contend that prohibition has negative public health consequences such as the spread of HIV from addicts who share dirty needles, accidental poisoning, and overdoses from impure drugs of variable potency. In 1994, more than one-third of new AIDS cases were among injection drug users who shared needles, cookers, cottons, rinse water, and other paraphernalia; many other individuals contracted AIDS by having sex, often while high, with infected injection drug users.[58]

Advocates of medicalization argue that while illicit drugs should not be freely available to all, doctors should be allowed to prescribe them (particularly heroin, but also cocaine) to addicts. They contend that giving addicts drugs assures purity and eliminates the need for addicts to steal in order to buy them.[59]

Giving addicts drugs like heroin, however, poses many problems. Providing them by prescription raises the danger of diversion for sale on the black market. The alternative—insisting that addicts take drugs on the prescriber's premises—entails at least two visits a day, thus interfering with the stated goal of many maintenance programs to enable addicts to hold jobs.

Heroin addicts require two to four shots each day in increasing doses as they build tolerance to its euphoric effect. On the other hand, methadone can be given at a constant dose since euphoria is not the objective. Addicts maintained on methadone need only a single dose each day and take it orally, eliminating the need for injection.[60] Because cocaine produces an intense, but short euphoria and an immediate desire for more,[61] addicts would have to be given the drug even more often than heroin in order to satisfy their craving sufficiently to prevent them from seeking additional cocaine on the street.

Other less radical harm reduction proposals also have serious flaws. Distributing free needles, for example, does not guarantee that addicts desperate for a high would refuse to share them. But to the extent that needle exchange programs are effective in reducing the spread of the AIDS virus and other diseases without increasing drug use, they can be adopted without legalizing drugs. Studies of whether needle exchange programs increase drug use have generally focused on periods of no longer than 12 months.[62] While use does not seem to increase in this period, data is lacking on the long-term effects of such programs and whether they prompt attitude shifts that in turn lead to increased drug use.

Some individuals do die as a result of drug impurities. But while drug purity could be assured in a government-regulated system (though not for those drugs sold on the black market), careful use could not. The increased numbers of users would probably produce a rising number of overdose deaths, similar to those caused by alcohol poisoning today.

The deaths and costs due to unregulated drug quality pale in comparison to the negative impact that legalization would have on drug users, their families, and society. Casual drug use is dangerous, not simply because it can lead to addiction or accidental overdoses, but because it is harmful per se, producing worker accidents, highway fatalities, and children born with physical and mental handicaps. Each year, roughly 500,000 newborns are exposed to illegal drugs in the womb; many others are never born because of drug-induced spontaneous abortions.[63] Newborns already exposed to drugs are far more likely to need intensive care and suffer the physical and mental consequences of low birth weight and premature birth, including early death.[64] The additional costs just to raise drug-exposed babies would outweigh any potential savings of legalization in criminal justice expenditures.[65]

Substance abuse aggravates medical conditions. Medicaid patients with a secondary diagnosis of substance abuse remain in hospitals twice as long as patients with the same primary diagnosis but with no substance abuse problems. Girls and boys under age 15 remain in the hospital three and four times as long, respectively, when they have a secondary diagnosis of substance abuse.[66] One-third to one-half of individuals with psychiatric problems are also substance abusers.[67] Young people who use drugs are at higher risk of mental health problems including depression, suicide, and personality disorders.[68] Teenagers who use illegal drugs are more likely to have sex[69] and are less likely to use a condom than those who do not use drugs.[70] Such sexual behavior exposes these teens to increased risk of pregnancy as well as AIDS and other sexually transmitted diseases.

In schools and families, drug abuse is devastating. Students who use drugs not only limit their own ability to learn, they also disrupt classrooms, interfering with the education of other students. Drug users tear apart families by failing to provide economic support, spending money on drugs, neglecting the emotional support of the spouse and guidance of children, and putting their children at greater risk of becoming substance abusers themselves.[71] With the advent of crack cocaine in the mid-1980s, foster care cases soared over 50 percent nationwide in five years; more than 70 percent of these cases involved families in which at least one parent abused drugs.[72]

Decreased coordination and impaired motor skills that result from drug use are dangerous. A recent study in Tennessee found that 59 percent of reckless drivers who, having been stopped by the police, test negative for alcohol on the breathalyzer, test positive for marijuana and/or cocaine.[73] Twenty percent of New York City drivers who die in automobile accidents test positive for cocaine use.[74] The extent of driving while high on marijuana and other illegal drugs is still not well known because usually the police do not have the same capability for roadside drug testing as they do for alcohol testing. . . .

Crime and Violence

Legalization advocates contend that *drug-related* violence is really *drug-trade-related* violence. They argue that what we have today is not a drug problem but a drug prohibition problem, that anti-drug laws spawn more violence and crime than the drugs themselves. Because illegality creates high prices for drugs and huge profits for dealers, advocates of legalization point out that users commit crimes to support their habit; drug pushers fight over turf; gangs and organized crime thrive; and users become criminals by coming into contact with the underworld.[75]

Legalization proponents argue that repeal of current laws, which criminalize drug use and sales, and wider availability of drugs at lower prices will end this black market and thus reduce the violence, crime, and incarceration associated with drugs.

Researchers divide drug-related violence into three types: systemic, economically compulsive, and psychopharmacological:[76]

- **Systemic violence** is that intrinsic to involvement with illegal drugs, including murders over drug turf, retribution for selling "bad" drugs, and fighting among users over drugs or drug paraphernalia.
- **Economically compulsive violence** results from addicts who engage in violent crime in order to support their addiction.
- **Psychopharmacological violence** is caused by the short or long-term use of certain drugs which lead to excitability, irrationality and violence, such as a brutal murder committed under the influence of cocaine.

Legalization of the drug trade and lower prices might decrease the first two types of violence, but higher use and abuse would increase the third. Dr. Mitchell Rosenthal, President of the Phoenix House treatment centers, warns, "What I and many other treatment professionals would expect to see in a drug-legalized America is a sharp rise in the amount of drug-related crime that is *not* committed for gain—homicide, assault, rape, and child abuse. Along with this, an increase in social disorder, due to rising levels of drug consumption and a growing number of drug abusers."[77]

In a study of 130 drug-related homicides, 60 percent resulted from the psychopharmacological effects of the drug; only 20 percent were found to be related to the drug trade; 3.1 percent were committed for economic reasons. (The remaining 17 percent either fell into more than one of these categories or were categorized as "other.")[78] U.S. Department of Justice statistics reveal that six times as many homicides, four times as many assaults, and almost one and a half times as many robberies are committed under the influence of drugs as are committed in order to get money to buy drugs.[79] Given these facts, any decreases in violent acts committed because of the current high cost of drugs would be more than offset by increases in psychopharmacological violence, such as that caused by cocaine psychosis.

The threat of rising violence is particularly serious in the case of cocaine, crack, methamphetamine, and PCP—drugs closely associated with violent behavior. Unlike marijuana or heroin, which depress activity, these drugs cause irritability and physical aggression. For instance, past increases in the New York City homicide rate have been tied to increases in cocaine use.[80]

Repeal of drug laws would not affect all addicts in the same way. Addicts engage in criminal behavior for different reasons. A small proportion of addicts is responsible for a disproportionately high number of drug-related crimes and arrests. Virtually all of these addicts committed crimes before abusing drugs and use crime to support themselves as well as their habits. Their criminal activity and drug use are symptomatic of chronic antisocial behavior and attitudes. Legally available drugs at lower prices would do little to discourage crime by this group. For a second group, criminal activity is associated with the high cost of illegal drugs. For these addicts, lower prices would decrease drug-related crimes. For a third group, legally available drugs would mean an opportunity to create illegal diversion markets, as some addicts currently do with methadone.[81]

Legalization advocates point to the exploding prison population and the failure of strict drug laws to lower crime rates.[82] Arrests for drug offenses doubled from 470,000 in 1980 to 1 million in 1993.[83] Some 60 percent of the 95,000 federal inmates are incarcerated for drug-law violations.[84]

Rising prison populations are generated in large part by stricter laws, tough enforcement, and mandatory minimum sentencing laws—policy choices of the public and Congress. But the growing number of prisoners is also a product of the high rate of recidivism—a phenomenon tied in good measure to the lack of treatment facilities, particularly in prison. Eighty percent of prisoners have prior convictions and 60 percent have served time before.[85] Despite the fact that more than 60 percent of all state inmates have used illegal drugs regularly and 30 percent were under the influence of drugs at the time they committed the crime for which they were incarcerated,[86] fewer than 20 percent of inmates with drug problems receive any treatment.[87] Many of these inmates also abuse alcohol, but there is little alcoholism treatment either for them or for those prisoners dependent only on alcohol.[88]

While strict laws and enforcement do not deter addicts from using drugs, the criminal justice system can be used to get them in treatment. Because of the nature of addiction, most drug abusers do not seek treatment voluntarily, but many respond to outside pressures including the threat of incarceration.[89]

Where the criminal justice system is used to encourage participation in treatment, addicts are more likely to complete treatment and stay off drugs. . . .[90]

Notes

1. Kurt Schmoke, "Decriminalizing Drugs: It Just Might Work—And Nothing Else Does," in *Drug Legalization: For and Against,* ed. Rod Evans and Irwin Berent (Lasalle: Open Court Press, 1992), p. 216; Merrill Smith, "The Drug Problem: Is There an Answer?" in Evans and Berent, eds., p. 84; Steven Wisotsky, "Statement Before the Select Committee on Narcotics Abuse and Control," in Evans and Berent, eds., p. 189.

2. National Commission on Marijuana and Drug Abuse, *Marijuana: Signal of Misunderstanding* (Washington, DC: GPO, 1972); Musto, p. 267.

3. U.S. Department of Health and Human Services, *Preliminary Estimates from the 1994 National Household Survey on Drug Abuse* (September 1995), pp. 2, 58.

4. Dept. of Health and Human Services (1995), p. 11.

5. Dept. of Health and Human Services (1995), p. 2.

6. Office of National Drug Control Policy (ONDCP), *National Drug Control Strategy: Strengthening Communities' Response to Drugs and Crime* (February 1995), p. 139.

7. ONDCP, *Breaking the Cycle of Drug Abuse* (September 1993), pp. 6–9.

8. Todd Austin Brenner, "The Legalization of Drugs: Why Prolong the Inevitable," in Evans and Berent, eds., p. 173; Schmoke, in Evans and Berent, eds., p. 218; Smith, in Evans and Berent, eds., p. 85.

9. Smith, in Evans and Berent, eds., pp. 83–86; Kevin Zeese, "Drug War Forever?" in *Searching for Alternatives: Drug-Control Policy in the United States,* eds. Melvyn Krauss and Edward Lazear (Stanford: Hoover Institute Press, 1992), p. 265.

10. Ethan Nadelmann, "The Case for Legalization," in *The Drug Legalization Debate,* ed. James Inciardi (Newbury Park: Sage Publications, 1991), pp. 39–40.

11. Michael Gazzaniga, "The Opium of the People: Crack in Perspective," in Evans and Berent, eds., p. 236.

12. Lloyd Johnston, Patrick O'Malley, and Jerald Bachman, *National Survey Results on Drug Use from The Monitoring the Future Study, 1975–1993* (Rockville: 1994), Vol. 1, p. 191 and Vol. 2, p. 144; Center on Addiction and Substance Abuse at Columbia University, *National Survey of American Attitudes on Substance Abuse* (July 1995).

13. Dept. of Health and Human Services *Preliminary Estimates from the 1993 National Household Survey: Press Release* (July 1994), p. 4.

14. Dept. of Health and Human Services (July 1994), p. 4.

15. See for example, Lester Grinspoon and James Bakalar, "The War on Drugs—A Peace Proposal," *The New England Journal of Medicine,* 330(5) 1994, pp. 357–60; Arnold Trebach, "For Legalization of Drugs" in *Legalize It? Debating American Drug Policy,* Arnold Trebach and James Inciardi, eds., (Washington: American University Press, 1993), p. 108.

16. Mark Moore, "Drugs: Getting a Fix on the Problem and the Solution," in Evans and Berent, eds., p. 152.

17. Johnston, O'Malley and Bachman, Vol. 1, p. 206.

18. Schmoke, in Evans and Berent, eds., p. 218; Brenner, in Evans and Berent, eds., p. 171; Wisotsky in Evans and Berent, eds., p. 210.

19. ONDCP (1995), p. 139; Centers for Disease Control, *Morbidity and Mortality Weekly Report,* 34(SS-3) 1994, p. 8.

20. Johnston, O'Malley and Bachman, Vol. 1, p. 79.

21. Moore in Evans and Berent, eds., p. 148; and Mark Moore, "Supply Reduction and Law Enforcement" in *Drugs and Crime,* Michael Tonry and James Wilson, eds., *Crime and Justice: A Review of Research,* Volume 13 (Chicago: University of Chicago Press, 1990), pp. 109–158; Michael Grossman, Gary Becker and Kevin Murphy, "Rational Addiction and the Effect of Price on Consumption," in Krauss and Lazear, eds., p. 83.

22. ONDCP (1995), p. 146.

23. Michael Farrell, John Strang and Peter Reuter, "The Non-Case for Legalization" in *Winning the War on Drugs: To Legalize or Not* (Institute of Economic Affairs: London, 1994).

24. Herbert Kleber, "Our Current Approach to Drug Abuse—Progress, Problems, Proposals," *The New England Journal of Medicine* 330(5), 1994, pp. 362–363; for higher estimates of the differences between illegal and legal costs see Moore, in Evans and Berent, eds., p. 148 and Wisotsky, in Evans and Berent, eds., p. 190.

25. Moore, in Evans and Berent, eds., pp. 129–130.

26. Center on Addiction and Substance Abuse at Columbia University, *National Survey of American Attitudes on Substance Abuse* (July 1995).

27. See for example, Wisotsky, in Evans and Berent, eds. p. 204.

28. Johnston, O'Malley and Bachman, Vol. 1, pp. 76–79.

29. K. Michael Cummings, Terry Pechacek and Donald Shopland, "The Illegal Sale of Cigarettes to US Minors: Estimates by State," *American Journal of Public Health,* 84(2) 1994, pp. 300–302.

30. Johnston, O'Malley and Bachman, Vol. 1, pp. 76–79.

31. Johnston, O'Malley and Bachman, Vol. 1, p. 79.

32. Lloyd Johnston, "A Synopsis of the Key Points in the 1994 Monitoring the Future Results" (December 1994), Table 1; Johnston, O'Malley and Bachman, Vol. 1, pp. 136–137.

33. Drug Strategies, *Keeping Score* (Washington, DC: 1995), p. 11.

34. Evelyn Cohen Reis et al, "The Impact of Anti-Drug Advertising: Perceptions of Middle and High School Students," *Archives of Pediatric and Adolescent Medicine,* 148, December 1994, pp. 1262–1268.

35. Johnston, O'Malley and Bachman, Vol. 1, p. 79.

36. "Hooked on Tobacco: The Teen Epidemic," *Consumer Reports,* March 1995, pp. 142–148.

37. Rodney Skager and Gregory Austin, *Fourth Biennial Statewide Survey of Drug and Alcohol Use Among California Students in Grades 7, 9, and 11,* Office

of the Attorney General, June 1993; Wayne Fisher, *Drug and Alcohol Use Among New Jersey High School Students,* New Jersey Department of Law and Public Safety, 1993.

38. David Peck, "Legal and Social Factors in the Deterrence of Adolescent Marijuana Use," *Journal of Alcohol and Drug Education,* 28(3) 1983, pp. 58–74.

39. Diedre Dupre, "Initiation and Progression of Alcohol, Marijuana and Cocaine Use Among Adolescent Abusers," *The American Journal on Addiction,* 4, 1995, pp. 43–48.

40. Ronald Simmons, Rand Conger and Leslie Whitbeck, "A Multistage Learning Model of the Influences of Family and Peers Upon Adolescent Substance Abuse," *Journal of Drug Issues* 18(3) 1988, pp. 293–315.

41. Simmons, Conger and Whitbeck, p. 304; Mark Moore, "Drugs: Getting a Fix on the Problem and the Solution," in Evans and Berent, eds., p. 143.

42. Musto, pp. 258–259.

43. Philip Cook, "The Effect of Liquor Taxes on Drinking, Cirrhosis, and Auto Accidents" in *Alcohol and Public Policy: Beyond the Shadow of Prohibition,* Mark Moore and Dean Gerstein, eds. (Washington, DC: National Academy Press, 1981), p. 256.

44. Jack Homer, "Projecting the Impact of Law Enforcement on Cocaine Prevalence: A System Dynamics Approach," *Journal of Drug Issues* 23(2) 1993, pp. 281–295.

45. Kleber, p. 361.

46. James Q. Wilson, "Against the Legalization of Drugs," *Commentary* (February 1990), pp. 21–28.

47. See for example, Schmoke in Evans and Berent, eds., p. 218.

48. ONDCP (1995), p. 138.

49. Bureau of Justice Statistics, *Survey of State Prison Inmates, 1991* (Washington, DC: 1993), p. 26.

50. Bureau of Justice Statistics, *Prisoners in 1994* (Washington, DC: 1995), p. 13.

51. Paul Aaron and David Musto, "Temperance and Prohibition in America: A Historical Overview," in Moore and Gerstein, eds., p. 172.

52. Drug Enforcement Administration (DEA), *How to Hold Your Own in a Drug Legalization Debate* (Washington, DC, 1994), p. 26, adjusted to 1995.

53. Center on Addiction and Substance Abuse at Columbia University (CASA), *The Cost of Substance Abuse to America's Health Care System, Final Report* (To be issued, 1995).

54. The Tobacco Institute (1994), adjusted to 1995.

55. CASA (To be issued, 1995).

56. Center on Addiction and Substance Abuse at Columbia University, *Substance Abuse and Federal Entitlement Programs* (February 1995).

57. CASA (To be issued, 1995).

58. Centers for Disease Control, National AIDS Clearinghouse (1994).

59. See for example, "Prescribing to Addicts Appears to Work in Britain: Interview with Dr. John Marks," *Psychiatric News,* December 17, 1993, pp. 8, 14.

60. Joyce Lowinson et al, "Methadone Maintenance," pp. 550–561; Jerome Jaffe, "Opiates: Clinical Aspects," pp. 186–194; and Eric Simon, "Opiates: Neurobiology," pp. 195–204 in *Substance Abuse: A Comprehensive Textbook*, 2nd ed., Joyce Lowinson, Pedro Ruiz and Robert Millman, eds. (Baltimore: Williams and Wilkins, 1992).

61. Mark Gold, "Cocaine (and Crack): Clinical Aspects," in Lowinson, Ruiz and Millman, eds., pp. 205–221.

62. Peter Lurie, Arthur Reingold et al, *The Public Health Impact of Needle Exchange Programs in the United States and Abroad*, 2 vols., (University of California, 1993).

63. Dept. of Justice (1992), p. 12; Paul Taubman, "Externalities and Decriminalization of Drugs," in Krauss and Lazear, eds., p. 99.

64. Dept. of Justice (1992), p. 12; Joel Hay, "The Harm They Do to Others," in Krauss and Lazear, eds., pp. 204–213.

65. Hay, in Krauss and Lazear, eds., p. 208.

66. Center on Addiction and Substance Abuse at Columbia University (CASA), *The Cost of Substance Abuse to America's Health Care System, Report 1: Medicaid Hospital Costs*, (July 1993), pp. 38–46.

67. Ronald Kessler et al, "Lifetime and 12-month prevalence of DSM-III-R psychiatric disorders in the United States: Results from the National Comorbidity Study," *Archives of General Psychiatry*, 51(1) 1994, pp. 8–19.

68. Dept. of Justice (1992), p. 11.

69. Centers for Disease Control, "Youth Risk Behavior Survey, 1991."

70. M. Lynne Cooper, Robert Pierce, and Rebecca Farmer Huselid, "Substance Abuse and Sexual Risk Taking Among Black Adolescents and White Adolescents," *Health Psychology* 13(3) 1994, pp. 251–262.

71. Dept. of Justice (1992), p. 9.

72. General Accounting Office, *Foster Care: Parental Drug Abuse Has Alarming Impact on Young Children* (Washington, DC: 1994).

73. Daniel Brookoff et al, "Testing Reckless Drivers for Cocaine and Marijuana" *The New England Journal of Medicine* 331(8) 1994, pp. 518–522.

74. Peter Marzuk, Kenneth Tardiff, et al, "Prevalence of Recent Cocaine Use among Motor Vehicle Fatalities in New York City," *Journal of the American Medical Association* 1990; 263, pp. 250–256.

75. See for example, Nadelmann, in Inciardi (1991), ed., pp. 31–32; Brenner, in Evans and Berent, eds., p. 174; Ira Glasser, "Drug Prohibition: An Engine for Crime," in Krauss and Lazear, eds., pp. 271–283; Milton Friedman, "The War We are Losing," in Krauss and Lazear, eds., pp. 53–57.

76. Paul J. Goldstein, "The Drugs/Violence Nexus: A Tripartite Conceptual Framework," *Journal of Drug Issues* (Fall 1985) pp. 493–516.

77. Mitchell Rosenthal, "Panacea or Chaos: The Legalization of Drugs in America," *Journal of Substance Abuse Treatment* 11(1) 1994, pp. 3–7.

78. Henry Brownstein and Paul J. Goldstein, "A Typology of Drug-Related Homicides" in *Drugs, Crime and the Criminal Justice System*, Ralph Weisheit, ed., (Cincinnati, OH: Anderson Publishing Co., 1990), pp. 171–191.

79. Bureau of Justice Statistics (1993), p. 22.

80. Kenneth Tardiff et al, "Homicide in New York City: Cocaine Use and Fire-arms," *Journal of the American Medical Association,* 272(1) 1994, pp. 43–46.

81. Jon Chaiken and Marcia Chaiken, "Varieties of Criminal Behavior," (Santa Monica: Rand, 1982); HK Wexler and George De Leon, "Criminals as Drug Abusers and Drug Abusers Who Are Criminals" Paper presented to the Annual Convention of the American Psychological Association, Washington, DC, 1980; cited in George De Leon, "Some Problems with the Anti-Prohibitionist Position on Legalization of Drugs," *Journal of Addictive Diseases,* 13(2) 1994, p. 38.

82. See for example, New York City Bar Association, "A Wiser Course: Ending Drug Prohibition," *The Record* 49(5) 1994, pp. 525–534.

83. Bureau of Justice Statistics (1995), p. 13.

84. Bureau of Justice Statistics (1995), pp. 1, 10.

85. Bureau of Justice Statistics (1993), p. 11.

86. Bureau of Justice Statistics (1993), p. 21.

87. General Accounting Office, *Drug Treatment: State Prisons Face Challenges in Providing Services* (Washington, DC: 1991).

88. Bureau of Justice Statistics (1993), p. 26.

89. De Leon, p. 38.

90. M. Douglas Anglin. "The Efficacy of Civil Commitment in Treating Narcotic Addiction" in *Compulsory Treatment of Drug Abuse: Research and Clinical Practice,* NIDA Research Monograph 86, 1988, pp. 8–34; Robert Hubbard et al, *Drug Abuse Treatment: A National Study of Effectiveness* (Chapel Hill: University of North Carolina Press, 1989).

Veteran Cops Against the Drug War

Howard Woolridge is outside of Utica, New York, heading east on horse-back on a beautiful late summer day. He's wearing a T-shirt with the slogan "Cops Say Legalize Drugs. Ask Me Why." For the last 3,000 miles, he's been switching off between his two horses, Misty and Sam. But the T-shirt slogan had stayed the same.

The rangy, good-looking guy is also talking on the cell phone to a reporter back in North Texas. But he interrupts that conversation to speak to someone who pulls up next to him in a car. "That's right—cops say legalize," he tells the newcomer in a deep voice. "Why? Because if we do, we just might be able to keep drugs out of the hands of your 14-year-old."

"Right on!" the motorist shouts, and drives off.

Woolridge is not a lunatic and he's not been out in the sun too long, even if he did cross the United States on horseback in the summer heat. He's a retired law enforcement officer with 18 years on the job who finally decided that the war on drugs was more of a problem than the illicit drugs it was purporting to fight.

He's also a serious long-distance horseman, on the road this time since March 4, when he left Los Angeles for the 3,400-mile ride to New York Harbor. It's the second time Woolridge has crossed the United States to publicize the campaign to repeal most of the drug laws in this country. In 2003 he rode from Georgia to Oregon. When he finished this trip on October 5, looking out at the Statue of Liberty, he was honored by the Long Riders' Guild as only the second person known to have ridden horseback all the way across the country in both directions. And he'll still be wearing one of his "Ask Me Why" T-shirts, the same shirts he's been wearing for six years.

"When I first started wearing it," he says, "people in Texas thought I was crazy. They thought my idea would destroy Texas and America. They believed the government propaganda that millions of people would pick up heroin or methamphetamines and become junkies overnight if you legalized it." But in the last two to three years, he's seen a sea change in the attitude of the American public regarding the war on drugs.

Jailed Over Medicinal Marijuana

"At any given Arby's, McDonald's, Rotary Club or veterans hall," he says, "people are overwhelmingly in favor of calling a halt to drug prohibition. Overwhelmingly."

Many of the houses Woolridge is riding past carry plaques attesting to the Utica area's involvement in the Underground Railroad that once funneled runaway slaves from the south up to Canada. It makes him think about Bernie Ellis, a fellow soldier in the war against the drug war, who has lost his own freedom.

"For 10 years he provided free medical marijuana to three oncologists in the Nashville, Tennessee, area for their patients undergoing chemotherapy. He never once met the doctors, of course; it was all cloak-and-dagger. He'd bring the marijuana to an office worker who'd get it to the patient.

"Well, he finally got busted last year. Now he's looking at five years mandatory federal prison time, though that might go up to 10 because he had a shotgun on his farm when he got busted. And of course his million-dollar farm has been forfeited because he grew the medical marijuana there."

The phone goes quiet for a minute, and there's the sound of a strangled sob. "Sorry. Got a little choked up for a second," he says. He pauses to explain his T-shirt to a motorist, then he's back on the phone talking about Bernie. "This is a guy who broke the law to help people and is now facing the consequences of that. Poor son of a bitch. Next time I see him he'll be in prison."

Woolridge is not a lone ranger in the fight to legalize drugs. He's a founding member of an organization called Law Enforcement Against Prohibition or LEAP, an organization made up entirely of current or former members of law enforcement who feel the drug war's a failure and believe legalization and regulation are preferable to the incarceration of drug users and control of the drug market by organized crime.

Founded in March 2002 by five police officers, LEAP now counts about 3,000 members, from the ranks of policemen, prison guards, Drug Enforcement Administration (DEA) agents, judges and even prosecutors in 48 states and 45 foreign countries. The idea behind LEAP is that, as with the Vietnam Veterans Against the War, the call for an end to the drug war carries more weight when it comes from folks who were in the trenches.

"We're the ones who fought the war," said Jack Cole, LEAP's executive director, who retired from the New Jersey state police as a detective lieutenant after 26 years, including 14 in their Narcotics Bureau, mostly undercover. "And I bear witness to the abject failure of the U.S. war on drugs and to the horrors these prohibitionist policies have produced."

The LEAP Web site provides the statistical backup for that argument. "After nearly four decades of fueling the U.S. policy of a war on drugs with over half a trillion tax dollars and increasingly punitive policies, our confined population has quadrupled," it says. "More than 2.2 million of our citizens are currently incarcerated and every year we arrest an additional 1.6 million for nonviolent drug offenses—more per capita than any country in the world. . . . Meanwhile, people continue dying in our streets while drug barons and terrorists continue to grow richer."

To get that message out, LEAP members have given nearly 1,500 speeches since 2003. And they don't preach to the choir. "We don't do hemp rallies or Million Man Marijuana Marches," said Woolridge. "We do Kiwanis Clubs and PTA meetings and cop conventions. That's where the people we've got to reach go."

To parents and teachers and Rotarians and other cops, LEAP members tell their own stories, about their work and about how they came to feel the drug war was not the answer.

Woolridge, for instance, was a street cop in Michigan for 15 of his 18 years of service, before moving up to the rank of detective. "I didn't work directly with the drug war, in that I wasn't in narcotics," he said. "Still, as a detective I was constantly working with felonies that touched on the drug war. Eight of 10 burglary suspects I dealt with were on crack at the time. They were stealing for drug money."

The burglary victims "were all in real pain," he said. "And I got so fed up with it I began saying, 'Why not let these guys have all the crack they want until they die?' Now I'd say, 'Have all you want for a dollar.' That makes it their choice to live or die. Either way, you don't have people breaking into houses for drug money anymore."

"Dehumanizing" Drug Users

To Cole, who did work directly in narcotics, the whole concept of the war on drugs is wrong. "You declare war, you need soldiers. You have soldiers, they need an enemy. So we've effectively taken a peacekeeping force—the police—and turned them into soldiers whose enemies are the 110 million people who have tried illegal substances in the U.S."

To be an effective soldier, you've got to dehumanize your enemy. "When I started out in narcotics I believed everything they told me," said Cole, a no-BS kind of guy. "Drugs were bad. The people who did them were less than human. I was all for locking them up."

Worse, he said, he and others often applied what they called a little "street justice" to the people they were arresting. "In our training we were taught to believe that drug users were the worst people in the world and whatever we did to them to try to stop their drug use was justified."

What they did was kick in home or apartment doors and have every man woman and child inside lie on the floor. If people didn't cooperate immediately, they were thrown to the floor. Then the place was ransacked. "When we searched for drugs we pretty much did as much damage as possible. We'd break bureaus, turn over beds, smash mirrors, throw things on the floor. Didn't matter, because the people there weren't humans, right? And then, if we did find any drugs, we'd arrest everyone in the house: parents, sisters, brothers. And since we'd already kicked the door down when we came in, it would be left open and anyone who wanted to enter could steal what they wanted. We never cared about that."

Street justice didn't stop there, said Cole. In court, he said officers routinely changed testimony to insure convictions—times, locations, amounts of drug, "anything that couldn't be checked to catch the officer in a lie."

It didn't take long for Cole to reach the conclusion that the drug war and its street justice weren't for him. He was mostly going after small-timers, and his job, he came to feel, was to insert himself into voluntary, private business transactions. "To do that, I had to become someone's confidant, their best friend. And once I was, I would bust them."

But he, too, got hooked—on the adrenaline high of the game. "By the time I came to my senses, I was working on big-timers, and pitting your mind against theirs was a great rush," he said. "Also, it was hard to quit because we were considered by the public and our peers as heroes. And then, given that I'd worked with a lot of cops who applied bad street justice, I let myself believe that at least if I was the one catching [the dopers] they'd be legally caught, and I'd tell the truth and justice would prevail."

He laughed. "Know what was the worst? When I realized that I liked and respected a lot of the bad guys much more than I liked or respected the guys I was working with."

Prohibition: Has It Worked by Its Own Standards?

The stated goals of the war on drugs are to lower drug consumption, reduce addiction and dependence, and decrease the quality and quantity of illegal drugs available on American streets. Those have been the goals since President Richard Nixon first declared the war as part of his attempt to look tough on crime during the presidential election in 1968.

Since then, the strategy of prohibition has been ramped up by every succeeding administration. Few people in this country—or anywhere—have escaped the effects of the U.S. drug war, from the toll of burglaries and car thefts committed to pay for drugs, to the tax bills for prisons to hold the increasing percentages of citizens locked up for nonviolent drug-related crimes, to the millions of kids who've grown up without one or both parents as a result of drug convictions and drug addictions. Drug-related murders reach into the tens of thousands in this country, and the toll is much higher in drug-producing and-shipping nations, from Colombia to Afghanistan to Jamaica. Thousands of peace officers have died fighting the drug war. Whole countries have found themselves under the boot of the illegal drug industry, their governments controlled or intimidated by drug cartels, their politicians and police forces infiltrated, and honest public servants assassinated.

The assumption in American drug policy has always been that those are the impacts of illegal drugs themselves. But LEAP members have come to believe those are the wages not of drugs, but of the war on drugs. And they want the rest of the country to look closely at the costs of that strategy and what they see as its failures.

Despite the billions of dollars spent on the fight in nearly 40 years, LEAP members point out, the drug war has failed on every one of its own stated goals.

Drug consumption, for instance, shows little sign of dropping. Whereas in 1965, according to the Drug Enforcement Administration, fewer than 4 million Americans had ever tried an illegal drug, the figure is now more than 110 million. In 2000, the federal government estimated that there were about 33 million people in this country who had used cocaine at least once—a more than 700 percent increase over the total number of people 35 years before who had used any illegal drug.

Dependence and addiction? According to the Office of National Drug Control Policy (ONDCP), the federal agency that sets and administers U.S. drug policy, in 2002 more than 7 million Americans were either dependent on or abusing illegal substances—nearly double the number of people who had even tried such drugs when Nixon declared his war. Heroin addicts have jumped from a few hundred thousand in the 1960s to between 750,000 and one million today according to the ONDCP.

Attempts to decrease the quality of available drugs also have failed. In 1970, average street heroin in this country had a potency of 1 to 2 percent. In 2000, according to the DEA, that purity figure was 36.8 percent—although U.S. drug czar John Walters did praise anti-drug forces recently for reducing the strength of street heroin coming from South America to 32.1 percent. Similarly, street cocaine was roughly 2 to 4 percent pure in 1968—and a whopping 56 percent in 2001, according to the ONDCP. The average strength of the active ingredient (THC) in marijuana sold in this country more than doubled between the late 1970s and 2001.

Nor is there much good news on drug quantities and availability, at least not judging by the numbers of users and the prices on the street. The ONDCP estimates that Americans' use of cocaine and crack has dropped from 447 tons in 1990 to 259 tons in 2000. But the price of cocaine has dropped from $100 per gram in 1970 to $25 to $50 per gram in 2002—for cocaine that was many times stronger. At the wholesale level, a kilogram of cocaine (2.2 pounds at roughly 25 percent purity) cost $45,000 in New York City in 1970. Today, in any large city in the U.S., it costs less than $15,000 and it's about 65 percent pure.

Only marijuana showed a price increase. In 1970, a bag of Mexican ditch-weed (roughly an ounce) cost $20. In 2005, that same bag costs nearly $50. But most Americans who can afford it don't smoke Mexican ditchweed. They smoke U.S.-grown sinsemilla, which runs up to $400 per ounce.

With availability, price, and quality making drugs as attractive as ever, the only other barometer of the success of the drug war might be if it's stopped anyone from trying drugs—an area where programs like DARE, a huge effort targeted at schoolkids—have had a noted lack of success. "It didn't stop George Bush, Bill Clinton, Al Gore or me from smoking pot," said Woolridge. "I don't think it probably ever stopped anyone."

Collateral Damage

The cops and prosecutors and judges who belong to LEAP think the bad results of the drug war go beyond its policy failures, even beyond the lives lost to drug violence and incarceration.

"Let's be honest," Cole said. "The war on drugs has taken an incredible toll in terms of the loss of our civil liberties, particularly in terms of the Fourth Amendment, from property forfeiture laws that fund law enforcement agencies to warrantless searches. It's promoted institutionalized racism, and it's created a systemic level of corruption among law enforcement unheard of prior to its initiation."

Law enforcement veterans like Cole and Woolridge believe the increase in institutional racism is one of the deepest wounds. They point out, for instance, that crack users (generally inner-city blacks) are subject to mandatory minimum sentences of five years for possession of five grams of crack, while powder cocaine users (generally middle-class whites) have to be caught with 500 grams to get the same mandatory sentence.

While ONDCP statistics show that whites use more than 70 percent of all illegal drugs, blacks are sentenced to prison for drug crimes seven times more often than whites.

"Imagine," said Cole, "one of the most racist places in the world: South Africa, 1993. At that time, the South African government was incarcerating black males at the rate of 859 per 100,000 population." And yet in 2004 in the United States—with more people and a higher percent of its population in prison than any country in the world—the incarceration rate for black males was 4,919 per 100,000 (compared to 726 overall).

He pointed to an FBI estimate that one in three black male babies born in the U.S. in 2004 have an expectation of going to prison during their lifetime. "That just blows my mind," he said.

LEAP members believe that a large percentage of the corruption found in U.S. police agencies is tied to drugs. In Texas, recent drug-related scandals included the Dallas fake-drugs operation, in which a snitch was paid more than $200,000 over a two-year period to provide local cops with drug dealers. The "dealers" turned out to be nearly all illegal immigrants; their "drugs" turned out to be crushed sheetrock and pool chalk.

And then there was Tulia, in the Texas Panhandle, in which a multi-county drug task force hired a corrupt deputy sheriff to rid the town of its drug problem; when it turned out there wasn't one, the deputy created one, and more than 40 people wound up arrested.

LEAP spokesmen see both of those high-profile Texas drug corruption cases as indicative of a much wider problem: officers cutting corners to get the arrest numbers that will keep the fuel line of federal and state anti-drug funding open. And those scandals don't begin to touch on the border patrol agents, police, and other law enforcement officials who have been corrupted because the drug money is so available.

More Law-Enforcement Corruption

Rusty White, another LEAP member, is a self-described redneck who grew up hard in east Texas and now, after many stops in other states and countries, lives just north of Fort Worth. At 13, he saw a friend shoot up black-tar heroin and decided he didn't like hard drugs. By 16, he'd been to juvenile detention five times and gotten kicked out of his high school "because I was traveling with an older crowd of bad-ass kids that I was trying to live up to."

In quick succession, he married, became a father, joined the Army and got divorced. After a second tour with the Army, he ended up in Florence, Arizona, where he went to work at the state penitentiary, which, he said, was "one of the most violent prisons in the United States at that time."

From 1973 to 1978, he worked as a guard on maximum security, death row, and administrative segregation cellblocks, dealing with horrors daily. "Life meant very little to those inside the walls," he said, noting that two prison guards were killed and mutilated by inmates in 1973. "And drugs were one of the biggest problems we had. They were the cause of most of the deaths and power struggles." And most of the drugs were brought in by family members of prison workers. "I got fed up with the corruption and left to go into the oil-drilling business in 1979," he said.

After working overseas for several years, White moved to Oklahoma. And there, he said, he got to see the war on drugs from a very different vantage point. "The county I lived in had a sheriff who controlled the drug market. And he did so with force. It was common knowledge that if you crossed him he could be—and had been—deadly."

But the same sheriff regularly flew around the county in National Guard helicopters, providing photo ops for news crews to show how tough he was on drugs. "The only thing he was getting rid of was the competition," said White disgustedly.

His only personal encounter with the sheriff and his machine occurred when White's brother-in-law, a small-time pot dealer, was busted. "He was poor, didn't have a car that ran, and was living off [government] commodities. Yet he was going to be played by the sheriff as a drug-dealing kingpin," the former prison guard said.

"Anyway, he's the father of three little ones, all younger than six, and when the police arrived, he offered to go with them willingly. But he asked that his kids be allowed to stay with an uncle who was there rather than dragging them down to the station. Well, you know how people feel about 'drug dealers.' The police said no, the kids were coming to the station to watch their father get busted, and then they'd be released to the uncle."

When the man's trial came up, White said, it turned out the district attorney didn't have any evidence against him as a big-time dealer. Nonetheless, he was offered a plea deal: Admit to being a big dealer and get a one- to three-year sentence. If he took it to trial, however, the prosecutor promised he'd ask for a full 10 years.

"He copped to the plea. But to see him struggle with having to lie in front of his kids and admit to something he hadn't done—well, I sort of snapped and screamed at the prosecutor and asked him if he'd thought he'd earned his money that day and why he was playing God, and he looked at me and answered, 'Because in this county, I am God.'"

A couple of years later, White said, the DA went back into private practice and shortly thereafter was arrested and convicted for dealing methamphetamines. "How the sheriff escaped that net, I don't know," White said. "But the thing to remember is that . . . this sort of thing is happening every day in the war on drugs, all over the country. And that abuse of trust and power is far more harmful to Americans than drugs could ever be."

No Place for "Anyone with a Conscience"

Shortly after his brother-in-law's conviction, White went back to work in the prison system, and became a drug-dog trainer and handler. It was the sort of work White said he was meant to do. "I tracked several escapees from the prison and even some cop killers using my track K-9s. We helped departments all over the state. I'd be sent to prisons to look for drugs—I had no problem with that. But the more we were used with other police organizations the more my conscience started to become a problem."

Two incidents stick in White's mind. Once while his partner was helping another officer, part of a joint was discovered in the ashtray of an old pickup belonging to an elderly man. The dogs were brought in, and in the camper shell on the back of the truck in which the old man lived the dogs sniffed out a brief-case with more than $9,000 in it. Because it was a drug dog that had alerted on it, the money was confiscated. "And they just stood around laughing as the old man begged them not to take his life savings. It just made me sick and ashamed. Heck, it's common knowledge that over 90 percent of the paper money in this country is tainted with a drug scent a dog can find. But using that to rob our people disgusts me. Heck, if you walk any K-9 into a bank vault the dog will mark on that money, too. How come that money isn't confiscated?"

The second incident occurred one night when White and his drug dog were called to help a local police department search a house for drugs. When he pulled up to the house, he asked to see the warrant. The officer told him it wasn't there yet but to go ahead and start the search, and it would be there shortly. "I told him that's just not how it works. I needed the warrant for the search to be legal. So I put my K-9 back into the truck and brought him back to the kennel. And then I got called on the carpet for refusing to assist."

White thought getting into trouble for following the law he'd sworn to uphold was just too much, so he quit. "Heck, there was so much corruption, even among K-9 handlers. If they didn't want someone with drugs caught they'd say the dog didn't mark. If they did, well, we heard of cases where guys went so far as to 'salt' the areas their dogs were searching to make sure some-one got busted. It was so bad that, being honest, you couldn't do it. . . . I don't think anyone with a conscience can be part of law enforcement anymore."

Richard Watkins saw the same corruption inside prison that White did, but from a unique perspective. A decorated Vietnam veteran with a Ph.D. in education, Watkins worked at Texas' Huntsville prison for 20 years; the last several as warden of Holiday Unit, a 2,100-bed facility housing a range of crim-inals from nonviolent to violent/maximum security.

He was originally hired to revamp and professionalize the correctional officers training program—something the prison system was forced to do by federal mandate, and which Watkins said was badly needed. "It was just hor-rible. Corrupt, bad, just plain horrible," he said.

Watkins had always had reservations about the war on drugs. He figured the drug dealers wouldn't go away as long as there was a market. And looking at this country's experience with Prohibition, "and how that created mobsters and criminal gangs," he figured that legalizing drugs made more sense. When selling and drinking booze became legal in this country again, he said, "you had so much more control of it. You had supporting laws that managed the use of alcohol."

Watkins was first exposed to drugs in Vietnam. He didn't use them—he preferred alcohol—but he saw a lot of other guys getting high on marijuana and other drugs. Many of those men wound up in prison when they came home with addiction problems. "And in prison, you could always get whatever drugs you wanted. Heck, we arrested a mom one time who was putting a lip-lock on her son to pass him a balloon full of heroin. But most of the drugs came in through the guards. Drugs are packaged so small, it's almost impossible to keep them out. Think about that: If you can't keep drugs out of a maximum-security prison, you can't keep them out of schools or anywhere else."

Once drugs lands someone in prison in Texas, he said, life's prospects get a lot dimmer. "We've got these minor players put in with professional criminals. If they weren't criminals going in they damn sure are when they get out. Imagine a system where we put people into a society that's really a training ground for criminals, then don't provide them with either schooling or treatment, then put them back on the streets where they came from. Do you really expect them to be reformed? Life doesn't work that way."

He wishes people wouldn't make the decision to use drugs. "But if they did use them, I wouldn't put them in prison. I'd rather see the money we spend on prisons going to give these kids the tools they need to make better choices."

Voices Opposing LEAP's Perspective

You might imagine that it would be easy to find law enforcement agencies and personnel who oppose LEAP's call for legalization and regulation as an alternative to the war on drugs. But neither the FBI nor the DEA would discuss the subject.

"Our job is to stop the flow of illegal drugs both at home and abroad, as well as to stop our citizens from wanting to use them, through education and prevention methods," said an ONDCP representative. "We will not discuss legalization or any organization which thinks that would be a solution."

Jack Cole wasn't surprised. "They're good soldiers," he said. "They're not allowed to question their commands. Our job is to simply have their commanders change their marching orders."

Mike Smithson, who runs LEAP's speakers bureau, said he's made more than 100 attempts to get law enforcement and drug policy officials to come out and debate LEAP, "and we've only been taken up on it five times. Policymakers generally say that debating us will lend us credence. We think they're just afraid. How can they defend a policy that is already being defended by every major drug dealer, cartel and drug-producing government worldwide?"

Woolridge says that on his entire ride from Los Angeles he's talked to only two officers who disagreed with LEAP's point of view. "One guy thought we'd destroy America if we legalized drugs. He was so angry when he couldn't find anything to write me a ticket for that he gave me the finger as he drove away. And there was a state trooper with 22 years on the job who told me to take off my shirt because it said "Cops say legalize drugs," and he didn't agree with that. I told him go make up his own shirt."

One person did agree to discuss his opposition to LEAP's stand was Sheriff John Cooke of Wells County in Colorado. Cooke is a member of a Rotary Club at which Howard Woolridge spoke. He was so taken aback by the idea of legalizing drugs that he demanded equal time and recently spoke to the Rotary Club himself.

"In my opinion, there are several reasons not to legalize drugs," Cooke told Fort Worth Weekly. First of all, when people say you're going to eliminate the black market, does that mean you're going to sell drugs to 12- and 15-year olds? Because if you don't, someone will. Law enforcement surely hasn't done a good job at keeping alcohol and cigarettes out of the hands of kids, so what makes them think they'll do any better with drugs? And if you don't sell drugs to them, there will be a black market created to sell to them. So I don't buy the end of the black market theory.

"Secondly, we already have social ills from the legal use of alcohol and tobacco. Why on earth would we want to turn other addictive substances loose on the public?

"Thirdly, these LEAP folks want to throw in the towel, say we've lost the drug war. But the thing is that I think we're winning the war on drugs. I think drug use is down. I think if we keep at it, we will win.

"Then there's the question of use. Right now, I believe that the threat of the hammer of law enforcement is keeping a great many people from doing drugs. The threat of prison time is a big hammer. I think if we legalized you'd see the number of people doing drugs in this country skyrocket. I believe we'd have a drug-dependent society . . . and I don't want to see America as a drug-dependent country."

Michael Gilbert, director of the Department of Criminal Justice at the University of Texas at San Antonio, said he doubted that there would be any sizeable black market aimed at teens if drugs were legalized. Gilbert is a LEAP member who worked in prisons—including Leavenworth—and with Justice Department agencies for more than 20 years.

"The reason there's so much money in the black market is not because of the small portion of destabilized street addicts we have, or even kids experimenting with drugs. It's because you have long-time productive millions [of people] who regularly purchase small quantities of the drugs of their choice but they don't use them in a way that becomes destructive to their lives," he said. "They're working, paying their taxes and so forth. The real money is from the enormous number of middle-class people who use drugs. So while you might still have a small market of teens purchasing drugs, it wouldn't be large enough to fund criminal enterprises as it does today."

While few policy makers will discuss the benefits of drug prohibition, several well-known former policy makers have come out against it. Among them are Nobel Prize-winning economist Milton Friedman, a former member of President Reagan's Economic Advisory Board; former Secretary of State (under Ronald Reagan) George P. Shultz; former governor of New Mexico Gary Johnson; former Baltimore Mayor Kurt Schmoke; and U.S. Rep. Dennis Kucinich of Ohio, a former presidential candidate.

Benefits of the LEAP Solution

None of the LEAP members interviewed for this article believes abusing drugs is a good choice. But that's different, they say, from the legal system further ruining people's lives because of that bad choice. They also figure that, like tattoos, hair color decisions, and bad marriages, drug use is a poor choice that society should only care about when it hurts other people. In town, running around in your yard naked and screaming at 4 a.m. breaks the social contract. On a ranch where no one else can see or hear, few people would care about it. Likewise, LEAP members figure, if you can do drugs and not break the social contract, go ahead. And in fact, the federal government figures that 72 percent of chronic drug users continue to function well in society, without harming others.

Even considering the harm that drugs can cause, however, LEAP members believe that the war on drugs is even more harmful. Legalizing drugs, on the other hand, would take profits out of the hands of criminals and hugely reduce the need for people to commit crime to pay for drugs, they say. Regulation would take drug manufacture out of the hands of bathtub chemists and put it into the hands of real chemists, eliminating many of the deaths from bad drugs—much like the end of Prohibition did for deaths from homemade booze. HIV and hepatitis C, rampant among needle-sharing junkies, could be significantly reduced with the availability of clean needles, reducing a major health-care burden for the country.

"Don't forget my favorite," Woolridge said. "If as Bush said, drug money funds terrorists, [then] legalizing drugs would take half a billion dollars a day out of Afghanistan alone, much of which is going to al Qaeda to buy weapons to be used to kill our boys. We could eliminate that overnight."

Legalization, in fact, would probably not increase drug use long-term, many believe—especially since nearly half the population has already tried it. "In all likelihood," Watkins said, "you would see a spike in use as we did with the end of alcohol prohibition. But that normalized pretty quickly, and would probably be the same with drugs. There would be a period of experimentation that would level out, and we'd be left with all the benefits and none of the negatives."

It was Sunday afternoon and Howard Woolridge and Misty were still in upstate New York, having made it from Utica to a ghetto in Schenectady. Woolridge was back on the phone again, when a woman approached him.

"What do you mean cops say legalize drugs?" she could be heard asking.

"Just that. Let's legalize drugs, take them off the street corner."

"What kind of drugs?"

"Heroin, crack, methamphetamine, anything you can think of."

"Are you crazy? I don't want my kids doing those drugs!"

"Neither do I," he told her. "They're no good. But that doesn't keep them from being sold on the corner in this very neighborhood, does it? I'd legalize them and get them into pharmacies. Keep your kids from being shot while walking down the street."

There was a pause and then she laughed. "I never thought of it that way before. You're making me think now."

POSTSCRIPT

Should Laws Against Drug Use Remain Restrictive?

Kleber and Califano assert that utilizing the criminal justice system to maintain the illegal nature of drugs is necessary to keep society free of the detrimental effects of drugs. Loosening drug laws is unwise and dangerous. They argue that international control efforts, interdiction, and domestic law enforcement are effective and that many problems associated with drug use are mitigated by drug regulation policies. They maintain that restrictive drug laws are a feasible and desirable means of dealing with the drug crisis.

Gorman charges that restrictive drug laws are highly destructive and discriminatory. He professes that if drug laws remain stringent, the result would be more drug users in prison and that drug abusers and addicts would engage in more criminal activity. Also, there is the possibility that more drug-related social problems would occur. Gorman concludes that society cannot afford to retain its intransigent position on drug legalization. The potential risks of the current federal policies on drug criminalization outweigh any potential benefits. Society suffers from harsh drug laws, says Gorman, by losing many of its civil liberties.

Proponents for less restrictive drug laws argue that such laws have not worked and that the drug battle has been lost. They believe that drug-related problems would diminish if more tolerant policies were implemented. Citing the legal drugs alcohol and tobacco as examples, legalization opponents argue that less restrictive drug laws would not decrease profits from the sale of drugs (the profits from cigarettes and alcohol are incredibly high). Moreover, opponents argue, relaxing drug laws does not make problems associated with drugs disappear (alcohol and tobacco have extremely high addiction rates as well as a myriad of other problems associated with their use).

Many European countries, such as the Netherlands and Switzerland, have a system of legalized drugs, and most have far fewer addiction rates and lower incidences of drug-related violence and crime than the United States. These countries make a distinction between soft drugs (those identified as less harmful) and hard drugs (those with serious consequences). However, would the outcomes of less restrictive laws in the United States be the same as in Europe? Relaxed drug laws in the United States could still be a tremendous risk because its drug problems could escalate and reimposing strict drug laws would be difficult. This was the case with Prohibition in the 1920s, which, in changing the status of alcohol from legal to illegal, produced numerous crime- and alcohol-related problems.

Many good articles debate the pros and cons of this issue. These include "Who's Using and Who's Doing Time: Incarceration, the War on Drugs, and

32

Public Health," by Lisa Moore and Amy Elkavich (*American Journal of Public Health,* September 2008); "Too Dangerous Not to Regulate," by Peter Moskos (*U.S. News and World Report,* August 4, 2008); "Reorienting U.S. Drug Policy," by Jonathon Caulkins and Peter Reuter (*Issues in Science and Technology,* Fall 2006); "No Surrender: The Drug War Saves Lives" by John Walters (*National Review,* September 27, 2004), the current director of the Office of National Drug Control Policy; "Lighting Up In Amsterdam," by John Tierney (*New York Times,* August 26, 2006); "What Drug Policies Cost. Estimating Government Drug Policy Expenditures," by Peter Reuter (*Addiction,* March 2006); "An Effective Drug Policy to Protect America's Youth and Communities," by Asa Hutchinson (*Fordham Urban Law Journal,* January 2003); and "The War at Home: Our Jails Overflow with Nonviolent Drug Offenders. Have We Reached the Point Where the Drug War Causes More Harm Than the Drugs Themselves," by Sanho Tree (*Sojourners,* May–June 2003).

ISSUE 2

Should the United States Put More Emphasis on Stopping the Importation of Drugs?

YES: Bureau of International Narcotics and Law Enforcement Affairs, from *2009 INCSR: Policy and Program Developments* (U.S. Department of State, 2009)

NO: Ethan Nadelmann, from "The Global War on Drugs Can Be Won," *Foreign Policy* (October 2007)

ISSUE SUMMARY

YES: Because the trafficking of drugs represents a direct threat to national security, the U.S. State Department maintains that more effort is needed to interdict drugs coming into the United States. Better cooperation with countries in Latin America, the Caribbean, Africa, and Asia, where drugs are grown and exported, is essential.

NO: Ethan Nadelmann, the executive director of the Drug Policy Alliance, contends that attempts to stem the flow of drugs are futile and that it is unrealistic to believe that the world can be made free of drugs. Nadelmann points out that global production is about the same as it was ten years earlier and that cocaine and heroin are purer and cheaper because producers have become more efficient.

Since the beginning of the 1990s, overall drug use in the United States has increased. Up to now, interdiction has not proven to be successful in slowing the flow of drugs into the United States. Drugs continue to cross U.S. borders at record levels. This may signal a need for stepped-up international efforts to stop the production and trafficking of drugs. Conversely, it may illustrate the inadequacy of the current strategy. Should the position of the U.S. government be to improve and strengthen current measures or to try an entirely new approach?

Some people contend that rather than attempting to limit illegal drugs from coming into the United States, more effort should be directed at reducing the demand for drugs and improving treatment for drug abusers. Foreign countries would not produce and transport drugs like heroin and cocaine into the United States if there was no market for them. Drug policies, some people maintain, should be aimed at the social and economic conditions underlying domestic drug problems, not at interfering with foreign governments.

Many U.S. government officials believe that other countries should assist in stopping the flow of drugs across their borders. Diminishing the supply of drugs by intercepting them before they reach the user is another way to eliminate or curtail drug use. Critical elements in the lucrative drug trade are multinational crime syndicates. One premise is that if the drug production, transportation, distribution, and processing functions as well as the money laundering operations of these criminal organizations can be interrupted and eventually crippled, then the drug problem would abate.

In South American countries such as Peru, Colombia, and Bolivia, where coca—from which cocaine is processed—is cultivated, economic aid has been made available to help the governments of these countries fight the cocaine kingpins. An alleged problem is that a number of government officials in these countries are corrupt or fearful of the cocaine cartel leaders. One proposed solution is to go directly to the farmers and offer them money to plant crops other than coca. This tactic, however, failed in the mid-1970s, when the U.S. government gave money to farmers in Turkey to stop growing opium poppy crops. After one year the program was discontinued due to the enormous expense, and opium poppy crops were once again planted.

Drug problems are not limited to the Americas. Since the breakup of the Soviet Union, for example, there has been a tremendous increase in opium production in many of the former republics. These republics are in dire need of money, and one source of income is opium production. Moreover, there is lax enforcement by police officials in these republics.

There are many reasons why people are dissatisfied with the current state of the war on drugs. For example, in the war on drugs, the casual user is generally the primary focus of drug use deterrence. This is viewed by many people as a form of discrimination because the vast majority of drug users and sellers who are arrested and prosecuted are poor, members of minorities, homeless, unemployed, and/or disenfranchised. Also, international drug dealers who are arrested are usually not the drug bosses but lower-level people working for them. Finally, some argue that the war on drugs should be redirected away from interdiction and enforcement because they feel that the worst drug problems in society today are caused by legal drugs, primarily alcohol and tobacco.

The following selections address the issue of whether or not the war on drugs should be fought on an international level. The U.S. Department of State takes the view that international cooperation is absolutely necessary if we are to stem the flow of drugs and reduce drug-related problems in the United States. Ethan Nadelmann argues that an international approach to dealing with drugs has been ineffective because the production of drugs has not been curtailed.

YES ⬅ Bureau of International Narcotics and Law Enforcement Affairs

2009 INCSR: Policy and Program Developments

Overview for 2008

International narcotics trafficking directly threatens the national security of the United States. Drugs sold on U.S. streets lead to overdose deaths and ruined lives, erode families, and foster criminality and violence. Trafficking organizations, looking to build their customer base, sometimes pay in drugs instead of cash, promoting drug abuse and its social consequences in source and transit countries in Latin America, the Caribbean, Africa, and Asia. Many of these same countries are besieged by narcotics criminals who corrupt and financially undermine legitimate law enforcement and government institutions. The environment is equally threatened, as drug producers hack down forests and dump toxic chemicals in fragile ecosystems.

The United States Government (USG) confronts the threat of international narcotics trafficking through a combination of law enforcement investigation, interdiction, diplomatic initiatives, targeted economic sanctions, financial programs and investigations, and institutional development initiatives focused on disrupting all segments of the illicit drug market, from the fields and clandestine laboratories where drugs are produced, through the transit zones, to our ports and borders. In 2008, U.S. federal law enforcement officials worked cooperatively with the police of partner nations to conduct international investigations that successfully apprehended, among others, Zhenli Ye Gon, Eduardo Arellano Felix, and Haji Juma Khan. Another international law enforcement operation involving the DEA, the Royal Thai Police, the Romanian Border Police, the Korps Politie Curacao of the Netherlands Antilles, and the Danish National Police Security Services led to the arrest of Victor Bout on charges of attempting to provide sophisticated weapons to the narco-terrorist organization the Fuerzas Armadas Revolucionarias de Colombia.[1]

The USG continued to provide partner nations with essential training assistance to strengthen their law enforcement and judicial systems and helped them improve their capacity to investigate, prosecute, and punish transnational criminal activity. Closer international cooperation among governments and financial institutions continues to close the loopholes that allow

From *2009 INCSR Report: Policy and Program Developments*, 2009. Published by Bureau of International Narcotics and Law Enforcement Affairs, U.S. Department of State.

narcotrafficking organizations to legitimize their enormous profits through sophisticated money laundering schemes.

Much of our cooperation with partner nations occurred under bilateral arrangements for mutual legal assistance, extraditions, and training programs. Multilateral efforts also continued to be a key component of the overall U.S. counternarcotics strategy. Through multilateral organizations, the United States has the opportunity to encourage contributions from other donors so that we can undertake counternarcotics assistance programs, jointly sharing costs and expertise. U.S. participation in multilateral programs also supports indigenous capabilities in regions where the United States is unable to operate bilaterally for political or logistical reasons. Counternarcotics assistance through international organizations promotes awareness that drug producing and transit countries inevitably become consuming nations; today it is clearly understood that drugs are not a U.S. problem, but a global challenge.

One example of working with partner donors is the Good Performers Initiative (GPI) in Afghanistan, a U.S.-UK-funded initiative launched in 2006 to reward provinces for successful counternarcotics performance. Based on the results of the UN Office on Drugs and Crime's annual Afghanistan Opium Cultivation Survey, this incentive program provides funds for development projects to provinces that were poppy-free or reduced their poppy cultivation by more than 10 percent from the previous year. In 2008, 29 of Afghanistan's 34 provinces qualified for over $39 million in GPI development assistance projects. To date, the U.S. government has contributed over $69 million to GPI and its predecessor the Good Performer's Fund, while the UK has provided approximately $12 million. In Nangarhar province, for example, four micro-hydro projects that generate electricity for rural villages have been completed with these funds and 20 more are scheduled to be built in 2009.

International treaties are another key tool in the fight against international narcotics trafficking. Three mutually reinforcing UN conventions are particularly important:

- The Single Convention on Narcotic Drugs—1961
- The Convention on Psychotropic Substances—1971, and
- The United Nations Convention against Illicit Traffic in Narcotic Drugs and Psychotropic Substances (the "1988 UN Drug Convention")

The 1988 UN Drug Convention is nearly universally accepted and serves as one of the bases for this report (For a full explanation, see the chapter titled "Legislative Basis for the INCSR"). A list of the countries that are parties to the 1988 UN Drug Convention is included in this report (source: UNODC). In 2008, there were no additional parties to the 1988 UN Drug Convention. Although the Convention does not contain a list of goals and objectives, it does set forth a number of obligations that the parties agree to undertake. Generally speaking, it requires the parties to take legal measures to outlaw and punish all forms of illicit drug production, trafficking, and drug money laundering; to control chemicals that can be used to process illicit drugs; and to cooperate in international efforts to these ends.

In addition to the UN conventions that are focused exclusively on drugs, newer international instruments, such as the United Nations Convention against Transnational Organized Crime and the United Nations Convention against Corruption, have helped in the fight against the international narcotics trade by making law enforcement cooperation, extraditions, border security, and tracking of illicit funds more efficient among the parties to the treaties.

While most countries are parties to the UN conventions, the ultimate success of international drug control efforts does not hinge completely on whether countries are parties to them. The vast majority of countries also have their own domestic laws and policies to support their obligations under the conventions. Success in international drug control depends on international political will to meet the commitments made when countries joined the UN conventions. Sustainable progress also requires sufficient capacities to enforce the rule of law and implementing the objectives of committed governments. To assist this process, the United States is committed to enhancing the capacity of partner governments to uphold their international commitments.

Controlling Supply

Cocaine, amphetamine-type stimulants (ATS), marijuana and heroin are the internationally trafficked drugs that most threaten the United States and our international allies. The United States is a producer of two of these drugs, marijuana and ATS. The USG is committed to confronting the illicit cultivation and manufacture of these drugs. In 2007, the DEA-initiated Domestic Cannabis Eradication/Suppression Program was responsible for the eradication of 6,600,000 cultivated outdoor cannabis plants and 430,000 indoor plants. In 2008, California alone eradicated 5,250,000 plants. Pharmaceutical preparations containing ephedrine and pseudoephedrine are the primary chemicals necessary for methamphetamine production. The Combat Methamphetamine Epidemic Act (CMEA), passed in 2005, established regulations for the sale of such products in the United States and became effective at the national level for the first time in late 2006. In 2008, the Methamphetamine Production Prevention Act was passed allowing states to institute computerized log books of purchases of methamphetamine precursor preparations. According to the National Clandestine Laboratory Database, methamphetamine lab incidents reported by all law enforcement agencies nationwide declined from more than 17,000 in 2005 to 5,900 in 2007 (2007 is the last complete year for which there are statistics, preliminary 2008 statistics are discussed later in this chapter, but the number in 2008 is expected to remain well below 50% of the 2005 figure). This dramatic decline is due to increased enforcement, the controls authorized by the two recent methamphetamine acts, and public and private demand reduction efforts.

In addition to eradicating marijuana crops found within the United States as part of our drug control strategy, the USG has provided assistance to countries that have made a policy decision to eradicate illicit crops as part of their own comprehensive drug control strategies. Crops in the ground are one of the critical nodes of production. Coca and poppy crops require adequate growing conditions, ample land, and time to reach maturity, all of which make them vulnerable to detection and eradication.

Perhaps the most acute and crucial challenge of achieving sustainable development in territories where drug cultivation takes place is the need to integrate otherwise marginalized regions into the economic and political mainstream of their country. The term that is most often used for this by the United States, the United Nations, and other international actors is "alternative development." Alternative development goes far beyond crop substitution, the usual assumed meaning. In some situations, crop substitution is neither feasible nor desirable. In some areas, the same soil that supports illicit drug crop cultivation does not have adequate nutrients to support licit crops. Licit crops rarely produce the same income as drug crops, and in some cases, farmers will need inducement to pursue non-agricultural pursuits. Anecdotal evidence suggests that in 2008 economic and environmental inducements caused many farmers in Afghanistan to plant wheat instead of poppy. One factor that possibly influenced this shift was the rise in global food prices, making wheat a more viable economic alternative to poppy. Other powerful inducements could include access to credit, improved security, and the provision of government services such as the building of roads, schools, and health centers, and a reliable supplying of basic services like electricity and water, and the threat of losing an investment in illicit crops to eradication or asset forfeiture. These programs are vulnerable to disruption from crime, corruption and non-state actors, such as the FARC in Colombia or the Taliban in Afghanistan. Establishing them on the ground is a lengthy, sometimes frustrating process; however, if implemented correctly, alternative development is an effective policy. Without it, crop eradication alone will never amount to more than a temporary palliative, and will not achieve sustainable reduction of illicit narcotic crops. However, without security and government control of outlaw areas, neither program can succeed.

For synthetic drugs, such as ATS, physical eradication is impossible. Instead, the United States and our allies must create a legal regime of chemical controls and law enforcement efforts aimed at thwarting those who divert key chemicals, and destroying the laboratories needed to create ATS. As with our domestic enforcement efforts, our international programs focus on all the links in the supply-to-consumer chain: processing, distribution, and transportation, as well as the money trail left by this illegal trade.

Cocaine

The rate of U.S. cocaine consumption has generally declined over the past decade. From 2002 to 2007, rates of past-year use among youths aged 12 to 17 declined significantly for cocaine as well as for illicit drugs overall (Source: SAMHSA, Office of Applied Studies, National Survey on Drug Use and Health). Despite the declines, cocaine continues to be a major domestic concern. Internationally, cocaine continues to pose considerable risk to societies in the Americas, and increasingly to fragile transit states in West Africa. The 2008 World Drug Report by the UN Office of Drugs and Crime noted, as it has in previous years, that the decline in cocaine consumption and demand in North America has been replaced by demand in Europe. The UN report is hopeful that demand in Europe is leveling off, but notes that, "the growth in markets which are either close to source (South America) or on emerging trafficking routes (Africa) indicate that further containment is still a challenge."

Since all cocaine originates in the Andean countries of Colombia, Peru, and Bolivia, the U.S. Government provides assistance to help these countries develop and implement comprehensive strategies to reduce the growing of coca, processing coca into cocaine, abuse of cocaine within their borders, and illegal transport of cocaine to other countries.

Coca Eradication/Alternative Development: The 2008 Interagency Assessment of Cocaine Movement (IACM) estimates that between 500 and 700 metric tons (MT) of cocaine departed South America toward the United States in 2007, slightly less than the previous year's estimate of 510 to 730 metric tons. We support efforts by these governments to eliminate illegal coca. Alternative development programs offer farmers opportunities to abandon illegal activities and join the legitimate economy, a key tool for countries seeking to free their agricultural sector from reliance on the drug trade. In the Andean countries, such programs play a vital role in providing funds and technical assistance to strengthen public and private institutions, expand rural infrastructure, improve natural resources management, introduce alternative legal crops, and develop local and international markets for these products.

In Colombia, USG alternative development (AD) initiatives supported the cultivation of over 238,000 hectares of legal crops and completed 1,212 social and productive infrastructure projects in the last seven years. More than 291,000 families in 18 departments have benefited from these programs, and the USG has worked with Colombia's private sector to create an additional 273,000 full-time equivalent jobs.

At the close of the sixth year of the Peru alternative development program, more than 756 communities have renounced coca cultivation and over 49,000 family farmers have received technical assistance on 61,000 hectares of licit crops (cacao, coffee, African palm oil, etc.). With many of these long-term crops now entering their most productive years, the alternative development program has expanded business development activities to link AD producers to local and world markets at optimum prices. The direct link between AD and eradication is successfully reducing coca cultivation and is a model for further progress against illicit cultivation.

In 2008, the annual value of USAID-promoted exports reached almost $35 million in Bolivia, assistance to farm communities and businesses helped generate 5,459 new jobs, new sales of AD products of nearly $28 million, and approximately 717 kilometers of roads were improved and 16 bridges constructed. However, these cooperative efforts were overshadowed by the Government of Bolivia's (GOB) ousting of USAID from the Chapare region.

The government of Colombia dedicates significant resources to reduce coca growing and cocaine production; however, its large territory and ideal climate conditions make Colombia the source of roughly 60 percent of the cocaine produced in the region and around 90 percent of the cocaine destined for the United States, with Peru and Bolivia a distant second and third respectively.

In 2008, the Colombian National Police (CNP) Anti-Narcotics Directorate reported aerial spraying of over 130,000 hectares of coca and manually eradicating over 96,000 hectares despite entrenched armed resistance by the FARC, a drug-trafficking organization that is also a designated Foreign Terrorist Organization. If harvested and refined, this eradicated coca could have yielded hundreds of metric tons of cocaine worth billions of dollars on U.S. streets.

In 2008, Peru exceeded its eradication goals for the second year in a row by eradicating more than 10,000 hectares. This success was achieved despite the continued targeting of eradication teams by the Shining Path, a designated Foreign Terrorist Organization (FTO). The Shining Path, which is reliant on drug trafficking for its funding, was reportedly responsible for attacks on police and military personnel in the Upper Huallaga Valley (UHV) and the Apurimac and Ene River Valleys and threatened eradication workers and other government authorities and alternative development teams. Coca growers in the UHV engaged in violent acts to resist eradication.

Bolivian President Evo Morales continued to promote his policy of "zero cocaine but not zero coca" and to push for legitimization of coca. His administration continues to pursue policies that would increase government-allowed coca cultivation from 12,000 to 20,000 hectares—a change that would violate current Bolivian law and contravene the 1988 UN Drug Convention, to which Bolivia is a party. On September 11, 2008, President Morales expelled the U.S. Ambassador to Bolivia. During 2008, President Morales also expelled the Drug Enforcement Administration (DEA) from Bolivia and the U.S. Agency for International Development from the coca-growing Chapare region. Coupled with continued increases in coca cultivation, cocaine production, and the Government of Bolivia's (GOB) unwillingness to regulate "licit" coca markets, President Bush determined on September 15 that Bolivia had "failed demonstrably" in meeting its international counterdrug obligations. For greater detail see the memorandum of justification in this report.

Cocaine Seizures: Colombian authorities reported seizing over 223 metric tons of cocaine in 2008, an all-time record, and destroyed 301 cocaine HCl labs and 3,238 cocaine base labs. Peru reported seizing over 22 metric tons of cocaine. In Bolivia, USG-supported counternarcotics units reported seizing 26 metric tons of cocaine base and cocaine hydrochloride (HCl) and destroying 6,535 cocaine labs and maceration pits.

Collectively, the eradication of coca and seizures of cocaine within the Andean source countries prevented hundreds of metric tons of cocaine from reaching U.S. streets and deprived international drug syndicates of billions of dollars in profits.

Interdiction in the Cocaine Transit Zone: The cocaine transit zone drug flow is of double importance for the United States: it threatens our borders, and it leaves a trail of corruption and addiction in its wake that undermines the social framework of societies in Central America, Mexico and the Caribbean. Helping our neighbors police transit zones has required a well-coordinated effort among the governments of the transit zone countries and the USG. With high levels of post-seizure intelligence collection, and cooperation with allied nations, we now have more actionable intelligence within the transit zone.

The U.S. Joint Inter-Agency Task Force—South (JIATF-S), working closely with international partners from throughout the Caribbean Basin, has focused its and regional partners' intelligence gathering efforts to detect, monitor, and seize maritime drug shipments. The USG's bilateral agreements with Caribbean and Latin American countries have eased the burden on these countries by allowing the United States to conduct boardings and search for contraband on their behalf. They also allow the USG to gain jurisdiction over cases, removing the coercive pressure from large drug trafficking organizations on some foreign governments.

Mexican law enforcement reported seizing 19 metric tons (MT) of cocaine in 2008.

Venezuela reported seizures of over 54 metric tons of cocaine in 2008. However, the Government of Venezuela does not allow the USG to confirm its seizures, and these figures include seizures made by other countries in international waters that were subsequently returned to Venezuela, the country of origin. According to the U.S. government's Consolidated Counterdrug Database, 239 non-commercial cocaine flights departed Venezuela in 2008, some bound for Caribbean islands in route to major markets.

Dominican authorities seized approximately 2.4 metric tons of cocaine. There was a fifteen percent increase in drug smuggling flights to Haiti in 2008. While Haitian law enforcement units worked to improve their response to air smuggling of cocaine, the seizure and arrest results were limited.

West Africa has become a hub for cocaine trafficking from South America to Europe. Although according the UNODC's 2008 *World Drug Report,* Africa accounts for less than 2 percent of global cocaine seizures, this number is expected to rise in future years. Seizures of cocaine in Africa reached 15 MT in 2006, but were below 1 MT between 1998 and 2002. Out of the total number of cocaine seizures made in Europe in 2007 (where the 'origin' had been identified), 22% were smuggled via Africa, up from 12% in 2006 and 5% in 2004. This onslaught is due to more effective interdiction along traditional trafficking routes, and the convenient location of West Africa between Andean cocaine suppliers and European consumers. It also reflects the vulnerability of West African countries to transnational organized crime.

Synthetic Drugs

Amphetamine-Type Stimulants (ATS): Abuse and trafficking in highly addictive amphetamine-type stimulants (ATS) remain among the more serious challenges in the drug-control arena. The 2008 edition of the UN Office of Drugs and Crime's World Drug Report notes that a stabilization in the ATS market over the past three years appears to have occurred in parallel with the implementation of precursor control programs and prevention programs. The report states that ATS abuse has decreased in the United States and increases in consumption have slowed in some other markets, such as Europe and Asia. Consumption, however, has increased in the Middle East and Africa.

Methamphetamine production and distribution are undergoing significant changes in the United States. The number of reported methamphetamine laboratory seizures in the United States decreased each year from 2004 through 2007; however, preliminary 2008 data and reporting indicate that domestic methamphetamine production, while still well below its peak, is increasing in some areas, and laboratory seizures for 2008 outpaced seizures in 2007. The pattern of decreased lab presence from 2004–2007 was probably due in part to increasingly effective domestic controls over the retail sale of licit pharmaceutical preparations containing ephedrine and pseudoephedrine, the primary chemicals necessary for methamphetamine. Regulations for the sale of such products in the United States became effective at the national level for the first time in late 2006 under the Combat Methamphetamine Epidemic Act (CMEA). To capitalize on these gains and prevent production from merely shifting ground, the U.S. Government enhanced the scale and pace of its law enforcement cooperation with the Government of Mexico to target the production and trafficking of methamphetamine. For its part, according to the National Drug Intelligence Center's 2009 National Drug Threat Assessment, ephedrine and pseudoephedrine import restrictions in Mexico contributed to a decrease in methamphetamine production in Mexico and reduced the flow of the drug from Mexico to the United States in 2007 and 2008. Methamphetamine shortages were reported in some drug markets in the Pacific, Southwest, and West Central Regions during much of 2007. In some drug markets, methamphetamine shortages continued through early 2008. In 2008, however, small-scale domestic methamphetamine production increased in many areas, and some Mexican drug trafficking organizations shifted their production operations from Mexico to the United States, particularly to California.

The United States is keenly aware that drug traffickers are adaptable, well-informed, and flexible. New precursor chemical trans-shipment routes may be emerging in Southeast Asia and Africa, and there is also ample evidence that organized criminal groups ship currently uncontrolled chemical analogues of ephedrine and pseudoephedrine for use in manufacturing illicit methamphetamine-type drugs. Some methamphetamine produced in Canada is distributed in U.S. drug markets and Canada is a source country for MDMA to U.S. markets as well as a transit or diversion point for precursor chemicals used to produce illicit synthetic drugs (notably MDMA, or ecstasy), according to the NDIC 2009 National Drug Threat Assessment.

The Netherlands remains an important producer of ecstasy as well, although the amount of this drug reaching the United States seems to have declined substantially in recent years, following new enforcement measures by the Dutch government. Labs in Poland and elsewhere in Eastern Europe are major suppliers of amphetamines to the European market, with the United Kingdom and the Nordic countries among the heaviest European consumers of ATS.

Pharmaceutical Abuse and the Internet: According to the National Drug Intelligence Center's December 2008 *National Drug Threat Assessment,* the number of Internet sites offering sales of controlled prescription drugs decreased in 2008, for the first time after several years of increase. It is not known what percentage of this abuse involves international sources. In the United States, the Ryan Haight Online Pharmacy Consumer Protection Act of 2008 was enacted in October 2008. The new federal law amends the Controlled Substances Act and prohibits the delivery, distribution, or dispensing of controlled prescription drugs over the Internet without a prescription written by a doctor who has conducted at least one in-person examination of the patient.

Cannabis (Marijuana)

Cannabis production and marijuana consumption continue to appear in nearly every world region, including in the United States. Marijuana still remains the most widely used of all of the illicit drugs. According to the December 2008 "Monitoring the Future" study, marijuana use among 8th, 10th, and 12th graders was not statistically different from the year before. However, since the peak years of the mid-1990s, annual use has fallen by over 40 percent among 8th graders, 30 percent among 10th graders, and nearly 20 percent among 12th graders. The prevalence rates for marijuana use in the prior year now stand at 11 percent, 24 percent, and 32 percent for grades 8, 10, and 12, respectively.

Drug organizations in Mexico produced more than 15,000 metric tons of marijuana in 2008, much of which was marketed to the more than 20 million users in the United States. Overall, Canada supplies a small proportion of the overall amount of marijuana consumed in the United States; however, large-scale cultivation of high potency marijuana is a thriving illicit industry in Canada. Other source countries for marijuana include Colombia, Jamaica, and possibly Nigeria. Production of marijuana within the United States may exceed that of foreign sources.

According to the U.S. Drug Enforcement Administration (DEA), marijuana potency has increased sharply. Of great concern is the high potency, indoor-grown cannabis produced on a large scale in Canada and the United States in laboratory conditions using specialized timers, ventilation, moveable lights on tracks, nutrients sprayed on exposed roots and special fertilizer that maximize THC levels. The result is a particularly powerful and dangerous drug.

Opium and Heroin

Opium poppy, the source of heroin, is cultivated mainly in Afghanistan, Southeast Asia, and on a smaller scale in Colombia and Mexico. In contrast to coca, a perennial which takes at least a year to mature into usable leaf, opium poppy is an easily planted annual crop. Opium gum can take less than 6 months from planting to harvest.

In Afghanistan, a combination of factors led to a reduction in the cultivation and production of opium for the first time in several years. Among these factors were: including Afghan government and international donor programs that rewarded entire provinces for decreasing or eliminating opium cultivation; increased prices for other commodities such as wheat; decreased prices for opium; and bad weather. Nangarhar province alone shifted from having the second highest area of poppy cultivation in 2007 to achieving poppy-free status in 2008. This was due in large part to the high-profile law enforcement and incentives campaign implemented by the provincial governor. Even with this limited progress, Afghanistan continues to be the source of more than 90% of the world's illicit opiates. This glut of narcotics has fueled increasing addiction rates in Afghanistan, Pakistan, and Iran. The narcotics trade thrives in the conditions created by insurgents and warlords, who exact a portion of the profits for protection of crops, labs, trucks, and drug markets. Exact figures for the black market economy are impossible to obtain, but the UN estimates that the Taliban and other anti-government forces have extorted $50 million to $70 million in protection payments from opium farmers and an additional $200 to $400 million of income in forced levies on the more-lucrative drug processing and trafficking in 2008.

Most of the heroin used in the United States comes from poppies grown in Colombia and Mexico, although both countries are minor producers in global terms. Mexico supplies most of the heroin found in the western United States while Colombia supplies most of the heroin east of the Mississippi. Long-standing joint eradication programs in both countries continue with our support. Colombian law enforcement reported eradicating 381 hectares of opium poppy in 2008. We estimate that poppy cultivation decreased 25 percent from 2006 to 2007 in directly comparable areas of Colombia. This led to a 27 percent drop in potential production of heroin and a 19 percent decrease in purity of Colombian heroin seized in the United States, according to the DEA. The Government of Mexico (GOM) reported eradicating 12,035 hectares of opium poppy.

Controlling Drug-Processing Chemicals

Cocaine and heroin are manufactured with certain critical chemicals, some of which also have licit uses but are diverted by criminals. The most commonly used chemicals in the manufacture of these illegal drugs are potassium permanganate (for cocaine) and acetic anhydride (for heroin). Government controls strive to differentiate between licit commercial use for these chemicals and illicit diversion to criminals. Governments must have efficient legal and regulatory regimes to control such chemicals, without placing undue burdens on legitimate commerce. Extensive international law enforcement cooperation is also required to prevent their diversion from licit commercial channels, and to investigate, arrest and dismantle the illegal networks engaged in their procurement. This topic is addressed in greater detail in the Chemical Control Chapter of this report.

Drugs and the Environment

Impact of Drug Cultivation and Processing: Illegal drug production usually takes place in remote areas far removed from the authority of central governments. Not surprisingly, drug criminals practice none of the environmental safeguards that are required for licit industry, and the toxic chemicals used to process raw organic materials into finished drugs are invariably dumped into sensitive ecosystems without regard for human health or the costs to the environment. Coca growers routinely slash and burn remote, virgin forestland in the Amazon to make way for their illegal crops; coca growers typically cut down up to 4 hectares of forest for every hectare of coca planted. Tropical rains quickly erode the thin topsoil of the fields, increasing soil runoff and depleting soil nutrients. By destroying timber and other resources, illicit coca cultivation decreases biological diversity in one of the most sensitive ecological areas in the world. In Colombia and elsewhere, traffickers also destroy jungle forests to build clandestine landing strips and laboratories for processing raw coca and poppy into cocaine and heroin.

Illicit coca growers use large quantities of highly toxic herbicides and fertilizers on their crops. These chemicals qualify under the U.S. Environmental Protection Agency's highest classification for toxicity (Category I) and are legally restricted for sale within Colombia and the United States. Production of the drugs requires large quantities of dangerous solvents and chemicals. One kilogram of cocaine base requires the use of three liters of concentrated sulfuric acid, 10 kilograms of lime, 60 to 80 liters of kerosene, 200 grams of potassium permanganate, and one liter of concentrated ammonia. These toxic pesticides, fertilizers, and processing chemicals are then dumped into the nearest waterway or on the ground. They saturate the soil and contaminate waterways and poison water systems upon which local human and animal populations rely. In the United States, marijuana-processing operations take place in national parks, especially in California and Texas near the border with Mexico. These marijuana growing operations leave behind tons of garbage, biohazard refuse, and toxic waste. They also contribute to erosion as land is compacted and small streams and other water sources are diverted for irrigating the illegal marijuana fields.

Methamphetamine is also alarming in its environmental impact. For each pound of methamphetamine produced in clandestine methamphetamine laboratories, five to six pounds of toxic, hazardous waste are generated, posing immediate and long-term environmental health risks, not only to individual homes but to neighborhoods. Poisonous vapors produced during synthesis permeate the walls and carpets of houses and buildings, often making them uninhabitable. Cleaning up these sites in the United States and Mexico requires specialized training and costs thousands of dollars per site.

Impact of Spray Eradication: Colombia is currently the only country that conducts regular aerial spraying of coca, although countries throughout the world regularly spray other crops with herbicides. The only active ingredient in the herbicide used in the aerial eradication program is glyphosate, which has been thoroughly tested in the United States, Colombia, and elsewhere. The U.S. Environmental Protection Agency (EPA) approved glyphosate for general use in 1974 and re-registered it in September 1993. EPA has approved its use on food croplands, forests, residential areas, and around aquatic areas. It is one of the most widely used herbicides in the world. Colombia's spray program represents a small fraction of total glyphosate use in the country. Biannual verification missions continue to show that aerial eradication causes no significant damage to the environment or human health. The eradication program follows strict environmental safeguards, monitored permanently by several Colombian government agencies, and adheres to all laws and regulations, including the Colombian Environmental Management Plan. In addition to the biannual verification missions, soil and water samples are taken before and after spray for analysis. The residues in these samples have never reached a level outside the established regulatory norms. The OAS, which published a study in 2005 positively assessing the chemicals and methodologies used in the aerial spray program, is currently conducting further investigations expected to be completed in early 2009 regarding spray drift and other issues.

Attacking Trafficking Organizations

Law enforcement tactics have grown more sophisticated over the past two decades to counter the ever-evolving tactics used by trafficking networks to transport large volumes of drugs internationally. Rather than measuring progress purely by seizures and numbers of arrests, international law enforcement authorities have increasingly targeted resources against the highest levels of drug trafficking organizations. Increasingly, international law enforcement authorities are learning the art of conspiracy investigations, using mutual legal assistance mechanisms and other advanced investigative techniques to follow the evidence to higher and higher levels of leadership within the syndicates, and cooperating on extradition so that the kingpins have no place to hide. These sophisticated law enforcement and legal tools are endorsed as recommended practices within both the 1988 UN Drug Control Convention and the UN Convention against Transnational Organized Crime.

The drug trade depends upon reliable and efficient distribution systems to get its product to market. While most illicit distribution systems have short-term back-up channels to compensate for temporary law enforcement disruptions, a network under intense enforcement pressure cannot function for long. In cooperation with law enforcement officials in other nations, our goal is to disrupt and dismantle these organizations, to remove the leadership and the facilitators who launder money and provide the chemicals needed for the production of illicit drugs, and to destroy their networks. By capturing the leaders of trafficking organizations, we demonstrate both to the criminals and to the governments fighting them that even the most powerful drug syndicates are vulnerable to concerted action by international law enforcement authorities.

Mexican drug syndicates continue to oversee much of the drug trafficking into the United States, with a strong presence in most of the primary U.S. distribution centers. President Calderon's counternarcotics programs seek to address some of the most basic institutional issues that have traditionally confounded Mexico's success against the cartels. The Government of Mexico is using the military to reestablish sovereign authority and counter the cartels' firepower, moving to establish integrity within the ranks of the police, and giving law enforcement officials and judicial authorities the resources and the legal underpinning they need to succeed.

To help Mexico achieve these goals, the United States Congress appropriated $465 million in June 2008 to provide inspection equipment to interdict trafficked drugs, arms, cash and persons; secure communications systems for law enforcement agencies; and technical advice and training to strengthen judicial institutions. Similarly, Congress has provided support to Central American countries, including the continued implementation of the USG's anti-gang strategy, support for specialized vetted units and judicial reforms, and enhanced land and maritime drug interdiction.

This appropriation will complement existing and planned initiatives of U.S. domestic law enforcement agencies engaged with counterparts in each participating country. On December 3, 2008, a Letter of Agreement (LOA) was signed with the Government of Mexico obligating $197 million of the funding for counternarcotics programs. On December 19, the governments of the United States and Mexico met to coordinate the implementation of the Mérida Initiative through a cabinet-level High Level Group, which underscored the urgency and importance of the Initiative. A working level inter-agency implementation meeting was held February 3 in Mexico City with the aim of accelerating the rollout of the 39 projects for Mexico under the Initiative. In addition, LOAs were signed with Honduras on January 9, El Salvador on January 12, Guatemala on February 5 and Belize on February 9.

Extradition

There are few legal sanctions that international criminals fear as much as extradition to the United States, where they can no longer use bribes and intimidation to manipulate the local judicial process. Governments willing to risk domestic political repercussions to extradite drug kingpins to the United States are finding that public acceptance of this measure has steadily increased.

Mexican authorities extradited 95 persons to the United States in 2008. Colombia has an outstanding record of extradition of drug criminals to the United States, and the numbers have increased even more in recent years. The Government of Colombia extradited a record 208 defendants in 2008. Since President Uribe assumed office in 2002, 789 individuals have been extradited.

Institutional Reform

Fighting Corruption: Among all criminal enterprises, the drug trade is best positioned to spread corruption and undermine the integrity and effectiveness of legitimate governments. Drugs generate illegal revenues on a scale without historical precedent. No commodity is so widely available, so cheap to produce, and as easily renewable as illegal drugs. A kilogram of cocaine can be sold in the United States for more than 15 times its value in Colombia, a return that dwarfs regular commodities and distorts the licit economy.

No government is completely safe from the threat of drug-related corruption, but fragile democracies in post-conflict situations are particularly vulnerable. The weakening of government institutions through bribery and intimidation ultimately poses just as great a danger to democratic governments as the challenge of armed insurgents. Drug syndicates seek to subvert governments in order to guarantee themselves a secure operating environment. Unchecked, the drug cartels have the wherewithal to buy their way into power. By keeping a focus on fighting corruption, we can help avoid the threat of a drug lord–controlled state.

Improving Criminal Justice Systems: A pivotal element of USG international drug control policy is to help strengthen enforcement, judicial, and financial institutions worldwide. Strong institutions limit the opportunities for infiltration and corruption by the drug trade. Corruption within a criminal justice system has an enormously detrimental impact; law enforcement agencies in drug source and transit countries may arrest influential drug criminals only to see them released following a questionable or inexplicable decision by a single judge, or a prosecutor may obtain an arrest warrant but be unable to find police who will execute it. Efforts by governments to enact basic reforms involving transparency, efficiency, and better pay for police and judges helps to build societies based on the rule of law.

Strengthening Border Security: Drug trafficking organizations must move their products across international borders. A key element in stopping the flow of narcotics is to help countries strengthen their border controls. Through training and technical assistance we improve the capability of countries to control the movement of people and goods across their borders. Effective border security can disrupt narcotics smuggling operations, forcing traffickers to adjust their methods and making them vulnerable to further detection and law enforcement action.

Note

1. The focus of this report is on the international aspects of drug trafficking, but we want also to acknowledge the hard work of law enforcement, drug prevention, and drug treatment professionals within the United States who work every day to reduce the demand for illicit drugs and to reduce the misery they bring to our own citizens. Federal, state, local, and tribal law enforcement agencies within the United States dedicate significant resources to confronting drug criminals. The United States has substantial public and private sector programs focused on drug prevention and treatment and has invested in cutting-edge medical and social research on how to decrease demand. We are proud of the results and have worked with the Organization of American States, the United Nations, and countries all over the world to share programs such as drug courts, early intervention, school and work-place drug testing coupled with counseling and other interventions, and medically sound treatment options that help addicted persons reclaim their lives. For more information about domestic drug control efforts, please see the National Drug Control Strategy of the White House Office of National Drug Control Policy, available on the . . . website.

Ethan Nadelmann  **NO**

The Global War on Drugs
Can Be Won

No, it can't. A "drug-free world," which the United Nations describes as a realistic goal, is no more attainable than an "alcohol-free world"—and no one has talked about that with a straight face since the repeal of Prohibition in the United States in 1933. Yet futile rhetoric about winning a "war on drugs" persists, despite mountains of evidence documenting its moral and ideological bankruptcy. When the U.N. General Assembly Special Session on drugs convened in 1998, it committed to "eliminating or significantly reducing the illicit cultivation of the coca bush, the cannabis plant and the opium poppy by the year 2008" and to "achieving significant and measurable results in the field of demand reduction." But today, global production and consumption of those drugs are roughly the same as they were a decade ago; meanwhile, many producers have become more efficient, and cocaine and heroin have become purer and cheaper.

It's always dangerous when rhetoric drives policy—and especially so when "war on drugs" rhetoric leads the public to accept collateral casualties that would never be permissible in civilian law enforcement, much less public health. Politicians still talk of eliminating drugs from the Earth as though their use is a plague on humanity. But drug control is not like disease control, for the simple reason that there's no popular demand for smallpox or polio. Cannabis and opium have been grown throughout much of the world for millennia. The same is true for coca in Latin America. Methamphetamine and other synthetic drugs can be produced anywhere. Demand for particular illicit drugs waxes and wanes, depending not just on availability but also fads, fashion, culture, and competition from alternative means of stimulation and distraction. The relative harshness of drug laws and the intensity of enforcement matter surprisingly little, except in totalitarian states. After all, rates of illegal drug use in the United States are the same as, or higher than, Europe, despite America's much more punitive policies.

We Can Reduce the Demand for Drugs

Good luck. Reducing the demand for illegal drugs seems to make sense. But the desire to alter one's state of consciousness, and to use psychoactive drugs to do so, is nearly universal—and mostly not a problem. There's virtually never been a drug-free society, and more drugs are discovered and devised every year.

Reprinted in entirety by McGraw-Hill with permission from *FOREIGN POLICY,* September/October 2007, pp. 24–26, 28–29. www.foreignpolicy.com. © 2007 Washingtonpost.Newsweek Interactive, LLC.

Demand-reduction efforts that rely on honest education and positive alternatives to drug use are helpful, but not when they devolve into unrealistic, "zero tolerance" policies.

As with sex, abstinence from drugs is the best way to avoid trouble, but one always needs a fallback strategy for those who can't or won't refrain. "Zero tolerance" policies deter some people, but they also dramatically increase the harms and costs for those who don't resist. Drugs become more potent, drug use becomes more hazardous, and people who use drugs are marginalized in ways that serve no one.

The better approach is not demand reduction but "harm reduction." Reducing drug use is fine, but it's not nearly as important as reducing the death, disease, crime, and suffering associated with both drug misuse and failed prohibitionist policies. With respect to legal drugs, such as alcohol and cigarettes, harm reduction means promoting responsible drinking and designated drivers, or persuading people to switch to nicotine patches, chewing gums, and smokeless tobacco. With respect to illegal drugs, it means reducing the transmission of infectious disease through syringe-exchange programs, reducing overdose fatalities by making antidotes readily available, and allowing people addicted to heroin and other illegal opiates to obtain methadone from doctors and even pharmaceutical heroin from clinics. Britain, Canada, Germany, the Netherlands, and Switzerland have already embraced this last option. There's no longer any question that these strategies decrease drug-related harms without increasing drug use. What blocks expansion of such programs is not cost; they typically save taxpayers' money that would otherwise go to criminal justice and healthcare. No, the roadblocks are abstinence-only ideologues and a cruel indifference to the lives and well-being of people who use drugs.

Reducing the Supply of Drugs Is the Answer

Not if history is any guide. Reducing supply makes as much sense as reducing demand; after all, if no one were planting cannabis, coca, and opium, there wouldn't be any heroin, cocaine, or marijuana to sell or consume. But the carrot and stick of crop eradication and substitution have been tried and failed, with rare exceptions, for half a century. These methods may succeed in targeted locales, but they usually simply shift production from one region to another: Opium production moves from Pakistan to Afghanistan; coca from Peru to Colombia; and cannabis from Mexico to the United States, while overall global production remains relatively constant or even increases.

The carrot, in the form of economic development and assistance in switching to legal crops, is typically both late and inadequate. The stick, often in the form of forced eradication, including aerial spraying, wipes out illegal and legal crops alike and can be hazardous to both people and local environments. The best thing to be said for emphasizing supply reduction is that it provides a rationale for wealthier nations to spend a little money on economic development in poorer countries. But, for the most part, crop eradication and substitution wreak havoc among impoverished farmers without diminishing overall global supply.

The global markets in cannabis, coca, and opium products operate essentially the same way that other global commodity markets do: If one source is compromised due to bad weather, rising production costs, or political difficulties, another emerges. If international drug control circles wanted to think strategically, the key question would no longer be how to reduce global supply, but rather: Where does illicit production cause the fewest problems (and the greatest benefits)? Think of it as a global vice control challenge. No one expects to eradicate vice, but it must be effectively zoned and regulated—even if it's illegal.

U.S. Drug Policy Is the World's Drug Policy

Sad, but true. Looking to the United States as a role model for drug control is like looking to apartheid-era South Africa for how to deal with race. The United States ranks first in the world in per capita incarceration—with less than 5 percent of the world's population, but almost 25 percent of the world's prisoners. The number of people locked up for U.S. drug-law violations has increased from roughly 50,000 in 1980 to almost 500,000 today; that's more than the number of people Western Europe locks up for everything. Even more deadly is U.S. resistance to syringe-exchange programs to reduce HIV/AIDS both at home and abroad. Who knows how many people might not have contracted HIV if the United States had implemented at home, and supported abroad, the sorts of syringe-exchange and other harm-reduction programs that have kept HIV/AIDS rates so low in Australia, Britain, the Netherlands, and elsewhere. Perhaps millions.

And yet, despite this dismal record, the United States has succeeded in constructing an international drug prohibition regime modeled after its own highly punitive and moralistic approach. It has dominated the drug control agencies of the United Nations and other international organizations, and its federal drug enforcement agency was the first national police organization to go global. Rarely has one nation so successfully promoted its own failed policies to the rest of the world.

But now, for the first time, U.S. hegemony in drug control is being challenged. The European Union is demanding rigorous assessment of drug control strategies. Exhausted by decades of service to the U.S.-led war on drugs, Latin Americans are far less inclined to collaborate closely with U.S. drug enforcement efforts. Finally waking up to the deadly threat of HIV/AIDS, China, Indonesia, Vietnam, and even Malaysia and Iran are increasingly accepting of syringe-exchange and other harm-reduction programs. In 2005, the ayatollah in charge of Iran's Ministry of Justice issued a *fatwa* declaring methadone maintenance and syringe-exchange programs compatible with *sharia* (Islamic) law. One only wishes his American counterpart were comparably enlightened.

Afghan Opium Production Must Be Curbed

Be careful what you wish for. It's easy to believe that eliminating record-high opium production in Afghanistan—which today accounts for roughly 90 percent of global supply, up from 50 percent 10 years ago—would solve everything from heroin abuse in Europe and Asia to the resurgence of the Taliban.

But assume for a moment that the United States, NATO, and Hamid Karzai's government were somehow able to cut opium production in Afghanistan. Who would benefit? Only the Taliban, warlords, and other black-market entrepreneurs whose stockpiles of opium would skyrocket in value. Hundreds of thousands of Afghan peasants would flock to cities, ill-prepared to find work. And many Afghans would return to their farms the following year to plant another illegal harvest, utilizing guerrilla farming methods to escape intensified eradication efforts. Except now, they'd soon be competing with poor farmers elsewhere in Central Asia, Latin America, or even Africa. This is, after all, a global commodities market.

And outside Afghanistan? Higher heroin prices typically translate into higher crime rates by addicts. They also invite cheaper but more dangerous means of consumption, such as switching from smoking to injecting heroin, which results in higher HIV and hepatitis C rates. All things considered, wiping out opium in Afghanistan would yield far fewer benefits than is commonly assumed.

So what's the solution? Some recommend buying up all the opium in Afghanistan, which would cost a lot less than is now being spent trying to eradicate it. But, given that farmers somewhere will produce opium so long as the demand for heroin persists, maybe the world is better off, all things considered, with 90 percent of it coming from just one country. And if that heresy becomes the new gospel, it opens up all sorts of possibilities for pursuing a new policy in Afghanistan that reconciles the interests of the United States, NATO, and millions of Afghan citizens.

Legalization Is the Best Approach

It might be. Global drug prohibition is clearly a costly disaster. The United Nations has estimated the value of the global market in illicit drugs at $400 billion, or 6 percent of global trade. The extraordinary profits available to those willing to assume the risks enrich criminals, terrorists, violent political insurgents, and corrupt politicians and governments. Many cities, states, and even countries in Latin America, the Caribbean, and Asia are reminiscent of Chicago under Al Capone—times 50. By bringing the market for drugs out into the open, legalization would radically change all that for the better.

More importantly, legalization would strip addiction down to what it really is: a health issue. Most people who use drugs are like the responsible alcohol consumer, causing no harm to themselves or anyone else. They would no longer be the state's business. But legalization would also benefit those who struggle with drugs by reducing the risks of overdose and disease associated with unregulated products, eliminating the need to obtain drugs from dangerous criminal markets, and allowing addiction problems to be treated as medical rather than criminal problems.

No one knows how much governments spend collectively on failing drug war policies, but it's probably at least $100 billion a year, with federal, state, and local governments in the United States accounting for almost half the total. Add to that the tens of billions of dollars to be gained annually in tax revenues from the sale of legalized drugs. Now imagine if just a third of that total were committed to reducing drug-related disease and addiction. Virtually everyone, except those who profit or gain politically from the current system, would benefit.

Some say legalization is immoral. That's nonsense, unless one believes there is some principled basis for discriminating against people based solely on what they put into their bodies, absent harm to others. Others say legalization would open the floodgates to huge increases in drug abuse. They forget that we already live in a world in which psychoactive drugs of all sorts are readily available—and in which people too poor to buy drugs resort to sniffing gasoline, glue, and other industrial products, which can be more harmful than any drug. No, the greatest downside to legalization may well be the fact that the legal markets would fall into the hands of the powerful alcohol, tobacco, and pharmaceutical companies. Still, legalization is a far more pragmatic option than living with the corruption, violence, and organized crime of the current system.

Legalization Will Never Happen

Never say never. Wholesale legalization may be a long way off—but partial legalization is not. If any drug stands a chance of being legalized, it's cannabis. Hundreds of millions of people have used it, the vast majority without suffering any harm or going on to use "harder" drugs. In Switzerland, for example, cannabis legalization was twice approved by one chamber of its parliament, but narrowly rejected by the other.

Elsewhere in Europe, support for the criminalization of cannabis is waning. In the United States, where roughly 40 percent of the country's 1.8 million annual drug arrests are for cannabis possession, typically of tiny amounts, 40 percent of Americans say that the drug should be taxed, controlled, and regulated like alcohol. Encouraged by Bolivian President Evo Morales, support is also growing in Latin America and Europe for removing coca from international antidrug conventions, given the absence of any credible health reason for keeping it there. Traditional growers would benefit economically, and there's some possibility that such products might compete favorably with more problematic substances, including alcohol.

The global war on drugs persists in part because so many people fail to distinguish between the harms of drug abuse and the harms of prohibition. Legalization forces that distinction to the forefront. The opium problem in Afghanistan is primarily a prohibition problem, not a drug problem. The same is true of the narcoviolence and corruption that has afflicted Latin America and the Caribbean for almost three decades—and that now threatens Africa. Governments can arrest and kill drug lord after drug lord, but the ultimate solution is a structural one, not a prosecutorial one. Few people doubt any longer that the war on drugs is lost, but courage and vision are needed to transcend the ignorance, fear, and vested interests that sustain it.

POSTSCRIPT

Should the United States Put More Emphasis on Stopping the Importation of Drugs?

The drug trade spawns violence: people die from using drugs or by dealing with people in the drug trade; families are ruined by the effects of drugs on family members; prisons are filled with tens of thousands of people who were and probably still are involved with illegal drugs; and drugs can devastate aspirations and careers. The adverse consequences of drugs can be seen everywhere in society. How should the government determine the best course of action to follow in remedying the negative effects of drugs? Would more people be helped by reducing the availability of drugs, or would more people benefit if they could be persuaded that drugs are harmful to them?

Two paths that are traditionally followed involve reducing either the supply of drugs or the demand for drugs. Four major agencies involved in the fight against drugs in the United States—the Drug Enforcement Administration (DEA), the Federal Bureau of Investigation (FBI), the U.S. Customs Service, and the U.S. Coast Guard—have seized thousands of pounds of marijuana, cocaine, and heroin during the past few years. Drug interdiction appears to be reducing the availability of drugs. But what effect does drug availability have on use? If a particular drug is not available, would other drugs be used in its place? Would the cost of drugs increase if there were a shortage of drugs? If costs increase, would violence due to drugs go up as well?

Annual surveys of 8th-, 10th-, and 12th-grade students indicate that availability is not a major factor in drug use. Throughout the 1980s drug use declined dramatically even though marijuana and cocaine could be easily obtained. According to the surveys, the perceived harm of these drugs, not their availability, is what affects students' drug use. As individuals' perceptions of drugs as harmful increase, usage decreases; as perceptions of harm decrease, usage increases. Generally, availability of drugs is a weak predictor of drug use.

Efforts to prevent drug use may prove fruitless if people have a natural desire to alter their consciousness. In his 1989 book *Intoxication: Life in the Pursuit of Artificial Paradise* (E. P. Dutton), Ronald Siegel contends that the urge to alter consciousness is as universal as the craving for food and sex.

A publication that examines trends in world drug markets is the *World Drug Report* (2006) by the United Nations Office on Drugs and Crime. Another publication that critically views current drug policies is *How Goes the War on Drugs? An Assessment of U.S. Drug Problems and Policy* by Jonathon Caulkins and associates (RAND Drug Policy Research Center, 2005).

Articles that examine international efforts to deal with the issue of drugs include "Latin America's Drug Problem," by Michael Shifter (*Current History,* February 2007); "End the Demand, End the Supply," by Lee P. Brown (*U.S. News and World Report,* August 4, 2008); "The New Opium War," by Matthew Quirk (*The Atlantic Monthly,* March 2005); and "The Price of Powder" (*The Economist,* November 7, 2004).

ISSUE 3

Should the United States Drinking Age Remain at 21?

YES: Kenneth P. Moritsugu, from *The Surgeon General's Call to Action to Prevent and Reduce Underage Drinking* (U.S. Department of Health and Human Services, 2007)

NO: Judith G. McMullen, from "Underage Drinking: Does Current Policy Make Sense?" *Lewis & Clark Law Review* (Summer 2006)

ISSUE SUMMARY

YES: Kenneth Moritsugu, the previous United States Surgeon General, maintains that underage drinking is fraught with numerous problems ranging from motor vehicle crashes to homicide and suicide. Underage drinking is also related to unhealthy risk-taking behaviors and poor academic performance. Rather than tolerate underage drinking, more effort should be placed on enforcing underage drinking laws.

NO: Judith McMullen, a law professor at Marquette University, argues that laws prohibiting underage drinking have been ineffective. Young adults between the ages of 18 and 21 who do not live at home have opportunities to drink alcohol without parental interference. In addition, this same age group has other legal rights, such as the right to marry, drive a car, or join the military. Enforcement of underage drinking laws, says McMullen, is destined for failure.

Over 90 percent of high school seniors consume alcohol and a significant percentage of those students engage in binge drinking. There is little doubt that many students drink to excess and that many young people drink alcohol irresponsibly. Regardless of the message that many underage drinkers receive, it is unhealthy, unlawful, and potentially dangerous for young people to drink alcohol, especially in excess. The question revolves around the best way to reduce the harms associated with alcohol use. Will reducing the drinking age make it easier to teach young people to drink responsibly? Or is reducing the drinking age simply capitulating to the realities that young people drink?

One important question is whether or not young people will respond to a message of responsible alcohol consumption if they are legally allowed to drink. Because it is a recognized fact that the vast majority of people under age 21 drink alcohol, simply telling young people to not drink does not stop that behavior. However, does it make more sense to teach young people how to drink alcohol responsibly so they do not endanger themselves, their friends, or innocent bystanders? The current message, that one should wait until age 21 to drink, is not being heard by the majority of people under that age. On the other hand, will someone be more amenable to being responsible if they are allowed to drink? Will reducing the drinking age result in very young people driving while under the influence? Will young people engage in less binge drinking?

Another relevant question deals with whether or not drinking laws discriminate against people under age 21. For example, one does not need to be age 21 to enter the military service. Obviously, being in the military can result in putting one's life in danger. Sixteen-year-olds are allowed to drive a car if they pass certain requirements. Driving a car safely requires one to be very responsible. However, should one be allowed to consume alcohol at age 16 simply because one can drive a car at age 16? Many young people become parents before age 21. Marriage is permitted before age 21. Again, if one can marry and have children, then should one not have the right to drink alcohol?

Whether or not young people under age 21 will drink responsibly if they are allowed legally to drink remains unclear. If the law were changed and the drinking age lowered, with the result that drinking rates increased or other problems surfaced, how easy would it be to change the law back to 21? Perhaps whether or not young people drink responsibly has nothing to do with the current drinking age. Some people are responsible regardless of the drinking age. There are many older people who drink irresponsibly. One might argue that one should pass certain requirements, besides age, before being allowed to drink. Maybe individuals with a history of substance abuse or some other type of unlawful or inappropriate behavior should not be allowed to drink.

In 2007, the United States surgeon general published a paper with suggestions to reduce underage drinking. In this paper, the surgeon general outlined numerous goals. One goal focused on societal changes that would reduce underage drinking. Another goal attempted to get parents, caregivers, schools, communities, and all social systems to work together to address this problem. The surgeon general recommended improving surveillance of underage drinking as well as additional research on adolescent alcohol use.

Kenneth Moritsugu believes that the risk of lowering the drinking age has too many potential problems and that it would be a grievous mistake to change the drinking age from 21. To reduce drinking-related problems, better enforcement of current laws is needed. Judith McMullen believes the law is hypocritical. Setting the drinking age at 21 is arbitrary and inconsistent. There are many activities one can engage in before age 21, and McMullen cites numerous examples.

YES

Kenneth P. Moritsugu

Underage Drinking in America: Scope of the Problem

Underage alcohol consumption in the United States is a widespread and persistent public health and safety problem that creates serious personal, social, and economic consequences for adolescents, their families, communities, and the Nation as a whole. Alcohol is the drug of choice among America's adolescents, used by more young people than tobacco or illicit drugs. The prevention and reduction of underage drinking and treatment of underage youth with alcohol use disorders (AUDs) are therefore important public health and safety goals. *The Surgeon General's Call to Action To Prevent and Reduce Underage Drinking* seeks to engage all levels of government as well as individuals and private sector institutions and organizations in a coordinated, multifaceted effort to prevent and reduce underage drinking and its adverse consequences.

The impetus for this *Call to Action* is the body of research demonstrating the potential negative consequences of underage alcohol use on human maturation, particularly on the brain, which recent studies show continues to develop into a person's twenties. Although considerable attention has been focused on the serious consequences of underage drinking and driving, accumulating evidence indicates that the range of adverse consequences is much more extensive than that and should also be comprehensively addressed. For example, the highest prevalence of alcohol dependence in the U.S. population is among 18- to 20-year-olds who typically began drinking years earlier. This finding underscores the need to consider problem drinking within a developmental framework. Furthermore, early and, especially, early heavy drinking are associated with increased risk for adverse lifetime alcohol-related consequences. Research also has provided a more complete understanding of how underage drinking is related to factors in the adolescent's environment, cultural issues, and an adolescent's individual characteristics. Taken together, these data demonstrate the compelling need to address alcohol problems early, continuously, and in the context of human development using a systematic approach that spans childhood through adolescence into adulthood.

Underage drinking remains a serious problem despite laws against it in all 50 States; decades of Federal, State, Tribal, and local programs aimed

From *The Surgeon General's Call to Action to Prevent and Reduce Underage Drinking* (U.S. Department of Health and Human Services, 2007), pp. 1–13.

at preventing and reducing underage drinking; and efforts by many private entities. Underage drinking is deeply embedded in the American culture, is often viewed as a rite of passage, is frequently facilitated by adults, and has proved stubbornly resistant to change. A new, more comprehensive and developmentally sensitive approach is warranted. The growing body of research in the developmental area, including identification of risk and protective factors for underage alcohol use, supports the more complex prevention and reduction strategies that are proposed in this *Call to Action.*

Underage Alcohol Use Increases With Age. Alcohol use is an age-related phenomenon. The percentage of the population who have drunk at least one whole drink rises steeply during adolescence until it plateaus at about age 21. By age 15, approximately 50 percent of boys and girls have had a whole drink of alcohol; by age 21, approximately 90 percent have done so.

There Is a High Prevalence of Alcohol Use Disorders Among the Young. Early alcohol consumption by some young people will result in an alcohol use disorder—that is, they will meet diagnostic criteria for either alcohol abuse or dependence. The highest prevalence of alcohol dependence is among people ages 18–20. In other words, the description these young people provide of their drinking behavior meets the criteria for alcohol dependence set forth in the most recent editions of the *Diagnostic and Statistical Manual of Mental Disorders (DSM)—DSM–IV* and *DSM–IV–TR.*

　　Even some youth younger than age 18 have an alcohol use disorder. According to data from the 2005 National Survey on Drug Use and Health (NSDUH), 5.5 percent of youth ages 12–17 meet the diagnostic criteria for alcohol abuse or dependence.

The Nature of Underage Drinking

Underage alcohol use is a pervasive problem with serious health and safety consequences for the Nation. The nature and gravity of the problem is best described in terms of the number of children and adolescents who drink, when and how they drink, and the negative consequences that result from drinking.

Alcohol Is the Most Widely Used Substance of Abuse Among America's Youth. A higher percentage of youth in 8th, 10th, and 12th grades used alcohol in the month prior to being surveyed than used tobacco or marijuana, the illicit drug most commonly used by adolescents.

A Substantial Number of Young People Begin Drinking at Very Young Ages. A number of surveys ask youth about the age at which they first used alcohol. Because the methodology in the various surveys differs, the data are not consistent across them. Nonetheless, they do show that a substantial number of youth begin drinking before the age of 13. For example, data from recent surveys indicate that:

- Approximately 10 percent of 9- to 10-year-olds have started drinking.
- Nearly one-third of youth begin drinking[3] before age 13.
- More than one-tenth of 12- or 13-year-olds and over one-third of 14- or 15-year-olds reported alcohol use (a whole drink) in the past year.
- The peak years of alcohol initiation are 7th and 8th grades.

Adolescents Drink Less Frequently Than Adults, But When They Do Drink, They Drink More Heavily Than Adults. When youth between the ages of 12 and 20 consume alcohol, they drink on average about five drinks per occasion about six times a month. This amount of alcohol puts an adolescent drinker in the binge range, which, depending on the study, is defined as "five or more drinks on one occasion" or "five or more drinks in a row for men and four or more drinks in a row for women." By comparison, adult drinkers age 26 and older consume on average two to three drinks per occasion about nine times a month.

Distinct age-related patterns are evident for both boys and girls, with a steady increase in binge drinking days for girls through age 18 and boys through age 20.

Differences in Underage Alcohol Use Exist Between the Sexes and Among Racial and Ethnic Groups. Despite differences between the sexes and among racial and ethnic groups, overall rates of drinking among most populations of adolescents are high. In multiple surveys, underage males generally report more alcohol use during the past month than underage females. Boys also tend to start drinking at an earlier age than girls, drink more frequently, and are more likely to binge drink. When youth ages 12–20 were asked about how old they were when they started drinking, the average age was 13.90 for boys and 14.36 for girls for those adolescents who reported drinking. Interestingly, the magnitude of the sex-related difference in the frequency of binge drinking varies substantially by age. Further, data from the Monitoring the Future survey show that while the percentages of boys and girls in the 8th and 10th grades who binge drink are similar (10.5 and 10.8, and 22.9 and 20.9, respectively), among 12th graders, boys have a higher prevalence of binge drinking compared to girls (29.8 compared to 22.8).

While the percentage of adolescents of all racial/ethnic subgroups who drink is high, Black or African-American and Asian youth tend to drink the least.

Binge Drinking by Teens Is Not Limited to the United States. In many European countries a significant proportion of young people ages 15–16 report binge drinking. In all of the countries listed, the minimum legal drinking age is lower than in the United States. These data call into question the suggestion that having a lower minimum legal drinking age, as they do in many European countries, results in less problem drinking by adolescents.

Adverse Consequences of Underage Drinking

The short- and long-term consequences that arise from underage alcohol consumption are astonishing in their range and magnitude, affecting adolescents, the people around them, and society as a whole. Adolescence is a time of life characterized by robust physical health and low incidence of disease, yet overall morbidity and mortality rates increase 200 percent between middle childhood and late adolescence/early adulthood. This dramatic rise is attributable in large part to the increase in risk-taking, sensation-seeking, and erratic behavior that follows the onset of puberty and which contributes to violence, unintentional injuries, risky sexual behavior, homicide, and suicide. Alcohol frequently plays a role in these adverse outcomes and the human tragedies they produce. Among the most prominent adverse consequences of underage alcohol use are those listed below. Underage drinking:

- Is a leading contributor to death from injuries, which are the main cause of death for people under age 21. Annually, about 5,000 people under age 21 die from alcohol-related injuries involving underage drinking. About 1,900 (38 percent) of the 5,000 deaths involve motor vehicle crashes, about 1,600 (32 percent) result from homicides, and about 300 (6 percent) result from suicides.
- Plays a significant role in risky sexual behavior, including unwanted, unintended, and unprotected sexual activity, and sex with multiple partners. Such behavior increases the risk for unplanned pregnancy and for contracting sexually transmitted diseases (STDs), including infection with HIV, the virus that causes AIDS.
- Increases the risk of physical and sexual assault.
- Is associated with academic failure.
- Is associated with illicit drug use.
- Is associated with tobacco use.
- Can cause a range of physical consequences, from hangovers to death from alcohol poisoning.
- Can cause alterations in the structure and function of the developing brain, which continues to mature into the mid- to late twenties, and may have consequences reaching far beyond adolescence.
- Creates secondhand effects that can put others at risk. Loud and unruly behavior, property destruction, unintentional injuries, violence, and even death because of underage alcohol use afflict innocent parties. For example, about 45 percent of people who die in crashes involving a drinking driver under the age of 21 are people other than the driver. Such secondhand effects often strike at random, making underage alcohol use truly everybody's problem.
- In conjunction with pregnancy, may result in fetal alcohol spectrum disorders, including fetal alcohol syndrome, which remains a leading cause of mental retardation.

Further, underage drinking is a risk factor for heavy drinking later in life, and continued heavy use of alcohol leads to increased risk across the lifespan for acute consequences and for medical problems such as cancers of the oral cavity, larynx, pharynx, and esophagus; liver cirrhosis; pancreatitis; and hemorrhagic stroke.

Early Onset of Drinking Can Be a Marker for Future Problems, Including Alcohol Dependence and Other Substance Abuse. Approximately 40 percent of individuals who report drinking before age 15 also describe their behavior and drinking at some point in their lives in ways consistent with a diagnosis for alcohol dependence. This is four times as many as among those who do not drink before age 21.

Besides experiencing a higher incidence of dependence later in life, youth who report drinking before the age of 15 are more likely than those who begin drinking later in life to have other substance abuse problems during adolescence; to engage in risky sexual behavior; and to be involved in car crashes, unintentional injuries, and physical fights after drinking both during adolescence and in adulthood. This is true for individuals from families both with and without a family history of alcohol dependence. Delaying the age of onset of first alcohol use as long as possible would ameliorate some of the negative consequences associated with underage alcohol consumption.

The Negative Consequences of Alcohol Use on College Campuses Are Widespread. Alcohol consumption by underage college students is commonplace, although it varies from campus to campus and from person to person. Indeed, many college students, as well as some parents and administrators, accept alcohol use as a normal part of student life. Studies consistently indicate that about 80 percent of college students drink alcohol, about 40 percent engage in binge drinking, and about 20 percent engage in frequent episodic heavy consumption, which is bingeing three or more times over the past 2 weeks. The negative consequences of alcohol use on college campuses are particularly serious and pervasive. For example:

- An estimated 1,700 college students between the ages of 18 and 24 die each year from alcohol-related unintentional injuries, including motor vehicle crashes.
- Approximately 600,000 students are unintentionally injured while under the influence of alcohol.
- Approximately 700,000 students are assaulted by other students who have been drinking.
- About 100,000 students are victims of alcohol-related sexual assault or date rape.

Underage Military Personnel Engage in Alcohol Use That Results in Negative Consequences. According to the most recent (2005) Department of Defense Survey of Health-Related Behaviors Among Military Personnel, 62.3 percent of underage military members drink at least once a year, with 21.3 percent reporting heavy alcohol use. Problems among underage military drinkers include: serious consequences (15.8 percent); alcohol-related productivity loss (19.5 percent); and as indicated by AUDIT scores, hazardous drinking (25.7 percent), harmful drinking (4.6 percent), or possible dependence (5.5 percent) (Bray et al, 2006).

Judith G. McMullen  **NO**

Underage Drinking: Does Current Policy Make Sense?

This Article examines the history of laws and policies regulating consumption of alcoholic beverages by young people in the United States, and examines youth drinking patterns that have emerged over time. Currently, all 50 states have a minimum drinking age of 21. Various rationales are offered for the 21 drinking age, such as the claim that earlier drinking hinders cognitive functions and the claim that earlier drinking increases the lifetime risk of becoming an alcoholic. While there is sufficient evidence to support the claim that it would be better for adolescents and young adults if they did not drink prior to age 21, research shows that vast numbers of underage persons consume alcoholic beverages, often in large quantities. The Article discusses the question of why underage drinking laws have not been able to effectively stop underage drinking.

Normally, discussions of underage drinking focus on persons under age 21 as one group. This Article breaks underage drinkers into two groups: minors (drinkers under the age of 18) and young adults (drinkers between the ages of 18 and 21). The Article goes on to separately analyze the two groups' drinking patterns and reasons for drinking. The Article concludes that prohibitions on drinking by minors could be made more effective because restrictions on activities by minors are expected and normally honored by parents, law, and society. The Article also concludes, however, that the enforcement of a drinking prohibition for young adults between the ages of 18 and 21 is doomed to remain largely ineffective because the drinking ban is wholly inconsistent with other legal policies aimed at that age group. The Article discusses three areas (health care decisions, educational decisions, and smoking) where persons over the age of 18 have virtually unfettered personal discretion, and applies the reasoning of those situations to the decision about whether to consume alcoholic beverages. The Article also compares the total drinking ban for young adults with the graduated privilege policies applied to drivers' licensing. The Article concludes that the total prohibition of alcohol consumption for young adults is inconsistent with other policies affecting young adults, and this inconsistency, coupled with harms that may come from the 21 drinking age, make the current policies ineffective and ill-advised for young adults between the age of 18 and 21.

Introduction

On the surface, youth alcohol policy is simple and straightforward: the legal age for alcohol consumption is 21 in all states, and drinking before then is illegal. As it happens, though, these laws are not terribly effective. Huge numbers of youngsters age 12 and up (and probably younger) consume alcoholic beverages, despite the law.[1] The numbers of underage drinkers skyrocket once kids are over 18, and college campuses are known hotbeds of underage consumption.[2] According to researchers, large numbers of young people drink alcohol, many heavily, before they attain the legal drinking age.[3]

This Article addresses the question of why underage drinking laws have not been able to effectively stop underage drinking. It examines some of the classic reasons: ambivalence among adults as to the law, feelings of entitlement by young people, and glorification of alcohol consumption by society as a whole. The Article argues that alcohol consumption by adolescents under the age of 18 could be reduced by stricter and more consistent enforcement. However, the Article goes on to conclude that the prohibition of alcohol consumption cannot ever be effective for the 18 to 21-year-old cohort, because it is wholly inconsistent with other legal policies aimed at that age group. Further, the Article argues that outlawing alcohol consumption for young adults[4] may cause harm because the policy may encourage unhealthy alcohol consumption patterns in young adults, and it carries the risk of engendering a lack of respect for the law in general.

Underage drinking laws need to be assessed in two parts. One policy is the prohibition of alcohol consumption for minors, i.e., persons under the age of 18. The second policy is prohibition of alcohol consumption for persons between the ages of 18 and 21. While similar justifications are offered for the restrictions on each of these groups, in fact, as we shall see, there are very different factors at play in terms of parental control, societal expectations, and overall consistency with other situations where the law asserts control over individual behaviors. Most articles on youth alcohol policy address whether the current policy is a good thing. This Article concedes that it might indeed be a good thing if persons under age 21 abstained from alcohol. However, the Article goes on to discuss how the youth alcohol policy fits—or does not fit—into the patchwork of laws and policies concerning state intervention into the lives of parents and their children.

This Article argues that banning alcohol consumption for the under-18 crowd is consistent with other child protective policies advanced by state laws, largely because the law does not accord many rights of self-determination to minors. Thus, the ban could be reasonably effective if enforcement were increased—perhaps with such measures as holding parents and other adults accountable for behaviors that facilitate illegal underage drinking. However, the Article also concludes that current alcohol policy for persons over age 18 is *not* consistent with analogous policies for persons who are legally adults: e.g., the right to refuse medical treatment or the right to smoke cigarettes. In fact, the alcohol laws governing young adults seem to substitute state policies for both parental judgment and the young person's self-determination on this single issue. Thus, the Article concludes that the policy cannot ever be widely effective with this group, and creates as many problems as it solves. This is despite the inarguable fact that alcohol consumption may well be harmful to persons in this disputed age group.

First, the Article gives an overview of drinking policies in the United States, from colonial times to the present.[5] Second, the Article discusses the current laws and the justifications offered for them.[6] Next, the Article examines the effectiveness of the laws and the drinking patterns among younger underage youths (up to age 18),[7] and older underage youths (ages 18 to 21).[8] The Article compares youth drinking policies with other policies affecting young adults and argues that the practical and philosophical differences between the drinking ban for 18- to 21-year-olds and other legal policies affecting that age group make the alcohol ban for young adults largely unenforceable.[9] The Article also discusses problems arguably caused by the prohibition of alcohol use by young adults and examines whether the drinking age law might have significant value despite its unenforceability.[10] Finally, the Article suggests that alcohol use by 18- to 21-year-olds might be more appropriately addressed in a manner analogous to drivers' licensing policies for young drivers: by providing a combination of alcohol education and supervision to young adults who choose to drink.

Assessing Current Policies and Patterns

A. Structure of Current Laws

Currently, all fifty states have a minimum legal drinking age of 21.[11] Enforcement is aimed at both underage drinkers and their suppliers. Underage drinkers may be penalized with municipal or state citations or drivers' license suspensions.[12] Parents or other individual adults who supply alcohol to underage persons may be held criminally responsible, which might result in assessment of a fine or a jail sentence, although several states do not impose these penalties on parents who are serving alcoholic beverages to their *own* children.[13] Adults who provide alcohol to minors may also be exposed to civil liability in the event of harm caused by the underage drinker.[14] Bar owners or storeowners may be hit with fines or may lose their liquor licenses.[15] Penalties for underage driving while under the influence are effectively more severe for young adults than for adults over the age of 21, because the offense is typically committed if the young driver has *any* detectable alcohol in her blood.[16]

B. Policy Objectives

There are two stated justifications for enforcing a minimum drinking age: protection of young people, and protection of society. Numerous studies and statistics are offered to support each justification.

The first argument, that a 21 drinking age protects young people from harm, is supported by recent research that suggests alcohol can have an especially detrimental effect on the developing brain. The American Medical Association released a report in 2002 stating that drinking by adolescents and young adults could result in long-term brain damage, including diminishment of memory, reasoning, and learning abilities.[17] Experts think that memory and learning impairment is worse in adolescents, who may experience adverse effects after consuming only half as much alcohol as adults.[18] Human research at the University of Pittsburgh showed that heavy-drinking girls between the ages of 14 and 21 had smaller hippocampi than girls of the same age who were non-drinkers.[19] Admittedly, this research does not prove whether it is the heavy drinking that causes changes in the hippocampus, or the reduced size of the hippocampus that causes the urge to engage in heavy drinking.[20] Moreover, teenage hormonal changes, eating habits, or abuse of other substances like marijuana could also be causes of learning and memory impairment.[21] However, research with rats has shown similar bad effects from alcohol consumption on the rodents' learning and memory, even extending into adulthood.[22]

In addition, some researchers contend that alcohol abuse in the teenage years is more likely to lead to alcohol dependence later in life than if the drinking had begun at a later age. A study released in 1998 by the National Institute of Alcohol Abuse and Alcoholism concluded that "[c]hildren who begin drinking regularly by age 13 are more than four times as likely to become alcoholics as those who delay consuming alcohol until age 21 or older. . . ."[23] The study found that children who started drinking regularly at age 13 faced a 47% lifetime risk of becoming an alcoholic, compared with a 25% risk for youth who began drinking at age 17, and a 10% risk for people who began drinking at age 21.[24] However, it is not clear why some children are prone to such early and heavy drinking and others are not. It may be, for example, that children who begin drinking heavily at age 13 do so because of some biological characteristic that also causes them to have more of a lifetime risk for alcoholism.[25] In other words, rather than the early drinking causing the later alcoholism, it may be a symptom of the existing vulnerability to alcoholism.

It is also claimed that withholding drinking privileges until a later age protects young people by reducing the number of fatal automobile accidents involving teenagers. Indeed, "[t]he National Highway Traffic Safety Administration estimates that since the '70s, the age-21 policy has saved 20,970 teenage lives from serious car crashes alone."[26] For example, "[i]n 1982, a study by the National Highway Traffic Safety Administration found that 5,380 persons between the ages of 15 and 20 had died in drunken driving accidents that year. . . . [By 1995] the number had been reduced to 2,206 nationwide. . . ."[27] However, drunk driving enforcement in general has been taken more seriously since the drinking age was changed, and this might also account for some of the improvement.[28]

The second argument, that a 21 drinking age protects society from the bad effects of underage drinking, is partly supported by data on traffic fatalities that could be caused by young drunk drivers.[29] In addition, there is another claimed benefit to society in banning underage drinking: the possible reduction of crime perpetrated by persons under age 21. Alcohol has been shown to be a major contributing factor in teen deaths from accidents, homicide, and suicide, and it has also been shown to increase the chances of juvenile delinquency and crime.[30] Alcohol abuse appears to increase the likelihood that young people will engage in unprotected sex or acquaintance rape, suicide, and other violent behavior.[31] Of course, alcohol is a known inhibition-reducer and is implicated in crimes for all age groups.[32] Moreover, both the drinking and other problem behaviors may be caused by the general turmoil of adolescence, which is characterized by impulsiveness, sensation seeking, and unconventionality.[33]

There is no doubt that a significant number of young people consume alcohol in violation of the minimum age laws. While state laws outlaw alcohol purchase and consumption for all persons under age 21, there are in fact two distinct groups of underage drinkers who present different issues. First of all are the minors (high school and younger drinkers), and second are the young adults or college age drinkers.[34]

C. Underage Drinking by Minors

Studies show that a significant minority of high school students consume alcohol on a regular basis: "According to 2002 Monitoring the Future (MTF) data, almost half (48.6 percent) of twelfth graders reported recent (within the past 30 days) alcohol use."[35] Although younger teens report lower incidences of alcohol use, "NHSDA[36] data indicate that the average age of self-reported first use of alcohol among individuals of all ages reporting any alcohol use decreased from 17.6 years to 15.9 years between 1965 and 1999."[37] Moreover, underage drinkers are more likely than adults to be heavy drinkers.[38]

Even for those minors who are not regular drinkers, certain rites of passage such as school dances, proms, and graduation can be the occasion of much alcoholic excess. A notorious incident that occurred in Scarsdale, New York in 2002 provides an excellent example of the dynamics. In the fall of 2002, *The New York Times* reported that the prestigious Scarsdale High School homecoming dance and pre-dance parties included widespread binge drinking "which left scores of students falling-down drunk, 27 with three-day school suspensions and five hospitalized with acute alcohol poisoning. . . ."[39] When the principal arrived at the dance shortly after its 8 pm start, he "found perhaps a third of the 600 students there in a stupor from drinking screwdrivers they had mixed at various homes. They had used vodka sneaked from their parents['] liquor cabinets and disguised in Poland Spring water bottles."[40]

While major high school events have precipitated underage drinking for generations, *The New York Times* cited differences noted by education and mental health experts. First, "[t]he drinking starts younger. . . . The quantity and speed of alcohol consumption are dangerously high and the goal seems to be total oblivion."[41] Second, certain psychological factors are different: baby boomer parents are less likely to be seen as authority figures by their children, and the children in upscale communities are in a super-competitive atmosphere with "enormous pressure to succeed."[42] If they don't meet parental expectations, they may drown their sorrows in drugs or alcohol. Finally, "[e]ducators and mental health professionals also say that affluence breeds a sense of entitlement in children. They're told from the time they're young that they're the prize of the community. . . . The conclusion an adolescent may draw is: 'I'm special. I get to do what I want.'"[43]

The Scarsdale incident also illustrates another phenomenon that has become common: placing much of the blame for underage drinking on adults, especially parents. According to Geraldine Greene, executive director of the Scarsdale Family Counseling Service, underage drinking is "an adult failure. In every case, an adult has let a child down. Somewhere along the way they haven't exercised due care."[44] Although Greene's comments could be directed at a large variety of adults, including parents, vendors, and teachers, she is most critical of affluent parents who she feels do not take enough time to raise their teenagers properly.[45] Adolescent psychologist Dr. Alan Tepp said that while parents hold their adolescents to ever-higher achievement standards, "at the same time, we're putting less restraint on them, watching them less. We push them, and then allow them out."[46]

Studies provide some support for these opinions. Large amounts of time free from adult supervision, including after-school time without parent contact, has been related to higher alcohol consumption among teens.[47] "'Hanging out' with friends in unstructured, unsupervised contexts is generally related to negative outcomes, while spending time with others in adult-sanctioned, structured contexts is generally related to positive outcomes."[48]

There is, of course, a more direct way in which parents can be responsible for youth drinking: they may provide the liquor consumed by high school–aged children. Some parents take the position that kids will drink anyway, and if the parents allow supervised drinking at home parties, this will reduce more dangerous binge drinking or drinking in cars, followed by driving while intoxicated.[49] For example, a 17-year-old graduate of Scarsdale High School said, "I know one of my friend's parents said, 'If you're staying in the house, then I don't have a problem with you drinking.' That's kind of promoting it. . . ."[50] Indeed, "having parents who sanction alcohol use (even in 'controlled' settings) is related to heavier drinking among adolescents."[51] A Westchester County District Attorney commented that the "number of kids getting drunk at home is on the increase, as is the frequency of alcohol being provided by an adult or older sibling. . . ."[52]

Herein lies part of the enforcement problem: some parents think drinking is a normal rite of passage for teenagers; others believe in zero-tolerance. A Scarsdale police detective, firmly in the latter camp, said, "Parents should send a clear message to their kids that this behavior will not be condoned. . . ."[53]

Yet even parents who might be willing to crack down are not always convinced that it will work. A principal in Chappaqua, New York quoted a parent who told him that "setting earlier curfews just makes the kids drink faster."[54] He added that since many parents feel powerless to stop their kids from drinking, they have adopted the view that "until society solves the problem, I want my kids alive."[55]

There are a number of different issues jumbled together here. First, we must consider whether it is reasonable for the state to prevent children under the age of 18 from consuming alcohol. Second, we must address whether we have consensus on this issue in this society. Finally, we must assess the reasonableness of the notion that parents can in large degree control the drinking behavior of their offspring.

Ever since *Prince v. Massachusetts*[56] upheld the state's right to protect a young Jehovah's Witness from the dangers of street preaching, it has been clear that a state can adopt reasonable policies to protect children, even over the heartfelt objections of their parents.[57] Unlike *Prince*, challenges to a state's protective alcohol policy do not rest on First Amendment free exercise claims; at best they depend upon arguments that reasonable parents might exercise their prerogative in favor of allowing their children to engage in moderate social drinking. A state's purposes of preventing traffic accidents, crime, and potential damage to a young imbiber's health or cognitive function would clearly survive any constitutional claim of infringement on parental authority. This is especially true in those few states that allow parents to serve alcohol to their own minor children while those children are in the parent's presence.[58] Even the most inconclusive of the scientific studies cited in Part III.B signals enough risk of harm that a state could reasonably prohibit alcohol consumption by minors.[59]

As to whether we have consensus about whether the absolute ban on consumption is a good thing, the answer is that we clearly do not. While a majority may favor the ban, a significant minority either thinks that it is counterproductive, or simply ineffective. These are the folks that may either look the other way or actually provide alcohol, on the theory that kids will drink anyway, and "I would rather know where they are."[60] In some national surveys, many parents admit to purchasing alcohol for their teenagers, in the hopes of providing a safe place for their kids to drink.[61] Ironically, these parents contribute to the fact that the ban is ineffective, and they make it ineffective not only for their own children, but for other people's children as well.

In fact, the combination of typical adolescent rebellion and readily available alcohol supplied by dissenting or indifferent adults makes it impossible for individual parents to completely control whether or not their children consume alcohol, unless the parents achieve round-the-clock supervision, amounting to lockdown, of their children.[62] Thus, penalizing parents for facilitating consumption, but not holding them accountable for the behavior of sneaky adolescent drinkers, makes good sense.

There are a myriad of situations where parents or the state effectively control situations involving persons under age 18. Parents are held responsible for the support and education of their minor children.[63] The law is generally structured to help parents in these endeavors, and to regulate parents who fall short. Thus, fit parents are generally entitled to custody of their minor children,[64] and deference is given to parental decisions about the incidents of that custody.[65] Laws that regulate minors' activities, such as truancy or curfew laws that may penalize errant children, are widely viewed as reinforcements to judicious parental controls.[66] Parents who stray from societal norms, such as parents who abuse their children or parents who are complicit in the truancy of their children, can be subjected to various penalties.[67]

Statutes and cases have attempted to strike a balance between parental prerogatives, children's rights, and societal interests in regulating minors' activities.[68] Where underage drinking is concerned, parents have an important role in restricting minors' access to alcohol.[69] Due to the fact that most minors live with at least one adult, greater adult consensus on the value of banning alcohol consumption by minors, as well as greater adult compliance with the laws, could combine to significantly reduce alcohol consumption by persons under age 18. Moreover, even if adolescent consumption is not reduced to zero, it could be reduced from current epidemic proportions, and abstinence from underage alcohol consumption could be internalized by minors as an important social norm.

D. Underage Drinking by Young Adults

Regulation of underage drinking becomes more problematic after a young person reaches the age of majority—usually 18—or moves away from home into a dorm or apartment. However imperfect parental supervision may have been before, it becomes nearly impossible at that time. Persons over the age of 18 are legally adults for any purpose *except* consuming alcohol. Even parents of economically dependent college students may not know whether their children are drinking, since schools have no obligation to notify parents when a young person violates underage drinking laws or school rules.[70]

Drinking in the 18 to 21 age group, however, is rampant. Young people in this age group who do not attend college drink less than those that do attend, but they are not teetotalers as a group.[71] And although not every child goes to college, these are the prime college age years for those that do, and college campuses are notorious for widespread alcohol consumption. According to one source, 44% of college students report binge drinking in the past two weeks, and 23% report frequent binge drinking.[72] Apparently, membership in fraternities and sororities greatly increases the likelihood of excessive drinking: a 2001 survey "showed that three-quarters of fraternity or sorority house residents (80 percent and 69 percent, respectively) are binge drinkers," an improvement over the 1993 figure of 83%.[73] Although binge drinking is typically defined as five or more drinks per occasion, the bingeing at many Greek organizations is reportedly far more extreme. One consultant stated:

> Our organization has worked extensively with Greek groups over the past twenty years and has found some chapters to report that more than 70 percent of their members consume thirteen or more drinks per occasion. We frequently hear from other professionals on campuses that fifteen to twenty drinks per occasion, though not the norm, is not uncommon among some groups of students.[74]

Theories abound as to why drinking is so extreme on college campuses. Researchers Wechsler and Wuethrich think one reason is that students "developed a sense of entitlement to alcohol" after the drinking age was lowered to 18 during the 1970s and then re-raised to 21.[75] They also point to the relaxation of dormitory supervision, the increasingly cultivated party images of fraternities and even schools themselves, and the rising importance of college sports as big business, with attendant alcohol industry sponsorships.[76] They also acknowledge alcohol's role in larger society as a factor.[77]

I believe that there is another important reason for widespread drinking among young adults: with the exception of alcohol, parental control over the young person's activities grinds to a halt after age 18, if not before then. Moreover, with the exception of alcohol, and to some extent drivers' licenses, state control of the activities of a person over 18 is no different for the 18 to 21 age group than for an adult of any age. Once a person attains age 18, he or she can legally marry without parental permission, join the military, enter contracts, smoke, make decisions concerning medical care, or drop out of school. These newfound freedoms occur at age 18, despite the fact that the young person may be immature or financially dependent on his parents, and despite the fact that he may have parents who disapprove of his decisions. It is this legal autonomy in other areas, I think, that makes enforcement of a 21 drinking age impossible.

For the sake of discussion, I will compare the 21 drinking age policy with policies aimed at the 18 to 21 age group in the areas of medical decision-making, decisions to forgo education, decisions about smoking, and regulations concerning driving. All of these represent adult privileges that can have serious consequences for the young person, and potentially for others around him. All also represent situations where a mistake in judgment, perhaps due to immaturity, can have dire consequences. Yet, unlike current alcohol policy, the policies in these areas defer to the judgment of the young person, for good or ill. If the main reason for forbidding alcohol consumption for persons under the age of 21 is protection from the adverse physical effects of youth drinking, such as greater likelihood of later alcoholism or greater damage to the brain, then the policy is entirely consistent with other policies for children under the age of 18. It is, however, completely unprecedented compared with other policies for young people in the 18 to 21 age group.

Problems Caused by the Prohibition of Alcohol Use by Young Adults

There are two potential problems that may result from the prohibition of alcohol use by young adults. The first problem is that the impossibility of enforcing the law will engender a lack of respect for the law in general among young adults. The second problem is that, for those who choose to violate the law, the necessity of sneaking around to drink may lead to more dangerous drinking patterns and may preclude access to avenues that might imbue healthier drinking habits.

A. The Difficulty of an Unenforceable Law

Laws that are difficult or impossible to enforce have always been problematic. Of course, no law is one hundred percent enforceable: history is replete with unsolved crimes and unpunished offenders of every sort.[78] However, laws may serve a useful symbolic or deterrent function despite sporadic enforcement. Indeed, "the effectiveness of symbolic laws depends on public affirmation rather than legal enforcement. 'People obey symbolic laws not for fear of legal sanction, but because they are backed by the consensus of society and the force of major social institutions.' "[79] As Lawrence Friedman has pointed out, even laws that are imperfectly enforced may reduce a given behavior by making it more costly: "[P]olicy choices are essentially selections among various techniques and means of encouraging or discouraging behavior, by making that behavior safer, cheaper, and more pleasant; or more expensive, more aversive."[80]

When we examine the 21 drinking age in this context, it can be argued that the current law reduces drinking by young adults and conveys important social values to all young adults, even those who violate the law. Advocates of the 21 drinking age claim that the law has resulted in more college-age students who abstain from alcohol use (and are willing to admit it), which thereby reduces alcohol-related problems of all sorts.[81] Not everyone credits the 21 drinking age with this progress, however. Richard Keeling, a physician and former director of health services at the University of Wisconsin-Madison, believes that enforcement methods such as crackdowns on house parties and increased fines for alcohol-related offenses are more likely reasons for changes in young adult behavior.[82]

The argument that a 21 drinking age conveys important societal values to teenagers and young adults is less persuasive in light of the fact, already discussed,[83] that the drinking ban for young adults does not seem to be backed by a broad consensus of society. As we have seen, many parents and other adults disagree with the law in principle.[84] These adults may view drinking as a rite of passage, or may believe that an earlier drinking age would be conducive to more moderate drinking habits later. Such adults may not only ignore violations of the drinking ban by young adults, but they may enable the young adults to commit the violations by supplying alcohol or hosting drinking parties.[85] In these circumstances, where the social consensus on youth drinking is divided at best, it is harder to claim that a strong moral message is being delivered to underage drinkers.

In addition, alcohol continues to be glorified in sports sponsorships and advertising, making it unclear exactly what social message teenagers and young adults are getting about alcohol. Research has shown that adolescents who are exposed to alcohol advertising are more likely to consume alcohol and to consume it in greater amounts.[86] It is clear that vast numbers of adolescents are in fact exposed to alcohol advertising. Voluntary conduct codes adopted in the late 1990s by the Distilled Spirits Council of the United States suggest that ads should only run in media outlets having no more than 30% of their audience under the age of 21.[87] However, 30% of a broadcast such as a sporting event can be a substantial number of underage viewers.

Sporting events often have alcohol companies as sponsors, such as the sponsorship of NASCAR driver Dale Earnhardt by Budweiser beer and the Busch beer sponsorship of the NASCAR Busch series.[88] Stadiums such as Miller Park in Wisconsin and Coors Field in Colorado associate their corporate sponsors with sports. College sports are no exception, with the NCAA allowing one minute per hour of alcohol ads during broadcast of NCAA events.[89] In a recent report, the Center for Science in the Public Interest argued that because the

NCAA has many underage followers (including kids as young as 9 or 10), the NCAA is effectively helping brewers to recruit kids to beer drinking in general, as well as to particular brands of beer.[90] The American Medical Association recently joined the Center for Science in the Public Interest in urging the NCAA to ban alcohol advertising during events,[91] but the NCAA decided to retain its existing policy.[92]

B. Potential Harmful Effects of a 21-Year-Old Drinking Age

Mixed messages sent to young drinkers are only part of the problem. In addition, it is possible that the drinking ban for young adults may have harmful effects.[93] We have seen that even during Prohibition, commentators bemoaned the lack of respect for the law that came from the widely flaunted ban.[94] Some argue that Prohibition may have exacerbated alcohol abuse, at least for some consumers:

> It's the same pattern observed during Prohibition, when illicit stills would blow up, and there was a rise in deaths from alcohol poisoning. Far from instilling virtue in Americans, Prohibition caused them to switch from beer and wine to hard liquor. Overall consumption of alcohol might even have increased.[95]

In modern times, many parents and adults fear that banning alcohol outright leads rebellious young adults to drink in more dangerous ways: "The pattern for underage students is more dangerous. . . . Afraid of being caught, they drink a lot in a short period of time. They do it less often but more intensely."[96]

The legal ban on drinking before age 21 also eliminates the possibility of teaching responsible drinking behaviors to young adults who, because of relative economic dependence, are often accessible to parents, college administrators, and others. The president of Middlebury College in Vermont, John McCardell, believes that the lack of supervised drinking experience for young adults causes much of the problem.[97] He argues that colleges should play an active role in teaching students how to drink responsibly.[98] Says McCardell: "You have to give them some exposure. . . . That doesn't mean sending everybody out to get drunk. But if you're serious about teaching somebody biology, you're going to include a laboratory. College campuses could be little laboratories of progressiveness."[99]

Nor is McCardell alone in his views. A recent article in the student newspaper at Tufts University quoted several University administrators who expressed similar concerns. "It's very complicated when you're living in a country where the legal drinking age forces you to bury your head in the sand," said Margot Abels, Director of Drug and Alcohol Education Services.[100] Tufts Dean of Students, Bruce Reitman, regrets that the 21 drinking age makes it impossible for faculty members to "model responsible drinking," as they did when an 18 drinking age allowed Friday afternoon student-faculty sherry hours where alcohol was used in a civilized, non-abusive manner.[101] Nowadays, Reitman notes, it is "naive" to tell freshmen that he expects them to never touch alcohol, especially in light of a recent survey of Tufts freshmen that indicated that more than 80% of respondents had tried alcohol before arriving at the University.[102]

The notion of allowing young adults to drink, at least in supervised settings such as college-sponsored parties, has some parallels with the grant of driving privileges to young drivers. Combining education and supervision with probationary privileges allows young drivers to acquire necessary skills. If they proceed through their probationary period without incident, they may obtain regular drivers' licenses. If they have violations, they may face delays or lose their licenses altogether.[103] Likewise, college campuses could sponsor parties where adult supervision is provided. Alcohol education could be incorporated into the mandatory curriculum. Nor are colleges the only institutions that could institute this approach. Churches, community centers, or other organizations frequented by young people could also provide much needed education and supervision to young adults who choose to drink. Otherwise, the furtive, excessive drinking patterns exhibited by a significant percentage of young adults may cause far greater problems than would come from lowering the drinking age.

Conclusion

This Article has attempted to show that prohibiting alcohol consumption by young adults aged 18 to 21 is a policy that is neither currently effective, nor likely to be effective in the future. This failure is partly due to the fact that parents, who are key players in the control of minors, no longer have legally enforceable control over offspring who have attained the age of majority. The failure of policy is also due to the fact that an outright ban on drinking by young adults is philosophically different from policies governing analogous decisions that may be made by adults in our society. Whereas adults may make questionable decisions in areas such as education, health, or smoking, decisions about alcohol are uniquely restricted. Due to this dichotomy, I believe that prohibition of alcohol use by young adults will never be widely effective, no matter how desirable a teetotaler young adult population might be.

Notes

1. *See, e.g.*, NAT'L RES. COUNCIL INST. OF MED., REDUCING UNDER-AGE DRINKING: A COLLECTIVE RESPONSIBILITY 35–57 (Richard J. Bonnie & Mary Ellen O'Connel eds., 2004).
2. *Id.* at 43–48.
3. *Id.* at 40–42.
4. Throughout the Article, I will use the term "young adults" to denote persons in the 18- to 21-year-old age group.
5. *See infra* Part II.

6. *See infra* Part III.A–B.

7. *See infra* Part III.C.

8. *See infra* Part III.D.

9. *See infra* Part IV.

10. *See infra* Part V.

11. Shelley, *supra* note 19, at 709.

12. *See, e.g.,* MNOOKIN & WEISBERG, *supra* note 29, at 663; WIS. STAT. § 125.07(4) (2004).

13. One Maryland father was charged with maintaining a disorderly house, "a misdemeanor subject to a fine of up to $300 or a maximum jail sentence of six months." Other possible charges include "contributing to the delinquency of a minor" and "drinking in prohibited places." Veronica T. Jennings, *Md. Parents Cited in Teen Drinking Crackdown,* WASH. POST, June 14, 1988, at B1. Some states impose criminal liability on persons who provide alcohol to minors, where the minor later dies or suffers bodily harm as a consequence of the drinking. *See, e.g.,* WIS. STAT. § 125.075 (2004). However, some states, such as Wisconsin and Texas, allow drinking in the presence of a minor's own parent. MNOOKIN & WEISBERG, *supra* note 29, at 664.

14. *See, e.g.,* WIS. STAT. § 125.035 (2004); Congini v. Portersville Valve Co., 470 A.2d 515 (Pa. 1983) (holding that guardian had a cause of action against the minor ward's employer where the employer served alcohol at a party, minor became drunk, drove away from the party with the knowledge of employer's agent, and the minor was subsequently injured in an automobile accident.). *But see* Charles v. Seigfried, 651 N.E.2d 154, 165 (Ill.1995) (holding that there is no common law right of action against social hosts who serve alcohol to minors).

15. *See, e.g.,* MNOOKIN & WEISBERG, *supra* note 29, at 663–64; WIS. STAT. § 125.07.

16. *See* JAMES H. HEDLUND & ANNE T. MCCARTT, DRUNK DRIVING: SEEKING ADDITIONAL SOLUTIONS 8 (2002). . . .

17. Michael Stroh, *Younger Drinkers Risk Damaging Brain Cells,* BALTIMORE SUN, Dec. 10, 2002, at 1A.

18. Joseph A. Califano, Jr., Editorial, *Don't Make Teen Drinking Easier,* WASH. POST, May 11, 2003, at B7.

19. Stroh, *supra* note 51. The hippocampus is a part of the brain involved in memory and learning.

20. *Id.*

21. *Id.*

22. *Id.*; Kathleen Fackelmann, *Teen Drinking, Thinking Don't Mix; Alcohol Appears to Damage Young Brains, Early Research Finds,* USA TODAY, Oct. 18, 2000, at 1D (citing Aaron M. White et al., *Binge Pattern Ethanol Exposure in Adolescent and Adult Rats: Differential Impact on Subsequent Responsiveness to Ethanol,* 24 ALCOHOLISM: CLINICAL & EXPERIMENTAL RES. 1251 (2000)).

23. Sally Squires, *Early Drinking Said to Increase Alcoholism Risk,* WASH. POST, Jan. 20, 1998, at Z7 (These findings "are drawn from the National

Longitudinal Alcohol Epidemiologic Survey, a national sample that included face-to-face interviews with nearly 28,000 current and former drinkers aged 18 years and older.").

24. *Id.* However, there were some gender and racial variations in these risk statistics: "Early drinking is especially risky for boys. Those who began drinking by age 13 had a 50 percent lifetime risk of alcoholism. For girls, the risk was 43 percent for those who began drinking at age 13. Among blacks, those who were drinking alcohol at age 13 had a 44 percent lifetime risk of alcoholism, while nonblack children the same age had a 48 percent lifetime risk." *Id.*

25. *Id.*

26. Alexander Wagenaar, Letter to the Editor, *Teenage Drinking: Rites and Wrongs*, WASH. POST, May 9, 2003, at A34.

27. Kevin Cullen & Karen Avenoso, *Deaths Show Backsliding on Alcohol; Teenage Drinking May Undo Progress*, BOSTON GLOBE, Aug. 6, 1996, at B1.

28. *See* HEDLUND & MCCARTT, *supra* note 50, at 7–9 (citing several examples of improved public awareness and enforcement of drunk driving laws throughout the 1980s and 1990s, including mandatory driver's license suspension, mandatory jail time, administrative license revocation, widely used breath test equipment, training in field sobriety testing, sobriety checkpoints, special drunk driving saturation patrols, zero tolerance for youth, and lowering of BAC limits to 0.08 by many states). *See also* Glen Martin, *Holiday Sees Rise in DUI Arrests; 3,000 Officers Join Effort to Prevent Highway Deaths*, S.F. CHRON., May 31, 2005, at B1 (California Highway Patrol Officer Mike Wright said, "Each year we've been able to throw more and more resources at the problem, so we're getting more and more arrests. . . . Bigger is better. We have more people looking for drunks, so we're catching more drunks.").

29. Cullen & Avenoso, *supra* note 61.

30. Califano, Jr., *supra* note 52.

31. Cullen & Avenoso, *supra* note 61.

32. Nat'l Council on Alcoholism and Drug Dependence, FYI: Alcohol & Crime. . . .

33. Nat'l Inst. on Alcohol Abuse and Alcoholism, *Youth Drinking: Risk Factors and Consequences*, ALCOHOL ALERT NO. 37, July 1997. . . .

34. I am using the terms "college age" and "young adult" to refer to persons between the ages of 18 and 21. Of course, some kids are only 17 when they enter college, many young people in that age group do not attend college, and many people attending colleges and universities are over age 21. However, many studies and discussions of underage drinking concern college students and refer to drinking patterns among persons of "college age," perhaps because there is a significant drinking culture on many college campuses.

35. NAT'L RES. COUNCIL INST. OF MED., *supra* note 1, at 35.

36. *See id.* at 36 (now called the National Survey on Drug Use and Health).

37. *Id.* at 38.

38. *Id.* at 39 (This was true even among the 7% of 12–14–year-olds who reported drinking at all. "With increasing age, more youth drink and more drinkers are heavy drinkers.").

39. Jane Gross, *Teenagers' Binge Leads Scarsdale to Painful Self-Reflection*, N.Y. TIMES, Oct. 8, 2002, at B1.
40. *Id.*
41. *Id.*
42. *Id.*
43. *Id.*
44. *Id.*
45. *Id.*
46. *Scarsdale School Suspends 28 Students for Drunkenness*, N.Y. TIMES, Sept. 27, 2002, at B6.
47. NAT'L RES. COUNCIL INST. OF MED., *supra* note 1, at 82.
48. *Id.*
49. *Id.*
50. Elizabeth Nesoff, *A Prim Suburb Rallies to Curb Teen Drinking*, CHRISTIAN SCI. MONITOR, July 22, 2003, at 2.
51. NAT'L RES. COUNCIL INST. OF MED., *supra* note 1, at 82.
52. Corey Kilgannon, *Drinking Young*, N.Y. TIMES, Oct. 27, 2002, at WE1.
53. Nesoff, *supra* note 84.
54. Kilgannon, *supra* note 86.
55. *Id.*
56. 321 U.S. 158 (1944).
57. *Prince v. Massachusetts* was an appeal from convictions for violation of Massachusetts' child labor laws by Sarah Prince, who had allowed her 9-year-old niece to offer Jehovah's Witness literature for sale one evening, shortly before 9 pm. Mrs. Prince argued that her right to religious freedom coupled with her right to raise her children as she saw fit made the enforcement of the statute unconstitutional. However, the U.S. Supreme Court upheld the statute and the convictions, stating that the State's power to protect children from the dangers of street preaching was not foreclosed by the presence of parents, who could reduce, but not eliminate, the possible dangers. The Court famously proclaimed: "Parents may be free to become martyrs themselves. But it does not follow they are free, in identical circumstances, to make martyrs of their children before they have reached the age of full and legal discretion when they can make that choice for themselves." *Id.* at 170.
58. Several states allow parents to supply alcoholic beverages to their own children. *See* MNOOKIN & WEISBERG, *supra* note 29, at 664; WIS. STAT. § 125.07 (2004).
59. *See* NAT'L RES. COUNCIL INST. OF MED., *supra* note 1, at 64–65; Stroh, *supra* note 51; Fackelmann, *supra* note 56.
60. *See* NAT'L RES. COUNCIL INST. OF MED., *supra* note 1, at 82; Kilgannon, *supra* note 86.
61. Karina Bland, *Crackdown on Teen Keggers; Don't Buy Liquor, Parents Warned*, ARIZ. REPUBLIC, May 26, 2004, at A1.
62. In another context, I have noted that advocates of such an extreme form of parental supervision are few. *See* Judith G. McMullen, *"You Can't Make*

Me!": How Expectations of Parental Control over Adolescents Influence the Law, 35 LOY. U. CHI. L.J. 603 (2003) [hereinafter McMullen, *"You Can't Make Me!"*]. In his 1995 book, *Parent in Control*, author Gregory Bodenhamer advises close monitoring of difficult children and teens, including following them, accompanying them on every outing, and physically forcing or restraining actions. GREGORY BODENHAMER, PARENT IN CONTROL 102–07 (1995). I could find no other authors who advocate such an extreme hands-on approach, although most parenting experts advocate discipline, persuasion, and communication.

63. *See* MNOOKIN & WEISBERG, *supra* note 29, at 144–46 (quoting WILLIAM BLACKSTONE, 2 COMMENTARIES *446, *446–51).

64. *See* MICHAEL GROSSBERG, GOVERNING THE HEARTH: LAW AND THE FAMILY IN NINETEENTH-CENTURY AMERICA 234–59 (1985) (discussing the historical evolution of parental fitness as the basis of custody).

65. Troxel v. Granville, 530 U.S. 57, 65–66 (2000).

66. *See* Ginsberg v. New York, 390 U.S. 629, 639 (1968) (stating that the "legislature could properly conclude that parents and others, teachers for example, who have this primary responsibility for children's well-being are entitled to the support of laws designed to aid discharge of that responsibility"). *Ginsberg* upheld a New York statute that restricted access of minors to sexually suggestive publications, in this case "girlie magazines." *Id.* at 631–33.

67. McMullen, *"You Can't Make Me!"*, *supra* note 96, at 622–25.

68. *See Ginsberg*, 390 U.S. at 639 (The Court balanced parental prerogatives in allowing children access to pornographic literature with the State's interest in limiting such access. The Court concluded that the State had an interest in restricting minor's access to sexually suggestive publications, but noted that the New York statute, which forbade the *sale* of such literature to persons under the age of 17, did not preclude a parent from allowing his own child to view such literature purchased by the parent.). *See also* Wisconsin v. Yoder, 406 U.S. 205, 214, 234 (1972) (The Court balanced the social interest in an educated citizenry with the right of parents to bring up children according to the parents' own religious beliefs. Here, the Court found that the state interest did not justify enforcing compulsory education rules requiring formal education until 16 against Amish parents whose religious convictions required them to remove their children from school after the eighth grade.).

69. *See* NAT'L RES. COUNCIL INST. OF MED., *supra* note 1, at 82 (stating that "both agesegregation and lack of adult supervision have been related to . . . greater alcohol consumption").

70. *Id.* at 204 (In the Higher Education Amendments of 1998, "Section 952 clarified that institutions of higher education are allowed (but not required) to notify parents if a student under the age of 21 at the time of notification commits a disciplinary violation involving alcohol or a controlled substance.").

71. *Id.* at 45 (The 2000 National Household Survey of Drug Abuse (NHSDA) reported that "41 percent of full-time college students aged 18 to 22 engaged in heavy drinking, compared with 36 percent of young adults who were attending college part time or not at all.").

72. *Providing Substance Abuse Prevention and Treatment Services to Adolescents: Hearing Before the Subcomm. on Substance Abuse and Mental Health Services of the Comm. on Health Education, Labor, and Pensions*, 108th Cong. 19 (2004) (prepared statement of Sandra A. Brown, Professor of Psychology and Psychiatry, Univ. of Cal.-San Diego).

73. WECHSLER & WUETHRICH, *supra* note 26, at 35.

74. *Id.* at 38 (quoting Mark Nason, prevention consultant with Prevention Research Institute, "a nonprofit organization that develops curricula to reduce the risk of alcohol and drug problems").

75. *Id.* at 30.

76. *Id.* at 30–31.

77. *Id.* at 31–32.

78. "Small" crimes, such as purse-snatching or low-level speeding while driving are examples of laws that often go unpunished because of the difficulty of apprehending every suspect. However, serious crimes sometimes go unpunished as well. The infamous and unsolved case of Jack the Ripper is but one example. L. PERRY CURTIS, JR., JACK THE RIPPER & THE LONDON PRESS 1 (2001).

79. Elizabeth A. Heaney, *Pennsylvania's Doctrine of Necessities: An Anachronism Demanding Abolishment*, 101 DICK. L. REV. 233, 259 (1996) (quoting Note, *The Unnecessary Doctrine of Necessaries*, 82 MICH. L. REV. 1767, 1798 (1984)).

80. Lawrence M. Friedman, *Two Faces of Law*, 1984 WIS. L. REV. 13, 14 (1984).

81. *See* Rutledge, *supra* note 158 (citing comments of Susan Crowley, director of PACE (Policy, Alternatives, Community and Education), a "10-year, $1.2 million program aimed at curtailing underage drinking" funded by the Robert Wood Johnson Foundation).

82. *Id.*

83. *See supra* Part III.C.

84. *See id.*

85. *See id.*

86. CTR. FOR SCI. IN THE PUBLIC INTEREST, TAKE A KID TO A BEER: HOW THE NCAA RECRUITS KIDS FOR THE BEER MARKET 10 (2005) . . . Alan W. Stacy et al., *Exposure to Televised Alcohol Ads and Subsequent Adolescent Alcohol Use*, 28 AM. J. OF HEALTH BEHAV. 498, 507–08 (2004); Susan E. Martin et al., *Alcohol Advertising and Youth*, 26 ALCOHOLISM: CLINICAL & EXPERIMENTAL RES. 900, 905 (2002).

87. Melanie Warner, *A Liquor Maker Keeps a Close Watch on Its Ads*, N.Y. TIMES, July 27, 2005, at C10.

88. *Id.*

89. CTR. FOR SCI. IN THE PUBLIC INTEREST, *supra* note 198, at 1.

90. *See generally id.* (The title of the report is a play on the NCAA's campaign to "Take a Kid to a Game.").

91. *NCAA Board OKs 12th Game; Decision Could Revive WVU-Herd Series*, CHARLESTON GAZETTE, Apr. 29, 2005, at P1B.

92. Jeff Miller, *NCAA Extends Brand's Deal; Board Also Approves Start of Academic Performance Guidelines*, DALLAS MORNING NEWS, Aug. 6, 2005, at 11C.

93. "Of course, many laws also produce side-effects and may do more harm than good. Policy choices should take these costs into account." Friedman, *supra* note 192, at 14.

94. *See* John Tierney, *Debunking the Drug War*, N.Y. TIMES, Aug. 9, 2005, at A19.

95. *Id.* (arguing that media exaggeration and law enforcement overreaction to amphetamine use makes the problem worse, not better).

96. Rutledge, *supra* note 158 (quoting Richard Keeling, physician and former director of health services at the University of Wisconsin-Madison).

97. *Id.*

98. *Id.*

99. *Id.*

100. Keith Barry, *Survey Offers Insight Into Freshman Substance Use*, TUFTS DAILY, Mar. 11, 2005. . . .

101. *Id.*

102. *Id.* (The administrators were commenting in light of an online questionnaire sent to freshmen. 600 students, or 47.1% of the Class of 2008, responded to the October, 2004 survey.)

103. MNOOKIN & WEISBERG, *supra* note 29, at 649.

POSTSCRIPT

Should the United States Drinking Age Remain at 21?

In view of the fact that the majority of youths consume alcohol, is it a worthwhile endeavor to try to teach young people how to drink responsibly? Are young people capable of drinking responsibly? Can young people learn to moderate their behavior, especially as those behaviors apply to alcohol consumption? Will lowering the drinking age produce positive results? In some areas, young people have shown that they are capable of being responsible. Despite the fact that many young people get into accidents when operating motor vehicles, most do not have accidents. Many parents trust their children with babysitters. Putting the care of our children into the hands of young people shows much trust. Many young people hold jobs and are very responsible in that regard. Young people are allowed to own firearms and most understand the importance of handling firearms responsibly.

In many ways young people are treated as adults. For example, one can join the military prior to age 21. Many young people are sent to war where they are placed in jeopardy. Eighteen-year-olds are allowed, and encouraged, to vote. One can marry and bear children long before age 21. If one can be legally allowed to go to war, get married, and produce children, one could ask the question whether it is hypocritical to prohibit those under age 21 from drinking alcohol.

Of course, there is a major difference between an 18-, 19-, or 20-year-old drinking alcohol and a 14- or 15-year-old drinking alcohol. An important consideration is the effect on teenagers age 15, 16, and 17 if the drinking age were lowered to 21. Would there be an increase in alcohol consumption among this age group? Would 18-year-olds provide alcohol to younger teens? If older teens are given the message that they can drink, then younger teens may interpret that it is more permissible for them to drink. It has been clearly shown that the younger one is when drinking is initiated, the greater the likelihood that dependency may develop. Besides the obvious physical problems associated with heavy alcohol abuse, such as those of the liver and endocrine system, young people who drink also have behavioral problems like being disruptive, aggressive, and rebellious. Anxiety and depression are also associated with youth drinking. According to statistics from the federal government, there are 1.4 million youth who meet the criteria for alcohol abuse or dependency.

To prevent youth drinking, the Surgeon General's report recommends that there should be stricter enforcement of laws. It is suggested that there should be zero tolerance for underage drinking and for those individuals and establishments that sell alcohol. Among those under age 21, approximately 1,900 die from motor vehicle crashes, 1,600 due to homicide, and 300 more from suicide. These statistics substantiate the need for preventing underage drinking. Judith McMullen points out the inconsistency in a policy that forbids alcohol consumption prior to age 21. Young people between ages 18 and 21 have discretion when it comes to health care decisions, educational decisions, and smoking.

Articles that address some of the problems and issues of underage drinking include "For MADD, the Legal Drinking Age Is Not Up for Debate," by Eric Hoover (*Chronicle of Higher Education*, November 11, 2008); "Taking on 21," by Paula Wasley (*Chronicle of Higher Education*, April 4, 2007); "Binge Drinking and Associated Health Risk Behaviors among High School Students," by Jacqueline Miller and others (*Pediatrics*, January 2007); and "Societal Cost of Underage Drinking," by Ted Miller and associates (*Journal of Studies on Alcohol*, July 2006).

ISSUE 4

Are the Dangers of Ecstasy (MDMA) Overstated?

YES: Leslie Iversen, from *Speed, ecstasy, Ritalin: The Science of Amphetamines* (Oxford University Press, 2006)

NO: National Institute on Drug Abuse, from "MDMA (ecstasy) Abuse," *National Institute on Drug Abuse Research Report* (March 2006)

ISSUE SUMMARY

YES: Author Leslie Iversen contends that ecstasy can result in adverse effects but that the drug has been unfairly demonized. Moreover, Iversen states that its negative consequences on the brain have not been proven conclusively. Iversen acknowledges that ecstasy may produce profound effects, although those effects are subject to an individual's perception.

NO: Club drugs such as ecstasy allow partygoers to dance and remain active for long periods of time according to the National Institute on Drug Abuse (NIDA). However, ecstasy may produce a number of adverse effects such as high blood pressure, panic attacks, loss of consciousness, seizures, and death. Moreover, ecstasy can produce negative effects on the brain, resulting in confusion, depression, memory impairment, and attention difficulties.

Although national surveys in the United States have shown a decrease in the use of ecstasy (MDMA), about 1 in 7 young adults between ages 19 and 30 have tried ecstasy. The number of people admitted to emergency rooms due to adverse reactions to ecstasy and other club drugs are also significant. In the year 2006, over 16,000 people visited emergency rooms due to ecstasy. As for other club drugs or hallucinogens, there were 4,002 emergency room visits attributed to LSD, 1,084 emergency room visits due to GHB, 270 visits due to Ketamine (Special K), and 21,960 visits due to PCP.

According to some drug experts, ecstasy use at rave parties and among gay and bisexual men is deeply embedded. One could argue that enforcing laws more tightly against club drugs like ecstasy increases the likelihood that adverse effects will occur because there would be no oversight on the purity of the drugs. This raises the question of whether it would be better to educate individuals about the potential harm of ecstasy or simply be more vigilant in preventing its use. One of the problems associated with buying illegal drugs is that they are not always what they are purported to be. One cannot be sure of the authenticity of the drug being purchased. Moreover, if one is sold a bogus drug, one has no legal recourse.

Because ecstasy is used at rave parties, attempts to make these parties and similar activities illegal are occurring on the national level as well as on the local level. A bipartisan bill was introduced into the Senate "to prohibit an individual from knowingly opening, maintaining, managing, controlling, renting, leasing, making available for use, or profiting from any place for the purpose of manufacturing, distributing, or using any controlled substance, and for other purposes." This act is referred to as the "Reducing Americans' Vulnerability to ecstasy Act of 2002" or the "RAVE Act." Penalties could include 20 years in prison or a fine of $250,000 or twice the gross receipts derived from each violation, whichever is more. One potential problem with the bill is that its language is broad enough to close down any business or establishment where any drug use or transaction occurs.

There is concern that ecstasy use will lead to adverse physical reactions as well as reckless behavior. One consequence of ecstasy use is dehydration due to a rise in body temperature (hyperthermia). According to the National Institute on Drug Abuse (NIDA), some of the other potential effects from ecstasy include profuse sweating, teeth grinding, high blood pressure, anxiety, aggressiveness, muscle cramping, panic attacks, nausea, loss of consciousness, and seizures. Whether or not ecstasy is addictive still remains a subject of debate. Similarly, whether or not ecstasy causes brain damage continues to be debated.

The following selections debate whether the dangers of ecstasy are overstated. The effects of ecstasy and other club drugs represent a serious threat to the physical and emotional well-being of young people according to the National Institute on Drug Abuse. Leslie Iversen acknowledges that drugs like ecstasy have the potential to cause harm. However, Iversen feels that warnings associated with drugs are blown out of proportion and that the dangers of ecstasy have not been conclusively proven.

YES

Leslie Iversen

Speed, Ecstasy, Ritalin: The Science of Amphetamines

In July 1985, the US DEA, apparently alarmed by accounts of increasing addiction to ecstasy and by scientific reports that the related drug MDA might cause brain damage, placed an immediate ban on ecstasy and MDA. They were placed in the most restrictive category of all, reserved for damaging and addictive drugs without medical use. The effect of prohibition was to curtail research into the drug without changing the attitudes of recreational users. Indeed, the DEA's action helped to promote awareness of the drug in the mass media because a small group of people who were convinced of the value of ecstasy in psychotherapy sued the US DEA to try to prevent them from outlawing the drug. The controversy provided free advertising which made ecstasy use spread like wildfire throughout the USA. The temporary ban only lasted for a year; meanwhile a hearing was set up to decide what permanent measures should be taken against the drug. The case received much publicity and was accompanied by press reports advancing the kind of scare stories now current in Europe, which added to the pressure to make the ban permanent. One widely publicized report from the laboratory of the scientist George Ricaurte referred to evidence that the related drug, MDA, caused brain damage in rats and concluded that MDMA could cause brain damage in humans. The media indulged in horror scenarios of 'our kids' brains rotting by the time they were thirty', although there was no evidence that ecstasy caused brain damage in rats at the dosage levels used by humans. On the other side were the psychotherapists who gave evidence of the benefits of the drug, but they had failed to prepare their ground by carrying out scientifically acceptable trials and so their evidence was regarded as 'anecdotal' (Holland 2001a).

The case ended with the judge recommending that MDMA be placed in a less restrictive category, Schedule 3, which would have allowed it to be manufactured, to be used on prescription, and to be the subject of research. However, the recommendation was ignored by the DEA, which refused to back down and instead placed MDMA permanently in Schedule 1, where it has remained ever since. Despite this, some continued to urge the virtues of the drug in psychiatry. As Ann Shulgin put it: 'MDMA is penicillin for the soul; you don't give up penicillin when you see what it can do'.

What is the ecstasy Experience Like?

The effects of psychedelic drugs are intensely subjective and by definition are hard to describe in words. Although at the doses used in humans there is not a fully developed 'serotonin syndrome', some elements are present, including hyperactivity. Ecstasy also causes a highly unusual series of changes in consciousness. It has been described as an 'empathogen' because it can promote an extraordinary clarity of introspective self-insight, together with a deep love of self and a no less emotionally intense empathetic love of others. MDMA also acts as a euphoriant. The euphoria is usually gentle and subtle; but is sometimes profound.

The experience is usually intensely pleasurable, with heightened awareness of sensory stimuli, a breakdown of normal social barriers and inhibitions, and increased empathy. In addition, there is an amphetamine-like stimulant effect which allows the user to stay awake and indulge in energetic activities for long periods of time. The onset of action can take 20–60 minutes, with peak effects usually occurring 60–90 minutes after ingestion, and the primary effects last for 3–5 hours. Alexander Shulgin was one of the first to describe the subjective effects of the drug, and he introduced many others to it. Shulgin experienced somewhat mixed results in testing the drug on himself, but described some of his experiences as follows. After taking a dose of 100 mg:

> My mood was light, happy, but with an underlying conviction that something significant was about to happen. There was a change in perspective both in the near visual field and in the distance. My usually poor vision was sharpened. I saw details in the distance that I could not normally see. After the peak experience had passed, my major state was one of deep relaxation. I felt that I could talk about deep or personal subjects with special clarity, and I experienced some of the feeling one has after the second martini, that one is discoursing brilliantly and with particularly acute analytical powers.

After taking 120 mg:

> I felt absolutely clean inside, and there is nothing but pure euphoria. I have never felt so great or believed this to be possible. The cleanliness, clarity and marvelous feeling of solid inner strength continued throughout the rest of the day, and evening, and through the next day. I am overcome by the profundity of the experience, and how much more powerful it was than previous experiences, for no apparent reason, other than a continually improving state of being. All the next day I felt like a 'citizen of the universe' rather than a citizen of the planet, completely disconnecting time and flowing easily from one activity to the next. (Shulgin and Shulgin 2000)

Some young ecstasy users also bound their first experience of the drug profoundly memorable:

> I'd have to say that in all of my eighteen years it was the most beautiful moment of my life.
> It was the most euphoric experience of my life.
> The peak was the most mind blowing experience I have ever had.
> It was as if I was in heaven. It was the best experience I have ever had!
> It was one of the greatest experiences of my life.
> I lived in a pure state of euphoria that night. It was the best feeling I had ever had in my life.

One of the unusual features of the MDMA experience is that the drug encourages social contacts and breaks down emotional barriers. This is the aspect most praised by those psychotherapists who have used the drug as an adjunct to normal therapy.

The MDMA experience in the context of a rave dance event has been well described by Simon Reynolds, whose book *The Energy Flash* (Reynolds 1998) gives an excellent account of the remarkable growth of the rave dance culture in the UK in the 1990s and the impact it had on youth culture.

> At a rave, the emotional outpouring and huggy demonstrativeness is a huge part of the MDMA experience (which is why ravers use the term 'loved up'), but the intimacy is dispersed into a general bonhomie: you bond with the gang you came with, but also people you've never met. . . .
> The blitz of noise and lights at a rave tilts the MDMA experience towards the drug's purely sensuous and sensational effects. With its mild trippy, pre-hallucinogenic feel, ecstasy makes colours, sounds, smells, tastes and tactile sensations more vivid. . . . The experience combines clarity and a limpid soft-focus radiance. . . .
> All music sounds better on E—crisper and more distinct, but also engulfing in its immediacy. House and techno sound especially fabulous. The music's emphasis on texture and timbre enhances the drug's mildly synaesthetic effects; so that sounds seem to caress the listener's skin. . . . Organised around the absence of crescendo or narrative progression, rave music instills a pleasurable tension, a rapt suspension that fits perfectly with the pre-orgasmic plateau of the MDMA high.

The effects of ecstasy on sexual function are subtle. MDMA is sensuous in its effects without being distinctively pro-sexual; it is more of a hug-drug than a love-drug. However, MDMA's capacity to dissolve a lifetime's social inhibitions, prudery, and sexual hang-ups means that lovemaking while under its spell is not uncommon. In men, orgasm is more intense than normal but is delayed; MDMA retains a residual sympathomimetic activity, triggering a detumescence of the male organ. To ease MDMA-induced performance difficulties, flagging Romeos increasingly combine ecstasy with Viagra.

It is easy to understand why ecstasy has proved so popular with young people. However, not every ecstasy experience is positive; some 25 percent of users report having had at least one adverse reaction, when unpleasant feelings and bodily sensations predominated (Davison and Parrott 1997). Minor adverse reactions are also common, but are generally short-lived. These include mydriasis (dilated pupils), photophobia (discomfort in bright lighting), headache, sweating, tachycardia (rapid heartbeat), bruxism (grinding of teeth), trismus (uncomfortable tightening of jaw muscles), and loss of appetite.

ecstasy-Related Deaths

Until the late 1980s the use of ecstasy was not controlled by legislation, but since then it has been portrayed as a dangerous narcotic on both sides of the Atlantic and placed in the highest category of harmful drugs, along with heroin and cocaine. This was a reaction partly to the widespread use of ecstasy on college campuses in the USA during the 1980s and partly to the first reports of ecstasy-related deaths among young people. The banning of legal ecstasy was later reinforced by scientific evidence which appeared to show that the drug could cause irreversible brain damage in both animals and humans.

The first reports of ecstasy-related deaths appeared in the USA in 1987 (Dowling *et al.* 1987) and in Europe a few years later (Milroy 1999). In the early cases drug-induced hyperthermia (abnormally elevated body temperature) appeared to be the principal cause. All those who died had been admitted to hospital with high temperatures (40–43 °C), which lead to damage to the liver, heart, and other organs. In an attempt at harm reduction, advice was given that dancers at rave events should take time out, go to a 'chill-out' area, and drink plenty of liquid. Unfortunately, some took this advice too literally; by 1993 deaths of ecstasy users from water intoxication began to be reported (Milroy 1999). Kalant (2001) surveyed reports on 87 ecstasy-related deaths in the world literature at that time and found that hyperthermia was the most common single cause (30 out of the total). An analysis of the true risks of fatal intoxication with ecstasy is difficult to make. The unnecessary death of each young person is of course a personal tragedy for their family and loved ones, and the media have given these events prominent cover and used them to convey the message that ecstasy is a deadly poison. However, the data need to be looked at in perspective. It has been estimated that more than 5000 elderly people die each year in the USA from gastric bleeding caused by over-use of aspirin-like medicines (Tamblyn *et al.* 1996). The rare deaths attributed to ecstasy need to be considered in relation to the very large number of users of the drug. During the 4-year period 1997–2000 a total of 81 deaths in England and Wales were reported to be related to ecstasy use (Schifano *et al.* 2003). However, post-mortem analysis revealed that most of those who died had been taking other drugs (prescribed and non-prescribed) at the same time as ecstasy; more than half (59 percent) had taken heroin or a related opiate. Indeed, most of the dead were known to the welfare or medical services as drug addicts, and typically they died at home rather than at a rave dance event. Only six of the total of 81 appeared to have died after taking only ecstasy. A case series in New York City studied 19,366 deaths between January 1997 and July 2000 for which post-mortem toxicological analysis was available (Gill *et al.* 2002). Only 22 of these were considered to be ecstasy related. As in the UK, the presence of other drugs was common in the ecstasy-related cases: heroin or other opiates in 32 percent, alcohol in 32 percent, ketamine in 27 percent, and cocaine in 22 percent.

A potentially serious adverse effect of ecstasy was pointed out by Setola *et al.* (2003) who reported that the drug had an appreciable affinity for 5-HT$_{2B}$ receptors and could promote a proliferation of cells in human heart valve tissue culture. Other drugs that have this property, notably the anti-obesity drug fenfluramine, have been found to be associated with potentially lethal heart valve disease. To date, however, there is no epidemiological evidence for an increased risk of heart valve disease in current or previous ecstasy users.

Tolerance and Dependence

In one of the first descriptions of human reactions to ecstasy, Shulgin (1986) commented: 'MDMA does not lend itself to overuse because its most desirable effects diminish with frequency of use'.

This proved to be an astute observation. Parrott (2005) reviewed his own surveys of ecstasy users and various reports published by others. It was apparent that there were clear differences in the pattern of drug consumption between novice users and those who were more experienced. Whereas novices used one or two tablets per session, more experienced users took two or three tablets and heavy users (lifetime use more than 100 tablets) took more than three tablets in each session. Although this provides evidence for tolerance, there was little to suggest that many ecstasy users become dependent on the drug, although for some users the association of the drug with the rave dance/club scene may become a way of life.

A more sinister aspect of tolerance to ecstasy is that the use of increasing doses may tend to exaggerate the psychostimulant effects of the drug, believed to be due largely to dopamine release in the brain. As one close observer of the ecstasy scene described it:

> By 1992, many hardcore 'veterans', who'd gotten into raving only a few years earlier and were often still in their teens, had increased their intake to three, four, five, or more pills per session. They were locked into a cycle of going raving once or twice a week, weekend after weekend. It was at this point that ecstasy's serotonin-depletion effect came into play. Even if you take pure MDMA each and every time, the drug's blissful effects fade fast, leaving only a jittery, amphetamine-like rush. In hardcore, this speedfreak effect was made worse as ravers necked more pills in a futile and misguided attempt to recover the long-lost bliss of yore. The physical side-effects—hypertension, racing heart—got worse, and so did the darkside paranoia. (Reynolds 1998, p. 192)

The author showed a remarkable insight into the possible neurochemistry underlying tolerance to ecstasy. Animal studies indeed show that the drug can cause a profound temporary impairment of serotonin function in the brain, while such changes do not occur to the same extent with dopamine-related functions (Green *et al.* 2003). The possibility that the amphetamine-like effects of ecstasy become more prominent in heavy users of the drug may explain why some heavy ecstasy users indulge in 'bingeing' (Parrott 2005). During a binge users may take several tablets at once, or take repeated tablets during a session, or both. The binge may last for up to 48 hours, usually without sleep or food, and can involve taking up to 20 ecstasy tablets. Some binge users 'snort' the powdered drug or inject it. These heavy users of ecstasy certainly show signs of becoming dependent on the drug, and many suffer harmful effects—days off with illness, loss of appetite, weight loss, and depressive experiences. Sumnall and Cole (2005) undertook a meta-analysis of 25 published surveys indicating self-reported depression in ecstasy users and concluded that it was a common phenomenon, although the effects were relatively small.

Animal studies have added little to our understanding of tolerance to and dependence on ecstasy. Whether experimental animals will readily self-administer a psychoactive drug is one widely used test of whether it is likely to prove addictive in humans. By this criterion ecstasy is not likely to be addictive, since animals do not usually self-administer it. However, under special experimental conditions animals can be taught to self-administer ecstasy. Fantegrossi *et al.* (2004) trained monkeys to self-administer ecstasy by first teaching them to self-administer cocaine (which they do very readily), and then switching to ecstasy. The animals continued to self-administer small doses of ecstasy for up to 18 months, although their consumption gradually went down during this period, which did not happen in animals trained to self-administer cocaine.

MDMA (ecstasy) Abuse

What Is MDMA?

MDMA is an illegal drug that acts as both a stimulant and psychedelic, producing an energizing effect, as well as distortions in time and perception and enhanced enjoyment from tactile experiences. Typically, MDMA (an acronym for its chemical name 3,4-methylenedioxymethamphetamine) is taken orally, usually in a tablet or capsule, and its effects last approximately 3 to 6 hours. The average reported dose is one to two tablets, with each tablet typically containing between 60 and 120 milligrams of MDMA. It is not uncommon for users to take a second dose of the drug as the effects of the first dose begin to fade.

MDMA can affect the brain by altering the activity of chemical messengers, or neurotransmitters, which enable nerve cells in the brain to communicate with one another. Research in animals has shown that MDMA in moderate to high doses can be toxic to nerve cells that contain serotonin and can cause long-lasting damage to them. Furthermore, MDMA raises body temperature. On rare but largely unpredictable occasions, this has led to severe medical consequences, including death. Also, MDMA causes the release of another neurotransmitter, norepinephrine, which is likely the cause of the increase in heart rate and blood pressure that often accompanies MDMA use.

Although MDMA is known universally among users as ecstasy, researchers have determined that many ecstasy tablets contain not only MDMA but also a number of other drugs or drug combinations that can be harmful as well. Adulterants found in MDMA tablets purchased on the street include methamphetamine, caffeine, the over-the-counter cough suppressant dextromethorphan, the diet drug ephedrine, and cocaine. Also, as with many other drugs of abuse, MDMA is rarely used alone. It is not uncommon for users to mix MDMA with other substances, such as alcohol and marijuana.

A Brief History of MDMA

MDMA was developed in Germany in the early 1900s as a parent compound to be used to synthesize other pharmaceuticals. During the 1970s, in the United States, some psychiatrists began using MDMA as a psychotherapeutic tool, despite the fact that the drug had never undergone formal clinical trials nor

From *National Institute on Drug Abuse Research Report,* March 2006, U. S. Department of Health and Human and Services.

FROM THE DIRECTOR

*T*he so-called "club drug" MDMA continues to be used by millions of Americans across the country, despite evidence of its potential harmful effects. 3,4-methylenedioxymethamphetamine (MDMA, or ecstasy) has gained a deceptive reputation as a "safe" drug among its users. This illegal drug, which has both stimulant and psychedelic properties, is often taken for the feelings of well-being, stimulation, and the distortions in time and sensory perceptions that it produces. MDMA first became popular in the "rave" and all-night party scene, but its use has now spread to a wide range of settings and demographic subgroups. According to the 2004 National Survey on Drug Use and Health, more than 11 million people have tried MDMA at least once.

Myths abound about both the acute effects and long-term consequences of this drug, often called ecstasy or "X." Indeed, one reason for the rapid rise in the drug's popularity is that many young people believe that MDMA is a new safe drug. But MDMA is not new to the scientific community, as many laboratories began investigating this drug in the 1980s, and the picture emerging from their efforts is of a drug that is far from benign. For example, MDMA can cause a dangerous increase in body temperature that can lead to kidney failure. MDMA can also increase heart rate, blood pressure, and heart wall stress. Animal studies show that MDMA can damage specific neurons in the brain. In humans, the research is not conclusive at this time; however, a number of studies show that long-term, heavy MDMA users suffer cognitive deficits, including problems with memory.

NIDA-supported research is developing a clearer picture of the potential dangers of MDMA, and this Research Report summarizes the latest findings. We hope that this compilation of scientific information will inform readers and help the public recognize the risks of MDMA use.

Nora D. Volkow, M.D.
Director
National Institute on Drug Abuse

received approval from the U.S. Food and Drug Administration (FDA) for use in humans. In fact, it was only in late 2000 that the FDA approved the first small clinical trial for MDMA that will determine if the drug can be used safely with 2 sessions of ongoing psychotherapy under carefully monitored conditions to treat post-traumatic stress disorder. Nevertheless, the drug gained a small following among psychiatrists in the late 1970s and early 1980s, with some even calling it "penicillin for the soul" because it was perceived to enhance communication in patient sessions and reportedly allowed users to achieve insights about their problems. It was also during this time that MDMA first started becoming available on the street. In 1985, the U.S. Drug Enforcement Administration (DEA) banned the drug, placing it on its list of Schedule I drugs, corresponding to those substances with no proven therapeutic value.

What Is the Scope of MDMA Abuse in the U.S.?

It is difficult to determine the exact scope of this problem because MDMA is often used in combination with other substances, and does not appear in some traditional data sources, such as treatment admission rates.

More than 11 million persons aged 12 or older reported using ecstasy at least once in their lifetimes, according to the 2004 National Survey on Drug Use and Health. The number of current (use in past month) users in 2004 was estimated to be 450,000.

The Drug Abuse Warning Network, maintained by the Substance Abuse and Mental Health Services Administration, reported that mentions of MDMA in drug abuse-related cases in hospital emergency departments were 2,221 for the third and fourth quarters of 2003. The majority of patients who came to emergency departments mentioning MDMA as a factor in their admissions during that time were aged 18–20.

There is, however, some encouraging news from NIDA's Monitoring the Future (MTF) survey, an annual survey used to track drug abuse trends among adolescents in middle and high schools across the country. Between 2001 and 2005, annual ecstasy use decreased by 52 percent in 8th-graders, 58 percent in 10th-graders, and 67 percent in 12th-graders. Rates of lifetime MDMA use decreased significantly from 2004 to 2005 among 12th-graders.

In 2005, 8th-graders reported a significant decrease in perceived harmfulness in using MDMA occasionally. The MTF data also show that MDMA use extends across many demographic sub-groups. Among 12th-graders in 2005, for example, 3.9 percent of Whites, 3.0 percent of Hispanic students, and 1.4 percent of African-Americans reported using MDMA in the year prior to the survey.

Who Is Abusing MDMA?

MDMA first gained popularity among adolescents and young adults in the night-club scene or weekend-long dance parties known as raves. However, the profile of the typical MDMA user has been changing. Community-level data from NIDA's Community Epidemiology Work Group (CEWG), continued to report that use of MDMA has spread among populations outside the nightclub scene.

Reports also indicate that use is spreading beyond predominantly White youth to a broader range of ethnic groups. In Chicago, the drug continues to be predominantly used by White youth, but there are increasing reports of its use by African-American adults in their twenties and thirties. Also, indicators in New York suggest that both the distribution and use of club drugs are becoming more common in non-White communities.

Other NIDA research shows that MDMA has also become a popular drug among urban gay males. Reports have shown that some gay and bisexual men take MDMA and other club drugs in myriad venues. This is concerning given that the use of club drugs has been linked to high-risk sexual behaviors that may lead to HIV or other sexually transmitted diseases. Many gay males in big cities report using MDMA as part of a multiple-drug experience that includes marijuana, cocaine, methamphetamine, ketamine, and other legal and illegal substances.

What Are the Effects of MDMA?

MDMA has become a popular drug, in part because of the positive effects that a person may experience within an hour or so after taking a single dose. Those effects include feelings of mental stimulation, emotional warmth, empathy toward others, a general sense of well being, and decreased anxiety. In addition, users report enhanced sensory perception as a hallmark of the MDMA experience. Because of the drug's stimulant properties, when used in club or dance settings, MDMA can also enable users to dance for extended periods. However, there are some users who report undesirable effects immediately, including anxiety, agitation, and recklessness.

As noted, MDMA is not a benign drug. MDMA can produce a variety of adverse health effects, including nausea, chills, sweating, involuntary teeth clenching, muscle cramping, and blurred vision. MDMA overdose can also occur—the symptoms can include high blood pressure, faintness, panic attacks, and in severe cases, a loss of consciousness and seizures.

Because of its stimulant properties and the environments in which it is often taken, MDMA is associated with vigorous physical activity for extended periods. This can lead to one of the most significant, although rare, acute adverse effects—a marked rise in body temperature (hyperthermia). Treatment of hyperthermia requires prompt medical attention, as it can rapidly lead to muscle breakdown, which can in turn result in kidney failure. In addition, dehydration, hypertension, and heart failure may occur in susceptible individuals. MDMA can also reduce the pumping efficiency of the heart, of particular concern during periods of increased physical activity, further complicating these problems.

MDMA is rapidly absorbed into the human bloodstream, but once in the body, MDMA metabolites interfere with the body's ability to metabolize, or break down, the drug. As a result, additional doses of MDMA can produce unexpectedly high blood levels, which could worsen the cardiovascular and other toxic effects of this drug. MDMA also interferes with the metabolism of other drugs, including some of the adulterants that may be found in MDMA tablets.

In the hours after taking the drug, MDMA produces significant reductions in mental abilities. These changes, particularly those affecting memory, can last for up to a week, and possibly longer in regular users. The fact that MDMA markedly impairs information processing emphasizes the potential dangers of performing complex or skilled activities, such as driving a car, while under the influence of this drug.

Over the course of a week following moderate use of the drug, many MDMA users report feeling a range of emotions, including anxiety, restlessness, irritability, and sadness that in some individuals can be as severe as true clinical depression. Similarly, elevated anxiety, impulsiveness, and aggression, as well as sleep disturbances, lack of appetite, and reduced interest in and pleasure from sex have been observed in regular MDMA users. Some of these disturbances may not be directly attributable to MDMA, but may be related to some of the

EFFECTS OF MDMA

Reported Undesirable Effects
(up to 1 week post-MDMA, or longer):
- Anxiety
- Restlessness
- Irritability
- Sadness
- Impulsiveness
- Aggression
- Sleep disturbances
- Lack of appetite
- Thirst
- Reduced interest in and pleasure from sex
- Significant reductions in mental abilities

Potential Adverse Health Effects:
- Nausea
- Chills
- Sweating
- Involuntary jaw clenching and teeth grinding
- Muscle cramping
- Blurred vision
- Marked rise in body temperature (hyperthermia)
- Dehydration
- High blood pressure
- Heart failure
- Kidney failure
- Arrhythmia

Symptoms of MDMA Overdose:
- High blood pressure
- Faintness
- Panic attacks
- Loss of consciousness
- Seizures

other drugs often used in combination with MDMA, such as cocaine or marijuana, or to adulterants commonly found in MDMA tablets.

What Does MDMA Do to the Brain?

MDMA affects the brain by increasing the activity of at least three neurotransmitters (the chemical messengers of brain cells): serotonin, dopamine, and norepinephrine. Like other amphetamines, MDMA causes these neurotransmitters to be released from their storage sites in neurons, resulting in increased neurotransmitter activity. Compared to the very potent stimulant, methamphetamine, MDMA causes greater serotonin release and somewhat lesser dopamine release. Serotonin is a neurotransmitter that plays an important role in the regulation of mood, sleep, pain, appetite, and other behaviors. The excess release of serotonin by MDMA likely causes the mood elevating effects experienced by MDMA users. However, by releasing large amounts of serotonin, MDMA causes the brain to become significantly depleted of this important neurotransmitter, contributing to the negative behavioral aftereffects that users often experience for several days after taking MDMA.

Numerous studies in animals have demonstrated that MDMA can damage serotonin-containing neurons; some of these studies have shown these effects to be long lasting. This suggests that such damage may occur in humans as well; however, measuring serotonin damage in humans is more difficult. Studies have shown that some heavy MDMA users experience long-lasting confusion, depression, and selective impairment of working memory and attention processes. Such memory impairments have been associated with a decrease in serotonin metabolites or other markers of serotonin function. Imaging studies in MDMA users have shown changes in brain activity in regions involved in cognition, emotion, and motor function. However, improved imaging technologies and more research are needed to confirm these findings and to elucidate the exact nature of the effects of MDMA on the human brain.

It is also important to keep in mind that many users of ecstasy may unknowingly be taking other drugs that are sold as ecstasy, and/or they may intentionally use other drugs, such as marijuana, which could contribute to these behavioral effects. Additionally, most studies in people do not have behavioral measures from before the users began taking drugs, making it difficult to rule out pre-existing conditions. Factors such as gender, dosage, frequency and intensity of use, age at which use began, the use of other drugs, as well as genetic and environmental factors all may play a role in some of the cognitive deficits that result from MDMA use and should be taken into consideration when studying the effects of MDMA in humans.

Given that most MDMA users are young and in their reproductive years, it is possible that some female users may be pregnant when they take MDMA, either inadvertently or intentionally because of the misperception that it is a safe drug. The potential adverse effects of MDMA on the developing fetus are of great concern. Behavioral studies in animals have found significant adverse effects on tests of learning and memory from exposure to MDMA during a developmental period equivalent to the third trimester in humans. However, the effects of MDMA on animals earlier in development are unclear; therefore, more research is needed to determine what the effects of MDMA are on the developing human nervous system.

Is MDMA Addictive?

For some people, MDMA can be addictive. A survey of young adult and adolescent MDMA users found that 43 percent of those who reported ecstasy use met the accepted diagnostic criteria for dependence, as evidenced by continued use despite knowledge of physical or psychological harm, withdrawal effects, and tolerance (or diminished response), and 34 percent met the criteria for drug abuse. Almost 60 percent of people who use MDMA report withdrawal symptoms, including fatigue, loss of appetite, depressed feelings, and trouble concentrating.

MDMA affects many of the same neurotransmitter systems in the brain that are targeted by other addictive drugs. Experiments have shown that animals prefer MDMA, much like they do cocaine, over other pleasurable stimuli, another hallmark of most addictive drugs.

What Do We Know About Preventing MDMA Abuse?

Because social context and networks seem to be an important component of MDMA use, the use of peer-led advocacy and drug prevention programs may be a promising approach to reduce MDMA use among adolescents and young adults. High schools and colleges can serve as important venues for delivering messages about the effects of MDMA use. Providing accurate scientific information regarding the effects of MDMA is important if we hope to reduce the damaging effects of this drug. Education is one of the most important tools for use in preventing MDMA abuse.

Are There Effective Treatments for MDMA Abuse?

There are no specific treatments for MDMA abuse. The most effective treatments for drug abuse and addiction are cognitive behavioral interventions that are designed to help modify the patient's thinking, expectancies, and behaviors, and to increase skills in coping with life's stressors. Drug abuse recovery support groups may be effective in combination with behavioral interventions to support long-term, drug-free recovery. There are currently no pharmacological treatments for dependence on MDMA.

Access Information on the Internet

- What's new on the NIDA Web site
- Information on drugs of abuse
- Publications and communications (including NIDA NOTES)
- Calendar of events
- Links to NIDA organizational units
- Funding information (including program announcements and deadlines)
- International activities
- Links to related Web sites (access to Web sites of many other organizations in the field)

Where Can I Get More Scientific Information on MDMA?

To learn more about MDMA and other drugs of abuse, contact the National Clearinghouse for Alcohol and Drug Information (NCADI) at 800-729-6686. Information specialists are available to help you locate information and resources.

Fact sheets, including *InfoFacts*, on the health effects of MDMA, other drugs of abuse, and other drug abuse topics are available on the NIDA Web site . . . and can be ordered free of charge in English and Spanish from NCADI. . . .

References

Bolla, K.I.; McCann, U.D.; and Ricaurte, G.A. Memory impairment in abstinent MDMA ("ecstasy") users. *Neurology* 51:1532–1537 (1998).

Broening, H.W.; Morford, L.L.; Inman-Wood, S.L.; Fukumura, M.; and Vorhees, C.V. 3,4-Methylenedioxymethamphetamine (ecstasy)-induced learning and memory impairments depend on the age of exposure during early development. *The Journal of Neuroscience* 21:3228–3235 (2001).

Colado, M.I.; O'Shea, E.; Granados, R.; Misra, A.; Murray, T.K.; and Green, A.R.; A study of the neurotoxic effect of MDMA ('ecstasy') on 5-HT neurons in the brains of mothers and neonates following administration of the drug during pregnancy. *British Journal of Pharmacology* 121:827–833 (1997).

Community Epidemiology Work Group. *Epidemiologic Trends in Drug Abuse: Volume I.* Bethesda, MD. June 2005.

Cottler, L.B.; Womack, S.B.; Compton, W.M.; and Ben-Abdallah, A. ecstasy abuse and dependence among adolescents and young adults: applicability and reliability of DSM-IV criteria. *Human Psychopharmacology* 16:599–606 (2001).

Curran, H.V.; and Travill, R.A. Mood and cognitive effects of ±3,4-methylenedioxymethamphetamine (MDMA, 'ecstasy'): week-end 'high' followed by mid-week low. *Addiction* 92:821–831 (1997).

Dafters, R.I.; and Lynch, E. Persistent loss of thermo-regulation in the rate induced by 3,4-methylenedioxymethamphetamine (MDMA or "ecstasy") but not by fenfluramine. *Psychopharmacology* 138:207–212 (1998).

Kish, S.J.; Furukawa, Y.; Ang, L.; Vorce, S.P.; and Kalasinsky, K.S. Striatal serotonin is depleted in brain of a human MDMA (ecstasy) user. *Neurology* 55:294–296 (2000).

Koprich, J.B.; Chen, E.-Y.; Kanaan, N.M.; Campbell, N.G.; Kordower, J.H.; and Lipton, J.W. Prenatal 3,4-methylenedioxymethamphetamine (ecstasy) alters exploratory behavior, reduces monoamine metabolism, and increases forebrain tyrosine hydroxylase fiber density of juvenile rats. *Neurotoxicology and Teratology* 25: 509–517 (2003).

Lester, S.J.; Baggott, M.; Welm, S.; Schiller, N.B.; Jones, R.T.; Foster, E.; and Mendelson, J. Cardiovascular effects of 3,4-methylenedioxymethamphetamine: a double-blind, placebo-controlled trial. *Annals of Internal Medicine* 133:969–973 (2000).

Liechti, M.E.; and Vollenweider, F.X. Which neuroreceptors mediate the subjective effects of MDMA in humans? A summary of mechanistic studies. *Human Psychopharmacology* 16:589–598 (2001).

Lyles, J.; and Cadet, J.L. Methylenedioxymethamphetamine (MDMA, ecstasy) neurotoxicity: cellular and molecular mechanisms. *Brain Research Reviews* 42:155–168 (2003).

McCann, U.D.; Eligulashvili, V.; and Ricaurte, G.A. (±)3,4-Methylenedioxymethamphetamine ('ecstasy')-induced serotonin neurotoxicity: clinical studies. *Neuropsychobiology* 42:11–16 (2000).

Morgan, M.J. ecstasy (MDMA): a review of its possible persistent psychological effects. *Psychopharmacology* 152:230–248 (2000).

Morgan, M.J. Memory deficits associated with recreational use of "ecstasy" (MDMA). *Psychopharmacology* 141:30–36 (1999).

National Institute on Drug Abuse. *Monitoring the Future: National Results on Adolescent Drug Use 2005*.

Obrocki, J.; Buchert, R.; Väterlein, O.; Thomasius, R.; Beyer, W.; and Schiemann, T. ecstasy—long-term effects on the human central nervous system revealed by positron emission tomography. *British Journal of Psychiatry* 175:186–188 (1999).

Parrott, A.C.; and Lasky, J. ecstasy (MDMA) effect upon mood and cognition: before, during and after a Saturday night dance. *Psychopharmacology* 139: 261–268 (1998).

Reneman, L.; Booij, J.; Schmand, B.; van den Brink, W.; and Gunning, B. Memory disturbances in "ecstasy" users are correlated with an altered brain serotonin neurotransmission. *Psychopharmacology* 148:322–324 (2000).

Schenk, S.; Gittings, D.; Johnstone, M.; and Daniela, E. Development, maintenance and temporal pattern of self-administration maintained by ecstasy (MDMA) in rats. *Psychopharmacology* 169:21–27 (2003).

Sherlock, K.; Wolff, K.; Hay, A.W.; and Conner, M. Analysis of illicit ecstasy tablets. *Journal of Accident and Emergency Medicine* 16:194–197 (1999).

Substance Abuse and Mental Health Services Administration, Office of Applied Studies. *Drug Abuse Warning Network, 2003: Interim National Estimates of Drug-Related Emergency Department Visits*. DAWN Series D-26, DHHS Publication No. (SMA) 04–3972. Rockville, MD (2004).

Thompson, M.R.; Li, K.M.; Clemens, K.J.; Gurtman, C.G.; Hunt, G.E.; Cornish, J.L.; and McGregor; I.S. Chronic fluoxetine treatment partly attenuates the long-term anxiety and depressive symptoms induced by MDMA ('ecstasy') in rats. *Neuropsychopharmacology* 29(40):694–704, 2004.

Verkes, R.J.; Gijsman, H.J.; Pieters, M.S.M.; Schoemaker, R.C.; de Visser, S.; Kuijpers, M.; Pennings, E.J.M.; de Bruin, D.; Van de Wijngaart, G.; Van Gerven, J.M.A.; and Cohen, A.F. Cognitive performance and serotonergic function in users of ecstasy. *Psychopharmacology* 153:196–202 (2001).

Wareing, M.; Fisk, J.E.; and Murphy, P.N. Working memory deficits in current and previous users of MDMA ('ecstasy'). *British Journal of Psychology* 91:181–188 (2000).

POSTSCRIPT

Are the Dangers of Ecstasy (MDMA) Overstated?

There is little argument that mind-altering drugs can cause physical and emotional havoc for the user. People may become less inhibited and become involved in behaviors they would not typically do if they were not on drugs. It is not uncommon for ecstasy users to open up emotionally. However, is one's use of ecstasy and other so-called club drugs likely to increase these behaviors? Perhaps individuals who use these drugs are the types of people who would engage in reckless behavior regardless. In other words, is ecstasy the reason people are more open or does ecstasy provide the excuse to be more open?

The National Institute on Drug Abuse (NIDA) contends that these ecstasy and other club drugs are deleterious. The fact that an increasing number of secondary students perceive ecstasy as harmful illustrates its potential harm. In recent years, there has been a slight decrease in ecstasy use by secondary students. Nonetheless, thousands of people visit emergency rooms as a result of an adverse reaction to ecstasy. NIDA admits that additional research still needs to be conducted into the effects of ecstasy, but that there is more than enough research to point to the dangers of ecstasy.

Some people argue that history shows that bringing attention to certain drugs results in their increased use. Young people would not know to alter their consciousness with certain drugs unless they were alerted to their effects. For example, how would one know that sniffing glue would affect one's consciousness unless that fact was established. However, if young people participate in an activity that is potentially harmful, one could argue that it is the government's responsibility to step in. At what point is too much information counterproductive? Balancing one's right to know about drugs with the publicity generated by informing the public about certain drugs is difficult.

The issue of whether or not we should be concerned about ecstasy and other club drugs raises a number of interesting questions. For example, how much danger must a drug represent before it is considered too dangerous? Is exaggerating the effects of drugs like ecstasy providing a disservice because other information about drugs that are especially harmful may be ignored? Should the government's focus be on prohibiting the use of ecstasy at all costs or should the government try to educate people about its potential adverse effects?

At one time ecstasy was used for therapeutic purposes. There has been a renewed interest in exploring the therapeutic benefits of ecstasy. If ecstasy has these types of benefits, can the drug be as bad as it is purported to be?

There are a number of articles that look at the benefits or dangers of ecstasy and similar drugs. Two good articles are "Researchers Explore New Visions for

Hallucinogens," by Susan Brown (*The Chronicle for Higher Education*, December 6, 2006) and "The Ups and Downs of ecstasy," by Erika Check (*Nature*, May 13, 2004). Other informative articles on this issue include "Evidence for Significant Polydrug Use Among ecstasy-Using College Students," by Eric Wish and colleagues (*Journal of American College Health*, 2006); "Treatment Implications for Young Adult Users of MDMA," by Brian Dew, Kirk Elifson, and Claire Sterk (*Journal of Addictions and Offender Counseling*, April 2006); and "Club Drug Use Among Young Adults Frequenting Dance Clubs and Other Social Venues in New York City," by Jeffrey Parsons, Perry Halkitis, and David Bimbi (*Journal of Child and Adolescent Substance Abuse*, 2006). One group that sponsors research into the therapeutic benefits of ecstasy and other drugs is the Multidisciplinary Association for Psychedelic Studies (MAPS). Its Web site is www.maps.org.

ISSUE 5

Should Pregnant Drug Users Be Prosecuted?

YES: Paul A. Logli, from "Drugs in the Womb: The Newest Battle-field in the War on Drugs," *Criminal Justice Ethics* (Winter/Spring 1990)

NO: Carolyn S. Carter, from "Perinatal Care for Women Who Are Addicted: Implications for Empowerment," *Health and Social Work* (August 2002)

ISSUE SUMMARY

YES: Paul A. Logli, an Illinois prosecuting attorney, argues that it is the government's duty to enforce every child's right to begin life with a healthy, drug-free mind and body. Logli maintains that pregnant women who use drugs should be prosecuted because they harm the life of their unborn children. He feels that it is the state's responsibility to ensure that every baby is born as healthy as possible.

NO: Carolyn Carter, a social work professor at Howard University, argues that the stigma of drug use during pregnancy has resulted in the avoidance of treatment. Carter asserts that the prosecution of pregnant drug users is unfair because poor women are more likely to be the targets of such prosecution. To enable pregnant women who use drugs to receive perinatal care, it is necessary to define their drug use as a health problem rather than as a legal problem.

The effects that drugs have on a fetus can be mild and temporary or severe and permanent, depending on the extent of drug use by the mother, the type of substance used, and the stage of fetal development at the time the drug crosses the placental barrier and enters the bloodstream of the fetus. Both ille-gal and legal drugs, such as cocaine, crack, marijuana, alcohol, and nicotine, are increasingly found to be responsible for incidents of premature births, con-genital abnormalities, fetal alcohol syndrome, mental retardation, and other serious birth defects. The exposure of the fetus to these substances and the long-term involuntary physical, intellectual, and emotional effects are disturb-ing. In addition, the medical, social, and economic costs to treat and care for babies who are exposed to or become addicted to drugs while in utero (in the uterus) warrant serious concern.

An important consideration regarding the prosecution of pregnant drug users is whether this is a legal problem or a medical problem. In recent years, attempts have been made to establish laws that would allow the incarceration of drug-using pregnant women on the basis of "fetal abuse." Some cases have been successfully prosecuted: Mothers have been denied custody of their infants until they enter appropriate treatment programs, and criminal charges have been brought against mothers whose children were born with drug-related complications. The underlying presumption is that the unborn fetus should be afforded protection against the harmful actions of another person, specifically the use of harmful drugs by the mother.

Those who profess that prosecuting pregnant women who use drugs is necessary insist that the health and welfare of the unborn child is the highest priority. They contend that the possibility that these women will avoid obtaining health care for themselves or their babies because they fear punishment does not absolve the state from the responsibility of protecting the babies. They also argue that criminalizing these acts is imperative to protect fetuses and newborns who cannot protect themselves. It is the duty of the legal system to deter pregnant women from engaging in future criminal drug use and to protect the best interests of infants.

Others maintain that drug use and dependency by pregnant women is a medical problem, not a criminal one. Many pregnant women seek treatment, but they often find that rehabilitation programs are limited or unavailable. Shortages of openings in chemical dependency programs may keep a prospective client waiting for months, during which time she will most likely continue to use the drugs to which she is addicted and prolong her fetus's drug exposure. Many low-income women do not receive drug treatment and adequate prenatal care due to financial constraints. Women who fear criminal prosecution because of their drug use may simply avoid prenatal care altogether.

Some suggest that medical intervention, drug prevention, and education—not prosecution—are needed for pregnant drug users. Prosecution, they contend, drives women who need medical attention away from the very help they and their babies need. Others respond that prosecuting pregnant women who use drugs will help identify those who need attention, at which point adequate medical and social welfare services can be provided to treat and protect the mother and child.

In the following selections, Paul A. Logli, arguing for the prosecution of pregnant drug users, contends that it is the state's responsibility to protect the unborn and the newborn because they are least able to protect themselves. He charges that it is the prosecutor's responsibility to deter future criminal drug use by mothers who he feels violate the rights of their potential newborns to have an opportunity for a healthy and normal life. Carolyn Carter contends that prosecuting pregnant drug users may be counterproductive to improving the quality of infant and maternal health. To help women who use drugs during pregnancy, it would be more helpful to identify the problem as a medical problem and not as a legal problem.

Drugs in the Womb: The Newest Battlefield in the War on Drugs

Introduction

The reported incidence of drug-related births has risen dramatically over the last several years. The legal system and, in particular, local prosecutors have attempted to properly respond to the suffering, death, and economic costs which result from a pregnant woman's use of drugs. The ensuing debate has raised serious constitutional and practical issues which are far from resolution.

Prosecutors have achieved mixed results in using current criminal and juvenile statutes as a basis for legal action intended to prosecute mothers and protect children. As a result, state and federal legislators have begun the difficult task of drafting appropriate laws to deal with the problem, while at the same time acknowledging the concerns of medical authorities, child protection groups, and advocates for individual rights.

The Problem

The plight of "cocaine babies," children addicted at birth to narcotic substances or otherwise affected by maternal drug use during pregnancy, has prompted prosecutors in some jurisdictions to bring criminal charges against drug-abusing mothers. Not only have these prosecutions generated heated debates both inside and outside of the nation's courtrooms, but they have also expanded the war on drugs to a controversial new battlefield—the mother's womb.

A 1988 survey of hospitals conducted by Dr. Ira Chasnoff, Associate Professor of Northwestern University Medical School and President of the National Association for Perinatal Addiction Research and Education (NAPARE) indicated that as many as 375,000 infants may be affected by maternal cocaine use during pregnancy each year. Chasnoff's survey included 36 hospitals across the country and showed incidence rates ranging from 1 percent to 27 percent. It also indicated that the problem was not restricted to urban populations or particular racial or socio-economic groups. More recently a study at Hutzel Hospital in Detroit's inner city found that 42.7 percent of its newborn babies were exposed to drugs while in their mothers' wombs.

Paul A. Logli, "Drugs in the Womb: The Newest Battlefield in the War on Drugs," as appeared in *Criminal Justice Ethics,* Volume 9, Number 1, [Winter/Spring 1990] pp. 23–29. Reprinted by permission of The Institute for Criminal Justice Ethics, 555 West 57th Street, Suite 607, New York, NY 10019-1029.

The effects of maternal use of cocaine and other drugs during pregnancy on the mother and her newborn child have by now been well-documented and will not be repeated here. The effects are severe and can cause numerous threats to the short-term health of the child. In a few cases it can even result in death.

Medical authorities have just begun to evaluate the long-term effects of cocaine exposure on children as they grow older. Early findings show that many of these infants show serious difficulties in relating and reacting to adults and environments, as well as in organizing creative play, and they appear similar to mildly autistic or personality-disordered children.

The human costs related to the pain, suffering, and deaths resulting from maternal cocaine use during pregnancy are simply incalculable. In economic terms, the typical intensive-care costs for treating babies exposed to drugs range from $7,500 to $31,000. In some cases medical bills go as high as $150,000.

The costs grow enormously as more and more hospitals encounter the problem of "boarder babies"—those children literally abandoned at the hospital by an addicted mother, and left to be cared for by the nursing staff. Future costs to society for simply educating a generation of drug-affected children can only be the object of speculation. It is clear, however, that besides pain, suffering, and death the economic costs to society of drug use by pregnant women is presently enormous and is certainly growing larger.

The Prosecutor's Response

It is against this backdrop and fueled by the evergrowing emphasis on an aggressively waged war on drugs that prosecutors have begun a number of actions against women who have given birth to drug-affected children. A review of at least two cases will illustrate the potential success or failure of attempts to use existing statutes.

People v. Melanie Green   On February 4, 1989, at a Rockford, Illinois hospital, two-day-old Bianca Green lost her brief struggle for life. At the time of Bianca's birth both she and her mother, twenty-four-year-old Melanie Green, tested positive for the presence of cocaine in their systems.

Pathologists in Rockford and Madison, Wisconsin, indicated that the death of the baby was the result of a prenatal injury related to cocaine used by the mother during the pregnancy. They asserted that maternal cocaine use had caused the placenta to prematurely rupture, which deprived the fetus of oxygen before and during delivery. As a result of oxygen deprivation, the child's brain began to swell and she eventually died.

After an investigation by the Rockford Police Department and the State of Illinois Department of Children and Family Services, prosecutors allowed a criminal complaint to be filed on May 9, 1989, charging Melanie Green with the offenses of Involuntary Manslaughter and Delivery of a Controlled Substance.

On May 25, 1989, testimony was presented to the Winnebago County Grand Jury by prosecutors seeking a formal indictment. The Grand Jury, however, declined to indict Green on either charge. Since Grand Jury proceedings in the State of Illinois are secret, as are the jurors' deliberations and votes, the reason for the decision of the Grand Jury in this case is determined more by conjecture than any direct knowledge. Prosecutors involved in the presentation observed that the jurors exhibited a certain amount of sympathy for the young woman who had been brought before the Grand Jury at the jurors' request. It is also likely that the jurors were uncomfortable with the use of statutes that were not intended to be used in these circumstances.

It would also be difficult to disregard the fact that, after the criminal complaints were announced on May 9th and prior to the Grand Jury deliberations of May 25th, a national debate had ensued revolving around the charges brought in Rockford, Illinois, and their implications for the ever-increasing problem of women who use drugs during pregnancy.

People v. Jennifer Clarise Johnson   On July 13, 1989, a Seminole County, Florida judge found Jennifer Johnson guilty of delivery of a controlled substance to a child. The judge found that delivery, for purposes of the statute, occurred through the umbilical cord after the birth of the child and before the cord was severed. Jeff Deen, the Assistant State's Attorney who prosecuted the case, has since pointed out that Johnson, age 23, had previously given birth to three other cocaine-affected babies, and in this case was arrested at a crack house. "We needed to make sure this woman does not give birth to another cocaine baby."

Johnson was sentenced to fifteen years of probation including strict supervision, drug treatment, random drug testing, educational and vocational training, and an intensive prenatal care program if she ever became pregnant again.

Support for the Prosecution of Maternal Drug Abuse

Both cases reported above relied on a single important fact as a basis for the prosecution of the drug-abusing mother: that the child was born alive and exhibited the consequences of prenatal injury.

In the Melanie Green case, Illinois prosecutors relied on the "born alive" rule set out earlier in *People v. Bolar*. In *Bolar* the defendant was convicted of the offense of reckless homicide. The case involved an accident between a car driven by the defendant, who was found to be drunk, and another automobile containing a pregnant woman. As a result, the woman delivered her baby by emergency caesarean section within hours of the collision. Although the newborn child exhibited only a few heartbeats and lived for approximately two minutes, the court found that the child was born alive and was therefore a person for purposes of the criminal statutes of the State of Illinois.

The Florida prosecution relied on a live birth in an entirely different fashion. The prosecutor argued in that case that the delivery of the controlled substance occurred after the live birth via the umbilical cord and prior to the cutting of the cord. Thus, it was argued, that the delivery of the controlled substance occurred not to a fetus but to a person who enjoyed the protection of the criminal code of the State of Florida.

Further support for the State's role in protecting the health of newborns even against prenatal injury is found in the statutes which provide protection for the fetus. These statutes proscribe actions by a person, usually other than the mother, which either intentionally or recklessly harm or kill a fetus. In other words, even in the absence of a live birth, most states afford protection to the unborn fetus against the harmful actions of another person. Arguably, the same protection should be afforded the infant against intentional harmful actions by a drug-abusing mother.

The state also receives support for a position in favor of the protection of the health of a newborn from a number of non-criminal cases. A line of civil cases in several states would appear to stand for the principle that a child has a right to begin life with a sound mind and body, and a person who interferes with that right may be subject to civil liability. In two cases decided within months of each other, the Supreme Court of Michigan upheld two actions for recovery of damages that were caused by the infliction of prenatal injury. In *Womack v. Buckhorn* the court upheld an action on behalf of an eight-year-old surviving child for prenatal brain injuries apparently suffered during the fourth month of the pregnancy in an automobile accident. The court adopted with approval the reasoning of a New Jersey Supreme Court decision and "recognized that a child has a legal right to begin life with a sound mind and body." Similarly, in *O'Neill v. Morse* the court found that a cause of action was allowed for prenatal injuries that caused the death of an eight-month-old viable fetus.

Illinois courts have allowed civil recovery on behalf of an infant for a negligently administered blood transfusion given to the mother prior to conception which resulted in damage to the child at birth. However, the same Illinois court would not extend a similar cause of action for prebirth injuries as between a child and its own mother. The court, however, went on to say that a right to such a cause of action could be statutorily enacted by the Legislature.

Additional support for the state's role in protecting the health of newborns is found in the principles annunciated in recent decisions of the United States Supreme Court. The often cited case of *Roe v. Wade* set out that although a woman's right of privacy is broad enough to cover the abortion decision, the right is not absolute and is subject to limitations, "and that at some point the state's interest as to protection of health, medical standards and prenatal life, becomes dominant."

More recently, in the case of *Webster v. Reproductive Health Services*, the court expanded the state's interest in protecting potential human life by setting aside viability as a rigid line that had previously allowed state regulation only after viability had been shown but prohibited it before viability. The court goes on to say that the "fundamental right" to abortion as described in *Roe* is now accorded the lesser status of a "liberty interest." Such language surely supports a prosecutor's argument that the state's compelling interest in potential human life would allow the criminalization of acts which if committed by a pregnant woman can damage not just a viable fetus but eventually a born-alive infant. It follows that, once a pregnant woman has abandoned her right to abort and has decided to carry the fetus to term, society can well impose a duty on the mother to insure that the fetus is born as healthy as possible.

A further argument in support of the state's interest in prosecuting women who engage in conduct which is damaging to the health of a newborn child is especially compelling in regard to maternal drug use during pregnancy. Simply put, there is no fundamental right or even a liberty interest in the use of psycho-active drugs. A perceived right of privacy has never formed an absolute barrier against state prosecutions of those who use or possess narcotics. Certainly no exception can be made simply because the person using drugs happens to be pregnant.

Critics of the prosecutor's role argue that any statute that would punish mothers who create a substantial risk of harm to their fetus will run afoul of constitutional requirements, including prohibitions on vagueness, guarantees of liberty and privacy, and rights of due process and equal protection. . . .

In spite of such criticism, the state's role in protecting those citizens who are least able to protect themselves, namely the newborn, mandates an aggressive posture. Much of the criticism of prosecutorial efforts is based on speculation as to the consequences of prosecution and ignores the basic tenet of criminal law that prosecutions deter the prosecuted and others from committing additional crimes. To assume that it will only drive persons further underground is to somehow argue that certain prosecutions of crime will only force perpetrators to make even more aggressive efforts to escape apprehension, thus making arrest and prosecution unadvisable. Neither could this be accepted as an argument justifying even the weakening of criminal sanctions. . . .

The concern that pregnant addicts will avoid obtaining health care for themselves or their infants because of the fear of prosecution cannot justify the absence of state action to protect the newborn. If the state were to accept such reasoning, then existing child abuse laws would have to be reconsidered since they might deter parents from obtaining medical care for physically or sexually abused children. That argument has not been accepted as a valid reason for abolishing child abuse laws or for not prosecuting child abusers. . . .

The far better policy is for the state to acknowledge its responsibility not only to provide a deterrant to criminal and destructive behavior by pregnant addicts but also to provide adequate opportunities for those who might seek help to discontinue their addiction. Prosecution has a role in its ability to deter future criminal behavior and to protect the best interests of the child. The medical and social welfare establishment must assume an even greater responsibility to encourage legislators to provide adequate funding and facilities so that no pregnant woman who is addicted to drugs will be denied the opportunity to seek appropriate prenatal care and treatment for her addiction.

One State's Response

The Legislature of the State of Illinois at the urging of local prosecutors moved quickly to amend its juvenile court act in order to provide protection to those children born drug-affected. Previously, Illinois law provided that a court could assume jurisdiction over addicted minors or a minor who is generally declared neglected or abused.

Effective January 1, 1990, the juvenile court act was amended to expand the definition of a neglected or abused minor. . . .

> those who are neglected include . . . any newborn infant whose blood or urine contains any amount of a controlled substance. . . .

The purpose of the new statute is to make it easier for the court to assert jurisdiction over a newborn infant born drug-affected. The state is not required to show either the addiction of the child or harmful effects on the child in order to remove the child from a drug-abusing mother. Used in this context, prosecutors can work with the mother in a rather coercive atmosphere to encourage her to enter into drug rehabilitation and, upon the successful completion of the program, be reunited with her child.

Additional legislation before the Illinois Legislature is House Bill 2835 sponsored by Representatives John Hallock (R-Rockford) and Edolo "Zeke" Giorgi (D-Rockford). This bill represents the first attempt to specifically address the prosecution of drug-abusing pregnant women. . . .

The statute provides for a class 4 felony disposition upon conviction. A class 4 felony is a probationable felony which can also result in a term of imprisonment from one to three years.

Subsequent paragraphs set out certain defenses available to the accused.

> It shall not be a violation of this section if a woman knowingly or intentionally uses a narcotic or dangerous drug in the first twelve weeks of pregnancy and: 1. She has no knowledge that she is pregnant; or 2. Subsequently, within the first twelve weeks of pregnancy, undergoes medical treatment for substance abuse or treatment or rehabilitation in a program or facility approved by the Illinois Department of Alcoholism and Substance Abuse, and thereafter discontinues any further use of drugs or narcotics as previously set forth.

. . . A woman, under this statute, could not be prosecuted for self-reporting her addiction in the early stages of the pregnancy. Nor could she be prosecuted under this statute if, even during the subsequent stages of the pregnancy, she discontinued her drug use to the extent that no drugs were present in her system or the baby's system at the time of birth. The statute, as drafted, is clearly intended to allow prosecutors to invoke the criminal statutes in the most serious of cases.

Conclusion

Local prosecutors have a legitimate role in responding to the increasing problem of drug-abusing pregnant women and their drug-affected children. Eliminating the pain, suffering and death resulting from drug exposure in newborns must be a prosecutor's priority. However, the use of existing statutes to address the problem may meet with limited success since they are burdened with numerous constitutional problems dealing with original intent, notice, vagueness, and due process.

The juvenile courts may offer perhaps the best initial response in working to protect the interests of a surviving child. However, in order to address more serious cases, legislative efforts may be required to provide new statutes that will specifically address the problem and hopefully deter future criminal conduct which deprives children of their important right to a healthy and normal birth.

The long-term solution does not rest with the prosecutor alone. Society, including the medical and social welfare establishment, must be more responsive in providing readily accessible prenatal care and treatment alternatives for pregnant addicts. In the short term however, prosecutors must be prepared to play a vital role in protecting children and deterring women from engaging in conduct which will harm the newborn child. If prosecutors fail to respond, then they are simply closing the doors of the criminal justice system to those persons, the newborn, who are least able to open the doors for themselves.

Carolyn S. Carter

 **NO**

Perinatal Care for Women Who Are Addicted: Implications for Empowerment

. . . Perinatal drug abuse is the use of alcohol and other drugs among women who are pregnant. The National Institute on Drug Abuse estimates that 5.5 percent of the women in the United States have used illicit drugs while pregnant, including cocaine, marijuana, heroin, and psychotherapeutic drugs that were not prescribed by a physician. More than 18 percent used alcohol during their pregnancy, and 20.4 percent smoked cigarettes.

Literature reports the increased use of drugs during pregnancy, using therapeutic communities and neighborhood context for addressing perinatal drug abuse; access barriers for low-income ethnic minority women who are addicted and pregnant; the importance of effective policy making; referrals to child protection services; and other responses to perinatal drug abuse.

Women who abuse drugs while pregnant face severe consequences, which include becoming stigmatized as immoral and deficient caregivers. A behavioral outcome of societal attitudes toward perinatal drug abuse is the degree to which the drug-taking behavior of pregnant women is criminalized. Criminalization refers to using legal approaches, such as incarceration, for medical problems of clients rather than referring them for treatment. Community response to the increasing number of women who give birth to infants addicted to crack cocaine, for example, has been to prosecute women for perinatal drug abuse. Similarly, the number of mentally ill inmates in jails and prisons is estimated as being twice that in state hospitals. Individuals in helping professions also display stigmatic attitudes toward perinatal drug abuse. Disparaging interactions with women in some perinatal care facilities, for example, include rude and judgmental comments to clients and violation of their confidentiality. Uncomfortable relationships with health care providers and fear of reprisal on the part of pregnant women who are addicted make women four times less likely to receive adequate care, thereby creating health risks for women who are addicted, their unborn fetuses, and their other children.

In this article I discuss contemporary responses to perinatal drug abuse, including ways in which the behavior of women who abuse drugs is criminalized or subjected to legal interventions. Vignettes from an ethnographic

From *Health and Social Work,* vol. 27, issue 3, August 2002, pp. 166–174. Copyright © 2002 by National Association of Social Workers, Inc. Reprinted by permission of NASW Press.

study of 120 women who used heroin, crack cocaine, and methamphetamine while pregnant depict the attitudes and behaviors of health care providers, society at large, and women themselves toward maternal drug abuse. This article demonstrates how poor women and women of color encounter legal interventions—such as prosecution or reports to city or state child protective services (CPS)—more frequently for using drugs during pregnancy than their more affluent, white counterparts. Because criminalizing perinatal drug abuse presents substantial risks to the health of women and children, empowering strategies are suggested for redefining perinatal drug abuse less as a legal issue and more as a health concern. The strategies are consistent with elements of the national health plan of the U.S. Department of Health and Human Services (DHHS), such as creating access to health care and minimizing risks to maternal, infant, and child health.

Societal Attitudes Toward Perinatal Drug Abuse

Over the past 100 years, there has been an overall shift in obstetric medicine to a focus on fetal protection. In cases involving maternal drug abuse, the shift has sometimes resulted in adversarial attitudes with sentiment favoring the well-being of fetuses and against pregnant women. The following excerpts offer three perspectives toward perinatal drug abuse that have primary emphasis on unborn fetuses: The first comment reflects the attitudes of some drug dealers; the second statement is a common reaction of partners of pregnant women; and the third depicts the attitude of society at large.

> They [crack dealers] tell me that I shouldn't be doing this in the first place, but I'm gonna do it anyway. And they go, "You know it. I shouldn't even really sell you anything. I shouldn't sell you anything cause you're pregnant. I'm not gonna contribute to that."
> My baby came home with crack in her system, and he [baby's father who is himself a crack dealer] don't want to claim her now.
> I know one girl. She just smokes [crack] and doesn't give a damn. Her stomach is way out there, so she shouldn't be out there [using crack] anyway, cause people be like, "man, look, a pregnant woman!"

Negative attitudes like the ones in the vignettes above are pervasive and often based on assumed medical and developmental consequences of drugs on fetuses. The concerns are both supported and refuted by research. Studies of the effects of drug use on fetal development cite problems such as low birthweight, small head size, prematurity, and small size for gestational age. A study of 11,000 infants conducted by the Brown University School of Medicine, however, showed no increase in abnormalities at birth among children who had been exposed to cocaine in utero. Although the latter study has not followed the children into school age and is therefore inconclusive, other studies of adjustment among drug-exposed children also challenge the notion of devastating effects resulting from cocaine use during pregnancy. Coles concluded that the effects of the social environment are too often ignored in studies of perinatal drug abuse.

In addition to the pejorative attitudes toward women who abuse drugs during pregnancy based on ideas about adverse fetal development is the belief that drug use compromises the reproductive and caregiver roles of women. It is believed that women who abuse substances are unfit mothers undeserving of their children. Society sanctions women for failing to live up to preconceived gender-role expectations by using legal interventions, particularly against poor women of color who use drugs while they are pregnant.

Legal Interventions

Legal interventions for perinatal drug abuse may be increasing in the United States. Since 1985, 240 women in 35 states have been prosecuted for using alcohol or illegal drugs while pregnant. Eleven states have developed specific gestational-abuse statutes. The most comprehensive reporting system is in Minnesota and includes toxicological screening and "involuntary civil commitment" to drug rehabilitation of pregnant women who have used drugs. Before March 2001, eight states mandated that health care workers report neonates' positive drug toxicology as evidence of child abuse and neglect, thus paving the way for court proceedings and actions affecting the parental rights of mothers. On March 21, 2001, the U.S. Supreme Court ruled that it is unlawful to involuntarily test pregnant women who are suspected of drug abuse. In Ferguson v. City of Charleston, Charleston, South Carolina was a litigant in the Supreme Court case and, along with Florida, enforced the greatest number of legal interventions.

It is informative to place the legal interventions that occurred before the March 2001 judicial ruling within a sociocultural context. In doing so, it becomes clear that although illegal drug use is similar across class and racial lines, poor and ethnic minority women were more likely to be criminalized. The manner in which drug screening occurred is an example. Screenings commonly occurred during routine prenatal care, and the stated purpose was protecting fetuses. However, drug screenings were often limited to facilities that served low socioeconomic populations and populations of color, thus making screenings more detrimental for poor and pregnant women from ethnic minority groups.

Reports to CPS were disparate across cultural groups as well. A review of mandatory reporting of perinatal drug addiction in Florida showed that positive drug screening rates were almost equal among white and African American women and among women seen in clinics and private offices. Yet, reporting rates were much higher for African American women than for white women.

The procedures for prosecuting pregnant women for substance use were discretionary and reflected disparities across demographic groups. A 1987 review of court-ordered obstetrical interventions showed that 81 percent of the women were African American, Hispanic, or Asian and 24 percent did not speak English as a primary language. More recent study results indicate that pregnant African American women were nine times more likely to be prosecuted for substance use than pregnant white women.

Incarceration, like other legal approaches to perinatal drug abuse, also discriminated against poor women and women of color. Women with low incomes generally gave birth in public health settings. Delivering in these facilities increased their chances of incarceration compared with middle-and upper-income women who gave birth in private hospitals that rarely screened for illicit drugs. Public hospitals were more likely to have mandatory drug screenings and protocols that included reporting positive toxicology to CPS. Disclosing positive toxicology to CPS could result in incarceration. Disparities in the rate of incarceration extended to ethnic minority groups, with African American women facing the greatest burden of being imprisoned. Of the 41 pregnant women arrested for abusing drugs in South Carolina from 1989 to 1993, 40 were African American.

The American Medical Association (AMA) stated that drug addiction was an illness that required medical rather than legal intervention, and prosecution did not prevent harm to infants but it often resulted in harm. For example, fear of reprisal was a barrier to outreach and often deterred addicted pregnant women from receiving medical care. Avoiding medical care increased the risk of drug exposure before birth and ineffective parenting later. Also, women who abused drugs were more likely to physically abuse their children.

Legal interventions disregarded the treatment and advocacy roles of health care providers. For example, medical personnel often performed drug screenings without the informed consent of female patients, and the results were then used as evidence during criminal prosecutions. Addressing perinatal drug abuse through legal intervention was punitive. In large part, it operated on the assumption that although drug treatment programs for women were available in sufficient numbers, women had not made use of the services, and the research conclusively attested to the effectiveness of current drug programs for women with children. In fact, drug programs for women, and particularly pregnant women, were largely unavailable. Less than 1 percent of the federal antidrug budget was targeted for women, yet this minimal amount was expected to include women who were pregnant. Also, most drug interventions were designed with men in mind and overlooked the needs of women. Residential treatment programs, for example, rarely provided child care even though 80 percent of the women entering residential drug rehabilitation had children and half had their children living with them at the time they entered treatment. Consequently, mothers who were addicted to drugs, had other children for whom they provided primary care, and had no familial support, risked losing custody of their children by entering treatment.

Interventions based on legal ideology distorted client–worker relationships. Salient features of ethical client–helper relationships are establishing trust and respecting the confidentiality, dignity, and uniqueness of individuals. Women entering perinatal care could not be assured of these aspects of treatment. In the following scenarios involving two African American woman who were addicted to drugs, the clients' dignity and confidentiality were each violated while they received perinatal services:

> They [health care providers] look at you, they look at you foul and they tell me [sarcastic voice], "Oh, you're a crack user." And then they want to look at your record, and then this nurse look at it and this other nurse look at it, then this other nurse look at it, then . . . They talking all loud, everybody around.

> I know a lot of mothers say that they don't get prenatal care cause they feel like as soon as they walk through the door, they will be judged. "Oh you're a crack head. So why . . . did you get pregnant anyway?" So they don't get prenatal care . . . they are thinking how they gonna be looked at when they walk in the hospital door, like they are not good enough to be pregnant.

Experiences such as the ones above not only diminished the quality of services, but also restricted access by causing women to retreat before obtaining the care they sought.

The strained client–worker relationships precipitated by legal interventions also created parallel care systems that were not in the best interest of clients. Prototypes were nontraditional birthing methods. Parallel care also delayed registering the birth of children and reduced opportunities for health care providers to assist women in obtaining required immunizations and other follow-up care for their infants. In these ways, parallel systems for perinatal care placed both mothers who are addicted and infants at risk.

> I'm gonna have my baby at home and then I'm gonna register the birth at three or four months.

Health-Related Interventions

Health-related approaches to perinatal drug abuse are notably unlike legal interventions. As the Healthy People 2010 plan states, useful approaches to improving health build community partnerships and are systemic, multidisciplinary, absent of disparities across population groups, and attuned to the reciprocal relationship between individual health and community health. Reciprocal means community health is affected by the beliefs, attitudes, and behaviors of everyone in a given community and vice versa.

Components of Healthy People 2010—the national plan for improving public health in the United States—include two discrete goals, 467 objectives, and 28 focal areas. Among the focal areas of the plan are maternal, infant, and child health and substance abuse. Healthy People 2010 proposes to improve maternal, infant, and child health by decreasing maternal drug abuse. Because of the relevant focal areas and strategies of Healthy People 2010 and because the plan creates opportunities for individuals to make healthy lifestyle choices for themselves and their families, it has implications for developing empowerment strategies in perinatal care settings.

Implications for Empowerment

Of concern to social workers is that perinatal drug abuse, a health-related issue of families and children, is often criminalized. Basing perinatal approaches on empowerment strategies that target women who are addicted and health care providers promises to overcome legal interventions and address disparaging attitudes toward perinatal drug abuse.

Empowerment refers to increasing clients' personal, social, and political power so that they can change their situations and prevent reoccurrence of problems. Because empowerment theory emerged from efforts to develop more effective and responsive services for women and people of color, it is highly relevant to perinatal drug abuse.

The empowerment practice goals are helping client systems achieve a sense of personal power, become more aware of the connection between individual and community problems, develop helpful skills, and work toward social change. Studies cite the usefulness of empowerment practice in improving the contexts of human services organizations in ethnically diverse metropolitan areas and helping women of color in oppressed neighborhoods overcome unequal access to resources. Empowerment strategies include role playing as a technique for skills training, raising self-esteem, and helping women see the impact of the political environment on issues in their own lives. In empowerment practice, power is shared, clients are helped to "experience a sense of power" within helping relationships, and professionals are collaborators rather than superiors.

Perhaps the most empowering perinatal service about which social workers and their clients who are addicted can collaborate is helping women become alcohol and drug free. The specific strategies for motivating clients to seek drug rehabilitation, attain sobriety, and use relapse prevention measures are documented in the literature but are not a focus of this article. This article is concerned with empowering strategies for addressing the adverse attitudes and practices to which pregnant women who are addicted are often subjected. Examples include

- teaching pregnant women who are addicted to make formal complaints when they receive unprofessional services in perinatal care settings
- improving access by overcoming scheduling issues and advocating for adequate resources
- enhancing communication skills among women who are pregnant and addicted to drugs
- conducting culturally sensitive in-service training for health care providers
- addressing the unique issues of women of color
- promoting gender-sensitive programs
- overcoming systemic factors that create barriers to health care
- developing community partnerships with relevant groups
- recommending national policies that redefine perinatal drug abuse as a health issue.

Addressing Professional Attitudes and Practices

Social workers can help addicted women become empowered in perinatal care settings in which existing professional attitudes and practices are esteem lowering and potentially disempowering by conveying their own positive regard for the worth and dignity of individuals. This includes validating with clients that rude, judgmental, and other unethical practices are oppressive and unacceptable in health care settings. Collaborating with women about the best ways to file formal complaints against perinatal care personnel who fail to meet professional standards enhances women's personal power and is a model for social change.

Two of the most insurmountable barriers for low-income women seeking perinatal care are (1) the pejorative attitudes of providers and (2) the distrust of the health care system. Stressful interactions with health care providers can adversely affect the drug abuse recovery of women in perinatal care, further damage their self-esteem, and be intimidating as well.

The health of individuals and communities depends on access to quality health care. Case management approaches in which social workers appropriately assist in referring women who require perinatal care are potentially empowering because they facilitate access to services. Social workers can enhance their referrals by becoming knowledgeable about the practices and expectations for clients in perinatal care agencies and using the increased knowledge to improve clients' involvement in their own perinatal care regime. Examples are raising clients' general awareness of an agency's intake procedures and working collaboratively to overcome access barriers that are common in some perinatal care facilities. Access barriers include long waiting periods in facilities and scheduling problems—for example, consistently busy telephone lines and too few available appointments. Short-term strategies for overcoming barriers could involve scheduling appointments far in advance and adequately planning for such support services as extended child care, transportation, and meals when clients are scheduled for appointments. Long-term strategies should include advocating for increased resources.

By means of role playing or related techniques, addicted clients who require perinatal care can be taught more assertive, and thus personally empowering, means of communicating in health care settings. For instance, it is more useful for both clients and services professionals if a woman states, "Hello, I am [name] and I am here for my 3:00 appointment or the results of my lab work" than for her to say, "Hello, I am here for my appointment." Improved client communication may increase access and signal to providers that clients expect dignified, respectful services.

Health-related approaches to perinatal care have informed views on diversity. In-service training in which social workers help providers become more culturally sensitive to poor and ethnic minority clients is empowering because it can improve the overall environment of perinatal care settings. Our knowledge of human diversity and ethical commitment to ethnic-sensitive practice can enhance our role as trainers. Social workers understand, for instance, the usefulness of community intervention and how to use natural helping networks and extended families when working with poor families and families of color. Natural helpers, such as neighbors who can offer transportation or child care, are invaluable to perinatal drug abuse services. Lack of child care and transportation are access barriers that are personally disempowering to many women who require perinatal care.

It is also important to address the unique issues of women of color. For example, HIV infections are common among women who abuse intravenous drugs, but African American women are seven times more likely to die from

HIV/AIDS. Patient education on preventing HIV infections and other sexually transmitted diseases and planning for loss of parents and other effects of AIDS on families are important topics of discussion during perinatal care to African American women.

Counteracting Legal Interventions

Some experts believe the current political climate produces gender-biased, racist, and classist policies. An example is contemporary policy defining perinatal drug abuse as if it were strictly a legal issue and then targeting for prosecution poor women and women of color. Because of social workers' mandate to promote social justice, it is important that we advocate on behalf of vulnerable populations, for example, pregnant women who are addicted and their unborn children.

In recommending policies that foster adequate income, health insurance, and education, we can raise the socioeconomic status of mothers and, in turn, enhance the health status of drug-exposed babies. Being poor and less educated are linked to systemic issues like restricted access to health care, living in unsafe neighborhoods, inadequate housing, and limited opportunities to engage in health promotion. Many contemporary drug policies, however, blame women and divert attention from systemic forces, such as poverty, that promote substance abuse. A study of 1,000 substance abuse cases in four large cities showed that a sizable number of the parents lost their children to custodial care because of inadequate housing and poverty rather than explicit drug abuse. Healthy People 2010 embraces the empowering strategy of focusing on systemic factors that affect the health status of addicted women and their unborn fetuses.

Although it is important that social workers advocate for health-related perinatal care policies, it is even more empowering if the resulting programs are gender sensitive. Gender-sensitive perinatal programs take into account, among other factors, protecting women's physical health, access issues, and the rate of depression among women who are addicted. Depression, for example, is strongly correlated with high levels of personal stress, inadequate housing, lack of money for basic needs, and other factors associated with poverty. Because depressive symptoms are predictable among women who abuse drugs and can deter health-seeking behaviors, assessing depression in perinatal care settings is gender sensitive. Assessing depression is also a biopsychosocial strategy that favors health promotion. By treating depression, social workers can help clients in perinatal care settings overcome feelings of helplessness and become more available to engage in social change. Therefore, examining depression in perinatal care settings is personally, politically, and socially empowering to clients.

Social workers can intensify their perinatal advocacy efforts by developing community partnerships with CPS and perinatal care programs that fulfill the programs' missions while also protecting families and children. Perinatal toxicology screenings are allegedly designed to protect children, and CPS's primary mission is protecting children. However, between 1982 and 1989, when the number of substance abuse-related CPS cases doubled, child welfare agencies began separating children from their mothers solely on the basis of positive toxicology, without attempts to apply preventive measures or family rehabilitation. It is expedient that social workers help CPS and perinatal care providers refocus their dialogue on the needs of families within social and political contexts. Partnering agencies may then stop relying heavily on legal strategies and instead advocate for financial and other resources that can improve the health status of all family members—for example, by locating medical facilities in local communities and providing culturally specific health education. Because advocating community partnerships highlights the relatedness of individuals' problems and environmental conditions, it fulfills tenets of empowerment practice and Healthy People 2010.

Community partnerships that reach out to nontraditional partners can be among the most effective tools for improving health in communities. Social workers can further strengthen their campaigns to eliminate legal interventions for perinatal drug abuse by broadening their community partnerships with CPS and perinatal care programs to incorporate women, private companies, and community-based organizations such as criminal justice agencies, legal clinics, employment agencies, and churches. By providing research data, social workers can demonstrate to partners how legal means of "protecting" families and children are, in fact, injurious to them. Incarceration, for example, complicates birth outcomes in various ways. When women are released from prison, their own as well as their children's Medicaid eligibility is compromised for at least a month or more. If women and their children have chronic illnesses such as diabetes, HIV/AIDS, or hypertension, treatment adherence is essential, but health care is inaccessible without medical coverage. Women with low incomes, already at the highest risk of poor birth outcomes, are at greater risk of incarceration.

Once community partners are better informed, they can then educate politicians and other policymakers and thereafter solicit their help in adopting national policies that redefine perinatal drug abuse as a health-related issue. One example of such a policy is greater incentives for private corporations to develop partnerships with community-based drug rehabilitation organizations that accommodate mothers who are addicted as well as their children. Another is a policy that rewards medical schools for teaching students how to identify risk factors for substance use during pregnancy. In a survey of primary care physicians, only 17 percent could diagnose illicit drug use, a mere 30 percent were prepared to diagnose misuse of prescription drugs, and only 20 percent could confidently diagnose alcoholism. On the other hand, 82 percent of the physicians could identify patients with diabetes, and 83 percent could diagnose patients with hypertension. Increasing physicians' ability to identify risk factors for drug use during pregnancy is not only a preventive measure for improving maternal, infant, and child health, but a means of reinforcing among physicians and other health care providers the health-related definition of perinatal drug abuse.

Conclusion

Health care professionals and society at large exhibit negative attitudes toward women who abuse drugs. By means of empowerment strategies, social workers can potentially help clients who are addicted and pregnant to seek and complete perinatal treatment programs, improve the environment in which perinatal care services are provided, and advocate for policies that define perinatal drug abuse more as a health problem than a legal issue. Desired outcomes of these efforts are improved health care access and quality of life for families in which perinatal drug abuse is an issue.

POSTSCRIPT

Should Pregnant Drug Users Be Prosecuted?

Babies born with health problems as a result of their mothers' drug use are a tragedy that needs to be rectified. The issue is not whether this problem needs to be addressed but what course of action is best. The need for medical intervention and specialized treatment programs serving pregnant women with drug problems has been recognized. The groundwork has been set for funding and developing such programs. The Office of Substance Abuse Prevention is funding chemical dependency programs specifically for pregnant women in several states.

It has been argued that drug use by pregnant women is a problem that requires medical, not criminal, attention. One can contend the notion that pregnant drug users and their drug-exposed infants are victims of drug abuse. Critics contend that there is an element of discrimination in the practice of prosecuting women who use drugs during pregnancy because these women are primarily low-income, single, members of minority groups, and recipients of public assistance. Possible factors leading to their drug use—poverty, unemployment, poor education, and lack of vocational training—are not addressed when the solution to drug use during pregnancy is incarceration. Moreover, many pregnant women are denied access to treatment programs.

Prosecution proponents contend that medical intervention is not adequate in preventing pregnant women from using drugs and that criminal prosecution is necessary. Logli argues that "eliminating the pain, suffering and death resulting from drug exposure in newborns must be a prosecutor's priority." He maintains that the criminal justice system should protect newborns and, if legal cause does exist for prosecution, then statutes should provide protection for the fetus. However, will prosecution result in more protection or less protection for the fetus? If a mother stops using drugs for fear of prosecution, then the fetus benefits. If the mother avoids prenatal care because of potential legal punishment, then the fetus suffers.

If women can be prosecuted for using illegal drugs such as cocaine and narcotics during pregnancy because they harm the fetus, then should women who smoke cigarettes and drink alcohol during pregnancy also be prosecuted? The evidence is clear that tobacco and alcohol place the fetus at great risk; however, most discussions of prosecuting pregnant drug users overlook women who use these drugs. Also, the adverse health effects from secondhand smoke are well documented. Should people be prosecuted if they smoke around pregnant women?

"The Legality of Drug-Testing Procedures for Pregnant Women" by Kristin Pulatie (*Virtual Mentor,* January 2008) provides a good review of the legal aspects of drug testing women while they are pregnant. The extent of alcohol use by pregnant women is highlighted in "Alcohol Use among Women and Recent Mothers: 2002 to 2007" (*The NSDUH Report,* September 11, 2008). The adverse effects of drug use during pregnancy are described in "Effects of Substance Abuse During Pregnancy," by Anne Greenough and Zainab Kassim (*The Journal of the Royal Society for the Promotion of Health,* September 2005).

An excellent review of the effects of prenatal exposure to alcohol is "Alcohol and Pregnancy, Highlights from Three Decades of Research," by Carrie L. Randall (*Journal of Studies on Alcohol,* vol. 62, 2001).

ISSUE 6

Is Drug Addiction a Brain Disease?

YES: National Institute on Drug Abuse, from *The Science of Addiction* (April 2007)

NO: Sally Satel, from "The Human Factor," *The American* (July/August 2007)

ISSUE SUMMARY

YES: Because there are biological and chemical changes in the brain following drug abuse, the National Institute on Drug Abuse (NIDA) claims that drug addiction is a disease of the brain. One may initially use drugs voluntarily, but addiction occurs after repeated drug use. NIDA acknowledges that environment plays a role in the development of drug addiction, but one's genes plays a major role as well.

NO: Psychiatrist Sally Satel maintains that drug addiction is not a disease of the brain. Satel asserts that there are individuals who are capable of stopping their drug addiction without medical intervention. Moreover, diseases have distinct characteristics, and drug addiction does not share these characteristics. Satel feels that addicts are done a disservice by calling addiction a brain disease.

Is drug addiction caused by a brain disease, or is it caused by inappropriate behavioral patterns? This distinction is important because it has both legal and medical implications. Should people be held accountable for behaviors that stem from a brain disease over which they have no control? For example, if a person cannot help being an alcoholic and hurts or kills someone as a result of being drunk, should that person be treated or incarcerated? Likewise, if an individual's addiction is due to lack of self-control, rather than due to a disease, should taxpayer money go to pay for that person's treatment?

It can be argued that the disease concept of drug addiction legitimizes or excuses behaviors. If addiction is an illness or disease of the brain, then blame for poor behavior can be shifted to the disease and away from the individual. Moreover, if drug addiction is incurable, can people ever be held responsible for their behavior?

The National Institute on Drug Abuse contends that addiction is caused by heredity, biochemistry, and environment influences. If drug addiction is the result of factors beyond the individual's control, then one should not be held responsible for one's behavior, and loss of control is not inevitable. Critics assert that many individuals have the ability of alcoholics to stop their abuse of drugs. For example, it has been shown that many cocaine and heroin users do not lose control while using these drugs. In their study of U.S. service personnel in Vietnam, epidemiologist Lee N. Robins and colleagues showed that most of the soldiers who used narcotics regularly during the war did not continue using them once they returned home. Many service personnel in Vietnam reportedly used drugs because they were in a situation they did not want to be in. Additionally, without the support of loved ones and society's constraints, they were free to gravitate to behaviors that would not be tolerated by their families and friends.

Attitudes toward treating drug abuse are affected by whether it is perceived as a brain disease or as an act of free will. The disease concept implies that one needs help in overcoming addiction. By calling drug addiction a medical condition, the body is viewed as a machine that needs fixing; character and free will become secondary. Also, by calling addiction a disease, the role of society in causing drug addiction is left unexplored. What roles do poverty, crime, unemployment, inadequate health care, and poor education have in drug addiction?

Opponents to the disease concept argue that the addictive qualities of drugs, especially heroin, are exaggerated. By claiming that certain drugs are highly addictive, it is easier to demonize those drugs and people who use them. It has been demonstrated that more people are dependent on legal drugs such as alcohol and tobacco. Some studies show that a number of heroin users are weekend users. This dispels the notion that heroin use always causes addiction.

According to the disease perspective, an important step for addicts to take in order to benefit from treatment is to admit that they are powerless against their addiction. They need to acknowledge that their drug addiction controls them and that drug addiction is a lifelong problem. The implication of this view is that addicts are never cured. Addicts must therefore abstain from drugs for their entire lives.

Is addiction caused by psychological or biological factors? Can drugs produce changes in the brain that result in drug addiction? How much control do drug addicts have over their use of drugs? In the following selections, the position of the National Institute on Drug Abuse is that addiction is a disease of the brain, while Satel contends that the concept of drug addiction is a social construct, not based in science.

The Science of Addiction

Drug Abuse and Addiction

What Is Drug Addiction?

Addiction is defined as a chronic, relapsing brain disease that is character- ized by compulsive drug seeking and use, despite harmful consequences. It is considered a brain disease because drugs change the brain—they change its structure and how it works. These brain changes can be long lasting, and can lead to the harmful behaviors seen in people who abuse drugs.

Is Continued Drug Abuse a Voluntary Behavior?

The initial decision to take drugs is mostly voluntary. However, when drug abuse takes over, a person's ability to exert self control can become seriously impaired. Brain imaging studies from drug-addicted individuals show physi- cal changes in areas of the brain that are critical to judgment, decisionmak- ing, learning and memory, and behavior control. Scientists believe that these changes alter the way the brain works, and may help explain the compulsive and destructive behaviors of addiction.

Why Do Some People Become Addicted to Drugs, While Others Do Not?

As with any other disease, vulnerability to addiction differs from person to per- son. In general, the more risk factors an individual has, the greater the chance that taking drugs will lead to abuse and addiction. "Protective" factors reduce a person's risk of developing addiction.

What Factors Determine If a Person Will Become Addicted?

No single factor determines whether a person will become addicted to drugs. The overall risk for addiction is impacted by the biological makeup of the individual—it can even be influenced by gender or ethnicity, his or her devel- opmental stage, and the surrounding social environment (e.g., conditions at home, at school, and in the neighborhood).

Published by National Institutes of Health, NIH Pun no. 07-5605, April 2007, pp. 5, 7–8, 1010, 15–20.

Which Biological Factors Increase Risk of Addiction?

Scientists estimate that genetic factors account for between 40 and 60 percent of a person's vulnerability to addiction, including the effects of environment on gene expression and function. Adolescents and individuals with mental disorders are at greater risk of drug abuse and addiction than the general population.

The Brain Continues to Develop into Adulthood and Undergoes Dramatic Changes During Adolescence

One of the brain areas still maturing during adolescence is the prefrontal cortex—the part of the brain that enables us to assess situations, make sound decisions, and keep our emotions and desires under control. The fact that this critical part of an adolescent's brain is still a work-in-progress puts them at increased risk for poor decisions (such as trying drugs or continued abuse). Thus, introducing drugs while the brain is still developing may have profound and long-lasting consequences.

Drugs and the Brain

Introducing the Human Brain

The human brain is the most complex organ in the body. This three-pound mass of gray and white matter sits at the center of all human activity—you need it to drive a car, to enjoy a meal, to breathe, to create an artistic masterpiece, and to enjoy everyday activities. In brief, the brain regulates your basic body functions; enables you to interpret and respond to everything you experience, and shapes your thoughts, emotions, and behavior.

The brain is made up of many parts that all work together as a team. Different parts of the brain are responsible for coordinating and performing specific functions. Drags can alter important brain areas that are necessary for life-sustaining functions and can drive the compulsive drug abuse that marks addiction. Brain areas affected by drug abuse—

- *The brain stem* controls basic functions critical to life, such as heart rate, breathing, and sleeping.   .
- *The limbic system* contains the brain's reward circuit—it links together a number of brain structures that control and regulate our ability to feel pleasure. Feeling pleasure motivates us to repeat behaviors such as eating—actions that are critical to our existence. The limbic system is activated when we perform these activities—and also by drugs of abuse. In addition, the limbic system is responsible for our perception of other emotions, both positive and negative, which explains the mood-altering properties of many drugs.
- *The cerebral cortex* is divided into areas that control specific functions. Different areas process information from our senses, enabling us to see, feel, hear, and taste. The front part of the cortex, the frontal cortex or forebrain, is the thinking center of the brain; it powers our ability to think, plan, solve problems, and make decisions.

How Does the Brain Communicate?

The brain is a communications center consisting of billions of neurons, or nerve cells. Networks of neurons pass messages back and forth to different structures within the brain, the spinal column, and the peripheral nervous system. These nerve networks coordinate and regulate everything we feel, think, and do.

- *Neuron to Neuron*
  Each nerve cell in the brain sends and receives messages in the form of electrical impulses. Once a cell receives and processes a message, it sends it on to other neurons.
- *Neurotransmitters—The Brain's Chemical Messengers*
  The messages are carried between neurons by chemicals called neurotransmitters. (They transmit messages between neurons.)
- *Receptors—The Brain's Chemical Receivers*
  The neurotransmitter attaches to a specialized site on the receiving cell called a receptor. A neurotransmitter and its receptor operate like a "key and lock," an exquisitely specific mechanism that ensures that each receptor will forward the appropriate message only after interacting with the right kind of neurotransmitter.
- *Transporters—The Brain's Chemical Recyclers*
  Located on the cell that releases the neurotransmitter, transporters recycle these neurotransmitters (i.e., bring them back into the cell that released them), thereby shutting off the signal between neurons.

How Do Drugs Work in the Brain?

Drugs are chemicals. They work in the brain by tapping into the brain's communication system and interfering with the way nerve cells normally send, receive, and process information. Some drugs, such as marijuana and heroin, can activate neurons because their chemical structure mimics that of a natural neurotransmitter. This similarity in structure "fools" receptors and allows the drugs to lock onto and activate the nerve cells. Although these drugs mimic brain chemicals, they don't activate nerve cells in the same way as a natural neurotransmitter, and they lead to abnormal messages being transmitted through the network.

Other drugs, such as amphetamine or cocaine, can cause the nerve cells to release abnormally large amounts of natural neurotransmitters or prevent the normal recycling of these brain chemicals. This disruption produces a greatly amplified message, ultimately disrupting communication channels. The difference in effect can be described as the difference between someone whispering into your ear and someone shouting into a microphone.

How Do Drugs Work in the Brain to Produce Pleasure?

All drugs of abuse directly or indirectly target the brain's reward system by flooding the circuit with dopamine. Dopamine is a neurotransmitter present in regions of the brain that regulate movement, emotion, cognition, motivation, and feelings of pleasure. The overstimulation of this system, which rewards our natural behaviors, produces the euphoric effects sought by people who abuse drugs and teaches them to repeat the behavior.

How Does Stimulation of the Brain's Pleasure Circuit Teach Us to Keep Taking Drugs?

Our brains are wired to ensure that we will repeat life-sustaining activities by associating those activities with pleasure or reward. Whenever this reward circuit is activated, the brain notes that something important is happening that needs to be remembered, and teaches us to do it again and again, without thinking about it. Because drugs of abuse stimulate the same circuit, we learn to abuse drugs in the same way.

Why Are Drugs More Addictive Than Natural Rewards?

When some drugs of abuse are taken, they can release 2 to 10 times the amount of dopamine that natural rewards do. In some cases, this occurs almost immediately (as when drugs are smoked or injected), and the effects can last much longer than those produced by natural rewards. The resulting effects on the brain's pleasure circuit dwarfs those produced by naturally rewarding behaviors such as eating and sex. The effect of such a powerful reward strongly motivates people to take drugs again and again. This is why scientists sometimes say that drug abuse is something we learn to do very, very well.

What Happens to Your Brain If You Keep Taking Drugs?

Just as we turn down the volume on a radio that is too loud, the brain adjusts to the overwhelming surges in dopamine (and other neurotransmitters) by producing less dopamine or by reducing the number of receptors that can receive and transmit signals. As a result, dopamine's impact on the reward circuit of a drug abuser's brain can become abnormally low, and the ability to experience any pleasure is reduced. This is why the abuser eventually feels flat, lifeless, and depressed, and is unable to enjoy things that previously brought them pleasure. Now, they need to take drugs just to bring their dopamine function back up to normal. And, they must take larger amounts of the drug than they first did to create the dopamine high—an effect known as tolerance.

How Does Long-Term Drug Taking Affect Brain Circuits?

We know that the same sort of mechanisms involved in the development of tolerance can eventually lead to profound changes in neurons and brain circuits, with the potential to severely compromise the long-term health of the brain. For example, glutamate is another neurotransmitter that influences the reward circuit and the ability to learn. When the optimal concentration of glutamate is altered by drug abuse, the brain attempts to compensate for this change, which can cause impairment in cognitive function. Similarly, long-term drug abuse can trigger adaptations in habit or nonconscious memory systems. Conditioning is one example of this type of learning, whereby environmental cues become associated with the drug experience and can trigger uncontrollable cravings if the individual is later exposed to these cues, even without the drug itself being available. This learned "reflex" is extremely robust and can emerge even after many years of abstinence.

What Other Brain Changes Occur with Abuse?

Chronic exposure to drugs of abuse disrupts the way critical brain structures interact to control behavior—behavior specifically related to drug abuse. Just as continued abuse may lead to tolerance or the need for higher drug dosages to produce an effect, it may also lead to addiction, which can drive an abuser to seek out and take drugs compulsively. Drug addiction erodes a person's self-control and ability to make sound decisions, while sending intense impulses to take drugs.

 **NO**

The Human Factor

Drug abuse causes hundreds of billions of dollars in economic losses and untold personal heartache. How to limit the damage? Sally Satel suggests we start by ditching the 'brain disease' model that's popular with scientists and focus on treating addicts as people with the power to reshape their own lives. Despite its own prejudices, an HBO series transmits just this message of responsibility and optimism.

For nearly a century, the United States government has been waging one unsuccessful anti-drug crusade after another. Today, more than 20 million Americans abuse drugs and alcohol. And while the users themselves pay a high price in stunted lives and heartache, the social and economic costs are staggering. The direct effects of addiction—homelessness, unemployment, and disease—and the costs of interdiction and incarceration are estimated at over $200 billion annually. The annual burden in lost productivity in the workplace, mainly from absenteeism and accidents, is another $129 billion, and employees' drug- and alcohol-related healthcare costs add $16 billion. In all, that's about 3 percent of our gross domestic product.

Addicts and their families—and the rest of us who help pick up the pieces—have it hard enough. The last thing we need is a confusing public health message about the nature of addiction. Yet that is exactly what was purveyed earlier in the year by an ambitious television series on HBO about substance abuse. While much of the series preached an ultra-medicalized philosophy of addiction—one I find woefully misleading—the broader message, paradoxically, was powerful and accurate: namely, that addicts are endowed with the ability to change their own lives.

Traditionally, efforts to cut drug abuse have been divided into two parts. Supply reduction tries to limit the availability of drugs. So far, despite enormous outlays of tax dollars and increased criminal penalties, results have been dismal. Meanwhile, demand reduction both tries to stop people from using drugs (prevention) and, if they start, tries to get them to stop (treatment). That's where I come in. I am a psychiatrist in a methadone clinic in Northeast Washington, D.C.

My job is to help addicts quit heroin and not go back to it in the future. If this is a challenge for the clinician, it's a monumental effort for the addict. Every so often a patient will ask me if I can "hypnotize" him out of his habit. One patient told me he wished there were an anti-addiction pill, "something

From *The American*, July/August 2007, pp. 92–102. Copyright © 2007 by American Enterprise Institute. Reprinted by permission. www.american.com

to make me not want." Indeed, that is the timeless quest of troubled addicts everywhere: not to want. It comes as no news to them, however, that recovery is very much a project of the heart and mind. Nor is it news that recovery is attainable.

This is why I chafe at the conventional scientific wisdom about addiction: namely, that it is "a chronic and relapsing brain disease." This view is much heralded by the National Institute on Drug Abuse, or NIDA, part of the National Institutes of Health. NIDA is funded at slightly over $1 billion a year and carries enormous authority on Capitol Hill, among grant-seeking scientists, and in medical schools. The "brain disease" idea is promoted at major rehab institutions such as the Betty Ford Center and Hazelden; it is now a staple of antidrug education in high schools and in counselor education. And, of course, lawyers play fast and loose with the brain disease rhetoric in courtrooms.

The brain disease concept sends a perilous public health message. First, it suggests that an addict's condition is amenable to a medical cure (much as pneumonia is cleared with antibiotics). Second, it misappropriates language more properly used to describe conditions such as multiple sclerosis or schizophrenia—afflictions that are neither brought on by the sufferer himself nor modifiable by his desire to be well. Third, it carries a fatalistic theme, implying that users can never free themselves of their drug or alcohol problems.

The brain disease rhetoric also threatens to obscure the vast role of personal agency in perpetuating the cycle of use and relapse to drugs and alcohol. It sends a mixed message that undermines the rationale for therapies and policies that depend on recognizing the addict's potential for self-governance.

Despite its worrisome implications, the scientists who forged the brain disease concept in the mid-1990s had good intentions. By placing addiction on equal footing with more conventional medical disorders, they sought to create an image of the addict as a hapless victim of his own wayward neurochemistry. They hoped this would inspire companies and politicians to allocate more funding for treatment. Also, by emphasizing dramatic scientific advances, such as brain imaging techniques, and applying them to addiction, they hoped researchers might reap more financial support for their work. Finally, promoting the idea of addiction as a brain disease would rehabilitate the addict's public image from that of a criminal who deserves punishment into a sympathetic figure who deserves treatment.

Within clinical and research circles, the brain disease narrative quickly made a powerful impression. "The majority of the biomedical community now considers addiction, in its essence, to be a brain disease," says Alan Leshner, the former director of NIDA, who now heads the American Association for the Advancement of Science. To the public, however, the notion has largely been unknown.

Until now. This spring, the "chronic and relapsing brain disease" message got a big boost from HBO's series called "Addiction," which featured nine full-length segments plus a "supplementary series" that included interviews with medical experts and researchers about treatment and recovery. There was also a "complementary series" that comprised intimate portraits of the lives of four people, plus an impressive educational website and a book entitled *Addiction: Why Can't They Just Stop?* Full-page ads with the tag line "Why can't they just stop?" were placed in major newspapers and magazines.

The series was produced in partnership with NIDA, the National Institute on Alcohol Abuse and Alcoholism, and the Robert Wood Johnson Foundation. Brain disease had center stage. As Nora Volkow, the neuroscientist who heads NIDA, explained in one episode, "Addiction is a disease of the brain that translates into abnormal behavior."

But what exactly does that assertion mean? It's no abstract question. The answer determines the extent to which we can and should hold addicts responsible for their actions—a matter which, in turn, determines to a significant degree our ability to reduce the effects of drug and alcohol abuse.

According to Volkow and other neuroscientists, "brain disease" refers to disruptions in the brain's motivational and reward circuitry that result from the cumulative effect of repeated use of certain substances. As these neural pathways become "hijacked," use that started as voluntary becomes less and less deliberate, harder and harder to control, and, in the most extreme cases, even automatic. The process unfolds through the action of a major neurotransmitter called dopamine, which, under normal circumstances, increases in the presence of any salient stimulus that is important or pleasurable, such as food, sex, or social bonding. It serves as a "learning signal." An organism, animal or human, comes to desire, again and again, any experience that causes dopamine's release.

When drugs, as opposed to food or sex, serve as the stimulus, the dopamine release is especially intense. Thus, each new infusion "teaches" the brain to desire drugs. Ultimately, the urge to use heroin or cocaine overrides a person's interest in once-enjoyable activities—let alone the basic chores of living, which now seem drab by comparison. After a while, however, many addicts report getting very little pleasure from drinking or using drugs. So why does the intense desire to consume persist? According to Volkow and her colleagues, persistent exposure to drugs and alcohol damages the parts of the brain that evaluate experiences and plan appropriate actions.

Addicts' brains, says Volkow, "have been modified by the drug in such a way that absence of the drug makes a signal to their brain that is equivalent to the signal of when you are starving. . . . [It is] as if the individual was in a state of deprivation, where taking the drug is indispensable for survival. It's as powerful as that."

What's so compelling about this model is that you can literally see it in action. Scientists use an imaging technique called positron emission tomography (PET) to produce a visual record of the brain on drugs. When a person is given a drug, or merely shown pictures of paraphernalia, a PET scan image will depict the brain's reward centers glowing red with a rush of dopamine-related metabolic activity.

Such PET scans are prominently featured in the HBO series, and they seem convincing. Biology, however, is not destiny. In fact, the brain of an addict who is experiencing a drug craving but fights it off also lights up like a Christmas tree—as brightly as the brain of a person who planned to obtain drugs to quell the craving—because resistance activates additional inhibitory centers in the brain.

Nor can scans permit scientists to predict reliably whether a person with a desire-activated brain will act on that desire. Indeed, researchers have noted that self-reported craving does not necessarily correlate with a greater chance of actually using cocaine. In other words, scans cannot distinguish between an impulse that is irresistible and an impulse that can be resisted but is not. "You can examine pictures of brains all day," says philosopher Daniel Shapiro of West Virginia University, "but you'd never call anyone an addict unless he acted like one."

We tend to think of the cocaine addict in the throes of a days-long binge. He frantically gouges himself with needles, jams a new rock into his pipe every 15 minutes, or hungrily snorts lines of powder. Or we think of the heroin junkie either nodding off or doubled over in misery from withdrawal, so desperate for the next hit that he'll get the money any way he can. In the grip of such forces, an addict cannot be expected blithely to get up and walk away. These tumultuous states—with neuronal function severely disrupted—are the closest drug use comes to being beyond the user's restraint.

Yet addicts rarely spend all of their time in conditions of such intense neurochemical siege. In the days between binges, for example, cocaine addicts make many decisions that have nothing to do with drug-seeking. Should they clean the apartment? Try to find a different job? Kick that freeloading cousin off their couch for good? Heroin-dependent individuals often function quite well as long as they have regular access to some form of opiate drug in order to prevent withdrawal symptoms. Most of my own patients even hold jobs while pursuing their heroin habits, which typically entail use about every six to eight hours.

In other words, there is room for other choices. These addicts could go to a Narcotics Anonymous meeting, for example, or enter treatment if they have private insurance, or register at a public clinic if they don't. And yes, they could even stop cold turkey. I've interviewed scores of opiate addicts who have done it. They take lots of Valium-type drugs to handle withdrawal and suffer through a few days of vomiting, diarrhea, and cramping.

When Jamie Lee Curtis, who abused painkillers, appeared on a recent Larry King show that was devoted to addiction (and plugged the HBO series), guest host Maria Shriver asked her, "What made you get clean?" She responded, "Well, you know what, that turning point was a—was really a moment between me and God. I never went to treatment. I walked into the door of a 12-step program and I have not walked out since." Apparently, Ms. Curtis never got the memo that addiction is a brain disease.

It is simply a fact that many people do stop spontaneously. It is also a fact that a lot of them will start up again weeks, months, or years later. But in the interim, they have command over whether or not they do.

The "chronic and relapsing" element of the brain disease narrative suggests that relapse is an inherent and virtually inevitable property of addiction. Volkow sums it up: "Just as an asthma attack can be triggered by smoke, or a person with diabetes can have a reaction if they eat too much sugar, a drug addict can be triggered to return to drug abuse." Scientists also explain the process in neurobiological terms. During the early phase of recovery, the brain's dopamine stores are still somewhat depleted from the recent period of heavy use, leading to feelings of apathy and "grayness," a state that can be temporarily reversed with more drugs.

What's more, according to this theory, the brain's dopamine-rich centers, even if they are less stoked than normal, remain hypersensitive, so that an encounter with an old drug buddy, say, or a whiff of whisky can provoke sharp craving, as Pavlov could have predicted.

Nonetheless, according to neuroscientist Steven Hyman, professor of neurobiology at Harvard Medical School, addicted individuals are not reduced to "zombies who are permanently controlled by external cues. As overvalued as drugs become, as potent as the effects of drug cues on behavior, other goals are not extirpated."

An important therapy for reducing the intensity of craving in newly abstinent patients is called "relapse prevention," a form of cognitive-behavioral therapy, a well-established and effective treatment for depression and other conditions. Patients are helped to identify cues that reliably trigger a burst of desire to use the drug. These cues are generally the "people, places, and things" that the addict associates with drug use, but some of the triggers are curiously idiosyncratic. For example, a teacher trying to recover from cocaine addiction might begin to think lovingly about cocaine, even tasting it in the back of his throat, when he sees the powdered residue of classroom chalk.

Internal cues, such as stress and boredom, can be powerful too. Patients rehearse strategies for avoiding the cues if they possibly can, and managing the craving when they cannot. They learn to observe themselves when they have an urge to use so they can buy enough time to talk themselves out of acting.

Perhaps one day we'll develop a medication to blunt craving—and I'm sure I would prescribe it—but the fact is that even intense urges need not be obeyed. And as a person begins to develop other sources of pleasure and interest, these will generate their own outpouring of dopamine, to put it in brain-speak. But an addict won't replace substances with more compelling preoccupations without a reason; something has to be at stake. Sometimes it's a threat that gets his attention—the risk of jail, of losing a job, a family, or a reputation. Sometimes it's the challenge of facing who he has become.

Author Jacob Sullum has interviewed many drug users who became aware that they were sliding down the path to full-blown addiction—and pulled themselves back. "It undermined their sense of themselves as individuals in control of their own destinies. And so they stopped," Sullum writes. "That doesn't mean that giving up cocaine might not be harder for different people in different circumstances, but it does show that the chemical does not neutralize free will."

Even among those who have not pulled themselves back from the brink, there is a broad range of behavior. Yes, some have held up gas stations to get money, but others have never stolen a cent. In fact, the shock of almost becoming a criminal, of stealing from a family member, or of sleeping through an infant's screams of pain was just what brought them in to our clinic. "My God, I almost robbed my own sister," one exclaimed in self-disgust. "What kind of mother am I?" asked another, incredulous at her dereliction.

During the most intense and troubled phase of their use, these patients had a spasm of self-reproach and a sudden flash of self-awareness that moved them to do something to fix their problem. It is epiphanies like these that make me wonder about the matter-of-fact pronouncement of several of the HBO experts that, in addiction, "the judgment part of the brain becomes completely nonfunctional." Granted, not every addict has an "aha!" moment—many are arm-twisted into our clinic by spouses, children, or the courts. But for those who do, it would be fascinating to know what their brain scans looked like at the time of revelation. Probably just as afire as those of addicts using cocaine.

Indeed, for those in recovery at any phase, the path back to use is well marked by scores of red flags—small, deliberate choices, made many times a day: with whom to spend time, which neighborhoods to visit, whether to allow oneself to become bored. With each choice, the addict makes himself more vulnerable to continued use. These small decisions, then, are critical to relapse.

The process also indicates why we should not hesitate to hold actor Mel Gibson responsible for his alcohol-soaked anti-Semitic rant last year. And why Representative Patrick Kennedy was suffering from far more than a "brain disease" when he crashed his car on Capitol Hill last year. After all, a remorseful substance abuser almost always has substantial knowledge of how he behaves when under the influence, yet, in spite of this insight, sets anew the stage on which history will repeat itself.

Yes, it is true than an addict is not responsible for his inborn vulnerabilities, but once he knows he has them—a point made vividly clear by having lived firsthand through one or more harrowing episodes of reckless use—he is fully responsible for his actions.

"If the brain is the core of the problem," wrote former NIDA head Alan Leshner, "attending to the brain needs to be the core of the solution." In a seminal 1997 article in the journal *Science* entitled "Addiction Is a Brain Disease, and It Matters," Leshner goes on to explain how: by using "medications or behavioral treatments to reverse or compensate for brain changes."

Fortunately, I have never met a flesh-and-blood clinician who talks this way. Nor, apparently, has HBO. For all the brain scans and the focus on brain disease, the series presented savvy clinicians giving edifying tutorials on treatments—therapies aimed first and foremost at the *person*, not his physical organ. A poignant array of stories showed why it makes more sense to address the human factor than to set out to change the brain's chemistry.

Consider the HBO episode on a drug court in South Boston. Drug courts are jail-diversion programs that offer intensive, supervised substance-abuse treatment to addicts who have committed nonviolent, drug-related crimes. Eligible offenders who choose drug court over routine court processing are closely monitored by a judge for roughly a year. If they fail a drug test or violate some other expectation, the judge administers swift and reliable sanctions, such as community service or a night in jail. Subsequent violations elicit more severe punishments, culminating in incarceration if the offender continues to flout the rules. The judge also rewards good behavior. A participant who does well for several months progresses to a new phase of treatment with less intense oversight.

Most patient-offenders respond well to this graduated behavioral approach. Swift response to infractions drives home the message that one's own actions are taken seriously—that the addict controls his fate. Dropout rates are significantly lower than in standard treatment, and criminal recidivism is reduced compared with standard court processing with probation. Contrary to conventional psychiatric wisdom, addicts don't have to want to change their lives for a treatment program to succeed. Gradually, they absorb the values of the program as they appreciate the benefits of drug-free living.

With the prospect of doing time hanging over his head, an offender is more likely to finish treatment. Leverage is crucial. "Drug court uses the power of the judge to get people to change their way of life," said the judge in the HBO documentary, Robert P. Ziemian. "The fact that [participants] have coercion keeps them facing their problems" in treatment. In short, the judge holds the person, not his brain, accountable for setbacks and progress.

Volumes of data attest to the fact that the longer addicts stay in treatment, the better their chances of turning their lives around. Holding people accountable for resuming use is not "blaming the victim," as the brain disease model implies. To the contrary, acknowledging their responsibility expresses faith in a human capacity for restraint and self-determination—a much more optimistic and realistic message than "young man, you have a chronic and relapsing brain disease."

By combining the moral and medical approaches to treatment—which work better together than either does alone—drug courts have proven an effective innovation. At the heart of drug courts (and there are now over 1,600 around the country) is a well-established practice called contingency management. A broad scientific literature shows that rewards and sanctions for behavior typically exert a dramatic effect on a person's drug use. By contrast, no amount of reinforcement or punishment can alter the course of a truly autonomous biological condition. Imagine bribing an Alzheimer's patient to keep her dementia from worsening, or threatening to impose a penalty on her if it did.

Another valuable intervention is self-help. An episode about Steamfitters Local Union 638 in Astoria, Queens, featured an employee-assistance program headed by a charismatic steamfitter, a recovering alcoholic who drove home the point that "we use brotherhood as a way of intervening." Borrowing from AA, the union program provided round-the-clock social support and a community of peers, some of whom have been sober for many years.

Unfortunately, the HBO series barely mentioned Alcoholics Anonymous itself, the most widely used and successful method for staying sober. "Well-done studies repeatedly find that AA is more effective in moving people to abstinence than any other form of outpatient treatment for alcoholism," says Keith Humphreys, professor of psychiatry at Stanford University and an expert in the field. "On additional measures, like reduced days missed at work, improvement in depression, and better family life, AA is comparable to other treatment. And, what's more, the price is right: it's free."

The omission by HBO, however, was not altogether surprising. After all, the AA fellowship extols the idea that the alcoholic must enter into nothing less than a crucible of character change—must become more humble, honest, and morally reflective by working through the program's 12 steps. This is not a philosophy that meshes well with the biological version of addiction.

One of the most riveting HBO episodes was a full-length profile of Lisa, a 37-year-old woman living in a run-down hotel room in Toronto and working as a call girl. For most of the show, we see her sitting on the bed talking to the filmmaker behind the camera. She is animated, engaging, and witty. Flipping her shiny brown hair and inspecting her well-kept nails, she talks eagerly about how much she makes selling sex, how much she spends on drugs, and what cocaine feels like ("someone coming up behind you and hugging you . . . warm").

Lisa's cell phone rings about every ten minutes, and she flirts with the prospective johns. Then it is time to use. "Wanna see me get high?" she asks the filmmaker. She injects cocaine in a very deliberate manner, and when she hits a dud vein in her arm, which happens four times, she moves on to another one unfazed.

Lisa has been through many rehabs, we are told. When she was filmed, she was healthy and engaging; in other words, she looked and talked like someone who was recently abstinent but is back in the early stages of her next downward spiral. She has no interest in stopping things at this point. "Right now, I am in no position to go into recovery. [This way of life] is working for me. . . . I have money, drugs, business. I'm O.K."

To say Lisa's problem is the effect of cocaine on her brain is to miss the true threat to her well-being: Lisa herself. "I always use for a reason. It's repressing what needs to be repressed," she says. She yearns for "oblivion" through drugs and calls her use "complete selfishness."

Lisa's saga is a stunning illustration of the shortcomings of the medicalized view of addiction, which is silent on the fact that many people are drawn to drugs in the first place because the substances temporarily help quell all manner of pain they endured before ever becoming addicted: persistent self-loathing, anxiety, alienation, deep-seated intolerance of stress or boredom, pervasive loneliness. When Lisa says she seeks "oblivion," I am reminded of screenwriter Jerry Stahl and his potent memoir of addiction, *Permanent Midnight*: "The point is, everything, good or bad, boils back to the decade on the needle, and the years before that imbibing everything from cocaine to Romilar, pot to percs, LSD to liquid meth and a pharmacy in between: a lifetime spent altering the single niggling fact that to be alive means being conscious."

Cocaine, heroin, or alcohol may provide relief, but it is temporary, and when the addict finally does stop, the raw vulnerabilities that prompted his devotion to drugs in the first place are still there, throbbing like a fresh surgical incision as the painkillers wear off.

High-quality long-term rehabilitation takes the personal dimension of drug abuse seriously. Phoenix House, a nonprofit institution based in New York, is the national leader in this approach, and HBO featured one of its rehab programs for adolescents. Phoenix Academy in Austin, Texas, provides up to 24 months of residential care with the underlying philosophy that the addict himself, not his drug or his brain, is the primary problem. Addiction is understood more as a symptom than a disease. The root pathology is the patient's failure to engage in purposeful activity and achievement, and to acquire a feeling of self-worth and a capacity for self-control. On top of this, a young person's heavy drug use derails him from completing the maturational tasks of adolescence. By age 18, he is lost when it comes to consolidating a personal identity, forming a concept of his future, or figuring out how to give his life meaning.

"Drugs cover up all your problems," says Ted, a teenager forced by his parents to attend the academy. "Here there are no drugs, so you are forced to deal with your problems. [It] makes you internalize wanting to have a schedule and needing to stay busy all the time."

All residents must work, get an education, or learn a skill. When patients are deterred from acting on every impulse, they can learn the basic psychological skills so many of us take for granted: how to delay gratification, develop relationships based on trust, devise internal strategies for coping, and accumulate the small successes that eventually coalesce into a sense of self-worth. They learn to live in cooperation with others and to accept authority and supervision—concepts essential to workplace success.

By the time I had finished watching episodes like the one on Phoenix Academy, I realized that the series had actually made most of the points I would want the public to know about addiction, potential treatments, and the dynamics of recovery. It showed the profound truth about drug abuse: that individuals have the power to shape their own lives. It was a notable conclusion that all of the featured scientists supported as well—even though the brain disease rhetoric would imply otherwise. To be sure, PET scans and tutorials on neurobiology have a part in any comprehensive examination of addiction but, in the end, it was hard to imagine that viewers could come away thinking that the addict's disembodied brain held the secrets to understanding or helping him. The human face of the series could not help but dispel such a narrow impression.

I am a clinician. I treat real-life patients. As a pragmatist, I can't see the advantage of conceptualizing addiction as a "chronic and relapsing brain disease." At the same time, no reasonable person would disagree that addiction is mediated through the dopamine system of the brain. Or that intense activation of the dopamine system makes it more difficult for users to quit. Or that genetic factors influence the intensity of the effect that users derive from substances, the rapidity with which they develop compulsive use, the potency of their cue-related craving, and the severity of withdrawal symptoms.

Nevertheless, I remain loyal to the more traditional understanding of the word "addiction," the one that I assume the general public holds: namely, that addiction is a condition in which people engage in damaging and compulsive use of mind-altering substances. To me, that definition casts *behavior* as the essence of the problem; it also stipulates that addicts themselves have the ability to change that behavior.

I prefer the language of self-agency because it is the one that translates best into efforts to prevent, treat, and overcome addiction. Perhaps one day discoveries unearthed by brain science will oblige me to reconsider, and talking about addiction in the idiom of neurobiology will be more fruitful in the clinical domain. But for now, people like me must engage a patient in a consideration of *himself*—his anxieties and aspirations—not his brain.

POSTSCRIPT

Is Drug Addiction a Brain Disease?

There is little debate that drug addiction is a major problem. Drug addiction wreaks havoc for society and ruins the lives of numerous individuals and people who care for them. Addressing the causes of drug addiction and what to do about people who become addicted is especially relevant. Views on whether or not drug addiction is a brain disease diverge. Because drug abuse can be viewed as a matter of free will or as a brain disorder, there are also different views on how society should deal with drug abusers. Should drug addicts be incarcerated or treated? Does it matter whether one is responsible for one's drug addiction?

One could argue that free will and the concept of a brain disorder both apply to drug addiction. What may start out as a matter of free will may turn into an illness. Likewise, drug use may start out as an occasional behavior that may become abusive. To illustrate this point, many people may use alcohol for recreational or social purposes, but their alcohol use may develop into a chronic, abusive pattern—one that the person cannot easily overcome. Initially, one can stop using alcohol without too much discomfort. As time passes, however, and alcohol consumption becomes more frequent and the amounts increase, stopping for many people becomes difficult. By its very definition, social drinkers can stop drinking at will. Alcoholics drink out of necessity.

Many people who use addictive drugs do not become dependent on them. Perhaps there are factors beyond free will and changes in the brain that account for these people to become dependent. Is it possible that social factors come into play? Can friends and colleagues and their attitudes about drugs influence whether a drug user becomes a drug abuser? In the final analysis, drug addiction may result from the interaction of numerous factors and not simply be a dichotomy between psychology and biology.

Two articles that discuss addiction as a disease are "What Addicts Need" by Jeneen Interlandi (*Newsweek,* March 3, 2008) and "The Science of Addiction" by Michael Lemonick and Alice Park (*Time,* July 16, 2007). Stanton Peele, an outspoken critic of the disease concept, discusses this issue in "The Surprising Truth About Addiction," (*Psychology Today,* May/June 2004). In his book *Addiction Is a Choice,* Jeffrey Schaler argues against addiction as a disease. Other articles that explore whether addiction is a matter of biology is "Addiction Is a Disease," by John Halpern (*Psychiatric Times,* October 1, 2002) and "Addiction and Responsibility," by Richard J. Bonnie (*Social Research,* Fall 2001).

ISSUE 7

Should the Federal Government Play a Larger Role in Regulating Steroid Use?

YES: National Institute on Drug Abuse, from "Anabolic Steroid Abuse," *National Institute on Drug Abuse Research Report* (August 2006)

NO: Laura K. Egendorf, from *Performance Enhancing Drugs* (Reference Point Press, 2007)

ISSUE SUMMARY

YES: The National Institute on Drug Abuse (NIDA) warns that anabolic steroids produce numerous harmful side effects that can lead to stunted growth, breast development in males, excessive hair growth on women, acne, complications of the liver, and infections from nonsterile needles. Behaviorally, anabolic steroids have been associated with rage and aggression. According to NIDA, simply teaching about steroids does not deter their use.

NO: In her book, author Laura Egendorf cites individuals who feel that athletes are aware of the risks of taking steroids and other performance-enhancing drugs. Competition and the desire to succeed drive individuals to improve their athletic performance. Allowing steroid use would essentially level the playing field for all athletes. In addition, some experts believe that the negative consequences are exaggerated.

Anabolic steroids are synthetic derivatives of the male hormone testosterone. Although they have legitimate medical uses, steroids are used increasingly by individuals to build up muscle quickly and to increase personal strength. Concerns over the potential negative effects of steroid use seem to be justified: an estimated 1 million Americans, including two out of every 100 high school seniors, use anabolic steroids. Anabolic steroids users span all ethnic groups, nationalities, and socioeconomic groups. The emphasis on winning has led many athletes to take risks with steroids that are potentially destructive. Despite the widespread belief that anabolic steroids are used primarily by athletes, up to one-third of users are nonathletes who use these drugs to improve their physiques and self-images.

Society places much emphasis on winning, and to come out on top, many individuals are willing to make sacrifices—sacrifices that might compromise their health. Some people will do anything for the sake of winning. The sports headlines in many newspapers mention how various professional and Olympic athletes have used steroids. Drug testing is a major issue every time the Olympic competition is held. Besides the adverse physical consequences of steroids, there is the ethical question regarding fair play. Do steroids give competitors an unfair advantage? Should they be banned even if the side effects are not harmful? Do non-steroid users feel pressured to use these drugs to keep up with the competition? Would there be better regulation of steroids if their use was permitted?

The short-term consequences of anabolic steroids are well documented. Possible short-term effects among men include testicular atrophy, sperm count reduction, impotency, baldness, difficulty urinating, and breast enlargement. Among women, some potential effects are deepening of the voice, breast reduction, menstrual irregularities, the growth of body hair, and clitoral enlargement. Both sexes may develop acne, swelling in the feet, reduced levels of high-density lipoproteins (the type of cholesterol that is good for the body), hypertension, and liver damage. Taking steroids as an adolescent will stunt one's growth. Also related to steroid use are psychological changes, including mood swings, paranoia and violent behavior.

Steroids' short-term effects have been researched thoroughly; however, their long-term effects have not been substantiated. The problem with identifying the long-term effects of anabolic steroids is the lack of systematic, long-term studies. Much of the information regarding steroids' long-term effects comes from personal reports, not well-conducted, well-controlled studies. However, personal stories and anecdotal evidence are often accepted as fact.

The American Medical Association opposes stricter regulation of anabolic steroids on two grounds. First, anabolic steroids have been used medically to improve growth and development, for certain types of anemia, breast cancer, endometriosis, and osteoporosis. If stricter regulations are imposed, people who may benefit medically from these drugs will have more difficulty acquiring them. Second, it is highly unlikely that illicit use of these drugs will cease if they are banned. By maintaining legal access to these drugs, more studies regarding their long-term consequences can be conducted.

In the following selections, the National Institute on Drug Abuse (NIDA) contends that people who use anabolic steroids are risking their mental and physical well-being. NIDA advocates more testing for anabolic steroids.

Anabolic Steroid Abuse

What Are Anabolic Steroids?

"Anabolic steroids" is the familiar name for synthetic substances related to the male sex hormones (e.g., testosterone). They promote the growth of skeletal muscle (anabolic effects) and the development of male sexual characteristics (androgenic effects) in both males and females. The term "anabolic steroids" will be used throughout this report because of its familiarity, although the proper term for these compounds is "anabolic-androgenic steroids."

Anabolic steroids were developed in the late 1930s primarily to treat hypogonadism, a condition in which the testes do not produce sufficient testosterone for normal growth, development, and sexual functioning. The primary medical uses of these compounds are to treat delayed puberty, some types of impotence, and wasting of the body caused by HIV infection or other diseases.

During the 1930s, scientists discovered that anabolic steroids could facilitate the growth of skeletal muscle in laboratory animals, which led to abuse of the compounds first by bodybuilders and weightlifters and then by athletes in other sports. Steroid abuse has become so widespread in athletics that it can affect the outcome of sports contests.

Illicit steroids are often sold at gyms, competitions, and through mail order operations after being smuggled into this country. Most illegal steroids in the United States are smuggled from countries that do not require a prescription for the purchase of steroids. Steroids are also illegally diverted from U.S. pharmacies or synthesized in clandestine laboratories.

What Are Steroidal Supplements?

In the United States, supplements such as tetrahydrogestrinone (THG) and androstenedione (street name "Andro") previously could be purchased legally without a prescription through many commercial sources, including health food stores. Steroidal supplements can be converted into testosterone or a similar compound in the body. Less is known about the side effects of steroidal supplements, but if large quantities of these compounds substantially increase testosterone levels in the body, then they also are likely to produce the same side effects as anabolic steroids themselves. The purchase of these supplements, with the notable exception of dehydroepiandrosterone (DHEA), became illegal after the passage in 2004 of amendments to the Controlled Substances Act.

From *National Institute on Drug Abuse Research Report,* August 2006. U. S. Department of Health and Human and Services.

What Is the Scope of Steroid Use in the United States?

The 2005 Monitoring the Future study, a NIDA-funded survey of drug use among adolescents in middle and high schools across the United States, reported that past-year use of steroids decreased significantly among 8th- and 10th-graders since peak use in 2000. Among 12th-graders, there was a different trend—from 2000 to 2004, past year steroid use increased, but in 2005 there was a significant decrease, from 2.5 percent to 1.5 percent.

Steroid abuse affects individuals of various ages. However, it is difficult to estimate the true prevalence of steroid abuse in the United States because many data sources that measure drug abuse do not include steroids. Scientific evidence indicates that anabolic steroid abuse among athletes may range between one and six percent.

Why Do People Abuse Anabolic Steroids?

One of the main reasons people give for abusing steroids is to improve their athletic performance. Among athletes, steroid abuse has been estimated to be less that 6 percent according to surveys, but anecdotal information suggests more widespread abuse. Although testing procedures are now in place to deter steroid abuse among professional and Olympic athletes, new designer drugs constantly become available that can escape detection and put athletes willing to cheat one step ahead of testing efforts. This dynamic, however, may be about to shift if the saving of urine and blood samples for retesting at a future date becomes the standard. The high probability of eventual detection of the newer designer steroids, once the technology becomes available, plus the fear of retroactive sanctions, should give athletes pause.

Another reason people give for taking steroids is to increase their muscle size or to reduce their body fat. This group includes people suffering from the behavioral syndrome called muscle dysmorphia, which causes them to have a distorted image of their bodies. Men with muscle dysmorphia think that they look small and weak, even if they are large and muscular. Similarly, women with this condition think that they look fat and flabby, even though they are actually lean and muscular.

Some people who abuse steroids to boost muscle size have experienced physical or sexual abuse. In one series of interviews with male weightlifters, 25 percent who abused steroids reported memories of childhood physical or sexual abuse. Similarly, female weightlifters who had been raped were found to be twice as likely to report use of anabolic steroids or another purported musclebuilding drug, compared with those who had not been raped. Moreover, almost all of those who had been raped reported that they markedly increased their bodybuilding activities after the attack. They believed that being bigger and stronger would discourage further attacks because men would find them either intimidating or unattractive.

Finally, some adolescents abuse steroids as part of a pattern of high-risk behaviors. These adolescents also take risks such as drinking and driving, carrying a gun, driving a motorcycle without a helmet, and abusing other illicit drugs. Conditions such as muscle dysmorphia, a history of physical or sexual abuse, or a history of engaging in high-risk behaviors have all been associated with an increased risk of initiating or continuing steroid abuse.

How Are Anabolic Steroids Abused?

Some anabolic steroids are taken orally, others are injected intramuscularly, and still others are provided in gels or creams that are applied to the skin. Doses taken by abusers can be 10 to 100 times higher than the doses used for medical conditions.

Cycling, Stacking, and Pyramiding

Steroids are often abused in patterns called "cycling," which involve taking multiple doses of steroids over a specific period of time, stopping for a period, and starting again. Users also frequently combine several different types of steroids in a process known as "stacking." Steroid abusers typically "stack" the drugs, meaning that they take two or more different anabolic steroids, mixing oral and/or injectable types, and sometimes even including compounds that are designed for veterinary use. Abusers think that the different steroids interact to produce an effect on muscle size that is greater than the effects of each drug individually, a theory that has not been tested scientifically.

Another mode of steroid abuse is referred to as "pyramiding." This is a process in which users slowly escalate steroid abuse (increasing the number of steroids or the dose and frequency of one or more steroids used at one time), reaching a peak amount at mid-cycle and gradually tapering the dose toward the end of the cycle. Often, steroid abusers pyramid their doses in cycles of 6 to 12 weeks. At the beginning of a cycle, the person starts with low doses of the drugs being stacked and then slowly increases the doses. In the second half of the cycle, the doses are slowly decreased to zero. This is sometimes followed by a second cycle in which the person continues to train but without drugs. Abusers believe that pyramiding allows the body time to adjust to the high doses, and the drug-free cycle allows the body's hormonal system time to recuperate. As with stacking, the perceived benefits of pyramiding and cycling have not been substantiated scientifically.

What Are the Health Consequences of Steroid Abuse?

Anabolic steroid abuse has been associated with a wide range of adverse side effects ranging from some that are physically unattractive, such as acne and breast development in men, to others that are life threatening, such as heart attacks and liver cancer. Most are reversible if the abuser stops taking the drugs, but some are permanent, such as voice deepening in females.

Most data on the long-term effects of anabolic steroids in humans come from case reports rather than formal epidemiological studies. From the case reports, the incidence of life-threatening effects appears to be low, but serious adverse effects may be underrecognized or underreported, especially since they may occur many years later. Data from animal studies seem to support this possibility. One study found that exposing male mice for one-fifth of their lifespan to steroid doses comparable to those taken by human athletes caused a high frequency of early deaths.

Hormonal System

Steroid abuse disrupts the normal production of hormones in the body, causing both reversible and irreversible changes. Changes that can be reversed include reduced sperm production and shrinking of the testicles (testicular atrophy). Irreversible changes include male-pattern baldness and breast development (gynecomastia) in men. In one study of male bodybuilders, more than half had testicular atrophy and/or gynecomastia.

In the female body, anabolic steroids cause masculinization. Breast size and body fat decrease, the skin becomes coarse, the clitoris enlarges, and the voice deepens. Women may experience excessive growth of body hair but lose scalp hair. With continued administration of steroids, some of these effects become irreversible.

Musculoskeletal System

Rising levels of testosterone and other sex hormones normally trigger the growth spurt that occurs during puberty and adolescence and provide the signals to stop growth as well. When a child or adolescent takes anabolic steroids, the resulting artificially high sex hormone levels can prematurely signal the bones to stop growing.

Cardiovascular System

Steroid abuse has been associated with cardiovascular diseases (CVD), including heart attacks and strokes, even in athletes younger than 30. Steroids contribute to the development of CVD, partly by changing the levels of lipoproteins that carry cholesterol in the blood. Steroids, particularly oral steroids, increase the level of low-density lipoprotein (LDL) and decrease the level of high-density lipoprotein (HDL). High LDL and low HDL levels increase the risk of atherosclerosis, a condition in which fatty substances are deposited inside arteries and disrupt blood flow. If blood is prevented from reaching the heart, the result can be a heart attack. If blood is prevented from reaching the brain, the result can be a stroke.

Steroids also increase the risk that blood clots will form in blood vessels, potentially disrupting blood flow and damaging the heart muscle so that it does not pump blood effectively.

Liver

Steroid abuse has been associated with liver tumors and a rare condition called peliosis hepatis, in which blood-filled cysts form in the liver. Both the tumors and the cysts can rupture, causing internal bleeding.

Skin

Steroid abuse can cause acne, cysts, and oily hair and skin.

Infections

Many abusers who inject anabolic steroids may use nonsterile injection techniques or share contaminated needles with other abusers. In addition, some steroid preparations are manufactured illegally under nonsterile conditions. These factors put abusers at risk for acquiring life-threatening viral infections, such as HIV and hepatitis B and C. Abusers also can develop endocarditis, a bacterial infection that causes a potentially fatal inflammation of the inner lining of the heart. Bacterial infections also can cause pain and abscess formation at injection sites.

What Effects Do Anabolic Steroids Have on Behavior?

Case reports and small studies indicate that anabolic steroids, when used in high doses, increase irritability and aggression. Some steroid abusers report that they have committed aggressive acts, such as physical fighting or armed robbery, theft, vandalism, or burglary. Abusers who have committed aggressive acts or property crimes generally report that they engage in these behaviors more often when they take steroids than when they are drug free. A recent study suggests that the mood and behavioral effects seen during anabolic-androgenic steroid abuse may result from secondary hormonal changes.

Scientists have attempted to test the association between anabolic steroids and aggression by administering high steroid doses or placebo for days or weeks to human volunteers and then asking the people to report on their behavioral symptoms. To date, four such studies have been conducted. In three, high steroid doses did produce greater feelings of irritability and aggression than did placebo, although the effects appear to be highly variable across individuals. In one study, the drugs did not have that effect. One possible explanation, according to the researchers, is that some but not all anabolic steroids increase irritability and aggression. Recent animal studies show an increase in aggression after steroid administration.

In a few controlled studies, aggression or adverse, overt behaviors resulting from the administration of anabolic steroid use have been reported by a minority of volunteers.

In summary, the extent to which steroid abuse contributes to violence and behavioral disorders is unknown. As with the health complications of steroid abuse, the prevalence of extreme cases of violence and behavioral disorders seems to be low, but it may be underreported or underrecognized.

Research also indicates that some users might turn to other drugs to alleviate some of the negative effects of anabolic steroids. For example, a

POSSIBLE HEALTH CONSEQUENCES
OF ANABOLIC STEROID ABUSE

Hormonal System
- men
  - infertility
  - breast development
  - shrinking of the testicles
  - male-pattern baldness
- women
  - enlargement of the clitoris
  - excessive growth of body hair
  - male-pattern baldness

Musculoskeletal System
- short stature (if taken by adolescents)
- tendon rupture

Cardiovascular System
- increases in LDL; decreases in HDL
- high blood pressure
- heart attacks
- enlargement of the heart's left ventricle

Liver
- cancer
- peliosis hepatis
- tumors

Skin
- severe acne and cysts
- oily scalp
- jaundice
- fluid retention

Infection
- HIV/AIDS
- hepatitis

Psychiatric Effects
- rage, aggression
- mania
- delusions

study of 227 men admitted in 1999 to a private treatment center for addiction to heroin or other opioids found that 9.3 percent had abused anabolic steroids before trying any other illicit drug. Of these 9.3 percent, 86 percent first used opioids to counteract insomnia and irritability resulting from anabolic steroids.

Are Anabolic Steroids Addictive?

An undetermined percentage of steroid abusers may become addicted to the drugs, as evidenced by their continued abuse despite physical problems and negative effects on social relations. Also, steroid abusers typically spend large amounts of time and money obtaining the drugs, which is another indication that they may be addicted. Individuals who abuse steroids can experience withdrawal symptoms when they stop taking steroids, such as mood swings, fatigue, restlessness, loss of appetite, insomnia, reduced sex drive, and steroid cravings. The most dangerous of the withdrawal symptoms is depression, because it sometimes leads to suicide attempts. If left untreated, some depressive symptoms associated with anabolic steroid withdrawal have been known to persist for a year or more after the abuser stops taking the drugs.

What Can Be Done to Prevent Steroid Abuse?

Most prevention efforts in the United States today focus on athletes involved with the Olympics and professional sports; few school districts test for abuse of illicit drugs. It has been estimated that close to 9 percent of secondary schools conduct some sort of drug testing program, presumably focused on athletes, and that less than 4 percent of the Nation's high schools test their athletes for steroids. Studies are currently under way to determine whether such testing reduces drug abuse.

Research on steroid educational programs has shown that simply teaching students about steroids' adverse effects does not convince adolescents that they can be adversely affected. Nor does such instruction discourage young people from taking steroids in the future. Presenting both the risks and benefits of anabolic steroid use is more effective in convincing adolescents about steroids' negative effects, apparently because the students find a balanced approach more credible, according to the researchers.

NIDA-Funded Prevention Research Helps Reduce Steroid Abuse

A more sophisticated approach has shown promise for preventing steroid abuse among players on high school sports teams. The Adolescents Training and Learning to Avoid Steroids (ATLAS) program is showing high school football players that they do not need steroids to build powerful muscles and improve athletic performance. By educating student athletes about the harmful effects of anabolic steroids and providing nutrition and weight-training alternatives to steroid use, the ATLAS program has increased football players' healthy behaviors and reduced their intentions to abuse steroids. In the program, coaches and team leaders teach the harmful effects of anabolic steroids and other illicit drugs on immediate sports performance, and discuss how to refuse offers of drugs.

Studies show that 1 year after completion of the program, compared with a control group, ATLAS-trained students in 15 high schools had:

- Half the incidence of new abuse of anabolic steroids and less intention to abuse them in the future;
- Less abuse of alcohol, marijuana, amphetamines, and narcotics;
- Less abuse of "athletic enhancing" supplements;
- Less likelihood of engaging in hazardous substance abuse behaviors such as drinking and driving;
- Increased protection against steroid and other substance abuse. Namely, less interest in trying steroids, less desire to abuse them, better knowledge of alternatives to steroid abuse, improved body image, and increased knowledge of diet supplements.

The Athletes Targeting Healthy Exercise and Nutrition Alternatives (ATHENA) program was patterned after the ATLAS program, but designed for adolescent girls on sports teams. Early testing of girls enrolled in the ATHENA program showed significant decreases in risky behaviors. While preseason risk behaviors were similar among controls and ATHENA participants, the control athletes were three times more likely to begin using diet pills and almost twice as likely to begin abuse of other body-shaping substances, including amphetamines, anabolic steroids, and muscle-building supplements during the sports season. The use of diet pills increased among control subjects, while use fell to approximately half of the preseason levels among ATHENA participants. In addition, ATHENA team members were less likely to be sexually active, more likely to wear seatbelts, less likely to ride in a car with a driver who had been drinking, and they experienced fewer injuries during the sports season.

Both Congress and the Substance Abuse and Mental Health Services Administration have endorsed ATLAS and ATHENA as model prevention programs. These Oregon Health & Science University programs have been awarded the 2006 annual *Sports Illustrated* magazine's first-ever "Champion Award."

What Treatments Are Effective for Anabolic Steroid Abuse?

Few studies of treatments for anabolic steroid abuse have been conducted. Current knowledge is based largely on the experiences of a small number of physicians who have worked with patients undergoing steroid withdrawal. The physicians have found that supportive therapy is sufficient in some cases. Patients are educated about what they may experience during withdrawal and are evaluated for suicidal thoughts. If symptoms are severe or prolonged, medications or hospitalization may be needed.

Some medications that have been used for treating steroid withdrawal restore the hormonal system after its disruption by steroid abuse. Other medications target specific withdrawal symptoms—for example, antidepressants to treat depression and analgesics for headaches and muscle and joint pains.

Some patients require assistance beyond pharmacological treatment of withdrawal symptoms and are treated with behavioral therapies.

Where Can I Get Further Scientific Information About Steroid Abuse?

To learn more about anabolic steroids and other drugs of abuse, contact the National Clearinghouse for Alcohol and Drug Information (NCADI) at 800-729-6686. Information specialists are available to help you locate information and resources.

Fact sheets, including *InfoFacts,* on the health effects of anabolic steroids, other drugs of abuse, and other drug topics are available on the NIDA Web site . . . and can be ordered free of charge in English and Spanish from NCADI. . . .

References

Bahrke MS, Yesalis CE, Wright JE. Psychological and behavioral effects of endogenous testosterone and anabolic-androgenic steroids: an update. *Sports Med* 22(6):367–390, 1996.

Berning JM, Adams KJ, Stamford BA. Anabolic steroid usage in athletics: facts, fiction, and public relations. *J Strength Conditioning Res* 18(4):908–917, 2004.

Blue JG, Lombardo JA. Steroids and steroid-like compounds. *Clin Sports Med* 18(3):667–689, 1999.

Bronson FH, Matherne CM. Exposure to anabolic-androgenic steroids shortens life span of male mice. *Med Sci Sports Exerc* 29(5):615–619, 1997.

Brower KJ. Withdrawal from anabolic steroids. *Curr Ther Endocrinol Metab* 6:338–343, 1997.

Daly RC, et al. Neuroendocrine and behavioral effects of high-dose anabolic steroid administration in male normal volunteers. *Psychoneuroendocrinology* 28(3): 317–331, 2003.

Elliot D, Goldberg L. Intervention and prevention of steroid use in adolescents. *Am J Sports Med* 24(6):S46–S47, 1996.

Goldberg L, et al. Anabolic steroid education and adolescents: Do scare tactics work? *Pediatrics* 87(3):283–286, 1991.

Goldberg L, et al. Effects of a multidimensional anabolic steroid prevention intervention: The Adolescents Training and Learning to Avoid Steroids (ATLAS) Program. *JAMA* 276(19):1555–1562, 1996.

Goldberg L, et al. The ATLAS program: Preventing drug use and promoting health behaviors. *Arch Pediatr Adolesc Med* 154(4):332–338, 2000.

Gottfredson GD, et al. *The national study of delinquency prevention in schools.* Ellicott City, MD: Gottfredson Associates, Inc., 2000.

Green et al. NCAA study of substance use and abuse habits of college student-athletes. *Clin J Sport Med* 11(1):51–56, 2001.

Gruber AJ, Pope HG Jr. Compulsive weight lifting and anabolic drug abuse among women rape victims. *Compr Psychiatry* 40(4):273–277, 1999.

Gruber AJ, Pope HG Jr. Psychiatric and medical effects of anabolic-androgenic steroid use in women. *Psychother Psychosom* 69:19–26, 2000.

Hoberman JM, Yesalis CE. The history of synthetic testosterone. *Sci Am* 272(2): 76–81, 1995.

Leder BZ, et al. Oral androstenedione administration and serum testosterone concentrations in young men. *JAMA* 283(6):779–782, 2000.

The Medical Letter on Drugs and Therapeutics. Creatine and androstenedione—two "dietary supplements." 40(1039):105–106. New Rochelle, NY: The Medical Letter, Inc., 1998.

Middleman AB, et al. High-risk behaviors among high school students in Massachusetts who use anabolic steroids. *Pediatrics* 96(2):268–272, 1995.

Pope HG Jr, Kouri EM, Hudson MD. Effects of supraphysiologic doses of testosterone on mood and aggression in normal men: a randomized controlled trial. *Arch Gen Psychiatry* 57(2):133–140, 2000.

Porcerelli JH, Sandler BA. Anabolic-androgenic steroid abuse and psychopathology. *Psychiatr Clin North Am* 21(4):829–833, 1998.

Rich JD, Dickinson BP, Flanigan TP, Valone SE. Abscess related to anabolic-androgenic steroid injection. *Med Sci Sports Exerc* 31(2):207–209, 1999.

Stilger VG, Yesalis CE. Anabolic-androgenic steroid use among high school football players. *J Community Health* 24(2):131–145, 1999.

Su T-P, et al. Neuropsychiatric effects of anabolic steroids in male normal volunteers. *JAMA* 269(21):2760–2764, 1993.

Sullivan ML, Martinez CM, Gennis P, Gallagher, EJ. The cardiac toxicity of anabolic steroids. *Prog Cardiovasc Dis* 41(1):1–15, 1998.

Verroken M. Hormones and Sport. Ethical aspects and the prevalence of hormone abuse in sport. *J Endocrinol* 170(1):49–54, 2001.

Yesalis CE. *Anabolic steroids in sports and exercise,* 2nd edition. Champaign, IL: Human Kinetics. 2000.

Yesalis CE. Androstenedione. Sport dietary supplements update, 2000, *E-SportMed.com*.

Yesalis CE. Trends in anabolic-androgenic steroid use among adolescents. *Arch Pediatr Adolesc Med* 151(12):1197–1206.

Yesalis CE, Kennedy NJ, Kopstein AN, Bahrke MS. Anabolic-androgenic steroid use in the United States. *JAMA* 270(10):1217–1221, 1993.

Zorpette G. Andro angst. *Sci Am* 279(6):22–26, 1998.

Is the Use of Performance Enhancing Drugs Cheating?

"Athletes chemically propelled to victory do not merely overvalue winning, they misunderstand why winning is properly valued."

—George F. Will, "Steroids Scandal Is Damaging to Baseball," *Conservative Chronicle,* December 2005.

Although modern-day athletes have used performance-enhancing drugs for decades, it was not until the 1960s that the leaders of the international and professional sports communities began to view the use of these drugs as cheating. The general disgust toward steroids and other performance-enhancing drugs has been especially strong since the late 1980s, following the discovery that Canadian sprinter Ben Johnson's world-record-setting victory in the 100-meter race in the 1988 Summer Olympics was fueled by his use of the steroid stanozolol. Before then, explains John Hoberman, a professor at the University of Texas and the author of several books on sports, "[the] use of performance enhancing substances was not viewed as cheating. It was simply a way of life for athletes of the times."

Athletes in the past did not deny their use of performance-enhancing drugs; for example, in the 1970s, Olympic weightlifters openly declared their use of steroids. Howard Bryant, in his book *Juicing the Game,* writes: "Drugs were part of the weightlifting world. . . . Gyms across America provided the conduits to information about which substances worked best and where illegal drugs could be obtained." The International Olympics Committee instituted drug testing in 1968 for narcotics and amphetamines, but steroids were not added to the list until 1975. Until then, Olympians were free to add muscle to their body through chemical means, and athletes with access to the best performance-enhancing drugs could continue to use them without fear of punishment.

Reasons for Using Performance-Enhancing Drugs

Athletes use performance-enhancing drugs for a variety of reasons. Steroids increase strength and reduce the time it takes to recover from injury. As a result, athletes who use them are able to push themselves harder and further than a clean athlete. Increased strength allows them to record more tackles, hit a ball farther, and grab more rebounds. Other drugs increase the red blood cell count, allowing the blood to carry more oxygen and thus enabling the athlete to run or bike over long distances without tiring.

Yet no matter what sport they play, athletes know that their salaries are dependent on their statistics. It is therefore not surprising that so many would choose to artificially enhance their talents with performance-enhancing drugs. Few baseball fans can remember who hit the most singles in any given year, but almost all of them know that Barry Bonds set the MLB single-season home-run record with 73 home runs in 2001. Olympic medalists are famous for life; the athlete who finishes in fourth place in the 100-meter dash is soon forgotten, even if he or she was only a few hundredths of a second behind the gold medalist.

Changing Views Toward Performance-Enhancing Drugs

Prior to the 1980s the lack of testing, other than in the Olympic Games, gave tacit approval to performance-enhancing drugs. The stories of rampant drug use in various professional sports leagues reveal a lackadaisical response that created a culture of acceptance and led to more and more athletes experimenting with drugs because they knew they could use whatever substances they wished without suffering any consequences. For example, Major League Baseball did not ban steroids until 2003, and once it did so, the penalty for failing a drug test was only a 10-game suspension.

However, the indifference toward performance-enhancing drugs that marked the 1960s through the middle of the 1980s began to be replaced by greater concerns as people became more aware of the health effects of these substances. Although the National Football League started testing for steroids in 1987, followers of the game likely did not recognize the dangerous effects of steroids until Lyle Alzado, a fearsome defensive end best know for his years with the Los Angeles Raiders, revealed in 1991 that he had brain cancer; he died the following year. Bryant writes, "Though many team doctors in the NFL doubted Lyle Alzado's claim that there was a direct connection between his steroid use and his brain cancer, his death in 1991 served as a sobering reminder of the influence of steroids in their sport."

People also began to consider the use of performance-enhancing drugs to be cheating, because athletes were using the drugs to enhance their abilities unnaturally. Such usage thus distorts the notion of a level playing field and misinterprets the importance of sports, many people argue. President George W. Bush has stated, "The use of performance-enhancing drugs . . . sends the wrong message . . . that there are shortcuts to accomplishment, and that performance is more important than character." Syndicated political columnist George Will suggests that the power of sports is diluted when winning becomes dependent on chemistry and not hard work.

Claims That Performance-Enhancing Drugs Have Limited Effects

One of the counterarguments to the idea that steroids cause a significant increase in athletic ability is that athletes still rely heavily on their natural ability; most people, no matter how hard they try, will never become professional or Olympic athletes. While performance-enhancing drugs can improve endurance and strength and speed up recovery, they cannot make a curve ball easier to hit or take seconds off of a sprinter's 100-meter time. As radio talk show host Steve Yuhas explains, "Popping a pill or injecting yourself with steroids, although harmful to the individual in the long run, does not make a person more athletically talented than anyone else."

Some people even argue that natural ability is as unfair an advantage as performance-enhancing drugs—perhaps even more so, because while the drugs are available to anyone, athletes cannot change the genes with which they were born. In fact, many people contend that the use of performance-enhancing drugs is simply a way to level the playing field. They argue that it is genetics, not drugs, that make a competition unfair; some people are simply better equipped to compete. One example is Finnish cross-country skier Eero Maentyranta, who won three gold medals in the 1964 Winter Olympics. Later tests revealed his blood naturally contained 40 to 50 percent more red blood cells than average. This gave him a significant advantage over his competitors because long-distance performance relies on delivery of oxygen to muscles, which is the job of red blood cells. His natural ability outmatched any benefit someone with an average level of red blood cells would receive from using drugs.

Similarly, one theory states that European distance runners lag behind their African counterparts because African runners, such as those from Kenya and Ethiopia, can resist fatigue longer and go farther on the same amount of oxygen. Studies also show that Kenyan runners tend to have slimmer legs than European runners, which means they do not need as much energy to run. Examination of this subject can be difficult, as it can lead to controversial conclusions on racial differences; however, physical evidence does suggest that body types are not universal—after all, no one would deny that the average man is too short to succeed in the National Basketball Association. As Julian Savulescu, Bennett Foddy, and Megan Clayton argue, "Sport discriminates against the genetically unfit. Sport is the province of the genetic elite."

At the same time, note people who disagree with that argument, performance-enhancing drugs can make a significant difference if taken by an elite athlete. If taking a steroid will enable a hitter to develop the arm strength needed to drive a baseball 15 feet farther, that could be the difference between a fly ball to the warning track and a home run. Using EPO might enable a world-class sprinter to shave enough time off his or her 100-meter dash to win an Olympic medal. Talent is essential for athletic success, but performance-enhancing drugs can provide a small but critical boost. At the topmost levels of sports, differences between athletic ability are minimal, save for a few exceptional athletes—the Michael Jordans and Wayne Gretzkys of the world.

Legalizing Performance-Enhancing Drugs

Some argue that the best way to even the playing field is by legalizing performance-enhancing drugs. Proponents of this view contend that legalization would eliminate any genetic advantages some athletes may possess. One writer even suggests that athletes who do not use steroids should be banned from competition. In the view of Sidney Gendin, "For all the money they have to lay out, fans are entitled to the best possible performances. Why, then, should they have to put up with the inferior performances of non-drug users?"

Legalizing drugs would bring with it a host of new complications. First, each major sports organization would have to decide which performance-enhancing drugs its athletes would be permitted to use. The drugs would have to be strictly regulated to ensure that they were not laced with banned substances. Athletes would need to be recompensed if they developed health problems as a result of using steroids or other drugs. Society would also need to decide whether performance-enhancing drugs should be legalized at the high school or college level. In addition, as Charles E. Yesalis, an expert on the history of drugs in sports, states, "Legalization of steroids in sport might lessen hypocrisy, but it would place an extremely heavy burden on individual athletes who then would be forced either to take drugs known to be harmful or compete at a disadvantage."

Whether using performance-enhancing drugs is a type of cheating or merely a way for athletes to create level playing fields is a matter of perspective. What is clear is that use of these drugs leads to considerable controversy and pointed debate. And as long as athletes come from different social and economic backgrounds and are of different shapes and sizes, athletic competitions can never take place between true equals.

How Dangerous Are Performance-Enhancing Drugs?

"The price of steroid abuse is high."

—Doug West, "Steroid Abuse—Getting Bigger,"
Youthculture@today, Fall 2002.

Steroids and other performance-enhancing drugs do more than improve athletic performance. They can also shorten or worsen the lives of the athletes who use them. The physical effects of performance-enhancing drugs have been well documented. Steroid users run the risk of heart attacks, liver cancer, and strokes. Less fatal but still troubling consequences include impotence and breast development for male users and breast reduction and facial hair for women. These gender-specific effects occur because steroids contain testosterone; too much testosterone gives women male characteristics, but it also changes the secondary sexual characteristics of men. Excessive levels of testosterone have also been found to kill brain cells, a discovery that researchers believe may be linked to behavior changes such as suicidal tendencies and hyperaggressiveness.

Consequences of Steroid Use

The fate of East German women athletes who were given steroids to improve their chances in the Olympic games shows that using these drugs can have unintended consequences. Howard Bryant writes, "In thousands of cases, the East German government had injected so much testosterone into its female athletes that some had essentially turned into men. Breast size shrank, facial hair grew, male pattern baldness developed, and the clitoris grew enlarged and deformed. A few, their bodies ravaged by years' worth of male hormones, would undergo sex-change operations."

Steroid users may also be more prone to injuries, in particular, tendon damage, because of their increased muscle mass. Some doctors believe this may be why Mark McGwire's home-run totals fell off rapidly after his record-setting season in 1998 and why injuries forced him to retire in 2001. Bryant suggests, "[Doctors] were . . . convinced that the types of injuries McGwire suffered were typical of a body affected by steroids, a by-product of overdevelopment, of joints weakened by anabolic substances, making his body far too powerful for his frame. McGwire grew so big his joints gave in."

Steroids and Organ Damage

Steroids can cause serious harm to the heart, liver, and kidneys. People who use steroids have an increased chance of blood clots and of enlargement and weakening of the heart. Androgen use has also been associated with heart attacks. Because the liver filters blood before it reaches the kidneys, it must constantly work to remove traces of drugs, such as steroids, from the blood. If too large an amount of drugs reaches the liver, the organ releases bile into the bloodstream. Bile causes the eyes and skin to turn yellow, a condition known as jaundice. Steroid use can also result in liver tumors and the condition peliosis hepatitis, in which blood-filled cysts form in the liver. These can rupture and lead to internal bleeding. Extensive steroid use can also cause kidney failure because every drug a person takes also has to be processed through the kidneys.

Performance-enhancing drugs also affect athletes emotionally and psychologically. The hyperaggressiveness associated with steroid use is known colloquially as "roid rage." Paranoia and antisocial behavior can also occur. Steroids can also be addictive, according to the Drug Enforcement Administration (DEA). The DEA explains, "An undetermined percentage of steroid abusers may become addicted to the drug, as evidenced by their continuing to take steroids in spite of physical problems, negative effects on social relations, or nervousness and irritability. Steroid users can experience withdrawal symptoms such as mood swings, fatigue, restlessness, and depression."

Have the Dangers of Performance-Enhancing Drugs Been Exaggerated?

Despite these effects, many people maintain that performance-enhancing drugs are not terribly dangerous. One person who has argued that the health risks of steroid use have been overstated is Rick Collins, a bodybuilder and attorney who has written extensively about steroids. He asserts, "A flawed 1988 study suggested that psychiatric disorders occur with unusual frequency among athletes using anabolics. But the conclusions of these researchers have been regarded with skepticism from other experts."

Furthermore, some performance-enhancing drugs have legitimate medical uses and thus, proponents say, should not be considered as wholly dangerous. Steroids speed the healing of injured muscles, help aging men build muscle mass, and increase libido. Human growth hormone has helped increase the height of thousands of children.

Would Legalization Reduce the Health Risks of Performance-Enhancing Drugs?

Some contend that one way to make sure that athletes do not experience health problems when they take performance-enhancing drugs is to legalize these drugs. If steroids and similar substances were legalized, athletes could take them under the supervision of doctors. Michael Le Page, writing for *New Scientist*, argues, "Allow the use of drugs, and have sports authorities focus on testing the health of athletes rather than their use of drugs. This is the suggestion of ethicists Julian Savulescu at the University of Oxford and Bennett Foddy at the University of Melbourne, Australia. They argue that any drugs that are safe should be permitted, whatever their effect on performance."

POSTSCRIPT

Should the Federal Government Play a Larger Role in Regulating Steroid Use?

There are several reasons why long-term research into the effects of anabolic steroids is lacking. First, it is unethical to give drugs to people that may prove harmful, even lethal. Also, the amount of steroids given to subjects in a laboratory setting may not replicate what illegal steroid users actually take. Users who take steroids illegally may take substantially more than what subjects are given in a clinical trial. It is not uncommon for steroid users to "stack" their drugs, meaning they take several different steroids.

Second, to determine the true effects of drugs, double-blind studies need to be conducted. This means that neither the researcher nor the people receiving the drugs know whether the subjects are receiving the steroids or the placebos (inert substances). This approach is not practical with steroids because subjects can always tell if they received the steroids or the placebos. The effects of steroids could be determined by following up with people who are known steroid users. However, this method lacks proper controls. If physical or psychological problems appear in a subject, for example, it cannot be determined whether the problems are due to the steroids or to other drugs the person may have been taking. Also, the type of person who uses steroids may be the kind of person who has emotional problems in the first place.

Even though the Drug Enforcement Administration estimates the black-market trade in anabolic steroids to be several hundred million dollars a year, one could argue that steroids are symptomatic of a much larger social problem. Society places much emphasis on appearance and performance. From the time we are children, we are bombarded with constant reminders that we must do better than the next person. If you want to make the varsity team, if you want that scholarship, if you want to be a professional athlete, then you need to do whatever it takes to get there. We are also constantly reminded of the importance of appearance—to either starve ourselves or pump ourselves up (or both) in order to satisfy the cultural ideal of beauty. If we cannot achieve these cultural standards through exercising, dieting, or drug use, then we can turn to surgery. Many males growing up are given the message that they should be "big and strong." One shortcut to achieving that look is through the use of steroids. Steroid use fits into the larger social problem of people not accepting themselves and their limitations.

The widespread use of performance-enhancing drugs in various sports is described in "The Doping Dilemma: Game Theory to Explain the Pervasive Abuse of Drugs in Cycling, Baseball and Other Sports" by Michael Shermer

(*Scientific American*, April 2008). In "Enhanced Athletes? It's Only Natural" (*Washington Post*, August 3, 2008), Andy Miah examines the use of technology, including steroids, in the development of the modern day athlete.

Testing for steroid use is discussed Scott Laffe's article "Steroids: To Test or to Educate? Several School Districts Find a Will and a Way to Examine Their Athletes for Illegal Substance Use" (*School Administrator,* June 2006). The use of steroids in sports is dealt with in "Chemical Edge: The Risks of Performance-Enhancing Drugs," by Marissa Saltzman (*Odyssey,* May 1, 2006) and "Drugs and the Olympics" (*The Economist,* August 7, 2004). The effects of tetrahydrogestrinone (THG), another performance-enhancing drug, are described in Deanna Franklin's article "FDA Warns About Dangers of THG: Banned Steroid" (*Pediatric News,* January 2004).

Internet References . . .

National Institute on Alcohol Abuse and Alcoholism (NIAAA)

This site provides research on the causes, consequences, treatment, and prevention of alcoholism and alcohol-related problems.

http://niaaa.nih.gov

American Medical Association (AMA)

Information regarding the development and promotion of standards in medical practice, research, and education are included through this website.

http://www.ama-assn.org

Columbia University College of Physicians and Surgeons Complete Home Medical Guide

This site provides information about health and medicine, including information dealing with psychotherapeutic drugs.

http://cpmcnet.columbia.edu/texts/guide/hmg06_005.html

American Psychological Association (APA)

Research concerning different psychological disorders and the various types of treatments, including drug treatments that are available, can be accessed through this site.

http://www.apa.org

CDC's Tobacco Information and Prevention Source

This location contains current information on smoking prevention programs. Much data regarding teen smoking can be found at this site.

http://www.cdc.gov/tobacco

Drugs and Social Policy

*E*xcept *for the debate over whether laws prohibiting marijuana use should be relaxed, each debate in this section focuses on drugs that are already legal. Despite concerns over the effects of illegal drugs, the most frequently used drugs in society are legal drugs. Because of their prevalence and legal status, the social, psychological, and physical impact of drugs like tobacco, caffeine, alcohol, and prescription drugs are often minimized or negated. However, tobacco and alcohol cause far more death and disability than all illegal drugs combined.*

The recent trend toward medical self-help raises questions of how much control one should have over one's health. The current tendency to identify nicotine as an addictive drug and to promote the moderate use of alcohol to reduce heart disease has generated much controversy. In the last several years the increase in consumers requesting prescription drugs for themselves and Ritalin for their children also has created much concern. Lastly, is it beneficial to the average consumer when prescription drugs are advertised?

- Should Employers Limit Secondhand Smoke?

- Should Marijuana be Legalized?

- Are Psychotherapeutic Drugs Overprescribed for Treating Mental Illness?

- Is Caffeine a Health Risk?

- Should School-age Children with Attention Deficit/Hyperactivity Disorder (ADHD) Be Treated with Ritalin and Other Stimulants?

- Do Consumers Benefit When Prescription Drugs Are Advertised?

ISSUE 8

Should Employers Limit Secondhand Smoke?

YES: Leslie Zellers, Meliah A. Thomas, and Marice Ashe, from "Legal Risks to Employers Who Allow Smoking in the Workplace," *American Journal of Public Health* (August 2007)

NO: Robert A. Levy and Rosalind B. Marimont, from "Lies, Damned Lies, and 400,000 Smoking-Related Deaths," *Regulation* (vol. 21, no. 4, 1998)

ISSUE SUMMARY

YES: Leslie Zellers and Marice Ashe, attorneys with Public Health Law and Policy of the Public Health Institute, and attorney Meliah Thomas maintain that employers should want to reduce their employees' exposure to secondhand smoke to reduce the risk of litigation and to decrease their premiums for workers' compensation. Moreover, eliminating secondhand smoke protects their employees from deleterious effects.

NO: Robert A. Levy, a senior fellow at the Cato Institute, and Rosalind B. Marimont, a mathematician and scientist who retired from the National Institute of Standards and Technology, claim that the government distorts and exaggerates the dangers associated with cigarette smoking. Levy and Marimont state that factors like poor nutrition and obesity are overlooked as causes of death among smokers. They note that cigarette smoking is harmful, but the misapplication of statistics should be regarded as "junk science."

Most people, including those who smoke, recognize that cigarette smoking is harmful. However, are nonsmokers in jeopardy due to secondhand smoke? Because of tobacco's reputation as a substance that jeopardizes people's health, many activists are requesting that more stringent restrictions be placed on it, including secondhand smoke. Cigarette packages are required to carry warnings describing the dangers of tobacco products but they do not mention the effects of secondhand smoke. In many countries tobacco products cannot be advertised on television or billboards. Laws that prevent minors from purchasing tobacco products are being more vigorously enforced. Should there not be greater regulation regarding secondhand smoke?

Defenders of the tobacco industry point to benefits associated with nicotine, the mild stimulant that is the chief active chemical in tobacco. In previous centuries, for example, tobacco was used to help people with a variety of ailments, including skin diseases; internal and external disorders; and diseases of the eyes, ears, mouth, and nose. Tobacco and its smoke were employed often by Native Americans for sacramental purposes. For users, smoking provides a sense of euphoria, and is a source of gratification that does not impair thinking or performance. One can drive a car, socialize, study for a test, and engage in a variety of activities while smoking. Nicotine can relieve anxiety and stress, and it can reduce weight by lessening one's appetite and by increasing metabolic activity. Many smokers assert that smoking cigarettes enables them to concentrate better and that abstaining from smoking impairs their concentration. One could ask the question as to how much secondhand smoke impairs others and whether smokers should be deprived of smoking.

Critics paint a very different picture of tobacco products, citing some of the following statistics: Tobacco is responsible for about 30 percent of deaths among people between ages 35 and 69, making it the single most prominent cause of premature death in the developed world. The relationship between cigarette smoking and cardiovascular disease, including heart attack, stroke, sudden death, peripheral vascular disease, and aortic aneurysm, is well documented. Even as few as one to four cigarettes daily can increase the risk of fatal coronary heart disease. Cigarettes have also been shown to reduce blood flow and the level of high-density lipoprotein cholesterol, which is the beneficial type of cholesterol.

According to the United States Surgeon General, exposure to secondhand smoke causes lung cancer, cardiovascular disease, damage to the respiratory tract, and middle-ear disease; exacerbates asthma in children; and is linked to sudden infant death syndrome (SIDS). Secondhand smoke contains more than 50 carcinogens.

According to smokers' rights advocates, the majority of smokers are already aware of the potential harm of tobacco products; in fact, most smokers tend to overestimate the dangers of smoking. Adults should therefore be allowed to smoke if that is their wish. Many promote the idea that the Food and Drug Administration (FDA) and a number of politicians are attempting to deny smokers the right to engage in a behavior that they freely choose. Balancing the rights of smokers and nonsmokers is difficult. The question remains as to whether employers should limit the exposure of secondhand smoke to nonsmokers. What would be the impact of limiting smoking on the morale of smokers and nonsmokers?

In the following selections, Leslie Zellers, Meliah Thomas and Marice Ashe argue that it is the responsibility of employers to protect employees from the effects of secondhand smoke. They maintain that employers also reduce their risk of litigation and reduce workers' compensation premiums by limiting exposure to secondhand smoke. Robert A. Levy and Rosalind B. Marimont argue that the scientific evidence demonstrating that tobacco use is harmful to smokers is disputable. Levy and Marimont state that smoking has been demonized unfairly. Cigarette smoking is not illegal and does not cause intoxication, violent behavior, or unemployment.

YES

Leslie Zellers, Meliah A. Thomas, and Marice Ashe

Legal Risks to Employers Who Allow *Smoking* in the Workplace

There is mounting evidence that documents the dangers of exposure to secondhand smoke, including in the workplace. In states that permit workplace *smoking,* employers face significant legal risks from employees who are exposed to secondhand smoke on the job. Employers have been held liable for employee exposure to secondhand smoke in numerous cases, including those based on workers' compensation, state and federal disability law, and the duty to provide a safe workplace. Given this liability risk, employers should voluntarily adopt smoke-free workplace policies. Such policies do more than fulfill an employer's legal obligation to provide a safe workplace; they also reduce the risk of litigation, potentially reduce workers' compensation premiums, and protect employees from harm. (Am J Public Health. 2007;97:1376–1382. doi: 10.2105/AJPH.2006.094102)

There is mounting evidence of the dangers of exposure to secondhand smoke. Several recent studies have shown that employees' exposure to secondhand smoke in the workplace causes significant increases in tobacco-specific carcinogens in the human body (M. Stark, PhD, unpublished data, April 2006).[1–6] *Smoking* in bars, restaurants, and other hospitality venues contributes substantially to poor indoor air quality in these workplaces and exposes employees to carcinogens and other toxic agents in tobacco smoke.[7] Specifically, nonsmokers who are exposed to secondhand smoke at work increase their risk of heart disease by 25%–30% and their risk of lung cancer by 20%–30%, and are susceptible to immediate damage to the cardiovascular system.[8] The only way to effectively eliminate secondhand smoke exposure in the workplace is to make the workplace a smoke-free environment.[9] Studies have shown immediate improvements in air quality,[10–11] and workers' respiratory health[12] when *smoking* is eliminated from workplaces, including hospitality venues.

To protect employees and patrons from the dangers of exposure to secondhand smoke, many state and local governments have passed laws creating smoke-free workplaces, including restaurants and bars.[13] In states without smoke-free workplace laws, employers still face significant legal risks from employees who are exposed to secondhand smoke on the job. Employers can reduce these legal risks by voluntarily prohibiting *smoking* at their worksites.

From *American Journal of Public Health,* August 2007, pp. 1376–1382. Copyright © 2007 by American Public Health Association. Reprinted by permission of American Public Health Association.

Scientific Evidence and Smoke-Free Laws

Research conducted during the past several decades clearly documents that exposure to secondhand smoke causes death and disease in nonsmokers. Some research indicates that secondhand smoke is more toxic and potentially more dangerous than the smoke that is directly inhaled by the smoker.[14-15] Nationally, the US Environmental Protection Agency has found secondhand smoke to be a risk to public health and has classified secondhand smoke as a group A carcinogen, the most dangerous class of carcinogen.[16] A recent report from the US surgeon general on the health consequences of involuntary exposure to tobacco smoke concluded that there is no safe level of exposure to secondhand smoke and neither separating smokers from nonsmokers nor installing ventilation systems effectively eliminates secondhand smoke.[9] In California, the state Air Resources Board declared secondhand smoke as a toxic air contaminant for which there is no known safe level of exposure.[17]

Additional research has focused on how exposure to secondhand smoke affects individual employees. For example, a major area of research has focused on biomarkers of secondhand smoke exposure in fluids such as urine and saliva. Several recent studies have shown that employees' exposure to secondhand smoke in the workplace causes significant increases in the uptake of tobacco-specific carcinogens.[1-6] In a national study of nonsmoking workers, exposure to secondhand smoke varied significantly by occupation.[5,18] Higher levels of exposure were observed in occupational groups that tend to be described as blue collar or service, such as waiters and bartenders, and lower levels in groups that tend to be described as white collar (e.g., office workers).[5]

Other studies have shown immediate improvements in air quality[10,11] and workers' respiratory health[12,19] when *smoking* is eliminated from hospitality venues. One such study monitored air quality in 7 different sites and documented an 80% reduction in indoor air pollution in venues that were required to be smoke free.[20] Policies that prohibit *smoking* in the workplace reduce exposure to secondhand smoke and significantly improve the health of employees.[21] In particular, the national association that sets engineering standards for indoor air quality has found that adverse health effects for the occupants of a smoking room cannot be controlled by ventilation and that the only way to effectively eliminate health risk associated with indoor exposure is to ban *smoking*.[22]

Research that documents the dangers of exposure to secondhand smoke has helped propel state and local action creating smoke-free workplace laws. Since the 1970s, the nonsmokers' rights movement has made significant progress toward clean indoor air. As of April 2006, more than 2000 municipalities nationwide had implemented laws that restrict where *smoking* is allowed. Of these, 461 municipalities have a 100% smoke-free provision in effect at the local level—in workplaces, restaurants, bars, or all 3.[13] On the state level, 11 states have laws in effect that require 100% smoke-free workplaces, including restaurants and bars.[23]

Nonetheless, many workers remain unprotected. For example, in some areas, a state law may preempt stricter local regulation.[24] In addition, some jurisdictions—either on the state or local level—may lack sufficient political will to pass such laws, or efforts to do so may be blocked by tobacco industry lobbying.[25]

Legal Risks

Workers who are not currently protected by state or local laws that create smoke-free workplaces nevertheless have legal options available. For example,

- an employee could file a workers' compensation claim against an employer for illness or injury attributable to exposure to secondhand smoke on the job. Such claims may increase an employer's workers' compensation premiums,
- an employee could file a disability discrimination claim that an employer failed to provide a "reasonable accommodation"—in this instance protection from exposure to secondhand smoke—if the worker has a disability (such as asthma) that is exacerbated by exposure to secondhand smoke, or
- an employee could file a claim that the employer failed to provide a safe workplace, based on a common law duty.

Employers may voluntarily adopt smoke-free workplace policies to reduce the threat of litigation in these areas. These 3 risks are examined in turn.

Workers' Compensation

State workers' compensation laws are designed to protect workers from injuries and illnesses that arise out of and in the course of employment. The state laws are not based on fault; an injured worker can recover benefits, including compensation for temporary or permanent loss of income and medical expenses, without proving that the employer was negligent. A state administrative agency usually oversees the workers' compensation system so that employees may recover benefits promptly. In most cases, the state workers' compensation system prevents the employee from also suing the employer in tort.[26]

Premiums

States generally require employers to provide workers' compensation insurance to their employees by contracting with a private company, with a fund provided by the state, or by self-insuring.[26] An employer's workers' compensation premiums may increase because of claims filed because of workers' exposure to secondhand smoke on the job. Conversely, employers may be able to reduce their workers' compensation premiums by implementing safety policies, including smoke-free workplace policies, to reduce workplace illnesses and injuries.

Workers' compensation premiums for employers are rated according to past worker injury experience (also known as "experience rating").[27] This means that if a firm's injury history is better than average for a firm of its size and class, its premiums will be reduced. If the firm's injury history is worse than the average, its premiums will be increased.[27] Because experience rating gives individual employers some influence over the final premiums they pay, it provides an incentive for employers to prevent occupational injuries and illnesses.[27] Studies have shown that firms with aggressive safety programs often have lower workers' compensation costs than those that do not and that the reduction in these costs more than offsets the cost of safety initiatives.[28-29] Although only 15% of firms in the United States are experience rated, these firms employ approximately 90% of those who work.[30]

By contrast, some firms in the United States are so small that they are not experience rated. For those firms, premiums are determined by class insurance rates, a practice that is sometimes referred to as manual rating.[27] These rates are applicable to a specific industry or occupational group.[27] The premiums for these firms are not subject to change based on a particular company's injury history.

There is little research on the potential impact of secondhand smoke—related injuries on workers' compensation premiums. However, at least 1 insurance underwriter has noted that

> Studies have shown that employees who work in a smoke-filled environment suffer higher absenteeism and lower productivity, while such firms experience increasing health insurance rates and liability claims. Given that reality, you would think insureds would recognize the overall value of changing their policies to assure a safer, lawsuit-proof workplace.[31(p25)]

In addition, workplaces that have instituted *smoking* bans have seen a reduction in *smoking* prevalence, which also could lead to a reduction in premiums.[32]

Litigation Under Workers' Compensation Statutes

Employees have won in individual workers' compensation cases involving secondhand smoke-related injuries when the employee suffered an asthmatic or allergic reaction as a result of exposure to secondhand smoke in the workplace and the employee had demonstrated exposure to a heavy concentration of secondhand smoke for several years.[33] Because the outcomes of workers' compensation cases have varied widely across states, an employee's ability to recover compensation will depend heavily upon the state in which the employer is located.

Asthmatic or Allergic Reactions

Employees have successfully asserted workers' compensation claims in which secondhand smoke caused an asthmatic or allergic reaction on the job. In 1 case, New York's Workers' Compensation Board awarded benefits to an employee who suffered asthma attacks at work as a result of exposure to secondhand smoke in a crowded office.[34] The board ruled that the employee had sustained an occupational injury as a result of the repeated exposure to smoke in the office.[34] There were many smokers in the vicinity of the employee's work station, and she had suffered 2 severe asthma attacks at work that required that she be taken to the emergency room.[34]

Similarly, a New Mexico court ruled that an employee's allergic reaction and collapse stemming from exposure to secondhand smoke at work constituted an accidental injury.[35] The employee claimed that constant exposure to cigarette smoke in the work environment triggered the allergies that, in turn, caused him to collapse.[35] The court stated that "the happenings may be gradual and may involve several different accidents which culminate in an accidental injury."[35(p284)]

Prolonged Exposure to Secondhand Smoke

In some instances, plaintiffs exposed to heavy concentrations of secondhand smoke in the workplace for extensive periods of time have been able to assert workers' compensation claims.[36] In a New Jersey case, the plaintiff shared an office with a chain-*smoking* coworker for 26 years and contracted tonsil cancer.[37] The plaintiff's secondhand smoke exposure at work was regular and long-standing, and he attempted to avoid smoke from every other source but his coworker.[37] A workers' compensation judge concluded that the plaintiffs tonsil cancer was a compensable occupational disease and ordered the employer to pay past and future medical expenses and temporary disability benefits.[37]

Although the New Jersey case is significant because the court recognized that secondhand smoke in the workplace can cause cancer, a review of workers' compensation cases shows that employees will be least likely to recover compensation in cases in which they suffer illnesses with long latency periods, such as cancer or lung disease. This is because of the possibility that the diseases could have been caused by a combination of secondhand smoke exposure on the job and factors outside of the workplace.[33,38–43]

As scientific evidence that supports the dangers of secondhand smoke exposure continues to mount, employees may be more likely to recover workers' compensation as courts are faced with increasing documentation of the actual harm to workers caused directly by exposure to secondhand smoke.

State and Federal Disability Laws

If an employee is considered "disabled" under state or federal disability laws and exposure to secondhand smoke exacerbates that disability, the employer may be required to make a "reasonable accommodation" to protect the employee from exposure to secondhand smoke.

In general, courts have held that an employee can be considered disabled under the Americans With Disabilities Act (ADA) or the federal Rehabilitation Act of 1973 (Rehab Act) if secondhand smoke substantially impairs the employee's ability to breathe and the impairment occurred both in and out of the workplace.[44–46] In determining whether an employer reasonably accommodated an employee's secondhand smoke-related disability, employees have prevailed where the employer made little or no effort to address the employee's request for a smoke-free workplace.

Disability

Determining whether an individual's condition legally qualifies as a disability is decided on a case-by-case basis.[47,48] In most instances, individuals bringing secondhand smoke-related lawsuits will claim that they are disabled under the ADA and the Rehab Act because they have a "physical or mental impairment that substantially limits" a "major life activity."[49]

Employees appear to have been most successful in ADA cases when they argued that secondhand smoke both on and off the job substantially limited their ability to breathe. Courts especially take note of whether the employee ever sought medical care, left work because of the condition, or continued to participate in activities of daily living.

For example, in *Service v. Union Pacific Railroad Company*, an employee had suffered several asthma attacks that required medical treatment while working in locomotive cabs in which coworkers had recently smoked.[44] The court rejected the employer's assertion that the employee's condition was temporary, noting that an employee "need not be in a constant state of distress or suffer an asthmatic attack to quality as disabled under the ADA."[44(p1192)] The court "easily" found that genuine issues of material fact existed as to whether the employee's asthma substantially limited his major life activity of breathing.[44(p1192)]

However, in some cases, courts have found that employees were not able to qualify as disabled under federal disability laws. For example, in some cases, the court found that the employee's impairment was not "substantial" if the employee's ability to breathe was not impaired both on and off the job.[50–51] Or, in some cases, courts have found that the employee did not qualify as substantially limited in the "major life activity" of working if the exposure to smoke impaired the employee's ability to work only in that particular job but not in a broad class of jobs.[50,52,53] Each case is evaluated by the court on the basis of the specific facts of the situation.

Also, courts must consider any factors that may mitigate the plaintiffs impairment, such as an inhaler or other medication.[54] However, the presence of mitigating measures does not mean that an individual is not covered by the ADA or Rehab Act. An individual still may be substantially limited in a major life activity, notwithstanding the use of a mitigating measure like medicine, which may only lessen the symptoms of an impairment.[54] For example, in *Service v. Union Pacific Railroad Company*, the court noted that the employee could not prevent his asthma attacks by using inhalers, and even when he used medicine, his asthma could not always be controlled.[44]

Reasonable Accommodations

In addition to disputing whether the employee can be classified as disabled, the second major area that is litigated in secondhand smoke cases brought under the ADA and Rehab Act is whether the employer's accommodations of the employee's impairment were reasonable. A reasonable accommodation includes "modifications or adjustments to the work environment . . . that would enable a qualified individual with a disability to perform the essential functions of that position."[55] An employer need not accommodate an employee if doing so would impose an "undue hardship,"[56] which is defined as "an action requiring significant difficulty or expense."[57]

Employees with secondhand smoke-related disabilities have prevailed on the issue of reasonable accommodation in cases in which the employer made little effort to address the employee's request for a smoke-free workplace. In *Service v. Union Pacific Railroad Company*, the court found that although the employer barred employees from *smoking* in the plaintiff's presence, it did nothing to accommodate the plaintiff's sensitivity to residual smoke.[44] The employer claimed that providing the employee with a smoke-free work environment would have constituted an undue hardship but offered no evidence of this.[44] In fact, studies have shown that smoke-free workplace policies and laws are inexpensive to implement and do not harm businesses that have implemented them.[58–60]

In cases in which the employer fails to make the reasonable accommodation requested under the ADA, a disabled employee may seek monetary damages, injunctive relief (a court order to prevent future harm), and attorneys' fees, with some exceptions.[61]

State Disability Rights Laws

A number of states have disability rights laws that provide broader protections than those found in the ADA and the Rehab Act. In New York, for example, state law does not require that an employee identify a major life activity substantially limited by his or her impairment to be categorized as disabled.[62] An individual may have a disability under New York law if the impairment is demonstrable by medically accepted techniques.[62] New Jersey law contains a similar provision.[63]

California's Fair Employment and Housing Act (FEHA) also provides broader protections than those provided under federal law.[64] For example, FEHA requires an impairment that limits a major life activity[64] rather than the ADA and Rehab Act requirement that an impairment substantially limits a major life activity.[49]

Sensitivity to secondhand smoke can constitute a disability under FEHA, and employers have been required to provide reasonable accommodations for employees with this disability.[65] In *County of Fresno v. Fair Employment and Housing Commission*, the employees demonstrated that because of respiratory disorders, exposure to tobacco smoke substantially limited their ability to breathe.[65] The court held that the employees were "physically handicapped within the meaning of [FEHA]."[65(p563)] The court then held that the employer's efforts to accommodate the employees were not reasonable.[65] The employer had placed smokers and nonsmokers at separate ends of the room, had asked smokers to be "considerate" of nonsmokers, and eventually moved the plaintiffs into an office adjacent to an office where employees smoked.[65] The court held that the county failed to make a reasonable accommodation because there was not a smoke-free environment in which the employees could work.[65]

As these cases illustrate, disability lawsuits can be an effective way for an individual who meets the legal definition of disabled to get relief from second-hand smoke exposure in the workplace. However, because the number of people who qualify for these federal protections is limited, disability lawsuits are not an ideal vehicle for advocates seeking workplace-*smoking* restrictions that protect a broad group of employees. Nonetheless, an accumulation of individual lawsuits could build a case for employers to voluntarily adopt smoke-free workplace policies in order to avoid future liability.

The Duty to Provide a Safe Workplace

In most jurisdictions, employers have a legal duty to provide employees a reasonably safe work environments.[66] This duty arises either from state law or from the common law, which refers to laws derived from court decisions rather than from laws or constitutions. Several courts have examined whether the employer's common law duty to provide a safe workplace includes a duty to provide a working environment reasonably free from tobacco smoke.[67] Some courts have held that such a duty existed in instances in which plaintiff—employees complained to their employers regarding illnesses caused by workplace secondhand smoke and the employers had the ability to remedy the situation.[42]

Court decisions that find that employers breached their duty to provide a safe workplace share common elements (e.g., the employer knew that second-hand smoke was harmful to the plaintiff-employee; the employer had authority, ability, and reasonable means to control secondhand smoke; and the employer failed to take reasonable measures to control secondhand smoke.)

In *Shimp v Bell Telephone Co.*,[68] an employee who worked in an open area where other employees were permitted to smoke sought an injunction to require her employer to prohibit *smoking* in the area. The employee was severely allergic to tobacco smoke and was forced to leave work on several occasions after becoming physically ill because of exposure to secondhand smoke.[68] The court took judicial notice of the extensive evidence submitted by the employee of the health hazards that secondhand smoke poses to nonsmokers as a whole.[68] Relying on the employer's common law duty to provide a safe work environment, the court granted the injunction and ordered the employer to restrict the *smoking* of other employees to nonwork areas.[68] The court found that the injunction would not pose a hardship for the employer, because the company already had a rule barring employees from *smoking* around telephone equipment.[68]

Before arguing that an employer has breached the duty to provide a reasonably safe work environment, advocates should determine whether (1) the potential plaintiff informed the employer about the detrimental effects that secondhand smoke had on the employee's health, (2) the employer had the ability to implement reasonable restrictions on *smoking* in the workplace, and (3) the secondhand smoke in the employer's workplace was potentially harmful not only to the plaintiff but also to nonsmoking employees in general. Some courts have found no duty to provide a smoke-free workplace in cases in which individual employees failed to provide evidence of secondhand smoke's effects upon nonsmokers in general.[69]

However, since the 1976 decision in *Shimp v. Bell Telephone Co.*, decades of additional research on the effects of exposure to secondhand smoke has convincingly demonstrated the risk such exposure has for workers. In other cases decided more recently than *Shimp v. Bell Telephone Co.*, courts have agreed that employers can be found to have breached the duty to provide a safe workplace if they failed to maintain a smoke-free work environment.[43,70,71] The accumulation of evidence that documents the dangers of exposure to secondhand smoke should support plaintiffs in proving the potential harm of secondhand smoke exposure to all employees.

Advocates should note that, in most cases, the state workers' compensation system is the exclusive remedy for obtaining individual financial awards for job-related injuries and illnesses. In these states, employees should use the workers' compensation system to recover monetary damages for their injuries. However, if an employee is not seeking monetary damages but instead is seeking an injunction (e.g., a court order requiring a smoke-free workplace), the employee may pursue a claim on the basis of the common law duly to provide a safe workplace.[68,72] In addition, some state courts have ruled that workers' compensation laws do not provide coverage for injuries resulting from secondhand smoke in the workplace.[43] In those states, an employee may be able to pursue a claim based on the common law duty to provide a safe workplace and seek both monetary damages for the employee's injury and an injunction to prevent future harm.

Conclusion

Employers have been held liable for exposure of their employees to secondhand smoke on the job in numerous cases, including those based on workers' compensation, state and federal disability law, and the duty to provide a safe workplace. In addition, mounting scientific evidence that documents the dangers of exposure to secondhand smoke may increasingly persuade courts to assign liability to businesses that continue to allow workplace exposure to second-hand smoke. Given this liability risk, employers and insurance carriers should voluntarily adopt smoke-free workplace policies and support state or local legislation requiring smoke-free workplaces. Such policies not only will help fulfill an employer's legal obligation to provide a safe workplace and protect employees from harm but also make good business sense by potentially reducing workers' compensation premiums and reducing the risk of litigation.

References

1. Abrams SM, Mahoney MC, Hyland A, Cummings KM, Davis W, Song L. Early evidence on the effectiveness of clean indoor air legislation in New York State. Am] Public Health. 2006;96:296–298.

2. Hedley AJ, McGhee SM, Repace JL, et al. Risks for heart disease and lung cancer from *passive smoking* by workers in the catering industry. Toxicol Sci. 2006;90:539–548.

3. Tulunay OE, Hecht SS, Carmella SG, et al. Urinary metabolites of a tobacco-specific lung carcinogen in nonsmoking hospitality workers. Cancer Epidemiol Biomarkers Prev. 2005;14:1283–1286.

4. Bates MN, Fawcett J, Dickson S, Berezowski R, Garrett N. Exposure of hospitality workers to environmental tobacco smoke. Tob Control. 2002;11:125–129.

5. Wortley PM, Caraballo RS, Pederson LL, Pechacek TF. Exposure to second-hand smoke in the workplace: serum cotinitie by occupation. J Occup Environ Med 2002;44:503–509.

6. Maskarinep MP, Jenkins RA, Counts RW, Dindal AB. Determination of exposure to environmental tobacco smoke in restaurant and tavern workers in one US city. J Expo Anal Environ Epidemiol. 2000; 10(1):36–49.

7. Hoffmann, D, Hoffmann, I. Cigars: health effects and trends. In: *Smoking* and Tobacco Control Monograph No. 9. Bethesda, Md: National Institutes of Health, National Cancer Institute; 1998. NIH Pub. No. 98–4302.

8. Centers for Disease Control and Prevention. Secondhand smoke fact sheet (2006). Available at . . . Accessed September 14, 2006.

9. US Department of Health and Human Services. The Health Consequences of Involuntary Exposure to Tobacco Smoke: A Report of the Surgeon General. Atlanta, GA: US Department of Health and Human Services, Centers for Disease Control and Prevention: 2006. Available at: . . . Accessed September 14, 2006.

10. Travers MJ, Cummings KM, Hyland A, et al. Indoor air quality in hospitality venues before and after implementation of a clean indoor air law— western New York, 2003. MMWR Morb Mortal Wkly Rep. 2004;53:1038–1041.

11. Replace J. An air quality survey of respirable particles and particulate carcinogens in Boston pubs before and after a *smoking* ban. Available at: . . . . Accessed September 14, 2006.

12. Eisner MD, Smith AK, Blanc PD. Bartenders' respiratory health after establishment of smoke-free bars and taverns. JAMA. 1998;280:1909–1914.

13. American Nonsmokers' Rights Foundation. Overview list—how many smokefree laws? Available at: . . . . Accessed April 20, 2006.

14. Schick S, Glantz S. Philip Morris toxicological experiments with fresh sidestream smoke: more toxic than mainstream smoke. Tob Control. 2005;14:396–404.

15. Barnoya J, Glantx S. Cardiovascular effects of secondhand smoke: nearly as large as *smoking*. Circulation 2005:111:2684–2698.

16. Centers for Disease Control and Prevention. Clean indoor air regulations fact sheet. Available at: . . . . Accessed September 14, 2006.

17. California Environmental Protection Agency. California identifies second-hand smoke as a "toxic air contaminant." Available at: . . . . Accessed September 14, 2006.

18. Shopland DR, Anderson CM, Bums DM, Gerlach KK. Disparities in smoke-free workplace policies among food service workers. J Occup Environ Med 2004;46:347–356.

19. Eagan TML, Hetland J, Aaro LE. Decline in respiratory symptoms in service workers five months after a public *smoking* ban. Tob Control. 2006; 15:242–246.

20. Hyland A, Travers M, Repace J. 7 city air monitoring study (7CAM), March-April 2004. Available at: . . . . Accessed September 14, 2006.

21. Connolly CN, Carpenter CM, Travers M, et al. How smoke-free laws improve air quality: a global study of Irish pubs. Available at . . . . Accessed September 14, 2006.

22. American Society of Heating, Refrigerating and Air-Conditioning Engineers (ASHRAE). ASHRAE ETS positon document: engineers should follow local codes in regard to *smoking*. Available at: . . . . Accessed September 14, 2006.

23. Cherner J. Hawaii likely to become next smokefree workplace state. Available at: . . . . Accessed May 3, 2006.

24. American Medical Association. Preemption: Taking the local out of tobacco control, 2003. Available at: . . . . Accessed April 26, 2006.

25. Landman A, Bialick P. Tobacco industry involvement in Colorado. Available at: . . . . Accessed April 20, 2006.

26. Jacobs AJ, Surette EC, Lerning T, Shampo JJ, Martin L. American Jurisprudence. 2nd ed. Rochester NY: Lawyers Corp; 2006.

27. National Council on Compensation Insurance. ABCs of experience rating 2004. Available at: . . . . Accessed April 20, 2006.

28. Spieler EA. Perpetuating risk? Workers' compensation and the persistence of occupational injuries. Houston Law Rev. 1994;31:119–264.

29. Fefer MD. Taking control of your workers' comp costs. Fortune. Oct. 3, 1994; 131.

30. Worrall JD, Butler RJ. Experience rating matters. In: Appel D, Borba PS, eds. Workers' Compensation Insurance Pricing Bston, Mass: Kluwer Academic Publishers; 1988:81–94.

31. Reardon B. Second-hand smoke: the next black lung? National Underwriter Property and Casualty-Risk & Benefits Management. June 30, 2003:25.

32. Farrelly MC, Evans WN, Sfekas AE. The impact of workplace *smoking* baas: results from a national survey. Tob Control. 1999;8:272–277.

33. Fox JC. An assessment of the current legal climate concerning *smoking* in the workplace. St Louis U Pub Law Rev 1994;13:591–634.

34. Johannesen v Department of Housing Preservation and Development, 638 NE2d 981, 982–983 (NY 1994).

35. Schober v Mountain Dell Telephone, 600 P2d 283,284 (NM 1978).

36. Associated Press. Husband Wins Claim in Secondhand Smoke Death. *New York Times*. December 17, 1995;A28.

37. Magaw v Board of Education, 731 A2d 1196, 1199–1204 (NJ Superior Ct App Div 1999).

38. Palmer v Del Webb's High Sierra. 838 P2d 435 (Nev 1992).

39. ATE Fixture Fab v Wagner, 559 So 2d 635 (Fla Dist Ct App 1990).

40. Kellogg v Mayfield, 595 NE2d 465 (Ohio Ct App 1991).

41. Appellant v Respondent, No. 93744 Hex Workers' Comp Comm Oct. 1, 1993).

42. Vallone M. Employer liability for workplace environmental tobacco smoke: get out of the fog. Valparaiso U Law Rev. 1996;30:811–858.

43. McCarthy v Department of Social and Health Services, 759 P2d 351 (Wash Ct App 1986).

44. Service v Union Pacific RR Co. 153 F Supp 2d 1187,1188 (ED Cal 2001).

45. Bond v Sheahan, 152 F Supp 2d 1055, 1065 (ED III 2001).

46. Hendler v Intelecom USA, Inc, 963 F Supp 200, 207 (ED NY 1997).

47. Bragdon v Abbott, 524 US 624, 631 (1998).

48. 29 CFR §1630.2(j) (2000).

49. 42 USC §12102(2).

50. Muller v Costello, 187 F3d 298, 303 (2d Cir 1999).

51. Chan v Sprint Corp., 351 F Supp 2d 1197, 1207 (D Kan 2005).

52. Keck v Office of Alcoholism and Substance Abuse Services, 10 F Supp 2d 194, 199 (ND NY 1998).

53. Gupton v Commonwealth of Virginia, 14 F3d 203 (4th Cir 1994).

54. Sutton v. United Airlines, Inc., 527 US 471, 488 (1999).

55. 29 CFR §1630.2 (o) (ii) (2000).

56. 42 USC §12112 (b)(5)(A) (2000).

57. 42 USC §12111 (10)(A) (2000).

58. Scollo M, Lal A, Hyland A, Glantz S. Review of the quality of studies on the economic effects of smoke-free policies on the hospitality industry. Tob Control. 2003;12:13–20.

59. Glantz SA. Smoke-free restaurant ordinances do not affect restaurant business. J Public Health Manag Pract 1999;5(1):vi–ix.

60. Alamar BC, Glantz SA. Smokefree ordinances increase restaurant profit and values. Contemp Econ Policy 2004;22:520–525.

61. Topliff ML. Remedies available under Americans with Disabilities Act (42 U.S.C.A. §§ 12101 et seq.). Am Law Rep. 1997;136:63.

62. NY Exec law § 296 (McKinney 2005).

63. NJ Slat Ann §10:5-5 (West 2004).

64. Cal Government Code §12926.1 (West 2000).

65. County of Fresno v Fair Employment and Housing Commission, 277 Cal Rptr 557, 563-66 (1991).

66. American Law Institute. Restatement of the Lam, Second, Agency. Philadelphia, Penn: American Law Institute Publishers; 1958;§492.

67. Fischer TG. Employer's liability to employee for failure to provide work environment free from tobacco smoke. Am Law Rep. 2003;63:1021.

68. Skimp v Bell Telephone Co. 368 A2d 408, 410-16 (NJ Superior Ct Chancery Div 1976).

69. Gordon v Ravern Systems and Research. Inc. 462 A2d 10. 15 (DC 1983).

70. Wilhelm v CSX Transp, Inc. 65 F Appx 973, 978 (6th Cir 2003).

71. Smith v W Elec Co, 643 SW2d 10, 13 (Mo App 1982).

72. Rothstein MA. Occupational Safety and Health Law. 4th ed. St. Paul, Minn: West Group; 1998:§483.

Robert A. Levy and
Rosalind B. Marimont

 **NO**

Lies, Damned Lies, and 400,000 Smoking-Related Deaths

T ruth was an early victim in the battle against tobacco. The big lie, repeated ad nauseam in anti-tobacco circles, is that smoking causes more than 400,000 premature deaths each year in the United States. That mantra is the principal justification for all manner of tobacco regulations and legislation, not to mention lawsuits by dozens of states for Medicaid recovery, class actions by seventy-five to eighty union health funds, similar litigation by thirty-five Blue Cross plans, twenty-four class suits by smokers who are not yet ill, sixty class actions by allegedly ill smokers, five hundred suits for damages from secondhand smoke, and health-related litigation by twelve cities and counties—an explosion of adjudication never before experienced in this country or elsewhere.

The war on smoking started with a kernel of truth—that cigarettes are a high risk factor for lung cancer—but has grown into a monster of deceit and greed, eroding the credibility of government and subverting the rule of law. Junk science has replaced honest science and propaganda parades as fact. Our legislators and judges, in need of dispassionate analysis, are instead smothered by an avalanche of statistics—tendentious, inadequately documented, and unchecked by even rudimentary notions of objectivity. Meanwhile, Americans are indoctrinated by health "professionals" bent on imposing their lifestyle choices on the rest of us and brainwashed by politicians eager to tap the deep pockets of a pariah industry.

The aim of this paper is to dissect the granddaddy of all tobacco lies—that smoking causes 400,000 deaths each year. To set the stage, let's look at two of the many exaggerations, misstatements, and outright fabrications that have dominated the tobacco debate from the outset.

Third-Rate Thinking About Secondhand Smoke

"Passive Smoking Does Cause Lung Cancer, Do Not Let Them Fool You," states the headline of a March 1998 press release from the World Health Organization. The release begins by noting that WHO had been accused of suppressing its own study because it "failed to scientifically prove that there is an association between passive smoking . . . and a number of diseases, lung cancer in particular." Not true, insisted WHO. Smokers themselves are not the only ones who suffer health problems because of their habit; secondhand smoke can be fatal as well.

The press release went on to report that WHO researchers found "an estimated 16 percent increased risk of lung cancer among nonsmoking spouses of smokers. For workplace exposure the estimated increase in risk was 17 percent." Remarkably, the very next line warned: "Due to small sample size, neither increased risk was statistically significant." Contrast that conclusion with the hype in the headline: "Passive Smoking Does Cause Lung Cancer." Spoken often enough, the lie becomes its own evidence.

The full study would not see the light of day for seven more months, until October 1998, when it was finally published in the *Journal of the National Cancer Institute*. News reports omitted any mention of statistical insignificance. Instead, they again trumpeted relative risks of 1.16 and 1.17, corresponding to 16 and 17 percent increases, as if those ratios were meaningful. Somehow lost in WHO's media blitz was the National Cancer Institute's own guideline: "Relative risks of less than 2 [that is, a 100 percent increase] are considered small. . . . Such increases may be due to chance, statistical bias, or effects of confounding factors that are sometimes not evident." To put the WHO results in their proper perspective, note that the relative risk of lung cancer for persons who drink whole milk is 2.4. That is, the increased risk of contracting lung cancer from whole milk is 140 percent—more than eight times the 17 percent increase from secondhand smoke.

What should have mattered most to government officials, the health community and concerned parents is the following pronouncement from the WHO study: After examining 650 lung cancer patients and 1,500 healthy adults in seven European countries, WHO concluded that the "results indicate no association between childhood exposure to environmental tobacco smoke and lung cancer risk."

EPA's Junk Science

Another example of anti-tobacco misinformation is the landmark 1993 report in which the Environmental Protection Agency declared that environmental tobacco smoke (ETS) is a dangerous carcinogen that kills three thousand Americans yearly. Five years later, in July 1998, federal judge William L. Osteen lambasted the EPA for "cherry picking" the data, excluding studies that "demonstrated no association between ETS and cancer," and withholding "significant portions of its findings and reasoning in striving to confirm its *a priori* hypothesis." Both "the record and EPA's explanation," concluded the court, "make it clear that using standard methodology, EPA could not produce statistically significant results." A more damning assessment is difficult to imagine, but here are the court's conclusions at greater length, in its own words.

EPA publicly committed to a conclusion before research had begun; excluded industry [input thereby] violating the [Radon Research] Act's procedural requirements; adjusted established procedure and scientific norms to validate the Agency's public conclusion, and aggressively utilized the Act's authority to disseminate findings to establish a de facto regulatory scheme intended to restrict Plaintiff's products and to influence public opinion. In conducting the ETS Risk Assessment, EPA disregarded information and made findings on selective information; did not disseminate significant epidemiologic information; deviated from its Risk Assessment Guidelines; failed to disclose important findings and reasoning; and left significant questions without answers. EPA's conduct left substantial holes in the administrative record. While so doing, EPA produced limited evidence, then claimed the weight of the Agency's research evidence demonstrated ETS causes cancer.

—*Flue-Cured Tobacco Coop. Stabilization Corp. v. United States Environmental Protection Agency,* 4 F. Supp. 2d 435, 465–66 (M.D.N.C. 1998)

Hundreds of states, cities, and counties have banned indoor smoking—many in reaction to the EPA report. California even prohibits smoking in bars. According to Matthew L. Myers, general counsel of the Campaign for Tobacco-Free Kids, "the release of the original risk assessment gave an enormous boost to efforts to restrict smoking." Now that the study has been thoroughly debunked, one would think that many of the bans would be lifted. Don't hold your breath. When science is adulterated and debased for political ends, the culprits are unlikely to reverse course merely because they have been unmasked.

In reaction to the federal court's criticism EPA administrator Carol M. Browner said, "It's so widely accepted that secondhand smoke causes very real problems for kids and adults. Protecting people from the health hazards of secondhand smoke should be a national imperative." Like *Alice in Wonderland,* sentence first, evidence afterward. Browner reiterates: "We believe the health threats . . . from breathing secondhand smoke are very real." Never mind science; it is Browner's beliefs that control. The research can be suitably tailored.

For the EPA to alter results, disregard evidence, and adjust its procedures and standards to satisfy agency prejudices is unacceptable behavior, even to a first-year science student. Those criticisms are about honesty, carefulness, and rigor—the very essence of science.

Classifying Diseases as Smoking-Related

With that record of distortion, it should come as no surprise that anti-tobacco crusaders misrepresent the number of deaths due to smoking. Start by considering the diseases that are incorrectly classified as smoking-related. The Centers for Disease Control and Prevention (CDC) prepares and distributes information on smoking-attributable mortality, morbidity and economic costs (SAMMEC). In its *Morbidity and Mortality Weekly Report* for 27 August 1993, the

CDC states that 418,690 Americans died in 1990 of various diseases that they contracted because, according to the government, they smoked.

Diseases are categorized as smoking-related if the risk of death for smokers exceeds that for nonsmokers. In the jargon of epidemiology, a relative risk that is greater than 1 indicates a connection between exposure (smoking) and effect (death). Recall, however, the National Cancer Institute's guideline: "Relative risks of less than two are considered small. . . . Such increases may be due to chance, statistical bias, or effects of confounding factors that are sometimes not evident." And the *Federal Reference Manual on Scientific Evidence* confirms that the threshold test for legal significance is a relative risk of two or higher. At any ratio below two, the results are insufficiently reliable to conclude that a particular agent (e.g., tobacco) caused a particular disease.

What would happen if the SAMMEC data were to exclude deaths from those diseases that had a relative risk of less than two for current or former smokers? Table 1 shows that 163,071 deaths reported by CDC were from diseases that should not have been included in the report. Add to that another 1,362 deaths from burn injuries—unless one believes that Philip Morris is responsible when a smoker falls asleep with a lit cigarette. That is a total of 164,433 misreported deaths out of 418,690. When the report is properly limited to diseases that have a significant relationship with smoking, the death total declines to 254,257. Thus, on this count alone, SAMMEC overstates the number of deaths by 65 percent.

Calculating Excess Deaths

But there is more. Writing on "Risk Attribution and Tobacco-Related Deaths" in the 1993 *American Journal of Epidemiology,* T. D. Sterling, W. L. Rosenbaum, and J. J. Weinkam expose another overstatement—exceeding 65 percent—that flows from using the American Cancer Society's Cancer Prevention Survey (CPS) as a baseline against which excess deaths are computed. Here is how one government agency, the Office of Technology Assessment (OTA), calculates the number of deaths caused by smoking:

The OTA first determines the death rate for persons who were part of the CPS sample and never smoked. Next, that rate is applied to the total U.S. population in order to estimate the number of Americans who would have died if no one ever smoked. Finally, the hypothetical number of deaths for assumed never-smokers is subtracted from the actual number of U.S. deaths, and the difference is ascribed to smoking. That approach seems reasonable if one important condition is satisfied: The CPS sample must be roughly the same as the overall U.S. population with respect to those factors, other than smoking, that could be associated with the death rate. But as Sterling, Rosenbaum, and Weinkam point out, nothing could be further from the truth.

The American Cancer Society bases its CPS study on a million men and women volunteers, drawn from the ranks of the Society's members, friends, and acquaintances. The persons who participate are more affluent than average, overwhelmingly white, married, college graduates, who generally do not have hazardous jobs. Each of those characteristics tends to reduce the death

Table 1

Disease Category	Relative Risk	Deaths From Smoking
Cancer of pancreas	1.1–1.8	2,931*
Cancer of cervix	1.9	647*
Cancer of bladder	1.9	2,348*
Cancer of kidney, other urinary	1.2–1.4	353
Hypertension	1.2–1.9	5,450
Ischemic heart disease (age 35–64)	1.4–1.8	15,535*
Ischemic heart disease (age 65+)	1.3–1.6	64,789
Other heart disease	1.2–1.9	35,314
Cerebrovascular disease (age 35–64)	1.4	2,681*
Cerebrovascular disease (age 65+)	1.0–1.9	14,610
Atherosclerosis	1.3	1,267*
Aortic aneurysm	1.3	448*
Other arterial disease	1.3	372*
Pneumonia and influenza	1.4–1.6	10,552*
Other respiratory diseases	1.4–1.6	1,063*
Pediatric diseases	1.5–1.8	1,711
Sub-total		160,071
Environmental tobacco smoke	1.2	3,000
Total		163,071

* Number of deaths for this category assumes population deaths distributed between current and former smokers in same proportion as in Cancer Prevention Survey CPS-II, provided by the American Cancer Society.

rate of the CPS sample which, as a result, enjoys an average life expectancy that is substantially longer than the typical American enjoys.

Because OTA starts with an atypically low death rate for never-smokers in the CPS sample, then applies that rate to the whole population, its baseline for determining excess deaths is grossly underestimated. By comparing actual deaths with a baseline that is far too low, OTA creates the illusion that a large number of deaths are due to smoking.

That same illusion pervades the statistics released by the U.S. Surgeon General, who in his 1989 report estimated that 335,600 deaths were caused by smoking. When Sterling, Rosenbaum, and Weinkam recalculated the Surgeon General's numbers, replacing the distorted CPS sample with a more representative baseline from large surveys conducted by the National Center for Health Statistics, they found that the number of smoking-related deaths declined to 203,200. Thus, the Surgeon General's report overstated the number of deaths by more than 65 percent simply by choosing the wrong standard of comparison.

Sterling and his coauthors report that not only is the death rate considerably lower for the CPS sample than for the entire U.S. but, astonishingly, even smokers in the CPS sample have a lower death rate than the national average for both smokers and nonsmokers. As a result, if OTA were to have used the CPS death rate for smokers, applied that rate to the total population, then subtracted the actual number of deaths for all Americans, it would have found that smoking saves 277,621 lives each year. The authors caution, of course, that their calculation is sheer nonsense, not a medical miracle. Those "lives would be saved only if the U.S. population would die with the death rate of smokers in the affluent CPS sample."

Unhappily, the death rate for Americans is considerably higher than that for the CPS sample. Nearly as disturbing, researchers like Sterling, Rosenbaum, and Weinkam identified that statistical predicament many years ago; yet the government persists in publishing data on smoking-related deaths that are known to be greatly inflated.

Controlling for Confounding Variables

Even if actual deaths were compared against an appropriate baseline for non-smokers, the excess deaths could not properly be attributed to smoking alone. It cannot be assumed that the only difference between smokers and nonsmokers is that the former smoke. The two groups are dissimilar in many other respects, some of which affect their propensity to contract diseases that have been identified as smoking-related. For instance, smokers have higher rates of alcoholism, exercise less on average, eat fewer green vegetables, are more likely to be exposed to workplace carcinogens, and are poorer than nonsmokers. Each of those factors can be a "cause" of death from a so-called smoking-related disease; and each must be statistically controlled for if the impact of a single factor, like smoking, is to be reliably determined.

Sterling, Rosenbaum, and Weinkam found that adjusting their calculations for just two lifestyle differences—in income and alcohol consumption—between smokers and nonsmokers had the effect of reducing the Surgeon General's smoking-related death count still further, from 203,200 to 150,000. That means the combined effect of using a proper standard of comparison coupled with controls for income and alcohol was to lower the Surgeon General's estimate 55 percent—from 335,600 to 150,000. Thus, the original estimate was a disquieting 124 percent too high, even without adjustments for important variables like occupation, exercise, and nutritional habits.

What if smokers got plenty of exercise and had healthy diets while non-smokers were couch potatoes who consumed buckets of fast food? Naturally, there are some smokers and nonsmokers who satisfy those criteria. Dr. William E. Wecker, a consulting statistician who has testified for the tobacco industry, scanned the CPS database and found thousands of smokers with relatively low risk factors and thousands of never-smokers with high risk factors. Comparing the mortality rates of the two groups, Dr. Wecker discovered that the smokers were "healthier and die less often by a factor of three than the never-smokers." Obviously, other risk factors matter, and any study that ignores them is utterly worthless.

Yet, if a smoker who is obese; has a family history of high cholesterol, diabetes, and heart problems; and never exercises dies of a heart attack, the government attributes his death to smoking alone. That procedure, if applied to the other causal factors identified in the CPS study, would produce more than twice as many "attributed" deaths as there are actual deaths, according to Dr. Wecker. For example, the same calculations that yield 400,000 smoking-related deaths suggest that 504,000 people die each year because they engage in little or no exercise. Employing an identical formula, bad nutritional habits can be shown to account for 649,000 excess deaths annually. That is nearly 1.6 million deaths from only three causes—without considering alcoholism, accidents, poverty, etc.—out of 2.3 million deaths in 1995 from all causes combined. And on it goes—computer-generated phantom deaths, not real deaths—constrained neither by accepted statistical methods, by common sense, nor by the number of people who die each year.

Adjusting for Age at Death

Next and last, we turn to a different sort of deceit—one pertaining not to the number of smoking-related deaths but rather to the misperception that those deaths are somehow associated with kids and young adults. For purposes of this discussion, we will work with the far-fetched statistics published by CDC—an annual average from 1990 through 1994 of 427,743 deaths attributable to tobacco. Is the problem as serious as it sounds?

At first blush, it would seem that more than 400,000 annual deaths is an extremely serious problem. But suppose that all of the people died at age ninety-nine. Surely then, the seriousness of the problem would be tempered by the fact that the decedents would have died soon from some other cause in any event. That is not far from the truth: while tobacco does not kill people at an average age of ninety-nine, it does kill people at an average age of roughly seventy-two—far closer to ninety-nine than to childhood or even young adulthood. Indeed, according to a 1991 RAND study, smoking "reduces the life expectancy of a twenty-year-old by about 4.3 years"—not a trivial concern to be sure, but not the horror that is sometimes portrayed.

Consider Table 2, which shows the number of deaths and age at death for various causes of death: The three nonsmoking categories total nearly 97,000 deaths—probably not much different than the correctly calculated number of smoking-related deaths—but the average age at death is only thirty-nine. As contrasted with a seventy-two-year life expectancy for smokers, each of those nonsmoking deaths snuffs out thirty-three years of life—our most productive years, from both an economic and child-rearing perspective.

Table 2

Cause of Death	Number of Deaths per Year	Mean Age at Death
Smoking-attributed	427,743	72
Motor vehicle accidents	40,982	39
Suicide	30,484	45
Homicide	25,488	32

Source: Centers for Disease Control and Prevention

Table 3

Cause	Deaths	YPLL
Alcohol-related	99,247	1,795,458
Gaps in primary care*	132,593	1,771,133
Injuries (excluding alcohol-related)	64,169	1,755,720
Tobacco-related	338,022	1,497,161

* Inadequate access, screening and preventive interventions.

Perhaps that is why the Carter Center's "Closing the Gap" project at Emory University examined "years of potential life lost" (YPLL) for selected diseases, to identify those causes of death that were of greatest severity and consequence. The results were reported by R.W. Amler and D.L. Eddins, "Cross-Sectional Analysis: Precursors of Premature Death in the United States," in the 1987 *American Journal of Preventive Medicine*. First, the authors determined for each disease the annual number of deaths by age group. Second, they multiplied for each age group the number of deaths times the average number of years remaining before customary retirement at age sixty-five. Then they computed YPLL by summing the products for each disease across age groups.

Thus, if smoking were deemed to have killed, say, fifty thousand people from age sixty through sixty-four, a total of 150,000 years of life were lost in that age group—i.e., fifty thousand lives times an average of three years remaining to age sixty-five. YPLL for smoking would be the accumulation of lost years for all age groups up to sixty-five.

Amler and Eddins identified nine major precursors of preventable deaths. Measured by YPLL, tobacco was about halfway down the list—ranked four out of nine in terms of years lost—not "the number one killer in America" as alarmists have exclaimed. Table 3 shows the four most destructive causes of death, based on 1980 YPLL statistics. Bear in mind that the starting point for the YPLL calculation is the number of deaths, which for tobacco is grossly magnified for all of the reasons discussed above.

Table 4

U.S. Smoking-Attributable Mortality by Cause and Age of Death 1990–1994 Annual Average

Age at Death	Pediatric Diseases	Burn Victims	All Other Diseases	Total
Under 1	1,591	19	0	1,610
1–34	0	300	0	300
35–49	0	221	21,773	21,994
50–69	0	286	148,936	149,222
70–74	0	96	62,154	62,250
75–84	0	133	120,537	120,670
85+	0	45	71,652	71,697
Totals	1,591	1,100	425,052	427,743

Source: Private communication from the Centers for Disease Control and Prevention

According to Amler and Eddins, even if we were to look at medical treatment—measured by days of hospital care—nonalcohol-related injuries impose a 58 percent greater burden than tobacco, and nutrition-related diseases are more burdensome as well.

Another statistic that more accurately reflects the real health repercussions of smoking is the age distribution of the 427,743 deaths that CDC mistakenly traces to tobacco. No doubt most readers will be surprised to learn that—aside from burn victims and pediatric diseases—*tobacco does not kill a single person below the age of 35.*

Each year from 1990 through 1994, as shown in Table 4, only 1,910 tobacco-related deaths—less than half of 1 percent of the total—were persons below age thirty-five. Of those, 319 were burn victims and the rest were infants whose parents smoked. But the relationship between parental smoking and pediatric diseases carries a risk ratio of less than 2, and thus is statistically insignificant. Unless better evidence is produced, those deaths should not be associated with smoking.

On the other hand, the National Center for Health Statistics reports that more than twenty-one thousand persons below age thirty-five died from motor vehicle accidents in 1992, more than eleven thousand died from suicide, and nearly seventeen thousand died from homicide. Over half of those deaths were connected with alcohol or drug abuse. That should put smoking-related deaths in a somewhat different light.

Most revealing of all, almost 255,000 of the smoking-related deaths— nearly 60 percent of the total—occurred at age seventy or above. More than 192,000 deaths—nearly 45 percent of the total—occurred at age seventy-five or higher. And roughly 72,000 deaths—almost 17 percent of the total—occurred at the age of 85 or above. Still, the public health community disingenuously refers to "premature" deaths from smoking, as if there is no upper age limit to the computation.

The vast overestimate of the dangers of smoking has had disastrous results for the health of young people. Risky behavior does not exist in a vacuum; people compare uncertainties and apportion their time, effort, and money according to the perceived severity of the risk. Each year, alcohol and drug abuse kills tens of thousands of people under the age of thirty-five. Yet according to a 1995 survey by the U.S. Department of Health and Human Services, high school seniors thought smoking a pack a day was more dangerous than daily consumption of four to five alcoholic beverages or using barbiturates. And the CDC reports that the number of pregnant women who drank frequently quadrupled between 1991 and 1995—notwithstanding that fetal alcohol syndrome is the largest cause of preventable mental retardation, occurring in one out of every one thousand births.

Can anyone doubt that the drumbeat of antismoking propaganda from the White House and the health establishment has deluded Americans into thinking that tobacco is the real danger to our children? In truth, alcohol and drug abuse poses an immensely greater risk and antismoking zealots bear a heavy burden for their duplicity.

Conclusion

The unvarnished fact is that children do not die of tobacco-related diseases, correctly determined. If they smoke heavily during their teens, they may die of lung cancer in their old age, fifty or sixty years later, assuming lung cancer is still a threat then.

Meanwhile, do not expect consistency or even common sense from public officials. Alcoholism contributes to crime, violence, spousal abuse, and child neglect. Children are dying by the thousands in accidents, suicides, and homicides. But states go to war against nicotine—which is not an intoxicant, has no causal connection with crime, and poses little danger to young adults or family members.

The campaign against cigarettes is not entirely dishonest. After all, a seasoning of truth makes the lie more digestible. Evidence does suggest that cigarettes substantially increase the risk of lung cancer, bronchitis, and emphysema. The relationship between smoking and other diseases is not nearly so clear, however; and the scare-mongering that has passed for science is appalling. Not only is tobacco far less pernicious than Americans are led to believe, but its destructive effect is amplified by all manner of statistical legerdemain—counting diseases that should not be counted, using the wrong sample as a standard of comparison, and failing to control for obvious confounding variables.

To be blunt, there is no credible evidence that 400,000 deaths per year—or any number remotely close to 400,000—are caused by tobacco. Nor has that estimate been adjusted for the positive effects of smoking—less obesity, colitis, depression, Alzheimer's disease, Parkinson's disease and, for some women, a lower incidence of breast cancer. The actual damage from smoking is neither known nor knowable with precision. Responsible statisticians agree that it is impossible to attribute causation to a single variable, like tobacco, when there are multiple causal factors that are correlated with one another. The damage from cigarettes is far less than it is made out to be.

Most important, the government should stop lying and stop pretending that smoking-related deaths are anything but a statistical artifact. The unifying bond of all science is that truth is its aim. When that goal yields to politics, tainting science in order to advance predetermined ends, we are all at risk. Sadly, that is exactly what has transpired as our public officials fabricate evidence to promote their crusade against big tobacco.

POSTSCRIPT

Should Employers Limit Secondhand Smoke?

Much data indicate that smoking cigarettes and secondhand smoke are injurious to human health. For example, more than 400,000 people die from tobacco-related illnesses each year in the United States, costing the United States health care system billions of dollars annually. Exposure to secondhand smoke is estimated to increase the risk of heart disease 25% to 30% and lung cancer 20% to 30% for nonsmokers.

Thousands of people develop debilitating conditions such as chronic bronchitis and emphysema from cigarette smoking. Levy and Marimont, however, question the accuracy of the data. How the data are presented and interpreted may affect how one feels about the issue of placing more restrictions on tobacco products and secondhand smoke. If cigarette smoking is demonized, as Levy and Marimont suggest, it is not difficult to influence people's positions on regulating tobacco. There is currently a great deal of antismoking sentiment in society because of how the statistics are presented. Levy and Marimont do not recommend that people use tobacco products; however, they state only that the consequences linked to it are exaggerated. If the health effects of cigarette smoking were not deemed as hazardous as they are, would people feel differently about smoking as well as secondhand smoke?

Despite the hazards of tobacco smoking and secondhand smoke, should companies be responsible for the effects of secondhand smoke on its employees? What responsibility does a company have to its smokers who claim that they are dependent on tobacco? One could contend that the decision to start smoking is a matter of choice, but once tobacco dependency occurs, most smokers are in effect deprived of the choice to stop smoking. Many companies are faced with an ethical dilemma in that they may alienate workers who smoke by restricting their freedom to smoke. On the other hand, companies may alienate workers who do not want to be exposed to secondhand smoke.

Tobacco proponents maintain that people make all types of choices, and if the choices that people make are ultimately harmful, then that is their responsibility. A basic question is "do people have the right to engage in self-destructive behavior?" Does one have the right to expose others, such as co-workers, to their self-destructive behavior? If people are looked down upon because they smoke cigarettes, then should people be looked down upon if they eat too much or exercise too little? Does one have the right to eat a half dozen double cheeseburgers, to be a couch potato, to drink until one passes out? At what point does one lose the right to engage in deleterious behaviors—assuming that the rights of others are not adversely affected?

Changes in exposure to secondhand smoke are described in "Disparities in Secondhand Smoke Exposure—United States, 1988–1994 and 1999–2004," by S. E. Schober, C. Zhang, D. J. Brody, and C. Marano (*MMWR: Morbidity and Mortality Weekly Report,* July 11, 2008). Exposure of children to secondhand smoke is discussed in "Children's Secondhand Smoke Exposure in Private Homes and Cars: An Ethical Analysis," by Jill Jarvie and Ruth Malone (*American Journal of Public Health,* December 2008). An article that researches women in developing nations who are exposed to secondhand smoke is "Tobacco Use and Secondhand Smoke Exposure During Pregnancy: An Investigative Survey of Women in 9 Developing Nations," by Michele Bloch and associates (*American Journal of Public Health,* October 2008).

ISSUE 9

Should Marijuana be Legalized?

YES: Peter Cohen, from "The Culture of the Ban on Cannabis: Is It Political Laziness and Lack of Interest That Keeps This Farcical Blunder Afloat?" *Drugs and Alcohol Today* (June 2008)

NO: Office of National Drug Control Policy, from *Marijuana Myths and Facts: The Truth Behind 10 Popular Misconceptions* (2004)

ISSUE SUMMARY

YES: Author Peter Cohen argues that many assumptions about the effects of marijuana are untrue. Cohen indicates that research supports his claim but that there is little interest by public officials in the research. Cohen maintains that marijuana does not lead to the use of other drugs, nor does it result in mental illness or addiction. He also asserts that certain groups, such as police departments, benefit from the perpetuation of myths surrounding the use of marijuana.

NO: The Office of National Drug Control Policy (ONDCP) contends that marijuana is not a harmless drug. Besides causing physical problems, marijuana affects academic performance and emotional adjustment. Moreover, dealers who grow and sell marijuana may become violent to protect their commodity.

Despite the fact that marijuana is the most commonly used illegal drug in the United States, the federal government maintains that it is a potentially dangerous substance. Also, its use represents a danger, not just to the user, but to others. The government claims that marijuana can be addictive and that more young people are in treatment for marijuana than for other illegal drugs. Thus, the federal government does not advocate the legalization of marijuana.

The federal government argues that relaxing laws against marijuana use, even for medical purposes, is unwarranted. However, since the mid-1990s voters in California, Arizona, Oregon, Colorado, and other states have passed referenda to legalize marijuana for medical purposes. Despite the position of these voters, however, the federal government does not support the medical use of marijuana, and federal laws take precedence over state laws. A major concern of opponents of these referenda is that legalization of marijuana for medicinal purposes will lead to its use for recreational purposes.

The use of marijuana dates back at least 5,000 years. It was utilized medically as far back as 2737 BC, when Chinese emperor Shen Nung recommended marijuana, or cannabis, for medical use. By the 1890s some medical reports stated that cannabis was useful as a pain reliever. However, despite its historical significance, the use of marijuana for medical treatment is still a widely debated and controversial topic. The easing of marijuana laws, despite the drug's possible medical benefits, is viewed as a slippery slope. If marijuana is used medically, then its non-medical use may increase. Opponents argue that there has not been an increase in recreational marijuana use in those states where marijuana has been legalized for medical purposes.

Many of the concerns about the effects of marijuana date back to the 1930s when movies such as *Reefer Madness* were produced. Marijuana was painted as a drug that caused sexual perversions and violent behavior. In the absence of research, many people believed that marijuana was an evil drug that resulted in horrendous acts. When the Marijuana Tax Act was enacted in 1937, there was only small opposition to the law.

In more current times, marijuana is purported to cause mental illness and addiction. It is believed that marijuana affects academic achievement. Moreover, it is considered a gateway drug leading to other and more dangerous drugs. Cohen argues that these assumptions are untrue. He maintains that the federal government has not scientifically proven these assumptions to be valid. The research, says Cohen, is lacking. Proponents of marijuana legalization indicate that marijuana does not cause significant problems for individuals in European countries where marijuana is used.

Advocates for relaxing marijuana laws feel that the drug is unfairly labeled as a dangerous drug. For example, many more people throughout the world die from tobacco smoking and alcohol than from marijuana. Yet adults using those products do not go to jail, nor are they deprived of rights that other citizens enjoy. There are as many people in jail today for marijuana offenses as from cocaine, heroin, methamphetamine, Ecstasy, and all other illegal drugs combined.

Another point raised by those people in favor of relaxing marijuana laws is that it would be easier to educate young people about marijuana's effects if it was legal. By simply keeping the drug illegal, the message is "Don't use marijuana," rather than how to reduce harms associated with it. Marijuana proponents do not advocate the unregulated use of marijuana. They favor a more reasoned, controlled approach. They feel that too many people are arrested for marijuana possession and that governmental resources could be better used on stopping serious criminal activity.

In the following selections, Peter Cohen asserts that the federal government is overzealous in its enforcement of marijuana laws. The federal government, according to Cohen, continues to perpetuate myths regarding the dangers of marijuana use, and he also claims that local police departments have a vested interest in maintaining marijuana's illegal status. The Office of National Drug Control Policy (ONDCP) argues that marijuana is far more dangerous than many young people realize. The ONDCP tries to dispel many of the myths associated with marijuana. The ONDCP maintains that marijuana should not be used for legal medical purposes because the current research on marijuana's medicinal benefits is inconclusive. Other drugs are available that preclude the need to use marijuana.

YES

Peter Cohen

The Culture of the Ban on Cannabis: Is it Political Laziness and Lack of Interest that Keep this Farcical Blunder Afloat?

The subject I want to address here is the culture of the ban on cannabis. My main aim is not so much to explore how this culture came about as to explore the reasons for its continued existence. The ban, created long ago as a side issue during consultations about opium in the League of Nations in the 1920s, has endured over the years, through all the various upturns and downturns in culture or the economy.

My original plan was to give you a detailed account of those old deliberations in Geneva. But later I decided that they no longer matter. What does matter is that the ban is still in place and it is fair to assume that it achieves certain goals. So I shall make an effort to define these goals.

My primary aim is not to answer questions relating to the supposed dangers attached to the use of cannabis. Clearly, these dangers may not be the same in Greece as they are in Sweden or Belgium, and they may have changed in a variety of ways within specific countries or political cultures between 1936 and 2007. I shall return to the alleged dangers of cannabis in a moment, and report what some of the researchers I have consulted in Sweden, France and the UK have told me about how these dangers are defined in their own countries.

But as I have just said, describing these dangers and refuting them is not my main aim today. What I want to do here is to give a general description of the primary function of the ban on cannabis, regardless of geographical area, which is ostensibly justified by invoking a version of the dangers that is in fashion at a particular time.

Let me start by explaining that I am using the phrase "the culture of the ban on cannabis" to refer to a cluster of stories about the evils of cannabis, which are assumed to be true, which are not allowed to be tested seriously to check their validity, which are passed on and repeated within the various political systems and structures that we have in the world, and which culminate everywhere in some form of active enforcement of the ban on cannabis.

In this process, stories are mixed together in all sorts of ways, depending on complex historical developments in the various political systems. Tim

From *Drugs and Alcohol Today* by Peter Cohen, vol. 8, issue 2, June 2008, pp. 34+. Copyright © 2008 by Pavilion Journals Ltd. Reprinted by permission.

Boekhout van Solinge's (2004) dissertation, Dealing with Drugs in Europe demonstrated this convincingly for Sweden, France and the Netherlands.

Jerome Himmelstein has made another fascinating observation regarding the nature of these stories about the dangers of cannabis. In his well-known article, "From killer-weed to drop-out drug," he describes the fairly short period during which the cannabis ban has been in place in the United States, and discusses the arguments used to justify it. While in the early years of the ban, the 1930s, Americans blamed cannabis for causing violence, rape and sexual perversion, in the 1960s it was defined as one of the foundations of the cultural rebellion of that era. In that era it was identified as the primary cause of "dropping out," the lack of enthusiasm for America's dominant culture of consumption (Himmelstein, 1983). In other words, Himmelstein shows that within the space of a few decades, the scientific and social reasons for the ban, as invoked in the United States, have changed dramatically. To me these changes are interesting because of the way in which they relate to my subject here today, the survival of the culture of the ban.

I hope to convince you that the only thing that is relevant to the ban on cannabis is the ban itself and its survival, rather than the stories that are told about cannabis in a particular period of time. Why the ban was first imposed, and who benefits from it—and how—are of course significant questions, and interesting things to know. In a moment, for instance, I will show how the New York Police Department benefits from it. But the main point I want to make today is that the ban on cannabis has a certain status that shields it from rational and functional evaluation. The ban on cannabis has transcended the bounds of reason, and fulfils spiritual needs of a different nature than those for which it was created. That is why I decided that it was important to present this paper here, at an academic conference. There is a fair chance that I may meet people here who believe that sound research on the consumption and production of cannabis could conceivably influence the way in which the cannabis ban is retained, modified or perhaps even withdrawn! I hope that my words will explode that illusion, by showing that the ban on cannabis has acquired a sacred significance that places it beyond the pale of what we call scientific discourse. My use of the word "sacred" derives from the Dutch word sacraal as used by the anthropologist JojadaVerrips, whose work displays a certain fascination with the sacred origin of ritual murders in the early 20th century Netherlands. The need to commit these murders was experienced as a divine commandment; the murders were believed to purge the perpetrators, to liberate them from forms of defilement that were first transferred to the victims. According to Verrips, not only people but plants too may be victims! (Verrips, 1987). So my story is about the sacred nature of the ban on cannabis, its link to "purging" and the faith in this process, which removes it from the realm of ordinary debate about policy, or about scientific or economic issues. But let me first review some of the more banal aspects of the ban.

The example I promised to give you a moment ago about the organisations that benefit from the culture of the ban on cannabis comes from Harry Levine's current research on cannabis arrests in New York City (Levme & Small,

2008). He maintains that the driving force behind the arrests of large and ever-increasing numbers of people for the possession of cannabis in New York City is not the actual use of cannabis or any possible increase in that use. The driving force is the local police department. Levine concludes from the count-less interviews he has conducted that there are certain advantages attached to these arrests. I shall mention three of them.

1. It is a great boost to production figures. The police need these high figures because of its management style, in which "production" of statistics are required.
2. It provides police officers with opportunities for much-needed over-time, involving work that is relatively easy and free of danger.
3. Arresting, making official reports on, placing in police custody, try-ing, fining and releasing over 30,000 cannabis users a year—not to mention chasing up their fines—keeps a substantial number of police officers occupied, officers who can easily be deployed elsewhere if the need arises. Let me put it like this: it keeps a large force of officers on stand-by without leaving them to twiddle their thumbs without yielding any measurable "production."

I give this example to show that agencies involved in implementing the ban may derive significant advantages from it; it fulfils an important function. In addition, a major industry has grown up around the enforced treatment of cannabis users, not only in the United States. But this does not explain why these agencies can derive such enormous benefits from the ban without attracting the slightest criticism from politicians, and without being subjected to any checks. The explanation lies in the culture of the ban itself, of which the benefits listed above are merely a consequence.

Stories in Sweden, France and Britain

While preparing this paper, I asked five European researchers to answer the question of why the use of cannabis was prohibited in their country according to the most important agencies of their national enforcement systems. All five responded. The first Swedish respondent said that the ban was thought neces-sary because cannabis was a stepping-stone to other drugs, because it fostered apathy, and because it could cause schizophrenia. The second Swede said that cannabis was a stepping-stone to other drugs, that it caused dependency, and that it induced all sorts of psychoses.

One of the British researchers answered much more briefly. He said that it was universally believed that cannabis could cause madness, especially because of the popularity of the current strong species of marijuana. None of these researchers asserted that there was any scientific validity to these claims.

The Frenchman, who, like the others, had been conducting research on drugs for a very long time, replied that cannabis was "simply regarded as bad" for people in all sorts of ways, and that it was universally regarded as a step-ping-stone to the use of other drugs.

There are similarities and differences between the responses, and the story about cannabis as a source of violence is now found only in Britain. All these stories are known to be, scientifically speaking, either untrue or highly questionable. The notion that cannabis leads to other drugs—the story encountered everywhere—is really no longer tenable, as many studies, including those conducted by CEDRO, have shown. One of the most detailed calculations ever devoted to the matter, using two large, random samples of the population of Amsterdam, confirms Kandel's findings that drug use begins with tobacco, followed by alcohol (Kandel, 1975, 1978; Zie ook Golub & Johnson, 2001). For the minority of the population in Amsterdam aged 12 and older who go on to use cannabis after alcohol and tobacco, no significant pattern of other drug use can be demonstrated, except in the case of a small minority, and in this minority of cases generally for only a brief period of their time as drug users. I do not want to go into any more detail here regarding the debate on cannabis as a stepping-stone to other drugs, beyond saying that a vast body of epidemiological evidence could be published refuting this theory if there were any desire to see this evidence. The same applies to the propositions that cannabis induces violent behaviour, madness or apathy—maladies that were all, incidentally, attributed to masturbation in the 18th and 19th centuries. And potential adverse effects that are allegedly caused by intensive, frequent patterns of consumption (such as lung cancer) are almost always discussed in relation to all patterns of consumption. Hypotheses about physical or psychological consequences may perhaps apply to a small minority of highly specific cannabis users, but that applies to all propositions, however outlandish: such associations can always be found if one starts from biased presuppositions, or if one uses a carefully selected sample of people, such as those who use cannabis extremely frequently, or the inmates of psychiatric hospitals and prisons. For the vast majority of cannabis users, measured in random samples, these hypotheses are invalid. If the dominant political forces had adopted a different attitude to cannabis consumption, more money might have been available for research—and the publication of research—which demonstrate this invalidity. (We should not, however, overestimate the effect this might have had).

Clearly, there is something odd about the ban on cannabis. The changing stories that are evoked to prolong it again and again are untenable. But what is actually going on? The second British researcher I consulted added that leaving aside the many different problems related to cannabis, the ban also represents a moral standard imposed in society's name. It conveys a message to the population that using cannabis is not right. I'm sure that is true. It conveys that message. But does anyone listen to it? Some do, no doubt. But the Netherlands, Portugal and Greece, countries with substantially fewer users than Britain, receive the same message. Britain has more cannabis users than any other country in Europe aside from the Czech Republic. But the authorities in the countries with far lower levels of use also think that this message should be conveyed. This is regardless of the fact that after almost a century of cannabis use, no one knows whether this message is listened to or has the desired effect. Nor are there—and this is very revealing—any scientific analyses or serious attempts to explain the large discrepancies in cannabis use that exist not only within Europe but even within individual countries.

The lowest level of cannabis use in Europe, about seven percent of the population of Portugal, and the highest, 30% in the UK, differ by a factor of four. No one knows why this is the case. No one knows the determinants of these consumption figures, or whether they can be influenced—and if so by what. In the case of an ordinary problem, puzzles like this would be at the top of the list of research questions, but this does not apply to cannabis consumption. No one wants to know why the Portuguese smoke so little dope and the British smoke so much of it. No one wants to know why the Dutch occupy an intermediate position, between the Portuguese and the British, in spite of over 30 years of cannabis shops and free access to hashish and marijuana. In the Netherlands, for many years, anyone aged 16 and over could buy marijuana. The age limit was later raised to 18. People aged over 18 can still buy as much marijuana as they want. In other words, a situation that the British say, and the French and the Swedes say, would spell disaster, or at least lead to very high consumption figures, simply doesn't!

No one wants to know why not. People do not want to know, because it is not considered relevant. In the culture of the ban on cannabis, there is no platform for scientific argument. The political theatre of this ban is not produced for a critical public.

A Matter of Faith

In 17th-century Italy, the Catholic faith was embarrassed by Galileo Galilei's calculations of the motions of the sun and the moon, which made him guilty of a mortal sin. No one wanted to see such calculations. Galileo survived only because he and the Pope were old acquaintances. I often refer to Galileo's fate to illustrate the importance of faith in drug policy, but not to refer to faith in general. The 17th century Church was not opposed to scientific advances; only when such advances seemed to be undermining the basis of religious faith did science become a precarious business.

Galileo was not a heretic because he practised science, but because his undesirable science threatened one of the central dogmas of the religious authorities of the day, and the secular authorities deriving from them—namely, the dogma that the bible was based in its entirety on the word of God, and hence was wholly true. If that central dogma were to be undermined by calculations conflicting with the biblical text, this would undermine not only the Christian faith, but the very institution of the Church! And without the Church, the people could not attain salvation! It may be added that no one knew in those days whether a belief in the infallibility of the bible was the core value underlying adherence to the Catholic Church. Would people really have left the Church if they had realised that Galileo's astronomy was altogether sounder than that of the bible and Rome? Would people tend to use cannabis more than now if its use were depicted in the media as posing virtually no risk to the vast majority of users and if it did not incur the marginalisation that inevitably accompanies its illegality? We cannot answer these questions with certainty, but on the basis of many years of experience with legal access to cannabis in the Netherlands I tend to think not, on both counts. People who use cannabis learn to do so from other users, who set a certain example that they wish to follow. The existence of people outside their own circle who condemn cannabis and insist on retaining the ban on it may make a little difference, but not much. In Sweden, where the ban is strictly enforced and where children are told enormously exaggerated nonsense about cannabis at primary school, twice as many people use cannabis as in Portugal, where this practice does not exist and users are not even criminalised. In the Netherlands, where adults can purchase as much cannabis as they want perfectly legally, people living in rural areas use as little as in Sweden, while city folk use just as much as in Britain, even though the same message is propagated in all part of the Netherlands. In San Francisco, far more people, including cannabis users, consume cocaine than in Amsterdam, and at least twice as many people smoke dope in San Francisco as in Amsterdam. This is in spite of the low prices in Amsterdam, where customers can buy very small quantities in easily accessible shops with a wide assortment of wares, a distribution network that does not exist in San Francisco.

Cannabis is banned everywhere, notwithstanding differences in the degree to which the ban is enforced. Nowhere has it been demonstrated, however, that this ban has any impact on the drug's use. In large countries such as Australia or the United States, or Britain or France, which have harsh enforcement regimes, large sections of the population ignore the ban altogether. In the major cities of North America, there are few people who have never tried cannabis. But far fewer people use it on a weekly basis, let alone every day. That people do not become attached to it appears to be not because it is banned, but because they do not particularly like it or because it is linked to a limited number of social contexts. The social and physical context that determines whether people use cannabis, and if so how much, is described in detail in the comparative study on patterns of cannabis use that we carried out in Amsterdam, Bremen and San Francisco (Remarman et al, 2004).

The culture of the ban on cannabis censures any argument demonstrating the irrelevancy of the policy regime as a deviant and undesirable mode of reasoning, in much the same way that the culture of the infallibility of the bible—that is, of the Church—pronounced Galileo a heretic. Precisely where Galileo excelled, in observations of celestial bodies and calculations showing their motions to be strangely inconsistent with holy scripture, was where his reasoning was deemed to pose the greatest danger to the power of the Church. The idea that this argument regarding the risk posed to the Church might be erroneous was unthinkable! People were certain that if the Church allowed Galileo to study and teach without restriction, the institution of the Church, and therefore the salvation of human beings, would be harmed. The culture of the ban on cannabis is upheld with a similar dogmatic certainty. It is believed that if the state were to cease enforcing the ban, the physical and mental health of the population (or of those who are "weak") would be harmed.

All this means that the culture of the ban on cannabis is not susceptible to observations or data proving the ban to be incompatible with human rights, dangerous, destructive, impossible to enforce, inhumane, expensive, crime-inducing, and dysfunctional—even in its own terms. The ban was a blunder conceived in Geneva in or around 1924. Since then, an entire culture has grown up around it, and acquired near-saintly status. Let me try to define it more precisely. The culture of the ban on cannabis represents a way of thinking about the value of human beings, namely of the individual human being as the centre of things, and the highest good that the state must protect. The culture of the ban on cannabis can therefore be said to reflect a fossilised and misunderstood version of humanism. Misunderstood, because within the culture of the ban, politicians pursue the repressive and paternalist aspiration to protect citizens from "calamity." The state, here, is the secular successor to the Church as the protector of our spiritual and physical well-being. And in fact it does not really place the individual human being at the centre, but only a pale shadow of the individual. Within this culture, human beings are seen as weak creatures in need of protection, creatures who would be lost if the ban on cannabis were withdrawn.

The ban on cannabis has acquired sacred significance as a protective and purgative instrument, and is hence unassailable. So most politicians continue to support it and have nothing to gain from questioning it. Raising the matter of the follies and atrocities that are committed in the name of the ban is counterproductive. Proclaiming that the ban on cannabis cannot, and does not, protect citizens is rather like proclaiming in 17th-century Rome that the Church is a clown and that people are quite mature enough to take care of their own spiritual welfare.

As long as the culture of the ban on cannabis is the living symbol of the state's protection of its citizens, not a single argument is of the slightest relevance. The culture of the ban is protected from information, covered with a smooth conceptual armour that easily deflects or distorts reasoned argument. So it is my contention that the ban exists not for any tenable reason, but because of its sacred significance.

The Prohibition of Cannabis: An Auto-Da-Fé

I should like to close with a few observations on the lack of necessity to furnish religious rules with any rational grounds. An article on the significance of "kosher" posted to an American website called "Judaism 101" quotes a rabbi as saying that there is no reason whatsoever for the culture of kosher food aside the fact that the rules are mentioned in the Old Testament, the Jewish bible. Another rabbi also observes that there are no reasons for them aside from the requirement to obey the divine rules: "The ability to distinguish between right and wrong, good and evil, pure and defiled, the sacred and the profane, is very important in Judaism. Imposing rules on what you can and cannot eat ingrains that kind of self-control, requiring us to learn to control even our most basic, primal instincts."

In other words, there is a certain intrinsic value in the mere prescription and protection of rules. If the ban's provenance is, or is believed to be, good, no other reason is needed to corroborate this value. In a religious (or ideological) world view, obeying and protecting such rules is indicative of true faith, and is thus required. The substance and consequences of the rule cannot be questioned, since this would be to subject the faith itself to reason, and hence to doubt. Doubt means the end of faith.

In the culture of the ban on cannabis, its enforcement is a sign of faith in both the importance and the weakness of modern human beings, together with a belief in the capacity of the strong state to protect weak human beings. And this makes the ban unassailable.

The culture of the ban on cannabis, of eating kosher, of constantly affirming the infallibility of the bible, are all examples of imaginary rules based on faith, preserved by a long line of institutions and prelates. That would not matter all that much, were it not that the culture of the ban on cannabis, like any hunt for heretics, is attended by degrading injustice and the continuation of magical, infantile, contradictory and in some cases utterly insane practices. No price is too high for enforcing a ban once a culture has invested it with sacred value.

Office of National
Drug Control Policy

 **NO**

Marijuana & the Truth Behind
10 Popular Misperceptions

Introduction

Marijuana is the most widely used illicit drug in the United States. According to the National Survey on Drug Use and Health (formerly called the National Household Survey on Drug Abuse), 95 million Americans age 12 and older have tried "pot" at least once, and three out of every four illicit-drug users reported using marijuana within the previous 30 days.

Use of marijuana has adverse health, safety, social, academic, economic, and behavioral consequences. And yet, astonishingly, many people view the drug as "harmless." The widespread perception of marijuana as a benign natural herb seriously detracts from the most basic message our society needs to deliver: It is not OK for anyone—especially young people—to use this or any other illicit drug.

Marijuana became popular among the general youth population in the 1960s. Back then, many people who would become the parents and grandparents of teenage kids today smoked marijuana without significant adverse effects, so now they may see no harm in its use. But most of the marijuana available today is considerably more potent than the "weed" of the Woodstock era, and its users tend to be younger than those of past generations. Since the late 1960s, the average age of marijuana users has dropped from around 19 to just over 17. People are also lighting up at an earlier age. Fewer than half of those using marijuana for the first time in the late 1960s were under 18. By 2001, however, the proportion of under-18 initiates had increased to about two-thirds (67 percent).

Today's young people live in a world vastly different from that of their parents and grandparents. Kids these days, for instance, are bombarded constantly with pro-drug messages in print, on screen, and on CD. They also have easy access to the Internet, which abounds with sites promoting the wonders of marijuana, offering kits for beating drug tests, and, in some cases, advertising pot for sale. Meanwhile, the prevalence of higher potency marijuana, measured by levels of the chemical delta-9-tetrahydrocannabinol (THC), is increasing. Average THC levels rose from less than 1 percent in the mid-1970s to more than 6 percent in 2002. Sinsemilla potency increased in the past two decades from 6 percent to more than 13 percent, with some samples containing THC levels of up to 33 percent. . . .

From a report of Office of The National Drug Control Policy, 2004.

Myth 1: Marijuana Is Harmless

Marijuana harms in many ways, and kids are the most vulnerable to its damaging effects. Use of the drug can lead to significant health, safety, social, and learning or behavioral problems, especially for young users. . . .

Short-term effects of marijuana use include memory loss, distorted perception, trouble with thinking and problem-solving, and anxiety. Students who use marijuana may find it hard to learn, thus jeopardizing their ability to achieve their full potential.

Cognitive Impairment

That marijuana can cause problems with concentration and thinking has been shown in research funded by the National Institute on Drug Abuse (NIDA), the federal agency that brings the power of science to bear on drug abuse and addiction. A NIDA-funded study at McLean Hospital in Belmont, Massachusetts, is part of the growing body of research documenting cognitive impairment among heavy marijuana users. The study found that college students who used marijuana regularly had impaired skills related to attention, memory, and learning 24 hours after they last used the drug.

Another study, conducted at the University of Iowa College of Medicine, found that people who used marijuana frequently (7 or more times weekly for an extended period) showed deficits in mathematical skills and verbal expression, as well as selective impairments in memory-retrieval processes. These findings clearly have significant implications for young people, since reductions in cognitive function can lead to poor performance in school. . . .

Mental Health Problems

Smoking marijuana leads to changes in the brain similar to those caused by cocaine, heroin, and alcohol. All of these drugs disrupt the flow of chemical neurotransmitters, and all have specific receptor sites in the brain that have been linked to feelings of pleasure and, over time, addiction. Cannabinoid receptors are affected by THC, the active ingredient in marijuana, and many of these sites are found in the parts of the brain that influence pleasure, memory, thought, concentration, sensory and time perception, and coordinated movement.

Particularly for young people, marijuana use can lead to increased anxiety, panic attacks, depression, and other mental health problems. One study linked social withdrawal, anxiety, depression, attention problems, and thoughts of suicide in adolescents with past-year marijuana use. Other research shows that kids age 12 to 17 who smoke marijuana weekly are three times more likely than non-users to have thoughts about committing suicide. A recently published longitudinal study showed that use of cannabis increased the risk of major depression fourfold, and researchers in Sweden found a link between marijuana use and an increased risk of developing schizophrenia.

According to the American Society of Addiction Medicine, addiction and psychiatric disorders often occur together. The latest National Survey on Drug Use and Health reported that adults who use illicit drugs were more than twice as likely to have serious mental illness as adults who did not use an illicit drug.

Researchers conducting a longitudinal study of psychiatric disorders and substance use (including alcohol, marijuana, and other illicit drugs) have suggested several possible links between the two: (1) people may use drugs to feel better and alleviate symptoms of a mental disorder; (2) the use of the drug and the disorder share certain biological, social, or other risk factors; or (3) use of the drug can lead to anxiety, depression, or other disorders. . . .

Long-Term Consequences

The consequences of marijuana use can last long after the drug's effects have worn off. Studies show that early use of marijuana is strongly associated with later use of other illicit drugs and with a greater risk of illicit drug dependence or abuse. In fact, an analysis of data from the National Household Survey on Drug Abuse showed that the age of initiation for marijuana use was the most important predictor of later need for drug treatment.

Regular marijuana use has been shown to be associated with other long-term problems, including poor academic performance, poor job performance and increased absences from work, cognitive deficits, and lung damage. Marijuana use is also associated with a number of risky sexual behaviors, including having multiple sex partners, initiating sex at an early age, and failing to use condoms consistently.

Myth 2: Marijuana Is Not Addictive

. . . According to the 2002 National Survey on Drug Use and Health, 4.3 million Americans were classified with dependence on or abuse of marijuana. That figure represents 1.8 percent of the total U.S. population and 60.3 percent of those classified as individuals who abuse or are dependent on illicit drugs.

The desire for marijuana exerts a powerful pull on those who use it, and this desire, coupled with withdrawal symptoms, can make it hard for long-term smokers to stop using the drug. Users trying to quit often report irritability, anxiety, and difficulty sleeping. On psychological tests they also display increased aggression, which peaks approximately one week after they last used the drug.

Many people use marijuana compulsively even though it interferes with family, school, work, and recreational activities. What makes this all the more disturbing is that marijuana use has been shown to be three times more likely to lead to dependence among adolescents than among adults. Research indicates that the earlier kids start using marijuana, the more likely they are to become dependent on this or other illicit drugs later in life. . . .

Myth 3: Marijuana Is Not as Harmful to Your Health as Tobacco

Although some people think of marijuana as a benign natural herb, the drug actually contains many of the same cancer-causing chemicals found in tobacco. Puff for puff, the amount of tar inhaled and the level of carbon monoxide absorbed by those who smoke marijuana, regardless of THC content, are three to five times greater than among tobacco smokers.

Consequently, people who use marijuana on a regular basis often have the same breathing problems as tobacco users, such as chronic coughing and wheezing, more frequent acute chest illnesses, and a tendency toward obstructed airways. And because respiratory problems can affect athletic performance, smoking marijuana may be particularly harmful to kids involved in sports.

Researchers at the University of California, Los Angeles, have determined that marijuana smoking can cause potentially serious damage to the respiratory system at a relatively early age. Moreover, in a review of research on the health effects of marijuana use, the researchers cited findings that show "the daily smoking of relatively small amounts of marijuana (3 to 4 joints) has at least a comparable, if not greater effect" on the respiratory system than the smoking of more than 20 tobacco cigarettes.

Recently, scientists in England produced further evidence linking marijuana use to respiratory problems in young people. A research team at the University of Birmingham found that regular use of marijuana, even for less than six years, causes a marked deterioration in lung function. . . .

Myth 4: Marijuana Makes You Mellow

. . . Research shows that kids who use marijuana weekly are nearly four times more likely than non-users to report they engage in violent behavior. One study found that young people who had used marijuana in the past year were more likely than non-users to report aggressive behavior. According to that study, incidences of physically attacking people, stealing, and destroying property increased in proportion to the number of days marijuana was smoked in the past year. Users were also twice as likely as non-users to report they disobey at school and destroy their own things.

In another study, researchers looking into the relationship between ten illicit drugs and eight criminal offenses found that a greater frequency of marijuana use was associated with a greater likelihood to commit weapons offenses; except for alcohol, none of the other drugs showed such a connection. . . .

Myth 5: Marijuana Is Used to Treat Cancer and Other Diseases

Under the Comprehensive Drug Abuse Prevention and Control Act of 1970, marijuana was established as a Schedule I controlled substance. In other words, it is a dangerous drug that has no recognized medical value.

Whether marijuana can provide relief for people with certain medical conditions, including cancer, is a subject of intense national debate. It is true that THC, the primary active chemical in marijuana, can be useful for treating some medical problems. Synthetic THC is the main ingredient in Marinol®, an FDA-approved medication used to control nausea in cancer chemotherapy patients and to stimulate appetite in people with AIDS. Marinol, a legal and safe version of medical marijuana, has been available by prescription since 1985.

However, marijuana as a smoked product has never proven to be medically beneficial and, in fact, is much more likely to harm one's health; marijuana smoke is a crude THC delivery system that also sends many harmful substances into the body. In 1999, the Institute of Medicine (IOM) published a review of the available scientific evidence in an effort to assess the potential health benefits of marijuana and its constituent cannabinoids. The review concluded that smoking marijuana is not recommended for any long-term medical use, and a subsequent IOM report declared, "marijuana is not a modern medicine.". . .

Myth 6: Marijuana Is Not as Popular as MDMA (Ecstasy) or Other Drugs among Teens Today

Recent survey data show that about 15 million people—6.2 percent of the U.S. population—are current marijuana users, and that nearly a third of them (4.8 million people) used the drug on 20 or more days in the past month. Among kids age 12 to 17, more than two million (8.2 percent) reported past-month marijuana use. By contrast, fewer than 250,000 young people (1 percent) reported past-month use of hallucinogens, and of that number, only half (124,000) had used MDMA.

The 2003 Monitoring the Future Study showed that marijuana is not only popular today, it has been the most widely used illicit drug among high school seniors for the entire 29 years of the study. Meanwhile, Ecstasy use among American teens appears to be declining after record increases. Between 2001 and 2003, past-month use of MDMA among students in the three grades surveyed dropped by more than half, from 1.8 percent to 0.7 percent (8th grade), 2.6 percent to 1.1 percent (10th grade), and 2.8 percent to 1.3 percent (12th grade). . . .

Myth 7: If I Buy Marijuana, I'm Not Hurting Anyone Else
Violence at Home

. . . The trade in domestically grown marijuana often turns violent when dealers have conflicts or when growers feel their crops are threatened. But drug criminals are not the only ones threatened by the violence of the marijuana trade.

Much of the marijuana produced in America is grown on public lands, including our national forests and parks—areas set aside to preserve wildlife habitats, provide playgrounds for our children, and serve as natural refuges for recreation. Traffickers grow their crops in these areas because the land is free and accessible, crop ownership is hard to document, and because growers are immune to asset forfeiture laws. Law enforcement officials report that many marijuana growers, seeking to protect their crops from busybodies and rival "pot pirates," surround their plots with crude booby traps, including fishhooks dangling at eye level, bear traps, punji sticks, and rat traps rigged with shotgun shells.

Most of the marijuana on America's public lands is grown in the vast national forests of California, where more than 540,000 plants were seized or eradicated on land managed by the U.S. Forest Service in 2003 alone. This figure does not include the 309,000 marijuana plants taken from Forest Service land in other states, nor does it take into account the hundreds of thousands of plants removed from land managed by other government agencies. For example, in 2003 more than 134,000 marijuana plants were seized or eradicated from areas in California administered by the U.S. Department of the Interior's Bureau of Land Management.

According to officers with the Forest Service and other agencies, many of California's illegal marijuana fields are controlled not by peace-loving flower children but by employees of Mexican drug-trafficking organizations carrying high-powered assault weapons. During the growing season, the officers say, the cartels smuggle hundreds of undocumented Mexican nationals into the U.S. to work the fields, bringing with them pesticides, equipment, and guns. Hunters, campers, and others have been threatened at gunpoint or fired upon after stumbling into these illegal gardens. . . .

Myth 8: My Kids Won't Be Exposed to Marijuana

. . . More than half (55 percent) of youths age 12 to 17 responding to the National Survey on Drug Use and Health in 2002 reported that marijuana would be easy to obtain. The survey indicated that most marijuana users got the drug from a friend, and that almost nine percent of youths who bought marijuana did so inside a school building. Moreover, nearly 17 percent of the young people surveyed said they had been approached by someone selling drugs in the past month. In the 2000 survey, more than a quarter of 12- to 17-year-olds (26.6 percent) reported that drug-selling occurs frequently in their neighborhoods.

Kids are also exposed to a relentless barrage of marijuana messages in the popular culture—in the music they listen to, the movies they watch, and the magazines they read. And then there's the Internet, a crowded landscape of pro-marijuana and drug legalization Web sites. More often than not, the culture glamorizes or trivializes marijuana use and fails to show the serious harm it can cause. . . .

Not Just an Inner-City Problem

Some people have the impression that kids in the inner city are those most likely to get involved with drugs. Research shows, however, that marijuana use among youth in cities, rural areas, and the suburbs is roughly the same, and that use rates are similar regardless of population density. For example, annual prevalence rates of marijuana use among 10th graders are 28 percent in non-urban areas, 29 percent in large metropolitan statistical areas, and 32 percent in other metropolitan areas.

Myth 9: There's Not Much Parents Can Do to Stop Their Kids from Experimenting with Marijuana

Many people are surprised to learn that parents are the most powerful influence on their children when it comes to drugs. By staying involved, knowing what their kids are doing, and setting limits with clear rules and consequences, parents can increase the chances their kids will stay drug free. Research shows that appropriate parental monitoring can reduce future drug use even among adolescents who may be prone to marijuana use, such as those who are rebellious, cannot control their emotions, and experience internal distress. . . .

Parental Involvement

Kids who learn about the risks of drugs from their parents or caregivers are less likely to use drugs than kids who do not. Parents can create situations that help them connect with their children and stay involved in their lives. Experts suggest that parents try to be home with their kids after school, if possible, because evidence indicates that the riskiest time for kids with regard to drug involvement is between the hours of 3 p.m. and 6 p.m. Parents who can't be home with their children should consider enrolling them in after-school programs, sports, or other activities, or arrange for a trusted adult to oversee them.

It's also important for families to participate in activities such as eating meals together; holding meetings in which each person gets a chance to talk; and establishing regular routines of doing something special (like taking a walk) that allow parents to talk to their kids. Opening channels of communication between parents and children, as well as between families and the greater community, gives young people greater confidence and helps them make healthy choices.

Myth 10: The Government Sends Otherwise Innocent People to Prison for Casual Marijuana Use

On the contrary, it is extremely rare for anyone, particularly first-time offenders, to get sent to prison just for possessing a small amount of marijuana. In most states, possession of an ounce or less of pot is a misdemeanor offense, and some states have gone so far as to downgrade simple possession of marijuana to a civil offense akin to a traffic violation.

. . . In 1997, according to the U.S. Department of Justice's Bureau of Justice Statistics (BJS), only 1.6 percent of the state inmate population had been convicted of a marijuana-only crime, including trafficking. An even smaller percentage of state inmates were imprisoned with marijuana *possession* as the only charge (0.7 percent). And only 0.3 percent of those imprisoned just for marijuana possession were first-time offenders.

More recent estimates from the BJS show that at midyear 2002, approximately 8,400 state prisoners were serving time for possessing marijuana in any amount. Fewer than half of that group, or about 3,600 inmates, were incarcerated on a first offense. In other words, of the more than 1.2 million people doing time in state prisons across America, only a small fraction were first-time offenders sentenced just for marijuana possession. And again, this figure includes possession of *any* amount.

On the federal level, prosecutors focus largely on traffickers, kingpins, and other major drug criminals, so federal marijuana cases often involve hundreds of pounds of the drug. Cases involving smaller amounts are typically handled on the state level. This is part of the reason why hardly anyone ends up in federal prison for simple possession of marijuana. The fact is, of all drug defendants sentenced in federal court for marijuana offenses in 2001, the vast majority were convicted of trafficking. Only 2.3 percent—186 people—were sentenced for simple possession, and of the 174 for whom sentencing information is known, just 63 actually served time behind bars. . . .

Conclusion

The clutter of messages about marijuana in the popular culture creates an atmosphere of confusion and sends kids mixed signals about the drug. But what should be clear is that no responsible person thinks young people should use marijuana. . . .

Parents can help keep their children away from marijuana by letting them know its dangers, and by monitoring their activities and staying involved in their lives. . . . Both of these Web sites are supported by the Office of National Drug Control Policy.

Schools and communities can also play an important role by providing activities that keep kids interested and involved in healthy, drug-free programs.

If you want to help dispel misperceptions and spread the truth about marijuana to help kids grow up drug-free, you can:

- Educate yourself about the dangers of marijuana and keep up with scientific research into its harmful effects. For a wealth of good information, visit the Web site for the National Institute on Drug Abuse. . . .
- Help kids in trouble with marijuana get into drug treatment programs
- Be an advocate for better, more informed drugged-driving laws
- Support after-school programs and get involved in local anti-drug coalitions
- Stay informed about the marijuana laws in your state, and take a stand against changes in legislation that would increase the drug's availability in your community
- Support efforts to launch a student drug-testing program in your local schools

- See "What You Need to Know About Drug Testing in Schools," available by calling 800-666-3332. . . .
- To learn more about drug and alcohol abuse, visit the Substance Abuse & Mental Health Services Administration's National Clearinghouse for Alcohol and Drug Information at . . . or call its 24-hour hotline: 1-800-729-6686 or 1-800-788-2800

POSTSCRIPT

Should Marijuana be Legalized?

The restrictive laws against marijuana, according to Cohen, have resulted in a burgeoning number of people in prison for marijuana offenses. Cohen maintains that the scientific proof demonstrating that marijuana is harmful is lacking. Nonetheless, politicians have shown little interest in overturning the laws banning marijuana. The government's objection to marijuana, says Cohen, is based more on politics than scientific evidence.

Legalizing marijuana would raise a number of questions. If legalization resulted in much abuse and physical or psychological problems, how easy would it be to re-criminalize marijuana? For example, if there is a significant increase in the number of people using marijuana, could the law be rescinded? How would users react? If marijuana was legalized, what restrictions would apply to its legalization? Would there be a limit on how much one could possess? Would the age of consent be 18, 21, or some other age? Would there be restrictions on the secondhand effects of marijuana smoke? What kind of penalties would apply to adults supplying marijuana to minors?

Despite its popularity, the federal government notes that parents should and can assert more influence on their children's desire to use marijuana. The government claims that marijuana is not the harmless drug that many proponents believe. Marijuana can have adverse effects on mental health, physical well-being, and on academic performance. In addition, thousands of young people enter substance abuse treatment for their addiction to marijuana. It is important, states the Office of National Drug Control Policy, to counteract how culture trivializes the dangers of marijuana use.

Many marijuana proponents contend that the effort to prevent the legalization of marijuana for medical and non-medical use is purely a political battle. Detractors maintain that the issue is purely scientific—that the data supporting marijuana's medical usefulness are inconclusive and scientifically unsubstantiated. And although the chief administrative law judge of the Drug Enforcement Administration (DEA) made a recommendation to change the status of marijuana from Schedule I to Schedule II, the DEA and other federal agencies are not compelled to do so, and they have resisted any change in the law.

An extensive review of marijuana usage and effects is discussed in *Non-Medical Marijuana: Rite of Passage or Russian Roulette?* (The National Center on Addiction and Substance Abuse at Columbia University, June 2008). Two papers that examine the effects of marijuana are *Teen Marijuana Use Worsens Depression: An Analysis of Recent Data Shows "Self-Medicating" Could Actually Make Things Worse* (Office of National Drug Control Policy, May 2008) and "Prospective Associations Between Cannabis Use, Abuse, and Dependence and Panic Attacks and Disorder," by Michael Zvolensky and associates (*Journal of Psychiatric Research,* 2007).

ISSUE 10

Are Psychotherapeutic Drugs Overprescribed for Treating Mental Illness?

YES: Leemon McHenry, from "Ethical Issues in Psychopharmacology," *Journal of Medical Ethics* (July 2006)

NO: Bruce M. Cohen, from "Mind and Medicine: Drug Treatments for Psychiatric Illness," *Social Research* (Fall 2001)

ISSUE SUMMARY

YES: Professor Leemon McHenry, a professor with the Philosophy Department at the California State University at Northridge, questions the effectiveness of psychiatric drugs, especially antidepressant drugs known as selective serotonin reuptake inhibitors (SSRIs). McHenry maintains that the increase in the prescribing of antidepressant drugs results from their promotion by the pharmaceutical industry. McHenry also argues that pharmaceutical companies should be more forthright in the efficacy of these drugs.

NO: Medical doctor Bruce M. Cohen maintains that psychiatric medicines are very beneficial in enabling individuals with a variety of illnesses to return to normal aspects of consciousness. Cohen points out that people with conditions such as anxiety, depression, and psychosis respond very well to medications. These types of drugs have been utilized successfully for hundreds of years.

One of the most common emotional problems in America is mental illness, especially depression. It is estimated that approximately 10 percent of Americans experience some type of depression during their lives. Although some of the newer antidepressant drugs such as Prozac, Paxil, and Zoloft have not been available that long, they account for billions of dollars in sales. Does this mean that more people are becoming mentally ill or only that today people are more likely to be diagnosed with mental illness?

Although antidepressant drugs were originally developed to treat depression—for which they are believed to be about 60 percent effective—these drugs are now prescribed for an array of other conditions. Some of these conditions include eating disorders like bulimia and obesity, obsessive-compulsive disorders, panic attacks, and anxiety. An important question about these drugs is currently under debate: Are they prescribed too casually? Some experts feel that physicians are giving psychotherapeutic drugs to patients who do not need chemical treatment to overcome their afflictions. Yale University professor Sherwin Nuland has argued that drugs like Prozac are relatively safe for its approved applications but that they are inappropriate for less severe problems.

As with most other drugs, psychotherapeutic drugs like antidepressants produce a number of adverse side effects. These effects include hypotension (low blood pressure), weight gain, and irregular heart rhythms. Other side effects that may be experienced are headaches, fatigue, profuse sweating, anxiety, reduced appetite, jitteriness, dizziness, stomach discomfort, nausea, sexual dysfunction, and insomnia. Because these drugs are relatively new, long-term side effects have yet to be determined.

Soon after Prozac was introduced, several lawsuits were filed against Eli Lilly and Company, the drug's manufacturer, due to Prozac's side effects. The drug was linked to violent and suicidal behavior. Some individuals charged with violent crimes have used the defense that Prozac made them act violently and that they should not be held accountable for their actions while on the drug. Prozac also has been implicated in a number of suicides, although it is unclear whether Prozac caused these individuals to commit suicide or whether they would have committed suicide anyway. Paxil and Zoloft, which were introduced after Prozac, reportedly have fewer side effects.

Psychiatrist Peter R. Breggin, who feels that antidepressant drugs are prescribed too frequently, has argued that they are used to replace traditional psychotherapy. Breggin claims that psychiatry has given in to the pharmaceutical companies. In contrast to psychiatry, antidepressant drugs are less expensive and more convenient. However, do these drugs get at the root of the problems that many people have? The United States Public Health Service recommends drug therapy for severe cases of depression but psychotherapy for mild or moderate cases of depression.

One may accept the use of drug therapy when one's medical condition is caused by a chemical imbalance. However, should drugs be employed to alter one's personality, to help someone become more confident and less introverted? One could argue that if drugs help people with these personal qualities, then that is a healthy use of these drugs. Is using these drugs any different than people using cigarettes to relax or using alcohol to overcome shyness?

In the following selections, Leemon McHenry believes that psychotherapeutic drugs are overprescribed and that this is due to their heavy promotion by the pharmaceutical industry. Bruce M. Cohen argues that drugs such as antidepressants are invaluable drugs because they effectively treat anxiety, depression, and psychosis. The benefits of these drugs, claims Cohen, outweigh their potential side effects.

YES

Leemon McHenry

Ethical Issues in Psychopharmacology

Now more than ever the moral and scientific integrity of psychopharmacology deserves close scrutiny. A behemoth pharmaceutical industry has created corporate psychiatry along with industry-sponsored clinical research, direct to consumer marketing of antidepressants, ghost writing for medical journals and a major war for the market share. All the trappings are in place for marketing the disease rather than the cure. An illness intervention industry with no serious ethical commitment to health care threatens the most basic imperative of the medical art—"first, do no harm"—and demonstrates the weakness in the corporate model of medicine.

The Serotonin Hypothesis

The controversy over the serotonin hypothesis of depression lies at the very heart of the matter. Since, however, the pharmaceutical industry has an enormous financial interest in protecting the hypothesis, the problems with the theory are seldom discussed and less likely to reach publication. The epistemological virtue of science as the rigorous pursuit of truth has been corrupted by an industry that manipulates the process to its own advantage. Corporate psychiatrists become coconspirators by accepting a paradigm uncritically and by adopting the language game of chemical imbalance that entirely satisfies this purpose.

The serotonin hypothesis is a monoamine theory that advances the view that depression is caused by neurotransmitter system deficits. It was originally proposed in the late 1950s by George Ashcroft and Donald Eccleston at Edinburgh and gained further support from Alex Coppen at Surrey and Herman van Praag at Utrecht in the groundswell of early developments in biological psychiatry.[1-2] Low concentrations of serotonin, 5HT (5-hydroxytryptamine) or its main metabolite, 5-HIAA (5-hydroxyindole acetic acid), were found in autopsy studies of brains from suicide victims and in studies of cerebrospinal fluid from depressed patients.[3-6]

Although it might appear that the development of the new psychotropic drugs, the selective serotonin reuptake inhibitors (SSRIs), was the next logical step from the idea of serotonin deficiency, the actual history shows otherwise. The norepinephrine hypothesis of depression (another monoamine theory),

From *Journal of Medical Ethics*, vol. 32, no. 7, July 2006, pp. 405–410. Copyright © 2006 by Institute of Medical Ethics. Reprinted by permission of BMJ Publishing Group via Rightslink.

not the serotonin hypothesis, was the leading idea that guided research in psychopharmacology at the time, especially in the United States. The SSRIs were created when it became clear that drugs with an action on the serotonin system had a recognisably different effect from drugs active on the norepinephrine system. SSRIs function in the brain by blocking the breakdown or reuptake of serotonin from the synapse into the transmitting cell, thus leaving the serotonin active in the synapse for a longer period. "Selective" in "SSRI" suggests that the drug's action is clean or precise, but this is misleading as the drug has effects on a range of other neurotransmitter systems.

Although the serotonin theory might offer a compelling view within our physiochemical model of the brain, its main problem is oversimplicity in the overall neurochemical scenario. Even more to the point, however, it is probably false. The fact of the matter is that there never was a consistent body of evidence to support the theory. George Ashcroft, who was one of the pioneers in serotonin research, abandoned the idea of lowered serotonin levels by 1970. Ashcroft makes the crucial point: "What we believed was that 5-HIAA levels were probably a measure of functional activity of the systems and not a cause. It could just as well have been that people with depression had low activity in their system and that 5-HIAA was mirroring that and then when they got better it didn't necessarily go up."[9] With regard to Popperian and Kuhnian models of scientific advance, David Healy explains the survival of the monoamine theories despite a wealth of negative evidence. He describes them as erected on a quicksand of mistaken assumptions and apparently lacking in the mortar of supporting evidence.[10] Although there seems to be no question about the fact that SSRIs act on the serotonin system, what has not been established is an abnormality of serotonin metabolism in depression or that SSRIs correct a chemical Imbalance. Instead of going back to the proverbial drawing board with Ashcroft, however, the pharmaceutical company marketing departments revived the serotonin theory in the late 1980s and channelled all their financial might into promoting the SSRIs. It was a triumph of marketing over science.[11]

There are few neuroscientists today who would embrace the serotonin hypothesis. Whether this is true for prescribing physicians and psychiatrists is less clear. There are certainly those, perhaps the majority, who recognise that there are factors other than neurobiology involved in the aetiology, course and outcome of depressive disorders. My case against the serotonin hypothesis targets the manner in which this theory has been presented to the public by pharmaceutical Industry marketing.

The success of the SSRIs no more demonstrates the causal relationship between serotonin deficiency and depression than the relief provided by aspirin for the cause of a fever. The aspirin might treat the symptoms, but this does not provide any important information about the cause of the fever. Similarly, the fact that a patient's depression might be treated by an SSRI tells us nothing about the cause of the depression. Most of the supporting evidence for the serotonin hypothesis after the 1980s has been just exactly this. From the patients' response to the SSRIs, the inference is drawn that the cause of the disorder is a lack of serotonin. Drugs are used to probe and understand mental disorders yet this method functions entirely within the realm of symptomology. Nature refuses to reveal her true causes from the mere control of symptoms.

Depression is a complex mental disorder. Whether it is a disease with an organic origin is another matter. Nonetheless, the current focus on neurochemical abnormality has produced a "depression puzzle," in which the pieces simply do not add up. First, reserpine, an antipsychotic, produces depressive symptoms by depleting the brain of complex amines. This should cause depression in all patients if the serotonin hypothesis were true, but it does not. Less than 20% of patients will become depressed. Second, Max Lurie and Harry Salzer used the antidepressant drug, isoniazid, in the 1950s with two out of three patients responding, but isoniazid has no action on the serotonin system (Healy,[8] p 52). So, the same kind of evidence (drug action) that is used in support of the serotonin hypothesis also counts against it. Third, there has been a gradual increase in depression around the world, culminating in what has been called the "era of depression" in the 1990s.[14] If, however, the serotonin hypothesis is true, this must be because there is a corresponding gradual increase in defective serotonergic systems around the world. There is no evidence for this implausible idea. Finally, twice as many women as men are likely to become depressed, which must mean that women are born with a less effective serotonergic system. Again there is no evidence for this either.

Suppose that we dispose altogether of the serotonin hypothesis as an attempt to understand the aetiology of depression. What counts most in medicine are statistical correlations establishing varying degrees of reliability, and according to the advocates of SSRIs, their reliability (effectiveness and safety) is clearly established. The plain and simple fact of the matter (so it is said) is that millions of patients have been relieved of their debilitating depression, some of them in dramatic and unmistakable ways. How could this possibly be explained if the SSRIs are not effective treatments?

The clinical trials that form the basis of Food and Drug Administration (FDA) approval of SSRIs demonstrate repeatedly that these drugs show a clinically negligible advantage over inert placebo (sugar pills) in the treatment of depression. Here we must keep in mind that the data from clinical trials rank at the top of the hierarchy of evidence in the world of psychopharmacology. FDA approval, however, only requires that the drugs are better than nothing. According to the best data available, there is a less than 10% difference in the effect of FDA-approved antidepressants versus placebo.[15-16] In some studies, placebo control groups duplicated 80% of the response to medication.[17-19] The studies that provide the desired results, embarrassingly minimal as they are, reach publication and appear in the databases of the pharmaceutical companies and the FDA. What the general public barely sees are many of the failures of clinical trials around the world and the clinical trials that are prematurely terminated due to adverse side effects. These failed studies never see the light of day because the pharmaceutical companies that fund the studies own the data that is produced from the contract research organisations and site management organisations. The control over the data also enables the companies to provide the spin on the data that favours their drugs.[20 21]

Marketing Depression

No one knows exactly how SSRIs work, if indeed they really do work at all. One plausible explanation is that they mask symptoms of depression in moderate cases that resolve themselves spontaneously. It is also well known that the more a drug is hyped in the mainstream media as a "miracle drug," the greater is the likelihood of a strong placebo effect. What is, however, fundamentally problematic from an ethical point of view is the over inflation of SSRI effectiveness and safety, questionable marketing strategies, and the megadose prescriptions that can alter brain chemistry and behaviour for the worse.

Pharmaceutical companies in their direct to consumer marketing continue to promote SSRIs in television advertisements with the catchy suggestion: "While the cause of depression is not known, you might be suffering from a chemical imbalance. Ask your physician about [SSRI trade name]." Website advertisements for certain SSRIs claim their non-habit-forming drugs "correct the chemical imbalance believed to cause the disorder" and include diagrams of how this "science" works. In this manner, the companies "grow the market" by increasing consumer awareness of depression and target larger populations for their drugs. Direct to consumer advertising increases the request rates of the drugs and brand choices as well the likelihood that these drugs will be prescribed by physicians and psychiatrists.

The idea of selling us depression, whether we are truly ill or not, has become an immensely lucrative strategy for selling SSRIs, a large part of which succeeds on the basis of the idea of chemical imbalance. The range of prescriptions for SSRIs has included severe, chronic depression (completely non-functional human beings); moderate cases of depression (precipitated by stress, loss of loved ones, rape, divorce, professional failure), and the completely ludicrous (the angst-ridden, ill-adjusted child, personality sculpting, and psychotherapeutic fashion). The marketing strategy plays on the public's desire for a quick fix for all the vicissitudes of life and the power of the suggestion contained in the easy to understand model of chemical imbalance. This phenomenon has been dubbed the "medicalisation of society"—a phrase coined to describe the belief that every problem requires medical treatment, which is particularly relevant in the case of antidepressants. A report by the UK House of Commons health committee attributes this to the activities of the pharmaceutical industry.[23] However, the strategy also works so well because of the public's ignorance of, and trust in, the institution of science—there will always be those who know these marvellous things beyond the reach of ordinary people and they offer these amazing solutions to problems that just yesterday we did not understand. SSRIs have been abused as lifestyle drugs or performance enhancement drugs in the manner of LSD, Viagra, or anabolic steroids. The pharmaceutical companies have benefited from this trend to the tune of ten billion dollars per year from sales of all SSRIs. The problem begins here. The industry is marketing the condition and then the lifelong commitment to their products.[24] [25] Although patients might gain a short-term solution from SSRI prescriptions, the long-term harm is only just starting to come into focus for both individuals and the institution of medicine.

Marketing departments employ a strategy they call "evergreening" by beginning with one indication of a use for an SSRI and then moving on to explore other "green" pastures for potential markets. In order to convince people something is wrong with them that requires SSRI therapy, the marketing departments hire public relations firms to raise awareness of a newly approved indication, sometimes using celebrity spokespersons to pitch the idea. SSRIs were first marketed for depression, then for panic disorder, obsessive compulsive disorder, post-traumatic stress disorder, seasonal affective disorder, generalised anxiety disorder, and social anxiety disorder. Other potential indications in the marketing strategy that show up in clinical trials include premature ejaculation and paedophilia (since we know SSRIs cause sexual dysfunction), premenstrual syndrome, writer's block, obesity, alcoholism, cocaine addiction, compulsive shopping, and smoking cessation.

Healy explains how the so called "depression epidemic" developed from psychiatric concerns over unrecognised and untreated depression in the 1960s and 1970s. National depression campaigns were mounted in the United States and the United Kingdom. These involved alerting physicians and third party payers in health care to the huge economic burdens of untreated depression and educational campaigns to shame physicians for failing to detect and treat depression (Healy,[8] p 43). The infusion of industry money into psychiatry means influence on the very definitions of psychological disorder that determine how a patient will be diagnosed and treated. In this manner, depression is understood to be a physiological disease that is treated by drugs like SSRIs and thereby gains the imprimatur of organisations like the American Psychiatric Association.

Pharmaceutical companies effectively control many professional conferences and medical journal publications, employ psychiatrists as "key opinion leaders" and pay them handsomely to sign on to publications ghost written by their own staff or medical communication agencies employed by the company. The practice of for profit, industry-sponsored ghost writing has become a major concern since scientific journals are meant to be neutral arbiters of merit via the critical peer review process.[27-28] Marketing interests have, however, tainted some of the most distinguished journals in medicine, especially psychiatry. The marketing of depression has spread to the very highest levels now that the distinction between promotional materials and scientific objectivity has been blurred. Academics who are expected to be the legitimate authors of journal articles turn out to be little more than ornaments to a business rushing to gain blockbuster status for its drugs or instruments used in the competition between the various companies to dominate the market share.[29]

Is life really so much more stressful today than it was 20 or 30 years ago or has the marketing strategy of the pharmaceutical companies succeeded in convincing us that we are depressed and cannot cope without their drugs? Approximately 50 to 100 people per million were thought to be depressed before the creation of antidepressants; today our best estimates put the figure at 100,000 to 200,000 people per million (Healy,[8] p 20). A third possibility is that all these depressed people were previously walking the streets undiagnosed. If this was the idea of well-intentioned psychiatrists forty years ago, it has been exploited with maximum financial results by pharmaceutical marketing departments.

Hidden Dangers

Within the controlled environment of clinical trials it is possible to limit variables to determine the efficacy of the study drug versus placebo and identify the likely cause of adverse reactions. With regard to the latter, this typically comes down to two possibilities: the underlying disorder or the study drug. Despite many cases in which the investigator identifies the study drug as the definite or probable cause of the adverse reaction, the pharmaceutical companies consistently blame the underlying disorder rather than the treatment. In the parlance of the industry, this is known as "defending the molecule." The more serious adverse reactions that show up in clinical trials and spontaneous reports include: akathisia; aggression; self mutilation; emotional blunting; worsening depression; withdrawal symptoms; and suicidality. The latter two were a major concern with the introduction of the SSRIs and have been the focus of considerable debate in the medical literature.

Given that the serotonin hypothesis of depression emerged partly from an examination of serotonin levels in suicide victims, there has been a theoretical resistance from the start to the very idea that SSRIs could be responsible for some cases of suicide. While it is clear that depressed patients are at a higher risk of suicide, what is particularly problematic for the claim that any suicidal thoughts or attempts while on an SSRI are always caused by the underlying disorder is the lack of any suicidal history in many of these patients. Moreover, some patients on SSRIs for indications other than depression or in healthy volunteer studies become suicidal. Numerous cases of this sort caused alarm among researchers in the early 1990s.[32-33] A common side effect of SSRIs is akathisia—a drug-induced condition of extreme restlessness, insomnia, and agitation that is accompanied by compulsions to commit violence to oneself or to others.[34-36] Many patients will say that they "feel like a video on fast forward" or that they "just want to jump out of their skin" and see suicide as the only relief. The most disturbing cases on record concern functional individuals with moderate depression caused by some change of life who are prescribed an SSRI, become extremely agitated and restless, and then commit suicide within a matter of days or weeks—this being completely out of character with anything in their past. Patients of this sort are more than likely to be seen by primary care physicians who have not been trained to recognise the problem of akathisia. Their doctors will typically misdiagnose the symptoms as worsening depression and the suicides as a result of the underlying disorder—consistently with the approach of the marketing departments of the pharmaceutical companies.

The FDA and the drug companies have constantly argued that no causal relationship has been established between suicide and SSRIs despite the existence of many adverse drug experience reports. There are, however, indications that the sheer volume of these reports together with the ones from clinical trials are starting to command attention in psychiatry and general practice. Studies have been done by pharmaceutical companies that provide evidence for the causal relationship—namely, the method of determining causality: challenge, dechallenge, rechallenge. In this process a patient is given a drug and experiences a side effect (challenge), then the drug is discontinued and the side effect disappears (dechallenge), and finally the drug is reintroduced and the same side effect appears again (rechallenge). Suicidality is regularly coded as caused by the study drug by the investigators and the sponsor. What is even more revealing about the extent to which the pharmaceutical companies are willing to press the point is that discussions about side effects of drugs take on the character of something approaching a rigorous Humean scepticism with regard to the very meaning of the term "cause," but when the issue is efficacy the term suddenly has a perfectly clear meaning. SSRIs, we are told, do cause relief of depression. The serious side effects, such as suicidality, are merely unproved "associations."

In regulatory actions that were long overdue, the FDA issued a pair of warnings for SSRIs, both of which concern suicidality. On 22 March 2004, the FDA required antidepressant manufacturers to include in their label a warning statement that recommends close observation of adult and paediatric patients treated with these agents for worsening depression or the emergence of suicidality, "especially at the beginning of therapy or when the dose either increases or decreases." Then on 15 October 2004, the FDA, faced with public pressure from a recent action by UK regulators, followed up with the strongest warning possible—the "black box" warning—which describes the increased risk of suicidality in children and adolescents on SSRIs.[38] [39]

Determining causality in SSRI/suicide cases is enormously complex. According to some studies we must distinguish between SSRI-induced suicidality in children or adolescents, and adults: the former indicates a risk of suicide probably increased under SSRI therapy whereas the latter shows no increased risk.[40] The main evidence focuses attention on (1) the data comparing SSRI and tricyclics, which shows that users of SSRIs are not at any more risk of suicidality than those on tricyclics,[41] and (2) the failure of the SSRI/suicide cases to reach a statistical significance compared to placebo/suicide cases.[42–44] According to other studies the data from adult studies shows a twofold increase in the risk of fatal and non-fatal suicidal attempts in users of SSRIs compared to users of placebo, and this has been exactly what the data has shown since the introduction of the SSRIs.[45] Aursnes *et al* argue that Cipriani *et al* failed to convey the unanimous conclusion in the reviewed studies of an increased risk of suicidal attempts in adult patients on SSRIs.[46]

Many patients on SSRIs describe their experience as a "chemical prison." Once started on a regime, the attempt to reduce the dosage or discontinue the drug without experiencing severe adverse events can be very difficult. These include jolting electric zaps (paraesthesia); confusion; headaches; vomiting; dizziness; nausea; worsening depression; insomnia; irritability; emotional lability, including suicidality; and agitation that, when severe, can resemble a manic episode. A small percentage of patients claim they literally cannot get off the drugs even if they try and taper off the dosage. Pharmaceutical companies have vigorously maintained that SSRIs are not addictive and that what is believed to be withdrawal symptoms is really evidence that the drug is working. Since the adverse events that result from cessation of drug therapy are often confused with the re-emergence of the depressive illness, physicians typically advise their patients to continue their regime or increase the dosage. The most compelling evidence against the drugs, however, comes in the form of withdrawal symptoms in neonatals whose mothers were on SSRIs during pregnancy. In such cases, it is not possible to blame the adverse events on re-emergence of depression.[47–49]

The problem of withdrawal emerged first with paroxetine because of the great volume of reports on the adverse event reporting system. Paroxetine has a relatively short half life (21–24 hours) and shorter washout period compared to fluoxetine (4 to 16 days), so the withdrawal symptoms tend to be more severe upon abrupt discontinuation. In a feat of semantic opportunism, the maker of fluoxetine, Eli Lilly, launched a public relations campaign to replace "withdrawal symptoms" with "discontinuation symptoms." The alleged difference is that the latter does not imply addiction as with the case of alcohol or barbiturates. Over time, however, it has become more and more difficult to maintain this position despite the enormous amount of money that funded conferences and medical journal supplements on the topic.

The crux of the matter concerns the very meaning of "addiction." Psychiatrists who framed the definition in the third and fourth editions of *The Diagnostic and Statistical Manual of Mental Disorders* (DSM III and IV) had in mind diagnostic criteria identifying substance dependence—namely, maladaptive behaviour, euphoria, or compulsive drug seeking.[50] The classic cases of iatrogenic dependence in which the chemical system of the brain attempts to regain equilibrium no longer counts as addiction. This allowed the manufacturer of paroxetine, SmithKline Beecham (now GlaxoSmithKline), to claim in the patient's leaflet and in advertising that paroxetine is not addictive or habit forming. However, to patients suffering from withdrawal symptoms after discontinuing the drug, their physical dependence accorded with the common dictionary meaning of "addiction." In the *Oxford English Dictionary,* for example, "addiction" is defined as "the condition of taking drugs excessively and being unable to cease doing so without adverse effects".[51] In this latter sense, one can become "hooked" on SSRIs without exhibiting drug seeking behaviour or becoming completely non-functional.

For those who have followed the rise and fall of drugs in the marketplace, the SSRIs merely repeat a familiar pattern. The drug companies and regulators had claimed that benzodiazepines were not addictive for well over a decade, but eventually it was admitted that tranquilisers such as diazepam (Valium) were indeed addictive.[16] Glenmullen describes a "10–20–30" year pattern typical of side effects of popular psychiatric drugs—ten years for side effects to be identified, twenty years for enough data to accumulate to make the problem undeniable, and then thirty years for bureaucracies of regulatory agencies to make changes.[52] Of course, it still remains to be seen whether the SSRIs will follow this pattern to the same conclusion.

Conclusion

It is often claimed that corporations that are profit driven could not be expected to behave in any other manner than they do. The nature of business demands maximisation of the market share and shareholder value. Pharmaceutical companies, however, present themselves as responsible producers of health-care products. The very nature of the product involves trust in the science that produced it and an ethical commitment to the well-being of the patients who are their consumers. Despite appearances, nothing of this sort is true in the pharmaceutical industry.

As we have seen above, the serotonin hypothesis sold to consumers of pharmaceuticals is flawed. Making questionable claims for the efficacy and safety of SSRIs involves the pharmaceutical companies in further deception. Expanding the market for these drugs by creating dubious disease categories and then luring vulnerable individuals into SSRI therapy by direct to consumer advertising would represent, if perpetrated by a doctor, an abuse of the trust implicit in the relationship between patient and doctor.

I do not argue that SSRIs should be withdrawn from the market thus depriving clinicians and patients of this therapeutic option. Rather I argue that full disclosure of the data for efficacy and safety is a basic moral obligation of the pharmaceutical industry. Until such data is available to the public, prescribing clinicians and patients are relying on drug promotion rather than rigorous science. When Kant discusses the motivation of acting from duty as opposed to the motivation of self interest, he mentions the case of the merchant who keeps a fixed price for everyone so that a child who buys from him pays the same price as everyone else.[53] The only actions that have moral worth are those done from the motive of duty alone. And similarly, only when the pharmaceutical companies act from the motive of duty in fully disclosing all information they possess about the risks and benefits of their drugs do their actions have any moral worth.

The SSRI marketing story provides a lens through which we can view a much larger problem. The integrity of medicine is endangered by an industry that profits from illness and distorts the process of scientific inquiry by marketing strategy, public relations campaigns, and the sheer power of buying influence in high places. The House of Commons health committee in the UK has made the point: "It is not in the long-term interest of industry for prescribers and the public to lose faith in it. We need an industry which is led by the values of scientists not those of its marketing force" (House of Commons health committee,[23] p 6). Medicine desperately needs to win back the territory lost to business. If and when it does, it is not likely to be a result of industry and government regulators facing up to the problems, but rather a matter of the sheer weight of legal actions filed by victims and public outcry about the moral concerns of the sort raised in this paper.

References

1. Healy D. *The antidepressant era.* Cambridge: Harvard University Press, 1997: 155– 69.
2. Healy D. *The psychopharmacologists* [vols 1 and 3]. London: Altman, 2000.
3. Ashcroft GW, Sharman DF. 5-Hydroxyindoles in human cerebrospinal fluids. *Nature* 1960;**186**:1050–1.

4. Ashcroft GW, Crawford TBB, Stanton JB, *et al.* 5-Hydroxyindole compounds in the cerebrospinal fluid of patients with psychiatric or neurological diseases. *Lancet* 1966;**2**:1049–52.

5. Ashcroft GW, Eccleston D, Murry LG, *et al.* Modified amine hypothesis for the aetiology of affective illness. *Lancet* 1972;**2**:573–7.

6. Asberg M, Eriksson B, Martensson B, *et al.* Therapeutic effects of serotonin uptake inhibitors in depression. *J Clin Psychiatry* 1986;**47**(suppl 4): 23–35S.

7. Kramer PD. *Listening to prozac.* New York: Penguin Books, 1993, especially ch 3.

8. Healy D. *Let them eat Prozac: the unhealthy relationship between the pharmaceutical industry and depression.* Toronto: James Lorimer, 2003.

9. Ashcroft G. The receptor enters psychiatry. In: Healy D, eds. *The psychopharmacologists* [vol 3]. London: Arnold, 2000:194.

10. Healy D. The structure of psychopharmacological revolutions. *Psychiatr Dev* 1987;**4**:349–76.

11. Antonuccio DO, Burns DD, Donton WG. Antidepressants: a triumph of marketing over science? *Prevention & Treatment.* . . .

12. Flores BH, Musselman DL, DeBattista C, *et al.* Biology of mood disorders. In: Schatzberg AF, Nameroff CB, eds. *Textbook of psychopharmacology* [3rd ed]. Washington DC: American Psychatric Publishing, 2004:718.

13. Nemeroff CB. The neurobiology of depression. *Scientific American* 1998; **278**:2–9.

14. Healy D. Psychopharmacology and the government of the self. . . .

15. Smith DC. Antidepressant efficacy. *Ethical Hum Sci Serv* 2000;**2/3**:215–16.

16. Medawar C. The antidepressant web: marketing depression and making medicines work. *Int J Risk Safety Med* 1997;**10**:86–91.

17. Kirsch I, Moore TJ, Scoboria A, *et al.* The emperor's new drugs: an analysis of antidepressant medication data submitted to the US Food and Drug Administration. *Prevention and Treatment.* . . .

18. Carroll BJ. Sertraline and the Cheshire cat in geriatric depression. *AM J Psychiatry* 2004;**161**:759.

19. Kirsch I, Moncrieff J. Efficacy of antidepressants in adults. *BMJ* 2005;**331**:155–7.

20. Bodenheimer T. Uneasy alliance: clinical investigators and the pharmaceutical industry. *N Engl J Med* 2000;**342**:1539– 44 at 1541.

21. Whittington CJ, Kendall T, Fonagy P, *et al.* Selective serotonin reuptake inhibitors in childhood depression: systematic review of published versus unpublished data. *Lancet* 2004;**363**:1341–5.

22. Angell M. *The truth about the drug companies: how they deceive us and what to do about it.* New York: Random House, 2004:125.

23. House of Commons Health Committee. *The influence of the pharmaceutical industry vol 1.* London: The Stationery Office, 2005:100.

24. Wolfe SM. Profitably inventing new diseases. *Health Letter;* 2003;**19**:2–3.

25. Moynihan R, Cassels A. *Selling sickness: how the world's biggest pharmaceutical companies are turning us all into patients.* New York: Nation, 2005.

26. *SmithKlineBeecham's business plan guide December 1 1997—May 31, 1998.* . . .

27. Davidoff F, DeAngelis CD, Drazen JM, *et al.* Sponsorship, authorship, and accountability. *N Engl J Med* 2001;**345**:825–7.

28. Flanagin A, Carey LA, Fontanarosa PB, *et al.* Honorary authors and ghost authors in peer reviewed medical journals. *JAMA* 1998;**280**:222–4.

29. Healy D, Cattell D. Interface between authorship, industry and science in the domain of therapeutics. *Br J Psychiatry* 2003;**183**:22–7.

30. McHenry L. On the origin of great ideas: science in the age of big pharma. *Hastings Cent Rep* 2005;**35**:17–19.

31. Flynn P. *House of Commons official report:* col 1038. . . .

32. Teicher MH, Glod C, Cole JO. Suicidal preoccupation during fluoxetine treatment. *Am J Psychiatry* 1990;**147**:1380–1.

33. Masand P, Gupata S, Dewan M. Suicidal ideation related to fluoxetine treatment. *N Engl J Med* 1991;**324**:420.

34. LaPorta L. Sertraline-induced akathisia. *J Clin Psychopharmacology* 1993; **13**:219–20.

35. Healy D, Langmack C, Savage M. Suicide in the course of treatment of depression. *J Clin Psychopharmacology* 1999;**13**:94–9.

36. Breggin PR. *Toxic psychiatry: why therapy, empathy and love must replace the drugs, electroshock, and biochemical theories of the "new psychiatry."* New York: St Martin's Press, 1991:167.

37. Maris RRM. Suicide and neuropsychiatric adverse effects of SSRI medications: methodological issues. . . .

38. . . .

39. . . .

40. Cipriani A, Barbui C, Geddes JR. Suicide, depression, and antidepressants. *BMJ* 2005;**330**:373– 4.

41. Martinez C, Riebrock S, Wise L, *et al.* Antidepressant treatment and the risk of fatal and non-fatal self harm in first episode depression: nested case control study. *BMJ* 2005;**330**:389–93.

42. Kahn A, Warner HA, Brown WA. Symptom reduction and suicide risk in patients treated with placebo in antidepressant clinical trials. *Arch Gen Psychiatry* 2000;**57**:311–17.

43. Khan A, Khan S, Kolts R, *et al.* Suicide rates in clinical trials of SSRIs, other antidepressants, and placebo: an analysis of FDA reports. *Am J Psychiatry* 2003;**160**:790–2.

44. Gunnell D, Saperia J, Ashby D. Selective serotonin reuptake inhibitors (SSRIs) and suicide in adults: meta-analysis of drug company data from placebo controlled, randomised controlled trials submitted to the MHRA's safety review. *BMJ* 2005;**330**:385– 8.

45. Fergusson D, Doucette S, Glass KC, *et al.* Association between suicide attempts and selective serotonin reuptake inhibitors: systematic review of randomised controlled trials. *BMJ* 2005;**330**:396–9.

46. Aursnes I, Tvete IF, Goasemyr J, *et al.* Suicide attempts in clinical trials with paroxetine randomised against placebo. *BMC Medicine* 2005;**3**:14.

47. Nordeng H, Lindemann R, Perminov KV, *et al.* Neonatal withdrawal syndrome after in utero exposure to selective serotonin reuptake inhibitors. *Acta Poediatr* 2001;**90**:288–91.

48. Sanz EJ, De-las-Cuevas C, Kiuru A, *et al.* Selective serotonin reuptake inhibitors in pregnant women and neonatal withdrawal syndrome: a database analysis. *Lancet* 2005;**365**:482–7.

49. Medawar C, Hardon A. Medicines out of control? *Antidepressants and the conspiracy of goodwill.* Amsterdam: Aksant Academic Press, 2004:84.

50. American Psychiatric Association. *Diagnostic and statistical manual of mental disorders* [4th ed]. Washington, DC: APA, 2000:192–9.

51. Sykes JB. *The concise Oxford dictionary of current English.* Oxford: Clarendon Press, 1984:11.

52. Glenmullen J. *The antidepressant solution: a step by step guide to safely overcoming antidepressant withdrawal, dependence and "addiction."* New York: The Free Press, 2005:190–1.

53. Kant I. *The fundamental principles of the metaphysic of morals* [trans Abbott TK]. London: Longmans, Green and Co, 1946:15.

Bruce M. Cohen

Mind and Medicine: Drug Treatments for Psychiatric Illness

Psychiatric Disorders as Medical Illnesses

Psychiatric illnesses are conditions of the brain that lead to alternations in thinking, mood, and behavior. These illnesses are observed in cultures throughout the world and are probably at least as old as human beings. Recognizable features of psychiatric disorders are described in the texts of many early societies, including those of ancient Egypt, Israel, Greece, India, and China. Also ancient are attempts to treat people with disorders of cognition and emotion by what today would be called psychosocial therapies (including counseling, asylum, and exploration of thought) and psychopharmacologic therapies (that is, plant products or other drugs).

The most common symptoms experienced by those with psychiatric disorders fall into a few categories. Mood may be abnormally high or low. Irritability and anxiety are often felt. Thinking, and its expression in speech and other behaviors, may be illogical. Delusions, which are patently false beliefs not shared by others, can be present. Obsessions and compulsions may continuously haunt the sufferers. Prominent perceptual abnormalities may occur, the most common being hallucinations, which are false sensory percepts, usually the hearing of voices within one's own head. Finally, psychiatric disorders often are associated with changes of physiologic rhythms and the basic drives of life, with disrupted sleep, appetite, and energy.

Some symptoms of psychiatric disorders, notably depression or anxiety, seem to be extremes of normal states, just as hypertension is an extreme of blood pressure. Others, such as hallucinations, appear more distinct from normal experience, although most of us have occasionally thought we heard a voice when we were alone or saw a person when no one was there. These normal experiences are fleeting, while the symptoms of psychiatric disorders last from months to a lifetime.

Symptoms rarely occur alone. Rather, they tend to occur in recognizable clusters, called syndromes. Common syndromes in internal medicine include the pneumonias or congestive heart failure. The most common psychiatric syndromes include the depressive disorders, the anxiety disorders, and the

From *Social Research*, vol. 68, no. 3, Fall 2001, pp. 697–713. Copyright © 2001 by New School for Social Research. Reprinted by permission.

psychotic disorders, such as bipolar disorders and schizophrenia. It is the latter that are most frequently associated with hallucinations and delusions.

Psychiatric disorders are medical illnesses. Like other medical disorders, they are due to the interaction of inherited and environmental factors that, together, lead to the development of illness. While the specific genes that predispose to psychiatric disorders have not yet been identified, the presence of these genes is thoroughly and convincingly documented from family, twin, and adoption studies. Similarly, subtle but repeatedly observed differences in the brain between those with and without psychiatric disorders are now documented by post-mortem studies and observation of the brain during life using technologies such as magnetic resonance imaging (MRI), positron emission tomography (PET), and single photon emission computerized tomography (SPECT).

The explicit causes of most current cases of psychiatric disorder are not yet known, but numerous medical conditions that can cause psychiatric disorders are well documented. Over a century ago, many of the patients in psychiatric hospitals had infectious, nutritional, toxic, and hormonal conditions, such as syphilis, pellagra, lead poisoning, and hyper- and hypothyroidism which affected their thinking and mood. Today these medical disorders have responded well to preventive measures, based on diet and environmental advances, or to treatment with medications.

Psychiatric illnesses of unknown cause also tend to respond well to treatment, with success rates as high as those seen in other branches of medicine. Psychotherapeutic medication can restore to normal aspects of consciousness, including feeling, perception, and cognition. For this reason medication is at the core of treatment for most psychiatric disorders.

Drugs and the Brain

Taking drugs with the intent to change aspects of consciousness is very old and quite common. Alcohol, cocaine, opiates, and peyote have been used for thousands of years. These drugs appear to act on systems built into the brain to modulate behaviors associated with eating, sleeping, sexual activity, or other drives and rewards. Co-opting receptors and processes developed to respond to internal chemical messages, these external agents alter arousal, attention, emotional state, and thinking.

Foods can have effects on mood and cognition as well. Deficiencies of some nutrients, as noted, can lead to psychiatric illness, and the oldest recreational drugs are in essence food products or derivatives. Based on this history, numerous nutritional substances are currently being examined as possible treatments for psychiatric disorders.

Hormones, including thyroid, adrenal, and sex hormones, can have profound effects on brain function, drive, cognition, and feelings, and hormonal abnormalities, as was noted, can cause psychiatric symptoms. Hormone replacement—using hormones as drugs—can restore or, occasionally, disrupt mental function.

Further links between physiology, pharmacology, and psychology are evident from the effects of drugs given for purposes unrelated to brain function, but with unwanted actions there. For example, older antihistamines for allergies, which reached receptors throughout the body (including the brain), affected alertness, concentration, and memory. Newer agents were designed that were not absorbed into brain and, therefore, have few mental side effects.

These examples provide compelling evidence that drugs can change all the aspects of consciousness. This knowledge has been used for religious, recreational, and medicinal purposes for generations. With the revolution in organic chemistry, biochemistry, and molecular biology over the past hundred years, the development of new drugs targeted to specific illnesses, such as psychiatric disorders, has become more sophisticated and more successful.

Medication for Psychiatric Disorders

Medicinal treatments for psychiatric disorders are used throughout the world and have their origins in many ancient societies. The oldest documented of these medicinal preparations, made from the plant *Rauwolfia serpentina*, appears in Ayurmedic texts of India over 2,000 years ago. It was recommended for several medical illnesses including those whose description sounds much like the psychotic disorders: the schizophrenias and bipolar disorders. The active ingredient of this preparation was likely reserpine, which was isolated in the 1930s and used briefly but effectively to treat psychotic disorders in the 1950s. It was superseded by easier to use agents, the neuroleptic antipsychotic drugs (which will be described later), in the same decade.

Another "modern" treatment for psychiatric disorders, lithium, prescribed to patients with bipolar disorders, may also have been used in ancient times. Lithium is an element related to sodium and potassium. Like these elements, it most frequently occurs in nature as a salt, often appearing in spring waters. Between A.D. 100 and 300, during the Roman Empire, Arataeus, a physician from Cappadocia, and Soranus of Ephesus recommended waters from particular alkaline springs, which probably contained lithium, for the treatment of mania. While dose could not have been carefully controlled, their advice accords with the use of lithium today.

Eastern Hemisphere plant preparations containing opium have been used to alleviate pain for centuries, and in the late nineteenth and early twentieth centuries, opiate compounds isolated from these plants were used with limited efficacy for the treatment of psychotic disorders and severe depression. Similarly, coca leaves from the Western Hemisphere, chewed by generations for their energizing effects, yielded cocaine, used by Freud and others around 1900 for its stimulating and short-lived antidepressant effects.

None of these older medicinal preparations had strong and reliable enough therapeutic effects or tolerable toxicity for the routine treatment of patients with psychiatric disorders. Breakthroughs leading to the discovery of drugs currently in use, which have good safety and efficacy, occurred in the 1950s, with the introduction of the so-called tricyclic antidepressants, such as Tofranil (imipramine); neuroleptic antipsychotic drugs, such as Thorazine (chlorpromazine); and benzodiazepine anti-anxiety agents, such as Librium (chlordiazepoxide). These drugs revolutionized the care of people with psychiatric disorders, leading to the release of many patients from institutions and the return of others to productive lives.

These first modern medications were followed by many copies and by newer generations of psychotherapeutic drugs in the 1980s and 1990s. Examples include the serotonin specific re-uptake inhibitors, such as Prozac (fluoxetine), for depression; the atypical antipsychotic agents, such as Zyprex (olanzapine), for psychotic disorders; and the mood-stabilizing anticonvulsants, such as Depakote (valproate), for bipolar disorder.

The efficacy of these medications has been proved in numerous studies, including a large number of double-blind, placebo-controlled trials in which the drug being tested is compared to inactive substances, as well as compounds that have effects on the brain, such as sedation, that are not believed to address the key symptoms of psychiatric disorders. Neither the clinical investigator nor the patient knows which drug the patient is receiving. Few drugs in medicine have ever been as thoroughly tested and proven effective.

The proper use of these drugs leads to the successful treatment of most people with depressive disorders, anxiety disorders, schizophrenias and bipolar disorders, restoring them to their proper state of mind. As with all medications, there are side effects as well as therapeutic effects, but with careful use, beneficial effects far outweigh side effects for most people. The physical mechanisms underlying these drug effects and the return to normal consciousness are beginning to be understood, providing important information on the nature of psychiatric disorders and the relationship between brain and psyche.

Medications for Anxiety

In a lifetime, nearly one in six of us will experience a disorder in which anxiety is a prominent symptom. Current anti-anxiety medications, or anxiolytics, grew out of a recognition that alcohol, prized for the comfort and disinhibition it brought, could ease feelings of anxiety. Alcohol relieves distress or discomfort whether or not these feelings are pathological, as indicated by its common social use to relax couples on an evening out or large groups at a party.

Alcohol can provide some relief for those with disorders whose cardinal symptoms include anxiety. In these illnesses, feelings of anxiety may be nearly constant or may occur in attacks of panic. In either case the degree of anxiety is out of proportion to and may even bear no relationship to life events. Unfortunately, the relief is limited by the fast metabolism of alcohol and the tendency of the body to become tolerant to its effects. In fact, as the immediate action of alcohol fades, and as tolerance develops, those who drink for recreation or to medicate themselves for anxiety can find that a physiologic rebound opposite to the effects of alcohol occurs, and they become even more anxious.

From about 1900 on, recognizing the beneficial and toxic effects of alcohol, repeated attempts have been made to find chemical agents that share the calming or sedative effects of alcohol but lack its addictive qualities and the rebound that follows its use. These efforts have been only partially successful.

Early attempts to find safer and more effective compounds than alcohol for anxiety disorders and sedation led to discovery of the barbiturates. They were successful in producing anxiolytic effects, but toxic doses have tended to be close to therapeutic doses and tolerance and addiction are common. Barbiturates are still used for epilepsy and for sedation, but rarely in psychiatry for anxiety disorders.

In the 1950s, derivatives of mephenesin, chemically related to barbiturates, were developed and marketed under the names Miltown (meprobamate) and Equanil (tybamate). All these medications were superseded by compounds called benzodiazepine anxiolytics, which were developed in the late 1950s. The earliest of these, Librium (chlordiazepoxide) and Valium (diazepam), became exceedingly popular drugs, were felt to have low risk of poisoning and to be associated only rarely with tolerance and addiction.

Today, a large number of long- and short-acting benzodiazepines are on the market as anxiolytics and sedatives. They are good and effective drugs that are neither as dangerous as alcohol or barbiturates nor as safe as early hopes and claims suggested. Tolerance is common and addiction not rare.

Like alcohol, benzodiazepines reduce anxiety whether or not an individual has an anxiety disorder. Used continuously, their anxiolytic effect tends to fade. While they often blunt the attacks or nagging presence of pathological anxiety, they rarely eliminate these symptoms entirely when used alone. Nevertheless, their powerful and consistent ability to reduce anxiety soon after they are ingested or injected suggests they may work by altering the very brain mechanisms that mediate anxiety.

Following years of fruitful study, the likely site through which the benzodiazepine anxiolytics have their clinical effects is known. Nerve cells (called neurons in the brain) process signals by both electrical and chemical means. Each cell receives chemical messages from other cells, sends electrical messages down its length, and secretes its own chemical compound or compounds, called neurotransmitters, on the cells it contacts. Neurotransmitters produce their effects by binding to specific proteins, called neurotransmitter receptors, which induce a cascade of chemical reactions in the cell to stimulate or reduce electrical activity each time a chemical signal is received.

Eighty to ninety percent of the neuron to neuron contacts in the brain involve one of two neurotransmitters: gama amino butyric acid (GABA) or glutamate. Glutamate is an excitatory neurotransmitter; its message makes a neuron more likely to fire an electrical signal. GABA is an inhibitory neurotransmitter; it quiets cells, making them less likely to fire a signal.

Benzodiazepines attach to some of the same receptors that bind the neurotransmitter GABA and change their characteristics, making them more sensitive to GABA. In this way, benzodiazepines amplify the GABA signal, shifting the overall balance between excitation and inhibition in the brain toward inhibition. At low doses, benzodiazepines may produce their calming anti-anxiety effect through this shift to inhibition. At high doses, inhibition becomes great enough to induce sleep, or at doses higher still, to cause coma.

GABA is used as a neurotransmitter throughout the brain, and benzodiazepines enhance its inhibitory effects globally in the brain. It is not known if such a widespread effect is needed for relief of anxiety in humans, or if a local effect in specific regions would suffice. Medical technology is not yet ready routinely to deliver drugs solely to where they are needed. This is a common problem in using drugs in patients. Brain cells can deliver chemicals precisely, but medications go throughout the body, both to where they are needed and where they are not.

Medication for Depression

Like anxiety disorders, depressive disorders are quite common, affecting over one in eight of the population, worldwide, in a lifetime. Symptoms of depression and anxiety often occur together, and for many people, so-called antidepressant drugs are a better long-term treatment of anxiety than are the anxiolytic drugs. In chemical structure and mechanism of action, however, the two classes of drugs are unrelated.

One might think that antidepressant drugs would be derived from stimulants, such as the amphetamines. Stimulants can raise mood in almost anyone and can be helpful in some cases of depression. Unfortunately, they are more often not helpful and even when they improve mood, only do so transiently. Like anxiolytics, their short-lived effects can lead to tolerance, craving, and addiction.

The earliest current antidepressants were discovered serendipitously in patients with tuberculosis who were treated with an antibiotic called iproniazide. Some of the patients not only had TB, but were severely depressed, until they received iproniazide. Tests in patients without TB, who suffered from depression, indicated that iproniazide was an effective therapeutic agent in relieving depression and restoring abnormalities of appetite, energy, and sleep that usually accompany this illness.

Pharmacologic studies determined that iproniazide was an inhibitor of an enzyme called monoamine oxidase, which metabolizes, and thereby inactivates, a group of chemical messengers that include norepinephrine (also called noradrenaline), serotonin, and dopamine. Like GABA, these compounds, which chemically are called monoamines, are used in the brain as neurotransmitters. Unlike GABA, the effects of which are rapid, appearing nearly instantaneously and ending as quickly, the effects of the monoamine neurotransmitters are slow by the standards of the brain, lasting seconds or longer once they are released. For this reason, it has been hypothesized that the monoamines set the "tone" of activity by region in the brain.

Inhibiting the breakdown of monoamines leads to a higher concentration of these neurotransmitters in the brain, which might be the means by which iproniazide relieved depression. Evidence supportive of this speculation arises from the mechanisms by which stimulants act to more transiently elevate mood. Specifically, stimulants cause the release of monoamine neurotransmitters in the brain; block the re-uptake of these neurotransmitters back into the cell that released them; or mimic the effects of the monoamine neurotransmitters at the receptor proteins that recognize their presence. Based on the success of iproniazide, more monoamine oxidase inhibitor drugs (all called by the acronym MAOI) like iproniazid were developed, tested, and proved to be effective antidepressants.

Soon after the introduction of MAOIs, a new and different class of antidepressants was independently discovered. These compounds were observed in a search for agents to treat psychotic disorders, such as schizophrenia. In the early 1950s, the first modern drugs for psychosis became available. They had a structure containing three rings of carbon and occasional nitrogen, sulfur, and oxygen atoms. Many such compounds were designed, synthesized, and tested, and a clever observer noted that one compound in particular, while it lacked effects to treat psychosis, seemed to brighten mood substantially in depressed patients. The compound, imipramine, proved to be a greatly successful antidepressant, still on the market over 40 years later. Other compounds structurally similar, with three rings and, therefore, called tricyclic antidepressants, or TCAs, were developed to treat depression. Like the MAOIs, they relieve all the symptoms of depression, not just the dysphoric mood of patients.

Also like MAOIs, TCAs appear to produce their effects through actions on monoamine neurotransmitters. Specifically, they inhibit the uptake of norepinephrine back into the cells that released it. This increases the amount of norepinephrine interacting with neurons and prolongs the time over which norepinephrine acts. They have a similar, but weaker, effect on the re-uptake of serotonin. They have little effect on dopamine, which is the reverse of stimulants, which have their greatest effects on dopamine release and re-uptake.

In the late 1980s, based on the success of the TCAs but searching for a new class of antidepressants, pharmaceutical companies designed drugs that preferentially blocked the re-uptake of serotonin, rather than norepinephrine. The first of these so-called serotonin-specific re-uptake inhibitors, or SSRIs, was Prozac (fluoxetine). It and other SSRIs developed later have been extraordinarily successful, in part because they have different side effects than the TCAs, being safer and seeming to be more comfortable for most people to take. This comfort has led to an increase in the prescription of antidepressants by primary care practitioners as well as psychiatrists, with many newly treated individuals feeling relief from depression and anxiety.

Antidepressants, whether MAOIs, TCAs, or SSRIs, do not seem to benefit those who do not have symptoms of a depressive disorder. The broad use and success of the SSRIs has suggested to some that they have mood-elevating effects in people whether or not the people treated are ill. This is unlikely, as most healthy people only suffer side effects from antidepressants. Rather, as depression is a common illness, like colds in children or high blood pressure in the elderly, and physicians more readily prescribe SSRIs than previous antidepressants, more people with depressive disorders, including milder disorders, are being treated and benefiting from treatment.

Looking to why the brain responds to antidepressants, the available evidence points strongly to drug effects mediated through the monoamine neurotransmitters norepinephrine and serotonin. Two classes of drugs, the MAOIs and the TCAs, discovered independently and serendipitously, have potent actions affecting these chemical signals. A third class of agents, the SSRIs, was developed on the theory that increased serotonin messages would relieve depression. Their success helps confirm the theory. Due to crosstalk, changes in either the serotonin or norepinephrine neurotransmitter system lead to changes in the other system. Furthermore, a role for both norepinephrine and serotonin is suggested by the fact that individual antidepressant drugs whose potency is specific to one or the other monoamine appear equally efficacious in the majority of people.

It is important to note that, while drug effects on serotonin and nore-pinephrine can relieve depression, this outcome is not direct and immediate. Unlike benzodiazepines for anxiety, or aspirin for headache, the therapeutic effects of antidepressants do not occur in minutes or hours. They require weeks of continued use. Somehow, the brain changes its state in response to the continued presence of drug and the consequent higher levels of monoamine neurotransmitters. Brain-imaging studies suggest that depression fades as regional brain activity changes in response to altered levels of monoamine neurotransmitters induced by antidepressant drugs.

Medications for Psychosis

Psychotic disorders are among the most disabling of illnesses, disturbing thinking, perception, mood, and their interconnections, and diminishing normal human interactions. Fortunately, modern antipsychotic medications are among the more efficacious treatments in medicine today, reversing all or most symptoms in the majority of people with psychotic disorders. The effect is so dramatic that some have called antipsychotic medications the penicillin of psychiatry.

The two most common psychotic illnesses, the schizophrenias and bipolar disorders, affect over one in one hundred people. They often strike the young and can prevent a normal life or reduce successful people to homelessness. Even milder forms or episodes of psychotic illnesses can disrupt relationships among spouses, relatives, and friends. Despite obvious symptoms, including delusions, hallucinations, disrupted speech and thinking, and disorganized behavior, those in the midst of psychosis often do not realize they are ill. This peculiar lack of insight, even in those who have had multiple episodes of illness and been well in between, is another aspect of the unusual state of mind and awareness accompanying these psychotic disorders.

Many patients understand their illnesses and understand the benefits and risks of treatment. In others, lack of insight leads to considerable discussion and debate between the patient and clinicians. When there is an immediate risk of harm to the patient or others due to the symptoms of illness, medication may be started even if the patient does not accept the need for treatment. This is not common. Occasionally, patients who know medications will ameliorate their symptoms choose not to be treated. This, too, is not common, as the symptoms of psychosis are extremely uncomfortable for most people.

Others observe the symptoms of illness, of course, and for many years physicians have tried to help those with psychotic disorders. Reserpine, given in *Rauwolfia serpentina* or as the isolated chemical, had beneficial effects, but at the risk of dangerously low blood pressure and strong sedation. Opiates were used to calm patients, but had minimal effects on the key symptoms of psychosis.

It was not until the early 1950s that the first specific, well-tolerated and effective medication for psychosis, Thorazine (chlorpromazine), was introduced. This medication, and others modeled after it, were so effective that the number of patients with psychotic disorders in hospitals began to drop substantially. With the development of even newer agents that had similar therapeutic effects but fewer side effects, decreases in hospitalization continue, despite a growing population.

The antipsychotic medications were discovered by design, partly from modifying known sedatives, but mostly by looking for agents related to anesthetics, which produced a profound calming effect but not loss of consciousness. The antipsychotic drugs, however, are not all sedatives and are not, as they were once called, major tranquilizers. Some are sedative and some not. Some reduce anxiety, and some can increase it. All work similarly in reducing the symptoms of psychosis, including disrupted thinking, mood, perception, and behavior. Only one, Clozaril (clozapine), may be on average modestly more efficacious than other antipsychotic drugs.

Those without psychotic disorders gain nothing but side effects from these drugs. The drugs have little effect on people with odd or idiosyncratic ideas and behaviors, unless they have the symptoms of schizophrenia or bipolar disorder.

Given that antipsychotic medications all tend to produce a similar therapeutic outcome and were designed to be pharmacologically similar to chlorpromazine, the original antipsychotic drug, it is not surprising that they share common mechanisms of action at a molecular level. Specifically, all antipsychotic drugs block signals at some but not all receptors for the chemical messengers dopamine, norepinephrine, and serotonin.

By blocking signals at these receptors, the antipsychotic drugs produce effects in several key areas of the brain. They change activity in the nucleus accumbens, which is involved, in part, in mediating a sense of reward; the amygdala, which is involved in determining a sense of threat, disquiet, or safety; the thalamus, which appears to be involved in coordinating aspects of thought, perception, and emotion; and the prefrontal cortex, which is the most developed of all areas of the human brain and is involved in attention, decision making, and keeping thoughts in consciousness.

Like the antidepressants, therapeutic effects of antipsychotic drugs can take weeks to develop. How the immediate effects of the antipsychotic drugs become longer term effects is not known. However, there is growing evidence that modulation of signals through the monoamine receptors affected by antipsychotic drugs leads to changes in the activity of GABAergic and glutaminergic cells, which mediate much of the function of the brain.

It is not surprising that even though the antipsychotic drugs have effects on only a few specific receptors in the brain, their use would change activity at many sites. Neurons that employ dopamine, norepinephrine, and serotonin as their chemical messengers are few, but they contact vast numbers of cells throughout the brain. In addition, because cells in the brain are interconnected in a dense network, a limited direct effect can translate into a broad distributed effect.

Most well-described functions of the brain, such as the processing of visual information or the control of movement, are handled by cells distributed across many different, but sometimes overlapping, areas of the brain. It is possible, and even likely, that emotions and thoughts are also a consequence of changes in the activity of specific groups of cells linked to one another but representing different aspects of feeling or cognition and existing in different locations within the brain. The wide distribution of neurons responding to antipsychotic drugs, and mediating their effects, illustrates this point.

Psychiatric Disorders, Psychotherapeutic Medication, and Consciousness

Medications are a key component of the treatment of most psychiatric disorders. They are not, of course, the sole treatment. Proper care requires attention to the psychological and social aspects of illness. These may represent environmental stressors that, unaddressed, can trigger illness in those predisposed. Also, psychological and social problems are frequently consequences of the disruption of mood, thought, and behavior caused by illness. Patients need support in reconstituting their lives and sense of self once their symptoms fade.

It is remarkable, however, just how powerful medications are in relieving the symptoms of psychiatric disorders. Along with genetic, structural, and functional evidence, the effects of drugs are compelling findings suggesting that psychiatric illnesses arise from abnormal activity of the brain; that is, they are medical disorders of the brain.

Arguments can be made for and against the recreational use of drugs. Society accepts some, such as alcohol, and not others, such as marijuana. By comparison, there is little basis for argument about the treatment of psychiatric disorders with medication. For most people, the benefits clearly outweigh the risks.

The effects of psychotherapeutic medications also speak to questions beyond that of the origin and nature of psychiatric disorders. They speak to the nature of consciousness.

Drugs can disturb all aspects of consciousness and drugs can restore aspects of consciousness. As drugs act on the structure, chemistry, and electrical activity of the brain, it is logical to conclude that all aspects of consciousness depend on physical states of the brain.

Evidence is growing as to the precise molecular sites at which drugs act, as well as on the specific changes that occur in cellular metabolism and the state of neural circuits during drug treatment. Pharmacologic studies point to particular regions of the brain or particular distributed groups of nerve cells as being involved in mediating mood, awareness, cognition, or the integration of experience. Studies of the consequences of lesions associated with epilepsy, tumors, strokes, and trauma also suggest that particular parts of the brain are necessary, if not sufficient, to determine aspects of consciousness. Results from pharmacology and pathology agree strongly on which areas are associated with which aspects of consciousness.

No simple connections are likely to exist between a molecule and a thought or a nerve cell and a mood. However, it is reasonable to expect that the state of networks of nerve cells in the brain may be closely related to conscious states of thinking or feeling. Drugs and medications can change the patterns of firing in neural circuits and the tone of neural activity in the brain. By doing so, they can alter those aspects of consciousness that make us most human. The study of drug effects will remain an important tool for designing and testing models of how mind may arise from brain. Equally or more important, the use of currently available drugs and the arrival of new drugs under development will continue to provide good treatments, and someday cures, for the devastating illnesses classified as psychiatric disorders.

POSTSCRIPT

Are Psychotherapeutic Drugs Overprescribed for Treating Mental Illness?

Many mental health practitioners maintain that psychotherapeutic drugs can be effective in treating the majority of people suffering from mental illness. However, there is a sharp disagreement about whether these drugs are prescribed too readily and whether they are taking the place of traditional talk therapy. Of course, this debate does not need focus on which type of treatment is best. Many people receive both drug therapy and psychotherapy. In addition, it has been shown that drug therapy and psychotherapy work best in conjunction with each other.

The debate regarding psychotherapeutic drugs has spurned other concerns. Should they be prescribed for common problems that people encounter on a daily basis, such as stress, feelings of anxiety, phobias, shyness, and obsessive-compulsive behavior? Many people experience these problems. A certain degree of anxiety, shyness, and compulsivity is not unusual. Should people rid themselves of these conditions even if they may incur adverse side effects?

The pursuit of happiness seems to be of paramount importance in our society. Yet, can one find happiness in a pill? Should one turn to pills to find happiness? Do these drugs represent a quick and easy fix and is it ethical to chemically alter an individual's mood and personality in order to be happy? Will psychopharmacology replace traditional psychotherapy? Is the rapid growth of antidepressant drugs a well-conceived promotion on the part of pharmaceutical companies? In a society that values solving problems quickly and easily, these drugs seem to effectively fulfill a need. However, do their advantages outweigh their disadvantages?

A popular slogan many years ago referred to "better living through chemistry." If a drug is available that will make people happier, more confident, and more socially adept, should that drug be available for people who would derive some degree of benefit from it? One concern is that some individuals may rely on drugs to remedy many of their problems rather than to work through those issues that caused the problems in the first place. It is much easier to drop a pill than to engage in self-exploration and self-reflection. One could make some analogy between psychotherapeutic drugs and other drugs. Many people now use alcohol, tobacco, over-the-counter medicines, and illegal drugs to cope with life's problems. Drugs, whether they are legal or illegal, are used increasingly for dealing with our daily problems.

One article that looked at the extensiveness of mood disorders is "Prevalence and Effects of Mood Disorders on Work Performance in a Nationally

Representative Sample of U.S. Workers," by Ronald Kessler and others (*American Journal of Psychiatry*, September 2006). Algis Valiunas comments on the role of drugs and the role of therapy in treating mental illness in "Sadness, Gladness—and Serotonin" (*Commentary*, January 2006). *Consumer Reports* magazine (October 2004) assessed the advantages of drug therapy versus talk therapy and found that they work best when used in conjunction. Gordon Marino argues against psychotherapeutic drugs in "Altered States: Pills Alone Won't Cure the Blues" (*Commonweal*, May 21, 2004). The negative publicity regarding psychotherapeutic drugs may prevent young people from deriving their benefits according to Nancy Shute in "Teens, Drugs, and Sadness" (*U.S. News and World Report*, August 30, 2004). In his article "Is It Really Our Chemicals That Need Balancing?" (*Journal of American College Health*, July 2002), Christopher Bailey argues that society is falling into the trap of making minor problems into mental illnesses.

ISSUE 11

Is Caffeine a Health Risk?

YES: Nancy Shute, from "Over the Limit? Americans Young and Old Crave High-Octane Fuel, and Doctors Are Jittery," *U.S. News and World Report* (April 23, 2007)

NO: Sally Satel, from "Is Caffeine Addictive? A Review of the Literature," *American Journal of Drug and Alcohol Abuse* (November 2006)

ISSUE SUMMARY

YES: Writer Nancy Shute contends that many individuals, especially young people, are consuming high levels of caffeine to make up for their lack of rest. Although Shute acknowledges that caffeine has some benefits, she also notes that caffeine may cause anxiety, jitteriness, and heart palpitations as well as increase the risk of miscarriages and low–birth-weight babies.

NO: According to medical doctor Sally Satel, caffeine may have addictive qualities, but its dangers are overstated. Caffeine's addictive qualities are modest. Most caffeine users are able to moderate their consumption of caffeine. Headaches are one byproduct of caffeine cessation. Very few people consume caffeine compulsively. Moreover, individuals who have difficulty moderating their caffeine use often have other psychiatric problems.

Caffeine is one of the most widely consumed legal drugs in the world. In the United States, more than 9 out of every 10 people drink some type of caffeinated beverage, mostly for its stimulating effects. Caffeine elevates mood, reduces fatigue, increases work capacity, and stimulates respiration. Caffeine often provides the lift people need to start the day. Although many people associate caffeine primarily with coffee, caffeine also is found in numerous soft drinks, over-the-counter medications, chocolate, and tea. Because caffeinated drinks are common in society and there are very few legal controls regarding the use of caffeine, its physical and psychological effects frequently are overlooked, ignored, or minimized.

In recent years coffee consumption has declined; however, the amount of caffeine being consumed has not declined appreciably because of the increase in caffeinated soft drink consumption. To reduce their levels of caffeine intake, many people have switched to decaffeinated drinks and coffee. Although this results in less caffeine intake, decaffeinated coffee still contains small amounts of caffeine.

Research studies evaluating the effects of caffeine consumption on personal health date back to the 1960s. In particular, the medical community has conducted numerous studies to determine whether or not there is a relationship between caffeine consumption and cardiovascular disease, because heart disease is the leading cause of death in many countries, including the United States. In spite of the many studies on this subject, a clear relationship between heart disease and caffeine is not yet apparent. Studies have yielded conflicting results. Rather than clarifying the debate regarding the consequences of caffeine, the research only added to the confusion. As a result, studies suggesting that there is a connection between caffeine consumption and adverse physical and psychological effects have come under scrutiny by both the general public and health professions.

One serious limitation of previous research indicating that caffeine does have deleterious effects is that the research focused primarily on coffee use. There may be other ingredients in coffee besides caffeine that produce harmful effects. Moreover, an increasing percentage of the caffeine being consumed comes from other sources, such as soft drinks, tea, chocolate, antihistamines, and diet pills. Therefore, caffeine studies involving only coffee are not truly representative of the amount of caffeine that people ingest.

Another important criticism of caffeine research, especially studies linking caffeine use and heart disease, is gender bias. Until recently, research has focused primarily on the caffeine consumption of men. The bias in medical research is not limited to caffeine studies; men have traditionally been the primary group studied regarding many facets of health. This situation is changing. There is increasing research into the potential consequences of caffeine use on the fetus and nursing mother.

People who believe that drinking caffeine in moderation does not pose a significant health threat are critical of previous and current studies. This is particularly true of those studies that demonstrate a relationship between caffeine and heart disease. Critics contend that it is difficult to establish a definitive relationship between caffeine and heart disease due to myriad confounding variables. For example, cardiovascular disease has been linked to family history, a sedentary lifestyle, cigarette smoking, obesity, fat intake, and stress. Many individuals who consume large amounts of coffee also smoke cigarettes, drink alcohol, and are hard-driven. Several factors also affect caffeine's excretion from the body. Cigarette smoking increases caffeine metabolization, whereas the use of oral contraceptives and pregnancy slow down metabolization. Therefore, determining the extent to which caffeine use causes heart disease while adjusting for the influence of these other factors is difficult.

In the following selections, Nancy Shute cautions readers about the use of caffeine, even in moderate amounts. Shute claims that caffeine can cause panic and anxiety as well as miscarriages and low birth weight babies. In contrast, Sally Satel casts doubt on the negative effects associated with caffeine intake and believes that the effects of caffeine may not be as harmful as many people speculate.

YES

Nancy Shute

Over the Limit? Americans Young and Old Crave High-Octane Fuel, and Doctors Are Jittery

In the past three years alone, the number of 18-to-24-year-olds who drink coffee daily has doubled, from 16 percent to 31 percent—and some of them go on to pop prescription stimulants such as Adderall or Ritalin for late-night study sessions.

Linleigh Hawk starts the day at 5:30 a.m. by downing her first cup of coffee. She then stops at Starbucks for a grande vanilla skim latte on the way to Winston Churchill High School in Potomac, Md., where she's a senior. At 3 p.m., it's time for a jumbo iced tea to power her through hip-hop dance rehearsals and yearbook meetings. Homework, which often keeps her up past 1 a.m., requires more coffee. "I've got so much to do," she says. "I've got to have the caffeine." The java-fired schedule has paid off, says Hawk: She's been accepted by 15 of her 16 college choices, including first pick Wake Forest.

Hawk may sound like an anomaly, but she isn't. Overworked and sleep-deprived Americans young and old so crave a buzz these days that even alcoholic drinks come loaded with caffeine, and doctors are getting worried. In the past three years alone, the number of 18-to-24-year-olds who drink coffee daily has doubled, from 16 percent to 31 percent—and some of them go on to pop prescription stimulants such as Adderall or Ritalin for late-night study sessions. Energy drinks like Red Bull and Cocaine, with several times the buzz of a can of Coke, have mushroomed into a $3.5 billion-a-year industry.

"l can't go out and keep up with these 20-year-olds without it," says Jeremy Freer, a 29-year-old music teacher from Virginia Beach, Va., of his Saturday-night beverage of choice: vodka with Red Bull. (Partyers can opt instead for the new double espresso-double caffeinated Van Gogh vodka or a Bud Extra, a caffeinated beer.)

Wired

Health experts understand all too well why Americans gotta get wired. People of all ages are chronically sleep deprived, from teens who catch the bus before sunrise to working mothers who report they spend less than six hours a night in bed, according to a poll released in March by the National Sleep Foundation. But we may be pushing the limits of self-medication. Poison control centers and emergency room doctors report increasing numbers of people suffering from the rapid heartbeat and nausea of a caffeine overdose—like the 14-year-old boy who earlier this year showed up at a Minneapolis emergency room in respiratory distress after washing down caffeine pills with energy drinks so he could play video games all night. Instead, he spent the night in the pediatric intensive care unit, intubated, until the caffeine exited his system. They're also seeing more teens and young adults in distress after having bought or "borrowed" stimulant drugs from friends.

And, in the extreme, there are tragedies like that of James Stone, a 19-year-old from Wallingford, Conn., who died last November of cardiac arrest after taking nearly two dozen caffeine pills. His parents say he had been putting in long hours on a job search.

Doctors are particularly troubled to see youngsters forming the caffeine habit, even as toddlers. Children's consumption of soft drinks has doubled in the past 35 years, with sodas supplanting milk. A 2003 study of Columbus, Ohio, middle schoolers found some taking in 800 milligrams of caffeine a day—more than twice the recommended maximum for adults of 300 milligrams. "Their body weight is low," says Wahida Karmally, director of nutrition for the Irving Center for Clinical Research at Columbia University Medical Center. "They can't tolerate as much caffeine as adults."

Since scientists have never studied how caffeine affects growing bodies and brains, children who go through the day guzzling soda after iced tea after energy drink are serving as tiny guinea pigs. "This is something that nobody is looking at carefully," says Nora Volkow, a psychiatrist who directs the National Institute on Drug Abuse. "We really have no idea how it affects development long term."

The appeal to kids of high-octane energy drinks has some officials concerned enough to act. Just last week, the Food and Drug Administration announced it had sent a warning letter to the manufacturer of Cocaine Energy Drink, Redux Beverages LLC of Las Vegas, for marketing the beverage "as an alternative to an illicit street drug." Until last week, the manufacturer's website boasted "Cocaine-instant rush." Hyping the performance enhancements caffeine offers at the time you're introducing the drug to children "is a terrible message. It has implications for drug use in the future," says Roland Griffiths, a professor of behavioral biology at Johns Hopkins University Medical Center who has studied caffeine's effects for more than 30 years.

And last month, Doherty High School in Colorado Springs, Colo., banned a drink called Spike Shooter. Two students were taken to the hospital complaining of nausea, vomiting, and heart palpitations after drinking an 8-ounce can, which packs 300 mg of caffeine—the same as almost four Red Bulls.

For adults, and in reasonable doses—the equivalent of three 8-ounce cups of coffee, six Excedrin Migraine, or a half-dozen 12-ounce colas a day—caffeine has much to recommend it. As the world's most popular habit-forming drug, it fights fatigue, brightens mood, and eases pain while it's forestalling sleep. Test subjects dosed with the amount found in a cup of coffee come out ahead on problem-solving tasks. And by triggering the release of adrenaline to help muscles work harder and longer, caffeine so clearly enhances athletic perform- ance that until 2004 it was considered a controlled substance by the Interna- tional Olympic Committee. Supercaffeinated energy drinks like Redline RTD are marketed to bodybuilders.

Elixir of Life

The latest findings on coffee suggest that it even staves off disease. Caffeine reduces the risk of Parkinson's disease, for example, by blocking receptors for adenosine, a neurotransmitter that plays a role in motor function. It is now being tested as a Parkinson's treatment. Caffeine also heads off migraines by contracting blood vessels in the brain.

And probably because coffee, like blueberries and broccoli, contains potent antioxidants, it appears to reduce the risk of colon cancer, gallstones, and liver cancer, among other illnesses. In 2005, Harvard researchers found that drinking six cups of coffee or more daily cut the risk of getting type 2 dia- betes by half in men and 30 percent in women. One study of 80,000 women showed that those who drank more than two or three cups of coffee daily reduced their risk of suicide over 10 years by a third.

Alas, that glorious rush of energy isn't entirely benign. Numerous stud- ies have found no link between caffeine and cardiovascular disease. But it can cause anxiety, jitters, and heart palpitations, particularly in people who are sensitive to it. It also can cause stomach pain and gastrointestinal reflux, may make it harder for a woman to get pregnant, and may increase the risk of mis- carriage or a low-birth-weight baby. Doctors advise pregnant women to give up caffeine, or keep consumption down to a cup or two of coffee daily.

Sleeplessness, not surprisingly, is a notorious side effect of caffeine. In recent years, as the number of people taking prescription sleeping pills has soared, more than a few doctors have wondered if people should reconsider their use of caffeine before downing an Ambien or Lunesta. According to Medco Health Solutions of Franklin Lakes, N.J., use of such medications by adults ages 20 to 44 increased 114 percent from 2000 to 2005.

In kids, lack of sleep is both a worrisome cause and effect of the caffeine craze. Wilkie Wilson, a professor of pharmacology at Duke University Medi- cal Center and coauthor of *Buzzed,* a guide to commonly used drugs, says he's stunned by how little sleep kids get these days. Teenagers, he says, need at least nine hours of sleep a night; grade schoolers, 10 to 12 hours. Very few get close to that much—either, as in Linleigh Hawk's case, because they're actively fight- ing sleep, or because they're so jazzed from caffeine that they can't settle down at bedtime. The downside: "I'm exhausted. I can't remember simple things," Hawk says. But she gets the work done.

Indeed, lack of sleep interferes with concentration, says William Kohler, medical director of the Florida Sleep Institute in Spring Hill. It also can make kids fidgety. Since inattention and restlessness are signs of attention deficit hyperactivity disorder as well, sleep researchers increasingly believe that some kids diagnosed with ADHD are actually sleep deprived.

The caffeine itself makes kids fidgety, too, of course. Just ask Maya Thompson, a Sacramento, Calif., mother. "It's like two totally different extremes," she says of how much more aggressive her son Jordan, 12, becomes with even a sip of a caffeinated drink. Jordan, for his part, says that lots of kids in his sixth-grade class pull Monster or Rock Star energy drinks out of their backpacks and drink them before PE class. "Oh my gosh!" says Maya, 30. "I'm shocked by that—that is crazy!"

The young adult crowd who favor caffeine with their alcohol appear to be putting themselves at some risk, too. The stimulant does mitigate the effects of alcohol by improving response time, according to Mark Fillmore, a psychologist at the University of Kentucky who has been testing the combination on student volunteers. But it fails to reduce the number of errors that a person under the influence makes. "Caffeine seems to restore the speed of your behavior but not the accuracy," Fillmore says.

Until the advent of caffeine pills and highly caffeinated energy drinks, caffeine overdoses were exceedingly rare, because people became anxious, shaky, and nauseated before they could imbibe enough. Now, people are sometimes shocked to find out how few servings equal too much "I'm a strong, 47-year-old man, and I tell you what, that stuff put me on my knees," says Scott Silliman, a construction worker from Citrus Heights, Calif., who recently grabbed two cans of Redline RTD energy drink at 7-Eleven when he picked up lunch for the crew.

Silliman pounded down the drinks, then ate a burrito. Twenty minutes later, "I was sweating, I was shaking, I was freezing cold. I never felt anything like that in my life." Silliman thought he was having a heart attack. Actually, he had drunk 500 mg of caffeine in a few minutes, the equivalent of five cups of coffee. "The government should put some kind of regulations on this, or at least warning labels."

Consumer watchdog groups think so, too. The government puts caffeine in its category of "generally recognized as safe" and so doesn't require food and drink manufacturers to list caffeine content. For more than a decade, the American Medical Association and the Center for Science in the Public Interest have been lobbying the Food and Drug Administration to require caffeine content labels, as well as the words "not appropriate for children." Meantime, soft drink manufacturers, seeing growing concern in Congress and among local politicians about children's access to energy drinks, announced in February that they'll now list caffeine content on drinks. The Coca-Cola Co. has already relabeled Full Throttle energy drink (141 mg per 16 ounces) and its new Enviga sparkling green tea (100 mg in 12 ounces); classic Coke will reveal its 34 milligrams in May. PepsiCo will have caffeine content on Pepsi and other drinks this summer.

Even as they're upping their dosage of caffeine, many high schoolers and college students are seeking a stronger boost than it can give. Prescription stimulants such as Ritalin, Concerta, and Adderall, widely prescribed to treat the inattention of ADHD, have become a source of alertness and energy for studying, and for late-night parties. About 3 percent of college students say they've used prescription stimulants illegally, according to a March 2007 study by the National Center on Addiction and Substance Abuse at Columbia University. The number is small compared with students' use of alcohol, marijuana, and tobacco, but stimulant abuse is increasing faster, almost doubling between 1993 and 2005, according to Susan Foster, vice president and director of policy research and analysis.

The drugs are "universal performance enhancers," says Lawrence Diller, a pediatrician in Walnut Creek, Calif., and author of *The Last Normal Child*. He thinks doctors, including himself, overprescribe drugs for mild ADHD. About 1.5 million adults and 2.5 million children—some 10 percent of all 10-year-old boys—now have prescriptions.

That means just about everybody under age 20 knows someone with a potential source of Adderall or Ritalin. (Most nonmedical users prefer Adderall to the slower-acting Ritalin.) On college campuses, prices rise as exams approach, from $7 to $15 for a 10-mg pill.

Marshall Dines, 23, a senior at the University of Michigan, even had strangers E-mailing him to sell them medicine after he joined a Facebook group about Adderall. (He refused and later left the group.)

Prescription stimulants can be big trouble when used to excess; that's been apparent since World War II, when both the Axis and Allies gave troops amphetamines like Dexedrine to keep them alert on the front lines and many soldiers came home addicted (Adolf Hitler was reportedly a fan). More recently, stimulants have been popular with truck drivers and dieters. In 1971, the federal government added amphetamines (Adderall and other brands) and methylphenidates (Ritalin, Concerta, and other brands) to its Schedule II list of controlled substances—drugs with legitimate medical uses that also have a high potential for abuse. Stimulants account for just 1 percent of drug-related emergency room visits. But the number of people showing up with symptoms like confusion and convulsions after nonmedical use rose 33 percent from 2004 to 2005, according to a Substance Abuse and Mental Health Services Administration survey. Visits due to Ritalin and other methylphenidates more than doubled.

All stimulant medications work by increasing the amount of dopamine in the brain, a neurotransmitter that's a major player in the pleasure response to food, say, or sex. Cocaine and methamphetamine, a powerful (and illegal) cousin of the amphetamine in Adderall, create sharp upward spikes in dopamine, causing an intensely pleasurable rush. The equally quick crash, and the memory of the euphoric high, are powerful spurs to addiction. Prescription amphetamines raise dopamine levels slowly and lose their effect gradually. Thus, they're less likely to prompt a high and crash and be addictive.

But the reality is that people can become addicted to prescription stimulants, and repeated overuse can lead to hostility, paranoia, confusion, hallucinations, psychotic episodes, depression, and seizures. "There's an optimal level of dopamine in your brain," says NIDA's Volkow, who studies how drugs of abuse remodel the brain. Go beyond that level, and the brain, in effect, gets stuck.

These days, the impetus on campus is often less the urge for a high than the desire to get more done. "I saw no point in sleeping," says Derek Simeone, now 22, who was prescribed stimulant medication while in high school—and took it more often as a freshman at Syracuse University. "Adderall allows me to do more with my life in a certain amount of time." Beyond studying, the medication helped him stay up and play video games, party, and hang out. He finally cut back after a week without sleep left him hot, pale, and sweaty, and he eventually gave up Adderall altogether. Now a programmer in New Jersey, Simeone relies on coffee.

Heart Risks

Stimulant drugs also increase the chance of heart attacks and strokes, a risk that's well documented in abuse of drugs like cocaine and methamphetamine. In February 2006, after studies revealed 25 cases of fatal strokes or heart attacks in children and adults taking stimulant medication for ADHD, the FDA ordered manufacturers to put warnings on all prescription stimulants, including Ritalin, Adderall, and Concerta. Those complications are rare. But Steven Nissen, chairman of the department of cardiovascular medicine at the Cleveland Clinic, thinks the agency should go further, particularly since so many people are taking stimulants to treat only mild symptoms of ADHD.

"Can it possibly be that 10 percent of all the sixth-grade boys in America have a disease that requires amphetamines?" Nissen asks. "I'm unwilling to accept that that's an appropriate use of a psychotropic agent, particularly one that has well-known cardiovascular risks." He also worries about the rapidly increasing use of ADHD drugs by adults. "Ten percent of them are over age 55," Nissen says. "That's a potential disaster."

The popularity of stimulants on campus has not escaped the notice of university health officials. Although they are far more concerned about the dangers of binge drinking—a much more widespread problem—schools are becoming considerably more cautious about handing out stimulant medications. Two years ago, Indiana University initiated a screening process for students claiming to need stimulants that includes standardized tests, evaluation of a student's records as far back as elementary school, and a survey sent to parents, according to Hugh Jessop, director of the IU Health Center. Of the 283 students who scheduled appointments to get medication at Indiana in the past couple years, only 47 completed the process. The University of Wisconsin no longer even fills prescriptions from family doctors back home.

The lure of prescription stimulants may well fade, as it has in decades past, when the ugly effects of abuse and addiction become clear. (Hippies in the late 1960s graffitied the walls of San Francisco's Haight-Ashbury district with "Speed kills," a testament to the fact that overuse was no summer of love.) But the $4 minivacation from the stresses of daily life appears to be a destination with real staying power. "Coffee culture" has become so much a part of American culture that 36-year-old Starbucks, once considered a gourmet's treat, now boasts 9,401 stores nationwide and has focused growth on economically struggling neighborhoods far from the yuppified precincts of its early success.

Even McDonald's hawks a premium blend; Dunkin' Donuts sells lattes. "It's like a miniature splurge," says Tracy Allen, vice president for Zoka Coffee

Roaster and Tea Co. in Seattle, which markets a barista-brewed cup of organic Ethiopian Yirgacheffe as if it were a fine wine. "The coffee shop is the 21st-century version of the 1950s malt shop," says Joseph DeRupo, director of communications for the National Coffee Association. "It's where kids go to meet friends and socialize."

What's next? Richard Holschen, a police officer in Kaktovik, Alaska, couldn't tote around coffee in the subzero temperatures above the Arctic Circle, so he invented caffeinated SpazzStick lip balm. "I needed to stay awake if I was on duty three days straight," Holschen, 34, says. "Caffeine and lip balm were a logical conclusion for me." Internet sales have been brisk, he says.

Robert Bohannon's phone started ringing off the hook in January, when the Durham, N.C.-based inventor announced that he'd perfected a recipe for caffeinated doughnuts and bagels. "I feel completely overwhelmed," he says. He hasn't yet produced the pastry on a commercial scale but plans to license his invention this year.

Sally Satel  **NO**

Is Caffeine Addictive?—A Review of the Literature

Introduction

In July 2005, the Center for Science in the Public Interest, a Washington-based consumer advocacy group, called for the Food and Drug Administration (FDA) to mandate warning labels on caffeinated soda. The group's main concern was not only the association between soda and childhood obesity; it also judged caffeine to be a potentially dangerous substance. The Center suggested that "[C]affeinated drinks should bear a notice that reads 'This drink contains x grams of caffeine, which is a mildly addictive stimulant drug. Not appropriate for children'" (1).

Is caffeine addictive? Is it a harmful substance that compels the consumer to use at the risk of his well-being and despite a stated desire to refrain? Is it a "model drug of abuse" as the National Institute on Drug Abuse put it? (2). The answer is no. This paper summarizes evidence justifying this conclusion.

Impairment and Reinforcement

How does caffeine use fit into the DSM-IVR drug abuse schema? (3). A significant level of impairment is rarely a consequence of its consumption. Caffeine can be a factor in poor sleep, jitteriness, and arrhythmias in adults. Its effects on children, especially hyperactive ones, are not well known. However, in adults, too much caffeine produces sensations that are unpleasant (e.g., tremulousness, jitteriness) and may put a break on its consumption. Moreover, if caffeine were so intensely desirable, some individuals would likely self-administer caffeine supplements—available in 200 mg tablets—in doses exceeding the average caffeine intake of about 200–300 mg/day.

What about DSM IV-R dependence criteria? (4). Caffeine consumers do not display an inability to control consumption. Coffee drinking is weakly reinforcing, but this is not the same as saying that caffeine, as a substance, is reinforcing. Nehlig states that "the conditions under which caffeine functions as a reinforcer still are not clearly understood" (5).

First, the possible reinforcing effects of coffee may not be the caffeine per se, but rather the pleasurable aroma and taste of coffee as well as the social

From *American Journal of Drug and Alcohol Abuse,* vol. 32, issue 4, November 2006, pp. 493–502.

environment that usually accompanies coffee consumption. Second, the desire to use repeatedly is most marked in heavy caffeine consumers (>1000 mg/day) who also had histories of alcohol or drug abuse. For moderate caffeine users (130600 mg/day), caffeine reinforcement occurs in a smaller subset of consumers (6).

The author could find no reports of use that bear analogy to alcoholic-style drinking or chain smoking. Theoretically, an individual might be exquisitely sensitive to the effects of caffeine and be at risk for a more classical addiction, but if so, his sensitivity to caffeine would make the stimulating effects of the drug itself (e.g., jitteriness) too unpleasant to tolerate. Case reports of toxic levels involve deliberate or accidental overdoses of caffeine pills, not compulsive consumption of those pills or of coffee. In short, coffee drinking resembles more a dedicated habit than a compulsive addiction. (7)

Animal studies permit analysis of the effects of caffeine on the brain. Nehlig has examined this question in depth and discovered that caffeine levels approximating human consumption do not activate brain reward circuits as do classic stimulants (8). Amphetamines, cocaine, and nicotine stimulate the release of dopamine in the shell of the nucleus accumbens, the key structure in the brain for reward, motivation, and addiction. However, caffeine has no effect on the shell of the nucleus accumbens. Moreover, the experimental rats received caffeine intravenously, a route well known to be more reinforcing than oral use.

An important question about the reinforcing properties of caffeine is whether ongoing use is a function of a drinker's enjoyment of caffeine-containing beverages—in which case, it is more like a loyal, pleasurable habit than a compulsion—or whether users consume it to avoid subtle withdrawal effects.

Caffeine Tolerance and Withdrawal

People use caffeine in a regular pattern—every morning or after dinner—but there is little evidence that such behavior is of a compulsive nature. Rather, caffeine drinkers are often dedicated to their coffee—they seek its warmth, flavor, aroma, and, sometimes, mildly stimulating benefits. They do not feel intense distress if it is unavailable; though, some will drink it in order to suppress **withdrawal** symptoms.

Tolerance. Daily caffeine drinkers quickly develop tolerance to the jitteriness, anxiety, and edginess occasionally reported by first time users of the substance. Rather than becoming tolerant to caffeine's desirable effects (wakefulness, alertness), most drinkers become tolerant to the negative ones. Notably, with standard drugs of abuse it generally takes additional drugs to achieve the desired effect of a high or a feeling of tranquility.

Withdrawal. Also called discontinuation syndroms, withdrawal occurs upon abruptly stopping the use of a drug (including some prescribed medications). This phenomenon occurs because the user's central nervous system has adapted to regular exposure to the substance.

Such physical dependence is a product of "neuroadaptation"—that is, central nervous system neurons adapt to compensate for the continuous presence of a substance in the brain tissue. In the case of opiate addiction, when the level drops below a certain point, the neurons "rebound" and the user experiences physical symptoms such as chills, shakes, stomach cramps, or vomiting. After a period of regular use, a person might "crave" opiates simply to stop the sickness, and not because he desires the high. By contrast, the essence of addiction (psychological dependence) is a craving for the drug and its compulsive use.

Caffeine withdrawal includes headache, lethargy, irritability, and mental fuzzy-headedness. Some or all can occur among many daily caffeine consumers who abruptly stop their intake (9). Sometimes doses as low as 100 mg/d can provoke these symptoms, though daily caffeine consumption among Americans is estimated at about 280 mg/d or the equivalent of 2–3 cups of coffee (10, 11). Symptoms begin twelve to twenty-four hours after sudden cessation of continuous use, reach a peak at twenty to forty-eight hours, and resolve after ingesting caffeine (12–14).

Thus, physical dependence denotes the need for a substance to achieve physiological homeostasis; the classic signs of this phenomenon are tolerance and withdrawal. It differs from addiction (also called psychological dependence or just "**dependence**" in DSM IV) in that the latter entails compulsive engagement in a behavior with negative consequences.

Studies on Withdrawal. Researchers use two standard techniques to assess the nature and frequency of withdrawal. One is to ask daily caffeine consumers whether they have ever stopped use abruptly and the effects of cessation. However, the problem with retrospective surveys is that recall is often unreliable and difficult to validate.

The second kind of study entails observation of regular consumers of caffeine who are switched, without their knowledge or the awareness of the rater, to a caffeine-free diet during a study period. Such double-blinded, prospective clinical studies assess experience in real-time by objective observers.

Survey Studies. There are ten published random surveys of caffeine withdrawal, with four of them involving hospitalized patients. Of the remaining six, two specifically recruited subjects who identified themselves as experiencing caffeine-withdrawal while two others simply recruited coffee drinkers (15, 16). In the first, Goldstein and Kaiser reported that 58 percent of the eighteen people in their survey who drank 5–10 cups of coffee per day felt "half awake" when they stopped and another 8 percent reported headaches after stopping (17). Hughes and colleagues found that 11 percent of those who had given up or reduced caffeine use in the past year experienced headache plus one other symptom which together produced "significant distress or impairment in social, occupational, or other important areas of functioning" (18).

The remaining two of the six surveys were both random samples of over 1000 participants who were not surveyed specifically for their caffeine use. Dews and colleagues reported on 11,112 subjects who responded to an ad unrelated to caffeine consumption. Sixty-one percent (6,815) claimed to be daily caffeine consumers and of these, 11 percent reported that they experienced symptoms such as headaches, irritability, and sleepiness when they stopped using caffeine abruptly (19). In the second survey, Kendler and Prescott reported on 1,642 women in a twin-registry study of genetic aspects of various conditions. Twenty-four percent claimed that in stopping or decreasing use, they developed a headache and at least one other symptom (20).

Experimental studies. In 2004, Juliano and Griffiths summarized forty-two double-blind trials (21). In these trials, subjects typically underwent placebo replacement for caffeine for various periods of time. The researchers then compare withdrawal symptoms in those who received a placebo versus those who continued to receive caffeine. The bulk of the studies showed that caffeine abstention resulted in the placebo group reporting higher rates of lethargy, fuzziness, and headache.

Three studies made a special effort to recruit subjects who were naive to the purpose of the study.

Hughes and colleagues recruited moderate to heavy coffee drinkers (about 5–7 cups/d) to participate in a study of the effects of different coffee strengths on mood, general performance, and preference for each beverage (22). The study was administered over a four-day period. Twenty-two subjects with no history of substance abuse or mental illness participated. Subjects consumed either 4 cups of decaf coffee only on Day 1 or caffeinated coffee only on Day 2 or vice versa. On Days 3 and 4, subjects were allowed to choose between decaf and caffeinated coffees. There were six 4-day sessions total. Overall, subjects preferred caffeinated coffee on the days they could chose. On experimental days when they were given decaf, 41 percent reported drowsiness, fatigue, and headache, though baseline levels of these symptoms were not reported.

Silverman and coworkers recruited sixty-two adults through ads promoting a study of the effect of foods—including caffeine on behavior and mood (23). The participants' average daily intake of caffeine was 235 mg/d. No participants with a history of psychiatric disorder were enrolled. The subjects participated in 2 two-day study periods that were one week apart. During each two-day period, they received either their usual caffeine dose in pill form or placebo pills. Fifty-two percent of those in the placebo condition reported moderate or severe headaches (2 percent baseline), while 8–11 percent complained about depression and anxiety.

Dews and his team used subjects who responded to an ad for various medical studies (24). Over half (6,815) of the 11,112 subjects were daily caffeine drinkers and of these, fifty-seven said they experienced difficulty in the past when they stopped use. Subjects for an experimental phase were selected from the fifty-seven; subjects with a psychiatric disorder within the last twelve months were excluded.

The fifty-seven subjects consumed an average of 200–300 mg caffeine/day with a maximum consumption of 550 mg. They were divided, randomly, into three experimental groups. The first (n = 18) was kept on a constant dose of caffeine throughout the observation period. In the second (n = 18), coffee was replaced with decaf, without their knowledge, after the first five days of the fourteen-day study. Only six reported any symptoms within the first forty-eight hours of caffeine abstinence (one of them specifically reporting a "caffeine deprivation headache" on the first four days of withdrawal). Five others reported headache and lethargy on days 10 and 11.

Members of the third group (n = 20) were given progressively lower concentrations of caffeine (80 percent, 60, 40, 20, 0) on days 6–12. In that group, no consistent pattern of symptoms could be discerned. In many instances, the magnitude of the change registered was one-third of a point on a scale in which a single point indicated the change from "same as usual" to "slightly less than usual."

In Dews' study, three of seven subjects who claimed to experience "severe" withdrawal during the interview portion of the study, did not report any discomfort during the experimentally induced withdrawal segment of the trial. As the authors state: "It would appear that self-reports are an unreliable indicator of what is recognized by the same subject under double-blind conditions" (25). They conclude that caffeine withdrawal is not a clinically significant phenomenon and that many of the symptoms appear because subjects expect them to do so.

Methodological Problems

A number of methodological issues, in addition to the relatively small samples routinely used, complicate interpretation of clinical trials data. Foremost is whether the blind can be maintained, given the ability of drinkers to detect the presence of caffeine (26). Because blinding requires that neither the tester nor the participant know which drinks contain the active ingredient, the distinctive taste may make it impossible to preserve a blind. Additionally, there is evidence that research subjects will report in the desired direction of the person administering the study if it is known to them thus making it very difficult to obtain accurate data about caffeine effects and especially when reported withdrawal symptoms cannot be verified through a physical exam (27).

Second, it is important for studies to examine subjects who are representative of normal caffeine consumers. Particularly, a 1994 study by Strain and others, published in the prestigious *Journal of the American Medical Association* and one of the most widely cited studies on caffeine withdrawal, is problematic in this regard (28).

Not only was the study's sample size of eleven very small, the individuals were recruited through a newspaper ad specifically seeking subjects who deemed themselves "psychologically or physically dependent" upon caffeine. Therefore, the researchers chose an unrepresentative sample. Furthermore, the subjects' consent-to-participate form laid out the specific withdrawal symptoms, thus contaminating the blind and introducing expectation bias. In short, when the authors report that eight of the eleven subjects displayed "functional impairment" during the course of 2 two-day abstinence periods which were separated by one week, the finding is not obviously applicable to most caffeine consumers.

In addition, almost half of the subjects in the Strain study consumed their caffeine in the form of soft drinks. Given an average caffeine consumption of 300 mg/d, this means the subjects drank about ten cans of soda per day.

Additionally, the majority of the subjects had previous psychiatric problems, either alcohol or drug abuse and/or mood disorders. Such subjects may use caffeine to self-medicate depression-related lethargy and thus could experi-ence an exaggerated withdrawal. They are more sensitive to the effects of caf-feine, and may be prone to experience distress, to find strong emotional states hard to manage, and to act impulsively.

Lastly, the nature of a caffeine withdrawal syndrome is highly variable. For example, two studies examining the cardiovascular effects of abrupt caf-feine cessation elicited reports of no symptoms (29, 30). In another study from Johns Hopkins, Suzette Evans and Roland Griffiths noted that twenty-four hours after cessation of high doses of caffeine (900 mg/d), subjects reported no withdrawal (31). Numerous other studies yield inconsistent observations and self-report (32–40).

Clinical Relevance: Should We Be Worried?

The American Psychiatric Association does not recognize caffeine dependence. Only caffeine withdrawal is mentioned in the Diagnostic and Statistical Manual; not as a formal diagnosis but rather as a diagnosis worthy of further study. However, the 5th edition of the manual is under construction—the final text is not expected until at least 2010—and some researchers such as Griffiths claim that dependence is a valid diagnosis and presumably seek its inclusion (41). Nonetheless, clinical indicators of dependence, such as difficulty curtailing or stopping the use of caffeine intake and consumption despite harm, have not been demonstrated let alone replicated (42).

The prevalence of caffeine withdrawal syndrome is unknown. Nonetheless, a clinician should keep in mind that the symptoms can appear in a patient who has abruptly stopped intake of food and fluids. The symptoms can be mistaken for depression or tension headache. Better yet, he can advise patients how to avoid symptoms by tapering caffeine before an elective procedure. If withdrawal has begun and is unpleasant, the clinician can administer caffeine tablets.

Conclusion

Caffeine is a mild stimulant that restores mental alertness or wakefulness during fatigue or drowsiness. Its use is widely acceptable because caffeine is rarely medically harmful (except perhaps in people who have particular physical conditions) and does not lead to social disruption of any kind. Abrupt discontinuation of a moderate amount (generally at least 3 cups of coffee per day; 7 cans of cola soft drink per day) can lead to bothersome symptoms, most notably headache, in some but not all people (43). These effects can be readily avoided by tapering the amount consumed. The only study in which withdrawal-related impairment appeared to be problematic was conducted using a small sample of patients chosen specifically because they believed they were dependent on caffeine and had high rates of remit-ted substance abuse and mood disorders. In short, these subjects did not represent a random sample of caffeine drinkers and it is not possible to infer typical discontinuation symptoms from them.

Some have argued that continued caffeine use represents an attempt to suppress low grade withdrawal symptoms such as sleepiness and lethargy. In some moderate users, this is possible; however, in experimental contexts, the phenomenon is too inconsistent to constitute a reliably valid syndrome.

The common-sense use of the term addiction is that regular consumption is irresistible and that it creates problems. Caffeine use does not fit this profile. First, there is no harm to individuals or to society. Second, there is rarely a strong compulsion to use; more correctly the pattern of use can be described as a dedicated habit. Cessation of regular use may result in symptoms such as headache and lethargy. These are easily and reliably reversed by ingestion of caffeine. Avoidance of such symptoms, when they do occur, is easily accomplished by ingesting successively smaller doses of caffeine over about a week-long period.

Thus, caffeine use meets neither the common sense nor the scientific definitions of an addictive substance.

References

1. Center for Science in the Public Interest. CSPI Calls on FDA to Require Health Warnings on Sodas. . . .

2. Caffeine: A Model Drug of Abuse. National Institute on Drug Abuse, Research Monograph 1996; 162:73–75.

3. American Psychiatric Association. Diagnostic and Statistical Manual. 4th ed. 199.

4. American Psychiatric Association. Diagnostic and Statistical Manual. 4th ed. 197.

5. Nehlig A. Does caffeine lead to psychological dependence? Chemtech 1999; 29:30–35.

6. Nehlig A. Are we dependent upon coffee and caffeine? A review on human and animal data. Neuroscience and Biobehavioral Reviews 1999; 23: 563–576.

7. Daly JW. Caffeine has weak reinforcing properties, but with little or no evidence for upward dose adjustment possible because of the adverse effects of higher doses. Drug and Alcohol Dependence 1998; 51:199–206.

8. Juliano LM, Griffiths RR. A critical review of caffeine withdrawal: Empirical validation of symptoms and signs, incidence, severity, and associated features. Psychopharmacology 2004; 176:1–29.

9. Griffiths RR, Evans SM, Heishman SJ, Preston KL, Sannerud CA, Wolf B, Woodson PP. Low dose caffeine physical dependence in humans. Journal of Pharmacology and Experimental Therapeutics 1990; 255:1123–32.

10. Barone JJ, Roberts HR. Caffeine consumption. Food Chem Toxicol 1996; 34:119–129.

11. Dreisbach RH, Pfieffer C. Caffeine-withdrawal headache. The Journal of Laboratory and Clinical Medicine 1943; 28:1212–19.

12. Goldstein A, Kaiser S, Whitby O. Psychotropic effects of caffeine in man, IV: Quantitative and qualitative differences associated with habituation to coffee. Clinical Pharmacology and Therapeutics 1969; 10:489–97.

13. Strain EC, Mumford GK, Silverman K, Griffiths, RR. Caffeine dependence syndrome: Evidence from case histories and experimental evaluations. The Journal of the American Medical Association 1994; 272:1043–48.

14. Oberstar JV, Bernstein GA, Thuras PD. Caffeine use and dependence in adolescents: One year follow-up. Journal of Child & Adolescent Psychopharmacology 2002; 109:85–91.

15. Goldstein A, Kaizer S. Psychotropic effects of caffeine in man: A questionnaire survey of coffee drinking and its effects in a group of housewives. Clinical Pharmacology and Therapeutics 1969; 10:477–88.

16. Hughes JR, Oliveto AH, Liguori A, Carpenter J, Howard, T. Endorsement of DSM-IV dependence criteria among caffeine users. Drug and Alcohol Dependence 1998; 52:99–107.

17. Dews PB, Curtis G, Hanford K, O'Brien, CP. The frequency of caffeine withdrawal in a population-based survey and in a controlled, blinded pilot experiment. Psychopharmacology 1999; 39:1221–32.

18. Kendler KS, Prescott, CA. Caffeine intake, tolerance, and withdrawal in women: A population-based twin study. American Journal of Psychiatry 1999; 156:223–228.

19. Hughes J, Higgins S, Bickel WW, Hunt K, Fenwick JW, Gulliver SB, Mireault GC. Caffeine self-administration, withdrawal, and adverse effects among coffee drinkers. Archives of General Psychiatry 1991; 48:611–17.

20. Silverman K, Evans SM, Strain EC, Griffiths RR. Withdrawal syndrome after the double-blind cessation of caffeine consumption. New England Journal of Medicine 1992; 327:1109–1114.

21. Ibid., 1230.

22. Rosnthal R. Covert communication in the psychological experiment. Psychological Bulletin 1967; 67:356–67.

23. Robertson D, Wade D, Workman R, Woolsey R, Oates JA. Tolerance to the humoral and hemodynamic effects of caffeine in man. Journal of Clinical Investigation 1981; 67:1111–1117.

24. Ammon H, Bieck P, Mandalaz D, Verspohl E. Adaptation of blood pressure to continuous heavy coffee drinking in young volunteers. A double-blind crossover study. British Journal of Clinical Pharmacology 1983; 15:701–706.

25. Evans SM, Griffiths RR. Caffeine tolerance and choice in humans. Psychopharmacology 1992; 108:51–59.

26. Hughes JR, Oliveto AH, Higgins ST. Caffeine self-administration and subjective effects in adolescents. Experimental and Clinical Psychopharmacology 1995; 3:364–70.

27. Liguori A, Hughes JR, Oliveto AH. Caffeine self-administration in humans: 1. Efficacy of cola vehicle. Experimental and Clinical Psychopharmacology 1997; 5:286–94.

28. Dews PB, O'Brien CP, Bergman J. Behavioral effects of caffeine: Dependence and related issues. 1998. (Unpublished version)

29. Hughes JR, Oliveto AH, Bickel WK, Higgins ST, Badger GJ. Caffeine self-administration and withdrawal: Incidence, individual differences and interrelationships. Drug and Alcohol Dependence 1993; 32:239–46.

30. Ibid., 614.

31. Juliano LM, Griffiths RR. Is caffeine a drug of dependence? Psychiatric Times 2001; 18(2).

32. Hughes JR, Oliveto AH, Helzer JE, Higgins ST, Bickel WK. Should caffeine abuse, dependence, or withdrawal be added to DSM-IV and ICD-10? American Journal of Psychiatry 1992; 149:33–40.

POSTSCRIPT

Is Caffeine a Health Risk?

Although caffeine is commonly consumed by millions of people without much regard to its physical and psychological effects, many studies have questioned its safety. However, other studies have reported very few hazards. The basic question is whether or not people who drink several cups of coffee or other caffeinated beverages daily should be more concerned than they are. Are the claims of caffeine's benefits or hazards exaggerated?

Determining if certain foods or beverages promote disease or have health benefits can be trying because the research is unclear. Sometimes the research is contradictory. Many people become frustrated because quite a few of the things that we eat or drink are suspected of being unhealthy. For example, various reports indicate that the fat in beef can lead to various forms of cancer and heart disease, that we should consume less salt and sugar, that processed foods should be avoided, and that whole milk, butter, and margarine should be reduced or eliminated from our diets. If people paid attention to every report about the harmful effects of the foods and beverages they consumed, then they would not be able to eat much at all. What is the average consumer supposed to do?

A legitimate question is whether or not food studies are worth pursuing because so many of the products that are reportedly bad are enjoyed by millions of people. Some people claim they cannot start their day without caffeine. Caffeine is simply one more example of a commonly used product that has come under scrutiny. In addition, although the research is vast, it is inconclusive. One study, for instance, linked caffeine to pancreatic cancer, only to find later that the culprit was not caffeine but cigarette smoking. Research on caffeine's effects on cancers of the bladder, urinary tract, and kidney has also proven to be inconsistent and inconclusive. Because caffeinated products are consumed by millions of people, it is important to know if its dangers are significant or exaggerated. However, if professional researchers cannot agree about whether a product is safe or harmful, how can the average person know what to believe?

Critics of caffeine claim that caffeine may cause dependence because it shares some of the same characteristics of cocaine, alcohol, and nicotine. They state that too much caffeine causes tolerance as well as withdrawal symptoms. Despite their concern, there are not support groups for people addicted to caffeine. Sally Satel counters that caffeine's adverse effects are overstated. Satel indicates that caffeine is a mild stimulant and not a dangerous drug that requires regulation. Furthermore, she indicates that caffeine may have possible benefits such as increased mental alertness and wakefulness.

The effects of caffeine during pregnancy are addressed in "Maternal Caffeine Intake during Pregnancy and Risk of Fetal Growth Restriction: A Large Prospective Observational Study," by Justin Konje and others (*BMJ*,

November 3, 2008) and "Does Caffeine in Pregnancy Cause Birth Defects?" (*Child Health Alert,* June 2006). Jackie Berning looks at the implications for athletes using caffeinated products in "Caffeine and Athletic Performance" (*Clinical Reference Systems,* May 24, 2006). Other articles that examine caffeine's psychological and physical effects are "Caffeine: The Good, the Bad, and the Maybe," in *Nutrition Action* (March 2008) and "Night-time Thoughts in High and Low Worriers: Reaction to Caffeine-induced Sleeplessness," by Siri Omvik, Stale Pallesen, and Bjorn Bjorvatn (*Behaviour Research and Therapy,* April 2007). (March 2008).

ISSUE 12

Should School-Age Children with Attention Deficit/Hyperactivity Disorder (ADHD) Be Treated with Ritalin and Other Stimulants?

YES: Michael Fumento, from "Trick Question," *The New Republic* (February 3, 2003)

NO: Lawrence H. Diller, from *The Last Normal Child: Essays on the Intersection of Kids, Culture and Psychiatric Drugs* (Prager, 2006)

ISSUE SUMMARY

YES: Writer Michael Fumento disputes the idea that Ritalin is overprescribed. He notes that there are many myths associated with Ritalin. It does not lead to abuse and addiction. Fumento argues that Ritalin is an excellent medication for ADHD. One reason it is not as accepted is because it has been demonized by various groups. It is possible that the drug is underutilized. Fumento contends that more students would benefit from Ritalin and other stimulants.

NO: Behavioral pediatrician Lawrence Diller contends that Ritalin is overused and that many school districts advocate the use of Ritalin and other stimulants so that they do not have to provide other services. Diller acknowledges that Ritalin can moderate behavior, but that the drug does not help youngsters overcome learning problems. Another concern, states Diller, is that legal stimulants like Ritalin are being used illegally.

T he number one childhood psychiatric disorder in the United States is attention deficit/hyperactivity disorder, which affects approximately 6 million American school children. ADHD is characterized by inattentiveness, hyperactivity, and impulsivity. Many children are diagnosed as having only attention deficit disorder (ADD), which is ADHD without the hyperactivity. One commonly prescribed drug for ADHD is the stimulant Ritalin (generic name methylphenidate). American children consume 90 percent of all Ritalin produced worldwide. Only a very small percentage of European children are diagnosed with ADHD. Ritalin is therefore much less likely to be prescribed in Europe.

The use of stimulants to treat such behavioral disorders dates back to 1937. The practice of prescribing stimulants for behavioral problems increased dramatically beginning in 1970, when it was estimated that 150,000 American children were taking stimulant medications. It seems paradoxical for physicians to be prescribing a stimulant such as Ritalin for a behavioral disorder that already involves hyperactivity. However, Ritalin appears to be effective with many children, as well as with many adults, who suffer from this condition. Looking at this issue from a broader perspective, one needs to ask whether behavioral problems should be treated as a disease. Also, does Ritalin really address the problem? Or could it be covering up other maladies that otherwise should be treated?

Ritalin enhances the functioning of the brain's reticular activating system, which helps one to focus attention and to filter out extraneous stimuli. The drug has been shown to improve short-term learning. Ritalin also produces adverse effects such as insomnia, headaches, irritability, nausea, dizziness, weight loss, and growth retardation. Psychological dependence may develop, but physical dependence is unlikely. The effects of long-term Ritalin use are unknown.

Since 1990 the number of children receiving Ritalin has increased 500 percent. This large increase in the number of children diagnosed with ADHD may be attributed to a broader application of the criteria for diagnosing ADHD, heightened public awareness, and changes in American educational policy regarding schools' identifying children with the disorder. Some people feel that the increase in prescriptions for Ritalin reflects an increased effort to satisfy the needs of parents whose children exhibit behavioral problems. Ritalin has been referred to as "mother's little helper." Regardless of the reasons for the increase, many people question whether Ritalin is overprescribed and children are overmedicated or whether these stimulants are miracle drugs.

One problem with the increased prevalence of Ritalin prescriptions is that illegal use of the drug has also risen. There are accounts of some parents getting prescriptions for their children and then selling the drugs illegally. On a number of college campuses there are reports of students using Ritalin to get high or to stay awake in order to study. Historically, illegal use of Ritalin has been minimal, although officials of the Drug Enforcement Administration (DEA) are now concerned that its illegal use is proliferating. Problems with its use are unlikely to rival those of cocaine because the effects of Ritalin and other stimulants are more moderate than those of cocaine or amphetamines.

The fact is that children now receive prescriptions for Ritalin and other stimulants rather readily. Frequently, parents will pressure their pediatricians into writing the prescriptions. One survey found that almost one-half of all pediatricians spent less than an hour assessing children before prescribing Ritalin. On the other hand, if there is a medication available that would remedy a problem, shouldn't it be prescribed? If a child's academic performance can improve through the use of Ritalin, should that child be denied the drug?

In the following selections, Michael Fumento maintains that ADHD is underdiagnosed in many instances. He asserts that Ritalin's bad reputation arises from many misconceptions regarding the drug. Lawrence Diller questions the use and effectiveness of Ritalin. He contends that it is overprescribed because of the way the drug is marketed and that Ritalin does not improve learning.

YES

Michael Fumento

Trick Question

It's both right-wing and vast, but it's not a conspiracy. Actually, it's more of an anti-conspiracy. The subject is Attention Deficit Disorder (ADD) and Attention Deficit Hyperactivity Disorder (ADHD), closely related ailments (henceforth referred to in this article simply as ADHD). Rush Limbaugh declares it "may all be a hoax." Francis Fukuyama devotes much of one chapter in his latest book, *Our Posthuman Future,* to attacking Ritalin, the top-selling drug used to treat ADHD. Columnist Thomas Sowell writes, "The motto used to be: 'Boys will be boys.' Today, the motto seems to be: 'Boys will be medicated." And Phyllis Schlafly explains, "The old excuse of 'my dog ate my homework' has been replaced by 'I got an ADHD diagnosis.'" A March 2002 article in *The Weekly Standard* summed up the conservative line on ADHD with this rhetorical question: "Are we really prepared to redefine childhood as an ailment, and medicate it until it goes away?"

Many conservative writers, myself included, have criticized the growing tendency to pathologize every undesirable behavior—especially where children are concerned. But, when it comes to ADHD, this skepticism is misplaced. As even a cursory examination of the existing literature or, for that matter, simply talking to the parents and teachers of children with ADHD reveals, the condition is real, and it is treatable. And, if you don't believe me, you can ask conservatives who've come face to face with it themselves.

Myth: ADHD Isn't a Real Disorder

The most common argument against ADHD on the right is also the simplest: It doesn't exist. Conservative columnist Jonah Goldberg thus reduces ADHD to "ants in the pants." Sowell equates it with "being bored and restless." Fukuyama protests, "No one has been able to identify a cause of ADD/ADHD. It is a pathology recognized only by its symptoms." And a conservative columnist approvingly quotes Thomas Armstrong, Ritalin opponent and author, when he declares, "ADD is a disorder that cannot be authoritatively identified in the same way as polio, heart disease or other legitimate illnesses."

The Armstrong and Fukuyama observations are as correct as they are worthless. "Half of all medical disorders are diagnosed without benefit of a lab

From *The New Republic,* Vol. 228, no. 4, February 3, 2003, pp. 18–21. Copyright © 2003 by New Republic. Reprinted by permission.

procedure," notes Dr. Russell Barkley, professor of psychology at the College of Health Professionals at the Medical University of South Carolina. "Where are the lab tests for headaches and multiple sclerosis and Alzheimer's?" he asks. "Such a standard would virtually eliminate all mental disorders."

Often the best diagnostic test for an ailment is how it responds to treatment. And, by that standard, it doesn't get much more real than ADHD. The beneficial effects of administering stimulants to treat the disorder were first reported in 1937. And today medication for the disorder is reported to be 75 to 90 percent successful. "In our trials it was close to ninety percent," says Dr. Judith Rapoport, director of the National Institute of Mental Health's Child Psychiatry Branch, who has published about 100 papers on ADHD. "This means there was a significant difference in the children's ability to function in the classroom or at home."

Additionally, epidemiological evidence indicates that ADHD has a powerful genetic component. University of Colorado researchers have found that a child whose identical twin has the disorder is between eleven and 18 times more likely to also have it than is a non-twin sibling. For these reasons, the American Psychiatric Association (APA), American Medical Association, American Academy of Pediatrics, American Academy of Child Adolescent Psychiatry, the surgeon general's office, and other major medical bodies all acknowledge ADHD as both real and treatable.

Myth: ADHD Is Part of a Feminist Conspiracy to Make Little Boys More Like Little Girls

Many conservatives observe that boys receive ADHD diagnoses in much higher numbers than girls and find in this evidence of a feminist conspiracy. (This, despite the fact that genetic diseases are often heavily weighted more toward one gender or the other.) Sowell refers to "a growing tendency to treat boyhood as a pathological condition that requires a new three R's—repression, reeducation and Ritalin." Fukuyama claims Prozac is being used to give women "more of the alpha-male feeling," while Ritalin is making boys act more like girls. "Together, the two sexes are gently nudged toward that androgynous median personality. . . that is the current politically correct outcome in American society." George Will, while acknowledging that Ritalin can be helpful, nonetheless writes of the "androgyny agenda" of "drugging children because they are behaving like children, especially boy children." Anti-Ritalin conservatives frequently invoke Christina Hoff Sommers's best-selling 2000 book, *The War Against Boys*. You'd never know that the drug isn't mentioned in her book—or why.

"Originally I was going to have a chapter on it," Sommers tells me. "It seemed to fit the thesis." What stopped her was both her survey of the medical literature and her own empirical findings. Of one child she personally came to know she says, "He was utterly miserable, as was everybody around him. The drugs saved his life."

Myth: ADHD Is Part of the Public School System's Efforts to Warehouse Kids Rather Than to Discipline and Teach Them

"No doubt life is easier for teachers when everyone sits around quietly," writes Sowell. Use of ADHD drugs is "in the school's interest to deal with behavioral and discipline problems [because] it's so easy to use Ritalin to make kids compliant: to get them to sit down, shut up, and do what they're told," declares Schlafly. The word "zombies" to describe children under the effects of Ritalin is tossed around more than in a B-grade voodoo movie.

Kerri Houston, national field director for the American Conservative Union and the mother of two ADHD children on medication, agrees with much of the criticism of public schools. "But don't blame ADHD on crummy curricula and lazy teachers," she says. "If you've worked with these children, you know they have a serious neurological problem." In any case, Ritalin, when taken as prescribed, hardly stupefies children. To the extent the medicine works, it simply turns ADHD children into normal children. "ADHD is like having thirty televisions on at one time, and the medicine turns off twenty-nine so you can concentrate on the one," Houston describes. "This zombie stuff drives me nuts! My kids are both as lively and as fun as can be."

Myth: Parents Who Give Their Kids Anti-ADHD Drugs Are Merely Doping Up Problem Children

Limbaugh calls ADHD "the perfect way to explain the inattention, incompetence, and inability of adults to control their kids." Addressing parents directly, he lectures, "It helped you mask your own failings by doping up your children to calm them down."

Such charges blast the parents of ADHD kids into high orbit. That includes my Hudson Institute colleague (and fellow conservative) Mona Charen, the mother of an eleven-year-old with the disorder. "I have two non-ADHD children, so it's not a matter of parenting technique," says Charen. "People without such children have no idea what it's like. I can tell the difference between boyish high spirits and pathological hyperactivity. . . . These kids bounce off the walls. Their lives are chaos; their rooms are chaos. And nothing replaces the drugs."

Barkley and Rapoport say research backs her up. Randomized, controlled studies in both the United States and Sweden have tried combining medication with behavioral interventions and then dropped either one or the other. For those trying to go on without medicine, "the behavioral interventions maintained nothing," Barkley says. Rapoport concurs: "Unfortunately, behavior modification doesn't seem to help with ADHD." (Both doctors are quick to add that ADHD is often accompanied by other disorders that are treatable through behavior modification in tandem with medicine.)

Myth: Ritalin Is "Kiddie Cocaine"

One of the paradoxes of conservative attacks on Ritalin is that the drug is alternately accused of turning children into brain-dead zombies and of making them Mach-speed cocaine junkies. Indeed, Ritalin is widely disparaged as "kiddie cocaine." Writers who have sought to lump the two drugs together include Schlafly, talk-show host and columnist Armstrong Williams, and others whom I hesitate to name because of my long-standing personal relationships with them.

Mary Eberstadt wrote the "authoritative" Ritalin-cocaine piece for the April 1999 issue of *Policy Review,* then owned by the Heritage Foundation. The article, "Why Ritalin Rules," employs the word "cocaine" no fewer than twelve times. Eberstadt quotes from a 1995 Drug Enforcement Agency (DEA) background paper declaring methylphenidate, the active ingredient in Ritalin, "a central nervous system (CNS) stimulant [that] shares many of the pharmacological effects of amphetamine, methamphetamine, and cocaine." Further, it "produces behavioral, psychological, subjective, and reinforcing effects similar to those of d-amphetamine including increases in rating of euphoria, drug liking and activity, and decreases in sedation." Add to this the fact that the Controlled Substances Act lists it as a Schedule II drug, imposing on it the same tight prescription controls as morphine, and Ritalin starts to sound spooky indeed.

What Eberstadt fails to tell readers is that the DEA description concerns methylphenidate *abuse.* It's tautological to say abuse is harmful. According to the DEA, the drugs in question are comparable when "administered the same way at comparable doses." But ADHD stimulants, when taken as prescribed, are neither administered in the same way as cocaine nor at comparable doses. "What really counts," says Barkley "is the speed with which the drugs enter and clear the brain. With cocaine, because it's snorted, this happens tremendously quickly, giving users the characteristic addictive high." (Ever seen anyone pop a cocaine tablet?) Further, he says, "There's no evidence anywhere in literature of [Ritalin's] addictiveness when taken as prescribed." As to the Schedule II listing, again this is because of the potential for it to fall into the hands of abusers, not because of its effects on persons for whom it is prescribed. Ritalin and the other anti-ADHD drugs, says Barkley, "are the safest drugs in all of psychiatry." (And they may be getting even safer: A new medicine just released called Strattera represents the first true non-stimulant ADHD treatment.)

Indeed, a study just released in the journal *Pediatrics* found that children who take Ritalin or other stimulants to control ADHD cut their risk of future substance abuse by 50 percent compared with untreated ADHD children. The lead author speculated that "by treating ADHD you're reducing the demoralization that accompanies this disorder, and you're improving the academic functioning and well-being of adolescents and young adults during the critical times when substance abuse starts."

Myth: Ritalin Is Overprescribed Across the Country

Some call it "the Ritalin craze." In *The Weekly Standard,* Melana Zyla Vickers informs us that "Ritalin use has exploded," while Eberstadt writes that "Ritalin use more than doubled in the first half of the decade alone, [and] the number of schoolchildren taking the drug may now, by some estimates, be approaching the *4 million mark.*"

A report in the January 2003 issue of *Archives of Pediatrics and Adolescent Medicine* did find a large increase in the use of ADHD medicines from 1987 to 1996, an increase that doesn't appear to be slowing. Yet nobody thinks it's a problem that routine screening for high blood pressure has produced a big increase in the use of hypertension medicine. "Today, children suffering from ADHD are simply less likely to slip through the cracks," says Dr. Sally Satel, a psychiatrist, AEI fellow, and author of *PC, M.D.: How Political Correctness Is Corrupting Medicine.*

Satel agrees that some community studies, by the standards laid down in the APA's *Diagnostic and Statistical Manual of Mental Disorders (DSM)*, indicate that ADHD may often be over-diagnosed. On the other hand, she says, additional evidence shows that in some communities ADHD is *under*-diagnosed and *under*-treated. "I'm quite concerned with children who need the medication and aren't getting it," she says.

There *are* tremendous disparities in the percentage of children taking ADHD drugs when comparing small geographical areas. Psychologist Gretchen LeFever, for example, has compared the number of prescriptions in mostly white Virginia Beach, Virginia, with other, more heavily African American areas in the southeastern part of the state. Conservatives have latched onto her higher numbers—20 percent of white fifth-grade boys in Virginia Beach are being treated for ADHD—as evidence that something is horribly wrong. But others, such as Barkley, worry about the lower numbers. According to LeFever's study, black children are only half as likely to get medication as white children. "Black people don't get the care of white people; children of well-off parents get far better care than those of poorer parents," says Barkley.

Myth: States Should Pass Laws That Restrict Schools From Recommending Ritalin

Conservative writers have expressed delight that several states, led by Connecticut, have passed or are considering laws ostensibly protecting students from schools that allegedly pass out Ritalin like candy. Representative Lenny Winkler, lead sponsor of the Connecticut measure, told *Reuters Health*, "If the diagnosis is made, and it's an appropriate diagnosis that Ritalin be used, that's fine. But I have also heard of many families approached by the school system [who are told] that their child cannot attend school if they're not put on Ritalin."

Two attorneys I interviewed who specialize in child-disability issues, including one from the liberal Bazelon Center for Mental Health Law in Washington, D.C., acknowledge that school personnel have in some cases stepped over the line. But legislation can go too far in the other direction by declaring, as Connecticut's law does, that "any school personnel [shall be prohibited] from recommending the use of psychotropic drugs for any child." The law appears to offer an exemption by declaring, "The provisions of this section shall not prohibit *school medical staff* from recommending that a child be evaluated by an appropriate medical practitioner, or prohibit school personnel from consulting with such practitioner, with the consent of the parent or guardian of such child." [Emphasis added.] But of course many, if not most, schools have perhaps one nurse on regular "staff." That nurse will have limited contact with children in the classroom situations where ADHD is likely to be most evident. And, given the wording of the statute, a teacher who believed a student was suffering from ADHD would arguably be prohibited from referring that student to the nurse. Such ambiguity is sure to have a chilling effect on any form of intervention or recommendation by school personnel. Moreover, 20-year special-education veteran Sandra Rief said in an interview with the National Education Association that "recommending medical intervention for a student's behavior could lead to personal liability issues." Teachers, in other words, could be forced to choose between what they think is best for the health of their students and the possible risk of losing not only their jobs but their personal assets as well.

"Certainly it's not within the purview of a school to say kids can't attend if they don't take drugs," says Houston. "On the other hand, certainly teachers should be able to advise parents as to problems and potential solutions. . . . [T]hey may see things parents don't. My own son is an angel at home but was a demon at school."

If the real worry is "take the medicine or take a hike" ultimatums, legislation can be narrowly tailored to prevent them; broad-based gag orders, such as Connecticut's, are a solution that's worse than the problem.

The Conservative Case for ADHD Drugs

There are kernels of truth to every conservative suspicion about ADHD. Who among us has not had lapses of attention? And isn't hyperactivity a normal condition of childhood when compared with deskbound adults? Certainly there are lazy teachers, warehousing schools, androgyny-pushing feminists, and far too many parents unwilling or unable to expend the time and effort to raise their children properly, even by their own standards. Where conservatives go wrong is in making ADHD a scapegoat for frustration over what we perceive as a breakdown in the order of society and family. In a column in *The Boston Herald,* Boston University Chancellor John Silber rails that Ritalin is "a classic example of a cheap fix: low-cost, simple and purely superficial."

Exactly. Like most headaches, ADHD is a neurological problem that can usually be successfully treated with a chemical. Those who recommend or prescribe ADHD medicines do not, as *The Weekly Standard* put it, see them as "discipline in pill-form." They see them as pills.

In fact, it can be argued that the use of those pills, far from being liable for or symptomatic of the Decline of the West, reflects and reinforces conservative values. For one thing, they increase personal responsibility by removing an excuse that children (and their parents) can fall back on to explain misbehavior and poor performance. "Too many psychologists and psychiatrists focus on allowing patients to justify to themselves their troubling behavior," says Satel. "But something like Ritalin actually encourages greater autonomy because you're treating a compulsion to behave in a certain way. Also, by treating ADHD, you remove an opportunity to explain away bad behavior"

Moreover, unlike liberals, who tend to downplay differences between the sexes, conservatives are inclined to believe that there are substantial physiological differences—differences such as boys' greater tendency to suffer ADHD. "Conservatives celebrate the physiological differences between boys and girls and eschew the radical-feminist notion that gender differences are created by societal pressures," says Houston regarding the fuss over the boy-girl disparity among ADHD diagnoses. "ADHD is no exception."

But, however compatible conservatism may be with taking ADHD seriously, the truth is that most conservatives remain skeptics. "I'm sure I would have been one of those smug conservatives saying it's a made-up disease," admits Charen, "if I hadn't found out the hard way." Here's hoping other conservatives find an easier route to accepting the truth.

Lawrence H. Diller

The Last Normal Child: Essays on the Intersection of Kids, Culture, and Psychiatric Drugs

Ritalin Works! Great?

"Annie's grades and behavior have improved so much that she no longer qual-ifies for special education," the school psychologist announced decisively. I was attending nine-year-old Annie's annual Individualized Educational Plan (IEP) review at her school as her behavioral pediatrician. The school psycholo-gist sounded congratulatory almost triumphant. Wasn't Annie an example of the goal of special education—to return a child to as normal a class setting as possible? Why then was I so uneasy about the school's decision to no longer provide services to this girl? As I left the school grounds, I shuddered while pondering the national implications of little Annie's "triumph."

As recently as three months ago, third-grader Annie was struggling with distractibility and inattention in her classroom. Getting her homework done and turned in on time was a nightly two-hour monumental effort on the part of her single-parent mother, Gail. Daily temper tantrums over rules and chores were also part of Annie's behavioral repertoire. Before coming to see me, Annie had been identified as learning disabled by the school in the first grade and had been enrolled in a special education program. Annie's pediatrician started her on Concerta, a long-acting version of the better-known stimulant drug Ritalin, for attention-deficit/hyperactivity disorder (ADHD), inattentive type.

Despite the confusion caused by its name, this kind of ADHD does not include hyperactivity or even much impulsivity, two of the three cardinal symptoms of ADHD. Simply the child must appear inattentive, distractible, and disorganized with poor task completion. Virtually all children with inat-tentive ADHD have learning or processing problems, and their cognition has been described as "sluggish."

I coached Gail to respond to Annie much more quickly at home with rewards and punishments. I suggested to Annie's teacher that she handle Annie in a similar fashion. I also doubled Annie's medication dose for school. Annie responded beautifully, and within three months the school was ready to eliminate her tutoring and behavioral plan. So why was I unhappy?

Everyone in the room, including Annie's mother and me, believed increasing Annie's medication was the single intervention that was making the difference so quickly. Study after study has demonstrated that stimulants such as Ritalin, Concerta, and Adderall improve, on the short term, the performance and behavior of ADHD children. I was certain that if Annie stopped the medication, most of her problems would return—I doubted she could have changed that quickly solely with the behavioral program.

But with the medication improving Annie's performance, the school was no longer obligated to provide services to Annie, as the law was interpreted by school district's attorneys. In 1999, in *Sutton v. United Airlines,* the U.S. Supreme Court ruled that when persons with the use of mitigating measures are no longer functionally disabled, they then no longer qualify for services under the American with Disabilities Act. Thus, for example, if glasses can correct a visual impairment, then the individual no longer is eligible for services.

John N. Hartson, a pediatric psychologist, is the national consultant to the American College of Testing Program for students with ADHD requesting accommodations or services for disabilities. His interpretation of the law goes beyond even this school district's policies. If Dr. Hartson's suggestions were followed, Annie might never have received any special education from her school in the first place.

Dr. Hartson believes, under his interpretation of federal guidelines coming from these court decisions, that if a school psychologist diagnoses ADHD along with co-occurring problems (such as a learning disability or processing disorder), the child should first be given a trial of Ritalin or its equivalent before any services for that child are proposed by the school. Hartson expands on the Ritalin-glasses analogy with the following straw man case report to illustrate the question "Why offer services when glasses will correct all the problems?":

> A child presents at an optometrists' office and is evaluated for visual problems. The child is diagnosed with a problem with visual acuity and the doctor suggests that the child be prescribed glasses. The optometrist then sends the child to an educational specialist who evaluates the child. The educational specialist sees the child without glasses and notes that the child has a great deal of difficulty with reading and with correctly seeing items on a page. A number of recommendations are then offered including the need for preferential seating, larger print books . . . and additional time to complete reading and other visual tasks.

Following Dr. Hartson's analogy, if a child like Annie with learning problems and ADHD demonstrates few or no problems in the classroom while on medication, then she should receive no services from the school. Only if she continued to have problems while on medication should she then be retested and offered appropriate educational services and accommodations. To offer services first or even simultaneously with medication is not consistent with federal guidelines according to Dr. Hartson.

But if we consider *all* federal guidelines, I'm confused. It would appear, given the interpretation of Annie's school district and Dr. Hartson, that a school could deny services and accommodations to a child with ADHD if the child was not first medicated. Yet Congress, reacting to perceived school pressure on families to medicate their children, added an amendment to the most recent authorization of the Individuals with Disability Education Act (IDEA) of 2004 that specifically prohibits schools from insisting that a child be medicated in order to attend classes in that district.

I'm not sure in the end how the government and the courts will reconcile what appears to be a conflict in "federal guidelines." In the short run, though, I suspect more and more school districts will try the medication-first approach and reconsider only if there is resistance from the family.

Dr. Hartson and others make an analogy between glasses for visual acuity and medication for ADHD. But is Ritalin the same as glasses? Apparently school districts continually looking to save money think so. Therefore, even inexpensive behavioral interventions, such as preferential seating in the front of the class, use of contingency rewards (e.g., stars, stickers, M&M's), and discipline contracts that have been shown to improve ADHD children's behavior and reduce the necessary dosage and frequency of medication, will not be offered if the medication alone "works."

In many children with the symptoms of ADHD (especially the inattentive type) who also have learning problems, who's to say which problem came first or what is causing what? In other words, might the learning or processing problems be contributing to the child's inattention and distractibility? Could addressing the educational needs of the child first without medication reduce or eliminate the need for drugs?

Furthermore, there's no evidence that just medication makes a difference in the *long-term* outcome of ADHD or learning problems. Ritalin teaches a child nothing. ADHD children "learn" to improve their behavior with appropriate behavioral and educational interventions. Yet the pressure on parents coming from schools to medicate their children will only grow when school districts look for legal ways to save money.

Dr. Hartson, like many other ADHD experts, considers two different types of interventions, medical interventions and nondrug interventions, equivalent if they both "work." However, the two types of interventions are not *morally* equivalent. The best way to make clear this error, called a "logical fallacy of the means," is to also use an analogy, this one, literary. In the eighteenth century, the famous satirist Jonathan Swift wrote an essay entitled "A Modest Proposal." In it he offers a "solution" to the Irish potato famine crisis by suggesting Irish children be fed to their parents, providing nutrition while simultaneously decreasing the number of mouths to feed in one stroke.

My "modest proposal" goes as follows. Currently about four million children take Ritalin or its equivalent, and classroom size averages about twenty-nine children per class. It is well know that Ritalin improves the performance of children with ADHD, with borderline ADHD, or even without ADHD. I propose we increase the number of children taking Ritalin to seven million. We could do this by continuing to broaden the criteria for ADHD (a process that's already been going on for fifteen years). Perhaps any child who performs below the median in a class might be referred for an ADHD evaluation and medication?

In any case, by increasing the number of children taking medication to seven million, we could enlarge class size to forty children, hire fewer teachers, and save school districts and tax payers a bundle of money. If, indeed, the medication–glasses analogy is valid and medication is the same as addressing the individual educational needs of children, there should be many educators and politicians ready to support my "modest proposal."

No takers? I wonder why not—because in a way we already substitute medication for nondrug services at school (in the cases of Annie and thousands of children like her). Until we are clear that a child's success while on Ritalin is not morally equivalent to a child's success with educational support, my proposal has a chance. But in all seriousness, we need to take a closer look at our priorities, the moral implications of our policies, and the way we determine which children get what help at school and at home.

Getting Up to Speed for the SAT

American children are taking stimulants and other psychiatric drugs at an unprecedented rate. The reasons for this phenomenon are complex and widespread. But stories that I've been hearing for years and that are now confirmed by research data illuminate at least one part of the answer. My first clue came in 2002, when a television news producer called me about a Manhattan doctor who was giving her high school son Ritalin before important exams. She asked me if I had ever heard of such a practice. I had not, but I wasn't shocked. It seemed, rather inevitable that parents would use Ritalin that way to boost their kids' performance.

Indeed, about six months later, I too directly received a telephone call from a psychiatrist parent who asked me if I would consider medicating her teenager son just for exam taking. He had previously tried Concerta and found that it cut down on his "sociability" and wanted to take it just for exams. She could write the prescriptions herself, but she thought it would be better if her son was managed by someone other than his mother. I knew I would never agree to such a plan, but I was intrigued. I suggested that she, her husband, and her son come in, but I never heard back from them.

People are still surprised to learn that Ritalin, Adderall, and Concerta, along with all the other new stimulant drug formulations prescribed ostensibly to treat ADHD, also work in "normal" children and adults. A myth continues, which began with the very first case reports in the 1930s, that stimulants work "paradoxically" to calm hyperactive children. In reality, stimulant drugs have the same effect on everybody—low doses (such as those for ADHD) improve everyone's concentration and get people to be more methodical. The hyperactivity of ADHD decreases because the kids stick longer with tasks that used to bore them quickly.

Experts have known about the universal enhancing effects of the stimulants for years. The army explored the routine use of stimulants on GIs in the 1950s. (The Allies widely distributed amphetamine to soldiers in World War II after learning that the German general Rommel was giving stimulants to his famed Afrika Corps.) Although stimulants regularly improved the soldiers' alertness and performance on boring tasks, there were enough episodes of "erratic" behavior that the generals decided that giving amphetamine routinely to guys with guns was not a good idea.

In the late 1970s, the National Institute of Mental Health (NIMH) proved irrefutably that stimulants improve the performance of normal men and boys as much as they do for those with ADHD. College students have also known about the performance-enhancing effects of Ritalin, and since the 1990s boom in ADHD diagnosis, prescription stimulants have been freely traded or sold on campus, often crushed and snorted, for "power" studying or to get high. Recent reports have up to one in four students on some college campuses using prescription stimulants illegally. A specter of misuse of, tolerance of, and addiction to prescription stimulants hangs over such use.

But I was not especially surprised by these stories I'd heard or by the call I received about Ritalin being considered for children just to improve performance on tests. Of course, that mother-physician was acting unethically when prescribing the drug to her own son. Regardless of the ethics of performance enhancement, treating members of your own family for any reason is considered a "no-no" in all of medicine.

But what is disturbing is that many kids are probably getting stimulants from their doctors for alleged ADHD (or are taking them on their own) and using them just "as needed." This isn't necessarily because doctors are bad or lousy diagnosticians. Teenage and adult ADHD, except in extreme cases, is actually difficult to delineate. The line between the unmotivated or learning impaired and those with ADHD is very much in the eye of the beholder. Doctors already routinely prescribe stimulants like Ritalin or Adderall "just for school." Several of my college-age patients take Concerta only three days a week—on the days they have classes. They say they don't need the drug otherwise.

I draw the line though with people who want the drug only for occasional use—even if they meet my criteria for ADHD. Such intermittent use enables the procrastination and last minute panic typical of an ADHD lifestyle. But Ritalin for the ADHD diagnosis is a slippery slope, and many of the kids getting Ritalin from their doctors look pretty normal to me. Still they will do "better than normal" on Ritalin.

Unlike young children who never become addicted, teens and adults do run the risk of abuse, tolerance, and addiction with prescription stimulants. Just recently, in February of 2006, I received phone calls within two weeks of each other from parents who had discovered that their teenagers were abusing Adderall. (I predict we will ultimately learn that Adderall and Adderall XR are the prescription stimulant drugs most abused by teens and young adults in comparison with Ritalin or Concerta. That's because Adderall is amphetamine, and the other two are methylphenidate-based. And although the two chemicals are very similar, I feel that amphetamine is the more intense experience, even when used therapeutically, and therefore it will attract the greater number of abusers.)

One of these kids, a seventeen-year-old senior at the local high school told his mother that he had taken "a hit" of Adderall just before taking the SAT exam. He thought it was very helpful, and indeed he received a perfect 800 in the verbal part of the three-part exam. He had always "underperformed" in school according to his mother, and now both she and her son were interested in his trying the drug on a more regular basis. Unfortunately, as I learned more about this boy—his daily marijuana use, his selling it at school, and the general chaos of his home life—I knew that neither he nor his mother had the organizational responsibility necessary to safely handle a drug with the abuse potential of Adderall (or Concerta for that matter).

These individual stories of illegal use and abuse of prescription stimulants and the many more anecdotes reported nationally were finally confirmed by a statistical study of misuse of these drugs that appeared in the journal *Drug and Alcohol Dependence* in early 2006. The authors analyzed government-collected data of face-to-face interviews with 54,000 people in 2002. Taking into account U.S. 2000 census data, the researchers estimated that over seven million people have misused prescription stimulants. Of children between twelve and seventeen years old, 2.6 percent reported misusing stimulants, and in the age group of eighteen to twenty-five, 5.9 percent admitted to illegal prescription stimulant use.

More sobering are the stories of those younger kids who acknowledged use of these drugs and who met *DSM-IV* criteria for drug dependency or drug abuse. A little more than one in ten children who begin with casual use of these drugs go on to become stimulant addicts. This translates to about 75,000 teens and young adults in 2002 addicted to prescription stimulants. And annual production quota rates from the Drug Enforcement Administration (DEA) indicate that more legal speed has been produced in our country since that time.

A couple of doctors like me and officials from the Chemical Diversion Division of the DEA have fretted for years about the likelihood of a fourth wave of doctor-prescribed stimulant abuse. I earlier mentioned the Allies' use of these drugs with American GIs during World War II. Many of these soldiers came back to the States addicted to amphetamine. The early 1960s were marked by an era of "Dr. Feelgoods" who went so far as to inject amphetamine intravenously into their patients for a variety of ill-defined medical and emotional problems. The last wave of doctor-prescribed stimulant abuse (until this current one) took place in the 1970s and only ended when Congress and the states set limits and penalties on the use of prescription amphetamine for weight loss and control.

Repeatedly, American doctors and American society seem to lose their collective memory over these drugs and find another reason to prescribe them. "America Taking 'Uppers'," legal or illegal, ran a headline of a UN Narcotic Control Report in 1999. These drugs "work," no doubt, but at least in adults, whether they are used for losing weight or concentrating better, the evidence is only for short-term benefits. When the long-term data on weight loss and stimulants was examined by doctors and public officials in the 1970s, it was clear that in the long term, the medications were ineffective, and development of tolerance (needing increasing doses for the same effect) was common.

The longest study on the effects of prescription stimulants among teens and adults ran only two to three months. There are no long-term studies of, say, five years. In my experience of treating about fifteen older teens and adults for over five years, I'd estimate that in only three or four cases has the drug really made a difference in the quality of their lives (e.g., improved their employment status or family life). Ominously, tolerance has developed in four of these patients (my limit with them is 90 mg of Adderall XR daily).

The downside of prescription stimulants has been well known to researchers for decades, but for example, as of early 2006, I had still not found one research article on the development of tolerance with the use of prescription stimulants in adults. To some extent, doctors and the public have been misled by the excellent safety record of the use of these drugs in the preteen population. No child under thirteen has ever been reported to be addicted to Ritalin. Children don't have access to the medication and interestingly don't like higher doses ("I feel nervous. I feel weird" is what they tell their parents when the dose gets too high for them.). But access to the medication and response to higher doses ("I feel powerful. I feel grand.") are different in older teens and adults.

Ironically, the first study that analyzed the government data on prescription stimulant abuse was funded by Eli Lilly, the makers of Strattera, the only nonstimulant, non-abusable drug approved for the treatment of ADHD. Lilly's strategy is obvious. Lilly hopes this study will raise further concerns about drugs such as Adderall and Concerta that clearly work better than Strattera for ADHD but that have abuse potential. It seems in America that if there isn't money to be made, no one will do the work necessary to find out if any drug is safe or works long-term.

But in fact, most people can use prescription stimulants occasionally without much trouble. As word of the "benefits" of these drugs continues to spread, we will hear more about the use of Ritalin (and the other prescription stimulants) in questionable situations. In sports competition, the use of performance enhancing drugs is banned. In athletics we value not just the performance itself but also the effort involved in the achievement. Taking a drug somehow cheapens that performance.

These drugs are also banned because if we permit one athlete to take performance drugs, then we actually put pressure on all the other competing athletes to take the drug too, just in order to stay even. My seventeen-year-old son, a junior in high school, tells me about rampant Adderall use at his school during exam time for studying or test taking. We've talked about it at home and agree that improved performance by taking a drug isn't worth the improvement or the risk, but I still wonder if he isn't feeling some pressure to take these drugs too.

But isn't school different from sports anyway? Well, yes and no, yet there's certainly a competitive element to academics, especially with exams like the SAX GREs, MCATs, and LSATs. Without a clear line for diagnosis, how do we really know who legitimately "has or doesn't have" ADHD and who can benefit from Ritalin? And with so much available prescription stimulant medication out there anyway, you don't really need to go to a doctor to get your pills for the test.

It sounds incredible at this moment to consider, but will we in the near future need to require students to submit to random drug urine testing before they take important exams? Our national obsession with performance continues, and Ritalin will only complicate the race. But ultimately, a society that chooses to cope with life's challenges by turning to drugs does so at its own peril.

POSTSCRIPT

Should School-Age Children with Attention Deficit/Hyperactivity Disorder (ADHD) Be Treated with Ritalin and Other Stimulants?

To satisfy their own emotional needs, many parents push their physicians into diagnosing their children with ADHD. Some of these parents believe that their children will benefit if they are labeled ADHD. The pressure for children to do well academically in order to get into the right college and graduate school is intense. Some parents feel that if their children are diagnosed with ADHD, then they may be provided special circumstances or allowances such as additional time when taking college entrance examinations. Some parents also realize that if their children are identified as having ADHD, then they will be eligible for extra services in school. In some instances, the only way to receive such extra help is to be labeled with a disorder. Also, some teachers favor the use of Ritalin and other stimulants to control students' behavior. During the last few years, there has been increasing emphasis on controlling school budgets. The result is larger class sizes and higher student-to-teacher ratios. Thus, it should not be surprising that many teachers welcome the calming effect of Ritalin and other stimulants on students whose hyperactivity is disruptive to the class.

Whether or not drug therapy should be applied to behavioral problems raises another concern. What is the message that children are receiving about the role of drugs in society? Perhaps children will generalize the benefits of using legal drugs like Ritalin to remedy life's problems to using alcohol or illegal drugs to deal with other problems that they may be experiencing. Children may find that it is easier to drink alcohol or ingest a pill rather than to put the time and effort into resolving personal problems. For many adults, drugs seem to represent a shortcut to correcting life's difficulties. Through its reliance on drugs, is American society creating a wrong impression for its children, an illusion of believing that there is a pill for every ill?

When to prescribe Ritalin and other stimulants for children also places physicians in a quandary. They may see the benefit of helping students function more effectively in school. However, are physicians who readily prescribe Ritalin unintentionally promoting an antihumanistic, competitive environment in which performance matters regardless of cost? On the other hand, is it the place of physicians to dictate to parents what is best for their children? Should physicians acquiesce to the desires of parents who want to place their children on these drugs? In the final analysis, will the increase in prescriptions for Ritalin and other stimulants result in benefits for the child, for the parents, and for society?

Two articles that question the validity of attention deficit/hyperactivity disorder are "The Myth of ADHD and the Scandal of Ritalin: Helping John Dewey Students Succeed in Medicine-Free College Preparatory and Therapeutic High School" by Thomas Bratter (*International Journal of Reality Therapy,* Fall 2007); Rachel Ragg's "School Uniformity," in *Ecologist* (November 2006); and Jonathon Leo's "Broken Brains or Flawed Studies? A Critical Review of ADHD Neuroimaging Research," in *The Journal of Mind and Behavior* (Winter 2003). An article that addresses how individuals with attention deficit disorder are portrayed in popular culture is "Media Representations of Attention Deficit Disorder: Portrayals of Cultural Skepticism in Popular Media" by Elizabeth Kennedy (*The Journal of Popular Culture,* 2008). The use of Ritalin and Adderall on college campuses is discussed in "High and Mighty" by Abigail Rasminsky (*Dance Spirit,* September 2008). The effects of Ritalin are examined in "ADHD: A Research Study," by Judy Broadway in *Education Today* (2006).

ISSUE 13

Do Consumers Benefit When Prescription Drugs Are Advertised?

YES: **Merrill Matthews Jr.**, from "Advertising Drugs Is Good for Patients," *Consumers' Research Magazine* (August 2001)

NO: **Dominick L. Frosch, Patrick M. Krueger, Robert C. Hornik, Peter F. Cronholm and Frances K. Barg**, from "Creating Demand for Prescription Drugs: A Content Analysis of Television Direct-to-Consumer Advertising," *Annals of Family Medicine* (January/February 2007)

ISSUE SUMMARY

YES: Merrill Matthews, a health policy advisor with the American Legislative Exchange Council, argues that the advertising of prescription drugs directly to consumers will result in better-informed consumers. Additionally, communication between doctors and patients may improve because patients will be more knowledgeable about drugs.

NO: Dominic Frosch of the UCLA School of Medicine and his colleagues maintain that direct-to-consumer drug advertisements provide limited educational value to consumers. Moreover, the benefits of some prescription drugs are exaggerated. Frosch and associates feel that the drug advertisements dissuade individuals from engaging in health-promoting activities.

One of the most lucrative businesses in the world today is the prescription drug business. Billions of dollars are spent every year for prescription drugs in the United States alone. But, the *only* way for consumers to obtain a prescribed drug is through a physician. In the early 1980s drug companies in the United States began to advertise directly to the consumer. It is logical for drug companies to advertise to physicians because they are responsible for writing prescriptions. However, is it logical for pharmaceutical manufacturers to advertise their drugs directly to consumers? Are consumers capable of making informed, rational decisions regarding their pharmaceutical needs? Do consumers derive any benefits when prescription drugs are advertised?

An increasing number of individuals are assuming more responsibility for their own health care. In the United States, over one-third of all prescriptions are written at the request of patients. Also, many patients do not take their doctors' prescriptions to pharmacies to be filled. Both of these scenarios raise the question of whether consumers are adequately educated to make decisions pertaining to their pharmaceutical needs or to assess risks associated with prescription drugs. Evidence suggests that many are not. Prescription drugs, for example, cause more worksite accidents than illegal drugs do.

Some commentators, however, argue that there are several advantages to directly advertising drugs to consumers. One advantage is that direct advertisements make consumers better informed about the benefits and risks of certain drugs. For example, it is not unusual for a person to experience side effects from a drug without knowing that the drug was responsible for the side effects. Advertisements can provide this information. Another advantage for consumers is that they may learn about medications that they might not have known existed. Furthermore, advertising lowers the cost of prescription drugs because consumers are able to ask their physicians to prescribe less expensive drugs than the physician might be inclined to recommend. Finally, prescription drug advertising allows consumers to become more involved in choosing the medications that they need or want.

Critics argue that there are a number of risks associated with the direct advertising of prescription drugs. One concern is with the content of drug advertisements. Consumers may not pay enough attention to information detailing a drug's adverse effects. Also, sometimes a drug's benefits are exaggerated. Another problem is that there are many instances in which drugs that have been approved by the Food and Drug Administration (FDA) for one purpose have been promoted for other purposes. Is the average consumer capable of understanding the purposes of the drugs that are being advertised?

Opponents of direct-to-consumer drug advertisements express concern with the way in which the information in the advertisements is presented. Promotions for drugs that appear as objective reports are often actually slick publicity material. In such promotions, medical experts are shown providing testimony regarding a particular drug. Many consumers may not be aware that these physicians have financial ties to the pharmaceutical companies. Celebrities—in whom the public often places its trust despite their lack of medical expertise—are used to promote drugs also. Finally, the cost of the drugs advertised, a major concern to most consumers, is seldom mentioned in the advertisements.

In the following selections, Merrill Matthews argues that the marketing of prescription drugs helps consumers because it lowers the cost of drugs and effectively informs consumers about the benefits of new drugs. Dominic Frosch and associates do not believe the advertising of pharmaceutical drugs is beneficial to consumers. Individuals may rely on drugs for their health needs rather than engage in health-promoting activities.

YES

Merrill Matthews Jr.

Advertising Drugs Is Good for Patients

Many health policy experts believe that direct-to-consumer (DTC) advertising by pharmaceutical companies misinforms gullible consumers, encourages drug overconsumption, increases health care costs, strains doctor-patient relationships and undermines the quality of patient care. For example:

- The American College of Physicians and the American Society of Internal Medicine, in a joint policy statement, wrote: "We are concerned that advertising will result in increased consumption of these highly advertised drugs; though their use may be neither appropriate nor necessary." The organizations also wrote: "Many times, physicians will give in to the demand and when they don't, often patients will 'doctor shop' until they find a physician who will prescribe the medication."
- Sen. Tim Johnson (D-S.D.) also questioned the growth of DTC. "Is the information value worth the yearly increases in drug costs that advertising inevitably causes? Are patients getting the best individual choices of medicines or just the best advertised ones? Are generic drugs, often an excellent cost-effective alternative, getting equal consideration?"
- Finally, members of the Committee on Bioethical Issues of the Medical Society of the State of New York wrote: "Direct drug advertising provides no real benefit to patients, is potentially harmful, and is costly. We therefore urge the U.S. Food and Drug Administration to review and strengthen its policies concerning this practice."

Are these criticisms accurate? In some cases, yes. For example, DTC advertising does encourage more drug consumption—which can lower some health care costs when drug therapy precludes the need for other, more expensive therapies.

However, the above-mentioned concerns largely are misdirected. They focus on the evolving pharmaceutical marketplace when in fact the whole health care system is in transition. And direct-to-consumer pharmaceutical ads are a response to the transitional process, not the cause of it.

The U.S. health care system has reached a cross-roads, and the direction the country takes will determine the type, availability and quality of care for years to come. Pharmaceutical advertising pre-supposes that health care consumers can make choices for themselves—and that's the type of health care system people want. Those who have no choice in health care have no need of advertising.

A health care system in transition   America is in the forefront of the information economy. One of the hallmarks of this new economy is access to much more information by many more people. Patients have much greater access to health care information, especially through the Internet and through advertising. Indeed, the most important change occurring in the health care system is this access to information. According to health care consultant Lyn Siegel:

- About 25% of on-line information is related to health;
- More than 50% of adults who go on the Web use it for health care information; and
- More than 26% of people who go to disease-oriented Web sites ask their doctors for a specific brand of medication. Thus information is driving the transition to a patient-directed health care system.

A generation ago physicians were the possessors of all medical information. Patients went to physicians and accepted evaluations and diagnoses almost without question. Patients who want second opinions and physicians who gracefully accede to their wishes are relatively new phenomena.

In a physician-directed health care system:

- Physicians have all the extant medical knowledge and skills;
- Physicians perform all patient examinations;
- Patients accept their physicians' diagnoses and insurers pay for the care;
- Hospitals admit patients based on physicians' orders and pharmacists fill the prescriptions; and,
- Drug and medical device companies market to the physicians who control all access to patients.

In this model, no one reaches patients without a physician's consent. The physician-directed system worked well for several decades. The vast majority of working Americans had good health insurance benefits that protected them, their families and their assets from catastrophic losses due to a major accident or illness. Third-party payers were generous in their reimbursement policies while doctors and hospitals could do only so much. Whatever doctors recommended, insurers covered.

Once the amazing medical advances of the 1970s and 1980s began to appear, health care costs began to soar. Insured workers and seniors on Medicare were insulated from the cost of care, and so had little incentive to control health care spending. Employers and the government, who paid most health care bills, desperately sought cost-control mechanisms. That's when managed care came in. Its proponents claimed that managed care could lower the cost of comprehensive health care coverage, in part by controlling utilization. While the arguments continue over how well managed care controlled costs and whether it sacrificed quality to achieve savings, the growth in health care spending did slow during the 1990s. Recently, though, the rate of growth has escalated and engendered fears of more double-digit increases in health care spending.

Meanwhile, the expansion of managed care helped to undermine the physician-directed health care system. Insurers and employers gained the power to question and even override doctors' decisions, which put doctors in an uncomfortable and unsatisfactory position.

Patients also reacted negatively. Many believed their doctors were willing or able to give them only the level of care their insurers would cover. This distrust undermined the doctor-patient relationship and spurred patients to seek health care information directly, rather than from their doctor or insurer. Thus health care consumers began to exploit the information economy.

Increasingly, patients are entering the health care system armed with information—and sometimes misinformation. They may not know how to practice medicine, but many know something about their medical condition and the options available to them. And they raise questions if the doctor follows a different path from the one they expect.

As Dr. Thomas R. Reardon, past president of the American Medical Association, has insightfully noted: "Patients themselves are also creating a strong impetus for change. Disillusioned by restrictions on coverage and care, they are increasingly demanding choice of physician, hospital, and even type of health plan. More than ever, patients see physicians as the essential point of trust in a changing system, and demand choice and stability in their vital relationships with their doctors. . . . At the same time, patients themselves are becoming better educated, not only about insurance options but also about medical treatments. Today, thanks to the Internet, trends in product advertising, and the massive proliferation of medical information, patients are better equipped to take part in their care than ever before. Rather than simplifying the physician's job, however, this increased patient knowledge base is creating new challenges."

We are transitioning toward a patient-directed health care system—if the federal and state governments don't intervene—in which all of the components cater to the patient, rather than the physician. It is impossible to overstate the magnitude of the change. We aren't there yet, but the system is moving—or being pulled—in that direction.

In the new system, insurers and employers, doctors and other health care providers, researchers and pharmaceutical companies will view the patient rather than the provider as the primary consumer. And in the new system:

- Insurers will have to create products that consumers rather than their employers want;
- Doctors will have to please their patients rather than insurers, reinvigorating the weakened doctor-patient relationship; and
- Pharmaceutical and medical device companies increasingly will market directly to the consumers who use their products.

Because health care consumers are becoming better informed, they will, on balance, make better decisions. And they will want even more information.

But how do companies and providers reach individuals with the information the latter want and need? One way is through advertising.

Every Sunday newspaper is filled with advertising flyers for department stores, office products, computers, cars, food and clothing. Yet people don't complain they can't afford food because all the grocery stores advertise. And does anyone really think they would be able to get a computer for less money if none of the computer manufacturers and retail outlets advertised?

In virtually every sector of the economy, those with products or services to sell must get information to those who will buy. Advertising is the vehicle for getting information to the intended customers. It tells prospective customers about product availability, quality and cost—the information those prospects need in order to make comparisons. While some people may consider it annoying if they are not looking for a particular product, those in the market for the advertised item often will pay close attention to ads and other marketing techniques such as direct mail and communication from sales representatives.

The general assumption is that advertising raises the costs of products. This assumption recently has entered the debate over the impact of drug companies' advertisements aimed at consumers. But advertising can—and should—lower costs. For example, according to economist John Calfee of the American Enterprise Institute:

> A pioneering study compared the prices of eye-glasses in states that either permitted or restricted advertising for eyeglass services. Prices were about 25% higher where advertising was restricted or banned (and prices were highest for the least educated consumers). A later study by the Federal Trade Commission (FTC) staff showed that product quality in the states without advertising was not higher despite the higher prices. Studies also found higher prices in the absence of advertising for such diverse products as gasoline, prescription drugs and legal services.

How is it that advertising can actually lower prices? Most products have certain fixed costs, plus some variable costs. While variable costs are imputed to each item produced, fixed costs are divided by the number of products sold. The goal of advertising is to expand consumer awareness and increase sales. The more items sold, the greater the economies of scale and the lower the fixed costs per consumer.

Holman Jenkins of the *Wall Street Journal* explains the rationale: "The media also complain about advertising as if this were an extra cost borne by drug users. Drug companies spend on advertising because it's profitable—it pays for itself by generating additional sales, allowing development costs to be spread over a larger number of users. The average price to each user is lower."

In the absence of competition, advertising might raise prices. But in the absence of competition, vendors would likely raise prices whether they advertised or not. Competition keeps manufacturers from charging as much as they would like, except in cases where there is an unusually high demand for a particular product (as when everyone decides they want a Cabbage Patch doll, a Tickle Me Elmo or a Furby for Christmas). Thus, even when advertising doesn't increase sales, vendors cannot add the cost on top of the product if there are other competitively priced alternatives on the market.

DTC ads and the health care system   Putting information in the hands of consumers who didn't have that information before is a revolutionary business—and revolutions engender change. Critics know this and raise concerns that DTC advertising will increase health care spending, strain doctor-patient relationships and confuse consumers and patients. Worst of all, they believe going directly to the consumer is only a drug company technique to increase prices and therefore profits. Are any of these concerns valid?

Will DTC advertising increase health care spending?   Probably, but that is not necessarily bad. Increased health care spending is bad only when it is wasteful and inefficient. For example, if doctors were to prescribe medicines for patients who had no medical need, that would be wasteful—and unethical. However, very few doctors would prescribe medicines their patients do not need. In fact, a new *Prevention* magazine survey found that about half of those who talk to a doctor as a result of a DTC ad receive no drug therapy.

A greater concern is that patients, having seen an expensive brand-name drug advertised, will want it rather than a generic equivalent. When patients or their doctors choose brand names over generics, their choices may increase total health care spending. But, again, that may not be bad. The brand name may be higher in quality or slightly different in composition. And it may have fewer side effects. Thus it may offer additional benefits, in which case the additional cost may be justified.

If an expansion of DTC advertising means that we are treating more people who otherwise might have just suffered in pain or endured a debilitating condition, then increased medical spending is positive. Some have argued that increased drug spending may lower total health care costs if less expensive drug therapy replaces more expensive surgery or other procedures. This may be true for individual patients, but it cannot be aggregated to apply to the whole health care system. Total spending will continue to rise because the American health care system will continue to do more and more for patients.

Will DTC advertising strain the doctor-patient relationship?   Historically, doctors informed and patients performed. That is, doctors diagnosed and issued instructions that patients followed—or at least were supposed to. With more information at the patients' fingertips, that relationship is changing. Patients are asking questions, and doctors are beginning to see the questions as opportunities to enhance patients' understanding and sense of responsibility about their own health. (The author himself has asked a physician about an advertised prescription drug, and neither he nor the doctor saw anything unusual or unethical about the exchange.)

Doctors may have to take more time to discuss with their patients why Drug A, which the patient saw advertised on TV, would not in the doctor's opinion be as good a choice as Drug B. Cost, efficacy and suitability all may play a role in that discussion. Some irascible patients may refuse to accept the doctor's advice. But this occurs even without DTC advertising. Indeed, current DTC advertising is very subtle. No announcer tells the audience to demand Drug A from a doctor because it has been clinically proven to be better than Drug B. DTC ads tend to convey too little information rather than too much. This may change, but the medical community already is learning to deal with people who come to the doctor not just as patients but as consumers.

Will DTC ads confuse patients?   Economist John Calfee contends that three decades of research on advertising has led to two basic understandings:

> First, advertising has an unsuspected power to improve consumer wel-fare. As a market-perfecting mechanism, advertising arises spontaneously to attack serious defects in the marketplace. Advertising is an efficient and sometimes irreplaceable mechanism for bringing consumers infor-mation that would otherwise languish on the sidelines. Advertising's promise of more and better information also generates ripple effects in the market. These include enhanced incentives to create new informa-tion and develop better products. Theoretical and empirical research has demonstrated what generations of astute observers had known intuitively, that markets with advertising are far superior to markets without advertising.
>
> The second finding is that competitive advertising is fundamen-tally a self-correcting process. Some people may find this surprising. Well-informed observers once thought that unregulated advertising would bring massive distortion of consumer information and decisions. Careful research, however, has shown these fears to be groundless. Self-correcting competitive forces in advertising generate markets in which information is richer and more fundamentally balanced than can be achieved through detailed controls over advertising and information.

Is DTC just a way to increase drug prices?   Drug companies advertise for the same reason every other company and industry advertises: to increase sales with a view to increasing profits. The consumer benefit is that, as competi-tion grows, prices usually fall. By contrast, in the absence of marketing, prices would not go down, but up. Just consider under which scenario a manufac-turer is more likely to charge high prices for low quality: where there is no advertising and consumers have no way to comparison-shop without taking their own time to go from store to store to compare price and quality, or where advertising takes that information directly to the consumer? It is not advertis-ing that increases the price of products, it's the lack of it. High prices thrive in an atmosphere of ignorance. If critics want to see the price of prescription drugs fall, they should encourage even more advertising and competition.

The missing ingredient: value   As long as patients are insulated from the cost of medical care and doctors stand between patients and their prescrip-tions, the health care marketplace cannot work exactly like a normal market in which consumers demand from vendors quality, service and reasonable prices—that is, value.

But the U.S. health care system can take on some of the dynamics of a market, and in fact is already doing so. There is some competition; there is some DTC advertising; and prices at least for some health care products and services are relatively low.

As we continue to move into a patient-directed system, market forces may become more apparent. For example, if most people chose to combine a Medical Savings Account (MSA) for small expenses with a catastrophic health insurance policy for large expenses, patients would pay for their prescription drugs out of the MSA and thus be more cost-conscious.

In addition, the realization is growing in Washington that the current tax subsidy for health insurance causes problems. As a result, Congress may pass a tax credit that will help the uninsured purchase a policy. This in turn may lead to a fundamental shift in the type of health insurance policy people purchase—and facilitate the move to a patient-directed system.

Dominick L. Frosch, Patrick
M. Krueger, Robert C. Hornik, Peter
F. Cronholm, and Frances K. Barg

Creating Demand for Prescription Drugs: A Content Analysis of Television Direct-to-Consumer Advertising

Introduction

The United States and New Zealand are the only developed countries that permit direct-to-consumer advertising (DTCA) of prescription drugs. Average American television viewers see as many as 16 hours of prescription drug advertisements (ads) per year, far exceeding the average time spent with a primary care physician. Since the Food and Drug Administration (FDA) relaxed DTCA regulations in 1997, a polarized debate around the practice has ensued.

Opponents argue that ads mislead consumers and prompt requests for products that are unneeded or more expensive than other equally effective drugs or nonpharmacologic treatment options. Proponents counter that DTCA educates people about health conditions and available treatments and empowers them to become more active participants in their own care, thereby strengthening the health care system.

Television advertising now comprises most of the consumer-directed prescription pharmaceutical marketing expenditures. Previous research has examined print ads, but unlike print ads, television ads combine visual imagery, music, and spoken words to create complex stories that may provide more information and appeal to a wider range of consumer emotions. To date, no one has analyzed systematically what television ads claim about health conditions, how they attempt to appeal to consumers, or how they portray the role of lifestyle behaviors and medication in achieving good health. These questions are critically important given evidence that DTCA prompts consumers to request prescriptions for advertised products from their physicians, and that many of those requests are fulfilled despite being judged clinically inappropriate.

The goal of our study was to analyze the content of television DTCA messages to lay the foundation for future studies that examine the consequences of DTCA exposure. Little is known about how DTCA affects people's health-related beliefs and behaviors beyond prescription requests, even though television

From *Annals of Family Medicine*, January/February 2007, pp. 6–12. Copyright © 2007 by American Academy of Family Physicians. Reprinted by permission.

pharmaceutical ads are among the most common forms of mediated health communication in the United States. Content analysis is a well-established method of inquiry for generating research questions and hypotheses for future experimental and observational studies that examine the effects of advertising on consumers' beliefs and behaviors.

Methods
Sampling Strategy

We focused on ads that have the largest audiences, drawing a sample from peak television viewing times (prime time, 8:00-11:00 PM) and the evening news on channels with the most viewers (ABC, CBS, NBC, and Fox). We recorded programming for 4 consecutive weeks (June 30, 2004, to July 27, 2004), randomly selecting a different channel each day but never recording the same channel on 2 consecutive days. Each day of the week was represented for each network.

The FDA regulations distinguish between product claim ads and reminder ads. Product claim ads must include the name and indication of the drug, as well as a major statement of product risks, and they must direct consumers to a detailed summary of product risks and benefits accessible through a toll-free telephone number, an Internet site, or a concurrent print ad. We limited our analysis to television ads, rather than Internet, print, or telephone sources, because television ads reach a wider audience, and people might seek further information only if the ads are sufficiently compelling. Reminder ads are shorter and can mention the product name, but may not discuss indications, efficacy, or dosage recommendations. Our programming sample captured a total 103 ads comprising 31 unique product claim ads and 7 unique reminder ads, which provided the basis for our analysis (Table 1).

For each reminder ad we also had a corresponding product claim ad. We included reminder ads in our sample to describe how the messages and themes being communicated were affected by the shorter length of these ads. Our sample captured ads for 7 of the 10 topselling prescription drugs in 2004.

Ad Coding

We used 2 strategies to code the ads. First, to code the ads for the types of factual claims about the target condition (excluding product risk information) and the types of appeals to viewers, we drew on categories previously developed for print ads. The specific factual claim categories we coded are shown in Table 2. Proponents of DTCA have argued that ads serve in part to educate the public about diseases. Hence, our goal was to enumerate the frequency with which television ads made factual claims, regardless of the accuracy of this information. We drew on categories previously applied to print ads to code how the ads attempted to appeal to viewers with (1) rational appeals—providing information about product use, features, or comparison with similar products; (2) positive emotional appeals—evoking favorable affect, for example, by showing happiness; (3) negative emotional appeals—evoking negative affect

Table 1

Drug Advertisements Captured in Sample

Brand name	Generic Product Name	Manufacturer	Advertised indication
Actonel *	Risedronate	Procter & Gamble, Cincinnati, Ohio	Osteoporosis
Allegra *	Fexofenadine	Aventis, Bridgewater, NJ	Allergy
Ambien[†]	Zolpidem	Sanofi-Synthelabo, New York, NY	Insomnia
Celebrex[†]	Celecoxib	Pfizer, New York, NY	Osteoarthritis, rheumatoid arthritis
Cialis[†]	Tadalafil	Lilly ICOS, Indianapolis, Ind	Erectile dysfunction
Crestor*	Rosuvastatin	AstraZeneca, Wilmington, Del	Hypercholesterolemia
Detrol LA*	Tolterodine	Pfizer, New York, NY	Overactive bladder
Enbrel*	Etanercept	Immunex, Thousand Oaks, Calif	Rheumatoid arthritis
Fosamax*	Alendronate	Merck, Whitehouse Station, NJ	Osteoporosis
Lamisil*	Terbinafine	Novartis, East Hanover, NJ	Onychomycosis
Levitra*	Vardenafil	Bayer, West Haven, Conn	Erectile dysfunction
Lipitor[†]	Atorvastatin	Pfizer, New York, NY	Hypercholesterolemia
Nexium*	Esomeprazole	AstraZeneca, Wilmington, Del	Gastroesophageal reflux disease
Diovan*[†]	Valsartan	Novartis, East Hanover, NJ	Hypertension
Diovan HCT	Valsartan & HCT	Novartis, East Hanover, NJ	Hypertension
Lotrel	Amlodipine & Benazepril	Novartis, East Hanover, NJ	Hypertension
Plavix*	Clopidogrel	Bristol-Myers Squibb, Princeton, NJ	Acute coronary syndrome
Prevacid[†]	Lansoprazole	TAP, Lake Forest, Ill	Gastroesophageal reflux disease
Procrit[†]	Epoetin Alfa	Amgen, Thousand Oaks, Calif	Chemotherapy-related anemia
Singulair*	Montelukast	Merck, Whitehouse Station, NJ	Allergy
Valtrex[†]	Valacyclovir	GlaxoSmithKline, Middlesex, UK	Genital herpes
Zelnorm*	Tegaserod	Novartis, East Hanover, NJ	Irritable bowel syndrome with constipation
Zocor*	Simvastatin	Merck, Whitehouse Station, NJ	Hypercholesterolemia
Zoloft*	Sertraline	Pfizer, New York, NY	Depression, social anxiety disorder

* Product claim advertisement only.

† Product claim and reminder advertisement.

‡ Advertisement promoted unnamed products that were identified on corresponding Web site.

by portraying fear, regret, or other negative emotions; (4) humor appeals—using puns, jokes, or satire; (5) fantasy appeals—depicting an unrealistic or surreal scene; (6) sex appeals—showing characters in an intimate encounter, scantily clad, or using provocative gestures; and (7) nostalgic appeals—using images from an earlier time, or black-and-white or sepia tone visuals.

Second, we developed inductive codes by approaching our sample with 2 research questions: (1) How do the ads portray the role of medication in the lives of characters? and (2) How do the ads portray the role of healthy lifestyle behavior in the lives of characters? We used grounded theory coding procedures to inductively develop common thematic categories and refine their definitions and properties. Because our study was descriptive and did not aim to produce a theory, we limited our use of grounded theory procedures to open and axial coding. Open coding refers to the analytical process of examining, comparing, and categorizing qualitative data to develop thematic concepts. Axial coding involves coding similar data sequences to foster connections between emerging thematic concepts. Both coding procedures permit a thematic analysis of content data in mixed methods research projects. The first author (DLF) led the analytical process in frequent consultation with the coauthors, a team whose disciplinary backgrounds included clinical psychology (DLF), sociology (PMK), communication (RCH), medicine (PFC) and anthropology (FKB). The authors discussed the thematic concepts that emerged when viewing a sample of the ads. The defining properties of the concepts were gradually refined to create specific coding categories, whereupon 2 bachelor's level research assistants were trained to code all of the ads independently.

Coding Reliability and Frequency Presentation

We had good aggregate interrater reliability for our coding categories, as indicated by κ values ranging from .76 to .88. Coding disagreements between the research assistants were resolved through consensus. We report weighted frequencies that reflect the overall prevalence of the codes among the ads captured in the programming we recorded. The weights equal the total number of times each of the 38 ads was captured in our sample (mean = 2.7, SD = 2.3, range 1–12). Thus, ads that were captured more often in our sample had a proportionately greater impact on the prevalence of different coding categories. The unweighted data (not shown) reflected similar frequencies and patterns of the codes.

Results

Ad Length and Story Structure

The average ad length was 44.9 seconds (SD 18.6 seconds, range 14–62 seconds); product claim ads (mean = 51.8, SD 12.7) were significantly longer than reminder ads (mean = 14.4, SD 0.5; Mann-Whitney U = 5.0; P <.001). We identified 3 story structures for the ads. Almost one half (44.7%) of the ads showed characters before and after taking the product. A smaller proportion (39.5%) showed characters only after taking the product, and a minority showed characters only before taking the product (7.9%). Three ads (7.9%) did not use any characters or did not clearly depict whether characters had taken the product.

Factual Claims About the Target Condition

Because reminder ads cannot legally present factual information, we focused on product claim ads. Most of the ads made some factual claims about the target condition of the product, typically by mentioning condition symptoms (Table 2). More than one half the ads made a claim about the biological nature or mechanism of the disease, but only 26% made claims about risk factors or causes of the condition. Almost 25% made claims about the population prevalence of the condition, but among these ads, only 25% gave specific information (eg, 1 in 9). The remaining ads used vague terms, such as "millions." Only 8% of the ads identified specific subpopulations at increased risk of having the condition. Consistent with FDA regulations, all product claim ads, but none of the reminder ads, included information about major risks and side-effects. This information was always provided in the latter part of the ad, but never at the end, always leaving the final frames for a promotional message.

Table 2

Proportion of Advertisements That Present Factual Claims, Appeals, Lifestyle, and Medication Themes

	Weighted Percentages		
Categories of Content	All Ads	Product Claim Ads	Reminder Ads
Factual claims*			
Any factual information (eg, symptoms)	—	82.0	—
Biological nature or mechanism of disease	—	53.9	—
Risk factors or cause of condition	—	25.8	—
Prevalence of condition	—	24.7	—
Subpopulation at risk of the condition		7.9	
Appeals			
Rational	86.4	100.0	0.0
Positive emotional	95.1	94.4	100.0
Negative emotional	68.9	75.3	28.6
Humor	32.0	36.0	7.1
Fantasy	20.4	22.5	7.1
Sex	5.8	4.5	14.3
Nostalgia	3.9	3.4	7.1
Lifestyle portrayals			
Condition interferes with healthy or recreational activities	26.2	30.3	0.0
Product enables healthy or recreational activities	56.3	56.2	57.1
Lifestyle change is alternative to product use	0.0	0.0	0.0
Lifestyle change is insufficient	18.4	21.3	0.0
Lifestyle change is adjunct to product	19.4	22.5	0.0
Medication portrayals			
Loss of control caused by condition	58.3	67.4	0.0
Regaining control as result of product use	85.4	88.8	64.3
Social approval as a result of product use	77.7	83.1	42.9
Distress caused by condition	47.6	53.9	7.1
Breakthrough	58.3	67.4	0.0
Endurance increased as a result of product use	17.5	12.4	50.0
Protection as a result of product use	9.7	11.2	0.0

Note: Total unweighted N = 38, product claim ads n = 31, reminder ads n = 7.

* The Food and Drug Administration does not permit the presentation of factual information in reminder ads.

Appeals

Table 2 shows that all product claim ads used rational appeals, such as describing the product indication. Consistent with FDA regulations, reminder ads never used rational appeals. Almost 95% of product claim ads and 100% of the reminder ads used positive emotional appeals, often by depicting a happy character after taking a product. Sixty-nine percent of the ads used negative emotional appeals, such as showing a character in a fearful state before using the product. Almost one third of the ads used humor to appeal to viewers, sometimes by making fun of the character before taking the product.

Lifestyle Portrayals

Our inductive coding procedures identified 5 themes related to lifestyle portrayals of the ad characters (Table 2). Twenty-six percent of the ads suggested that the target condition may interfere with healthy or recreational activities, and 56% of the ads suggested that the product enables healthy or recreational activities. We coded the physical activities portrayed in the ads, distinguishing among mild, moderate, and vigorous physical activity (results not tabled). More than one half of the ads (52.7%) showed the primary character engaging in some physical activity. Eighty percent of these ads showed characters engaging in moderate or vigorous physical activity.

Several of the products advertised for our sample of ads target conditions (eg, hypercholesterolemia, insomnia, hypertension) that have nonpharmacological treatment alternatives which involve behavior change. None of these ads explicitly mentioned behavior changes as an alternative to the product. More than 18% of the ads suggested that lifestyle change is insufficient to manage the condition, implying that using the product was a superior alternative. Nineteen percent of the ads suggested that lifestyle change may be an adjunct to using the product.

Medication Portrayals

We inductively identified 7 themes related to medication portrayals in the ads: (1) loss of control—the characters have lost control of some biological process, function, or ability as a result of their condition; (2) regaining control—the characters have resumed control of some biological process, function, or ability by using the advertised product; (3) social approval—the characters are viewed favorably by others because they used the product, or that people frequently use the product; (4) distress—the ad shows a character in physical, emotional, or social distress; (5) breakthrough—the ad suggests the product represents a breakthrough in medical science or progress in treating or curing a disease; (6) endurance—the ad suggests the product could increase endurance for some activity; and (7) protection—the ad suggests the product could protect individuals from some health risk.

As shown in Table 2, many ads framed their products around loss of control, which often had a profound detrimental effect on the character's life. Further, most ads suggested that characters can regain control of lost functions or abilities by using the product. All ads that showed a loss of control subsequently showed regaining control through product use. Nearly 78% of the ads showed characters who received social approval for using and benefiting from the product. Given the complexity of these themes, Table 3 displays selected examples of how the ads depicted loss of control, regaining control, and subsequent social approval.

More than 58% of the ads claimed that the advertised products represented a medical or scientific breakthrough, often in such statements as "[the product] goes beyond what you were previously taking," "now you can . . . ," ". . . only [the product] can. . . ." Smaller percentages of ads indicated that the product enhances endurance in some activity, such as being able to work, or protects against some health risk, such as blood clots or herpes outbreaks.

Sample Television Ad

The Supplemental Figure . . . illustrates the application of the codes to an ad for rosuvastatin. The ad narrative provides a complete transcript of the spoken content, except for the statement of risks. For each frame, we note the codes we applied. Using black humor, the first 2 frames show "Joe" running through the "Land of No," a grim and deserted urban setting. Joe has lost control over his cholesterol, and the narrator suggests that lifestyle changes alone are not enough to keep him healthy. In the next 2 frames, Joe visits his doctor, who welcomes him approvingly and encourages him to take rosuvastatin. In the final 2 frames, Joe leaves the doctor's office and enters into sunny suburbia, or the "Land of Success," where his smiling neighbor waves as he walks home to enjoy a picnic with his smiling family.

Discussion

We found that most product claim ads made some factual claims about the target conditions, and more than one half made claims about the disease mechanisms. Even so, similar to print ads, television ads were often ambiguous about whether viewers might legitimately need the product. They offered limited information about risk factors, prevalence of the condition, or the subpopulations at greatest risk. By ambiguously defining who might need or benefit from the products, DTCA implicitly focuses on convincing people that they may be at risk for a wide array of health conditions that product consumption might ameliorate, rather than providing education about who may truly benefit from treatment. It has been suggested that DTCA contributes to the medicalization of what was previously considered part of the normal range of human experience.

All the product claim ads provided important information to viewers through rational arguments that detail either product use or the potential risks and benefits of the product use. The FDA limits the educational value of reminder ads, however, by prohibiting them from using rational appeals. Almost all ads used positive emotional appeals, and more than two thirds used negative emotional appeals. Emotional appeals may prompt viewers to

Table 3

Typical Examples of How Loss of Control, Regaining Control, and Social Approval Were Depicted in Selected Advertisements (Ads)

Product	Central Character(s)	Domain of Control	Loss of Control	Regaining Control	Social Approval
Zolpidem	Photographer, female, middle-aged, white Basketball referee, male, middle-aged, white Vacationing male, middle-aged, white	Amount of sleep each night; ability to engage in and enjoy work and leisure activities during the day	Ad states, "A funny thing happens when your body doesn't sleep at night. Your mind zones out during the day. It's like going through life on autopilot. Out of synch with the world around you." The ad shows each character engaging in professional and recreational activities, whereupon a ghostlike figure steps out of their body and makes sleeplike gestures	Ad shows a new character going to bed and waking up refreshed next morning, as narration continues, "To help you sleep there's Ambien, the number 1 prescribed sleep aid in America. Ambien helps you fall asleep fast and stay asleep longer. So you wake up refreshed, not groggy." Ad shows the photographer at work in the studio, smiling at her coworker, followed by a stern focus on her professional task Ad shows the basketball referee entertaining guests in a backyard barbecue, simultaneously serving food and socializing Ad shows the vacationing man with his children in a boat, visiting waterfalls, being cheerful	Coworkers are interested in the photographer's activities Guests are enjoying themselves at the hands of their host, and offer a toast with beverages The children are laughing with their father and photographing their enjoyable vacation activities
Esomeprazole	Wife/mother, middle-aged, white (Ad 1) Husband/father, middle-aged, African American (Ad 2)	Health of esophagus, enjoyment of specific foods, and participation in family dinner	Both ads show characters at the dinner table with a large family, as food is served. Other family members are engaged in animated conversation. Orange juice transforms into bubbling and steaming green acid as the husband pours it into the woman's glass. She briefly raises the glass, and her eyes grow wide with distress (Ad 1) Gravy transforms into thumbtacks as the wife pours it onto a slice of meat on the man's plate. His face turns from smile to frown (Ad 2)	The narrator states, "Next time, Nexium, the healing purple pill. For many, one prescription Nexium not only gets rid of heartburn, more importantly, it also heals acid reflux erosions. And healing is such a great feeling." The mother raises her glass for more orange juice and says, "I'll take that." (Ad 1) The father happily receives a serving dish from his wife and says, "I'll take that." (Ad 2)	As the wife/mother takes the orange juice, she begins talking with her family for the first time in the ad (Ad 1) As the husband/father takes the serving dish, he smiles at his wife and begins participating in the family meal (Ad 2)

Valacyclovir	Young adult, female, white	Ability to enjoy romantic encounters, and vacation	The character sits in a hammock and states, "Living with genital herpes can be a hassle." The next scene shows her sitting on the beach with a male romantic partner, as her voice narrates, "Each outbreak felt like it took days out of my life." The days of the week scroll across the bottom of the screen and disappear	The camera returns to her sitting in the hammock saying, "So I talked to my doctor and found out about Valtrex. Just 1 pill a day helps reduce the number of outbreaks. In fact, I've been outbreak-free for almost a year." She concludes, "My days are mine, and that's the way it should be."	The male romantic partner smiles and laughs with the primary character. They dance, sail, bike, and finally kiss and hug in the surf with Rio de Janeiro in the background
Sertraline	Red egglike cartoon character	Ability to feel comfortable in social settings	The main character enters a party and appears unhappy, uncomfortable, and isolated. Other characters, depicted in white, are dancing and talking. Narration states "You know that feeling of suddenly being very nervous? Maybe you're scared of being criticized, or imagine that others are judging you. You're embarrassed and don't know why. Your heart thumps and races. So you stay back. You worry that you're the only one whoever feels this way."	Narration states, "Zoloft prescription medicine can help. It works to correct a chemical imbalance in the brain which may be related to symptoms of social anxiety disorder." Animation shows neurotransmitter levels increasing across a synapse. The red character gradually fades to white and begins to smile, giggle, and jump up and down with the other characters as narration continues, "In time you could overcome those nervous anxious moments.... Zoloft, when you know more about what's wrong, you can help make it right."	After taking Zoloft, the primary character interacts with the other characters, smiles, giggles, and bounces up and down. The other characters smile approvingly and bounce as well

discount information about risks and benefits that is important when considering medication use, while they sway consumers in favor of a product. This approach may encourage viewers, some of whom may not be at risk of the condition, to seek treatment for clinically inappropriate reasons, such as fear, anticipated regret from not using the product, or expectations of happiness if they do use the product.

We identified several themes about the role of lifestyle in achieving and maintaining health. One quarter of the ads suggested that the target condition interferes with healthy or recreational activities. Although 19% of ads mentioned that healthy behaviors could be useful in combination with the product, they never described behaviors as a reasonable alternative. Several ads for cholesterol-lowering drugs appeared to suggest that nonpharmacological approaches were almost futile. One ad for atorvastatin showed an athletic middle-aged woman coaching basketball while images and text noted that she had been coaching for 25 years, ran 3 miles every day, and ate 50-calorie salads for lunch. Then we learn that her total cholesterol level is 277 mg/dL. Viewers may interpret the ad to mean that the product can improve health if lifestyle change is unsuccessful, or possibly that healthy behaviors are largely ineffective. In contrast, more than 56% of the ads showed the product enabling healthy or recreational activities. Thus, DTCA suggests that health improvement comes from taking the medication alone or in combination with healthy activities, never from behavior modification alone.

Portrayal of healthy lifestyles in the ads, however, may offer some public health benefits. The frequent exposure to DTCA in the United States could promote health because the ads often model people engaging in physical activity, and public health campaigns are most effective when they repeatedly expose people to a healthful message.

We also examined how the ads portrayed the role of medication in achieving health. Most ads showed characters who lost control of their lives as a result of their conditions and used medication to regain control. This loss of control extended beyond specific medical problems and often included an inability to participate in social, leisure, or work activities. Characters typically regained complete control over their lives after using the product, whereupon they also received social approval from friends or family. The target conditions for many of these products can impair function, but the ads may not portray the average benefit of product use. Some individuals might experience considerable relief, but others will likely achieve more modest benefits from product use. Most ads also suggest that their products reflect scientific or medical breakthroughs, a claim that others dispute. DTCA often presents best-case scenarios that can distort and inflate consumers' expectations about what prescription drugs can accomplish.

Our study has several limitations. First, television viewers might not interpret these ads in the same way we did. We watched each ad closely and repeatedly, whereas viewers in their homes might have numerous distractions. Viewers are also likely to interpret DTCA based on their own beliefs about the power of medication and the role of lifestyle change. Future work could examine how viewers interpret the ads in the context of their own homes, as well as the relationships among exposure to these ads, health beliefs and behaviors, and over- and underprescribing of the advertised drugs. Second, even though most ads run for several months, our sample came from 1 month of programming, and these findings might not reflect ad content throughout the year. Finally, we focused on the content of ads shown during times with the largest audiences. Future studies could examine the relationship between ad content and the demographics of the audience during different periods of programming throughout the day.

Senator William Frist recently called on the pharmaceutical industry to voluntarily refrain from advertising new products for 2 years after market introduction to permit a better assessment of a product's risks and benefits than can be obtained from the trials required for initial FDA approval. Previously, Bristol-Myers Squibb announced it would refrain from advertising new products for their first year on the market. These proposed reforms, however, deal with the issue of advertising products whose effects are uncertain; they do not address the concerns raised here about the content of the ads. Instead of (or in addition to) delays in advertising, the ads could more effectively convey the risks of taking new drugs for which we have limited knowledge about their long-term health consequences.

The Pharmaceutical Research and Manufacturers of America recently issued guidelines on DTCA for its members. Although the guidelines may address some of the concerns raised by our analysis (eg, "DTC advertising should reflect the seriousness of health conditions and the medicine being advertised"), they are, perhaps purposefully, vague. Furthermore, compliance with the guidelines is voluntary. Critics responded that the guidelines do not go far enough. Congress could pass legislation that requires specific content in pharmaceutical ads, including clearly specifying who may be at risk of the disease, detailing nonpharmacological treatment options, and describing the likely efficacy of alternative treatments based on current scientific evidence.

The enforcement of current and future laws rests with the FDA, which may require more staff to fulfill this mandate. At present, FDA regulatory action typically occurs long after an ad has begun airing on television. Alternatively, the New Zealand government is considering an outright ban of DTCA.

We found that DTCA often attempts to persuade viewers on grounds other than rational consideration of medical costs and benefits. Our findings suggest the need to reconsider the distinction between selling soap or other consumer products and selling prescription drugs. Poor judgment among soap brands may have few health consequences; DTCA influence on drug preferences and the resultant importuning of physicians to prescribe cost-ineffective (or even inappropriate) drugs are a much more substantial concern for health care expenditures and population health.

POSTSCRIPT

Do Consumers Benefit When Prescription Drugs Are Advertised?

Opponents of prescription drug advertising contend that drug companies' promotions are frequently inaccurate or deceptive. Furthermore, they maintain that drug companies are more interested in increasing their profits, not in truly providing additional medical benefit to the average consumer. Drug companies do not deny that they seek to make profits from their drugs, but they argue that they are offering an important public service by educating the public about new drugs through their advertisements. Also, after investing millions of dollars into developing and testing new drugs, should not pharmaceutical companies profit from the sale of these drugs?

An important issue is whether or not the average consumer is capable of discerning information distributed by pharmaceutical companies. Are people without a background in medicine, medical terminology, or research methods sufficiently knowledgeable to understand literature disseminated by drug companies? With the help of the Internet and other media, prescription drug advertising proponents maintain that the average consumer is capable of understanding information about various drugs. On the other hand, will most people take the time to follow up on drugs that are advertised? And, if people do not take the time to read about drugs they see advertised in the media, is that the fault of the drug companies?

Some critics argue that restricting drug advertisements is a moot point because consumers cannot obtain prescriptions without the approval of their physicians. Yet, in numerous instances physicians acquiesce to the wishes of their patients and write prescriptions upon the request of the patient. If in this way patients receive prescriptions that are not appropriate for their needs, who is responsible: the patient, the physician, or the drug manufacturer and advertiser? Is the role of the physician to dictate to the patient what drugs are appropriate or is it the role of the physician to explain to the patient the various options and then let the patient decide what to do?

When drug manufacturers introduce a new drug, they get a patent on the drug to protect their investment. Drug companies, therefore, receive financial rewards for introducing new drugs. Of course, drug companies also take financial risks when developing new drugs. One could argue that drug companies should be awarded for the financial risks they take. However, some critics maintain that many of these new drugs are merely "me-too" drugs that are similar to existing drugs and that they do not provide any additional benefit. Are consumers being fooled into requesting more expensive drugs that are no better than drugs already on the market?

Whether or not advertising prescription drugs is a matter of free speech is discussed in "Drug Risks and Free Speech: Can Congress Ban Consumer Drug Ads?" by Miriam Shuchman (*The New England Journal of Medicine*, May 31, 2007). A retrospective look into the advertising of prescription drugs is described in "A Decade of Direct-to-Consumer Advertising of Prescription Drugs" by Julie Donohue, Marisa Cevasco, and Meredith Rosenthal (*The New England Journal of Medicine*, August 16, 2007). Two additional articles that address this issue are "Time to Ban Direct-to-Consumer Prescription Drug Marketing" by Kurt Strange (*Annals of Family Medicine*, 2007) and "Will the Democrats Kill Direct-to-Consumer Drug Ads?" by Sean Gregory (*Time*, February 4, 2009).

Internet References . . .

National Clearinghouse for Alcohol and Drug Information (NCADI)

Information regarding a variety of drugs as well as research published by the federal government is available through this site. Up-to-date developments in drug use are available through NCADI.

http://www.health.org

The Weiner Nusim Foundation

This private foundation located in Connecticut publishes information regarding drug education. The information is free.

http://www.weinernusim.com

DrugHelp

This site, a service of the American Council for Drug Education (an affiliate of Phoenix House Foundation), provides information, counsel and referral to treatment centers.

http://www.drughelp.org

Partnership for a Drug-Free America

Extensive information on the effects of drugs and the extent of drug use by young people are discussed at this website.

http://www.drugfreeamerica.org

National Council on Alcoholism and Drug Dependence

This site contains objective information and referral for individuals, families and others seeking intervention and treatment.

http://www.ncadd.org

Drug Prevention and Treatment

*I*n spite of their legal consequences and the government's interdiction efforts, drugs are widely available and used. Two common ways of dealing with drug abuse are to incarcerate drug users and to intercept drugs before they enter the country. However, many drug experts believe that more energy should be put into preventing and treating drug abuse. An important step toward prevention and treatment is to find out what contributes to drug abuse and how to nullify these factors.

By educating young people about the potential hazards of drugs and by developing an awareness of social influences that contribute to drug use, many drug-related problems may be averted. The debates in this section focus on different prevention and treatment issues such as promoting smokeless tobacco as an alternative to cigarette smoking, the benefits and risks of legalizing marijuana for medical purposes, the effectiveness of drug abuse treatment, and whether schools should adopt a zero tolerance drug policy.

- Should Smokeless Tobacco Be Promoted as an Alternative to Cigarette Smoking?
- Is Alcoholism Hereditary?
- Should Marijuana Be Approved for Medical Use?
- Should Schools Drug Test Students?
- Does Drug Abuse Treatment Work?
- Is Abstinence an Effective Strategy for Drug Education?

ISSUE 14

Should Smokeless Tobacco Be Promoted as an Alternative to Cigarette Smoking?

YES: John Britton and Richard Edwards, from "Tobacco Smoking, Harm Reduction, and Nicotine Product Regulation," *The Lancet* (February 2, 2008)

NO: David A. Savitz, Roger E. Meyer, Jason M. Tanzer, Sidney S. Mirvish, and Freddi Lewin, from "Public Health Implications of Smokeless Tobacco as a Harm Reduction Strategy," *American Journal of Public Health* (November 2006)

ISSUE SUMMARY

YES: Professors John Britton and Richard Edwards advocate the use of smokeless tobacco as an alternative to tobacco smoking because the harm from tobacco is rooted more in the act of smoking than from nicotine. They recognize that smokeless tobacco carries certain risks, although they note that nicotine is not a known carcinogen nor does it reduce birthweight as much as tobacco smoking.

NO: David Savitz of the Mount Sinai School of Medicine and his colleagues raise concerns about the promotion of smokeless tobacco in lieu of tobacco smoking because there are numerous health concerns associated with smokeless tobacco. They are concerned about the products used in smokeless tobacco as well as the effects of smokeless tobacco on oral health, cardiovascular disease, and reproductive health.

T here is no debate as to whether cigarette smoking is deadly. On a worldwide basis, it is estimated that 100 million people die annually from this addiction. In the United States, over 400,000 die each year from cigarette smoking. Besides causing premature death, millions more people are afflicted with disabilities such as bronchitis, lung cancer, and emphysema. Cigarette tobacco emits secondhand smoke which has an impact on coworkers as well as spouses and children living with smokers. Health care professionals are adamant about the need to reduce cigarette smoking. Clearly, cigarette smoking interferes with one's quality of life. The issue being debated is not whether smokeless tobacco is beneficial, but whether or not should it be promoted as an alternative to cigarette smoking.

There are a number of adverse health effects associated with smokeless tobacco. Because there is more nicotine in smokeless tobacco than in cigarettes, the potential for addiction is high. Conversely, frequent use of smokeless tobacco greatly hinders one's ability to stop its use. According to its detractors, smokeless tobacco can be carcinogenic. Oral cancer has been associated with its use, although the risk of lung cancer from cigarette smoking is greater. Other oral health effects include dental cavities, gingivitis, and periodontitis.

Proponents of smokeless tobacco as an alternative to cigarette smoking agree that it is best for smokers to stop smoking altogether. However, in light of the fact that many people cannot quit smoking, despite numerous attempts, they maintain that smokeless tobacco is less harmful. In essence, the use of smokeless tobacco is a harm reduction strategy. Cigarette smoking is simply more deleterious than using smokeless tobacco. Smokeless tobacco is the lesser of two evils.

Those individuals who support smokeless tobacco as an alternative to cigarette smoking note that nicotine is not a recognized carcinogen and that it does not impair lung functioning. As noted previously, opponents of smokeless tobacco claim that smokeless tobacco may cause cancer. Currently, many people use nicotine patches and gums to reduce cigarette smoking. One could argue that smokeless tobacco is another example of nicotine replacement.

Opponents of the harm reduction strategy argue that smokeless tobacco use discourages individuals from stopping all tobacco use. Their position is that although smokeless tobacco may be less harmful than cigarette smoking, all tobacco use should be discouraged. Opponents dispel the notion of "harmful but safer" when discussing the use of smokeless tobacco. Any tobacco use is a public health problem. To stop or reduce the level of cigarette smoking, opponents would rather increase the tax on cigarettes or place other restrictions on its use.

It is believed that young people who start out using smokeless tobacco may eventually smoke cigarettes. Also, one could question whether young people get the wrong message if smokeless tobacco is advocated in lieu of cigarette smoking. Teenagers are influenced by the media. It has been shown that movies portraying cigarette smoking result in an increase in the number of adolescents smoking. Young people may get the impression that it is okay to use smokeless tobacco if it is advocated as an alternative to cigarette smoking.

In the following selections, John Britton and Richard Edwards advocate the use of smokeless tobacco as a safer alternative to cigarette smoking. They maintain that the hazards associated with smokeless tobacco may be exaggerated. David Savitz and his colleagues argue that that smokeless tobacco should not be promoted as a safer alternative to cigarette smoking. They believe that the potential dangers of smokeless tobacco outweigh its use.

YES  John Britton and Richard Edwards

Tobacco Smoking, Harm Reduction, and Nicotine Product Regulation

Cigarette smoking is highly addictive, widely prevalent, and very hazardous. Smoking killed 100 million people in the 20th century, and is predicted to kill 1 billion in the 21st century. Worldwide, there are about 1·1 billion smokers, and there are expected to be 1·6 billion by 2025. Half of all smokers will die prematurely, unless they stop smoking.

In the 50 years since the health risks of smoking first became widely recognised, the political and public health responses to smoking at national and international levels have been grossly inadequate. Although the main components of current recommended tobacco control policy (panel 1) have changed little from those first proposed in 1962, they have still not been widely applied and, in any case, achieve a reduction in smoking prevalence of typically about 0·5, and at best 1·0, percentage point per year. Full implementation of these policies might be sufficient to prevent smoking in countries in which the smoking epidemic has yet to take hold, but this is only part of the necessary solution for countries with an established smoking population. In the UK, for example, where 24% of adults still smoke, at a reduction rate of 0·5 percentage point per year it would take more than 20 years to reduce the prevalence of smoking by half. Even then, there will be more than 5 million smokers in the UK alone, predominantly from the most socioeconomically disadvantaged sectors of society, bearing a vast burden of avoidable morbidity and mortality. In fact most of the 150 million deaths from smoking that are expected over the next 20 years will occur in current smokers who are alive today. Since millions of these are unlikely to stop smoking in the near future, we argue, on the basis of a new report from the Royal College of Physicians, that in addition to conventional tobacco control policies, the application of harm reduction principles to nicotine and tobacco use could deliver substantial reductions in the morbidity and mortality currently caused by tobacco consumption. However, achievement of these reductions will require radical structural reform of the way in which nicotine and tobacco products are regulated and used.

From *The Lancet,* February 2-February 8, 2008, pp. 441–444 (refs. omitted). Copyright © 2008 by Elsevier Health Sciences. Reprinted by permission via Rightslink.

Panel 1: Essential components of tobacco control policy

- Use of price, tax increases, or both to reduce consumption
- Prevent smoking in public places and in workplaces
- Health warnings on packets of tobacco products
- Health promotion and public information campaigns
- Prohibition of advertising and other promotion
- Provision of smoking cessation services
- Prevention of smuggling
- Prohibition of sales and reduction of availability to people under age 18 years

Most people continue to smoke because they are addicted to nicotine. Inhaled tobacco smoke is especially addictive because it delivers high doses of nicotine to the brain very rapidly, and because nicotine confers rewarding properties on other stimuli associated with smoking. Exposure to high nicotine concentrations at an early age might also determine the intensity of addiction through effects on nicotinic receptor numbers in the brain.

Nicotine is available from a wide range of products: smoked tobacco, of which the cigarette is pre-eminent; medicinal nicotine, currently available as nicotine replacement therapy; and smokeless tobacco products, of which oral tobacco is the most widely used. Cigarettes and other smoked tobacco products, such as cigars and pipes, are by far the most harmful because they deliver nicotine in conjunction with hundreds of other toxins and carcinogens. It is these toxins and carcinogens that are mainly responsible for the major adverse health effects of smoking—particularly lung cancer, chronic obstructive pulmonary disease (COPD), heart disease, and stroke. By contrast, the safety record of medicinal nicotine products is very good.

Nicotine is not a recognised carcinogen and does not cause COPD. It has effects on blood pressure and heart rate that might be expected to increase risk of cardiovascular disease, but these effects are not seen in practice. Nicotine reduces placental blood flow, but medicinal nicotine does not reduce birthweight as much as smoking does. Therefore, although medicinal nicotine is not wholly safe, for practical purposes, and certainly when compared with smoking, the hazard associated with medicinal nicotine use is very low.

The risk profile of smokeless tobacco products is more wide ranging and includes oral cancer, other gastrointestinal cancers, and heart disease. These risks vary substantially between different smokeless products, but are low for products low in nitrosamine, such as Swedish snus. Snus use increases the risk of pancreatic cancer, but not of lung and oral cancers, or COPD. Use of other smokeless products has been linked to an increased risk of cardiovascular disease, but snus has little, if any, effect. The risk of adverse effects associated with snus use is lower than that associated with smoking, overall by an estimated 90%. Whatever the true overall hazard, use of low nitrosamine smokeless products is clearly substantially less harmful than tobacco smoking.

The rationale behind harm reduction is that although the best option would be to avoid the harmful behaviour completely, the next best option, if the behaviour is likely to continue, is to ensure that the harm caused is kept to a minimum. A logical harm reduction approach for the millions of smokers who are unlikely to achieve complete abstinence in the short-term or medium-term future is to promote the substitution of tobacco smoking with an alternative, less hazardous means of obtaining nicotine.

The least hazardous alternative is medicinal nicotine. Since their development around 20 years ago, medicinal nicotine products have been promoted as cessation therapies, for use as short-term substitutes for smoking in the context of attempts to stop smoking. In clinical trials, use of medicinal nicotine increases the likelihood of stopping smoking by around 80%, but the absolute increase in quit rates is modest because the baseline success rates are low. Thus, in a quit attempt using medicinal nicotine in conjunction with best-practice behavioural support, only about one in five smokers succeed in stopping for 6 months. These products are not strongly effective or competitive substitutes for smoking because they deliver nicotine in lower doses and more slowly than do cigarettes. Medicinal nicotine products are also much less available than cigarettes in most countries; are marketed and advertised as smoking cessation therapies (rather than long-term smoking substitutes); are expensive to buy; and are widely perceived as harmful by smokers.

Anecdotally, smokeless tobacco products have a history of use as temporary substitutes for smoking by occupational groups, such as coal miners, who cannot smoke while at work. In Sweden at least some of the substantial reduction in daily smoking prevalence in the past 20 years or so seems attributable to substitution of smoking by snus use, especially by men. Although there has been uptake of regular smoking by smokeless users who might not otherwise have smoked (gateway progression), the extent to which this progression has happened is much less than that from regular smoking to snus. However, this pattern of use has not been replicated elsewhere. In the USA, where other forms of smokeless tobacco have also been available for some time, the prevalence of smokeless tobacco use has fallen progressively in conjunction with that of smoking—to below 5% in men and 1% in women by 2000. In Norway, snus use has increased recently to about 11% of all men, and 18% of men aged 16–24 years, with no evidence yet of effect on the rate of decline in smoking prevalence [Erik Dybing, personal communication].

The effectiveness of smokeless tobacco as a substitute for smoking, and the relative extent to which wider availability and promotion of smokeless products would result in gateway progression into or out of smoking, are controversial topics. Some argue that health professionals should not condone any use of nicotine, and also that encouraging use of alternative nicotine products, particularly smokeless tobacco, would invite abuse of the market by their commercial producers. Others argue that if smokeless products are an effective and less hazardous substitute for smoking it would be in the public interest to harness that potential to public health benefit, particularly if the Swedish pattern of predominant gateway progression from smoking to smokeless use could be realised in other countries.

The arguments are finely balanced. However, on the basis of the Swedish data we believe that the potential role of smokeless products at least merits further consideration and investigation to find out whether and to what extent these products can act as substitutes for smoking; whether tobacco products are more effective smoking substitutes than medicinal nicotine; and, if so, whether the product characteristics responsible can be identified and used to develop more acceptable low-risk medicinal products. We also believe that the development of such products should happen only within an overall strategy of radical reform of the regulatory systems that apply to nicotine products, including much stronger regulation of smoked tobacco, to ensure that the harm caused by all nicotine use is kept to a minimum.

Effective harm reduction strategies, and particularly the option of providing nicotine without smoke as an acceptable long-term or even lifelong substitute for smoking, have not been widely applied to tobacco smoking. The pharmaceutical companies have not evidently engaged in the development of medicinal devices that are strongly competitive with cigarettes. Use of smokeless tobacco is actively discouraged by many health professionals and by WHO. This opposition to smokeless products is despite predicted benefits from modelling studies. If a product such as snus were marketed in the USA with a health warning stating that it is addictive and might increase risk of disease, but that it is substantially less harmful than cigarettes, the prevalence of smoking in the USA would be reduced by an estimated additional 1·3% to 3·1% over 5 years (ie, by about 0·44% per year). In a study modelling the effect of the introduction of snus as an alternative to smoking in Australia, the investigators concluded that the overall net effect would be beneficial to public health.

We believe that the absence of effective harm reduction options for smokers is perverse, unjust, and acts against the rights and best interests of smokers and the public health. Addicted smokers have a right to choose from a range of safer nicotine products, as well as accurate and unbiased information to guide that choice. There are, however, several obstacles to the development of an effective harm reduction strategy for tobacco smoking in the UK and many other countries, and particularly to the development and marketing of more effective medicinal products. Paramount among these is the current system of regulations that apply to different nicotine products in most countries.

A major reason why tobacco products have remained exempt from consumer protection regulation in most countries is that the logical and proportionate application of existing regulations would result in their immediate withdrawal from sale. Thus, the most dangerous and addictive nicotine products remain only slightly regulated, in great disproportion to their hazard, and are freely available and widely used. Tobacco companies are also free to develop or modify, and bring to market, new smoked tobacco products and other tobacco derivatives with little regulatory control.

By contrast, medicinal nicotine products, which are the safest source of nicotine, are generally subject to the highest levels of regulation since they are generally classified as drugs. This is almost certainly a major disincentive to new product development and innovation, and to market competition to create better and more effective cigarette substitutes. The present regulatory system also discourages innovation through the real or perceived likelihood that most effective smoking substitutes, which would almost certainly be more addictive than the present range of medicinal products, would be subject to even stricter controls on marketing and supply, or perhaps even prevented from coming to market.

Current regulation of smokeless tobacco products is also inconsistent, since most products are subject to minimal regulatory controls, whereas the supply of snus, which is one of the least hazardous of such products, is prohibited in most European countries. Extention of that prohibition across the range of smokeless products would resolve this inconsistency, but at the expense of the loss of a potentially effective alternative to smoking. On the other hand, removing the prohibition on snus would deal the tobacco industry a free hand to exploit the smokeless tobacco market with apparent endorsement by legislators. Neither of these options is ideal; hence, an alternative approach, designed to benefit public health rather than industry profit, is needed.

Our argument is that nicotine products should all be regulated rationally in relation to each other, in proportion to their level of hazard, in a system designed to reduce the overall harm caused by nicotine dependence and use. The regulatory framework should promote complete cessation of nicotine product use as the preferred option, but also encourage existing smokers who are unable to stop smoking to adopt a less hazardous source of the drug. An obvious prerequisite of this change would be an acceptance by society in general, and particularly by health professionals, that use of low-hazard nicotine products might be prevalent for many years.

Achievement of a rational nicotine regulatory framework needs a radical overhaul of existing systems to encourage the innovation, development, and use of new medicinal nicotine products at the least hazardous end of the spectrum, and to achieve the fastest possible reductions in use of products at the smoked tobacco extreme. The regulatory framework should therefore apply the levers of affordability, promotion, and availability in direct inverse relation to the hazard of the product, thus creating the most favourable market environment for the least hazardous products while also strongly discouraging the use of smoked tobacco. The anomalies that inhibit market competition to develop new and better rapid delivery, user-friendly medicinal nicotine products (eg, inhaled nicotine) that can compete with cigarettes for long-term use need to be removed; and there needs to be more widespread promotion and sale of existing or new lower-hazard products. The regulatory system should include a robust surveillance function so that potentially counterproductive trends in marketing or use of all nicotine products—particularly those that are tobacco-based—are promptly detected and resolved. The regulatory system should ensure that alternative nicotine products, medicinal or tobacco-based, are marketed with appropriate health information and, where appropriate, professional endorsement. Nicotine product regulation should also be applied over time to ensure that smoked tobacco products are subject to progressively increased restrictions—on availability and marketing, with the long-term objective of reducing and, in due course, eradicating all smoked tobacco use.

The options for rationalising nicotine regulation include making all nicotine product regulation the responsibility of an existing agency, such as a food or drug regulation agency, or by coordination and rationalisation of the activities of the different agencies that regulate nicotine products. We conclude, however, that meeting the challenges of implementing effective tobacco control and nicotine harm reduction policies (panel 2), both nationally and internationally, needs the creation of dedicated, autonomous, and fully resourced national (and where appropriate international) nicotine and tobacco product regulatory authorities. This approach might be unrealistic in many resource-poor countries, and less of a priority in those at the earliest stages of the smoking epidemic, but that is certainly not the case in those that already have a substantial population of established smokers, and hence the most to gain from this strategy.

Panel 2: Suggested roles and functions of a national nicotine regulatory authority

Functions at initiation
- Baseline measurement of all current nicotine product use
- Ensure full implementation of conventional tobacco control policies (panel 1)
- Permissive licensing of medicinal nicotine products for use as smoking substitutes
- Substantial relaxation of restrictions on marketing and sale of medicinal nicotine products
- Removal of tax on medicinal nicotine products
- Communication of objective health risk information for nicotine products and promotion of harm reduction principles to smokers and the public
- Establishment of ground rules for monitoring the use of health messages in promoting the use of lower hazard nicotine products as substitutes for smoking
- Imposition of generic packaging for all tobacco products
- Prohibition of retail display of smoked tobacco products
- Strong graphic health warnings on smoked tobacco products
- Setting of tax and consequently retail price of all nicotine products in relation to their probable relative risk to health
- Prohibition of all sale of nicotine products to individuals under age 18 years
- Introduce licensing of retailers of all smoked tobacco products
- Assume responsibility for overseeing nicotine product delivery and toxicity monitoring
- Mandate the introduction of reduced ignition propensity cigarettes
- Take expert advice on how current restrictions on smokeless nicotine products could be reformed to public health benefit

Continuing functions
- Regular monitoring of trends in nicotine product use, promotion, and availability
- Monitoring of effect of licensing and marketing relaxation on medicinal nicotine use, and revision as necessary to promote public health
- Progressive increases in tax on the most hazardous products
- Continued promotion of health information on different nicotine products and development and monitoring of mass communication strategies to prevent uptake, promote cessation, and reduce harm
- Progressive reduction in retail licences for smoked tobacco products
- Monitoring and policing of illicit and underage tobacco and nicotine trade
- Work with the commercial sector to promote competition and innovation in the medicinal nicotine market
- Monitoring and prevention of smoked product placement and new methods of marketing (eg internet, viral marketing)
- Act on expert advice to set framework for licensing of low-hazard smokeless products and possible test marketing
- Progressively incentivise minority, high risk smokeless tobacco users to quit or else migrate to safer products
- Identify and respond to new developments or threats to health from new or existing product development or promotion
- Control of expenditure on tobacco control interventions to ensure evidence-based and cost-effective interventions are used
- Support nicotine regulation and tobacco control approaches in resource-poor countries

The consequence of failing to intensify tobacco control efforts, and to address the current imbalance in nicotine product regulation, will be the unnecessary perpetuation of current smoking by millions of people, especially in disadvantaged communities, and a continued epidemic of avoidable death and disability. Specifically, cigarettes and other smoked tobacco products will continue to be freely available with few restrictions on their safety or content; the medicinal nicotine market will continue to focus on low-addiction, low-dose, low-effectiveness products while also stifling competition and innovation; and the current irrational regulation of smokeless products will continue. Most of the millions of smokers alive today will therefore continue to smoke tobacco, and half will die as a result.

David A. Savitz et al.  **NO**

Public Health Implications of Smokeless Tobacco Use as a Harm Reduction Strategy

Harm reduction strategies involve promoting a product that has adverse health consequences as a substitute for one that has more severe adverse health consequences. Smokeless tobacco low in nitrosamine content offers potential benefits in reducing smoking prevalence rates. Possible harm arises from the potential for such products to serve as a gateway to more harmful tobacco products, public misinterpretation of "less harmful" as "safe," distraction from the public health goal of tobacco elimination, and ethical issues involved in advising those marketing these harmful products. We offer a research agenda to provide a stronger basis for evaluating the risks and benefits of smokeless tobacco as a means of reducing the adverse health effects of tobacco. (*Am J Public Health.* 2006;96:1934–1939. doi:10.2105/AJPH.2005. 075499)

The use of tobacco products, especially cigarettes, results in exposure to hundreds of chemicals, many of which have adverse health consequences. The primary agents of concern in smoked tobacco are polycyclic aromatic hydrocarbons, carbon monoxide, nicotine, and N-nitroso compounds, along with smaller amounts of polonium, radon, arsenic, and cadmium. Polycyclic aromatic hydrocarbons are produced by the high temperatures reached in the burning of tobacco. N-nitroso compounds, including nitrosamines, are found in tobacco leaves themselves, may be formed to some extent during combustion, and are transported to cigarette smoke. Smoked tobacco is the most prevalent and harmful tobacco product, with overwhelming evidence showing substantially increased risks of a variety of cancers; chronic obstructive pulmonary, cardiovascular, and oral diseases; and adverse reproductive outcomes.

Recognition by leaders in some developed countries of these well-documented harmful consequences of smoking has resulted in increasingly effective actions, such as political action, taken to curtail the epidemic of tobacco-related diseases. Yet, the epidemic continues unabated and is even accelerating in many parts of the world. Tools for combating the epidemic

From *American Journal of Public Health,* vol. 96, no. 11, November 2006, pp. 1934-1938. Copyright © 2006 by American Public Health Association. Reprinted by permission of American Public Health Association.

include public policies intended to discourage tobacco use through taxation and restrictions on promotion, media campaigns designed to prevent smoking initiation and encourage cessation, individual counseling techniques[1] and medications designed to promote and maintain smoking cessation, modification of tobacco products to reduce harmfulness, and substitution of less harmful for more harmful products (e.g., pharmaceutical nicotine for smoked tobacco).

Harm Reduction Strategies

The underlying principle of harm reduction is that a product that has adverse health consequences is promoted as a substitute for one that has more severe adverse health consequences.[2] The addictive features of nicotine are central to the problem of continuing use of tobacco. Even nicotine as a pure pharmaceutical agent has short-term adverse cardiovascular effects, although it has none of the health effects associated with other agents in cigarette smoke or smokeless tobacco. Smokeless tobacco products offer a potential harm reduction strategy for which the magnitude of health risk to an individual user would be expected to fall between pharmaceutical-grade nicotine (1 of smokeless tobacco's constituents) and smoking (which includes all the toxic constituents of smokeless tobacco as well as others).

The primary agents of concern in smokeless tobacco are the strongly carcinogenic tobacco-specific nitrosamines, especially N'-nitrosonornicotine (NNN), 4-(methylnitrosamino)-1-(3-pyridyl)-1-butanone (NNK), and nicotine itself. Although the exact magnitude of reduction in risk gained from substituting use of smokeless tobacco (particularly a low-nitrosamine product) for cigarette smoking is not easily quantified, a panel of experts estimated reductions in total mortality in the range of 90% to 95%.[3] Despite such a large estimated benefit relative to smoking, important scientific and ethical questions arise.

Use of high-dose methadone maintenance treatment among heroin addicts has remained controversial despite 40 years of clear clinical evidence that it is moderately effective in rehabilitating opiate injection drug users and preventing the spread of HIV/AIDS. The price of this harm reduction is acceptance of continued addiction to a narcotic. Similar questions have been raised with regard to needle exchange programs designed to prevent the spread of HIV/AIDS among injection drug users. Parallel concerns arise with the substitution of less harmful for more harmful tobacco products: might this practice "sanitize" or even unintentionally initiate the harmful behavior? Does accommodating the harmful behavior suggest that society now condones or accepts it, discouraging more definitive solutions?

In Sweden the widespread use of Swedish snuff, called *snus,* a moist smokeless tobacco product placed under the upper lip, has been viewed as a possible model for successful harm reduction,[4,5] although not without controversy.[6] Sweden has achieved the lowest smoking prevalence rate in all of Europe, approximately 17% of adult men in 2000; an estimated 19% of adult men and 1% of adult women use *snus* daily.[5] Furthermore, *snus* appears to be a component of successful smoking cessation.[7] The low smoking prevalence rate and high rate of use of *snus* in Sweden may be related, but this association has not been established with certainty.

As recommended in the Institute of Medicine report *Clearing the Smote*,[8] manufacturers have now begun to develop and market tobacco products that reduce but do not eliminate exposure to tobacco-related toxicants. The report also called for consumers to be fully informed of the adverse consequences associated with these products and for surveillance to be conducted on health effects subsequent to marketing.

Star Scientific, a small tobacco company located in Chester, Va, began to market 2 smokeless tobacco products with very low levels of tobacco-specific nitrosamines and sought expert advice to better define the health risks associated with use of its products relative to smoked and conventional smokeless tobaccos. The company sought answers to the following questions: do smokeless tobacco products pose risks to health? If so, what is the nature of these risks, are there special populations at higher risk, and how do the risks compare with those of cigarette smoking? Are there physical or chemical characteristics of specific smokeless tobacco products or different uses that influence health risks?

Star Scientific provided an unrestricted grant to Best Practice Project Management Inc, a consulting and project management company located in Bethesda, Md, to convene a consensus conference to respond to these questions. A panel was convened in May 2003 with the agreement that it would respond to the questions and would, in addition, prepare a report for publication independent of the sponsor (the present article). The panel conducted a literature search on the topic and enlisted a range of experts with and without previous experience in tobacco research as members.

Evidence on the Health Effects of Smokeless Tobacco

Exposures Associated with Smokeless Tobacco

Smokeless tobacco products contain air- or fire-cured tobacco that is powdered or ground for use as nasal or oral snuff, cut and grated for use as chewing or oral snuff, or stripped and compacted for use as chewing tobacco. Such products may include sugars (sucrose, fructose, sorbitol, molasses, dried fruit), water, sodium chloride, ammonium chloride, licorice, menthol, paraffin oil, and glycerol. Tobacco-specific nitrosamines in smokeless products are derived from leaf nitrates that were reduced to nitrites, primarily via bacterial fermentation. Nitrites and amines in the tobacco react to form nitrosamines that are clearly carcinogenic in animals and probably carcinogenic in humans.[9] Trace metals occur at low levels and probably do not contribute to cartinogenesis in the smokeless tobacco products marketed in the United States and Sweden.[10]

Certain smokeless tobacco products have low levels of formaldehyde, and those that are smoke-cured also have significant amounts of polycydic aromatic hydrocarbons, some of which, such as benzo[a]pyrene, are carcinogens.[10] Swedish *snus* is composed of air-cured and fire-cured tobaccos. Since 1981, no fermentation has been used in its production, and a heating step sharply reduces microorganism content. Additives and flavors presumed to be safe are used in the process, and the net result is a product low in tobacco-specific nitrosamines (10 mg/kg or less).

The magnitude of the health risk associated with smokeless products appears to be associated with the type of tobacco and method of cultivation used. Greater potential for harm is associated with fire-curing (resulting in deposits of polycyclic aromatic hydrocarbons on the leaf), bacterial contamination, fermentation during production (which may favor the activity of microorganisms that reduce nitrates to nitrites, leading to formation of nitrosamines),[11] inclusion of certain additives in Asian products (e.g., areca nuts),[12] and particular methods of product storage (some of which may promote continued bacterial formation of nitrosamines). Behavioral influences on health risks include amount of smokeless tobacco consumed and frequency of use, length of application, surface of application, oral hygiene, and rates of salivating, swallowing, and spitting. Risk associated with use may be modified by other exposures such as diet, alcohol consumption, and genetics.[13–15]

Carcinogenicity

Evidence that smokeless tobacco, which includes moist and dry snuff, causes oral cancer in humans is persuasive, given biological plausibility, specificity for buccal mucosa and gingiva (sites of contact), and the strength and consistency of epidemiological evidence across populations and geographic locations.[16–18] The carcinogens NNN and NNK are found in the saliva of snuff dippers, and measurements of urinary excretions of NNK metabolites have been found to be similar among users of snuff and chewing tobacco and smokers.[10]

Reducing the nitrosamine content of smokeless tobacco (as in *snus*) should reduce carcinogenicity. Nonetheless, nitrosamines can be produced in vivo from nicotine itself and from tobacco-specific or other amines.[9] Reports on the carcinogenicity of *snus* in the Scandinavian and other literature[18–22] suggest minimal risk of oral or other cancers among users. However, as is the case with any smokeless tobacco product, *snus* contains carcinogenic nitrosamines, albeit at markedly lower levels than those found in the types of smokeless tobacco used in the United States and most other parts of the world; pharmaceutical nicotine does not contain these nitrosamines.[23]

American smokeless tobaccos can be divided into chewing tobacco, moist snuff, and dry snuff. In 1 review of different types of smokeless tobacco[24] that evaluated 23 studies published between 1957 and 1998, no clear epidemiological evidence was uncovered that indicated chewing tobacco increases the risk of head or neck cancer. There was evidence of an increased risk of oral cancer associated with use of American dry snuff, but there were small or no clear risks of oral cancer associated with use of moist snuff, despite the presence of elevated nitrosamine levels in such products.

Cardiovascular Disease

Smokeless tobacco use produces a much slower onset and much lower peak concentration of nicotine in the blood supplying the heart and brain than does smoked tobacco, even with the same total daily dose of nicotine. Use of chewing tobacco or snuff for 30 minutes leads to a gradual rise in blood nicotine concentration followed by a sustained level of concentration that continues for up to 2 hours.[25,26] The systemic dose from a single exposure to snuff or chewing tobacco is estimated at 2 to 3 mg.

Studies comparing cigarette smoking, snuff use, and use of chewing tobacco have demonstrated qualitatively similar effects on the sympathetic nervous system from nicotine.[26] For all 3 products, the heart rate is increased, although its elevation is sharper and persists for a shorter interval with smoking than with snuff, consistent with the time course of blood concentrations. During most of the day, circadian heart rates are approximately 7 beats per minute higher among those who smoke cigarettes, chew tobacco, or use oral snuff than among those who are abstinent.

Epidemiological studies of snuff users have revealed no increased risk of myocardial infarction[27] or increased atherosclerosis[28] relative to non-users. Although the acute nicotine-related effects of all tobacco products and pharmaceutical nicotine are essentially the same, the risk of clinically significant cardiovascular disease is clearly linked to smoking and not to use of smokeless tobacco.[28] Similarly, risks associated with chronic obstructive pulmonary disease are a consequence of smoking but not of smokeless tobacco use.[29]

Oral Health Effects of Smokeless Tobacco

In addition to cancers, oral health concerns related to smokeless tobacco include leukoplakia, gingivitis, periodontitis, and dental caries as well as cosmetic concerns such as tooth staining, malodor, and tooth loss with resultant disfigurement. Leukoplakia is strongly associated with the use and placement position of smokeless tobacco and appears and disappears with changes in use.[30] A Swedish study of mucosal and other leukoplakic lesions among snuff dippers showed reversible histological changes and suggested that Swedish *snus* produces less severe lesions than American snuff.[31]

Gingivitis and periodontitis are common infectious diseases in which bacteria colonize the tooth surface, with resulting gingival (gum) inflammation; recession from the tooth surface, exposing the roots; and accompanying destruction of the bony sockets of the teeth (periodontitis). Some data suggest that tobacco products adversely influence periodontitis-associated flora[32,33] and host immune responses to inflammatory agents.[34] There is no evidence of an association of smokeless tobacco with recession of the gums independent of preexisting gingivitis. However, periodontitis is clearly more rapidly destructive among smokers and perhaps among smokeless tobacco users. Periodontitis also responds more poorly to treatment in smokers.[35,36]

One study conducted in the United States showed that caries (decay) of the root surfaces of teeth was associated with use of chewing tobacco but not snuff.[37] Amount of decay was associated with intensity and duration of use and was probably a function of the high levels of sugar contained in chewing tobacco products.

Reproductive Health

The primary reproductive health concern with smokeless tobacco is nicotine itself, which has vasoconstrictive effects that can have an adverse influence on fetal growth and development. In rodents, nicotine exposure during pregnancy resulted in reduced birthweights, increased fetal mortality, abnormal bone development, and reduced activity levels.[38] Among smokers, carbon monoxide also contributes to adverse effects on growth and brain development.[38,39]

One study focusing on infant birthweight suggested that women given nicotine patches usually continued to smoke but smoked less, and those who smoked less had improved birthweights.[40] Few studies of reproductive health among women who use smokeless tobacco are available from Western countries, because historically not many women of reproductive age have used such products. Some research has been conducted in India among women using chewing tobacco; although these studies are of limited relevance because of the differences between that country's products and those used in the United States and Sweden, there were indications of increases in stillbirths[41] and reductions in birthweights among the participants.[41,42] A more recent study of Swedish *snus* users revealed decreases in birthweights and increased risks of preterm delivery (relative risk [RR]= 1.6) and preeclampsia (RR= 1.6)[43]; these results call for corroboration.

Public Health Concerns with Smokeless Tobacco

A public health approach to tobacco addiction should include preventing initiation of use, facilitating smoking cessation, and promoting abstinence from all tobacco products by current users. Policymakers understandably disagree on the risks and benefits of harm reduction strategies aimed at those who are unable (or unwilling) to stop using tobacco products. Any product that delivers nicotine confers health risks, yet smoked tobacco clearly confers far greater risks than smokeless tobacco. Reduction of nitrosamine levels in smokeless tobacco should markedly reduce carcinogenicity.

However, whereas scientists and public health experts acknowledge a gradient of harmfulness, the public may dichotomize products and behaviors as "harmful" or "safe." Applying the "harmful but safer" concept to the use of smokeless tobacco in comparison with active smoking poses a challenge to health educators and advertisers. Overstatement of harm could prevent smokers from switching to smokeless tobacco.[44] Understatement of harm could lead nonusers to adopt use of smokeless tobacco. Thus, the issue is not merely whether policymakers can agree on the *potential* value of risk reduction strategies but whether, in practice, the "harmful but safer" message can be effectively conveyed to the public.

The intense promotion of smokeless tobacco products to young men is clearly intended to foster initiation of use among this population. The legitimacy of harm reduction is predicated on effective targeting of *active* smokers and users of smokeless tobacco high in nitrosamine content Ideally, a product should not be promoted or adopted among either nonusers of tobacco or active smokers capable of quitting. The Swedish experience indicates that *snus* does not serve as a gateway to smoking and appears to have contributed to dramatic declines in smoking as its use increased,[22] but the response to such products may well differ in the United States. If it is not possible to isolate and market to the group of smokers who could benefit, there may be net harm from these products.

Given the financial incentive to market smokeless tobacco products on a wide scale, the success of a public health–based harm reduction strategy will depend in part on effective regulation. The complex regulatory environment affecting tobacco advertising and sales and the marketing of nicotine delivery products is applicable as well to the marketing of smokeless tobacco products low in nitrosamine content. Restrictions on advertising and sales to minors, reporting of constituents, and mandatory warning labels would be among the key considerations.

If a harm reduction strategy is adopted, it will require a clear definition of relative health risks associated with low-nitrosamine smokeless tobacco products, perhaps coupled with further limitations on advertising of more dangerous products. A comprehensive strategy is needed from the outset to ensure that the product is marketed solely as a harm reduction tool. The ultimate test of any regulatory approach to these new tobacco products is its impact on public health; thus, careful documentation of patterns and consequences of use is required.

Some public health advocates note that harm reduction strategies run counter to the ultimate goal of a tobacco-free society, confusing the public health message advocating abstinence from all forms of tobacco use. Furthermore, they argue, marketing one tobacco product as a substitute for another may divert attention and resources from policies designed to discourage or eliminate use altogether. Weakening the political will to aggressively pursue such proven strategies as increasing cigarette taxes, restricting public smoking, and enforcing age restrictions on purchasing tobacco may be an unintended consequence of promotion of harm reduction. Moreover, an attractive substitute in the form of smokeless tobacco could discourage active smokers from completely discontinuing their tobacco use.

A final concern facing researchers and public health advocates is ethical: whether and how to advise those who seek to market smokeless tobacco products. Manufacturers of smokeless tobacco would clearly be seeking profits through sales of a harmful product, albeit one that may have net public health benefits. These companies need scientific expertise if they are to address health concerns, devise marketing strategies consistent with the goal of harm reduction, and monitor the effectiveness of those strategies. The long history of dishonesty by the tobacco industry and by some of the researchers supported by that industry raises ethical concerns.

Proactively addressing the concerns expressed here should be helpful to policymakers and corporations contemplating the development and marketing of harm reduction products. If these issues can be raised objectively in advance, in an open forum, reputable scientists would have the opportunity to contribute their knowledge to policymakers, who would benefit from access to the best available information. Despite much success in eliminating tobacco use, we need more, not fewer, tools in the multifaceted effort to address this public health issue. Motivated current smokers who are unable to quit should be a specific target audience for harm reduction strategies.

As a result of the limited effectiveness of smoking cessation programs, recalcitrant smokers represent a sizable proportion of tobacco users both in the United States and around the world. Smokeless tobacco products low in nitrosamine content may represent a beneficial alternative for this group of smokers who have not been helped by other available tobacco control strategies.

Questions Concerning Smokeless Tobacco

Questions that need to be answered about smokeless tobacco products focus on whether these products have a place in the array of tobacco control tools. We propose that the following questions be addressed in research efforts:

- How do the constituents of concern change between manufacturer and consumer? In the process of storage and distribution, chemical changes can occur that could lead to increased levels of harmful compounds,[11] calling for evaluation of the effects of storage time and temperature after realistic estimates of distribution and storage have been taken into account
- What is the dose–response relationship between specific smokeless tobacco constituents and health outcomes? Quantitative uncertainties in such relationships call for additional toxicological and epidemiological research.
- What are the short- and long-term clinical consequences of switching from tobacco smoking to use of smokeless tobacco products? Although there are abundant data to predict physiological and clinical effects of switching, detailed studies characterizing cardiovascular, oral health, and related effects would improve the extent to which consequences of changes in patterns of tobacco use could be accurately predicted at the population level.
- What effect does use of smokeless tobacco products have on the success of smoking cessation interventions? What is the impact of using smokeless tobacco on amount of smoking among continuing smokers? Among current smokers who are unlikely to discontinue use, how effective is smokeless tobacco relative to pharmaceutical nicotine?
- What regulations are needed to ensure that the marketing and adoption of smokeless tobacco products yield public health benefits (i.e., helping recalcitrant smokers quit) as opposed to producing harmful outcomes (i.e., leading to use of these products by nonsmokers or those who could otherwise quit smoking)?
- What are the demographic characteristics and tobacco use histories of those who are initiating use of smokeless tobacco? To what extent is marketing leading to initiation of smokeless tobacco use among current smokers, as intended, or adoption by nonusers, possibly even leading to the use of more dangerous smokeless tobacco products or smoking? Research is also needed to estimate the proportion of active smokers who would have quit smoking but instead switched to a less

harmful smokeless tobacco product, as opposed to the proportion who would have continued smoking but switched. The proportion of current smokers who continue to smoke and simply add smokeless tobacco would be of interest as well.

Although many important issues remain unresolved, we believe that a harm reduction strategy needs to be considered as one of the elements of a broad program aimed at tobacco control. Finally, it is our belief that an effective harm reduction strategy merits the same rigorous assessment and critical evaluation as any other policy intended to advance public health.

About the Authors

At the time of the study, David A. Savitz was with the Department of Epidemiology, School of Public Health, University of North Carolina, Chapel Hill. Roger E. Meyer is with the Department of Psychiatry, Georgetown University School of Medicine, Washington, DC, and the Department of Psychiatry, University of Pennsylvania School of Medicine, Philadelphia. Jason M. Tanzer is with the Department of Oral Diagnosis, School of Dental Medicine, and the Department of Laboratory Medicine, School of Medicine, University of Connecticut Health Center, Farmington. Sidney S. Mirvish is with the Eppley Institute for Research in Cancer, University of Nebraska Medical Center, Omaha. Freddi Lewin is with the Department of Oncology, Karolinska Institute, Stockholm, Sweden.

Requests for reprints should be sent to David A. Savitz, PhD, Department of Community and Preventive Medicine, Mount Sinai School of Medicine, One Gustave L. Levy Place, Box 1057, New York, NY 10029 (e-mail: david.savitz@mssm.edu).

This article was accepted November 6, 2005.

Contributors

D.A. Savitz chaired the panel discussion on which this article was based and was the principal author of the article. R.E. Meyer, J.M. Tanzer, S.S. Mirvish, and F. Lewin participated in generating ideas, wrote sections of the article, and reviewed and edited multiple drafts of the article.

Acknowledgments

Star Scientific provided an unrestricted grant to Best Practice Management Inc (Bethesda, Md) to convene a panel to address specific questions concerning the health effects of smokeless tobacco.

The author acknowledge the participation of the following individuals: Neal Benowitz and Martin Jarvis, who participated without compensation in the panel discussion on which this article was based, and Jerome Jaffe, Gio Gori, Herbert Severson, Stephen Hecht, Lars Ramstrom, and David Sweanor, who made presentations to the panel on the first day of deliberations.

References

1. Fiore M, Bailey W, Cohen SJ, et al. *Treating Tobacco Use and Dependence: Clinical Practice Guideline.* Rockville, Md: Public Health Service; 2000.

2. Hatsukami DK, Lemmonds C, Tomar SL. Smokeless tobacco use: harm reduction or induction approach? *Prev Med.* 2004;38:309–317.

3. Levy DT, Mumford EA, Cummings KM, et al. The relative risks of a low-nitrosamine smokeless tobacco product compared with smoking cigarettes: estimates of a panel of experts. *Cancer Epidemiol Biomarkers Prev.* 2004; 13:2035–2042.

4. Bates C, Fagerström K, Jarvis M, Kunze M, McNeill, Ramström L. European Union policy on smokeless tobacco: a statement in favour of evidence-based regulation for public health. Available at: . . . Accessed July 20, 2006.

5. Fagerström KO, Schildt E-B. Should the European Union lift the ban on snus? Evidence from the Swedish experience. *Addiction.* 2003;98: 1191–1195.

6. Bolinder G. Swedish snuff: a hazardous experiment when interpreting scientific data into public health ethics. *Addiction.* 2003;98:1201–1204.

7. Gilljam H, Galanti MR. Role of snus (oral moist snuff) in smoking cessation and smoking reduction in Sweden. *Addiction.* 2003;98:1183–1189.

8. Stratton S, Shetty P, Wallace R, Bondurant S. *Clearing the Smoke: Assessing the Science Base for Tobacco Harm Reduction.* Washington, DC: Institute of Medicine; 2001.

9. Mirvish SS. Formation of N-nitroso compounds: chemistry, kinetics, and in vivo occurrence. *Toxicol Appl Pharmacol.* 1975;31:325–351.

10. Hoffmann D, Adams JD, Lisk D, Fisenne I, Brunnemann KD. Toxic and carcinogenic agents in dry and moist snuff. *J Natl Cancer Inst.* 1987;79: 1281–1286.

11. Mirvish SS. Role of N-nitroso compounds (NOC) and N-nitrosation in etiology of gastric esophageal, nasopharyngeal and bladder cancer and contribution to cancer of known exposures to NOC. *Cancer Lett.* 1995;93:17–48.

12. Jeng JH, Chang MC, Hahn LJ. Role of areca nut in betel quid-associated chemical carcinogenesis: current awareness and future perspectives. *Oral Oncol.* 2001;37:477–492.

13. Boyle P, Macfarlane GJ, Maisonneuve P, et al. Epidemiology of mouth cancer in 1989: a review. *J R Soc Med.* 1990;83:724–730.

14. McLaughlin JK, Gridley G, Block G, et al. Dietary factors in oral and pharyngeal cancer. *J Natl Cancer Inst.* 1988;80:1237–1243.

15. Scully C. Oncogenes, tumor suppressors and viruses in oral squamous cell carcinoma. *J Oral Pathol Med.* 1993;22:337–347.

16. Preston-Martin S. Evaluation of the evidence that tobacco-specific nitrosamines (TSNA) cause cancer in humans. *Crit Rev Toxicol.* 1991;21: 295–298.

17. Winn DM. Epidemiology of cancer and other systemic effects associated with the use of smokeless tobacco. *Adv Dent Res.* 1997;11:313–321.

18. Critchley JA, Unal B. Health effects associated with smokeless tobacco: a systematic review. *Thorax.* 2003;58:435–443.

19. Ahlbom A, Olsson UA, Pershagen G. *Health Hazards of Moist Snuff.* Stockholm, Sweden: National Board of Health and Welfare; 1997.

20. Lewin F, Norell SE, Johansson H, et al. Smoking tobacco, oral snuff, and alcohol in the etiology of squamous cell carcinoma of the head and neck: a population-based case-referent study in Sweden. *Cancer.* 1998;82:1367–1375.

21. Schildt EB, Eriksson M, Hardell L, Magnuson A. Oral snuff, smoking habits and alcohol consumption in relation to oral cancer in a Swedish case-control study. *Int J Cancer.* 1998;77:341–346.

22. Foulds J, Ramstrom L, Burke M, Fagerström K. Effect of smokeless tobacco (snus) on smoking and public health in Sweden. *Tob Control.* 2003; 12:349–359.

23. Hatsukami DK, Lemmonds C, Zhang Y, et al. Evaluation of carcinogen exposure in people who used "reduced exposure" tobacco products. *J Natl Cancer Inst.* 2004;96:844–852.

24. Rodu B, Cole P. Smokeless tobacco use and cancer of the upper respiratory tract. *Oral Surg Oral Med Oral Pathol Oral Radiol Endod.* 2002;93:511–515.

25. Benowitz NL. Systemic absorption and effects of nicotine from smokeless tobacco. *Adv Dent Res.* 1997;11:336–341.

26. Benowitz NL. Cardiovascular toxicity of nicotine: pharmacokinetic and pharmacodynamic considerations. In: Benowitz NL, ed. *Nicotine Safety and Toxicity.* New York, NY: Oxford University Press Inc; 1998:19–28.

27. Asplund K. Smokeless tobacco and cardiovascular disease. *Prog Cardiovasc Dis.* 2003;45:383–394.

28. Huhtasaari F, Asplund K, Lundberg V, Stegmayr B, Westor PO. Tobacco and myocardial infarction: is snuff less dangerous than cigarettes? *BMJ.* 1992; 305:1252–1256.

29. Accortt NA, Waterbor JW, Beall C, Howard G. Chronic disease mortality in a cohort of smokeless tobacco users. *Am J Epidemid.* 2002;156:730–737.

30. Larsson A, Axell T, Andersson G. Reversibility of snuff dipper's lesion in Swedish moist snuff users: a clinical and histologic follow-up study. *J Oral Pathol Med.* 1991;20:258–264.

31. Andersson G, Axell T, Larsson A. Impact of consumption factors on soft tissue changes in Swedish moist snuff users: a histologic study. *J Oral Pathol Med.* 1990;19:453–458.

32. Grossi SG, Zambon J, Machtei EE, et al. Effects of smoking and smoking cessation on healing after mechanical periodontal therapy. *J Am Dent Assoc.* 1997;128:599–607.

33. Haffajee AD, Socransky SS. Relationship of cigarette smoking to the subgingival microbiota. *J Clin Periodontol.* 2001;28:377–388.

34. Bergström J, Preber H. The influence of cigarette smoking on the development of experimental gingivitis. *J Periodontal Res.* 1986;21:668–676.

35. Kinane DF, Chestnutt I. Smoking and periodontal disease. *Crit Rev Oral Biol Med.* 2000;11:356–365.

36. Novak MJ, Novak KF. Smoking and periodontal disease. In: Newman MG, Takei HH, Carranza FA, eds. *Carranza's Clinical Periodontology.* 9th ed. Philadelphia, Pa: WB Saunders Co; 2002:245–252.

37. Tomar SL, Winn DM. Chewing tobacco use and dental caries among US men. *J Am Dent Assoc.* 1999;130:1601–1610.

38. Dempsey DA, Benowitz NL. Risks and benefits of nicotine to aid smoking cessation in pregnancy. *Drug Safety.* 2001;24:277–322.

39. Benowitz NL, Dempsey DA. Pharmacotherapy for smoking cessation during pregnancy. *Nicotine Tob Res.* 2004;6:S189–S202.

40. Wisborg K, Henriksen TB, Jespersen LB, Secher NJ. Nicotine patches for pregnant smokers: a randomized controlled study. *Obstet Gynecol.* 2000;96:967–971.

41. Krishna K. Tobacco chewing in pregnancy. *Br J Obstet Gynaecol.* 1978; 85:726–728.

42. Verma RC, Chansoriya M, Kaul KK. Effect of tobacco chewing by mothers on fetal outcome. *Indian Pediatr.* 1983;20:105–111.

43. England LJ, Levine RJ, Qian C, et al. Smoking before pregnancy and risk of gestational hypertension and preeclampsia. *Am J Obstet Gynecol.* 2002;186:1035–1040.

44. Kozlowski LT, O'Connor RJ. Apply federal research rules on deception to misleading health information: an example of smokeless tobacco and cigarettes. *Public Health Rep.* 2003;118:187–192.

POSTSCRIPT

Should Smokeless Tobacco Be Promoted as an Alternative to Cigarette Smoking?

To address the problem of cigarette smoking and the numerous health consequences associated with it, some people advocate that smokeless tobacco be promoted as an alternative. Britton and Edwards believe that smokeless tobacco causes less harm and should be explored as a means to get people from continuing their addiction to cigarettes. They maintain that cigarette smoking represents an economic burden to society and that everyone would benefit from a reduction in cigarette smoking. They believe that smokers are deprived of the right to choose safer alternatives if that information is withheld. In addition, smokers who switch to smokeless tobacco may eventually cease use of all tobacco products.

From the perspective of Savitz and his associates, promoting smokeless tobacco as an alternative to cigarette smoking would be a mistake because any tobacco use is harmful. They maintain that the risks of smokeless tobacco outweigh its benefits. Their point is that all tobacco use should be eliminated. Moreover, they see an ethical dilemma in promoting smokeless tobacco. Although the health dangers of smokeless tobacco may be less significant than those of cigarette smoking, they feel that it is not a good alternative because it is addicting and carries health risks. Savitz and colleagues question whether the average person can distinguish between "safe" and "safer."

One concern of promoting smokeless tobacco is that some people may misinterpret its promotion as being a safe product. Marketing smokeless tobacco as a desirable alternative to cigarette smoking may give one the impression that it is safe. An additional concern is that the use of smokeless tobacco may lead to the use of other forms of tobacco. The use of any tobacco products, opponents argue, is antithetical to good health.

The concept of harm reduction is not new. For example, methadone has been given to heroin addicts as a way to wean them off of heroin. Giving drug addicts clean hypodermic needles as a way of preventing the spread of HIV/AIDS is another harm reduction strategy. Parents who agree to drive their children home after drinking alcohol, without interrogating their children, is a harm reduction strategy. Parents do not want their teenage children drinking alcohol, but they are also worried about their safety. When one balances out the pros and cons of giving children rides home after drinking, many parents opt for their children's safe return home. One weighs the relative harm of smokeless tobacco against that of cigarette smoking. Again, one is not in favor of a potentially unhealthy behavior, but one may be in favor of a less unhealthy behavior.

The extent of smokeless tobacco use is described in *The NSDUH Report* "Smokeless Tobacco Use, Initiation, and Relationship to Cigarette Smoking: 2002 to 2007" (May 5, 2009). The merits of promoting smokeless tobacco as an alternative to cigarette smoking are discussed in "You Might as Well Smoke: The Misleading and Harmful Public Message about Smokeless Tobacco," by Carl Phillips, Constance Wang, and Brian Guenzel (*BMC Public Health*, April 5, 2005) and "You Don't Smoke It, But It's Still Tobacco" (*Harvard Health Letter*, November 2007). The advertising of smokeless tobacco is the focus of "Under the Radar: Smokeless Tobacco Advertising in Magazine with Substantial Youth Readership," by Margaret Morrison, Dean Krugman, and Pumsoon Park (*American Journal of Public Health*, 2008).

ISSUE 15

Is Alcoholism Hereditary?

YES: Markus Heilig, from "Triggering Addiction," *The Scientist* (December 2008)

NO: Grazyna Zajdow, from "Alcoholism's Unnatural History: Alcoholism Is Not a Health Issue, But One of Personal and Existential Pain. Recognising This Would Force Us to Acknowledge One of the Most Successful Methods of Dealing With Alcohol Addiction," *Arena Magazine* (April–May 2004)

ISSUE SUMMARY

YES: Markus Heilig, Clinical Director of the National Institute on Alcohol Abuse and Alcoholism, argues that molecular changes in the brain result in positive reinforcement from alcohol. Heilig notes that alcoholism has a behavioral component, but certain genes may be responsible for individuals who abuse alcohol despite its adverse consequences.

NO: Grazyna Zajdow, a lecturer in sociology at Deakin University, maintains that the concept of alcoholism results from a social construct of what it means to be alcoholic. Because alcoholism is a social stigma, it is viewed as a disease rather than as a condition caused by personal and existential pain. Environmental conditions, especially consumerism, says Zajdow, are the root cause of alcoholism.

$\mathbf{A}$lcoholism is a serious health problem throughout the world. The number of people with an addiction to alcohol surpasses the number of addicts of any other drug. Estimates from the National Institute on Alcohol Abuse and Alcoholism indicate that there are approximately 10 to 20 million alcoholics in the United States and millions more that are problem drinkers. Yet, it is not fully understood what determines a person's disposition to alcoholism. For years scientists have been reporting that there is a genetic tendency towards alcoholism. Research shows that there may exist specific biochemical and behavioral differences in the way sons and daughters of alcoholics respond to alcohol that may be a key to why these children are more prone to becoming addicted to or abusive of the drug.

Children of alcoholics have been consistently shown to have higher rates of alcoholism than children of nonalcoholics. Children of alcoholics are two to four times more likely to become alcoholic than children of nonalcoholic parents, according to the National Council on Alcoholism. Thus, alcoholism has been called a "family disease" because it tends to run in families.

The degree to which hereditary and biological risk factors make some individuals more likely candidates for addiction once they begin drinking is unknown. Psychological forces and environmental influences may also play a major role in predisposing one to alcoholism. Certainly, there is agreement among experts that a combination and interplay of all three of these factors— biological, psychological, and environmental—are responsible for alcoholic behaviors.

In one of the largest studies ever conducted on females and alcoholism, the *Journal of the American Medical Association* reports that heredity plays a major role in determining whether a woman becomes an alcoholic. Researchers found that genes do not automatically cause alcoholism, but they do account for 50 to 61 percent of a woman's risk of becoming an alcoholic. The report mirrors the results for men. Another research group found that college-aged sons of alcoholics tend to have a lower hormonal response to alcohol and feel less drunk when they drink too much when compared to young men whose parents are not alcoholic. And, many adoption and twin studies indicate a genetic predisposition to alcoholism among children of alcoholic parents.

Although many scientists and psychologists believe that there is a genetic component of alcoholism for many people, genetic theories are still inconclusive. Researchers have not identified a single gene that carries a predisposition to alcohol abuse. Some argue that risk factors for alcoholism cannot be translated directly into genetic and biological terms and that factors such as personality traits, values, individual needs, attitudes, family upbringing, peers, and other sociocultural influences in a person's life affect one's use or abuse of alcohol.

Studies of family members show (1) common causal factors that are shared among relatives and (2) risk factors that are unique to an individual family member's life experiences and environment. In addition to sharing genes, many family members share similar environments, customs, culture, diet, and patterns of behavior. The interaction of these factors may be the foundation for a pattern of alcoholism in the family or individual family member. Thus, the conclusion that the sole cause of alcoholism is genetic is viewed skeptically because there are too many other psychological and environmental factors that play a key role in the onset of alcoholism.

Markus Heilig argues that alcoholism has a genetic component and is not the result of family environment. He maintains that changes within the brain reinforce the overuse of alcohol that may lead to alcoholism. Grazyna Zajdow contends that alcoholism is not based on genetics but on society's view of what constitutes alcoholism. Zajdow argues that addictive drinking is a choice.

YES

Markus Heilig

Triggering Addiction

Alcohol abuse is the third leading preventable cause of death (defined as death due to lifestyle choice or modifiable behavior). In the United States alone it accounts for more than 75,000 deaths annually. To put it another way, if all cancers were miraculously cured tomorrow, those lives and the life years saved would be a drop in the bucket compared to what would be achieved by eliminating alcohol-related death and morbidity. In contrast to many other common conditions, alcohol abuse affects people whose life expectancy would otherwise be considerable, robbing them of an average 30 potential life years. The unmet medical needs are enormous.

And yet, as striking as these numbers are, they don't begin to capture the despair and sorrow of alcohol problems. I had been teaching students about the pharmacology of addictive drugs for several years before I met my first patient as a clinician. Knowing alcoholic patients, and understanding their day to day struggle has shaped my thinking about the problem and informed the questions I have asked in the laboratory.

Beyond the tragedy of this disease, there is also a fascination. What makes people set aside their most obvious needs and continue to abuse alcohol? Why do they do this despite knowing that it will kill them, harm them, or destroy the lives of those they love? This puzzle offers a window on what makes us humans tick, whether addicted or not.

Fermented beverages have been used since the Neolithic period, through ancient Egypt and China down to the present. Alcohol is the one drug that remains socially and legally acceptable in most of the Western world. I, along with more than half of the adult population, drink—personally I enjoy a good wine. Even though alcohol use disorders are among the most common serious medical conditions, they still only affect about 10% of those who use alcohol.

The disease is not just about drinking too much. Nor is it just about physical dependence characterized by an increased tolerance over time and severe withdrawal when use is stopped. Neither of these phenomena are necessary or sufficient to capture the disease.

At its core, alcoholism is a behavioral disorder. Cravings lead to a narrowed behavioral repertoire, so that seeking and consuming the drug crowds out other normal behaviors. Then there is the loss of control that results in someone planning on having one glass of wine, but ending up passed out on the couch. The combination of craving, loss of control and impaired judgment results in compulsive use, despite an intimate knowledge of the harmful effects. For most—but not all—who reach this state, a return to moderation seems difficult if not impossible.

Modern approaches to treating this disease have focused on the behaviors associated with alcoholism. They help patients develop a set of skills to recognize and avoid situations carrying a high risk of relapse. Such situations involve stressors, primarily of a social nature, and exposure to alcohol-associated cues, such as environments and people. Although treatments based on these principles are clearly documented to provide some benefit, two-thirds of patients still relapse within a one-year period. So, while good behavioral methods should be available to patients, it is also painfully clear that we need something beyond that.

Thankfully, we are finally learning something about the molecular basis of the behavior and compulsion of alcoholism.

In the early 1990s, Charles O'Brien at the University of Pennsylvania, and later Stephanie O'Malley at Yale University, made a breakthrough. They showed that the opioid receptor blocker, naltrexone, could help prevent relapse to heavy drinking in alcohol-dependent patients. The logic, which has gathered considerable support since, goes like this: When you drink, your brain releases endogenous opioid-like substances, called endorphins. These act on opioid receptors and give the sensation of pleasure or, in psychological lingo, "positive reinforcement" of the effects of alcohol. The enjoyment of alcohol has long been thought important in driving excessive drinking. Naltrexone blocks the opioid signaling chain, helping make drinking less pleasant.

There had been some controversy regarding the efficacy of naltrexone, and not every study had replicated its beneficial actions. But 15 years and some 30 controlled studies later, there could be no question: Once all the data were put into a meta-analysis, it was clear that naltrexone could provide a benefit. However, the magnitude of the effect was not very impressive, leading some to dismiss the value of naltrexone as a treatment.

I always looked at opioid-mediated stimulation by alcohol with some degree of skepticism. Remember your high school or college class? There were always two or three guys who danced on the table, and did crazy things when they drank alcohol. Look closer and you'll find that many of them have a family history of alcoholism, and got in trouble themselves down the line. But the rest of us were more likely to experience a welcome relief of tension, followed, at higher doses, by an irresistible desire to fall asleep on the couch. Among that majority, quite a few still developed alcohol use disorders. And even among the people who started out by getting the characteristic kick out of alcohol, 10 years into alcoholism there is little if any pleasure or stimulation left. Clearly, there had to be other mechanisms at play in the development and maintenance of alcoholism besides chasing the buzz.

Clinicians began to notice that naltrexone had certain limitations, and that these matched broad behavior categories. In some patients, the treatment turns their lives around. For the majority, however, you'd have to work hard to convince yourself there was any effect at all.

These days, whenever a basic researcher sees these kinds of individual differences, we think "genetics." In this case, there was a particular reason to do so. Ten years ago, Mary-Jeanne Kreek at the Rockefeller University found genetic variation at the locus encoding the µ-opioid receptor, or OPRM1—the target for naltrexone's therapeutic action. Among Caucasians, about 15% carry at least one copy of a variant that might change the function of the receptor to make carriers more susceptible to both alcoholism and naltrexone therapy.

While researchers still debate what the variant does on the molecular level, carriers of the variant allele consistently experience more of a subjective high in response to alcohol. Human laboratory studies in which the effects of alcohol intake can be directly assessed are limited in the amount of alcohol that can be given to subjects. However, a functionally equivalent variant of OPRM1 has been found in rhesus macaques. Studies in our own program at the National Institute on Alcohol Abuse and Alcoholism (NIAAA) spearheaded by Christina Barr showed that carriers of the rhesus ORPM1 allele variant were much more stimulated by high doses of alcohol, and that these carriers—but not other monkeys—voluntarily consumed alcohol to intoxication when given the opportunity. This work suggests that pleasure-mediated reward from alcohol plays a particularly important role in carriers of the OPRM1 variant. A recent NIAAA sponsored COMBINE trial led by Raymond Anton, confirmed what had been suggested a few years ago by David Oslin and Charles O'Brien at the University of Pennsylvania. It showed that only carriers of the variant receptor benefit from naltrexone treatment. And that minority benefits quite a bit: Twice as many in that group achieved a good clinical outcome when treated with naltrexone compared to placebo.

We had a gene that contributed to differences in alcohol responses, and a drug that could treat the disease pharmacologically. But we had only scratched the surface. What happens in the brains of alcoholics in whom this mechanism is not driving the process?

In the last five years or so, research in experimental animals has shown that the brain undergoes long-term changes as a result of repeated exposure to cycles of pronounced intoxication and withdrawal. Data are consistent between our own laboratory, and those of George Koob at the Scripps Research Institute in La Jolla, Calif., George Breese at the University of North Carolina, Chapel Hill, and Howard Becker at the Medical University of South Carolina in Charleston.

The brain pathology induced by a history of dependence has three key features. One, a history of dependence established through repeated cycles of excessive alcohol intake and withdrawal leads to a long lasting, perhaps lifelong pattern of excessive alcohol intake. Two, there is an equally persistent increase in responses to fear and stress. Three, while stress doesn't affect voluntary alcohol intake in non-dependent animals, it does so potently in animals with a history of dependence.

These findings are closely in line with patient reports and clinical experience. Some of them have already been translated into human studies. For instance, exaggerated responsiveness of brain stress and fear systems in human alcoholics has been shown by Dan Hommer's group in our program.

This suggests that long-term neuro-adaptations occur in the alcohol-addicted brain which provide a very different motivation for relapse than the pleasure-seeking response of those who have that genetic susceptibility. In the absence of alcohol, the individual will now find himself in a negative emotional state, which in the short term can be relieved by renewed intake of alcohol. The big question is what underlying biology is driving this shift into what George Koob has labeled "the dark side of addiction."

Since stress and fear are at the core of this new model of alcoholism, we started to look for molecular targets within the neural circuitry of stress. Our best bet was corticotropin releasing hormone (CRH). Discovered in 1982 by Wylie Vale, CRH is now in every medical textbook as the top-level control signal for the hormonal stress response. Much less recognized was the fact that extensive CRH systems within the brain mediate behavioral stress responses that are in concert with, but distinct from the physiological stress effects. A key target for this extrahypothalamic CRH is the amygdala complex, and studies from many laboratories have shown that CRH acting on CRH1 receptors within this structure mediate many behavioral stress responses.

Our recent work has shown that a history of alcohol dependence leads to a persistent up-regulation of CRH1 receptor gene expression and binding within the amygdala. This is exactly the type of molecular plasticity we would expect to see in response to stress and stress-driven excessive alcohol intake. But of course the gene expression data are only correlative. The only way to demonstrate causality is by pharmacology: Only if a CRH1 antagonist rescues the behavioral phenotype of post-dependent animals, that is, makes them normal again, would causality be demonstrated. Working with colleagues at Eli Lilly, we were able to show just that. George Koob's group verified the finding using several other antagonists for the CRH1 receptor. All these molecules have the same signature: They don't do anything to non-dependent animals with low alcohol intake levels, but totally eliminate the excessive drinking that occurs in the post-dependent state.

Based on these observations, the CRH1 receptor appeared to be a very promising target for treatment of the "dark," relief-driven alcoholism. Human trials are now in the planning stages to test this prediction, but continue to face extensive obstacles with regard to the chemistry and toxicology. For instance, making molecules that will dissolve and enter the brain after having been taken as a pill, has turned out to be hard nut to crack.

While investigating the properties of CRH, we badly wanted to find some tool that would allow us to test these ideas in humans sooner. The answer came in the form of a category of compounds that had been collecting dust on many pharmaceutical companies' shelves for years. Substance P (SP), an 11 amino acid peptide discovered by Nobel Prize winner Ulf von Euler back in the 1930s, had for many years been implicated in pain and inflammation. In 1991 researchers at Pfizer developed a small molecule that blocked the main human SP receptor for the transmission of pain, called the neurokinin 1 receptor (NK1R). This was followed by the discovery of several other chemical series that successfully targeted this receptor. But to the disappointment of many, these turned out to be ineffective in treating any pain or inflammation-related clinical condition you can imagine.

Several research groups showed that SP is released in both rat and human amygdala upon exposure to stress, and mediates at least some behavioral effects of the stressor. In fact, several of the effects were identical to those induced by CRH, although its actions were not as general as those of CRH, and less pronounced. It was clear that these were converging systems that generated the same functional outcomes. Jokingly, we started calling SP "CRH light." We realized that an NK1R antagonist might allow us to assess some of our ideas and experimental approaches in humans.

What followed was a rare experience. By any measure we applied, the predictions held up. Mouse mutants that lacked the NK1R drank markedly lower amounts of alcohol, and didn't seem to obtain any reward from this drug. Moving into humans, we treated a group of recently detoxified alcoholics with an orally available, brain penetrating NK1R antagonist for three weeks. Treated subjects had fewer alcohol cravings, and reported markedly improved overall well-being when evaluated weekly by a blinded physician who followed a standard assessment questionnaire. During a challenge session, we mimicked a real-life situation with a high relapse risk: A social stressor, followed by exposure to handling and smelling a preferred alcoholic beverage. This procedure induces powerful craving in placebo-treated subjects, but those responses were markedly suppressed in patients given the NK1R blocker. In parallel with the suppressed cravings, we also found a marked suppression of the hormonal stress-response.

Surprisingly, we could see some of the most striking effects using functional magnetic resonance imaging (fMRI). By looking at the degree of oxygen use, fMRI can visualize activity of neurons in response to various stimuli. As expected based on prior work, placebo-treated alcoholics had exaggerated activation of brain circuits that process negative emotions when presented with unpleasant or scary pictures. This was particularly pronounced in the insula, a region of the brain that has been associated both with perception of aversive experience and with drug cravings. These negative responses were almost eliminated by the treatment. Conversely, placebo treated subjects had all but absent brain responses to pleasant pictures, which otherwise typically activate brain reward circuitry. Remarkably, when treated with the NK1R blocker, the patients could once again respond to pleasant stimuli.

That brain responses to aversive stimuli were dampened by an anti-stress treatment was according to our hypothesis. But the ability of the anti-stress treatment to restore reward responses was an interesting surprise. It is typically thought that stress and reward are mediated through distinct systems. Based on our findings, it would appear that there is cross-talk between the two.

NK1R antagonists are now heading into full-scale outpatient treatment trials. As promising as the early data appear, one should remember that drug development is a high stakes game. Even having reached this stage, only about 10–20% of candidates succeed. With very few exceptions, medical progress is incremental. There is no single achievement one could say has cured childhood cancer. Yet when the outcomes of 20 years ago are compared with those of today, survival has improved dramatically. The same will happen with alcoholism, and we are only in the early days of improving outcomes.

Once the new treatments are developed, a key challenge remains. Alcoholism is a chronic relapsing disease, not unlike asthma, diabetes or hypertension. None of these conditions may be possible to cure, but they can all be successfully managed. Our ability to do so will improve as the range of therapeutics expands, and knowledge about mechanisms allows us to tailor treatment to the specific characteristics of the individual patient. But for all of this to succeed, the naïve notion that alcoholism can be cured in a 28-day rehab session has to give way to a realization that our brains undergo complex and long-lasting changes in addiction.

Grazyna Zajdow  **NO**

Alcoholism's Unnatural History: Alcoholism Is Not a "Health" Issue, But One of Personal and Existential Pain. Recognising This Would Force Us to Acknowledge One of the Most Successful Methods of Dealing With Alcohol Addiction

Watching former Tasmanian premier Jim Bacon on TV, resigning himself to continuing a course of palliative care for lung cancer and urging young Australians not to be "idiots" and smoke, reminds one that there is such a thing as addiction. Bacon prefers to say he was stupid rather than addicted. And this is to a substance that is not mind-altering!

This example gives us an interesting view of how we deal with addictive substances on a social and personal level. Addiction is a problem for the late modern world because it questions the very basis of consumption and choice. In a wider social world, choice is everything; for the addict, choice can be death. Yet the Australian response to addiction is marked by ambivalence, particularly in the case of addiction to alcohol. Despite the widespread acknowledgement of the serious nature of this social problem, the attitude to one of the most successful ways of dealing with alcoholism—through Alcoholics Anonymous—is often one of downright antagonism. As a sociologist who reads the literature on addictions and problematic drug use, I often wonder why—and here I will try to unravel the mystery.

The most prominent narrative of addiction in the last few years in Australia and other places is the narrative of social construction. This narrative presents drug use as an integral part of the social world and cuts it loose from biology and physiology. Addiction only exists if there is a stigmatised role of "addict." Without this deviant category there would not be a notion of addiction. Thomas de Quincey wrote about his seventeen-year addiction to opium and even lengthier time with laudanum. He could write so openly because

From *Arena* Magazine, issue 70, April/May 2004, pp. 41–43. Copyright © 2004 by Arena Magazine.

there was no notion of addiction as a stigmatised social category at the time, but what he described was addiction nonetheless.

There is also the postmodern, discursive view of addiction as an extension of social constructionism. Discourses of addiction, in this view, are part of the Foucauldian notion of disciplinary power and knowledge. The addict is part of the "web of power" that plugs him/her into a network that constrains and limits the individual. This is a particularly abstract notion of addiction that rarely admits to material reality of the individual body, or even the social body. This narrative comes not from the sociological study of the experience of addiction, but cultural studies research on written texts such as the book *What's Wrong with Addiction* by Helen Keane.

These narratives of addiction often merge and become entangled in academic discussions. Combine these with the antagonism-towards-the-disease model of addiction that is sometimes—erroneously in my view—linked to Temperance and Prohibition and we might get an idea of why AA and its models have had such bad press, particularly on the social welfare Left. Take a typical example from a major textbook called *Drug Use in Australia,* in which one chapter refers to the AA model of addiction as the grand narrative of the "alcoholic as sinner." The evidence the authors present is one person's reported statements in an AA meeting from another academic text! Another chapter presents it as a disease model of addiction—but nowhere in the text is any of the large-scale and in-depth studies of AA referred to.

I would argue that the fundamental fact about alcoholism must be that this problem lies in the individual body as much as the social body and it is experienced as a highly individual pain. This pain is materially real and cannot be explained away as a form of discourse, amenable to the linguistic contortions of postmodernity or dismissed as simply a social construction. Alcoholics are different from non-alcoholics. The difference is not easy to distinguish—it only really becomes apparent in its most extreme manifestations—but it is there. I cannot say that my first drink of alcohol changed my life—I cannot even remember it—but I know plenty of alcoholics who say just that. They remember their first drink and how it made them feel. For some who always believed they were different or outsiders, their first drink made them feel part of humanity. For others, their natural shyness disappeared and they became loquacious and humorous. Again others just drank themselves into a stupor from the first moment because they hated the world so much and never seemed to leave this state, at least not until the pain became too great and they permanently left this world.

The sociologist Norman Denzin, in his opus *The Alcoholic Society,* wrote that every alcoholic he talked to drank "to escape an inner emptiness of self." Of course, many of us experience an inner emptiness at many times of our lives, but what Denzin talks about is an emptiness which is a constant. For Denzin, the "alcoholic self" is constantly in search of fulfilment through alcohol, but alcohol just pushes the alcoholic further away from him/herself and all others. No drug or cognitive therapy produces permanent fulfilment—only sobriety through the experience of likeminded others. One could suggest that the divided self produced by alcoholism precedes the first drink, and an existential pain must exist which is married to some physiological and biochemical response to alcohol. There is some genetic component, but what it is and how it works is not understood, and it is unlikely that any pharmaceutical therapy can ever offer a solution—though medical experts, along with pharmaceutical companies are always hinting at the possibility. For Denzin, the answer to the individual alcoholic's pain is the community of others, specifically the community of alcoholics. He is talking, of course, about Alcoholics Anonymous.

A Parallel World

Many years ago, I worked as a youth worker in what was known as the Community Youth Support Scheme. We worked out of an old house, but there was one room that we did not use and which was generally locked. One day I had to go in to do something and I felt that I had stumbled on the meeting room of a secret order, like the Masons. What struck me at first was the terrible odour of tobacco (this was in the days when we could smoke absolutely anywhere) and then I noticed the banners on the wall. They were full of strange language which included the terms God, higher power and surrender. It looked to me as if I had fallen through a hole in the floor and found myself in a parallel world. My stoned friends and I lived off jokes about it for years.

Thus, as a sociologist and a materialist, feminist and atheist, my first AA meeting—which I attended as a non-alcoholic—came as a shock to me. I imagined it had to be a cult, that it produced automatons who were close to born-again Christians. For me, the answer to alcohol and drug problems was to sweep away poverty and inequality; the social and personal body were indistinguishable—what was good for one was equally good for the other. After listening to the unmediated stories of pain, anguish and redemption, I came to believe that I was wrong. Not that poverty and inequality should not be swept away, but that alcoholism would be swept away with them. However, I did meet many stalwarts of the Left in those AA meetings and stalwarts they stayed. I know academics, unionists, politicians, writers, folk singers, musos from the 1970s who regularly maintain their sober conditions through AA. To get to this position and stay in AA, these people had to cross a line that would have been unimaginable, and the only explanation can be the intense, existential pain they experienced when they drank.

Many, whatever the drug of choice had originally been, ended up drinking themselves into oblivion. It may only have been because alcohol was the cheapest and most freely available. There are many paths into addiction and many different categories of addicts. In the end, I never truly understood what they were doing or what they were feeling. I could not understand, ever. I am not like them. I do not feel their pain, I could never cause pain to people the way they did, and nothing I do could ease their suffering. I suspect this is one of the reasons there is such a distrust of AA and its notion of alcoholism—that alcoholism produces a different category of individual, one not amenable to the niceties of living in the world as nonaddicts might do.

But I do know people who are like them. They come together in rooms (no longer smoke-ridden) and recite a prayer at the end of their meetings. Most of them have found some kind of religious understanding; many are still atheists; but all have some form of spiritual fulfilment. Those meetings are more egalitarian than almost any other community they may belong to, although sexism and racism still exist to some extent.

Here people seek to change the way they live in the world and it is a change in morality, as much as in alcohol consumption. We may find the way that television has taken up this public confession distasteful, but the AA meeting is not an episode of Oprah—it is not a mediated televisual experience. To the same extent as any conversation, it is unmediated. It also demands an ethical understanding of individual experience. Obviously some people are better at it than others. An old AA saying is that a sober horse-thief is still a horse-thief.

There are many well-known people who admit to membership of AA. Even in death, however, many people's friends and relatives often refuse to acknowledge the importance of AA in their lives. It is as if acknowledging AA is a recognition that some things (like sobriety) are more important than motherhood or friendship or other social roles.

Why are we so reluctant to recognise this state of addiction that some people find themselves in? There are strong cultural and economic forces that make alcoholism almost impossible to speak about. To recognise it would mean having to do something about it. In Australia at the moment, it would mean having to deal with the availability of help to overcome the problems of drunkenness, and it would mean facing up to the key issue of whether it should be portrayed to any degree as a "health" issue. While it has health consequences, it is not a health issue; it is an issue of personal and existential pain. Even after his public humiliation, Democrats leader Andrew Bartlett would not admit to an alcohol problem. He called it instead a "health" problem. More people are now willing to admit to problems with depression but few mention that they have been compulsively drinking a depressant for most of their adult lives. They are happy to admit to Prozac but not the sobriety (or lack of).

It is more than likely that it is a cultural distrust of AA, its religiosity and its American influence, that keeps many antagonistic to it. Ultimately, one of the most powerful arguments in AA's favour is that it works. A sixty-year follow-up by the writer George Vaillant—carried out fifteen years after the release of his *The Natural History of Alcoholism,* which looked at American men with clear alcohol problems in the 1940s—found that those who were still alive were most likely to be abstinent.

Beyond that, most alcohol-related problems in Australia are not connected to alcoholism or addiction, but to drunkenness and its consequences. Indeed, alcoholics or chronic heavy drinkers make up between 5 and 15 percent of the drinking population. Mixed with aggressive forms of masculinity, drunkenness contributes to all forms of violent crime, from the minor altercation in the pub between drunken bulls, to domestic assault and then to deaths of all sorts. It does not matter whether it is used as a form of excuse or "time-out"—without the intoxicating effects of alcohol, violent crime would be much reduced.

Large and small epidemiological studies show quite clearly that the cheaper and more readily available the alcohol is, and the greater the number of alcohol outlets, the greater the problems that exist. Some cultural factors may ameliorate or enhance its worst effects, but the reality is that humans, especially those in societies which are based on endless consumerism, will endlessly consume alcohol and other intoxicating substances. Attempting to minimise its most harmful effects without dealing with supply is to park an ambulance at the bottom of the cliff. I am not saying we should not provide the ambulance, but we cannot pretend that it is anything more than that. It is here that the abstract nature of academic discussions combines with libertarian constructions of personal choice. Resistance, then, to the restriction of the supply of alcohol means that we are really unable to effectively deal with the worst aspects of alcohol consumption.

POSTSCRIPT

Is Alcoholism Hereditary?

Is there a significant, substantiated relationship between heredity and alcoholism? The National Institute on Alcohol Abuse and Alcoholism (NIAAA) notes that numerous studies demonstrate a high probability of biological vulnerability to alcohol addiction. The NIAAA claims that there are differences in the brains of alcoholics compared to others. Critics agree that alcoholism runs in families, but they argue that there are critical environmental and psychological risk factors for alcoholism that cannot be overlooked. In the final analysis, this issue comes down to which research one chooses to accept.

Some experts have expressed concern for certain people who feel that alcoholism is a family legacy. An individual who believes that he or she is destined to become an alcoholic because his or her mother, father, aunt, uncle, or grandparent has suffered from alcoholism may become alcoholic to satisfy a self-fulfilling prophecy. Some psychologists believe this may have lamentable consequences for such individuals who feel that alcoholism is their destiny anyway. Although it is true that alcoholism tends to run in families, most children of alcoholics do not become alcoholics. A person whose parent or parents were alcoholic should be more wary of the possibility of becoming an alcoholic, but becoming an alcoholic is not a foregone conclusion for children of alcoholics.

Whether or not alcoholism is genetic or environmental has serious implications. For example, if a genetic predisposition to alcoholism was conclusively proven, then medical therapies could be designed to help those who had the hereditary risk. Second, if a person was diagnosed as having a genetic predisposition, then he or she could adopt behaviors that would help avoid problem drinking. That is, they would become aware of the hereditary factor and adjust their attitudes and actions accordingly. If alcoholism is environmental, then one's environment could be altered to influence drinking behavior.

Because of the lack of conclusive evidence identifying heredity as the primary cause for alcoholism, it may be wise to err on the side of caution with regard to consigning children of alcoholics to a fate of alcoholism. On the other hand, research that consistently finds higher rates of alcoholism and alcohol abuse among children of alcoholics cannot be dismissed. This link alone provides ample support for additional funding of research studies that may delineate the exact nature of and risk factors of alcoholism. Still, efforts against the perils of alcoholism via progressive alcohol prevention and education programs to meet the needs of children of alcoholics as well as the general public need to be strengthened.

Two technical publications from the National Institute on Alcohol Abuse and Alcoholism (NIAAA) that discuss the hereditary viability of alcoholism are "The Genetics of Alcohol and Other Drug Dependence" by Danielle Dick and Arpana Agrawal (2008) and "Systems Genetics of Alcoholism" by Chantel Sloan, Vicki Sayarath, and Jason Moore (2008). A less technical article that reviews the hereditary basis of alcoholism is "Unraveling the Genetics of Alcoholism" by Patrick Perry (*The Saturday Evening Post*, 2007). The psychosocial effects of alcoholism are examined in "Alcohol and the Burden of Disease" by Walter Gubinat (*Addiction Research and Theory*, December 2008).

ISSUE 16

Should Marijuana Be Approved for Medical Use?

YES: Peter J. Cohen, from "Medical Marijauna, Compassionate Use, and Public Policy: Expert Opinion and *Vox Populi?" Hastings Center Report* (May/June 2006)

NO: Drug Enforcement Administration, from *The DEA Position on Marijuana* (May 2006)

ISSUE SUMMARY

YES: Peter J. Cohen, an adjunct law professor at Georgetown University and a medical doctor, notes that marijuana has a long history of medicinal use. Cohen supports research to verify whether marijuana is a safe and effective therapeutic agent for various maladies. However, the federal government has presented barriers to conducting the necessary research.

NO: The Drug Enforcement Administration (DEA) states that marijuana has not been proven to have medical utility. The DEA cites the positions of the American Medical Association, the American Cancer Society, the American Academy of Pediatrics, and the National Multiple Sclerosis Society to support its position. The DEA feels that any benefits of medicinal marijuana are outweighed by its drawbacks.

Numerous states have passed referenda to legalize marijuana for medical pur-poses. Despite the position of these voters, however, the federal government does not support the medical use of marijuana, and federal laws take precedence over state laws. A major concern of opponents of these referenda is that legalization of marijuana for medicinal purposes will lead to its use for recreational purposes.

Marijuana's medicinal qualities have been recognized for centuries. Marijuana was utilized medically as far back as 2737 B.C., when Chinese emperor Shen Nung recommended marijuana, or cannabis, for medical use. By the 1890s some medical reports had stated that cannabis was useful as a pain reliever. However, despite its historical significance, the use of marijuana for medical treatment is still a widely debated and controversial topic.

Marijuana has been tested in the treatment of glaucoma, asthma, convulsions, epilepsy, and migraine headaches, and in the reduction of nausea, vomiting, and loss of appetite associated with chemotherapy treatments. Many medical professionals and patients believe that marijuana shows promise in the treatment of these disorders and others, including spasticity in amputees and multiple sclerosis. Yet others argue that there are alternative drugs and treatments available that are more specific and effective in treating these disorders than marijuana and that marijuana cannot be considered a medical replacement.

Because of the conflicting viewpoints and what many people argue is an absence of reliable, scientific research supporting the medicinal value of marijuana, the drug and its plant materials remain in Schedule I of the Controlled Substances Act of 1970. This act established five categories, or schedules, under which drugs are classified according to their potential for abuse and their medical usefulness, which in turn determines their availability. Drugs classified under Schedule I are those that have a high potential for abuse and no scientifically proven medical use. Many marijuana proponents have called for the Drug Enforcement Administration (DEA) to move marijuana from Schedule I to Schedule II, which classifies drugs as having a high potential for abuse but also having an established medical use. A switch to Schedule II would legally allow physicians to utilize marijuana and its components in certain treatment programs. To date, however, the DEA has refused.

Currently, marijuana is used medically but not legally. Most of the controversy surrounds whether marijuana and its plant properties are indeed of medical value and whether the risks associated with its use outweigh its proposed medical benefits. Research reports and scientific studies have been inconclusive. Some physicians and many cancer patients say that marijuana greatly reduces the side effects of chemotherapy. Many glaucoma patients believe that marijuana use has greatly improved their condition. In view of these reports by patients and the recommendations by some physicians to allow inclusion of marijuana in treatment, expectations have been raised with regard to marijuana's worth as a medical treatment.

Marijuana opponents argue that the evidence in support of marijuana as medically useful suffers from far too many deficiencies. The DEA, for example, believes that studies supporting the medical value of marijuana are scientifically limited, based on biased testimonies of ill individuals who have used marijuana and their families and friends, and grounded in the unscientific opinions of certain physicians, nurses, and other hospital personnel. Furthermore, marijuana opponents feel that the safety of marijuana has not been established by reliable scientific data weighing marijuana's possible therapeutic benefits against its known negative effects.

In the following selections, Peter J. Cohen notes that marijuana has a long history of medicinal use. He asserts that the federal government is unfairly putting up roadblocks which would validate marijuana's medicinal value. The Drug Enforcement Agency (DEA) argues that marijuana should not be used for legal medical purposes because the current research on marijuana's medicinal benefits is inconclusive. Other drugs are available that preclude the need to use marijuana.

YES

Peter J. Cohen

Medical Marijuana, Compassionate Use, and Public Policy: Expert Opinion or *Vox Populi?*

A recent article in the *Hastings Center Report* reviewed the Supreme Court's current (but undoubtedly not final) delineation of the boundaries of federal power as set forth by the Constitution's commerce clause.[1] The question before the Court was straightforward: Did federal authority asserted under the Controlled Substance Act of 1970 (CSA) trump California's legalization of "medical marijuana" when these plants were grown within the state and were not bought, sold, or transported into another state?[2] By a six to three vote, the Raich court held that the federal Drug Enforcement Administration could enforce the CSA against two individuals who were growing marijuana for their own medical use in full compliance with California's Compassionate Use Act (Proposition 215). At the same time, the Court's holding neither struck down Proposition 215 nor demanded that California bring criminal charges against its citizens who were using marijuana on the advice of their physicians.

Unfortunately, the far more significant policy question raised by Proposition 215 was never adjudicated. In effect, Proposition 215 declared that some compounds used to treat disease could be evaluated and approved by a vote of the people rather than "by experts qualified by scientific training and experience," as mandated by the Food, Drug, and Cosmetic Act.[3] But Proposition 215 was wrong as a matter of public policy. Anecdotes, Internet blogs, and advertisements do not provide a sound basis for assessing the safety and efficacy of pharmacologic agents.[4] "Medical marijuana" should be subjected to the same scientific scrutiny as any drug proposed for use in medical therapy, rather than made legal for medical use by popular will.

In *Raich* and other cases[5] involving Proposition 215, marijuana's advocates presented this compound to the courts as a drug, a pharmaceutical agent efficacious in the treatment of serious and even life-threatening illnesses:

> Indeed, for Raich, 39, a mother of two teenagers who says she has been suffering from a litany of disabling ailments since she was a teenager herself, medical cannabis has worked where scores of other prescribed drugs have failed. . . . It relieves pain, she said, from progressive

From *Hastings Center Report,* May/June 2006, pp. 19–22. Copyright © 2006 by The Hastings Center. Reprinted by permission of the publisher and Peter J. Cohen.

scoliosis, endometriosis and tumors in her uterus. Raich even believes it has something to do with arresting the growth of an inoperable brain tumor.

She is convinced that her use of medical marijuana, which began in 1997 after she had been using a wheelchair for two years, made her strong enough to stand up and learn to walk again. She said doctors could find no other explanation.[6]

These extravagant claims notwithstanding, marijuana has been used as a therapeutic agent throughout history, as Mathew W. Grey noted in a 1996 review of the use of medical marijuana:

> Cannabis, more commonly referred to as marijuana, has a long history of medical use in this country and worldwide. Accounts dating back as far as 2700 B.C. describe the Chinese using marijuana for maladies ranging from rheumatism to constipation. There are similar reports of Indians, Africans, ancient Greeks and medieval Europeans using the substance to treat fevers, dysentery and malaria. In the United States, physicians documented the therapeutic properties of the drug as early as 1840, and the drug was included in the United States Pharmacopoeia, the official list of recognized medical drugs, from 1850 through 1942. During this period, lack of appetite was one of the indications for marijuana prescription.[7]

Such anecdotal reports have been used by marijuana's adherents to support their wish to exempt the drug from the same scrutiny required for any other compound that is used to treat, ameliorate, or prevent human disease. Specifically, they have never campaigned vigorously for medical marijuana's evaluation by the Food and Drug Administration. Had those who favored the use of smoked marijuana as a drug elected not to circumvent the Food, Drug, and Cosmetic Act, and had smoked marijuana successfully traversed the same FDA regulatory process required for any drug proposed for use in medical treatment, it would have attained the status of an approved pharmaceutical. It could then have been purchased legally and used for medical purposes when prescribed by a properly licensed physician.

Why should PDA approval have been sought? Why should "medical marijuana" have been classified as a drug rather than a botanical, an herbal medication, or a folk remedy? The answer is in the Food, Drug, and Cosmetic Act itself: "The term 'drug' means articles intended for use in the diagnosis, cure, mitigation, treatment, or prevention of disease in man . . . and articles (other than food) intended to affect the structure or any function of the body of man."[8] That smoked marijuana is both a "controlled substance" and a plant product is extraneous to this discussion. Controlled substances have widespread use in legitimate medical practice. As an anesthesiologist, I have legally administered more narcotics (in the course of providing medical care) than many low-level illegal drug dealers. Plants and their derivatives can be potent medications. During my internship, I used digitalis leaf (derived from the foxglove plant) to treat congestive heart failure. Botanicals are the active ingredients in tincture of opium[9] and belladonna suppositories,[10] both of which are legal and FDA approved when employed for legitimate therapeutic use. Smoked marijuana could achieve the same status were the FDA to find it safe and effective for medical use.

A Consensus Conference convened by the National Institutes of Health on February 19–20,1997, to discuss the role of legitimate scientific research in evaluating the safety and efficacy of smoked marijuana reiterated the need for accurate and nonbiased scientific investigation of medical marijuana. The final report from the conference acknowledged that the FDA has approved a drug known as Marinol, which contains tetrahydrocannabinol (THC, the active psychotropic ingredient of *Cannabis sativa,* and a controlled substance), for oral use in treating both loss of appetite due to the AIDS-wasting syndrome and chemotherapy-induced nausea and vomiting, but then offered a caution:

> [This] does not fully satisfy the need to evaluate the potential medical utility of marijuana. The Expert Group noted that, although [THC] is the principal psychoactive component of the cannabis leaf, there may be other compounds in the leaf that have useful therapeutic properties. Furthermore, the bioavailability and pharmacokinetics of THC from smoked marijuana are substantially different than those of the oral dosage form.[11]

The Consensus Conference also observed that other pharmacologic agents had already been approved to treat many of the disorders for which marijuana's claims had not been scientifically substantiated. Yet, the report stated, "this does not mean, however, that the issue should be foreclosed. It simply means that in order to evaluate various hypotheses concerning the potential utility of marijuana in various therapeutic areas, more and better studies would be needed."[12]

Finally, the consultants felt that the evidence to date showed medical marijuana might have a significant role in the areas of appetite stimulation and cachexia (bodily wasting in the late stages of cancer), nausea and vomiting following anticancer therapy, neurological and movement disorders, analgesia, and glaucoma. At the same time, they made it clear that these possibilities would never reach fruition in the absence of scientific data:

> Until studies are done using scientifically acceptable clinical trial design and subjected to appropriate statistical analysis, the questions concerning the therapeutic utility of marijuana will likely remain much as they have to date—largely unanswered. To the extent that the NIH can facilitate the development of a scientifically rigorous and relevant database, the NIH should do so.[13]

The Food, Drug, and Cosmetic Act requires that drugs may not be advertised and sold in the absence of "evidence consisting of adequate and well controlled investigations, including clinical investigations, by experts qualified by scientific training and experience to evaluate the effectiveness of the drug involved."[14] However, the road to approval is not easy, and many investigators attempting to carry out scientific studies of marijuana have encountered political obstacles. Consider, for example, the difficulties faced by Donald Abrams, Professor of Medicine at the University of California, San Francisco, and chair of the Bay Area's Community Consortium on HIV research, in his attempts to study the effects of smoked marijuana on AIDS wasting. Abrams, a clinical pharmacologist, had proposed a study to provide objective data on whether smoked marijuana could ease the symptoms of AIDS wasting and produce gains in body weight. His university's institutional review board had approved the study, the FDA had approved it, and the university planned to fund it. Nonetheless, his request to import marijuana from the Netherlands was rejected.

Since the National Institute on Drug Abuse (NIDA) grows marijuana that is supplied to appropriate scientific investigators, the professor requested their assistance. However, because his funding had originated at his university, and not the NIH, of which NIDA is a part, he was denied access to the product. The NIH stated that its policy was to make marijuana available only to investigators who had received a peer-reviewed NIH grant to conduct the proposed study.

> In May of 1996, Dr. Abrams resubmitted his study proposal to the National Institute of Health, believing that he had addressed NIDA's concerns. At that time, the study was still approved and funded at the university level. In October 1996, four years after he had initiated requests to obtain marijuana legally, he was again informed that NIH's Mississippi marijuana "farm" would not supply the needed cannabis. . . . The following month, the people of California voters passed Proposition 215 by a wide margin.[15]

Political barriers to the performance of scientifically valid studies of medical marijuana do not obviate the argument that marijuana should be assessed in the same way as other drugs proposed for therapy. The sick still need medically sound treatments. In the case of Angel Raich, unfortunately, scientific evidence of this drug's efficacy in curing her inoperable brain tumor is simply nonexistent.

Decades ago, the Supreme Court gave an ample argument for protecting people from the vain hope of unproven therapy:

> Since the turn of the century, resourceful entrepreneurs have advertised a wide variety of purportedly simple and painless cures for cancer, including liniments of turpentine, mustard, oil, eggs, and ammonia; peat moss; arrangements of colored floodlamps; pastes made from glycerine and limburger cheese. . . . In citing these examples, we do not, of course, intend to deprecate the sincerity of Laetrile's current proponents, or to imply any opinion on whether that drug may ultimately prove safe and effective for cancer treatment. But this historical experience does suggest why Congress could reasonably have determined to protect the terminally ill, no less than other patients, from the vast range of self-styled panaceas that inventive minds can devise.[16]

Smoked marijuana ought not to be allowed to take the easy path to drug approval. Marinol, containing pure THC, has already been approved in the United States. Sativex, another formulation of THC, has been approved in Canada and is under consideration in the United States. Smoked marijuana might also be approved and legally prescribed for appropriate therapeutic uses.

I cannot resist a final thought. Had *Cannabis sativa* not been prescribed by the Controlled Substances Act (and been taxed and regulated, as are alcohol and tobacco, two substances that cause far more "societal pathology"), every "medical marijuana" case would have been moot. And under this scenario, as long as smoked marijuana was not advertised as an FDA-approved pharmaceutical (which would hardly have been necessary), it would undoubtedly have become one of this century's premier herbal medications.

References

1. C.E. Schneider, "A Government of Limited Powers," *Hastings Center Report* 35, no. 4 (2005): 11–12.

2. *Ashcroft v. Raich,* 124 S. Ct. 2909 (2004). "Medical marijuana" refers to any form of *Cannabis sativa* used to treat a wide variety of pathologic states and diseases. Its adherents claim (with pharmacologic justification) that smoking allows easy titration and rapid onset of its pharmacologic effects.

3. Section 505(d) of the Federal Food, Drug, and Cosmetic Act, United States Code, Title 21, as amended, sec. 321 et. seq. (2000).

4. See P.J. Cohen, "Science, Politics, and the Regulation of Dietary Supplements: It's Time to Repeal DSHEA," *American Journal of Law & Medicine* 31, nos. 2 and 3 (2005): 175–214.

5. *See United States v. Oakland Cannabis Buyers' Cooperative,* 121 S.Ct. 1711(2001).

6. E. Nieves, "User of Medical Marijuana Says She'll Continue to Fight," *The Washington Post,* June 7, 2005.

7. M.W. Grey, "Medical Use of Marijuana: Legal and Ethical Conflicts in the Patient/Physician Relationship " *University of Richmond Law Review* 30, no. 1 (1996): 249–74.

8. Food, Drug, and Cosmetic Act, United States Code, Title 21, as amended, sec. 201(g)(1)(B) and (C).

9. J.H. Jaffe and W.R. Martin, "Opioid Analgesics and Antagonists," in *The Pharmacological Basis of Therapeutics,* ed. A.G. Gilman, L.S. Goodman, and A. Gilman (New York: Macmillan, 1980), 494–534: Paregoric, U.S.P. (camphorated opium tincture) is a hydroalcoholic preparation in which there is also benzoic acid, camphor, and anise oil. The usual adult dose is 5 to 10 ml, which corresponds to 2 to 4 mg of morphine.

10. *Physicians' Desk Reference* (Montvale, NX: Thompson PDR, 2005), 2816.

11. National Institutes of Health, "Workshop on the Medical Utility of Marijuana," February 19-20,1997, Executive Summary; available at . . . p. 2.

12. Ibid., 4.

13. Ibid., 4.

14. Section 505(d) of the Federal Food, Drug, and Cosmetic Act.

15. P.J. Cohen, "The Politics of Marijuana," in *Drugs, Addiction, and the Law: Policy, Politics, and Public Health* (Durham, N.C.: Carolina Academic Press, 2004), 290–92.

16. *United States v. Rutherford,* 442 U.S. 544, 558 (1979).

Drug Enforcement Administration  **NO**

The DEA Position on Marijuana

The campaign to legitimize what is called "medical" marijuana is based on two propositions: that science views marijuana as medicine, and that DEA targets sick and dying people using the drug. Neither proposition is true. Smoked marijuana has not withstood the rigors of science—it is not medicine and it is not safe. DEA targets criminals engaged in cultivation and trafficking, not the sick and dying. No state has legalized the trafficking of marijuana, including the twelve states that have decriminalized certain marijuana use.[1]

Smoked Marijuana Is Not Medicine

There is no consensus of medical evidence that smoking marijuana helps patients. Congress enacted laws against marijuana in 1970 based in part on its conclusion that marijuana has no scientifically proven medical value. The Food and Drug Administration (FDA) is the federal agency responsible for approving drugs as safe and effective medicine based on valid scientific data. FDA has not approved smoked marijuana for any condition or disease. The FDA noted that "there is currently sound evidence that smoked marijuana is harmful," and "that no sound scientific studies supported medical use of marijuana for treatment in the United States, and no animal or human data supported the safety or efficacy of marijuana for general medical use."[2]

In 2001, the Supreme Court affirmed Congress's 1970 judgment about marijuana in *United States v. Oakland Cannabis Buyers' Cooperative et al.*, 532 U.S. 438 (2001), which held that, given the absence of medical usefulness, medical necessity is not a defense to marijuana prosecution. Furthermore, in *Gonzales v. Raich*, 125 S.Ct. 2195 (2005), the Supreme Court reaffirmed that the authority of Congress to regulate the use of potentially harmful substances through the federal Controlled Substances Act includes the authority to regulate marijuana of a purely intrastate character, regardless of a state law purporting to authorize "medical" use of marijuana.

The DEA and the federal government are not alone in viewing smoked marijuana as having no documented medical value. Voices in the medical community likewise do not accept smoked marijuana as medicine:

- The American Medical Association has rejected pleas to endorse marijuana as medicine, and instead has urged that marijuana remain a prohibited, Schedule I controlled substance, at least until more research is done.[3]

From a report issued by The Justice Department, May 2006.

350

- The American Cancer Society "does not advocate inhaling smoke, nor the legalization of marijuana," although the organization does support carefully controlled clinical studies for alternative delivery methods, specifically a THC skin patch.[4]
- The American Academy of Pediatrics (AAP) believes that "[a]ny change in the legal status of marijuana, even if limited to adults, could affect the prevalence of use among adolescents." While it supports scientific research on the possible medical use of cannabinoids as opposed to smoked marijuana, it opposes the legalization of marijuana.[5]
- The National Multiple Sclerosis Society (NMSS) states that studies done to date "have not provided convincing evidence that marijuana benefits people with MS," and thus marijuana is not a recommended treatment. Furthermore, the NMSS warns that the "long-term use of marijuana may be associated with significant serious side effects."[6]
- The British Medical Association (BMA) voiced extreme concern that down-grading the criminal status of marijuana would "mislead" the public into believing that the drug is safe. The BMA maintains that marijuana "has been linked to greater risk of heart disease, lung cancer, bronchitis and emphysema."[7] The 2004 Deputy Chairman of the BMA's Board of Science said that "[t]he public must be made aware of the harmful effects we know result from smoking this drug."[8]
- The American Academy of Pediatrics asserted that with regard to marijuana use, "from a public health perspective, even a small increase in use, whether attributable to increased availability or decreased perception of risk, would have significant ramifications."[9]

In 1999, The Institute of Medicine (IOM) released a landmark study reviewing the supposed medical properties of marijuana. The study is frequently cited by "medical" marijuana advocates, but in fact severely undermines their arguments.

- After release of the IOM study, the principal investigators cautioned that the active compounds in marijuana may have medicinal potential and therefore should be researched further. However, the study concluded that "there is little future in smoked marijuana as a medically approved medication."[10]
- For some ailments, the IOM found ". . . potential therapeutic value of cannabinoid drugs, primarily THC, for pain relief, control of nausea and vomiting, and appetite stimulation."[11] However, it pointed out that "[t]he effects of cannabinoids on the symptoms studied are generally modest, and in most cases there are more effective medications [than smoked marijuana]."[12]
- The study concluded that, at best, there is only anecdotal information on the medical benefits of smoked marijuana for some ailments, such as muscle spasticity. For other ailments, such as epilepsy and glaucoma, the study found no evidence of medical value and did not endorse further research.[13]
- The IOM study explained that "smoked marijuana . . . is a crude THC delivery system that also delivers harmful substances." In addition, "plants contain a variable mixture of biologically active compounds and cannot be expected to provide a precisely defined drug effect."

Therefore, the study concluded that "there is little future in smoked marijuana as a medically approved medication."[14]
- The principal investigators explicitly stated that using smoked marijuana in clinical trials "should not be designed to develop it as a licensed drug, but should be a stepping stone to the development of new, safe delivery systems of cannabinoids."[15]

Thus, even scientists and researchers who believe that certain active ingredients in marijuana may have potential medicinal value openly discount the notion that smoked marijuana is or can become "medicine."

DEA has approved and will continue to approve research into whether THC has any medicinal use. As of May 8, 2006, DEA had registered every one of the 163 researchers who requested to use marijuana in studies and who met Department of Health and Human Services standards.[16] One of those researchers, The Center for Medicinal Cannabis Research (CMCR), conducts studies "to ascertain the general medical safety and efficacy of cannabis and cannabis products and examine alternative forms of cannabis administration."[17] The CMCR currently has 11 on-going studies involving marijuana and the efficacy of cannabis and cannabis compounds as they relate to medical conditions such as HIV, cancer pain, MS, and nausea.[18]

At present, however, the clear weight of the evidence is that smoked marijuana is harmful. No matter what medical condition has been studied, other drugs already approved by the FDA, such as Marinol—a pill form of synthetic THC—have been proven to be safer and more effective than smoked marijuana.

Marijuana Is Dangerous to the User and Others

Legalization of marijuana, no matter how it begins, will come at the expense of our children and public safety. It will create dependency and treatment issues, and open the door to use of other drugs, impaired health, delinquent behavior, and drugged drivers.

This is not the marijuana of the 1970s; today's marijuana is far more powerful. Average THC levels of seized marijuana rose from less than one per cent in the mid-1970s to a national average of over eight per cent in 2004.[19] And the potency of "B.C. Bud" is roughly twice the national average—ranging from 15 percent to as high as 25 percent THC content.[20]

Dependency and Treatment:

- Adolescents are at highest risk for marijuana addiction, as they are "three times more likely than adults to develop dependency."[21] This is borne out by the fact that treatment admission rates for adolescents reporting marijuana as the primary substance of abuse increased from 32 to 65 percent between 1993 and 2003.[22] More young people ages 12–17 entered treatment in 2003 for marijuana dependency than for alcohol and all other illegal drugs combined.[23]

- "[R]esearch shows that use of [marijuana] can lead to dependence. Some heavy users of marijuana develop withdrawal symptoms when they have not used the drug for a period of time. Marijuana use, in fact, is often associated with behavior that meets the criteria for substance dependence established by the American Psychiatric Association."[24]
- Of the 19.1 million Americans aged 12 or older who used illicit drugs in the past 30 days in 2004, 14.6 million used marijuana, making it the most commonly used illicit drug in 2004.[25]
- Among all ages, marijuana was the most common illicit drug responsible for treatment admissions in 2003, accounting for 15 percent of all admissions—outdistancing heroin, the next most prevalent cause.[26]
- In 2003, 20 percent (185,239) of the 919,833 adults admitted to treatment for illegal drug abuse cited marijuana as their primary drug of abuse.[27]

Marijuana As a Precursor to Abuse of Other Drugs:

- Marijuana is a frequent precursor to the use of more dangerous drugs, and signals a significantly enhanced likelihood of drug problems in adult life. The *Journal of the American Medical Association* reported, based on a study of 300 sets of twins, "that marijuana-using twins were four times more likely than their siblings to use cocaine and crack cocaine, and five times more likely to use hallucinogens such as LSD."[28]
- Long-term studies on patterns of drug usage among young people show that very few of them use other drugs without first starting with marijuana. For example, one study found that among adults (age 26 and older) who had used cocaine, 62 percent had initiated marijuana use before age 15. By contrast, less than one percent of adults who never tried marijuana went on to use cocaine.[29]
- Columbia University's National Center on Addiction and Substance Abuse reports that teens who used marijuana at least once in the last month are 13 times likelier than other teens to use another drug like cocaine, heroin, or methamphetamine, and almost 26 times likelier than those teens who have never used marijuana to use another drug.[30]
- Marijuana use in early adolescence is particularly ominous. Adults who were early marijuana users were found to be five times more likely to become dependent on any drug, eight times more likely to use cocaine in the future, and fifteen times more likely to use heroin later in life.[31]
- In 2003, 3.1 million Americans aged 12 or older used marijuana daily or almost daily in the past year. Of those daily marijuana users, nearly two-thirds "used at least one other illicit drug in the past 12 months." More than half (53.3 percent) of daily marijuana users were also dependent on or abused alcohol or another illicit drug compared to those who were nonusers or used marijuana less than daily.[32]
- Healthcare workers, legal counsel, police and judges indicate that marijuana is a typical precursor to methamphetamine. For instance, Nancy Kneeland, a substance abuse counselor in Idaho, pointed out that "in almost all cases meth users began with alcohol and pot."[33]

Mental and Physical Health Issues Related to Marijuana:

- John Walters, Director of the Office of National Drug Control Policy, Charles G. Curie, Administrator of the Substance Abuse and Mental Health Services Administration, and experts and scientists from leading mental health organizations joined together in May 2005 to warn parents about the mental health dangers marijuana poses to teens. According to several recent studies, marijuana use has been linked with depression and suicidal thoughts, in addition to schizophrenia. These studies report that weekly marijuana use among teens doubles the risk of developing depression and triples the incidence of suicidal thoughts.[34]
- Dr. Andrew Campbell, a member of the New South Wales (Australia) Mental Health Review Tribunal, published a study in 2005 which revealed that four out of five individuals with schizophrenia were regular cannabis users when they were teenagers. Between 75–80 percent of the patients involved in the study used cannabis habitually between the ages of 12 and 21.[35] In addition, a laboratory-controlled study by Yale scientists, published in 2004, found that THC "transiently induced a range of schizophrenia-like effects in healthy people."[36]
- Smoked marijuana has also been associated with an increased risk of the same respiratory symptoms as tobacco, including coughing, phlegm production, chronic bronchitis, shortness of breath and wheezing. Because cannabis plants are contaminated with a range of fungal spores, smoking marijuana may also increase the risk of respiratory exposure by infectious organisms (i.e., molds and fungi).[37]
- Marijuana takes the risks of tobacco and raises them: marijuana smoke contains more than 400 chemicals and increases the risk of serious health consequences, including lung damage.[38]
- According to two studies, marijuana use narrows arteries in the brain, "similar to patients with high blood pressure and dementia," and may explain why memory tests are difficult for marijuana users. In addition, "chronic consumers of cannabis lose molecules called CB1 receptors in the brain's arteries," leading to blood flow problems in the brain which can cause memory loss, attention deficits, and impaired learning ability.[39]
- Carleton University researchers published a study in 2005 showing that current marijuana users who smoke at least five "joints" per week did significantly worse than non-users when tested on neurocognition tests such as processing speed, memory, and overall IQ.[40]

Delinquent Behaviors and Drugged Driving:

- In 2002, the percentage of young people engaging in delinquent behaviors "rose with [the] increasing frequency of marijuana use." For example, according to a National Survey on Drug Use and Health (NSDUH) report, 42.2 percent of youths who smoked marijuana 300 or more days per year and 37.1 percent of those who did so 50–99 days took part in serious fighting at school or work. Only 18.2 percent of those who did not use marijuana in the past year engaged in serious fighting.[41]

- A large shock trauma unit conducting an ongoing study found that 17 percent (one in six) of crash victims tested positive for marijuana. The rates were slightly higher for crash victims under the age of eighteen, 19 percent of whom tested positive for marijuana.[42]
- In a study of high school classes in 2000 and 2001, about 28,000 seniors each year admitted that they were in at least one accident after using marijuana.[43]
- Approximately 15 percent of teens reported driving under the influence of marijuana. This is almost equal to the percentage of teens who reported driving under the influence of alcohol (16 percent).[44]
- A study of motorists pulled over for reckless driving showed that, among those who were not impaired by alcohol, 45 percent tested positive for marijuana.[45]
- The National Highway Traffic Safety Administration (NHTSA) has found that marijuana significantly impairs one's ability to safely operate a motor vehicle. According to its report, "[e]pidemiology data from road traffic arrests and fatalities indicate that after alcohol, marijuana is the most frequently detected psychoactive substance among driving populations." Problems reported include: decreased car handling performance, inability to maintain headway, impaired time and distance estimation, increased reaction times, sleepiness, lack of motor coordination, and impaired sustained vigilance.[46]

Some of the consequences of marijuana-impaired driving are startling:

- The driver of a charter bus, whose 1999 accident resulted in the death of 22 people, had been fired from bus companies in 1989 and 1996 because he tested positive for marijuana four times. A federal investigator confirmed a report that the driver "tested positive for marijuana when he was hospitalized Sunday after the bus veered off a highway and plunged into an embankment."[47]
- In April 2002, four children and the driver of a van died when the van hit a concrete bridge abutment after veering off the freeway. Investigators reported that the children nicknamed the driver "Smokey" because he regularly smoked marijuana. The driver was found at the crash scene with marijuana in his pocket.[48]
- A former nurse's aide was convicted in 2003 of murder and sentenced to 50 years in prison for hitting a homeless man with her car and driving home with his mangled body "lodged in the windshield." The incident happened after a night of drinking and taking drugs, including marijuana. After arriving home, the woman parked her car, with the man still lodged in the windshield, and left him there until he died.[49]
- In April 2005, an eight-year-old boy was killed when he was run over by an unlicensed 16-year-old driver who police believed had been smoking marijuana just before the accident.[50]
- In 2001, George Lynard was convicted of driving with marijuana in his bloodstream, causing a head-on collision that killed a 73-year-old man and a 69-year-old woman. Lynard appealed this conviction because he allegedly had a "valid prescription" for marijuana. A Nevada judge agreed with Lynard and granted him a new trial.[51] The case has been appealed to the Nevada Supreme Court.[52]

- Duane Baehler, 47, of Tulsa, Okalahoma was "involved in a fiery crash that killed his teenage son" in 2003. Police reported that Baehler had methamphetamine, cocaine and marijuana in his system at the time of the accident.[53]

Marijuana also creates hazards that are not always predictable. In August 2004, two Philadelphia firefighters died battling a fire that started because of tangled wires and lamps used to grow marijuana in a basement closet.[54]

Marijuana and Incarceration

Federal marijuana investigations and prosecutions usually involve hundreds of pounds of marijuana. Few defendants are incarcerated in federal prison for simple possession of marijuana.

- In 2001, there were 24,299 offenders sentenced in federal court on drug charges. Of those, only 2.3 percent (186 people) were sentenced for simple possession.[55] In addition, it is important to recognize that many inmates were initially charged with more serious crimes but negotiated reduced charges to simple possession through plea agreements.[56]
- According to the latest survey data in a 2005 ONDCP study, marijuana accounted for 13 percent of all state drug offenders in 1997, and of the inmates convicted of marijuana offenses, only 0.7 percent were incarcerated for marijuana possession alone.[57]

The Foreign Experience

The Netherlands:

- Due to international pressure on permissive Dutch cannabis policy and domestic complaints over the spread of marijuana "coffee shops," the government of the Netherlands has reconsidered its legalization measures. After marijuana became normalized, consumption nearly tripled—from 15 percent to 44 percent—among 18- to 20-year-old Dutch youth.[58] As a result of stricter local government policies, the number of cannabis "coffeehouses" in the Netherlands was reduced—from 1,179 in 1997[59] to 737 in 2004, a 37 percent decrease in 7 years.[60]
- About 70 percent of Dutch towns have a zero-tolerance policy toward cannabis cafes.[61]
- In August 2004, after local governments began clamping down on cannabis "coffeehouses" seven years earlier, the government of the Netherlands formally announced a shift in its cannabis policy through the United National International Narcotics Control Board (INCB). According to "an inter-ministerial policy paper on cannabis, the government acknowledged that 'cannabis is not harmless'—neither for the abusers, nor for the community." Netherlands intends to reduce the number of coffee shops (especially those near border areas and schools), closely monitor drug tourism, and implement an action plan to discourage cannabis use. This public policy change brings the Netherlands "closer towards full compliance with the international drug control treaties with regard to cannabis."[62]

- Dr. Ernest Bunning, formerly with Holland's Ministry of Health and a principal proponent of that country's liberal drug philosophy, has acknowledged that, "[t]here are young people who abuse soft drugs . . . particularly those that have [a] high THC [content]. The place that cannabis takes in their lives becomes so dominant they don't have space for the other important things in life. They crawl out of bed in the morning, grab a joint, don't work, smoke another joint. They don't know what to do with their lives."[63]

Switzerland:

- Liberalization of marijuana laws in Switzerland has likewise produced damaging results. After liberalization, Switzerland became a magnet for drug users from many other countries. In 1987, Zurich permitted drug use and sales in a part of the city called Platzpitz, dubbed "Needle Park." By 1992, the number of regular drug users at the park reportedly swelled from a "few hundred at the outset in 1987 to about 20,000." The area around the park became crime-ridden, forcing closure of the park. The experiment has since been terminated.[64]

Canada:

- After a large decline in the 1980s, marijuana use among teens increased during the 1990s as young people became "confused about the state of federal pot law" in the wake of an aggressive decriminalization campaign, according to a special adviser to Health Canada's Director General of drug strategy. Several Canadian drug surveys show that marijuana use among Canadian youth has steadily climbed to surpass its 26-year peak, rising to 29.6 percent of youth in grades 7-12 in 2003.[65]

United Kingdom:

- In March 2005, British Home Secretary Charles Clarke took the unprecedented step of calling "for a rethink on Labour's legal downgrading of cannabis" from a Class B to a Class C substance. Mr. Clarke requested that the Advisory Council on the Misuse of Drugs complete a new report, taking into account recent studies showing a link between cannabis and psychosis and also considering the more potent cannabis referred to as "skunk."[66]
- In 2005, during a general election speech to concerned parents, British Prime Minister Tony Blair noted that medical evidence increasingly suggests that cannabis is not as harmless as people think and warned parents that young people who smoke cannabis could move on to harder drugs.[67]

The Legalization Lobby

The proposition that smoked marijuana is "medicine" is, in sum, false—trickery used by those promoting wholesale legalization. When a statute dramatically reducing penalties for "medical" marijuana took effect in Maryland in October

2003, a defense attorney noted that "[t]here are a whole bunch of people who like marijuana who can now try to use this defense." The attorney observed that lawyers would be "neglecting their clients if they did not try to find out what "physical, emotional or psychological" condition could be enlisted to develop a defense to justify a defendant's using the drug. "Sometimes people are self-medicating without even realizing it," he said.[68]

- Ed Rosenthal, senior editor of *High Times,* a pro-drug magazine, once revealed the legalizer strategy behind the "medical" marijuana movement. While addressing an effort to seek public sympathy for glaucoma patients, he said, "I have to tell you that I also use marijuana medically. I have a latent glaucoma which has never been diagnosed. The reason why it's never been diagnosed is because I've been treating it." He continued, "I have to be honest, there is another reason why I do use marijuana . . . and that is because I like to get high. Marijuana is fun."[69]
- A few billionaires—not broad grassroots support—started and sustain the "medical" marijuana and drug legalization movements in the United States. Without their money and influence, the drug legalization movement would shrivel. According to National Families in Action, four individuals—George Soros, Peter Lewis, George Zimmer and John Sperling—contributed $1,510,000 to the effort to pass a "medical" marijuana law in California in 1996, a sum representing nearly 60 percent of the total contributions.[70]
- In 2000, *The New York Times* interviewed Ethan Nadelmann, Director of the Lindesmith Center. Responding to criticism that the medical marijuana issue is a stalking horse for drug legalization, Mr. Nadelmann stated: "Will it help lead toward marijuana legalization? . . . I hope so."[71]
- In 2004, Alaska voters faced a ballot initiative that would have made it legal for adults age 21 and older to possess, grow, buy, or give away marijuana. The measure also called for state regulation and taxation of the drug. The campaign was funded almost entirely by the Washington, D.C.-based Marijuana Policy Project, which provided "almost all" the $857,000 taken in by the pro-marijuana campaign. Fortunately, Alaskan voters rejected the initiative.[72]
- In October 2005, Denver voters passed Initiative 100 decriminalizing marijuana based on incomplete and misleading campaign advertisements put forth by the Safer Alternative For Enjoyable Recreation (SAFER). A Denver City Councilman complained that the group used the slogan "Make Denver SAFER" on billboards and campaign signs to mislead the voters into thinking that the initiative supported increased police staffing. Indeed, the Denver voters were never informed of the initiative's true intent to decriminalize marijuana.[73]
- The legalization movement is not simply a harmless academic exercise. The mortal danger of thinking that marijuana is "medicine" was graphically illustrated by a story from California. In the spring of 2004, Irma Perez was "in the throes of her first experience with the drug ecstasy" when, after taking one ecstasy tablet, she became ill and told friends that she felt like she was "going to die." Two teenage acquaintances did not seek medical care and instead tried to get Perez to smoke

marijuana. When that failed due to her seizures, the friends tried to force-feed marijuana leaves to her, "apparently because [they] knew that drug is sometimes used to treat cancer patients." Irma Perez lost consciousness and died a few days later when she was taken off life support. She was 14 years old.[74]

Still, There's Good News
Continued Declines in Marijuana Use among Youth

In 2005, the *Monitoring the Future (MTF)* survey recorded an overall 19.1 percent decrease in current use of illegal drugs between 2001 and 2005, edging the nation closer to its five-year goal of a 25 percent reduction in illicit drug use in 2006. Specific to marijuana, the 2005 MTF survey showed:

- Between 2001 and 2005, marijuana use dropped in all three categories: lifetime (13%), past year (15%) and 30-day use (19%). Current marijuana use decreased 28 percent among 8th graders (from 9.2% to 6.6%), and 23 percent among 10th graders (from 19.8 percent to 15.2%).[75]

Increased Eradication

- As of September 20, 2005, DEA's Domestic Cannabis Eradication/Suppression Program supported the eradication of 3,054,336 plants in the top seven marijuana producing states (California, Hawaii, Kentucky, Oregon, Tennessee, Washington and West Virginia). This is an increase of 315,628 eradicated plants over the previous year.[76]
- For the 2005 eradication season, a total of 5 million marijuana plants have been eradicated across the United States. This is a one million plant increase over last year. The Departments of Agriculture and Interior combined have eradicated an estimated 1.2 million plants during this 2005 eradication season[77]

Appendix A
Acronyms Used in "The DEA Position on Marijuana"

AAP: American Academy of Pediatrics
ACS: American Cancer Society
AMA: American Medical Association
BBC: British Broadcasting Company
B.C.: Bud British Columbia Bud
BMA: British Medical Association
CB1: Cannabinoid Receptor 1: one of two receptors in the brain's endo-cannabinoid (EC) system associated with the intake of food and tobacco dependency.
CMCR: Center for Medicinal Cannabis Research
DASIS: Drug and Alcohol Services Information System
DEA: Drug Enforcement Administration

FDA: Food and Drug Administration
HIV: Human Immunodeficiency Virus
INCB: International Narcotics Control Board
IOM: Institute of Medicine
IOP: Intraocular Pressure
LSD: Diethylamide-Lysergic Acid
MS: Multiple Sclerosis
NHTSA: National Highway Traffic Safety Administration
NIDA: National Institute on Drug Abuse
NMSS: National Multiple Sclerosis Society
NORML: National Organization for the Reform of Marijuana Laws
NSDUH: National Survey of Drug Use and Health
ONDCP: Office of National Drug Control Policy
TEDS: Treatment Episode Data Set
THC: Tetrahydrocannabinol

Endnotes

1. As of April 2006, the eleven states that have decriminalized certain marijuana use are Arizona, Alaska, California, Colorado, Hawaii, Maine, Montana, Nevada, Oregon, Rhode Island, Vermont, and Washington. In addition, Maryland has enacted legislation that recognizes a "medical marijuana" defense.

2. "Inter-Agency Advisory Regarding Claims That Smoked Marijuana Is a Medicine." U.S. Food and Drug Administration, April 20, 2006. . . .

3. "Policy H-95.952 'Medical Marijuana.'" *American Medical Association.* See also, American Medical Association, Featured Council on Scientific Affairs. "Medical Marijuana (A-01)." June 2001. In 2001, the AMA updated their policy regarding medical marijuana reflecting the results of this study. It should be noted that a few medical organizations have offered limited support to the concept of "medical" marijuana. For example, the American Academy of Family Physicians has said that it opposes the use of marijuana "except under medical supervision and control, for specific medical indications." Largely at the urging of one activist—a lobbyist and former Board member of NORML—the American Nurses Association has endorsed "medical" marijuana under "appropriate prescriber supervision," and the American Academy of HIV Medicine, a group of about 1,800 members founded in 2000, has taken the view that marijuana should not only be made available for "medical" use, but should be excluded altogether as a Schedule I drug.

4. "Experts: Pot Smoking Is Not Best Choice to Treat Chemo Side-Effects." American Cancer Society. 22 May 2001. . . .

5. Committee on Substance Abuse and Committee on Adolescence. "Legalization of Marijuana: Potential Impact on Youth." *Pediatrics* Vol. 113, No. 6 (6 June 2004): 1825-1826. See also, Joffe, Alain, MD, MPH, and Yancy, Samuel, MD. "Legalization of Marijuana: Potential Impact on Youth." *Pediatrics* Vol. 113, No. 6 (6 June 2004): e632-e638h.

6. National MS Society. "Information Sourcebook." *National MS Society.* December 2004. . . .

7. "Doctors' Fears at Cannabis Change." BBC News. 21 January 2004.

8. Manchester Online. "Doctors Support Drive Against Cannabis." *Manchester News*. 21 January 2004. . . .

9. Joffe, Alain, MD, MPH, Yancy, Samuel W., MD, the Committee on Substance Abuse and the Committee on Adolescence, Technical Report: "Legalization of Marijuana: Potential Impact on Youth", American Academy of Pediatrics, 6 June 2004.

10. Institute of Medicine. "Marijuana and Medicine: Assessing the Science Base." (1999). Summary. (12 April 2005).

11. Id.

12. Institute of Medicine. "Marijuana and Medicine: Assessing the Science Base." (1999). Executive Summary. . . .

13. Institute of Medicine. "Marijuana and Medicine: Assessing the Science Base." (1999). Summary. . . .

14. Institute of Medicine. "Marijuana and Medicine: Assessing the Science Base." (1999). Summary. . . .

15. Benson, John A., Jr. and Watson, Stanley J., Jr. "Strike a Balance in the Marijuana Debate." *The Standard-Times*. 13 April 1999.

16. DEA, Office of Diversion Control. 8 May 2006.

17. "CMCR Mission Statement." *Center for Medicinal Cannabis Research*. . . .

18. DEA, Office of Diversion Control. 6 January 2006.

19. Marijuana Potency Monitoring Project. "Quarterly Report #87." *Marijuana Potency Monitoring Project*. 8 November 2004.

20. "BC Bud: Growth of the Canadian Marijuana Trade." *Drug Enforcement Administration, Intelligence Division*. December 2000.

21. "Teens at High Risk for Pot Addiction." *The Seattle Post-Intelligencer*. 6 January 2004.

22. Department of Health and Human Services, Substance Abuse and Mental Health Services Administration, Office of Applied Studies. *Treatment Episode Data Set (TEDS) 1993-2003: National Admissions to Substance Abuse Treatment Services*. November 2005, Table 5.1b. . . .

23. Id.

24. "Marijuana Myths & Facts: The Truth Behind 10 Popular Misperceptions." *Office of National Drug Control Policy*. . . .

25. Department of Health and Human Services, Substance Abuse and Mental Health Services Administration, Office of Applied Studies. *Overview of Findings from 2004 National Survey on Drug Use and Health*. September 2005.

26. Department of Health and Human Services, Substance Abuse and Mental Health Services Administration, Office of Applied Studies. Treatment Episode Data Set (TEDS) 1993-2003: *National Admissions to Substance Abuse Treatment Services*. November 2005. Page 74; Table 2.1b. . . .

27. Id., Tables 2.1a and 5.1a. There were 284,361 primary marijuana admissions in 2003, with 99,122 of those being juvenile marijuana admissions, meaning that there were 185,239 adult marijuana admissions.

28. "What Americans Need to Know about Marijuana." *Office of National Drug Control Policy*. October 2003.

29. Gfroerer, Joseph C., et al. "Initiation of Marijuana Use: Trends, Patterns and Implications." *Department of Health and Human Services, Substance Abuse and Mental Health Services Administration, Office of Applied Studies.* July 2002. Page 71.

30. "Non-Medical Marijuana II: Rite of Passage or Russian Roulette?" *CASA Reports.* April 2004. Chapter V, Page 15.

31. "What Americans Need to Know about Marijuana," 9.

32. Department of Health and Human Services, Substance Abuse and Mental Health Services Administration, Office of Applied Studies. "Daily Marijuana Users." *The NSDUH Report.* 26 November 2004.

33. Furber, Matt. "Threat of Meth-'the Devil's Drug'—increases." *Idaho Mountain Express and Guide.* 28 December 2005.

34. "Drug Abuse; Drug Czar, Others Warn Parents that Teen Marijuana Use can Lead to Depression." *Life Science Weekly.* 31 May 2005.

35. Kearney, Simon. "Cannabis is Worst Drug for Psychosis." *The Australian.* 21 November 2005.

36. Curtis, John. "Study Suggests Marijuana Induces Temporary Schizophrenia-Like Effects." *Yale Medicine.* Fall/Winter 2004.

37. "Marijuana Associated with Same Respiratory Symptoms as Tobacco," *YALE News Release.* 13 January 2005. . . . See also, "Marijuana Causes Same Respiratory Symptoms as Tobacco," January 13, 2005, . . .

38. "What Americans Need to Know about Marijuana," page 9.

39. "Marijuana Affects Brain Long-Term, Study Finds." Reuters. 8 February 2005. See also: "Marijuana Affects Blood Vessels." BBC News. 8 February 2005; "Marijuana Affects Blood Flow to Brain." *The Chicago Sun-Times. 8 February 2005; Querna, Elizabeth.* "Pot Head." *US News & World Report.* 8 February 2005.

40. "Neurotoxicology; Neurocognitive Effects of Chronic Marijuana Use Characterized." *Health & Medicine Week.* 16 May 2005.

41. Department of Health and Human Services, Substance Abuse and Mental Health Services Administration (SAMHSA), Office of Applied Sciences. "Marijuana Use and Delinquent Behaviors Among Youths." *The NSDUH Report.* 9 January 2004.

42. "Drugged Driving Poses Serious Safety Risk to Teens; Campaign to Urge Teens to 'Steer Clear of Pot' During National Drunk and Drugged Driving (3D) Prevention Month." *PR Newswire.* 2 December 2004.

43. O'Malley, Patrick and Johnston, Lloyd. "Unsafe Driving by High School Seniors: National Trends from 1976 to 2001 in Tickets and Accidents After Use of Alcohol, Marijuana and Other Illegal Drugs." *Journal of Studies on Alcohol.* May 2003.

44. Id.

45. "White House Drug Czar Launches Campaign to Stop Drugged Driving." *Office of National Drug Control Policy Press Release.* 19 November 2002.

46. Couper, Fiona, J., Ph.D., page 11.

47. Orange County Register. "Nation: Drug Test Positive for Driver in Deadly Crash." *Orange County Register.* 14 May 1999.

48. Edmondson, Aimee. "Drug Tests Required of Child Care Drivers—Fatal Crash Stirs Change; Many Already Test Positive." *The Commercial Appeal.* 2 July 2003.

49. McDonald, Melody and Boyd, Deanna. "Jury Gives Mallard 50 Years for Murder; Victim's Son Forgives but Says 'Restitution is Still Required.'" *Fort Worth Star Telegram.* 28 June 2003.

50. "Boy, 8, Who Was Struck While Riding Bike Dies." *The Dallas Morning News.* 25 April 2005.

51. "Lastest News in Brief from Northern Nevada." *The Associated Press State & Local Wire.* 30 April 2005.

52. Washoe County District Attorney's Office. 6 January 2006.

53. The Associated Press. "Police: Driver in Fatal Crash had Drugs in System." *The Associated Press.* 1 June 2003.

54. The Associated Press. "Murder Charges Filed in Blaze that Killed Two Firefighters." *The Associated Press.* 21 August 2004.

55. Office of National Drug Control Policy. "Who's Really in Prison for Marijuana?" May 2005. Page 22.

56. "Marijuana Myths & Facts." Page 22.

57. "Who's Really in Prison for Marijuana? Page 20.

58. "What Americans Need to Know about Marijuana," ONDCP, Page 10.

59. Dutch Health, Welfare and Sports Ministry Report. 23 April 2004.

60. INTRAVAL Bureau for Research & Consultancy. "Coffeeshops in the Netherlands 2004." *Dutch Ministry of Justice.* June 2005. . . .

61. Id.

62. International Narcotics Control Board. "INCB Welcomes 'Crucial and Significant Change in Dutch Cannabis Policy.'" *United Nations Information Service.* 2 March 2005. The action plan to discourage cannabis use includes elements such as drug prevention campaigns, mass-media anti-drugs campaign, increased treatment efforts to cannabis users, and encouragement of administrative and criminal law enforcement efforts. See also: "International Narcotics Control Board Annual Report Focuses on Need to Integrate Drug Demand, Supply Strategies." SOC/NAR/924 *Press Release.* 3 February 2005. . . . "Press Briefing by International Narcotics Control Board." 3 January 2005. . . .

63. Collins, Larry. "Holland's Half-Baked Drug Experiment." *Foreign Affairs* Vol. 73, No. 3. May-June 1999: Pages 87–88.

64. Cohen, Roger. "Amid Growing Crime, Zurich Closes a Park it Reserved for Drug Addicts." *The New York Times.* 11 February 1992.

65. Adlaf, Edward M. and Paglia-Boak, Angela, Center for Addiction and Mental Health, *Drug Use Among Ontario Students, 1977–2005,* CAMH Research Document Series No. 16. The study does not contain data on marijuana use among 12th graders prior to 1999. See also: *Canadian Addiction Survey, Highlights* (November 2004) and *Detailed Report* (March 2005), produced by Health Canada and the Canadian Executive Council on Addictions; *Youth and Marijuana Quantitative Research 2003 Final Report,* Health Canada; Tibbetts, Janice and Rogers, Dave. "Marijuana Tops Tobacco Among Teens,

Survey Says: Youth Cannabis Use Hits 25-Year Peak," *The Ottawa Citizen,* 29 October 2003.

66. Koster, Olinka, Doughty, Steve, and Wright, Stephen. "Cannabis Climbdown." *Daily Mail* (London). 19 March 2005. See also. Revill, Jo, and Bright, Martin. "Cannabis: the Questions that Remain Unanswered." *The Observer.* 20 March 2005; Steele, John and Helm, Toby. "Clarke Reviews 'Too Soft' Law on Cannabis." The Daily Telegraph (London). 19 March 2005; Brown, Colin. "Clarke Orders Review of Blunkett Move to Downgrade Cannabis." *The Independent (London).* 19 March 2005.

67. "Blair's 'Concern' on Cannabis." *The Irish Times.* 4 May 2005. See also, Russell, Ben. "Election 2005: Blair Rules Out National Insurance Rise." *The Independent (London).* 4 May 2005.

68. Craig, Tim. "Md. Starts to Allow Marijuana Court Plea; Penalty Can be Cut for Medicinal Use." *The Washington Post.* 1 October 2003, sec B.

69. From a videotape recording of Mr. Rosenthal's speech, as shown in "Medical Marijuana: A Smoke Screen."

70. "A Guide to Drug Related State Ballot Initiatives." *National Families in Action.* 23 April 2002. . . .

71. Wren, Christopher S. "Small But Forceful Coalition Works to Counter U.S. War on Drugs." *The New York Times,* 2 January 2000.

72. Brant, Tataboline. "Marijuana Campaign Draws in $857,000." *The Anchorage Daily News.* 30 October 2004.

73. Gathright, Alan. "Pot Backers Can't Stoke Hickenlooper." *Rocky Mountain News.* 27 October 2005.

74. Stannard, Matthew B. "Ecstasy Victim Told Friends She Felt Like She Was Going to Die." *The San Francisco Chronicle,* 4 May 2004. *The Chronicle* reported that Ms. Perez was given ibuprofen and "possibly marijuana," but DEA has confirmed that the drug given to her was indeed marijuana.

75. *Monitoring the Future,* 2005. Supplemented by information from the Office of National Drug Control Policy press release on the 2005 MTF Survey, December 19, 2005.

76. DEA Domestic Cannabis Eradication/Suppression Program, 2005 eradication season.

77. Id.

POSTSCRIPT

Should Marijuana Be Approved for Medical Use?

The delay in the medicalization of marijuana stems from arduous and restrictive procedures of the federal government according to many people who support marijuana's medical use. They argue that the federal government prevents research from being conducted that would validate the medical benefits of marijuana. Thus, they argue that the government blocks people in need from receiving medication that is both therapeutic and benign. The government's objection to marijuana, according to these supporters, is based more on politics than scientific evidence.

From the federal government's perspective, promoting marijuana as a medicinal agent would be a mistake because it has not been proven medically useful or safe. Moreover, it feels that the availability of marijuana should not be predicated on personal accounts of its benefits or whether the public supports its use. Also, the Drug Enforcement Agency (DEA) disputes that although those studies show that marijuana may have medical value, much of that research has been based on bad scientific methodology and other deficiencies. The results of previous research, the DEA contends, do not lend strong credence to marijuana's medicinal value.

Some people have expressed concern about what will happen if marijuana is approved for medicinal use. Would it then become more acceptable for nonmedical, recreational use? Would it not be easy for people to get prescriptions for marijuana even though they may not have a medical need for the drug? There is also a possibility that some people would misinterpret the government's message and think that marijuana cures cancer when, in fact, it would only be used to treat the side effects of the chemotherapy.

A central question is if physicians feel that marijuana use is justified to properly care for seriously ill patients, should they promote this form of medical treatment even though it falls outside the law? Does the relief of pain and suffering for patients warrant going beyond what federal legislation says is acceptable? Also, should physicians be prosecuted if they recommend marijuana to their patients? What about the unknown risks of using an illegal drug? Is it worthwhile to ignore the possibility that marijuana may produce harmful side effects in order to alleviate pain or to treat other ailments?

Many marijuana proponents contend that the effort to prevent the legalization of marijuana for medical use is purely a political battle. Detractors maintain that the issue is purely scientific—that the data supporting marijuana's medical usefulness are inconclusive and scientifically unsubstantiated. And although the chief administrative law judge of the Drug Enforcement

Administration (DEA) made a recommendation to change the status of marijuana from Schedule I to Schedule II, the DEA and other federal agencies are not compelled to do so, and they have resisted any change in the law.

Articles that discuss whether marijuana should be legalized as a medication include "Smoked Marijuana as Medicine: Not Much Future," by Harold Kalant (*Clinical Pharmacology and Therapeutics*, 2008); "Respectable Reefer," by Gary Greenberg in *Mother Jones* (November 2005); and "Medical Marijuana," in *The Economist* (April 27, 2006). Two additional articles that deal with specific medical uses of marijuana are "Cannabis Has Potential as a Drug to Relieve the Side Effects of Cancer and Its Treatment," by Donald Abrams in *Oncology News International* (March 1, 2006) and "Cannabis and AIDS" by Jule Klotter in *Townsend Letter for Doctors and Patients* (June 2006).

ISSUE 17

Should Schools Drug Test Students?

YES: Office of National Drug Control Policy, from *Strategies for Success: New Pathways to Drug Abuse Prevention* (Fall/Winter 2006)

NO: Jennifer Kern, Fatema Gunja, Alexandra Cox, Marsha Rosenbaum, Judith Appel, and Anjuli Verma, from *Making Sense of Student Drug Testing: Why Educators Are Saying No* (January 2006)

ISSUE SUMMARY

YES: The Office of National Drug Control Policy (ONDCP), an agency of the federal government, maintains that it is important to test students for illicit drugs because testing reduces drug use and improves the learning environment in schools. The ONDCP purports that the majority of students support drug testing. In addition, drug testing does not decrease participation in extracurricular activities.

NO: Jennifer Kern and associates maintain that drug testing is ineffective and that the threat of drug testing may dissuade students from participating in extracurricular activities. Moreover, drug testing is costly, it may make schools susceptible to litigation, and it undermines relationships of trust between students and teachers. Drug testing, according to Kern, does not effectively identify students who may have serious drug problems.

Attempting to reduce drug use by students is a desirable goal. Whether or not drug testing students is a means to achieve this goal is the subject of this debate. If it can be shown that drug testing results in less student drug use, then it is worthwhile. However, people on both sides of this issue do not agree on whether drug use is curtailed by drug testing.

According to the Office of National Drug Control Policy (ONDCP), drug testing acts as a deterrent to drug use. The threat of drug testing, states the ONDCP, has been shown to be extremely effective in reducing drug use by students in schools who participate in extracurricular activities as well as by individuals in the workplace. On the other hand, Jennifer Kern and associates believe that drug testing does not have an impact on drug use. They indicate that drug testing is counterproductive in that the threat of drug testing will cause many students to avoid extracurricular activities. Moreover, drug testing may lead to false positives in which students may be erroneously accused of using drugs.

Should the expense of drug testing be a factor in whether schools test students? Very few students are detected as having used illegal drugs. When school districts are strapped for funds, is drug testing a good use of funds? Critics maintain that a more effective strategy for reducing drug use would be better drug education programs that are geared to having students understand the hazards associated with drugs. Drug testing is geared to preventing drug use, not to reducing the harms that come from drug use.

An important question evolves around the legality of drug testing. Does drug testing unfairly discriminate against student athletes? In June 2002, the Supreme Court, in a 5 to 4 decision, ruled that random drug testing for all middle and high school students participating in extracurricular activities is allowable. Prior to 2002, only student athletes could be tested. Should students who participate in school government, band, plays, or other school-related activities undergo drug testing?

One reason the federal government supports drug testing is that students who use drugs do not perform as well academically as those students who do not use drugs. The point of drug testing, states the federal government, is to help students, not to punish them. One criticism of drug testing is that it focuses on illegal drugs. Teenagers are far more likely to use tobacco and alcohol than illegal drugs. Drug testing does not address the problem of tobacco and alcohol use. Tobacco and alcohol cause far more harm than illegal drugs. Drug testing proponents agree that tobacco and alcohol are not adequately addressed, but that does not mean that students should not be tested for illegal drugs.

In the following selections, the Office of National Drug Control Policy (ONDCP) advocates drug testing as a means of reducing illegal drug use by students. The ONDCP claims that the threat of drug testing is sufficient for stopping drug use or preventing drug use from occurring in the first place. Jennifer Kern and her associates question the effectiveness of drug testing. They maintain that drug testing has the opposite effect in that many students will choose not to participate in extracurricular activities for fear of testing positive for illegal drugs.

YES

Office of National Drug Control Policy

Strategies for Success: New Pathways to Drug Abuse Prevention

Principals Claim Testing Brings a Wealth of Benefits

Evidence suggesting the efficacy of random student drug testing as a tool to reduce drug use among youth is mounting. Results of a recent survey in Indiana corroborate what some educators and substance-abuse experts have maintained for years: drug testing is a promising drug prevention strategy.

Testing may not only reduce illicit drug use, the report suggests, it may also help improve the learning environment in schools by diminishing the culture of drugs. Principals participating in the survey indicated they believe drug testing has no negative effect on school morale or participation in sports or extracurricular activities, and that costs are minimal.

Published in the February 23 issue of *West's Education Law Reporter*, "The Effectiveness and Legality of Random Student Drug Testing Programs Revisited" presents findings from an April 2005 survey of principals at 65 Indiana high schools. Of the 56 schools that responded to the written survey, 54 used drug testing as part of their substance-abuse prevention programs. Two-thirds of the principals responding to the questionnaire said they based their answers on written student surveys.

The report, written by Joseph R. McKinney, chairman of the Department of Educational Leadership at Ball State University, is a follow-up to a survey conducted at the same high schools in 2002–2003, a time when the schools had either just begun or resumed their drug testing programs. Several years earlier, schools across Indiana had been forced to halt all drug testing because a ruling by a state appeals court had declared them unconstitutional. A landmark decision in June 2002 by the U.S. Supreme Court cleared the way by ruling that middle and high schools can conduct random drug tests of students participating in extracurricular activities.

The 2005 study is an attempt to learn about the effectiveness of drug testing programs by asking survey respondents what changes, if any, occurred in student drug use and other behavior at the target schools after nearly three years with testing programs in place. Its purpose, as stated in the report, is to shed light on two issues facing school districts trying to decide whether to

From the Office of National Drug Control Policy, *Pathways to Drug Abuse Prevention*, Fall/Winter 2006.

test students for drug use: Are drug testing programs effective in reducing and preventing drug use, and are they legal?

McKinney is optimistic on both counts. "The Supreme Court has spoken," he writes, "and so have several state and federal courts. Random student drug testing [RSDT] is legal with some limitations." In McKinney's opinion, "The research on RSDT also speaks volumes on the effectiveness of drug testing programs. RSDT programs are effective in deterring, reducing and detecting illegal drug use among students."

While some indicators remained constant between surveys, almost every reported change in drug-use behavior or related activities was a change for the better. For example, more than half (58 percent) of the principals in the 2005 study who relied on written student surveys for their responses said student drug use had decreased since the previous study. The rest said levels of use remained the same. Additionally, 41 percent of the full group of principals reported that the positive drug-test result rate—the percentage of students testing positive for drug use—had decreased, while 56 percent said the rate had not changed since the previous survey.

Among the encouraging results to emerge from the McKinney survey is that in no case was drug testing seen to have a negative impact on the classroom. Despite critics' concerns that drug testing erodes student morale, 100 percent of the responding Indiana principals whose schools have drug testing programs said their experiences showed these claims to be untrue. (One left the question blank.)

Reporting on data collected from the survey, McKinney also addresses charges that drug testing discourages participation in sports and other extra-curricular activities and is too costly. More than half of the high schools with drug testing programs reported that levels of participation in athletic programs remained the same from 2003 to 2005. The rest said participation increased. None reported that participation levels had gone down. As for the expense, the overwhelming majority (91 percent) of schools with testing programs reported that the per-test cost was only $30 or less. Almost two-thirds said the drug tests cost no more than $20 each.

Although overall youth drug use has decreased by nearly 20 percent Nationwide since 2001, illegal drugs remain a significant threat to young people. A 2005 survey of teens by the National Center on Addiction and Substance Abuse at Columbia University found that 62 percent of high schoolers and 28 percent of middle schoolers report that drugs are used, kept, or sold at their schools. According to the 2005 Youth Risk Behavior Survey, almost half of all students (47.6 percent) have used marijuana by the time they finish high school.

Results of the McKinney survey cannot, of course, be construed as a definitive measure of student drug use or attitudes, nor do they prove a causal relationship between drug testing and reduced levels of use. Still, taken as a whole, the survey data offer compelling evidence that random drug testing can be helpful in the effort to keep students drug free. The report bolsters the notion that random drug testing, used in conjunction with other methods as part of a comprehensive program for preventing and treating substance abuse, can be a useful and potentially effective drug abuse prevention tool.

KEY FINDINGS

Here are key findings of the McKinney report, which compares the results of an April 2005 survey of 65 Indiana high schools with data collected from the same schools in 2002–2003:

Principals Report:

Student Drug Use*
- Decreased: 58 percent
- Remained the same: 42 percent
- Increased: 0 percent

Per-Test Cost
- $30 or less: 91 percent of surveyed schools
- $20 or less: 63 percent of surveyed schools

Positive Drug-Test Result Rate
- Decreased: 41 percent
- Remained the same: 56 percent
- Increased: 3 percent

Effects of Drug Testing on Peer Pressure to Use Drugs
- Testing limits the effects of peer pressure: 91 percent
- Testing does not limit the effects of peer pressure: 9 percent

Participation in Athletic Programs
- Decreased: 0 percent
- Remained the same: 54 percent
- Increased: 46 percent

Participation in Extracurricular Activities
- Decreased: 0 percent
- Remained the same: 55 percent
- Increased: 45 percent

Impact Upon Morale
- Principals reporting that, based on their experiences, random drug testing does not have a negative impact in the classroom: 100 percent

* Responses based on written student surveys

Drugs and Testing: Looking at the Big Picture

Imagine a surgeon turning down the opportunity to use a powerful medical procedure that is government-approved, affordable, available, easy to use, and potentially life-saving.

It makes no sense.

The same could be said about schools that pass up a promising new technique for combating the scourge of substance abuse: random student drug testing. As any good surgeon knows, better methods bring better results.

Parents and educators have a responsibility to keep young people safe from drug use. In recent years we have made solid, measurable progress toward that end. According to the latest national survey in the Monitoring the Future series, the proportion of 8th-, 10th-, and 12th-grade students combined who use illicit drugs continued to fall in 2006, the fifth consecutive year of decline for these age groups. Similarly, results of the 2005 Youth Risk Behavior Survey show that rates of current marijuana use among high school students have dropped from a peak of 26.7 percent in 1999 to 20.2 percent.

This is good news, to be sure, but hardly reason to drop our guard. Consider: In 2006, according to Monitoring the Future, a fifth (21 percent) of today's 8th graders, over a third (36 percent) of 10th graders, and about half (48 percent) of 12th graders in America had tried illegal drugs at some point in their lives. Proportions indicating past-year drug use were 15 percent, 29 percent, and 37 percent, respectively, for the same grade levels.

Marijuana remains the greatest single drug threat facing our young people. Past-year marijuana use among 18- to 25-year-olds (the group with the highest drug-use rates) fell 6 percent from 2002 to 2005, according to the National Survey on Drug Use and Health. And yet, despite reduced rates in this and other user categories, marijuana still ranks as the most commonly used of all illicit drugs, with a rate of 6 percent—14.6 million current users—for the U.S. population age 12 and older. This is particularly disturbing because marijuana use can lead to significant health, safety, social, and learning or behavioral problems, and kids are the most vulnerable to its damaging effects.

Adding more cause for concern is the emergence of new threats, such as prescription-drug abuse. Over the past decade, youth populations have more than tripled their non-medical use of prescription drugs. Nearly one in five teens has taken prescription medications to get "high," according to a recent study by the Partnership for a Drug-Free America.

Our task, then, is to keep forging ahead and working to defeat drug abuse wherever it should arise. And to do this, we need all the help we can get. It is vital that we make use of the best tools at our disposal to protect young people from a behavior that destroys bodies and minds, impedes academic performance, and creates barriers to success.

Drug testing is just such a tool. For decades, drug testing has been used effectively to help reduce drug use in the U.S. Military and the Nation's workforce. Now this strategy is available to any school that understands the devastation of drug use and is determined to push back. Many of our schools urgently need effective ways to reinforce their anti-drug efforts. A random drug testing program can help them.

In June 2002, the U.S. Supreme Court broadened the authority of public schools to test students for illegal drugs. The ruling allows random drug tests not just for student athletes, but for all middle and high school students participating in competitive extracurricular activities. School administrators, however, need to consult with their counsels about any additional state law requirements regarding student drug testing.

Scientists know that drug use can interfere with brain function, learning, and the ability to retain information (see "The Biology of Drug Addiction," page 12). Any drug use at school disrupts the learning environment for all students. It spreads like a contagious disease from peer to peer and is, in this regard, nothing less than a public health threat. Schools routinely test for tuberculosis and other communicable diseases that jeopardize student health. Clearly, there is every reason to test for drugs as well.

It is important to understand that random student drug testing is not a panacea or an end in itself. Nor is it a substitute for other techniques or programs designed to reduce drug use by young people. Testing is only part of the solution and cannot do the job alone. For maximum effectiveness, it should be used in combination with other proven strategies in a comprehensive substance-abuse prevention and treatment program.

Schools considering adding a testing program to their current prevention efforts will find reassurance in knowing drug testing can be done in a way that is compassionate and respectful of students' privacy, pride, and dignity. The purpose of testing, after all, is not to punish or stigmatize kids who use drugs. Rather, it is to prevent drug use in the first place, and to make sure users get the help they need before the disease of addition can spread. Drug testing is also affordable. Discussions with individual schools indicate that, on average, a high school with 1,000 students will spend approximately $1,500 a year to test 70 students, or 10 percent of the pool of eligible students.

As the number of schools with testing programs grows, so does the body of evidence suggesting that random student drug testing can have beneficial effects on school morale. Students feel safer participating in an activity when they know their classmates are drug-free. As former drug users get and stay clean, they make healthier and better choices about how to spend leisure time, and they are more likely to engage in school activities. School pride and spirit increase as students, parents, and the school community become more involved in the school environment.

Our Road to Random

Robert Razzano

On October 2, 2003, a young man made the ultimate decision of his life. It was a decision that would affect his family, friends, and community. That young man's name was Michael Mikkanen.

Michael was a model high school student who had it all. He was an athlete, honor student, popular, and personable. His future was full of promise and opportunities. The pressure of his transition from high school to his first year in college led to severe anxiety, depression, and instability. His inability to cope led to drug use. Heroin was cheap and easy to get. Michael's addiction became so intense that it led to crime to feed his habit. Eventually Michael was arrested and jailed. On his first night behind bars, Michael made the fateful decision to take his own life.

ISSUE 17 / Should Schools Drug Test Students?

At the funeral home, Michael's mother pleaded with me to do something to help our young people with the drug problem in our city. As I sat there with my eldest son and watched Michael's friends walk up to the casket, I made a commitment to myself that I would try to fulfill the appeal of Michael's mother. Shortly thereafter I started my research on random and reasonable-suspicion drug testing.

As an administrator for the New Castle Area School District in Pennsylvania, I presented my research at our monthly administrative meetings. Superintendent George Gabriel asked me to select a committee and to present a proposal for drug testing to the school board. My committee included parents, coaches, the district attorney, school board members, the band director, and the athletic director. We spoke with many other school districts that already had a written drug testing policy. The committee spent six months working on the proposal, which Michael's mother and I presented to the school board. The board approved it, and the policy was implemented for the 2004/2005 school year.

The purpose of the random drug testing policy for the New Castle Area School District is to create a drug-free setting for all students and district employees. It is our belief that participation on any interscholastic athletic team or in any extracurricular activity is a privilege and not a right. The students who volunteer to take part in these programs are expected to accept the responsibilities granted to them by this privilege.

We recognized that drug use by school-age children is becoming more prevalent and dangerous in the community and believed the problem had to be addressed to ensure the health, safety, and welfare of all the students within the district. The need for a random drug testing policy is predicated upon the risk of immediate physical harm to drug users and to those with whom the users play sports or participate in extracurricular activities.

Drug use is not only a national problem, but a local problem. The objectives of our district's random drug testing program are to establish a deterrent to drug use and to take a proactive approach toward creating a truly safe and drug-free school. We believe the random drug testing policy undermines the effects of peer pressure by providing students with a legitimate reason to refuse to use illegal drugs. The policy also, we believe, will encourage students who use drugs to participate in drug treatment programs.

Over the past two years, we have administered 2,221 drug tests to our 7th- to 12th-grade students. Less than 1 percent tested positive for illegal drugs. Of the 1,112 students tested during the 2004/2005 school year, there were eight positive tests (five freshman and three seniors). In 2005/2006, we tested 1,109 students. Only two tested positive. The parents of all those students were notified, and each student was obligated to follow the consequence phase of the policy.

The consequences phase includes suspension from extracurricular or athletic activities, assessment from a certified drug and alcohol counselor, five consecutive weeks of drug testing, and an automatic referral to the student assistance program. Also included in our policy is a parental request referral: if parents request that their son or daughter be drug-tested, that student will be added to the random sample list on the next scheduled date.

AROUND THE U.S., HOPEFUL SIGNS AT SCHOOLS WITH TESTING

Drug testing programs have shown great promise in reducing student drug use. Here are some encouraging numbers from school districts around the country.

Community High School District #117 Lake Villa, Illinois

Results of the American Drug and Alcohol Survey for 9th through 12th graders in 2005–2006 show a 29 percent decrease in past-year drug use, down from 30 percent in 2002 to 21 percent in 2006; and a 33 percent decrease in past-month drug use, down from 18 percent in 2002 to 12 percent in 2006.

Oceanside Unified School District Oceanside, California

The Oceanside District saw an increase in drug use among student-athletes in 2004 after their drug testing program was eliminated. The school reinstated the program during the 2005–2006 school year. More than half of student athletes surveyed in 2006 said the school's current drug testing program made it easier for them to say no to drugs.

Eagle Mountain-Saginaw Independent School District Fort Worth, Texas

Ninth through 12th graders showed a decline in substance use in 8 of 13 substances from 2004 to 2005, according to a school substance use survey.

Paradise Unified School District Paradise, California

Paradise High School staff noted a decrease in school disciplinary actions for student drug use during the 2005–2006 school year after drug testing began. The California Healthy Kids Survey results for Paradise Valley indicate that past-month drug use by 11th graders decreased 12 percent since 2003.

Pulaski County Board of Education Somerset, Kentucky

The number of disciplinary infractions related to drug use decreased 26 percent from 76 incidents in 2004–05 to 56 incidents in 2005–06 after one year of student drug testing.

I am not under the illusion that drug testing is a panacea in the war on drugs. However, I unequivocally believe that a random drug testing policy is a strong deterrent and helps our young people say "no" to drugs. A drug testing program is worth the effort even if it saves only one life. I know Michael Mikkanen's family would agree.

British Educator Calls Testing Program a Success

Peter Walker is not the type to sit idly by and wait for others to find solutions. Beneath that jovial, self-effacing manner and soft English accent lies an iron determination. "In this world," the longtime educator told a group of ONDCP staffers and guests during a recent visit, "if you think there's a problem and you can do something about it—you do it."

Before stepping down last spring as headteacher (headmaster) of the Abbey School in Faversham, Kent County, England, Walker took his own advice to heart. He knew about the problem of drug abuse, about how drugs create barriers to education, burden society, and destroy young lives. So in a bold and historic move, he did something about it.

Early last year, Walker launched the first random student drug testing program at a public school in the United Kingdom. The program is open to all students but is entirely voluntary; both the student and parents must give their consent before testing can occur. And though more research must be done to determine the program's full impact, Walker needs no further convincing. For him, the signs of success are everywhere.

The Numbers

Walker spent nearly a year developing the testing program, consulting with students, parents, teachers, staff, government officials, local police, and others. "I was overwhelmed by the support," he said.

Particularly encouraging was the response of parents: 86 percent gave permission for their children to be tested.

From the time testing began in January 2005 until last spring, 600 of the nearly 1,000 students at the Abbey School had been tested for drug use (using the oral-fluids method). Only four refused when their names were called. And of all the samples tested that first year, just one was positive for drug use.

Academic Achievement

When the testing program began, Walker went on record with his belief that examination results would improve within the first year. It was a risky prediction, he said, "because in the UK, if a school doesn't meet its targets, the headteacher is the first to go." At year's end, however, he was able to report that the exam results were not only the best in the school's history, they beat out the previous record by a remarkable ten percent.

Reduced Crime

Levels of crime, too, have plunged since testing began, Walker said. Last winter, a policeman came to his office and asked why crime rates at Abbey School had dropped below those at the other area schools within the past year. Walker wouldn't go so far as to claim that drug testing alone was responsible for the decline. "But," he said, "I will claim that drug testing might have had an influence."

Improved Morale

And then there are the intangible signs of success. Morale, for instance, has improved noticeably throughout the school since testing began, Walker said. When the program was announced, more than half of the staff agreed to make themselves eligible for testing—"and they weren't even asked."

As for the students, they not only accept the program, Walker said, "They support it. They want it. They believe in it, and they're proud of it." For one thing, he continued, testing gives them a way to resist what he called the greatest motivation for taking drugs in the first place: peer pressure. Fear of being called up for a drug test gives students a convenient excuse to say no to drugs, he said. "If they can come up with their own reasons that their peer group will accept, you're on a winner."

A drug testing program, Walker explained, also shifts some of the emphasis away from the students who may be using drugs and focuses needed attention on those who strive to avoid them. From the start, he set out to achieve two main goals through drug testing. The first was to prevent drug use before it begins—by far the cheapest and most effective way to combat substance abuse.

The second main goal was to improve the quality of life for kids who choose not to take drugs. Indeed, gaining the cooperation of the non-using majority of students is vital to the program's success. "That's the trick," said

---

MYTH VS. FACT

Myth
Participation in extracurricular activities decreases when schools implement random student drug testing programs.

Fact
To date, more than 750 schools have implemented random student drug testing programs. A number of these schools indicate that the presence of a testing program does not appear to reduce levels of student participation in extracurricular activities; in fact, the levels have remained stable or actually increased. In Florida's Polk County schools, for example, where athletes are randomly drug-tested, 448 more students tried out for sports in 2005 than in 2004, and 319 more students tried out for sports in 2004 than in 2003.

Published studies support these findings. In Oregon, the Student Athlete Testing Using Random Notification (SATURN) study found that sport-activity participation increased by over 10 percent in schools with a random testing program. In addition, on a recent survey of high school principals in Indiana with 54 principals responding, 45 percent of principals in schools with random student drug testing programs reported increases in student participation, and no principals reported a decrease (see "Principals Claim Testing Brings a Wealth of Benefits,". . .).

Walker. One day last fall, he overheard a student telling a visiting reporter that she welcomed the program. With drug testing, she explained, "the kids now feel that they're being protected. They're feeling valued."

Any good drug-prevention program requires what Walker calls a "total package" of student support. "Do it in isolation," as he put it, "and you're on a loser." It is pointless to address substance abuse only occasionally or halfheartedly, such as during "drug awareness month," he said. Instead, it has to be part of a package that encompasses broad aspects of the students' lives, from academics and health education to sexual and financial matters.

Looking Ahead

The Abbey School's drug testing program has become a catalyst for big changes in England. Prompted by its success, the government is rolling out a pilot drug testing program this fall for all schools in Kent. If all goes well, the plan is to extend drug testing to schools throughout the country.

Walker, meanwhile, though retired as headteacher, remains nonetheless an educator, actively spreading the word as a government-appointed ambassador for random drug testing. "I'm not an evangelist," he said, "and I'm not selling anything. But I believe this can make a difference to young people."

Jennifer Kern et al.    **NO**

Making Sense of Student Drug Testing: Why Educators Are Saying No

Executive Summary

Comprehensive, rigorous and respected research shows there are many reasons why random student drug testing is not good policy:

- Drug testing is not effective in deterring drug use among young people;
- Drug testing is expensive, taking away scarce dollars from other, more effective programs that keep young people out of trouble with drugs;
- Drug testing can be legally risky, exposing schools to potentially costly litigation;
- Drug testing may drive students away from extracurricular activities, which are a proven means of helping students stay out of trouble with drugs;
- Drug testing can undermine trust between students and teachers, and between parents and children;
- Drug testing can result in false positives, leading to the punishment of innocent students;
- Drug testing does not effectively identify students who have serious problems with drugs; and
- Drug testing may lead to unintended consequences, such as students using drugs (like alcohol) that are more dangerous but less detectable by a drug test.

There *are* alternatives to drug testing that emphasize education, discussion, counseling and extracurricular activities, and that build trust between students and adults.

Random Drug Testing Does Not Deter Drug Use

Proponents assert the success of random student drug testing by citing a handful of reports from schools that anecdotally claim drug testing reduced drug use. The only formal study to claim a reduction in drug use was based on a snapshot of two schools and was suspended by the federal government for lack of sound methodology.[1, 2]

In a 2005 report evaluating the available evidence, Professor Neil McKeganey critiqued the methodology and biases of the studies repeatedly presented in support of random student drug testing, saying, "It is a matter of concern that student drug testing has been widely developed within the USA . . . on the basis of the slimmest available research evidence."[3]

Largest National Study Shows Drug Testing Fails

The first large-scale national study on student drug testing found virtually no difference in rates of drug use between schools that have drug testing programs and those that do not.[4] Based on data collected between 1998 and 2001 from 76,000 students nationwide in 8th, 10th and 12th grades, the study found that drug testing did not have an impact on illicit drug use among students, including athletes.

Dr. Lloyd D. Johnston, an author of the study, directs *Monitoring the Future,* the leading survey by the federal government of trends in student drug use and attitudes about drugs. According to Dr. Johnston, **"[The study] suggests that there really isn't an impact from drug testing as practiced . . . I don't think it brings about any constructive changes in their attitudes about drugs or their belief in the dangers associated with using them."**[5] Published in the April 2003 *Journal of School Health,* the study was conducted by researchers at the University of Michigan and funded in part by the National Institute on Drug Abuse (NIDA).

Follow-Up Study Confirms Results: Drug Testing Fails

The researchers at the University of Michigan conducted a more extensive study later that year with an enlarged sample of schools, an additional year of data and an increased focus on random testing programs.[6] The updated results reinforced their previous conclusions:

> **So, does drug testing prevent or inhibit student drug use? Our data suggest that, as practiced in recent years in American secondary schools, it does not . . . The two forms of drug testing that are generally assumed to be most promising for reducing student drug use—random testing applied to all students . . . and testing of athletes—did not produce encouraging results.**[7]

The follow-up study was published in 2003 as part of the Youth, Education and Society (YES) Occasional Papers Series sponsored by the Robert Wood Johnson Foundation.

The strongest predictor of student drug use, the studies' authors note, is students' attitudes toward drug use and their perceptions of peer use. The authors recommend policies that address "these key values, attitudes and perceptions" as effective alternatives to drug testing.[8] The results of these national studies are supported by numerous other surveys and studies that examine the effectiveness of various options for the prevention of student drug misuse.[9]

Who Says No to Random Drug Testing?

A groundswell of opposition has emerged to random drug testing among school officials, experts, parents and state legislatures.

School Officials and Parents Say No to Drug Testing

We stopped testing because "we didn't think it was the deterrent that we thought it would be . . . we didn't think it was as effective with the money we spent on it."

—Scot Dahl, President at school board in Guymon, Oklahoma[10]

We decided not to drug test because "it really is a parental responsibility . . . it is not our job to actually test [students]."

—Harry M. Ward, Superintendent in Mathews County, Virginia[11]

"The concerns of parents [in opposing a student drug testing proposal] have ranged from the budgetary issues to losing our focus on education to creating a threatening environment."

—Laura Rowe, President of Band Aids, a parent association of the high school band program in Oconomowoc, Wisconsin[12]

"We object to the urine-testing policy as an unwarranted invasion of privacy. We want school to teach our children to think critically, not to police them."

—Hans York, parent and Deputy Sheriff in Wahkiakum, Washington[13]

"I would have liked to see healthy community participation that stimulates thoughtful interaction among us. Instead, this [drug testing] policy was steamrolled into place, powered by mob thinking."

—Jackie Puccetti, parent in El Paso, Texas[14]

Educators and School Officials

The majority of school officials—including administrators, teachers, coaches, school counselors and school board members—have chosen not to implement drug testing programs. With their concerns rooted in knowledge and practical experience, school officials object to drug testing for a variety of reasons, including the cost of testing, the invasion of privacy and the unfair burden that student drug testing places on schools. For many educators and school officials, drug testing simply fails to reflect the reality of what works to establish safe school environments.

Experts

Physicians, social workers, substance abuse treatment providers and child advocates agree that student drug testing cannot replace pragmatic drug prevention measures, such as after-school activities. Many prominent national organizations representing these groups have come forward in court to oppose drug testing programs. These groups include the American Academy of Pediatrics, the National Education Association, the American Public Health Association, the National Association of Social Workers, and the National Council on Alcoholism and Drug Dependence. These experts have stated: **"Our experience—and a broad body of relevant research—convinces us that a policy [of random student drug testing]** *cannot* **work in the way it is hoped to and will, for many adolescents, interfere with more sound prevention and treatment processes."**[15]

Experts Say No to Drug Testing

"Social workers, concerned with a child's well-being, question whether [drug testing] will do more harm than good . . . What is most effective in keeping kids away from drugs and alcohol are substance abuse prevention programs based on scientific research."

—Elizabeth J. Clark, Ph.D., A.C.S.W., M.P.H., Executive Director of the National Association of Social Workers[16]

"Protecting America's youth from alcohol and drugs requires more than a simple drug test. We need a greater commitment to prevention and treatment . . . At-risk and marginal students need the support systems and mentoring relationships that extracurricular activities provide. Excluding students who test positive for drugs will likely exacerbate their problems."

—Bill Burnett, President, the Association for Addiction Professionals[17]

"Let us not rush to accept the illusory view that drug testing in schools is the silver bullet for the prevention of youth substance abuse . . . While [drug tests] are increasing in popularity, their efficacy is unproven and they are associated with significant technical concerns."

—Dr. John R. Knight, Director of the Center for Adolescent Substance Abuse Research at Children's Hospital in Boston and Dr. Sharon Levy, Director of Pediatrics for the Adolescent Substance Abuse Program at Children's Hospital in Boston[18]

The Oklahoma policy **"falls short doubly if deterrence is its aim: It invades the privacy of students who need deterrence least, and risks steering students at greatest risk for substance abuse away from extracurricular involvement that potentially may palliate drug problems."**

—U.S. Supreme Court Justice Ruth Bader Ginsburg's Dissenting Opinion in Board of Education of Pottawatomie v. Earls[19]

Parents

Many parents oppose drug testing for the same reasons as school staff and administrators. In addition, some parents believe that schools are misappropriating their roles when they initiate drug testing programs. They believe that it is the role of parents, not schools, to make decisions about their children's health.

State Governments

Since the U.S. Supreme Court's 2002 decision that schools may randomly drug test students participating in competitive extracurricular activities, several state legislatures have opposed student drug testing after hearing community and expert concerns about privacy, confidentiality, potential liability and overall effectiveness. For example, the Hawaii legislature tabled a bill that would have established a drug testing pilot program at several public high schools.[20] In Louisiana, a bill was defeated that would have mandated drug testing state scholarship recipients.[21]

Drug Testing Has a Negative Impact on the Classroom

Drug testing can undermine student-teacher relationships by pitting students against the teachers and coaches who test them, eroding trust and leaving students ashamed and resentful.

As educators know, student-teacher trust is critical to creating an atmosphere in which students can address their fears and concerns about drug use

---

THE HUMAN COSTS OF DRUG TESTING: A CASE IN POINT

Lori Brown of Texas felt her son was wronged by his school's random drug testing program. Seventeen-year-old Mike, an upstanding senior at Shallowater High School near Lubbock, Texas, was taking a number of medications for allergies, as well as some antibiotics, when his school randomly tested him. One of these antibiotics, his doctor later confirmed, can cause a false positive for cocaine. The school failed to properly follow their own policies by neglecting to ask Mike to list the medications he was taking. To make matters worse, South Plains Compliance, the drug testing company hired by the school to administer the tests, maintained that their procedures were 100 percent accurate despite the extenuating circumstances.

After the test came up positive for cocaine, Lori had Mike tested several times by their own physician for her own peace of mind. Each test confirmed what she already knew: Mike was not using cocaine. Lori defended her son, explaining to school authorities what she learned from Mike's doctor. But they refused to listen. Over the next six months, he was "randomly" picked for testing several more times and began to feel harassed and stigmatized as a result.

"In my opinion, schools are using the [drug] testing program as a tool to police students, when they should be concentrating on education," Lori says.

Finally, Lori and Mike had reached their emotional limit when a South Plains Compliance representative yelled at Mike for not producing enough urine for his sixth test. Together they decide to remove him from the drug testing program. As a result, Mike could no longer participate in extracurricular activities.

PROBLEMS WITH DIFFERENT TYPES OF TESTS[24]

School officials lack the expertise to determine which type of testing is more reliable.

Urine	Marijuana Cocaine Opiates Amphetamine PCP	$10–$50 per test	• Tests commonly used in schools often do not detect alcohol or tobacco • Since marijuana stays in the body longer than other drugs, drugs like cocaine, heroin and methamphetamine often go undetected • Test is invasive and embarrassing • Specimen can be adulterated
Hair	Marijuana Cocaine Opiates Amphetamine PCP MDMA/ [Ecstasy]	$60–$75 per test	• Expensive • Cannot detect alcohol use • Will not detect very recent drug use • The test is discriminatory: dark-haired people are more likely to test positive than blondes, and African Americans are more likely to test positive than Caucasians • Passive exposure to drugs in the environment, especially those that are smoked, may lead to false positive results
Sweat Patch	Marijuana Cocaine Opiates Amphetamine PCP	$20–$50 per test	• Limited number of labs able to process results • Passive exposure to drugs may contaminate patch and result in false-positives • People with skin eruptions, excessive hair, or cuts and abrasions cannot wear the patch
Saliva	Marijuana Cocaine Opiates Amphetamine PCP	$10–$50 per test	• Detects only very recent use and limited number of drugs • New technology; accuracy rates and testing guidelines not established

itself, as well as the issues that can lead to drug use, including depression, anxiety, peer pressure and unstable family life.[22] Trust is jeopardized if teachers act as confidants in some circumstances but as police in others.

Drug testing also results in missed classroom instruction. Officials at some schools with testing programs reported that many students would flagrantly ridicule the testing process by stalling for hours to produce a urine sample—during which time they remained absent from class.[23]

Drug Testing is Expensive and a Waste of School Resources

Drug testing costs schools an average of $42 per student tested, which amounts to $21,000 for a high school testing 500 students.[25] This figure is for the initial test alone and does not include the costs of other routine components of drug testing, such as additional tests throughout the year or follow-up testing.

The cost of drug testing often exceeds the total a school district spends on existing drug education, prevention and counseling programs combined. In fact, drug testing may actually take scarce resources away from the very health and treatment services needed by students who are misusing drugs.

The process for dealing with a positive test is usually long and involved; not only must a second test be done to rule out a false positive result, but treatment referral and follow-up systems must also be in place. In one school district, the cost of detecting the 11 students who tested positive amounted to $35,000.[26]

Beyond the initial costs, there are long-term operational and administrative expenses associated with student drug testing, including:

COST-BENEFIT ANALYSIS IN DUBLIN, OHIO[27]

In Dublin, Ohio, school administrators ended their drug testing program and hired two full time substance abuse counselors instead, concluding that drug testing reduces resources for more effective drug prevention programs.

	Drug Testing	Substance Abuse Counselor
Cost of program	$35,000 per school year	$32,000 annual starting salary per counselor
Number of students	Out of 1,473 students tested, 11 tested positive	Prevention programs for all 3,581 high school students incorporated in a weekly class curriculum
Cost per student	$24 per student for drug test $3,200 per student who tested positive	$18 per student for drug prevention, education and intervention Intervention programs for all targeted students who need help

---

U.S. SUPREME COURT DID NOT SAY . . .

- The Court DID NOT say that schools are required to test students involved in competitive extracurricular activities.
- The Court DID NOT say drug testing of all students or specific groups of students outside of those participating in competitive extracurricular activities (i.e. student drivers) is constitutional.
- The court DID NOT say it is constitutional to drug test elementary school children.
- The Court DID NOT say that it is constitutional to test by means other than urinalysis.
- The Court DID NOT say that schools are protected from lawsuits under their respective state laws.

- Monitoring students' urination to collect accurate samples;
- Documentation, bookkeeping and compliance with confidentiality requirements; and
- Tort or other insurance to safeguard against potential lawsuits.

Not All Drug Testing is Protected Under the Law

In 2002, by a margin of five to four, the U.S. Supreme Court in *Board of Education of Pottawatomie v. Earls* permitted public school districts to drug test students participating in competitive extracurricular activities. In its ruling, however, the Court only interpreted *federal* law. Schools are also subject to *state* law, which may provide greater protections for students' privacy rights. These laws vary greatly from state to state and, in many states, the law may not yet be well-defined by the courts.

Since the 2002 *Earls* decision, lawsuits have been filed in many states, including Indiana, New Jersey, Oregon, Pennsylvania, Texas and Washington, challenging school districts' drug testing policies.[28] Most of these school districts will spend thousands of taxpayer dollars battling these lawsuits with no guarantee of success.

What National Experts Said to the U.S. Supreme Court[29]

A mandatory drug testing policy "injects the school and its personnel, unnecessarily, into a realm where parental and medical judgment should be preeminent."

—American Academy of Pediatrics, et al.

School drug testing policies often operate "in disregard for prevention and treatment principles that doctors and substance abuse experts view as fundamental . . ."

—American Public Health Association, et al.

"There is growing recognition that extracurricular involvement plays a role in protecting students from substance abuse and other dangerous health behaviors."

—National Education Association, et al.

The risk that testing students for illicit drugs "will be understood to signal that alcohol and tobacco are of lesser danger is not an idle concern."

—National Council on Alcoholism and Drug Dependence, et al.

Random Drug Testing is a Barrier to Joining Extracurricular Activities

Random drug testing is typically directed at students who want to participate in extracurricular activities, including athletics, which have proven among the most effective pathways to preventing adolescent drug use. However, all too often drug testing policies actually prevent students from engaging in these activities.

Research shows a vastly disproportionate incidence of adolescent drug use and other dangerous behavior occurs during the unsupervised hours between the end of classes and parents' arrival home in the evening.[30]

Research also shows that students who participate in extracurricular activities are:

- Less likely to develop substance abuse problems;
- Less likely to engage in other dangerous behavior such as violent crime; and
- More likely to stay in school, earn higher grades, and set and achieve more ambitious educational goals.[31]

In addition, after-school programs offer students who are experimenting with or misusing drugs productive activities as well as contact with teachers, coaches and peers, who can help them identify and address problematic drug use.

The Tulia Independent School District, one of the many districts facing heightened public concerns about privacy and confidentiality, has seen a dramatic reduction in student participation in extracurricular activities since implementing drug testing.[32] . . .

Drug Testing Results in False Positives That Punish Innocent Students

A positive drug test can be a devastating accusation for an innocent student. The most widely used drug screening method, urinalysis, will falsely identify some students as illicit drug users when they are not actually using illicit drugs,

VIOLATING CONFIDENTIALITY

When Tecumseh High School in Oklahoma enacted its random drug testing program, the school failed to ensure the protection of private information concerning prescription drug use submitted under the testing policy. The choir teacher, for instance, looked at students' prescription drug lists and inadvertently left them where other students could see them. The result of a positive test, too, were disseminated to as many as 13 faculty members at a time. Other students figured out the results when a student was abruptly suspended from his/her activity shortly after the administration of a drug test.[36] This not only violates students' privacy rights, but can also lead to costly litigation.

because drug testing does not necessarily distinguish between drug metabolites with similar structures. For example:

- Over-the-counter decongestants may produce a positive result for amphetamine.[33]
- Codeine can produce a positive result for heroin.[34]
- Food products with poppy seeds can produce a positive result for opiates.[35]

Out of a desire to eliminate the possibility for false positives, schools often ask students to identify their prescription medications before taking a drug test. This both compromises students' privacy rights and creates an added burden for schools to ensure that students' private information is safely guarded.

Drug Testing is Not the Best Way to Identify Students With a Drug Problem

Drug testing says very little about who is misusing or abusing drugs. Thousands of students might be tested in order to detect a tiny fraction of those who may have used the drugs covered by the test. Additionally, students misusing other harmful substances not detected by drug tests will not be identified. If schools rely on drug testing, they may undervalue better ways of detecting young people who are having problems with drugs. Most often, problematic drug use is discovered by learning to recognize its common symptoms. Properly trained teachers, coaches and other school officials can identify symptoms of a potential drug problem by paying attention to such signs as student absences, erratic behavior, changes in grades and withdrawal from peers.

FIRST, ASK THESE HARD QUESTIONS

- Has the drug test been proven to identify students likely to have future problems and to clear those who will not?
- Have schools been proven to be more appropriate or cost-effective places to perform these tests than a doctor's office?
- Are resources in place to assist students who fail the test, regardless of health insurance status or parental income?
- Is the financial interest of a proprietary firm behind the test's promotion?
- Is the school staff using precious time to elicit parental permission, explain the test, make the referrals and assure follow-up?

Adapted from the American Association of School Administrators' website[37]

Drug Testing Has Unintended Consequences

Students may turn to more dangerous drugs or binge drinking   Because marijuana is the most detectable drug, with traces of THC remaining in the body for weeks, students may simply take drugs that exit the body quickly, like methamphetamine, MDMA (Ecstasy) or inhalants.[38] Knowing alcohol is less detectable, they may also engage in binge drinking, creating health and safety risks for students and the community as a whole.

Students can outsmart the drug test   Students who fear being caught by a drug test may find ways to cheat the test, often by purchasing products on the Internet. A quick Internet search for "pass drug test" yields nearly four million hits, linking students to websites selling drug-free replacement urine, herbal detoxifiers, hair follicle shampoo and other products designed to beat drug tests. Students may also try dangerous home remedies. The president of the school board for Guymon, Oklahoma, described a frantic parent who had caught her daughter drinking bleach;[39] the district's drug testing program was subsequently abandoned. In one Louisiana school district, students who were facing a hair test shaved their heads and body hair, making a mockery of the drug testing program.[40]

Students learn that they are guilty until proven innocent   Students are taught that under the U.S. Constitution people are presumed innocent until proven guilty and have a reasonable expectation of privacy. Random drug testing undermines both lessons; students are assumed guilty until they can produce a clean urine sample with no regard for their privacy rights.

Alternatives to Student Drug Testing

The current push to increase drug testing comes from the drug testing industry as well as well-intentioned educators and parents frustrated by the lack of success of drug prevention programs such as Drug Abuse Resistance Education (DARE).[41] However, there are more effective ways to keep teens out of trouble with drugs.

Engage Students in After-School Programs

Schools and local communities should help engage students in extracurricular activities and athletics, as these are among the best deterrents to drug misuse.

Incorporate Reality-Based Drug Education into the School Curriculum

Drugs of all sorts abound in our society. We are constantly confronted by a wide variety of substances with recreational and medicinal uses that can be purchased over-the-counter, by prescription and illegally. Since our decisions about drugs of all kinds should be based on complete, accurate information, quality drug education should be incorporated into a broad range of science disciplines, including physiology, chemistry and biology as well as psychology, history and sociology. Drug education should avoid dishonest scare tactics and should also recognize the wide spectrum of drug use and misuse, and the reasons why young people might choose to use (or not use) drugs.

Provide Counseling

Schools should provide counseling for students who are using drugs in a way that is causing harm to themselves or others. An emerging model that stresses relationships between students and counselors is that of a comprehensive Student Assistance Program (SAP).[42] Such a program advocates a mix of prevention, education and intervention. Counselors who teach about drugs can remain an important resource for students after the formal session ends, while trained student counselors can engage those students who feel more comfortable talking about their problems with peers.[43]

Allow Students to Be Assessed and Treated by Healthcare Professionals

Schools can refer students to healthcare professionals who can play a role in screening, intervening and referring adolescents to treatment. Several screening tools other than urinalysis, such as questionnaires, are available to healthcare professionals in diagnosing drug abuse among adolescents.[44]

Encourage Parents to Become Better Informed

Informed parents play a key role in preventing and detecting student drug misuse, so they should learn as much as they can. Schools can encourage parents to open a dialogue when adolescents are first confronted with alcohol and other intoxicating drugs, usually in middle school. At this point, "drug talks" should be two-way conversations. It is important for parents to teach, as well as learn from, their children.[45]

Cultivate Trust and Respect Among Students and Adults

Trust and respect are perhaps the most important elements of relationships with teens. Young people who enjoy the confidence of their parents and teachers, and who are expected to assume responsibility for their actions, are the most likely to act responsibly. They need to practice responsibility while in high school, where they have a crucial parental and school safety net.

The combination of these methods will help ensure that students:

- **Receive comprehensive, science-based information;**
- **Receive help when they need it; and**
- **Stay busy and involved in productive activities when the school day ends.**

Resources

Studies on Students, Drug Testing and/or After-School Activities

Neil McKeganey, *Random Drug Testing of Schoolchildren: A Shot in the Arm or a Shot in the Foot for Drug Prevention?* (York, UK: Joseph Rowntree Foundation, 2005). . . .

Ryoko Yamaguchi, Lloyd D. Johnston, and Patrick M. O'Malley, *Drug Testing in Schools: Policies, Practices, and Association With Student Drug Use,* Youth, Education, and Society (YES) Occasional Papers Series (Ann Arbor, MI: The Robert Wood Johnson Foundation, 2003). . . .

Ryoko Yamaguchi, Lloyd D. Johnston, and Patrick M. O'Malley, "Relationship Between Student Illicit Drug Use and School Drug-Testing Policies," *Journal of School Health* 73, no. 4 (2003): pp. 159–164. . . .

William J. Bailey, "Suspicionless Drug Testing in Schools," Indiana Prevention Resource Center (1998). . . .

Julie Pederson and others, "The Potential of After-School Programs" in *Safe and Smart: Making After-School Hours Work for Kids* (Washington, D.C.: U.S. Department of Education and U.S. Department of Justice, 1998). . . .

Nicholas Zill, Christine Winquist Nord, and Laura Spencer Loomis, "Adolescent Time Use, Risky Behavior and Outcomes: An Analysis of National Data," U.S. Department of Health and Human Services (1995). . . .

Recommended Reading and Viewing

Rodney Skager, Ph.D., *Beyond Zero Tolerance: A Reality-Based Approach to Drug Education and Student Assistance* (San Francisco, CA: Drug Policy Alliance, 2005). This 23-page booklet offers educators an approach to secondary school drug education that is honest, interactive and cost-effective. The booklet also addresses student assistance and restorative practices as an alternative to punitive zero tolerance policies. . . .

Brave New Films, *The ACLU Freedom Files: The Supreme Court* (2005) is a television show featuring the story of Lindsay Earls, the high school sophomore who opposed her school's drug testing policy for violating her privacy. Screen the half-hour program online and see how she stood up for her beliefs in front of the U.S. Supreme Court. Lindsay Earls was a student at Tecumseh High School, a member of the debate team and a performer in the choir, when a mandatory drug testing policy was instituted for anyone participating in extracurricular activities. She opposed the order as an unconstitutional invasion of her privacy in *Board of Education of Pottawatomie v. Earls*. The show traces the Earls' family experience and gives an insider's view of the high court and the justices who serve on it. . . .

Andrew Weil, M.D. and Winifred Rosen, *From Chocolate to Morphine: Everything You Need to Know About Mind-Altering Drugs* (Boston, MA: Houghton Mifflin, 2004).

Marsha Rosenbaum, Ph.D., *Safety First: A Reality-Based Approach to Teens, Drugs and Drug Education* (San Francisco, CA: Drug Policy Alliance, 2004). This 20-page booklet provides parents and educators with pragmatic ways to address teenage drug use. . . . The Safety First website also contains "fact sheets" about drugs, strategies for talking with teens, news about teen drug use and drug education, an "Ask the Experts" column containing questions submitted by parents and educators, links to relevant sites, ordering information and more.

Mark Birnbaum and Jim Schermbeck, *Larry v. Lockney* (Dallas, TX: Independent Television Service, KERA Unlimited and Public Broadcasting Service, 2003). This documentary follows a parent's fight against a student drug testing program in his son's school. The film's website includes lesson plans and other related resources. . . .

Friend-of-the-Court brief of the American Academy of Pediatrics, et al. in Support of Lindsay Earls, in *Earls*, 536 U.S. 822 (2002). . . .

American Bar Association, *Teaching about Drug Testing in Schools* adapted from Street Law, Inc. (1999). This lesson plan educates students about drug testing in schools and allows them to consider and discuss the consequences of a student drug testing policy. . . .

Recommended Websites

"Drug Testing Fails" provides resources for parents, educators, coaches, and other interested and concerned adults, who believe that safe and trusting learning environments are critical to our young people's health and safety, and that student drug testing programs get in the way of creating that kind of environment. . . .

"A Test You Can't Study For" is a special ACLU web feature on student drug testing that includes a guide for students, fact sheets, reports and other materials. . . .

Student for Sensible Drug Policy (SSDP), an organization with more than 115 college and high school chapters nationwide, is committed to providing education on harms caused by the war on drugs, working to involve youth in the political process, and promoting an open, honest and rational discussion of alternative solutions to our nation's drug problems. SSDP offers talking points, background materials and organizational assistance to students and families working to counteract drug testing programs in their school districts. . . .

Endnotes

1. Office for Human Research Protections to Peter O. Kohler, M.D., president, Oregon Health and Science University, determination letter, October 24, 2002; Adil E. Shamoo and Jonathan D. Moreno, "Ethics of Research Involving Mandatory Drug Testing of High School Athletes in Oregon," *The American Journal of Bioethics* 4, no. 1 (2004): pp. 25–31.

2. Linn Goldberg, the author of the study suspended by federal authorities, now agrees that "even his study did not prove that testing limits consumption. 'Schools should not implement a drug testing program until they're proven to work,' he added. 'They're too expensive. It's like having experimental surgery that's never been shown to work.'" Greg Winter, "Study Finds No Sign That Testing Deters Students' Drug Use," *New York Times,* May 17, 2003.

3. Neil McKeganey, *Random Drug Testing of Schoolchildren: A Shot in the Arm or a Shot in the Foot for Drug Prevention?* (York, UK: Joseph Rowntree Foundation, 2005), p. 12. . . .

4. Ryoko Yamaguchi, Lloyd D. Johnston, and Patrick M. O'Malley, "Relationship Between Student Illicit Drug Use and School Drug–Testing Policies," *Journal of School Health* 73, no. 4 (2003): pp. 159–164. . . .

5. Greg Winter, "Study Finds No Sign That Testing Deters Students' Drug Use," *New York Times,* May 17, 2003.

6. Ryoko Yamaguchi, Lloyd D. Johnston, and Patrick M. O'Malley, *Drug Testing in Schools, Policies, Practices, and Association With Student Drug Use,* Youth, Education, and Society (YES) Occasional Papers Series (Ann Arbor, MI: The Robert Wood Johnson Foundation, 2003). . . .

7. Ibid., p. 16.

8. Ryoko Yamaguchi, Lloyd D. Johnston, and Patrick M. O'Malley, "Relationship Between Student Illicit Drug Use and School Drug-Testing Policies," *Journal of School Health* 73, no. 4 (2003): p. 164.

9. See, for example: Nicholas Zill, Christine Winquist Nord, and Laura Spencer Loomis, "Adolescent Time Use, Risky Behavior and Outcomes: An Analysis of National Data," U.S. Department of Health and Human Services (1995). . . . Lee Shilts, "The Relationship of Early Adolescent Substance Use to Extracurricular Activities, Peer Influence, and Personal Attitudes," *Adolescence* 26, no. 103 (1991): pp. 613, 615; William J. Bailey, "Suspicionless Drug Testing in Schools," Indiana Prevention Resource Center (1998). . . . Robert Taylor, "Compensating Behavior and the Drug Testing of High School Athletes," *The Cato Journal* 16, No. 3 (1997). . . . and Rodney Skager, *Beyond Zero Tolerance: A Reality-Based Approach to Drug Education and Student Assistance* (San Francisco, CA: Drug Policy Alliance, 2005).

10. Jessica Raynor, "Guymon to Eliminate Drug Program," *Amarillo Globe-News Online,* August I5, 2002. . . .

11. Andrew Petkofsky, "School Scraps Drug Testing; but Mathews Will Make Kits Available," *Richmond Times Dispatch,* July 27, 2002.

12. Kay Nolan, "District Drops Random Drug Testing Plan; Proposal for Oconomowoc Schools Lacks Parents' Support," *Milwaukee Journal Sentinel,* October 22, 2003.

13. ACLU of Washington, "First Lawsuit Filed Challenging Suspicionless Student Urine-Testing in Washington," press release, December 17, 1999. . . .

14. Jackie Puccetti to Cathedral High School Community, February 28, 2003. . . .

15. Brief of Amici Curiae American Academy of Pediatrics, et al. at 1, *Board of Education of Independent School District No. 92 of Pottawatomie County, et al. v. Lindsay Earls, et al.,* 536 U.S. 822 (2002) (No. 01-332). . . .

16. National Association of Social Workers, "Social Workers Disagree with Supreme Court Decision to Test Students for Drug Use," press release, June 27, 2002. . . .

17. The Association for Addiction Professionals, "Supreme Court Ruling on Student Drug Testing Misguided: NAADAC Speaks Out Against Court's Approval of Random Drug Tests for Public School Students," press release, June 27, 2002. . . .

18. John R. Knight and Sharon Levy, "An F for School Drug Tests," *Boston Globe,* June 13, 2005.

19. *Board of Education of Independent School District No. 92 of Pottawatomie County, et al. v. Lindsay Earls, et al.,* 536 U.S. 822 (2002) (Ginsburg, R., dissenting).

20. Hawaii State Legislature, HB 273 "Relating to Education: Drug Testing Public School Students," Introduced January 21, 2005. . . .

21. Louisiana State Legislature, SB117 "Tuition Opportunity Program for Students," Considered April 24, 2003. . . .

22. See, for example: Clea A. McNeely, James M. Nonnemaker, and Robert W. Blum, "Promoting School Connectedness: Evidence from the National Longitudinal Study of Adolescent Health," *Journal of School Health* 72, no. 4 (2002): pp. 138-46; Rodney Skager, *Beyond Zero Tolerance: A Reality-Based Approach to Drug Education and Student Assistance* (San Francisco: Drug Policy Alliance, 2005).

23. "Proposed Random Drug Testing Plan Expected to Pass with Minor Changes," *Drug Detection Report,* 15 no. 10 (2005): p. 77.

24. "Student Drug Testing: An Investment in Fear," Drug Policy Alliance. . . .

25. Robert L. DuPont. Teresa G. Campbell and Jacqueline J. Mazza, *Report of a Preliminary Study: Elements of a Successful School-Based Student Drug Testing Program* (Rockville, MD: United States Department of Education, 2002), p. 8.

26. Mary Bridgman and Dean Narciso, "Dublin Halts Drug Tests; School District Stops Screening Athletes," *Columbus Dispatch,* June 26, 2002.

27. Mary Bridgman and Dean Narciso, "Dublin Halts Drug Tests; School District Stops Screening Athletes," *Columbus Dispatch,* June 26, 2002; Dublin Coffman High School Guidance Department, personal communication., July 2003; Richard Caster, Executive Director of Administration at the

Dublin Schools, personal communication, April 2005; "Student Drug Testing: An Investment in Fear," Drug Policy Alliance. . . .

28. "ACLU Drug Testing Cases Across the Nation," ACLU. . . .

29. Statements come from the Brief of Amici Curiae of the American Academy of Pediatrics, et al., *Board of Education of Independent School District No. 92 of Pottawatomie County. et al. v. Lindsay Earls*, 536 U.S. 822 (2002) (No. 01-332). . . .

30. Julie Pederson and others, "The Potential of After-School Programs" in *Safe and Smart: Making After-School Hours Work for Kids* (Washington, D.C.: U.S. Department of Education and U.S. Department of Justice, 1998). . . .

31. Maureen Glancy, F. K. Willits and Patricia Farrell, "Adolescent Activities and Adult Success and Happiness: Twenty-four years later," *Sociology and Social Research* 70, no. 3 (1986): p. 242.

32. Plaintiffs in the lawsuit *Bean v. Tulia Independent School District,* claim that, "In 1990-1991 participation of black seniors was 100% in extracurricular clubs and activities and 100% in sports; while the 2000–2001 participation rates [after student drug testing] of black seniors fell to 0% within both." Affidavit of Nancy Cozette Bean, p. 3, *Bean v. Tulia Independent School District,* 2003 WL 22004511 (N.D. Tex. Feb. 18, 2003).

33. American Civil Liberties Union, *Drug Testing: A Bad Investment* (New York: ACLU, 1999), p. 18. . . .

34. Ibid.

35. C. Meadway, S. George, and R. Braithwaite, "Opiate Concentrations Following the Ingestion of Poppy Seed Product: Evidence for 'The Poppy Seed Defense,'" *Forensic Science International* 96, no. 1 (1998): pp. 29–38; American Civil Liberties Union, *Drug Testing: A Bad Investment* (New York: ACLU, 1999), p. 18. . . .

36. Respondents' Brief at 3, *Board of Education of Independent School District No. 92 of Pottawatomie County, et al. v. Lindsay Earls. et al.,* 536 U.S. 822 (2002) (No. 01-332).

37. Howard Taras, "Maximizing Student Health Resources," American Association of School Administrators (2003). . . .

38. American Civil Liberties Union, *Drug Testing: A Bad Investment* (New York: ACLU, 1999), p. 13. . . .

39. Annette Fuentes, "Student Drug Tests Aren't the Answer" *USA Today,* June 10, 2005.

40. Rob Nelson, "Jeff Schools Trim Drug Test Loophole; Hair Samples Will be Required by Policy," *Times Picayune,* July 11, 2003.

41. U.S. General Accounting Office, *Youth Illicit Drug Use Prevention: DARE Long-Term Evaluations and Federal Efforts to Identify Effective Programs* (Washington, D.C.: January 15, 2003).

42. Student Assistance Programs (SAPs) are comprehensive models for the delivery of K-12 prevention, intervention and support services. SAPs are designed to reduce student risk factors, promote protective factors, and increase personal development and decision-making skills by students. For information about developing SAPs, see the National Student Assistance Association. . . .

43. See: Rodney Skager, *Beyond Zero Tolerance: A Reality-Based Approach to Drug Education and Student Assistance* (San Francisco, CA: Drug Policy Alliance, 2005). . . .

44. Physician Leadership on National Drug Policy, *Adolescent Substance Abuse: A Public Health Priority; An Evidence-Based. Comprehensive and Integrative Approach* (Providence, RI: Physician Leadership on National Drug Policy, 2002), pp. 23–31. . . . These tools include the Personal Experience Inventory (PEI), Drug Abuse Screening Test for Adolescents (DAST-A), and Adolescent Drug Involvement Scale (ADIS), among others.

45. See: Marsha Rosenbaum, *Safety First: A Reality-Based Approach to Teen, Drugs, and Drug Education* (San Francisco, CA: Drug Policy Alliance, 2004). . . .

POSTSCRIPT

Should Schools Drug Test Students?

Advocates for random drug testing and people opposed to drug testing do not agree on whether such programs reduce illegal drug use. Regardless of whether drug testing curtails the use of drugs, some critics are concerned that drug testing programs undermine relationships of trust between students and teachers. Teachers are often put in the position of enforcers.

An important question evolves around the role of parents regarding their children. Is it the responsibility of schools to test students for drug use? Should parents be responsible for their children's behavior? In addition, if students test positive for drugs, is it the school's or the parents' responsibility to deal with this problem?

Another concern regarding drug testing is that some schools may be susceptible to litigation. What is the school's role if a student is falsely identified as having used drugs? The federal government recognizes this risk and strongly supports that school districts who randomly drug test students have safeguards in the event that students test positive. Moreover, what actions should schools take if students test positive for drugs? Is the purpose to punish or help students who test positive? Lastly, which school personnel should have access to the results of drug tests? Generally, it is recommended that only school administrators and parents have access to this confidential information.

Some school administrators oppose drug testing on the grounds that such programs create a threatening environment. In addition, some administrators feel that drug testing represents an unwarranted invasion of privacy. Others maintain that whether or not students use drugs is the responsibility of parents, not schools. Proponents of drug testing point out that many parents abdicate their parental responsibilities. They claim that schools are the logical place to implement drug testing.

One concern is that students will try to outsmart the drug test. Whether or not one can fool a drug test is not the point. The point is that students may engage in unhealthy practices to avoid detection. One only has to surf the Internet to find hundreds of advertisements discussing ways to beat drug tests. One can purchase herbal detoxifiers, hair follicle shampoo, or drug-free replacement urine.

According to Supreme Court Justice Ruth Bader Ginsburg, drug testing "risks steering students at greater risk for substance abuse away from extracurricular involvement that potentially may palliate drug problems." At the present time, the vast majority of schools do not randomly drug test student athletes.

The Office of National Drug Control Policy (ONDCP) does not support that all schools drug test students. Its position is that a school should drug test if they or the community feels that there is a drug problem among its students. Without community support, drug testing is not advocated. Because the ONDCP recognizes that some students may test falsely positive, it recommends that reputable drug testing laboratories be used.

The legality of random drug testing is reviewed in "Respect Versus Surveillance: Drug Testing Our Students," by Larry Brendtro and Gordon Martin in *Reclaiming Children and Youth* (Summer 2006). Two articles that point to the effectiveness of drug testing programs to reduce drug use are "High School Drug Testing Program Dramatically Reduces Drug Use" in *Medical Letter on the CDC and FDA* (February 2, 2003) and Norm Brodsky's article "Street Smarts" in *INC Magazine* (November 2004). In their article "Relationship Between Student Illicit Drug Use and School-testing Policies" (*Journal of School Health*, April 2003), Ryoko Yamaguchi, Lloyd D. Johnston, and Patrick O'Malley argue that drug testing had no impact on whether high school students used illegal drugs.

ISSUE 18

Does Drug Abuse Treatment Work?

YES: Susan L. Ettner, David Huang, Elizabeth Evans, Danielle Rose Ash, Mary Hardy, Mickel Jourabchi, and Yih-Ing Hser, from "Benefit-Cost in the California Treatment Outcome Project: Does Substance Abuse Treatment 'Pay for Itself?'" *Health Services Research* (February 2006)

NO: United Nations, from *Investing in Drug Abuse Treatment* (2003)

ISSUE SUMMARY

YES: Author Susan L. Ettner and associates maintain that not only do people in substance abuse treatment benefit, but that taxpayers also benefit. They estimate that about seven dollars are saved for every dollar spent on treatment. Individuals in treatment are less likely to engage in criminal activity and they are more likely to be employed.

NO: The report from the United Nations Office on Drugs and Crime argues that drug abuse treatment does not cure drug abuse. Most people who go through drug treatment relapse. Drug abuse treatment does not get at the root causes of drug abuse: crime, family disruption, loss of economic productivity, and social decay. At best, treatment may minimize drug abuse.

Numerous drug experts feel that more funding should go toward preventing drug use from starting or escalating and toward treating individuals who are dependent on drugs. Today, when taxpayers dispute how their tax monies are spent, the question of whether government funds should be used to treat people who abuse drugs is especially relevant. Questions surrounding this debate include: Does drug abuse treatment reduce criminal activity associated with drugs? Will drug addicts stop their abusive behavior if they enter treatment? Will more drug addicts receive treatment than currently do if services are expanded? Will the availability and demand for illegal drugs decline?

The research on the effectiveness of drug treatment is mixed. In *The Effectiveness of Treatment for Drug Abusers Under Criminal Justice Supervision*

(National Institute of Justice, 1995), Douglas S. Lipton states that drug abuse treatment not only reduces the rate of arrests but also reduces crime and lowers the cost to taxpayers over the long run. Also, it has been shown that illicit drug use is curtailed by drug abuse treatment and that treated drug addicts are better able to function in society and to maintain employment. Perhaps most important, drug treatment may prove beneficial in curbing the escalation of HIV (human immunodeficiency virus), the virus that causes AIDS.

Some experts contend that reports regarding the effectiveness of drug treatment are not always accurate and that research on drug abuse has not been subjected to rigorous standards. Some question how effectiveness should be determined. If a person relapses after one year, should the treatment be considered ineffective? Would a reduction in an individual's illegal drug use indicate that the treatment was effective, or would an addict have to maintain complete abstinence? Also, if illegal drug use and criminal activity decline after treatment, it is possible that these results would have occurred anyway, regardless of whether the individual had been treated.

There are a variety of drug treatment programs. One type of treatment program developed in the 1960s is *therapeutic communities*. Therapeutic communities are usually residential facilities staffed by former drug addicts. Although there is no standard definition of what constitutes a therapeutic community, the program generally involves task assignments for addicts, group intervention techniques, vocational and educational counseling, and personal skill development. Inpatient treatment facilities are the most expensive type of treatment and are often based on a hospital model. These programs are very structured and include highly regimented schedules, demanding rules of conduct, and individual and group counseling.

Outpatient treatment, the most common drug treatment, is less expensive, less stigmatizing, and less disruptive to the abuser's family than other forms of treatment. Vocational, educational, and social counseling is provided. Outpatient treatment is often used after an addict leaves an inpatient program. One type of treatment that has proliferated in recent years is the self-help group. Members of self-help groups are bound by a common denominator, whether it is alcohol, cocaine, or narcotics. Due to the anonymous and confidential nature of self-help groups, however, it is difficult to conduct follow-up research to determine their effectiveness.

Individuals addicted to narcotics are often referred to methadone maintenance programs. Methadone is a synthetic narcotic that prevents narcotic addicts from getting high and eliminates withdrawal symptoms. Because methadone's effects last about 24 hours, addicts need to receive treatment frequently. Unfortunately, the relapse rate is high once addicts stop treatment. Because there is much demand for methadone maintenance in some areas, there are lengthy waiting lists. A newer, more effective drug for treating narcotic addiction is buprenorphine.

In the following selections, Susan Ettner and associates maintain that drug abuse treatment is beneficial and cost effective. The United Nations International Drug Control Program argues that drug abuse treatment is ineffective because treatment programs do not get at the root cause of addiction.

YES

Susan L. Ettner et al.

Benefit-Cost in the California Treatment Outcome Project: Does Substance Abuse Treatment "Pay for Itself"?

Objective. To examine costs and monetary benefits associated with substance abuse treatment.

Data Sources. Primary and administrative data on client outcomes and agency costs from 43 substance abuse treatment providers in 13 counties in California during 2000-2001.

Study Design. Using a social planner perspective, the estimated direct cost of treatment was compared with the associated monetary benefits, including the client's costs of medical care, mental health services, criminal activity, earnings, and (from the government's perspective) transfer program payments. The cost of the client's substance abuse treatment episode was estimated by multiplying the number of days that the client spent in each treatment modality by the estimated average per diem cost of that modality. Monetary benefits associated with treatment were estimated using a pre-post treatment admission study design, i.e., each client served as his or her own control.

Data Collection. Treatment cost data were collected from providers using the Drug Abuse Treatment Cost Analysis Program instrument. For the main sample of 2,567 clients, information on medical hospitalizations, emergency room visits, earnings, and transfer payments was obtained from baseline and 9-month follow-up interviews, and linked to information on inpatient and outpatient mental health services use and criminal activity from administrative databases. Sensitivity analyses examined administrative data outcomes for a larger cohort ($N = 6,545$) and longer time period (1 year).

Principal Findings. On average, substance abuse treatment costs $1,583 and is associated with a monetary benefit to society of $11,487, representing a greater than 7:1 ratio of benefits to costs. These benefits were primarily because of reduced costs of crime and increased employment earnings.

From *Health Services Research*, February 2006, pp. 192–197, 206–213. Copyright © 2006 by Health Research & Educational Trust (HRET). Reprinted by permission of Wiley-Blackwell.

Conclusions. Even without considering the direct value to clients of improved health and quality of life, allocating taxpayer dollars to substance abuse treatment may be a wise investment. . . .

In spite of advances in treatment and technology, successfully treating those addicted to alcohol and drugs and helping them maintain abstinence remains a challenge. Traditional health services research on these topics has focused on the effectiveness of treatments and access to treatment. In recent years, however, there has been greater focus on assessing the societal impact of addiction and substance abuse treatment. A substantial body of empirical evidence suggests that in addition to the cost of substance abuse treatment itself, drug and alcohol abuse are associated with increases in a wide range of costs (Harwood et al. 1998; Holder 1998a; French, Salome, and Carney 2002; McCollister and French 2003; Salome et al. 2003; Sindelar et al. 2004), including those associated with crime and the criminal justice system (Wall et al. 2000; Vencill and Sadjadi 2001); medical care, especially hospital and emergency room (ER) (French, Salome, Krupski et al. 2000; Wall et al. 2000; Hunkeler et al. 2001; Office of National Drug Control Policy 2001; Palepu et al. 2001; Sturm 2001, 2002); infectious diseases such as HIV/AIDS, hepatitis, and tuberculosis (Daley et al. 2000; Mark et al. 2001); pre- and postnatal care (Mark et al. 2001); mental disorders (Harwood et al. 1998); and government and private transfer payments and other social programs (Gresenz et al. 1998; Merrill and Fox 1998; Cook and Moore 2000; Mark et al. 2001), including unemployment benefits, welfare payments, disability benefits, and food stamps. Evidence on the effects of substance abuse on unemployment and impaired work productivity is somewhat more mixed, with some suggestion that drinking may not have the same adverse effects as alcohol or drug abuse (Mullahy and Sindelar 1998; Cook and Moore 2000; Wall et al. 2000; Feng et al. 2001; Mark et al. 2001; Vencill and Sadjadi 2001).

Successful substance abuse treatment can have an extraordinarily important impact on lives; yet, in many instances, these programs are needed by those who are indigent and hence dependent on services that are publicly financed. In a cost-cutting environment, public funding for substance abuse treatment competes more broadly with other uses of limited societal resources for improving population health. Given the stigma associated with substance abuse and perhaps an underlying skepticism about the value of rehabilitation, financing for substance abuse treatment may not be readily provided in the current policy climate. Pressure therefore exists for advocates to demonstrate that the benefits of substance abuse treatment can be explained not only in human terms but also in monetary terms. Policymakers are generally more inclined to support treatment programs if they "pay for themselves" through reductions in other types of costs, e.g., health care, criminal justice costs, etc. With one notable exception (Alexandre et al. 2002), the literature in this area has consistently suggested that substance abuse treatment is associated with net benefits.

Previous studies were, however, subject to certain limitations, including the inability to compare the benefits with the cost of the treatment; small sample sizes; potential lack of generalizability beyond randomized-controlled trial settings, populations, and interventions; inability to measure a comprehensive array of costs, including both health care and crime; and age of the data. For example, Holder's (1998a, b) reviews of the older literature identify the cost savings resulting from substance abuse treatment, but did not provide information on the cost of the treatment itself, so estimates of the benefit:cost ratio were not available. In the more recent literature, several studies looked at reductions in health care costs or use only (Zywiak et al. 1999; Goodman et al. 2000; Parthasa-rathy et al. 2001); conversely, other studies looked only at reductions in crime (Flynn et al. 1999; Daley et al. 2000; Aos et al. 2001). One study (Mauser et al. 1994) adopted a more comprehensive approach in exploring the monetary benefits associated with substance abuse treatment, including savings related to both health care and crime, but had a relatively small sample size that made detection of statistically significant differences challenging. Other studies incorporated multiple outcome measures like criminal activity, health services utilization, and employment status but were performed with narrowly defined populations (Daley et al. 2000; French et al. 2002b, 2003; Logan et al. 2004) or were focused on particular treatment modalities (Barnett and Hui 2000; French, Salome, and Carney 2002), or insured populations (French, Salome, Krupski et al. 2000; Goodman et al. 2000; Humphreys and Moos 2001; Parthasarathy et al. 2001).

A number of the other studies assessed the cost-benefit of one treatment modality only relative to another modality. For example, Flynn et al. (1999) compared long-term residential and outpatient drug-free treatment, while Salome et al. (2003) compared the results of one outpatient modality that initiated with inpatient treatment with another that did not. Weisner et al. (2000) compared outcomes from day hospital treatment to traditional outpatient regimens, and Holder et al. (2000) compared outcomes of cognitive behavior therapy, motivational enhancement therapy, or a Twelve-Step facilitation treatment. Still other studies compare enhanced interventions with standard ones. Hartz et al. (1998) evaluated the value of contingency contracting, while Avants et al. (1999) compared outcomes from a standard versus an enhanced treatment. Koenig et al. (2000a, b) looked at the marginal costs and benefits associated with increased treatment duration and intensity; French, McCollister et al. (2002a) compared a modified therapeutic community to treatment-as-usual for homeless mentally ill substance abusers; and Fleming et al. (2002) examined the benefit-cost of a brief intervention for problem drinkers.

In the present study, we address the benefit-cost question using data from the California Treatment Outcome Project (CalTOP), a large demonstration project that collected outcomes data on clients admitted to 43 substance abuse treatment providers in 13 counties in California. CalTOP was the successor to the California Drug and Alcohol Treatment Assessment Program (CalDATA), a large-scale study of the effects of alcohol and drug treatment on participant behavior, treatment costs, and economic benefits to society (Gerstein et al. 1994) that suggested that substance abuse treatment was associated with a 7:1 ratio of benefits to costs. CalDATA was conducted 10 years earlier than CalTOP, prior to a number of changes in the California substance abuse treatment system and treatment population, such as increased methamphetamine users, decreases in the average length of treatment, and concomitant increases in the number of prior treatment episodes (Urada 2000). CalTOP also improved upon other aspects of CalDATA, including its reliance on a discharge sample and 50 percent response rate; its lack of a baseline survey, which meant that analyses were based on self-reports of events occurring up to 3 years earlier; its reliance on self-reported crime; and its comparison of benefits with the cost of the initial treatment episode only (35 percent of clients reentered treatment during follow-up).

Methods

Study Design

As detailed in the CalTOP Final Report (Hser et al. 2002, 2003), the 43 CalTOP providers administered the ASI-Lite (McLellan et al. 1980, 1992) to all of their clients at intake. CalTOP subjects were comparable at intake to those entering treatment statewide, except that CalTOP had slightly fewer criminal justice clients, slightly more patients with a secondary drug problem, and fewer methadone programs. A consecutive census of intake clients was then asked to participate in follow-up surveys at 3 and 9 months, using the same instrument. At intake and 9 months post-intake, self-reported information was collected from clients on ER visits and hospital nights for medical problems during the past 30 days and 6 months, as well as money received from employment, unemployment, disability/retirement, and welfare during the past 30 days. Of the 3,314 clients targeted for the 3-month follow-up, 86 percent were interviewed, 8 percent were not found, 3 percent were incarcerated, 2 percent refused the interview, less than 1 percent were deceased, and less than 1 percent were not interviewed for other reasons. Of the 3,715 clients targeted for the 9-month follow-up, 73 percent were interviewed, 20 percent were not found, 5 percent were incarcerated, less than 1 percent refused the interview when contacted, less than 1 percent were deceased, and less than 1 percent were not interviewed for other reasons. An attrition analysis showed that clients who did and did not complete each follow-up interview were not statistically different in terms of age, ethnicity, marital and educational status, employment, primary drug, treatment history, and legal status at admission. The only significant difference was that 50 percent of the clients who completed the follow-up interviews were female, compared with 43 percent of those who did not.

To determine the ratio of costs to monetary benefits associated with substance abuse treatment, the estimated average direct cost of substance abuse treatment ("treatment cost") was compared with the average change in nontreatment costs associated with treatment (hereinafter referred to as the "monetary benefits"). Substance abuse treatment costs were calculated using a combination of cost data collected from providers and administrative data on days in treatment. Monetary benefit measures were derived from survey and administrative data, and depending on the study perspective taken, included medical care, mental health services, criminal activity, earnings, and government transfer payments. To estimate the monetary benefits, we compared nontreatment costs before and after admission with treatment, i.e., each client served as his or her own "control." All costs and benefits were adjusted to

2001 using the appropriate Consumer Price Index component. To the extent possible, the analyses follow the benefit-cost guidelines outlined in French, Salome, Sindelar et al. (2002). The main perspective adopted was that of the "social planner," in which all costs and benefits are included, regardless of the party to whom they accrue.

Study Cohort and Follow-up Period

The main analyses were based on the cohort of clients entering substance abuse treatment between January 4, 2000 and May 31, 2001, who also completed a 9-month follow-up survey (N = 2,567). These analyses utilized 3- and 9-month follow-up ASI data and administrative data. Because the follow-up period was only 9 months, the "look-back" period for the preadmission data was also 9 months. Sensitivity analyses were conducted using all clients entering substance abuse treatment between January 4, 2000 and May 31, 2001 (N = 6,545), using only administrative data and a 1-year follow-up period. The second cohort was larger and had a longer follow-up period, but the first cohort had more complete data on the benefits of substance abuse treatment. . . .

Discussion

Our best estimate is that on average, substance abuse treatment costs $1,583 and is associated with a societal benefit of $11,487, representing a 7:1 ratio of benefits to costs (9:1 when arrest data are "inflated" to proxy for actual crimes committed). This ratio is based on weighted average treatment costs, which reflect expected costs of treatment; 9-month follow-up of clients in all modalities with follow-up survey data, so that as many sources of benefit as possible could be included in the analysis; and benefit measures that demonstrate significant change, so that the estimates are robust to rare events. Sixty-five percent of the total benefit was attributable to reductions in crime costs, including incarceration. Twenty-nine percent was because of increased employment earnings, with the remaining 6 percent because of reduced medical and behavioral health care costs.

A review of 11 studies (McCollister and French 2003) found that the benefit-cost ratios associated with substance abuse treatment ranged from 1.33 to 23.33 and that benefits were overwhelmingly because of reductions in criminal activity, with smaller contributions of earnings, and averted health care. Our conclusion is similar, especially when inflating the arrest data. Our benefit-cost ratio is also similar to the CalDATA estimate, despite differences in study design and methodology. However, our estimates of substance abuse treatment costs tend to be lower than those in previous studies. An earlier literature review by Roebuck, French, and McLellan (2003) suggested that the average cost per treatment episode was $7,358 for MM, $1,944 for standard outpatient, and $9,426 for residential. Our estimates were $2,737, $838, and $2,791, respectively, based on weighted per diem estimates. The lower episode costs in CalTOP were because of shorter lengths of treatment for MM and residential, as the weekly cost of treatment was actually higher ($99 and $235, respectively, in CalTOP, compared with $91 and $194 in Roebuck et al.). For outpatient, lower episode costs were also attributable to lower weekly costs, around $48 versus $121 in Roebuck et al. These discrepancies might reflect geographic differences in the intensity and duration of treatment.

Our findings should be interpreted with caution, given a number of study limitations. The results may not generalize to non-CalTOP providers, especially those in other states. Attrition may have biased the estimated cost-benefit ratio among the "intake+follow-up" cohort if the clients who were women, incarcerated, or could not be located were more costly on average than the clients who were successfully tracked. Compared with the statewide data, the CalTOP sample slightly underrepresented methadone clients, although statewide methadone clients only account for 10 percent of the total treatment population. We may have slightly overestimated benefit-cost ratios if they were based on the average across CalTOP programs of all modalities. Reductions in nontreatment costs may be overstated because of regression to the mean, i.e., persons entering substance abuse treatment often have hit the bottom and "have nowhere to go but up." A related issue is whether clients who were court-mandated to enter treatment were deterred in the short run from committing further criminal activities. Unfortunately, randomization to treatment is neither logistically nor ethically possible in a large-scale, "realworld" study of this type, plus randomized-controlled studies lack the external validity of observational studies. The pre-post study design has strong advantages over observational studies comparing substance abusers who do and do not enter treatment, because of the selection bias inherent in the latter. The high ratio of benefits to costs makes it less plausible that the cost of substance abuse treatment would have outweighed its benefits if regression to the mean and deterrence effects could have been taken into account. Although it was not possible to study these effects using CalTOP data, we analyzed studies including a "no-treatment" control group from a published meta-analysis of drug abuse treatment outcomes (Prendergast et al. 2002). These analyses suggested that the controls had pre-post differences in outcomes that were about half as large as those in the treatment group. Applying this ratio to CalTOP, the $1,583 in treatment costs would be compared with a benefit of $5,744 ($11,487/2).

The relatively short 9-month follow-up period may understate the monetary benefits associated with treatment if its effects persist over the longer run; alternatively, the additional benefits accrued beyond the 9-month window might be offset by additional costs if the patients relapse and require further treatment. Most of the other study limitations are likely to lead to conservative biases, e.g., the inability to cost out certain crimes (especially those related to drug manufacture and sales, which showed the largest reductions following treatment) and to measure probation and parole costs and costs imposed on family members and friends. Systematic underreporting of hospitalizations, ER use, days incarcerated, and employment income would tend to understate the benefits of treatment as long as the under-reporting was similar for a given client before and after treatment. The lack of comprehensive outpatient medical care data could have induced either a conservative or liberal bias, depending on whether engagement in substance abuse treatment increased referrals to medical providers or primarily improved physical health so that less medical care was needed. Treatment costs may have been slightly underestimated because providers estimated the depreciated costs of their furniture to be zero.

The CalTOP study provided a number of important lessons for conducting future analyses of the cost-benefit of substance abuse treatment. Given concerns about respondent burden, use of a shorter version of the DATCAP is desirable and we do not believe much critical information would be lost. A brief version of the DATCAP has been pilot tested (French, Roebuck, and McLellan 2004). Similarly, the ASI-6 will be better suited for economic evaluation studies than the older version used for CalTOP. The most important sources of monetary benefits (crime, hospitalizations, and earnings) occurred in domains that can be measured using administrative data. As omission of many other sources of monetary benefit induces only a conservative bias, a reasonable cost-benefit analysis might be conducted without the time and expense of primary data collection from clients. Use of administrative data only has the added advantage of allowing the entire client population to be included in the analysis. Long administrative data lags suggest that cost-benefit analyses may need to be based on older data, but lags pose less of a threat to the validity of the findings if treatment systems or client populations do not change rapidly over time. If primary data collection is used as the primary or a supplementary source of information, an instrument designed specifically for cost-benefit analyses should be administered. For example, the most recent version of the Addiction Severity Index (the forthcoming ASI-6) has been redesigned to permit economic evaluation.

Nontrivial differences by treatment modality were observed. Although the benefits associated with outpatient treatment were lower than for residential treatment, the costs were also lower, so the net return on investment was actually higher for outpatient than for residential treatment. No statistically significant monetary benefits were identified among the MM clients, likely because of the small sample size and low power. Alternatively, benefits may be smaller for the MM clients, because of the long-term nature of methadone treatment. The strongest effects of treatment are likely to occur soon after the client becomes drug-free. The overwhelming majority of MM clients had prior treatment admissions, suggesting that many may have been on methadone for a long time and hence already realized any reductions in crime in past years. The baseline level of crime costs was much lower for MM clients than for either outpatient or residential clients, suggesting little room for additional improvement. In other words, our "pre" admission measurement period may not actually precede the receipt of treatment for these clients, but rather, reflect a phase in ongoing treatment. Again, however, the lack of precision in the estimates when looking separately at MM clients precludes us from drawing firm conclusions about the relative magnitudes of the effects for methadone versus outpatient or residential clients. In general, caution must be exercised in making comparisons across modalities, because substance abusers tend to move in and out of treatment and across treatment modalities during their life course. Furthermore, the modality comparisons were based on initial treatment modality, so attribution of benefits to a single modality may be misleading.

Taken as a whole, our findings suggest that even without considering the health and quality-of-life benefits to the clients themselves, spending taxpayer dollars on substance abuse treatment may be a wise investment. Further research is needed to establish a link between the monetary benefits of treatment and the duration and intensity of treatment. Challenges in identifying this relationship include collecting reliable data on the services received by clients and addressing selection bias (i.e., more acute clients probably receive more intensive services, at least to begin with, but more motivated clients are likely to have higher retention rates). Despite these challenges, such an analysis would seem to be the logical next step in building on the CalTOP findings. . . .

References

Alexandre, P., H. Salome, M. French, J. Rivers, and C. McCoy. 2002. "Consequences and Costs of Closing a Publicly Funded Methadone Maintenance Clinic." *Social Science Quarterly* 83 (2): 519–36.

Aos, S., P. Phipps, R. Barnoski, and R. Lieb. 2001. *The Comparative Costs and Benefits of Programs to Reduce Crime, Version 4.0 (Document No. 01-05-1201).* Olympia, WA: Washington State Institute for Public Policy.

Avants, S., M. Kelly, S. Arther, L. Jody, B. Rounsaville, R. Schottenfeld, S. Stine, N. Cooney, R. Rosencheck, S. Li, and T. Kosten. 1999. "Day Treatment versus Enhanced Standard Methadone Services for Opioid-Dependence Patients: A Comparison of Clinical Efficacy and Cost." *American Journal of Psychiatry* 156 (1): 27–33.

Barnett, P., and S. Hui. 2000. "The Cost-Effectiveness of Methadone Maintenance." *Mount Sinai Journal of Medicine* 67 (5 & 6): 365–74.

Beck, A., and B. Shipley. 1997. Bureau of Justice Statistics Special Report: Recidivism of Prisoners Released in 1983. U.S. Department of Justice, Office of Justice Programs.

California State Auditor. 1998. *California Department of Corrections: The Cost of Incarcerating Inmates in State-Run Prisons is Higher Than the Department's Published Cost.* Sacramento, CA: Bureau of State Audits.

Cohen, M. 2001. "Calculations for Cost of Gang-Related Crime" [accessed on September 17, 2003]. . . .

Cook, P., and M. Moore. 2000. "The Economics of Alcohol Abuse and Alcohol-Control Policies." *Health Affairs* 21 (2): 120–33.

Daley, M., M. Argeriou, D. McCarty, J. Callahan, D. Shephard, and C. Williams. 2000. "The Costs of Crime and the Benefits of Substance Abuse Treatment for Pregnant Women." *Journal of Substance Abuse Treatment* 19 (4): 445–58.

Feng, W., W. Zhou, J. Beutler, B. Booth, and M. French. 2001. "The Impact of Problem Drinking on Employment." *Health Economics* 10 (6): 509–21.

Fleming, M. F., M. P. Mundt, M. T. French, L. B. Manwell, E. A. Stauffacher, and K. L. Barry. 2002. "Brief Physician Advice for Problem Drinkers: Long-Term Efficacy and Benefit-Cost Analysis." *Alcoholism: Clinical and Experimental Research* 26 (1): 36–43.

Flynn, P., P. Kristiansen, J. Porto, and R. Hubbard. 1999. "Costs and Benefits of Treatment for Cocaine Addiction in DATOS." *Drug and Alcohol Dependence* 57 (2): 167–74.

French, M., and R. Martin. 1996. "The Costs of Drug Abuse Consequences: A Summary of Research Findings." *Journal of Substance Abuse Treatment* 13 (6): 453–66.

French, M. T., K. A. McCollister, S. Sacks, K. McKendrick, and G. DeLeon. 2002a. "Benefit Cost Analysis of a Modified Therapeutic Community for Mentally Ill Chemical Abusers." *Evaluation and Program Planning* 25 (2): 137–48.

———. 2002b. "Benefit-Cost Analysis of Addiction Treatment in Arkansas: Specialty and Standard Residential Programs for Pregnant and Parenting Women." *Substance Abuse* 23 (1): 31–51.

French, M. T., M. C. Roebuck, M. L. Dennis, S.H. Godley, H. Liddle, and F. M. Tims. 2003. "Outpatient Marijuana Treatment for Adolescents: Economic Evaluation of a Multisite Field Experiment." *Evaluation Review* 27 (4): 421–59.

French, M. T., M. C. Roebuck, and A. T. McLellan. 2004. "Cost Estimation When Time and Resources Are Limited: The Brief DATCAP." *Journal of Substance Abuse Treatment 27* (3): 187–93.

French, M. T., H. J. Salome, and M. Carney. 2002. "Using the DATCAP and ASI to Estimate the Costs and Benefits of Residential Addiction Treatment in the State of Washington." *Social Science and Medicine* 55 (12): 2267–82.

French, M., H. Salome, A. Krupski, J. McKay, D. Donovan, A. McLellan, and J. Durell. 2000. "Benefit-Cost Analysis of Residential and Outpatient Addiction of Treatment in the State of Washington." *Evaluation Review* 24 (6): 609–34.

French, M. T., H. J. Salome, J. L. Sindelar, and A. T. McLellan. 2002. "Benefit-Cost Analysis of Addiction Treatment: Methodological Guidelines and Application Using the DATCAP and ASI." *Health Services Research* 37 (2): 433–55.

Gerstein, D., R. Dean, R. Johnson, M. Foote, N. Suter, K. Jack, G. Merker, S. Turner, R. Bailey, K. Malloy, E. Williams, H. Harwood, and D. Fountain. 1994. Evaluating Recovery Services: The California Drug And Alcohol Treatment Assessment (CalDATA), Methodology Report (Control No. 92-00110). Department of Alcohol and Drug Programs, State of California.

Goodman, A., J. Tilford, J. Hankin, H. Holder, and E. Nishiura. 2000. "Alcoholism Treatment Offset Effects: An Insurance Perspective." *Medical Care Research and Review* 57 (1): 51–75.

Gresenz, C., K. Watkins, and D. Podus. 1998. "Supplemental Security Income (SSI), Disability Insurance (DI), and Substance Abusers." *Community Mental Health Journal* 34 (4): 337–50.

Hartz, D., P. Meek, N. Piotrowski, D. Tusel, C. Henke, K. Delucchi, K. Sees, and S. Hall. 1998. "A Cost-Effectiveness and Cost-Benefit Analysis of Contingency Contracting-Enhanced Methadone Detoxification Treatment." *American Journal of Drug and Alcohol Abuse* 25 (2): 207–18.

Harwood, H., D. Fountain, and G. Livermore. 1998. *The Economic Costs of Alcohol and Drug Abuse in the United States, 1992.* Rockville, MD: National Institute on Drug Abuse.

Holder, H. D. 1998a. "Cost Benefits of Substance Abuse Treatment: An Overview of Results from Alcohol and Drug Abuse." *Journal of Mental Health Policy and Economics* 1: 23–9.

——. 1998b. "The Cost Offsets of Alcoholism Treatment." *Recent Developments in Alcoholism* 14: 361–74.

Holder, H. D., R. A. Cisler, R. Longabaugh, R. L. Stout, A. J. Treno, and A. Zweben. 2000. "Alcoholism Treatment and Medical Care Costs from Project MATCH." *Addiction* 95: 999–1013.

Hser, Y., E. Evans, S. Ettner, D. Huang, and R. Picazo. 2003. *The California Treatment Outcome Project Supplement to the Pinal Report. Submitted to the California Department of Alcohol and Drug Programs.* Los Angeles, CA: UCLA Integrated Substance Abuse Programs.

Hser, Y., E. Evans, C. Teruya, M. Hardy, D. Urada, Y. Huang, R. Picazo, H. Shen, J. Hsieh, and D. Anglin. 2002. *The California Treatment Outcome Project (CalTOP) Final Report Submitted to the California Department of Alcohol and Drug Programs.* Los Angeles, CA: UCLA Integrated Substance Abuse Programs.

Humphreys, K., and R. Moos. 2001. "Can Encouraging Substance Abuse Patients to Participate in Self-Help Groups Reduce Demand for Health Care? A Quasi-Experimental Study." *Alcoholism Clinical and Experimental Research* 25 (5): 711–6.

Hunkeler, E., Y. Hung, D. Rice, C. Weisner, and T. Hu. 2001. "Alcohol Consumption Patterns and Health Care Costs in an HMO." *Drug and Alcohol Dependence* 64: 181–90.

Koenig, L., H. Harwood, J. Henrick, K. Sullivan, and N. Sen. 2000a. *Do the Benefits of More Intensive Substance Abuse Treatment Offset the Costs? (Caliber/NEDS Contract No. 270-97-7016).* Rockville, MD: Center for Substance Abuse Treatment, Substance Abuse and Mental Health Services Administration, Department of Health and Human Services.

Koenig, L., H. Harwood, K. Sullivan, and N. Sen. 2000b. "The Economic Benefits of Increased Treatment Duration and Intensity in Residential and Outpatient Substance Abuse Treatment Settings." *Journal of Psychopathology and Behavioral Assessment* 22 (4): 399–417.

Logan, T. K., W. Hoyt, K. E. McCollister, M. T. French, C. Leukefeld, and L. Minton. 2004. "Economic Evaluation of Drug Court: Methodology, Results, and Policy Implications." *Evaluation and Program Planning* 27: 381–96.

Mark, T., G. Woody, T. Juday, and H. Kleber. 2001. "The Economic Costs of Heroin Addiction." *Drug and Alcohol Dependence* 61: 195–206.

Mauser, E., K. VanStelle, and D. Moberg. 1994. "The Economic Impact of Diverting Substance-Abusing Offenders into Treatment." *Crime and Delinquency* 40 (4): 568–88.

McCollister, K. E., and M. T. French. 2003. "The Relative Contribution of Outcome Domains in the Total Economic Benefit of Addiction Interventions: A Review of First Findings." *Addiction* 98: 1647–59.

McLellan, A., H. Kushner, D. Metzger, R. Peters, I. Smith, G. Grissom, H. Pettinati, and M. Argeriou. 1992. "The Fifth Edition of the Addiction Severity Index." *Journal of Substance Abuse Treatment* 9: 199–213.

McLellan, A., L. Luborsky, G. Woody, and C. O'Brien. 1980. "An Improved Diagnostic Evaluation Instrument for Substance Abuse Patients: The Addiction Severity Index." *Journal of Nervous and Mental Disease* 168: 26–33.

Merrill, J., and K. Fox. 1998. *The Impact of Substance Abuse on Federal Spending. Cost-Benefit/Cost-Effectiveness Research of Drug Abuse Prevention: Implications for Programming and Policy (Report No. 76)*. Rockville, MD: National Institute on Drug Abuse.

Miller, T., M. Cohen, and B. Wiersama. 1996. *Victim Costs and Consequences: A New Look. Final Summary Report Presented to the National Institute of Justice, January, 1996*. Rockville, MD: National Institute of Justice.

Mullahy, J., and J. L. Sindelar. 1998. "Drinking, Problem Drinking, and Productivity." *Canadian Medical Association Journal* 165 (4): 415–20.

Office of National Drug Control Policy. 2001. *The Economic Costs of Drug Abuse in the United States, 1992–1998. (Publication No. NCJ-190636.)* Washington, DC: The Executive Office of the President.

Palepu, A., M. Tyndall, H. Leon, J. Muller, M. O'Shaughnessy, M. Schechter, and A. Anis. 2001. "Hospital Utilization and Costs in a Cohort of Injection Drug Users." *Canadian Medical Association Journal* 165 (4): 415–20.

Parthasarathy, S., C. Weisner, T. Hu, and C. Moore. 2001. "Association of Outpatient Alcohol and Drug Treatment with Health Care Utilization and Costs: Revisiting the Offset Hypothesis." *Journal of Studies on Alcohol* 62 (1): 89–97.

Prendergast, M. L., D. Podus, E. Chang, and D. Urada. 2002. "The Effectiveness of Drug Abuse Treatment: A Meta-Analysis of Comparison Group Studies." *Drug and Alcohol Dependence* 67 (1): 53–72.

Roebuck, M. C, M. T. French, and A. T. McLellan. 2003. "DATStats: Results from 85 Studies Using the Drug Abuse Treatment Cost Analysis Program (DAT-CAP)." *Journal of Substance Abuse Treatment* 25: 51–7.

Salome, H. J., M. T. French, C. Scott, M. Foss, and M. L. Dennis. 2003. "Investigating the Economic Costs and Benefits of Addiction Treatment: Econometric Analysis of the Chicago Target Cities Project." *Evaluation and Programming Planning* 26 (3): 325–38.

Sindelar, J. L., M. Jofre-Bonet, M. T. French, and A. T. McLellan. 2004. "Cost-Effectiveness Analysis of Addiction Treatment: Paradoxes of Multiple Outcomes." *Drug and Alcohol Dependence* 73: 41–50.

Sturm, R. 2001. *The Costs of Covering Mental Health and Substance Abuse as Medical Care in Private Insurance Plans (RAND Health Publication No. CT-180)*. Chicago: RAND.

—. 2002. "The Effects of Obesity, Smoking and Drinking on Medical Problems and Costs." *Health Affairs* 21 (2): 245–53.

Urada, D. 2000. *California State Treatment Needs Assessment Program Existing Service Utilization, and Outcomes: Interim Report (Under Contract No. 270-98-7052)*. Los Angeles, CA: California Department of Alcohol and Drug Programs.

Vencill, C, and Z. Sadjadi. 2001. "Allocation of the California War Costs: Direct Expenses, Externalities, Opportunity Costs, and Fiscal Losses." *Justice Policy Journal* 1 (1): 1–40.

Wall, R., J. Rehm, B. Fischer, B. Brands, L. Gliksman, J. Stweard, W. Medved, and J. Blacke. 2000. "Social Costs of Untreated Opioid Dependence." *Journal of Urban Health: Bulletin of the New York Academy of Medicine* 77 (4): 688–722.

Weisner, C, J. Mertens, S. Parthasarathy, C. Moore, E. Hunkleler, T. Hu, and J. Selby. 2000. "The Outcome and Cost of Alcohol and Drug Treatment in an HMO: Day Hospital versus Traditional Outpatient Regimens." *Health Services Research* 35 (4): 791–812.

Zywiak, W., N. Hoffman, R. Stout, S. Hagberg, A. Floyd, and S. DeHart. 1999. "Substance Abuse Treatment Cost-Offsets Vary with Gender, Age, and Abstinence Likelihood." *Journal of Health Care Financing* 26 (1): 33–9.

Investing in Drug Abuse Treatment

Summary

Drug addiction produces serious, pervasive and expensive social problems. Regardless of whether substance abuse is a sin, a crime, a bad habit or an illness, society has a right to expect that an effective public policy or approach to the "drug abuse problem" will reduce drug-related crime, unemployment, family dysfunction and disproportionate use of medical care.

Science has made great progress over the past several years, but it is still not possible to account fully for the physiological and psychological processes that transform controlled, voluntary "use" of alcohol and/or other drugs into uncontrolled, involuntary "dependence" on those substances, and there is still no cure. What can be done is to treat use "effectively" and to provide an attractive return on societal investment in treatment. . . .

Importantly, the research shows that while motivation for treatment plays an important role in maintaining treatment participation, most substance-abusing patients enter treatment with combinations of internal motivation and family, employment or legal pressure. Those pressures can be combined with treatment interventions for the benefit of the patient and society.

The evidence is compelling that, at the present state of knowledge, addiction is best considered a chronic relapsing condition. It is true that not all cases of addiction are chronic and some who meet diagnostic criteria for substance dependence recover completely without treatment. However, many of those who develop addiction disorders suffer multiple relapses following treatments and are thought to retain a continuing vulnerability to relapse for years or perhaps a lifetime. Like so many other illnesses, it is impossible to predict whether or when an acute care strategy is likely to achieve complete remission. For example, while change in diet, exercise and lifestyle can reduce high blood pressure in some patients without medication or continuing treatment, many others require sustained management with medications as well as regular monitoring of diet, stress and exercise. In considering addiction a chronic condition, it is no longer surprising that incarcerations or brief stabilizations are not effective.

Published by United Nations International Drug Control Programme, 2003.

The available research is quite clear on these points:

- Education does not correct drug dependence: it is not simply a problem of lack of knowledge.
- Consequences of drug use (e.g. hangovers, loss of job, arrest, etc.) appear to be important stimuli leading to entry into drug abuse treatment.
- Very few addicted individuals are able to profit from a corrections-oriented approach by itself. Relapse rates are over 70 percent from all forms of criminal justice interventions.
- Addiction is not simply a matter of becoming stabilized and getting the drugs out of one's system. Relapse rates following detoxifications are approximately the same as those following incarceration. . . .

Introduction

Problems of substance dependence produce dramatic costs to all societies in terms of lost productivity, transmission of infectious diseases, family and social disorder, crime and, of course, excessive utilization of health care. These alcohol and drug-related problems not only reduce the safety and quality of daily life, they are also a source of substantial expense. For example, it has been estimated that, in the United States of America, the total cost of alcohol abuse in 1990 was 99 billion United States dollars and drug abuse cost approximately US$ 67 billion, while the total cost of illicit drug abuse in Australia was estimated to be 1,684 million Australian dollars (or US$ 1,237 million) in 1992. In Canada, the total cost of alcohol abuse in 1992 was estimated to be 7,522 million Canadian dollars (US$ 6,223 million) and the total cost of illicit drug abuse Can$ 1,371 million (US$ 1,134).

Understandably, such problems also produce heated debates regarding what a family, a school, an employer, a government and/or a society should do to reduce the costs and the threats of substance abuse to the public health and safety of citizens.

There are few countries—regardless of their economic development—with a well-developed public treatment system designed to address different substances of abuse and different levels or manifestations of the addiction spectrum. Why have treatment options not been more favourably considered and better developed and disseminated to address the problems of substance dependence? Perhaps the first reason for this is the relative prominence of the social problems caused by drug and alcohol abuse. Crime, family disruption, loss of economic productivity and social decay are the most observable, potentially dangerous and expensive effects of drugs on the social systems of most countries. This is a powerful factor in shaping the general view that the "drug issue" is primarily a criminal problem requiring a social-judicial remedy rather than a health problem requiring prevention and treatment.

A second reason for a diminished role of treatment in most public policies regarding drug abuse is that most societies are skeptical about the effectiveness of substance abuse treatments and most governments question whether treatment is "worth it." Moreover, recent surveys show that even a majority of general practice physicians and nurses feel that the currently available medical or health-care interventions are not appropriate or effective in treating addiction.

A third reason why treatment options may not have received more attention in public policies regarding drug abuse is the pervasive view that a treatment approach to substance abuse conveys an implicit message that the addiction—and the addiction-related problems—are not the fault of the addicted person; that they "can't help themselves" and that they have no responsibility for the actions that led to—or resulted from—the addiction. In that regard, the view exists that treatments are designed exclusively to help the drug user but not society. Why should a society expend resources to help an individual who may have produced social harms? These are messages that many people find offensive and unfair.

Thus, treatment interventions that admittedly cannot cure addiction and that may be seen as focused only on helping socially stigmatized addicted individuals are not popular in many segments of society. Are those perceptions correct? Is there a role for addiction treatment in public policy aimed at reducing drug-related problems? In the text that follows the issue is considered from several perspectives. The first part of the paper considers the perspective of a Government or public agency questioning the value of any intervention aimed at "drug problems": What would an "effective" intervention do, regardless of whether the intervention were a punitive, criminal justice intervention, an educational intervention, a new social policy or a treatment intervention? Here the paper examines the characteristics of patients who enter addiction treatments—asking where they have come from, who or what agency has referred them to treatment and what goals are expected by those agencies and organizations. This examination is used to develop a set of outcome expectations that would make treatment "worth it" to a society that might be asked to support such an intervention or policy. . . .

Why Are Addiction Treatments Not as Effective as Treatments for Other Illnesses?

Implications for the Delivery and Evaluation of Addiction Treatment

The previous sections of this paper have examined the addiction treatment field from the perspective of its value to society. It would seem that this review would provide a relatively simple answer to what appears to be a direct question of cost and value. Yet it is not a direct question at all. This paper has tried to show that the reasonable expectations of a society regarding any form of intervention designed to "take care of the drug problem" must address many different issues, all typically related to the "addiction-related" problems that are so frightening and costly to society. Multiple perspectives on outcome are not typical in evaluations of medical illnesses. In the treatment of most chronic illnesses "effective" treatments are expected to reduce symptoms, increase function and prevent relapse, especially costly relapse. Thus, as a final perspective on the issue of the effectiveness and worth of addiction treatments, this section now considers an evaluation of the effectiveness of addiction treatments using the criteria typical for evaluations of other chronic illnesses.

Compliance, Symptom Remission and Relapse in Addiction Treatment

It is important to note that addiction does not need to be considered chronic. Many who meet diagnostic criteria for substance dependence recover completely even without treatment. Others have long remissions following treatment. However, many of those who develop addiction disorders suffer multiple relapses following treatments and are thought to retain a continuing vulnerability to relapse for years or perhaps a lifetime. It is possible to argue that as yet there is no reliable "cure" for drug dependence. For the reasons outlined above, those dependent upon alcohol and/or other drugs who attempt to continue but reduce their use are likely to have problems in maintaining "controlled use." Among those who become addicted, patients who comply with the recommended regimen of education, counselling and medication have favourable outcomes during and for at least 6-12 months following treatment. However, most of those who start any type of treatment drop out prior to completion or they ignore their physician's advice to remain on medication and to continue participation in aftercare or self-help groups. It is also well known that problems of low socio-economic status, co-morbid psychiatric conditions and lack of family or social supports are among the most important variables associated with lack of compliance in addiction treatment and with relapse following treatment. Because of multiple co-morbid medical and social conditions and because of poor compliance with the medical and behavioural components of the treatment regimen, one-year follow-up studies have typically shown that only about 40-60 percent of treated patients are abstinent, although an additional 15-30 percent have not resumed dependent use during that period.

It is quite discouraging to many in the addiction treatment field that so many drug- and alcohol-dependent patients fail to comply with the recommended course of treatment and that so many subsequently resume substance use. As indicated above, there are now several medications that have demonstrated effectiveness in the treatment of alcohol and opiate dependence. However, for those medications to be effective, they must be taken on a regular basis and lack of patient compliance has severely limited their impact. Ongoing clinical research in this area is focused upon the development of longer-acting or "depot" forms of these medications, as well as behavioural strategies to increase patient compliance.

Compliance, Symptom Remission and Relapse in the Treatment of Chronic Illnesses

Hypertension, diabetes and asthma are well-studied, chronic disorders, requiring continuing care for most if not all of a patient's life. At the same time, these disorders are not necessarily unremitting or unalterably lethal, as long as the treatment regimen of medication, diet and behavioural change is followed. This last point requires elaboration. Treatments for these medical disorders are heavily dependent upon behavioural change and medication compliance to achieve their potential effectiveness. In a recently published review of treatment outcome studies of these disorders, patient compliance with the recommended medical regimen was the most significant determinant of treatment outcome. However, studies have shown that less than 60 percent of type-1, insulin-dependent, adult diabetics fully comply with their medication schedule and less than 40 percent of hypertensive or asthmatic patients comply fully with their medication regimens. The problem is even worse for the behavioural and diet changes that are so important for the maintenance of short-term gains in these chronic illnesses. Again, a review of recent studies in the fields of adult-onset diabetes, hypertension and asthma indicates that less than 30 percent of patients in treatment for these disorders comply with prescribed diet and/or behavioural changes that are designed to increase functional status and to reduce risk factors for reoccurrence of the disorders. Across all three of these chronic medical illnesses, compliance, and ultimately outcome, is poorest among patients with low socio-economic status, low family and social supports or significant psychiatric co-morbidity, as summarized in Table 1.

This review of medication and behavioural compliance in the treatment of other chronic medical illnesses suggests important parallels with the treatment of drug dependence. In all these disorders, lack of patient compliance with the treatment regimen is a major contributor to the reoccurrence of symptoms; and in all these disorders compliance is poorest among those with co-morbid medical, psychiatric, family and social problems. Perhaps because of these similarities in treatment compliance there is also similarity in relapse or reoccurrence rates across all these disorders. In fact, outcome studies indicate that 30-50 percent of insulin-dependent adult diabetic patients and approximately 50-70 percent of adult hypertensive and asthmatic patients suffer reoccurrences of their symptoms each year to the point that they require, at least, re-stabilization of their medication and/or additional medical care to re-establish symptom remission. Many of these reoccurrences result in serious health complications. For example, limb amputations and blindness are common results of treatment non-compliance among diabetics. Stroke and cardiac disease are common problems associated with exacerbation of hypertension.

Table 1

Factors Associated with Relapse in Hypertension, Diabetes and Asthma

- Lack of adherence to prescribed medication, diet or behavioural change regimens
- Low socio-economic status
- Low family supports
- Psychiatric co-morbidity

A Chronic Illness Perspective on Treatment and Evaluation Designs

This section focuses on the question of whether the assumptions underlying interventions for acute conditions or those for chronic conditions are more appropriate for the treatment of addiction.

There are no definitive "cures" for any of the chronic medical illnesses reviewed here. Yet it is interesting that despite rather comparable rates of compliance and relapse across all of the disorders examined, there is no serious argument as to whether the treatments for diabetes, hypertension or asthma are "effective" or whether they should be supported by contemporary health insurance. However, this issue is very much in question with regard to treatments for drug dependence. In this regard, it is interesting that the relatively high relapse rates among diabetic, hypertensive and asthmatic patients following cessation of their medications have been considered evidence of the effectiveness of those medications and of the need for compliance enhancement strategies. In contrast, relapses to drug and alcohol use following cessation of addiction treatments has often been considered evidence of treatment failure.

Drug dependence treatments are not provided and especially are not evaluated under the same assumptions that pertain to other chronic illnesses. Particularly important in this regard is that drug dependence treatments are rarely delivered under a continuing care model that would be appropriate for a chronic illness. Indeed, with the exception of methadone maintenance and self-help groups most contemporary treatments for drug dependence are acute-care episodes. For example, it is common for a drug-dependent individual to be admitted to an outpatient rehabilitation programme lasting 30-90 days, rarely accompanied by medical monitoring or medication. This period of treatment is typically followed by discharge with referral to "community sources." While addiction treatment might be conceptualized as ongoing by those in the treatment field, from an operational perspective addiction treatments are delivered in much the same way as one might treat a surgical patient following a joint replacement. Outcome evaluations are typically conducted 6-12 months following treatment discharge, because addiction treatments have been expected to produce lasting reduction in symptoms following termination of treatment. Unlike the treatments for other chronic conditions, the reduction of symptoms during treatment has not been considered adequate to the expectations underlying addiction treatment.

This argument has nothing to do with whether addiction is fundamentally a disease, a bad habit, a social problem or all of the above. Moreover, it does not matter whether the essence of the intervention is the correction of some biological abnormality, the resolution of a psychological process, the teaching of some new behaviour or the development of some improved social support system. The expectations have been that some finite combination of medications, counselling and therapy, social services and/or social support systems should effect essential change in the root causes of addiction, remove those causal factors and result in lasting benefits.

A more realistic expectation is that the interventions currently availa-ble will not permanently correct the essence of the problem, only reduce the number and severity of the symptoms and improve personal function, as long as the patient participates in the intervention. This is precisely the same expec-tation that currently prevails in the treatment of chronic illnesses. Further, an "acute-care" expectation placed upon those types of treatment produces some perverse and even absurd results. For example, consider contemporary goals and the prevailing evaluation strategy for addiction treatments—applied to a hypertension treatment regimen. Patients who meet diagnostic criteria for hypertension would be admitted to an outpatient "hypertension rehabilita-tion" programme lasting 30–90 days in which they might receive medication, behavioural change therapy, dietary education and an exercise regimen. At the end of that period, the medication would be tapered during the last days of the treatment and the patients would be referred to community sources. The evaluation team would recontact the patient six months later and deter-mine whether the patient had been continuously normotensive throughout that post-treatment period. Only those patients who met that criterion would be considered "successfully treated." Obviously, this hypothetical treatment management strategy and its associated evaluation approach are absurd for any chronic illness, including drug dependence.

POSTSCRIPT

Does Drug Abuse Treatment Work?

Much of the research on drug abuse treatment effectiveness is inconclusive; furthermore, researchers do not agree on what the best way is to measure effectiveness. Determining the effectiveness of drug abuse treatment is extremely important because the federal government and a number of state governments debate how much drug treatment should be funded. Many experts in the drug field agree that much of the money that has been used to deal with problems related to drugs has not been wisely spent. To prevent further waste of taxpayer funds, it is essential to find out if drug abuse treatment works before funding for it is increased.

Another concern related to this issue is that addicts who wish to receive treatment often face many barriers. One of the most serious barriers is that there is a lack of available treatment facilities. Compounding the problem is the fact that many communities resist the idea of having a drug treatment center in the neighborhoods, even though there is little research on the effects of treatment facilities on property values and neighborhood crime rates. Another barrier to treatment is cost, which, with the exception of self-help groups, is expensive. Furthermore, some addicts avoid organized treatment altogether for fear that if they go for treatment, they will be identified as drug abusers by law enforcement agencies. Likewise, many female drug addicts avoid drug treatment because they fear they will lose custody of their children. Among adolescents in drug treatment, 31 percent were female.

Many addicts in treatment are there because they are given a choice of entering either prison or treatment. Are people who are required to enter treatment more or less likely to succeed than people who enter treatment voluntarily? Early studies showed that treatment was more effective for voluntary clients. However, a study conducted by the U.S. federal government of 12,000 clients enrolled in 41 publicly funded treatment centers found that clients referred by the criminal justice system fared as well as if not better than voluntary clients in terms of reduced criminal activity and drug use. People who enter treatment voluntarily have an easier time walking away from treatment. Typically, the longer one stays in treatment, the more likely the treatment will be effective.

One emerging trend is to provide drug treatment to people in prison. Prison-based drug treatment has increased in recent years. Drug abuse treatment to prison inmates has been shown to reduce recidivism.

The publication *Services Research Outcomes Study* by the Office of Applied Studies (U.S. Department of Health and Human Services, January 28, 2004) describes the benefits of drug abuse treatment. Two articles that support drug abuse treatment are "Drug Treatment: The Willard Option" in *Corrections*

Today (April 2004) and "Coming Clean; Drug Treatment" in *The Economist* (October 16, 2004). Donna Lyons examines whether drug addicts should be sent to prison or to treatment in "Conviction for Addiction: States Are Considering No-nonsense Drug Policy Should Mean Prison or Treatment" in *State Legislatures* (June 2002). The advantages of providing drug abuse treatment to addicts in prison are discussed in Peter Anderson's article "Treatment With Teeth: A Judge Explains Why Drug Courts That Mandate and Supervise Treatment Are an Effective Middle Ground to Help Addicts Stay Clean and Reduce Crime" in *The American Prospect* (December 2003).

ISSUE 19

Is Abstinence an Effective Strategy for Drug Education?

YES: Tracy J. Evans-Whipp, Lyndal Bond, John W. Toumbourou, and Richard F. Catalano, from "School, Parent, and Student Perspectives of School Drug Policies," *Journal of School Health* (March 2007)

NO: Rodney Skager, from "Beyond Zero Tolerance: A Reality-Based Approach to Drug Education and School Discipline" (*Drug Policy Alliance,* 2007)

ISSUE SUMMARY

YES: Tracy J. Evans-Whipp, of the Murdoch Children's Research Institute in Melbourne, Australia, and her colleagues maintain that an abstinence message coupled with harsh penalties is more effective at reducing drug use than a message aimed at minimizing the harms of drugs. They contend that an abstinence message is clear and that a harm reduction message may give a mixed message.

NO: Rodney Skager, formerly a professor at UCLA, argues that a zero tolerance drug policy does not change drug-taking behavior among young people. Instead of merely punishing drug offenders, Skager suggests that effective drug education is needed. Instances in which drug use presents a significant problem for the user may require intervention and treatment. Again, zero tolerance does very little to rectify behavior.

Drug education is arguably one of the most logical ways of dealing with the problems of drugs in American society. Drug-taking behavior has not been significantly affected by attempts to reduce the demand for drugs, and drug prohibition has not been successful either. One remaining option to explore is drug education. Drug education is not a panacea for eliminating drug problems. Rates of cigarette smoking are much lower today than they were thirty and forty years ago, but it took several decades of public health efforts to achieve this decline. If drug education is to ultimately prove successful, it too will take years. However, will a zero tolerance policy reduce drug use? Will students heed the message that they should abstain from drug use?

Many early drug education programs were misguided. One emphasis was on scare tactics. Experts erroneously believed that if young people saw the horrible consequences of drug use, then they would certainly abstain from drugs. Another faulty assumption was that drug use would be affected by knowledge about drugs, but knowledge is not enough. Over 400,000 people die each year from tobacco use, but many adults and teenagers continue to smoke even though most know the grim statistics about tobacco. Young people have a hard time relating to the potential problems like cancer and cirrhosis of the liver (which is caused by long-term alcohol abuse) because these problems take years to manifest themselves. Another problem with early drug education is that much of the information that teachers relayed concerning drugs was either incorrect or exaggerated. Teachers were therefore not seen as credible.

One could argue that a zero tolerance policy does not ultimately change behavior. Many people who go to prison for drug use return to using drugs after their release. A zero tolerance approach, according to some people, is a Band-Aid on a larger problem. One's unhealthy behavior, drug use, is not exchanged for a healthy behavior. Moreover, even if drug use is prevented in a school environment, drug use can occur outside of school. The zero tolerance approach overlooks the possibility that young people may turn to drugs because they want to be accepted by their peers, because drugs are forbidden, or simply because they enjoy the high that comes from drug use. Acceptance and euphoria provide more reward for some young people than abstinence.

The current emphasis in drug education is on primary prevention. It is easier to have young people not use drugs in the first place than to get them to stop after they have already started using drugs. One popular drug prevention program, Drug Abuse Resistance Education (DARE), attempts to get upper-elementary students to pledge not to use drugs. The rationale is that putting energy into teaching elementary students about drugs rather than high school students will be more likely to reduce drug use because the latter are more likely to have already begun using drugs. The program focuses mainly on tobacco, alcohol, and marijuana. These are considered gateway drugs, which means that students who use other drugs are most likely to have used these first. The longer students delay using tobacco, alcohol, and marijuana, the less likely they will be to use other drugs.

In the following selections, Tracy J. Evans-Whipp and her colleagues feel that the most effective message for reducing drug use is abstinence coupled with harsh punishment. Rodney Skager believes that an abstinence-only message is ineffective and that a zero tolerance policy is merely punitive. He advocates promoting drug education to reduce the harms associated with drug use.

YES ⬅ Tracy J. Evans-Whipp, Lyndal Bond, John W. Toumbourou, and Richard F. Catalano

School, Parent, and Student Perspectives of School Drug Policies

Introduction

Schools are now recognized as much more than centers for academic instruction, with their role in contributing to the health and social well-being of students and staff now widely accepted.(1–5) Schools acknowledge their important influence on preventing youth tobacco, alcohol, and illicit-drug use (and their associated harms) and implement a range of education programs and policy directives to this end.

School drug policies form an important component of school-wide drug prevention, acting to set normative values and expectancies for student behavior as well as documenting procedures for dealing with drug-related incidents. (6) However, it is not clear to what degree, if any, school drug policies influence student behavior and the mechanism by which any such influence occurs. (7,8) Thus, policy makers are provided with little empirical guidance for developing and implementing effective school drug policy. It is likely that schools develop drug policies that reflect the values of the community, state, and country in which they reside, and a recent cross-country comparison of school policies in the United States and Australia(9) indeed found this to be the case.

In working toward an understanding of what constitutes effective school policy, it is important to establish an effective method for collecting information about schools' current policies. Most descriptive accounts of school policies have used school personnel and/or higher level bodies (such as school districts or local education authorities) as informants.(10,11) However, implementation of school drug policy is likely to be a key determinant of policy impact, and investigation of student and parent perspectives of policy provides a broader insight into how policy is carried out in practice. Few studies of school drug policies and student substance-use behaviors have collected information from multiple school policy stakeholders. Where data have been collected from students, the focus has mostly been on student substance-use behaviors rather than on students' understanding of policy content and implementation. (7,12–14) One notable exception is a study by

From *Journal of School Health*, vol. 77, issue 3, March 2007, pp. 138–146. Copyright © 2007 by American School Health Association. Reprinted by permission of Wiley-Blackwell Publishing.

Griesbach et al (15) in which the impact of school drug policy components on student smoking at school was measured. This study found that student perceptions of smoking at school were significantly lower in schools where pupil smoking restrictions were consistently enforced, thereby highlighting the importance of measuring policy implementation in addition to documentation. It appears that no other studies have collected information on school drug policy from parents.

We have recently developed and tested a school drug policy survey questionnaire on schools in Victoria, Australia, and Washington State, USA. (9) These 2 states share many sociodemographic characteristics(16) but differ in their approach to drugs, alcohol, and illicit drugs. US drug policies tend to reflect an abstinence-only orientation, (17) whereas Australian policies are based on a combination of abstinence and harm-minimization principles.(17,18) In measuring school policies in states in 2 countries with contrasting policy approaches, a wide variety of policy descriptions and implementation procedures were observed. The survey collected responses from school personnel, usually school principals, who are considered to be knowledgeable about the policy content. The current paper extends the observations collected from school administrators by examining parent and student reports of school drug policy gathered in parallel surveys. Thus, it is possible to compare responses between the 3 groups of respondents to gain a more comprehensive picture of how school policy operates. In particular, cross-comparison of responses will enable us to (1) determine how effectively schools are communicating school drug policy information to parents and students, (2) gain insight into how school policies are implemented, and (3) investigate what policy variables impact students' drug use at school and their perceptions of other students' drug use at school.

Methods

Participants and Procedures

The surveys were conducted in 2003 as part of the International Youth Development Study (IYDS), a longitudinal research study of adolescent substance use and its predictors in Washington State and Victoria. Samples of public and private schools in both states were drawn to constitute representative samples of students at seventh and ninth grade. Procedures for the IYDS sampling, school administrator survey, and student survey have been described previously. (9,19)

This study used data collected from secondary schools and the grade 7 and 9 students (and their parents) attending them.

School administrator survey.   The 205 schools (104 from Washington and 101 from Victoria) represent 97.6% of participating secondary (grade 7 through to highest) and mixed (combination of pre- and postgrade 7) schools. The majority of respondents were principals or heads of school (72.1% in Washington and 46% in Victoria), or assistant/vice principals (13.5% in Washington and 22% in Victoria).

Student survey.   Students in grade 7 and grade 9 classes yielded a total of 5085 eligible students, of whom 3899 (76.7%) consented to and participated in the survey (1942 in Washington and 1957 in Victoria). Honesty criteria, which included student reports of being "not honest at all" when completing the survey, using a fictional drug, or using illicit drugs more than 120 times in the past 30 days, were used to remove surveys of 23 students from the sample (8 from Washington and 15 from Victoria).

Parent survey.   Concurrent with the student survey, a 15-minute telephone interview was administered to a parent/guardian of each participating student, using computer-assisted telephone interviewing technology. A total of 1886 Washington parents, representing 98% of the valid student sample, and 1858 Victorian parents (95% of the student sample) were successfully contacted and interviewed. The survey was administered in English for most respondents but also conducted in Vietnamese and Cantonese in Victoria and in Spanish, Korean, Vietnamese, and Russian in Washington. The majority of parents interviewed were biological parents (94% in Washington and 98% in Victoria) and female (74% in Washington and 81% in Victoria).

Measures

Parent awareness of policy and involvement.   School administrators were asked to report how aware they thought parents were of existing substance-use policies and how involved parents were in making decisions and setting substance-use policies at their school.

Awareness of school drug policies was assessed in the parent interview by asking to what degree parents were aware of what happened to a student caught smoking, drinking alcohol, or possessing or using illicit drugs at their child's school. A single construct for parental awareness of school drug policy was generated from the mean of the responses to all 3 items.

Communication methods.   School administrators were asked to indicate which of the following methods they use to communicate policy to parents: parent handbook, structured meetings with school staff (conferences), newsletters/bulletins, letters home to parents, orientation/parent night, or other.

Parents were asked in the interview whether or not details of school drug policies were communicated by their child's school via newsletters or bulletins, parent/teacher meetings, parent handbooks, or student diaries/handbooks, indirectly through their child, or through verbal communication with school staff.

Policy philosophy/orientation.   To index policy orientation toward abstinence-only and harm-minimization principles, administrators were asked to indicate the degree to which the following 2 statements described their school: "School policies emphasize total abstinence from drug use" and "School policies are based on the assumption that most youth will experiment with drugs." For school drug education orientation, administrators were asked to what degree they agreed with these statements: "Drug education programs emphasize total abstinence from drug use" and "Drug education programs emphasize safe drug use rather than no drug use."

To index policy and drug education orientation toward abstinence and harm minimization, respectively, students were asked to indicate the degree to which they agreed with the following two statements: "We are taught to say no to alcohol" and "We are taught to use alcohol safely."

Policy enforcement. Policy enforcement was measured in the school administrator survey by a series of items asking the likelihood of specific consequences for students caught using tobacco, alcohol, and illicit drugs on school grounds or at school events. These included referral to a school counselor or nurse, in-school or out-of-school suspension, expulsion from school, and referral to legal authorities (police).

In the student survey, policy enforcement was assessed by a series of items asking which consequences are used for students caught using tobacco, alcohol, and illicit drugs at school. The consequences given were: he or she would be talked to by a teacher about the dangers of smoking cigarettes/drinking alcohol/using drugs, he or she would be suspended, he or she would be expelled, or the police would be called.

Student drug use on school grounds. Two items in the student survey measured students' perceptions about tobacco and alcohol use at school: "Many students smoke on school grounds without getting caught" and "Many students drink alcohol on school grounds without getting caught."

Students were asked to report their own drug taking on school grounds with the following item: "How many times in the past year (12 months) have you been drunk or high at school?" Responses were dichotomized into "never" and "one or more times" categories.

Results

Parental Awareness of Policy

The percentage of parents aware of specific drug policies at their child's school was higher in Washington than in Victoria (81.6% aware of smoking policies, 86.7% aware of alcohol policies, and 88.8% aware of illicit-drug policies vs 72.1%, 70.3%, and 71.9%, respectively, for Victoria). . . . There was no significant difference between the 2 states in terms of school perceptions of parent awareness (82.5% in Washington vs 80.2% in Victoria), . . . but Victorian schools perceived greater parent awareness than was actually reported by parents.

It was hypothesized that schools that involved their parent body in the policy setting process would report higher levels of parental policy awareness. Less than 10% of schools in both states reported that parents were "very involved" in the policy setting process, and there was no significant difference in the levels of parental policy awareness between schools that did or did not involve parents in policy setting (89% vs 80%). . . .

Methods Used to Communicate Policy

. . . Schools in both states reported that the most commonly used method for communicating school drug policy information to parents was via newsletters/ bulletins and then orientation/parent night. Parents also rated newsletters/ bulletins as the most commonly used method, but in both states, it was reported that parent handbooks and student diaries/handbooks were other commonly used methods. Parent/teacher meetings were not as frequently used.

Washington parents reported the use of each of the communication methods more frequently than Victorian parents, whereas school administrators reported that only one of the communication methods (parent handbook) was used more frequently by Washington schools. . . .

Abstinence and Harm-Minimization Messages

Washington school administrators reported that their school policies placed more emphasis on total abstinence from drug use than policies of Victorian school administrators. . . . Washington school drug education programs also emphasized total abstinence from drug use, whereas Victorian administrators reported that school policies had a stronger abstinence message than did drug education curricula.

More Victorian than Washington school administrators (18% vs 5%) reported that their school drug policies were based on the assumption that most youth will experiment with drugs. Similarly, the harm-minimization concept was adopted within drug education curricula to a much greater extent by Victorian schools than by Washington schools (33% vs 2%) (table not shown). . . .

As with school administrator reports, an emphasis on abstinence was reported by more Washington students and an emphasis on harm minimization by Victorian students. . . .

Policy Enforcement

The most common consequences for all drug policy violations reported by school administrators in both states were referral of the student to a counselor/ nurse or suspension. . . . Highly punitive measures such as expulsion and contacting the police were more commonly used for illicit-drug offences than for tobacco and alcohol policy violations. Washington school administrators were more likely than Victorian administrators to use highly punitive measures.

More Washington than Victorian students reported that highly punitive measures were used for all drug-type violations. Students in both states agreed with school administrators that highly punitive measures were used for illicit-drug offences than for tobacco and alcohol policy violations. Students did not report that referral to a teacher was a common consequence, with only around 50% or less of students reporting use of this method. Victorian students were more likely than Washington students to report this consequence for all drug-type violations.

Policy and Student Drug Use on School Grounds

Students in Victoria were twice as likely to report that students smoke on school grounds without getting caught as students in Washington (61% vs

30%). . . . Perceptions of alcohol use on school grounds were lower than for smoking and similar in both states (12% in Victoria and 14% in Washington) . . . , as was student self-reported drug and/or alcohol use at school in the past year (5% in Victoria and 7% in Washington). . . .

Characteristics of students, including their being in ninth grade and recent use in the past month, increased their perceptions of smoking on school grounds, and living in Washington reduced the likelihood of perceptions of smoking on school grounds. Student perceptions of smoking on school grounds were lower where students reported having received a strong abstinence drug education message . . . or perceiving harsh penalties if caught smoking at school. . . , parents reported awareness of school drug policy. . . , and if the school reported using an abstinence-based policy . . . or strict policy enforcement. . . . Monitoring of school grounds and bathrooms was significantly associated with higher student perceptions of smoking on school grounds. . . .

Characteristics of students, including being in ninth grade and smoking in the last 30 days, increased the perceptions of drinking on school grounds. Student perceptions of drinking on school grounds were lower when students perceived harsh penalties if caught drinking at school . . . , and were higher if the school reported monitoring of bathrooms. . . .

Ninth grade students and those who used tobacco in the last 30 days reported more drinking or drug taking on school grounds. Student self-reported drinking or drug taking on school grounds was lower where students reported having received a strong abstinence drug education message or a strong harm-minimization drug education message. . . .

Adjusting for state, cohort, and recent (past 30 days) self-reported tobacco use, student perception of harsh penalties for drug policy violations continued to be statistically significantly associated with lower student perceptions of smoking . . . and drinking . . . at school. . . . Student perceptions of a strong abstinence drug education message continued to be statistically significantly associated with lower drug use at school. . . . Harm-minimization drug education continued to be statistically significantly associated with lower perceptions of smoking at school . . . , and marginally significant with self-report of being drunk or high at school. . . . The relationship between school report of monitoring bathrooms and school grounds and high levels of drinking at school also continued to be significant after adjusting for state, cohort, and recent tobacco use. . . . School reports for expulsion for alcohol violations continued to be associated with lower numbers of students reporting being drunk or high at school. . . .

Discussion

This study collected information on school drug policy from 3 different sources and provides detailed insight into policy implementation in schools from 2 countries that have different drug policy environments. Collecting parent reports on policy was important since schools are encouraged to involve their parent body in policy development and ensure that all relevant parties, including parents, are aware of the policy. The considerable investment on the part of schools to achieve this is considered acceptable, as parent involvement is expected to facilitate the school's ability to handle drug incidents in a manner consistent with community expectations, and parental involvement enables parents to enforce similar restrictions outside of school.(22-24) Parents' self-reported awareness of school drug policy in this study indicated that schools in Victoria tend to overestimate slightly how well they are communicating school drug policy information to parents. Interestingly, about 30% fewer Victorian parents reported receiving drug policy information via school newsletters, the most commonly used method, than schools reported using them. It is possible that schools are producing these materials, but that parents do not always receive or remember receiving them. In Washington, about 10% more parents recall receiving drug policy information via school newsletters than schools reported using them.

It is difficult to determine from this study any potential benefits from parent involvement in policy setting since less than 10% of schools reported high levels of parental involvement. This finding is in accordance with other studies in the United States and England that also found low levels of parent involvement in policy setting.(25,26)

How and if student drug use is influenced by school drug policy will be related to students' understanding of policy and their perceptions of its enforcement. This study assessed how well schools communicate their drug policy messages to their students. It appears that schools in both states are successfully communicating their stance on at least alcohol use since the observed differences in policy orientation between schools in the 2 states was also reported by students. By adopting an abstinence-based policy stance to drug issues, Washington schools are able to provide a more consistent message to their students with strong abstinence messages in both drug policy and drug education messages. The harm-minimization concept adopted by most Victorian schools takes a broader view, encouraging abstinence as a key method of reducing harms, but accepting some degree of experimentation and attempting to equip students with knowledge on safe levels of use. As a consequence, Victorian schools report that their policies place strong emphasis on abstinence (the use of drugs being inappropriate at school), while their drug education programs have a greater harm-minimization focus.

Students in both states were generally knowledgeable about the likely consequences for drug policy violations in their school. Students confirmed school reports that Washington schools were more likely than Victorian schools to use highly punitive measures such as expulsion and referral to the police. Students in both states believed that remedial consequences such as counseling were less likely to be used, especially for illicit-drug use, than was indicated by the schools. This disparity in responses might reflect a genuine difference between policy documentation and implementation (ie, schools overreport the use of counseling) or might result from students not being well informed about the remedial consequences of policy violations. It is possible that when communicating school drug policy, schools place more emphasis on the highly punitive consequences to enhance the deterrent effect. The impact of the perception of punitive measures for smoking and drinking is also associated with lower perceptions of smoking and drinking at school, but interestingly, it is less strongly associated with student reports of being drunk or high at school. This area warrants further investigation as there is emerging evidence that the use of education and counseling along with disciplinary sanctions is associated with lower student smoking rates than the use of punitive measures alone.(14,27) The finding that students are generally well aware of their school's policy implementation is an important one as there is strong evidence that school drug policy will only impact student behavior if it is perceived to be well enforced.(15,28,29)

Measuring the impact of school drug policies on student behaviors is a difficult task given the number of known influences on students' decisions to use tobacco, alcohol, and other drugs.(30) It was hypothesized that school policy would be expected to have the greatest effect on student drug use on school grounds. In this study, self-reported drug use on school grounds was measured as well as perceptions of smoking and drinking by other students at school without getting caught. Importantly, reductions in the ORs for these behaviors were observed in schools where students reported receiving an abstinence drug education message and perceived harsh penalties if caught using drugs at school, even when controlling for known influences (cohort, state, and recent tobacco use). Strong harm-minimization messages were also associated with lower levels of self-reported use, indicating that clearly delivered policy messages of either orientation can be effective in lowering levels of drug use at school.

Interestingly, monitoring drug use on school grounds or in bathrooms was associated with increases in perceptions of student smoking and alcohol use but not self-reports of being drunk or high at school. This suggests that monitoring may increase perceptions of student drug use whilst not serving to reduce actual use levels. This may be worrisome since perceptions of drug use are associated with higher levels of drug initiation. (31)

The current study has a number of limitations that should be noted. Only one school informant completed the School Administrator Survey, and it is possible that the responses might more accurately depict school policy if additional school respondents were surveyed. The wording of questions was not always consistent across student, parent, or administrator surveys. For example, when asking about the consequences for policy violations, schools were asked about student referral to a counselor or nurse, whereas students were asked about referral to a teacher. However, there are a number of key strengths to the study, namely its very large representative sample from 2 states with different national drug policy backgrounds, collection of data from 3 key school groups, and measures of actual and perceived student drug use on school grounds.

The implications of this study for school policy makers are preliminary but encouraging. Schools in the 2 study states generally have some impact in educating their students about drug policy. When delivered effectively, policy messages are associated with reduced student drug use at school. Abstinence messages and harsh penalties convey a coherent message to students associated with reduced student drug use at school. Strong harm-minimization messages delivered within a "no drugs at school" context are also associated with reduced drug use at school, but effects are weaker than those for abstinence messages. It is possible that the smaller impact of harm-minimization messages is a result of conflicting messages between policy (abstinence) and drug education (acceptance of experimentation). Harm-minimization advocates would argue that this smaller effect is acceptable given the anticipated reduction in the levels of current and future harmful use and school drop out within the student population. Given that nearly all schools invest substantial time and money developing and implementing policies for tobacco, alcohol, and illicit drugs and drug education, it is imperative that further research is conducted to evaluate which aspects of policy are important in reducing student drug use.

References

1. Commonwealth Department of Health and Family Services. A National Framework for Health Promoting Schools (2000–2003). Canberra Australia: Commonwealth Department of Health and Family Services and Australian Health Promoting Schools Association; 2001.

2. Rutter M, Maughan B, Mortimore P, Ouston J, Smith A. fifteen thousand hours: secondary schools and their effects on children. London: Open Books; 1979.

3. Resnick MD, Bearman PS, Blum RW, et al. Protecting adolescents from harm: findings from the National Longitudinal Study on Adolescent Health. JAMA. 1997;278(10):823–832.

4. Bond L, Patton G, Glover S, et al. The Gatehouse Project: can a multilevel school intervention affect emotional well-being and health risk behaviours? J Epidemiol Community Health. 2004;58(12):997–1003.

5. Patton G, Bond L, Butler H, Glover S. Changing schools, changing health? Design and implementation of the Gatehouse Project. J Adolesc Health. 2003;33(4):231–239.

6. Goodstadt MS. Substance abuse curricula vs. school drug policies. J Sch Health. 1989;59(6):246–250.

7. Evans-Whipp T, Beyers JM, Lloyd S, et al. A review of school drug policies and their impact on youth substance use. Health Promot Int. 2004; 19(2):227–234.

8. Flay BR. Approaches to substance use prevention utilizing school curriculum plus social environment change. Addict Behav 2000;25(6):861–885.

9. Beyers JM, Evans-Whipp T, Mathers M, Toumbourou JW, Catalano RF. A cross-national comparison of school drug policies in Washington State, United States, and Victoria, Australia. J Sch Health. 2005;75(4): 134–140.

10. Small ML, Jones SE, Barrios LC, et al. School policy and environment: results from the School Health Policies and Programs Study 2000. J Sch Health. 2001;71(7):325–334.

11. Ross JG, Einhaus KB, Hohenemser LK, Greene BZ, Kann L, Gold RS. School health policies prohibiting tobacco use, alcohol and other drug use, and violence. J Sch Health. 1995;65(8):333–338.

12. Pentz MA, Brannon BR, Charlin VL, Barrett EJ, MacKinnon DP, Flay BR. The power of policy: the relationship of smoking policy to adolescent smoking. Am J Public Health. 1989;79(7):857–862.

13. Charlton A, While D. Smoking prevalence among 16–19-year-olds related to staff and student smoking policies in sixth forms and further education. Health Educ J. 1994;53:28–39.

14. Hamilton G, Cross D, Lower T, Resnicow K, Williams P. School policy: what helps to reduce teenage smoking? Nicotine Tob Res. 2003;5(4):507–513.

15. Griesbach D, Inchley J, Currie C. More than words? The status and impact of smoking policies in Scottish schools. Health Promot Int. 2002;17(1):31–41.

16. McMorris BJ, Hemphill SA, Toumbourou JW, Catalano RF, Patton GC. Prevalence of substance use and delinquent behavior in adolescents from Victoria, Australia and Washington State, USA. Health Educ Behav. 2006.

17. Caulkins JP, Reuter P. Setting goals for drug policy: harm reduction or use reduction? Addiction. 1997;92(9):1143–1150.

18. Munro G, Midford R. "Zero tolerance" and drug education in Australian schools. Drug Alcohol Rev. 2001;20(1):105–109.

19. Patton GC, McMorris BJ, Toumbourou JW, Hemphill SA, Donath S, Catalano RF. Puberty and the onset of substance use and abuse. Pediatrics. 2004;114(3):e300–e306.

20. Stata statistical software: Release 8. College Station, TX: StataCorp; 2001.

21. Carlin JB, Wolfe R, Coffey C, Patton GC. Tutorial in biostatistics: analysis of binary outcomes in longitudinal studies using weighted estimating equations and discrete-time survival methods: prevalence and incidence of smoking in an adolescent cohort. Stat Med. 1999;18(19):2655–2679.

22. Peck DD, Acott C, Richard P, Hill S, Schuster C. The Colorado Tobacco-Free Schools and Communities Project. J Sch Health. 1993;63(5):214–217.

23. Commonwealth Department of Education Training and Youth Affairs. National School Drug Education Strategy, May 1999. . . .

24. Commonwealth Department of Education Science and Training. Innovation and Good Practice in Drug Education. Effective Communication. Canberra: Commonwealth of Australia; 2003: 10.

25. Brener ND, Dittus PJ, Hayes G. Family and community involvement in schools: results from the School Health Policies and Programs Study 2000. J Sch Health. 2001;71(7):340–344.

26. Denman S, Pearson J, Hopkins D, Wallbanks C, Skuriat V. The management and organisation of health promotion: a survey of school policies in Nottinghamshire. Health Educ J. 1999;58:165–176.

27. Hamilton G, Cross D, Resnicow K, Hall M. A school-based harm minimization smoking intervention trial: outcome results. Addiction. 2005; 100(5):689–700.

28. Moore L, Roberts C, Tudor-Smith C. School smoking policies and smoking prevalence among adolescents: multilevel analysis of cross-sectional data from Wales. Tob Control. 2001;10(2):117–123.

29. Wakefield MA, Chaloupka FJ, Kaufman NJ, Orleans CT, Barker DC, Ruel BE. Effect of restrictions on smoking at home, at school, and in public places on teenage smoking: cross sectional study. BMJ. 2000;321(7257):333–337.

30. Hawkins JD, Catalano RF, Miller JY. Risk and protective factors for alcohol and other drug problems in adolescence and early adulthood: implications for substance abuse prevention. Psychol Bull. 1992;112(1):64–105.

31. Hansen WB, Graham JW. Preventing alcohol, marijuana, and cigarette use among adolescents: peer pressure resistance training versus establishing conservative norms. Prey Med. 1991;20(3):414–430.

Beyond Zero Tolerance: A Reality-Based Approach to Drug Education & School Discipline

Beyond Zero Tolerance: A Reality-Based Model
Where We Are Today

Most American high schools do not offer effective drug education, nor do they provide interventions to assist students struggling with abuse of alcohol and other drugs. Instead, they rely primarily on deterrent punishment for students who are caught violating the rules. Proponents of the "big four" consequences —exclusion from extracurricular activities, transfer to another school, suspension, and expulsion—believe that harsh consequences for those who are caught will deter other students from committing similar offenses, and too often constitute the whole of prevention.

But research has shown that these punishments are not likely to change students' behavior. Ironically, rather than serving as an effective deterrent, drug education that lacks credibility and is backed by punitive measures often fosters resentment and oppositional behavior. The few secondary schools that offer drug education often repeat messages that may have had some credence for elementary school students but lack credibility for older, more experienced teenagers. Current "science-based" programs are more sophisticated than earlier "just say no" programs, but are still based on questionable assumptions about the reasons so many teens experiment with drugs.

Empowering Tomorrow: A Comprehensive Approach

A reality-based model incorporates three mutually reinforcing elements: *education, intervention/assistance,* and *restorative consequences.* The basic tenets, which are described later in more detail, are as follows:

- Drug education should be honest, balanced, interactive, and delivered in a way that involves full participation of students.
- Intervention for students who need assistance should be an integral part of drug education.
- A restorative process, in which offenders identify harms they have caused and then make amends, should replace most suspensions and expulsions.

Guiding Realities

The use of alcohol and marijuana is common among high school students, and most young people accept it as part of teenage social life.

For decades, alcohol and other drug use has been widely accepted among older teens. A majority of them, including those who choose abstinence, view the use of alcohol and marijuana as a common social activity rather than abhorrent behavior practiced only by outcasts and deviants. In the California Student Survey, most older teens consistently report that their peers try alcohol or marijuana because they are curious about the effects and that "having fun" is the main reason to continue. This social climate tolerates drug experimentation and occasional use, though not necessarily use that causes problems.

Throughout the '90s, my students at UCLA joined in lively class discussions and wrote reports based on anonymous interviews with other college students about the use of alcohol and other drugs in their high school communities. Findings from over 300 interviews included the following:

- Alcohol and other drugs were readily available to students in their high schools and most students, whether they used them or not, were tolerant of friends who did. Those who abstained did not condemn the user as a person even though they disapproved of the behavior.
- The interviewees did not remember much about prevention education in their elementary schools ("they just told us drugs were bad").
- Most denied that teenagers try drugs because of direct peer pressure.
- All were aware that use of alcohol or other drugs caused problems for some of their peers, but many also cited benefits associated with moderate use and others made it clear that they did not view users as immoral.

"Smoking pot for my friends was like watching TV for me. It was just normal."

"It's possible for someone to think that drug use is immoral, but to also not have a biased opinion of the user. I have friends who do it, but I'm still friends with them."

"Among my friends some people choose not to do it and others do. And nobody thinks less of any other person."

"The D.A.R.E. program made it seem like smoking bud was a horrible thing to do, but when I saw my friends do it they were having a blast, so I joined in."

"The people I knew were well informed on the consequences of drugs, but they didn't care. When they did drugs they were bonding with friends."

Over the last 30 years the national Monitoring the Future survey (. . .) has consistently shown that marijuana accounts for the lion's share of illegal drug use among teenagers. The results since 1991 continue to confirm its popularity.

- 42% of current high school seniors have smoked marijuana in their lifetime compared to a peak of 50% in 1999 and a 33% low in 1992.

- 27% used an illegal drug other than marijuana at least once compared to a peak of 31% in 2001 and a low of 25% in 1992.

Although underage drinking is at its lowest level in recent history (unlike use of illegal drugs), the great majority of older teens have tried alcohol at least once in their lives and substantial numbers drink heavily and frequently.

- 73% of high school seniors tried alcohol compared to a peak of 88% in 1991.
- 56% have been drunk at least once compared to a peak of 65% in 1991.

Use of pharmaceutical drugs without a doctor's prescription is on the increase, possibly explaining the decline for alcohol.

- 10% of high school seniors used pain-killers, such as Vicodin, in the last year, and 4% used OxyContin.
- 7% used tranquilizers, such as Xanax, and 7% used sedative barbiturates in the last year.

Use rates fluctuate from year to year, but they never come close to reflecting universal abstinence. Perhaps this is because young people live in a society where a range of legal substances, including alcohol, over-the-counter drugs, and pharmaceuticals are not only tolerated, but promoted through popular culture and the media.

As a result, drug prevention programs for preteens, instituted nationwide in the mid-80s, have not reduced widespread acceptance and use of alcohol and marijuana among contemporary high school populations. These savvy teens have easy access to these substances, and are skeptical of "just say no" messages.

Drug prevention programs designed to "inoculate" children against later alcohol and other drug experimentation have failed.
Most existing drug education programs are delivered with the assumption that elementary school students can be *inoculated* against later temptation. While a few of these programs offer secondary school "booster sessions," the curricula mainly recap the same messages heard in elementary school, even though little evidence supports the theory that early prevention education has been successful in reducing use of alcohol and other drugs by the mid-teen years.

Older teens become skeptical about the warning messages heard in elementary school prevention programs and can identify little or nothing of what they learned in their pre-teen years. Independent scientists have identified serious flaws in research ostensibly supporting even "science-based" elementary school programs. Given students' limited retention of the information taught in these programs, it seems the best time to *start* school-based drug education is at the beginning of the teenage years, immediately before experimentation escalates.

Those who have reared or taught children know they become adolescents rather suddenly at 11 or 12 years old, when physical and motivational changes are obvious. The equally important leap forward in mental capacity that occurs at this age is usually less apparent. "Formal reasoning" ability, as psychologists call it, enables teenagers to arrive at answers to problems in the same way as adults, by thinking of possible explanations and testing them out. However, in modern developed societies young people have been prevented from assuming responsibilities commensurate with their capabilities. The response to this "infantilizing" is often oppositional, with substance use an "in your face" example.

An adolescent's ability to reason helps to explain why early one-sided or factually inaccurate drug prevention messages are rejected by the mid-teen years. The information conveyed by adults often conflicts with knowledge teens have acquired on their own, through observation or personal experience. In a social climate of widespread acceptance of the use of alcohol and other drugs, underestimating teens' mental agility and delivering simplistic "drugs are bad" messages results in cynicism rather than obedience.

Given today's climate of government-sanctioned fear, I appreciate the difficulty adults may have delivering a balanced message. It can be professionally dangerous for teachers to acknowledge benign use and/or the positive aspects of alcohol and other drugs. By omitting these realities, we seriously compromise our ability to establish and maintain credibility. To go a step further and admit that most young people who do try alcohol or other drugs do not get into lifelong patterns of abuse provokes the accusation that, "you are sending the wrong message!" and thereby granting permission to use.

Teenagers do not ask adults whether they can drink alcohol, smoke cigarettes, or try marijuana. Instead, most young people respond to the norms of their own social world, just as they do for modes of talk, dress, sexual behavior, or music.

"Nothing about us without us!"—Drug education that ignores the views of young people is bound to fail.
Historically, drug prevention education has been a top-down enterprise that has ignored the experience and opinions of young people, resulting in cynicism.

Our society relies heavily on polling and other tools to gauge customer opinions. Drug prevention programs would benefit from the application of similar techniques: What do teenagers remember from the drug education they experienced as children? Do they later see inaccuracies or lack of balance in the information and messages? What about the information and images they have been bombarded with since then—do they ring true? Do young people view the programs as effective, or are they perceived as just more hypocritical indoctrination?

Students should also be involved in setting school policies regarding consequences for violating rules. The battle cry of the disability rights movement, "nothing about us without us!" applies with equal force to working with teenagers.

Severe punishment of those caught with alcohol and other drugs has not affected use rates among other high school students.

Most Americans believe education is the primary tool for preventing substance use among young people. However, in practice, *deterrent punishment* is the key component in prevention. Deterrent punishment refers generally to punitive measures such as expulsion, suspension, or exclusion from participation in student government, sports, and other extracurricular activities. These "consequences" are thought to insure abstinence among teens.

Yet, defying adults through oppositional behavior is a tactic frequently used in striking back at what many young people perceive as unreasonable and arbitrary rules and decisions. When it comes to the use of alcohol and other drugs, we have no proof that punishing the few who are caught actually deters others from predictable experimentation. Additionally, deterrent punishment undermines a sense of connection—among those caught and observers alike—leaving young people feeling isolated and believing that "the system" is uneven, unfair, and cruel.

Moreover, draconian punishments largely ignore the welfare of the students who are cast out of the school community.

Research has shown that young people who feel connected to family and school are more likely to make positive health choices, including abstinence. That's why the California State Parent Teacher Association passed an "Alternatives to Zero Tolerance" resolution at its annual convention in 2003.

Most high school students report that friends troubled by their use of alcohol or other drugs are not likely to find help at their schools. They are aware that these offenders are instead "disappeared" through suspension, expulsion, or transfer to another school where the process starts all over again. To most of them, this seems both callous and unwise.

From the UCLA interviewees:

"Expulsion just encourages the negative behavior. It leaves no alternative open to the kid."

"Expelling a student is getting rid of problem kids and not getting rid of the problem in those kids."

"You are continuing the problem with expulsion. A kid who comes to school high is obviously in need of some attention and guidance. By kicking him or her out of school, you may eliminate the only stability that he or she has in life."

"Kicking kids out of school is the dumbest thing ever. Then what are they going to do? Just sit home and smoke pot all the time?"

"If the school expels the student, he or she is just going to be transferred to another school . . . (and) repeat the same behaviors. The rest of the students don't care . . . because they think that they won't get caught and they're right, most students don't get caught."

The 2006 California Student Survey found that in any 30-day period almost 12% of 11th graders admit to having used alcohol or other drugs at least once on campus. A much smaller minority are actually caught selling drugs at school, with wide variability in administrative responses to such violations, although suspension or expulsion tends to be the norm.

REALITY: 12% The 2006 CALIFORNIA STUDENT SURVEY found that in any 30-day period almost 12% of 11th graders admit to having used alcohol or other drugs at least once on campus; that is one out of every eight students.

When dealing with offenders, I believe that consequences likely to *reform rather than disadvantage* the student will significantly reduce oppositional behavior, including drug possession and use on campus, while increasing the likelihood of ultimate success in school and work. "Restorative practices," alternative methods for dealing with offenders, are discussed beginning on page 13 of this booklet.

Some students are so seriously involved with alcohol and/or other drugs that they would benefit from *professional* intervention and treatment in lieu of expulsion. In one UCLA interview, a severely drug-involved student at a Catholic girls preparatory school told a story with a happy ending. She had been coming to school intoxicated on a daily basis. Eventually she was caught and suspended. Fortunately, teachers and counselors begged her to get help and managed to get her the resources to do just that.

This student desperately needed direct intervention and compassionate assistance, and was helped as a result.

As she said:
"Some days it would be vodka in my water bottle, other days I would pop speed in the girl's bathroom before class. If I were expelled, I never would have gotten a chance at life. I would have dropped out of high school, not gotten into rehab, and not been in college right now. Thank God for them (the counselors and teachers) and thank goodness for my friends."

Education or Surveillance?

In light of the deficiencies in current prevention approaches, the federal government advocates widespread implementation of random student drug testing. Unfortunately, this policy perpetuates many of the problematic aspects of zero tolerance strategies:

- Random drug testing erodes relationship of trust between students and adults at school, hindering open communication and damaging an essential component of a safe and rewarding learning environment.
- Drug testing programs are counter-productive, erecting barriers to participation in extracurricular activities—the very activities likely to increase students' connection to caring adults at school, and provide structure and supervision during the peak hours of adolescent drug use, from 3–6 pm.
- Drug testing programs do not effectively identify students who have serious problems with drugs and further marginalize at-risk students.

- Testing may trigger oppositional behavior by inadvertently encouraging more students to abuse alcohol—not included in many standard testing panels—or by motivating some drug-involved adolescents to switch to harder drugs that leave the system more quickly.
- Specimen collection is invasive and humiliating.
- Drug testing can result in false positives, leading to the punishment of innocent students.
- Drug testing is expensive, wasting scarce dollars that could be better spent on other, more effective programs that keep young people out of trouble with drugs.
- The scientific literature does not support the safety or effectiveness of random student drug testing. The only national peer-reviewed study conducted on the topic to date compared 94,000 students in almost 900 American schools with and without a drug testing program, and found virtually no difference in illegal drug use.
- Prominent national organizations representing experts on adolescent health oppose student drug testing, including the American Academy of Pediatrics, the Association for Addiction Professionals, the National Education Association, the American Public Health Association, the National Association of Social Workers and the National Council on Alcoholism and Drug Dependence, among others.
- Drug testing fails to reach students' key attitudes and beliefs. Instead, we should spend our scarce resources educating students through comprehensive, interactive and honest drug education with identification of, and assistance for, students whose lives are disrupted by substance use.

Schools should implement a policy of restorative practices in lieu of expulsion or suspension

The majority of youth who violate school rules involving drugs do not need formal treatment, suspension, or expulsion. Instead, they should be involved in a process likely to replace alienation with changed attitudes.

Restorative practices, as described by Dr. Francis Barnes, former school superintendent and current Pennsylvania Secretary of Education, are "a set of practical responses to student behavior and proactive strategies that strengthen accountability and improve school culture."

Young people are often unaware of the harmful impact of their behavior on themselves or others. A restorative experience, which is an interactive process rather than a punitive sentence, begins with awareness. The individual then finds ways to repair the damage, including service activities and making personal amends.

In the case of substance use, amends can include apologies to teachers disturbed and frustrated by disruptive or insultingly inattentive behavior, as well as to fellow students who want a serious and productive experience in their classrooms.

It is up to the offender to decide how he or she will make things right with others and the institution. This teaches accountability while repairing damage.

There is nothing new about restorative practices, which have a long history of effectiveness. Alcoholics Anonymous's ninth step, "making amends," provides an example. For young people, actively making amends rather than passively enduring punishment is likely to promote positive feelings, rather than resentment and alienation toward school, the adults who work there, and the community.

POSTSCRIPT

Is Abstinence an Effective Strategy for Drug Education?

Is it more desirable to promote an abstinence and zero tolerance approach or to promote drug education as a means of addressing drug use? Before the effectiveness of drug education programs can be determined, it is necessary to define the goals of drug education. Are the goals of drug education to prevent drug use from starting? To prevent drug abuse? To prevent drug dependency? Perhaps the goal of drug education is to teach young people how to protect themselves and others from harm *if* they are going to use drugs. Should the messages about drugs be tailored to different audiences? Without a clear understanding of the goals one wants to achieve in teaching about drugs, it is impossible to determine the effectiveness of drug education and whether it is better than an abstinence approach.

Before a drug education program can be designed, questions regarding what to include in the drug education curriculum needs to be addressed. Should the primary focus be on teaching abstinence or responsible use? Is it feasible to teach abstinence from some drugs and responsible use of other drugs? The vast majority of high school students have drunk alcohol; should they be taught that they should not drink at all, or should they be taught how to use alcohol responsibly? Is it ethical to teach responsible use of a substance that is illegal? Does the age of the children make a difference in what is taught? Do elementary students have the reasoning skills of high school students? Should the goal be for students to engage in a decision-making process or simply to adopt certain behaviors?

Surveys of drug use by secondary students over the past thirty years show that the rate of drug use is cyclical. Periods of high drug use are followed by periods of lower drug use. This fact could lead one to conclude that drug education has little bearing on whether drugs are used and that other factors contribute to the use, or nonuse, of drugs. It is possible that the availability of drugs is a factor in their use as well as stories in the media.

If drug prevention programs are going to be effective in reducing drug use, schools and other institutions will need to work together. Many young people drop out of school or simply do not attend, so community agencies and faith-based institutions need to become involved. The media have a large impact on young people. What is the best way to incorporate the media in the effort to reduce drug use? Are antidrug commercial spots shown during programs aimed at teenage audiences effective? Do movies and music videos in which drug use is depicted contribute to whether drugs are used?

The role of teachers in drug education is discussed in "Teaching Teachers to Just Say 'Know': Reflections on Drug Education" by Kenneth Tupper

(Teaching and Teacher Education, February 2008). Factors such as peers, family, psychological functioning, and stressful life events are described in "Risk Factors for Serious Alcohol and Drug Use: The Role of Psychosocial Variables in Predicting the Frequency of Substance Use Among Adolescents," by Maury Nation and Craig Anne Heflinger *(American Journal of Drug and Alcohol Abuse,* August 2006). Lastly, Marsha Rosenbaum of the Drug Policy Alliance addresses the importance of effective drug education in *Safety First: A Reality-Based Approach to Teens and Drugs* (2007).

Contributors to This Volume

EDITOR

RAYMOND GOLDBERG is the dean for health sciences for Vance-Granville Community College in Henderson, North Carolina. Previously, he served as the associate dean for the School of Professional Studies for the State University of New York at Cortland. In addition, he was the graduate coordinator for its graduate programs and a professor in its health department. He received his Ph.D. in health education from the University of Toledo, his master's degree from the University of South Carolina, and his bachelor's degree from the University of North Carolina at Pembroke. He is the author of *Drugs Across the Spectrum*, 6th edition (Cengage Publishers, Inc.). He has received over $750,000 in grants for his research in health and drug education.

AUTHORS

JUDITH APPEL is the executive director of the Our Family Coalition. Appel has more than 15 years of experience as a public interest lawyer involved in policy-based work. Appel previously was director of legal affairs for the Drug Policy Alliance, a national, nonprofit organization dedicated to reducing the harm caused by drugs and drug policies. She serves on the Boards of Directors of the Ella Baker Center for Human Rights, Oakland Civil Liberties Alliance, and the Coalition on Homelessness.

DANIELLE ROSE ASH is a doctoral student who is associated with the Division of General Internal Medicine and Health Services Research at the David Geffen School of Medicine at UCLA.

MARICE ASHE is the founder and director of Public Health Law & Policy (PHLP), part of the Public Health Institute in San Francisco. In addition to being a professor of public health law at the University of California at Berkeley School of Public Health, Ms. Ashe serves on the board of the California Center for Public Health Advocacy and has worked with the University of California Office of the President and the Contra Costa County Health Services Department. She graduated from the University of Notre Dame and received her law and public health degrees from the University of California at Berkeley.

FRANCES K. BARG is an Assistant Professor of Family Medicine and Community Health at the Hospital of the University of Pennsylvania. Professor Barg has studied the distribution of risk and disease among ethnic groups, the impact of culture in medicine, and depression in older adults. Professor Barg's doctorate in medical anthropology was earned at the University of Pennsylvania, her bachelor's degree was from George Washington University, and her master's degree was from the University of Pittsburgh.

LYNDAL BOND is the research director for the Adolescent Health and Social Environments Program, Centre for Adolescent Health, Murdoch Children's Research Institute, Melbourne, Australia.

JOHN BRITTON is a professor of Epidemiology at the University of Nottingham School of Community Health where he directs the UK Centre for Tobacco Control Studies. The Centre researches policies and practices to reduce the prevalence of smoking and the harm it causes through prevention of uptake of smoking, promotion of smoking cessation, and development of more effective harm reduction strategies for those currently unable to stop smoking.

JOSEPH A. CALIFANO, JR., is chairman of the National Center on Addiction and Substance Abuse at Columbia University. Califano has written several books, including *High Society: How Substance Abuse Ravages America and What to Do About It.*

CAROLYN S. CARTER is a social work professor at Howard University.

RICHARD F. CATALANO is professor and the associate director of the Social Development Research Group at the University of Washington's School of

Social Work in Seattle, Washington. For over 25 years, he has led research and program development to promote positive youth development and prevent problem behavior. His work has focused on discovering risk and protective factors for positive and problem behavior, and designing and evaluating programs to address these factors.

BRUCE M. COHEN is a clinical instructor of psychiatry and behavioral sciences at the University of Arkansas for Medical Sciences. He is director of the Child Study Center Clinic and Community Outreach Program in the Division of Pediatric Psychiatry as well as clinical director of Arkansas CARES. His clinical work has focused on children and adolescents with ADHD, learning problems, and depression, and he has extensive experience in school consultation. He earned his B.S. in psychology and his M.S. in clinical psychology (child clinical specialty) from Memphis State University.

PETER J. COHEN is an attorney, a physician, and an adjunct professor of law at Georgetown University. Dr. Cohen previously was a professor of anesthesiology at the University of Pennsylvania Medical Center and professor and chairman of anesthesiology at the Universities of Colorado and Michigan Medical Centers. Dr. Cohen worked in health care policy, serving as a special expert for the Medications Development Division in the National Institute on Drug Abuse (NIDA). He has written extensively on legal/medical ethical issues.

ALEXANDRA COX works for the Office of Legal Affairs for Drug Policy Alliance, which promotes alternatives to the war on drugs.

PETER F. CRONHOLM, a physician specializing in family health and community medicine, practices in Philadelphia. Dr. Cronholm is an assistant professor with the Department of Family Medicine and Community Health at the University of Pennsylvania. He received his medical degree in 1998 from the Temple University School of Medicine.

LAWRENCE DILLER practices behavioral-development pediatrics and family therapy in Walnut Creek, California. He is the author of *Running on Ritalin: A Physician Reflects on Children, Society, and Performance in a Pill.*

THE DRUG ENFORCEMENT ADMINISTRATION (DEA) has a mission to enforce the controlled substances laws and regulations of the United States and bring to the criminal and civil justice systems of the United States, or any other competent jurisdiction, those organizations and principal members of organizations, involved in the growing, manufacture, or distribution of controlled substances appearing in or destined for illicit traffic in the United States; and to recommend and support nonenforcement programs aimed at reducing the availability of illicit controlled substances on the domestic and international markets.

RICHARD EDWARDS trained as a public health physician in the United Kingdom. Dr. Edwards is a senior lecturer in epidemiology at New Zealand's University of Otago Wellington School of Medicine and Health Science. His research deals with tobacco use epidemiology and control, secondhand smoke and smoke-free policies and legislation, smoking and eye disease, and non-communicable diseases in sub-Saharan Africa.

LAURA K. EGENDORF is a writer and an editor of young adult books. Some of her publications include *Should Social Networking Websites Be Banned?* and *Smoking and Sexually Transmitted Diseases*. In addition, Laura Egendorf has written about the environment, anti-Semitism, terrorism, human rights, violence, aging, and chemical dependency.

SUSAN L. ETTNER is professor in the Division of General Internal Medicine and Health Services Research in the UCLA Department of Public Health. Dr. Ettner obtained her Ph.D. in economics at the Massachusetts Institute of Technology in 1991. She was on the faculty of Harvard Medical School in the Department of Health Care Policy prior to joining UCLA as a tenured associate professor in 1999.

ELIZABETH EVANS is affiliated with the UCLA Integrated Substance Abuse Programs in Los Angeles.

TRACY J. EVANS-WHIPP is a research manager for the Centre for Adolescent Health, Murdoch Children's Research Institute, Melbourne, Australia.

DOMINICK L. FROSCH is an Assistant Professor of Medicine at UCLA. He previously served as a Distinguished Visiting Fellow at Cardiff University (UK) and Senior Fellow at the Leonard Davis Institute of Health Economics, University of Pennsylvania. Professor Frosch received his undergraduate education from the University of Southern California and his Ph.D. in clinical health psychology from the University of California, San Diego. He completed a fellowship as a Robert Wood Johnson Health & Society Scholar at the University of Pennsylvania.

MICHAEL FUMENTO is an author, journalist, and attorney specializing in science and health issues. He is a science columnist for Scripps-Howard and a senior fellow of the Hudson Institute in Washington, D.C. He has also been a legal writer for the *Washington Times* and an editorial writer for the *Rocky Mountain News* in Denver, and he was the first "National Issues" reporter for *Investor's Business Daily*. Fumento has lectured on science and health issues throughout the world, including Great Britain, France, the Czech Republic, Greece, Austria, China, and South America. His publications include *BioEvolution: How Biotechnology Is Changing Our World* (Encounter Books, 2003).

PETER GORMAN is an investigative journalist and former editor-in-chief of *High Times* magazine. He spends at least three months of every year living in Peru, where he works with Ayahuasca and other plant-based medicines, as well as doing political work. Much of his writing, in both Peru and the United States, has focused on the ongoing war on drugs.

FATEMA GUNJA attended Cornell University. After graduating, she worked on drug policy issues, first as a communications coordinator at the American Civil Liberties Union and then as the first director of the Drug Policy Forum of Massachusetts. During her drug policy days, she became a passionate spokesperson and writer on racial justice and students' rights in the context of the war on drugs.

MARY HARDY is affiliated with the UCLA Integrated Substance Abuse Programs in Los Angeles.

MARKUS HEILIG is the Chief of the Laboratory of Clinical Studies (LCS) and Clinical Director in the National Institute on Alcohol Abuse and Alcoholism's Division of Intramural Clinical and Biological Research. Dr. Heilig received the M.D. degree from Sweden's Lund University and a Ph.D. in psychiatric neurochemistry from the same institution. He has been a leader in addiction research in the European Community, having organized a trans-European initiative in drug dependence as well as a number of conferences and other meetings.

ROBERT C. HORNIK is the Wilbur Schramm Professor of Communication and Health Policy at the Annenberg School for Communication, University of Pennsylvania. Professor Hornik was the principal investigator for USAID-sponsored evaluations of national AIDS education programs in four developing countries and a co-principal investigator for the NIDA-funded evaluation of the National Anti-Drug Media Campaign. He is editor of *Public Health Communication: Evidence for Behavior Change*, which addresses how public health communication influences health behavior and outcomes. Professor Hornik received his Ph.D. from Stanford University.

YIH-ING HSER is affiliated with the UCLA Integrated Substance Abuse Programs in Los Angeles.

DAVID HUANG is affiliated with the UCLA Integrated Substance Abuse Programs in Los Angeles.

LESLIE L. IVERSEN received his Ph.D. from the University of Cambridge. He is a Professor of Pharmacology at University of Oxford, England, where he has taught since 1995. Previously, Dr. Iversen was a Professor of Pharmacology at King's College, London, where he was Director of the Wolfson Centre for Age Related Diseases from 1999 until 2004. Dr. Iversen is noted for his contributions to the understanding of neurotransmission. He served as Vice President of Neuroscience Research for Merck Research Laboratories and as Director of the Neuroscience Research Center of Merck Research Laboratories in the UK.

MICKEL JOURABCHI is a resident of Encino, California.

JENNIFER KERN is a research associate at the Drug Policy Alliance's Office of Legal Affairs in Berkeley. Ms. Kern serves as the national campaign coordinator for DPA's "Drug Testing Fails Our Youth," a public education project. She has been interviewed by a wide range of national print and broadcast media, including *Newsweek, Reuters, the Associated Press, Washington Post, Christian Science Monitor, Houston Chronicle,* and *Milwaukee Journal Sentinel,* among others.

HERBERT KLEBER founded at Columbia University the Division on Substance Abuse, now one of the leading centers in the country. Dr. Kleber is the author of more than 200 papers, and the coeditor of the *American Psychiatric Press Textbook of Substance Abuse Treatment.*

PATRICK M. KRUEGER, an assistant professor at the University of Texas School of Public Health at Houston and a Faculty Research Associate at the Population Research Center at the University of Texas at Austin, studies how various factors such as race, ethnicity, neighborhoods, and families affect healthy lifestyles and mortality. Professor Krueger earned his Ph.D. from the University of Colorado and his undergraduate degree from Aquinas College in Grand Rapids, Michigan.

ROBERT A. LEVY, a senior fellow in constitutional studies, joined the Cato Institute in 1997 after 25 years in business. He is a director of the Institute for Justice and a member of the board of visitors of the Federalist Society. Levy received his Ph.D. in business from American University in 1996.

FREDDI LEWIN is a physician who previously held a position with the Department of Oncology at the Karolinska Institute in Stockholm, Sweden. Dr. Lewin currently serves as a health advisor for Swedish Match, a company that produces snus. He was medically responsible for training and research on the impact of moist snuff on public health. He is an experienced oncologist and has worked as both Section Manager and Director of Studies for the specialist oncology program at the Department of Oncology, Huddinge University Hospital.

PAUL A. LOGLI is state's attorney for Winnebago County, Illinois, and a lecturer at the National College of District Attorneys. A member of the Illinois State Bar since 1974, he is a nationally recognized advocate for prosecutorial involvement in the issue of substance-abused infants. He earned his J.D. from the University of Illinois.

ROSALIND B. MARIMONT is a retired mathematician and scientist, having done research and development for the National Institute of Standards and Technology (formerly the Bureau of Standards) for 18 years and for the National Institute of Health (NIH) for another 19. She started in electronics defense work during World War II, then went into the logical design of the early digital computers during the 1950s. At the NIH she studied and published papers on human vision, speech, and other biomathematical subjects. Since her retirement she has been active in health policy issues, particularly the war on smoking.

MERRILL MATTHEWS, JR., is a public policy analyst specializing in health care, social security, welfare, and Internet issues, and the author of numerous studies in health policy, as well as other public policy issues. Currently a visiting scholar with the Institute for Policy Innovation, he is former president of the Health Economics Roundtable for the National Association for Business Economics and former health policy adviser for the American Legislative Exchange Council. Matthews also serves as the medical ethicist for the University of Texas Southwestern Medical Center's Institutional Review Board for Human Experimentation. He earned his Ph.D. in philosophy and humanities from the University of Texas at Dallas.

LEEMAN McHENRY is a professor in the Philosophy Department at the California State University at Northridge.

JUDITH G. McMULLEN is a graduate of Yale Law School, who joined the faculty in 1987 and teaches in the areas of Family Law, Trusts & Estates, and Property. Her articles on family and children's issues have appeared in the *University of Michigan Journal of Law Reform*, the *Indiana Law Review*, and other publications.

ROGER E. MEYER is a physician who has written about substance abuse since the early 1970s. He has worked with the White House Special Action Office for Drug Abuse Prevention, the National Institute for Alcohol Abuse and Alcoholism, and the National Institute for Mental Health. Dr. Meyer is a partner and CEO of Best Practice Project Management, Inc. He is a Clinical Professor of Psychiatry at Georgetown University and Adjunct Professor of Psychiatry at the University of Pennsylvania. Dr. Meyer is a recipient of a MacArthur Foundation grant. He is a graduate of the Harvard Medical School.

SIDNEY S. MIRVISH is a professor in the Department of Biochemistry and Molecular Biology at the University of Nebraska at Omaha. At the university he is affiliated with the Eppley Institute for Research in Cancer. Professor Mirvish's research addresses the role of nitrosamines as a carcinogen, including the carcinogenic effects of nitrosamines in cigarettes. He received his Ph.D. from the University of Cambridge.

KENNETH P. MORITSUGU is a physician, a public health administrator, and a retired Rear Admiral who served with the Unites States Public Health Service until 2007. Dr. Moritsugu previously served as the acting Surgeon General. He earned his medical degree from the George Washington University School of Medicine and a master's degree in public health from the University of California, Berkeley.

ETHAN NADELMANN is the founder and executive director of the Drug Policy Alliance, the leading organization in the United States promoting alternatives to the war on drugs. Nadelmann received his B.A., J.D., and Ph.D. from Harvard, and a master's degree in international relations from the London School of Economics. In 1994, Nadelmann founded the Lindesmith Center, a drug policy institute created with the philanthropic support of George Soros. In 2000, the growing Center merged with another organization to form the Drug Policy Alliance, which advocates for drug policies grounded in science, compassion, health, and human rights.

THE NATIONAL INSTITUTE ON DRUG ABUSE (NIDA) has as its mission to lead our nation in bringing the power of science to bear on drug abuse and addiction.

THE OFFICE OF NATIONAL DRUG CONTROL POLICY establishes policies, priorities, and objectives for the nation's drug control program. The goals of the program are to reduce illicit drug use, manufacturing, and trafficking; drug-related crime and violence; and drug-related health consequences.

MARSHA ROSENBAUM is director of the Safety First project and director of the San Francisco office of the Drug Policy Alliance. She received her doctorate in medical sociology from the University of California at San Francisco in 1979. From 1977 to 1995, Rosenbaum was the principal investigator on NIDA-funded studies of heroin addiction, methadone maintenance treatment, MDMA (Ecstasy), cocaine, and drug use during pregnancy. She is author of three books: *Women on Heroin, Pursuit of Ecstasy: The MDMA Experience* (with Jerome E. Beck), and *Pregnant Women on Drugs: Combating Stereotypes and Stigma* (with Sheigla Murphy).

SALLY SATEL is the staff psychiatrist at the Oasis Clinic in Washington, D.C. She serves on the advisory committee of the Center for Mental Health Services of the Substance Abuse and Mental Health Services Administration. She has written widely in academic journals on topics in psychiatry and medicine, and has published articles on cultural aspects of medicine and science in numerous magazines and journals. Dr. Satel is author of *Drug Treatment: The Case for Coercion* (AEI Press, 1999) and *PC, M.D.: How Political Correctness Is Corrupting Medicine* (Basic Books, 2001), and is coauthor, with Christina Hoff Sommers, of *One Nation under Therapy* (St. Martin's Press, 2005).

DAVID A. SAVITZ joined the Mount Sinai School of Medicine in 2005. He has served as editor of the *American Journal of Epidemiology* and was president of both the Society for Epidemiologic Research and the Society for Pediatric and Perinatal Epidemiologic Research. Savitz received his undergraduate training at Brandeis University, a master's degree in Preventive Medicine at Ohio State University, and his Ph.D. in Epidemiology from the University of Pittsburgh Graduate School of Public Health. His primary research activities and interests are in reproductive, environmental, and cancer epidemiology.

NANCY SHUTE is an award-winning senior writer at *US News & World Report*, where she covers science and medicine. She has written numerous articles appearing in national publications such as *Outside, Smithsonian,* the *New York Times, New Republic,* and *National Journal.* Ms. Shute has been a guest on NPR, CNN, CBS, and NBC and serves on the executive board of the National Association of Science Writers. Ms. Shute traveled to Kamchatka, Russia, as a Fulbright Scholar. She has degrees from Washington University and Yale University.

RODNEY SKAGER retired as a Professor of Education Psychology from UCLA. He also served as the Director of the California Attorney General's annual Survey of Student Substance Use in California Public Schools. Professor Skager published extensively on prevention policy, comparative studies of national drug policies, and treatment and recovery from alcohol and illicit drug abuse, and was a member of the Board of Directors for the national therapeutic community Phoenix House in California. Professor Skager earned his graduate degrees at the University of California at Los Angeles.

JASON M. TANZER is a professor of Oral Health at the University of Connecticut Health Center where he has been affiliated for the past 30 years.

Dr. Tanzer is renowned for his research into the role of microorganisms and their role in dental caries. In addition to receiving his dental degree from Tufts University, Dr. Tanzer earned a Ph.D. from Georgetown University. In 2003 Dr. Tanzer was awarded an honorary degree by Sahlgrenska Academy of the University at Gothenburg (Sweden).

MELIAH A. THOMAS graduated from the University of California at Berkeley School of Law where she was a scholarship recipient. Ms. Thomas served as a senior supervising editor for the *California Law Review* while at UC Berkeley. Her undergraduate degree was earned at Gonzaga University.

JOHN W. TOUMBOUROU is associate professor at the Department of Paediatrics, University of Melbourne, and a senior researcher at the Center for Adolescent Health. He is a founding member and outgoing chair of the College of Health Psychologists within the Australian Psychological Society. Professor Toumbourou is a principal investigator on a number of studies investigating healthy youth development including the Australian Temperament Project (investigating the role of childhood temperament and behavior in the prediction of adolescent substance use, delinquency, and depression), and the International Youth Development study (a collaborative longitudinal study with the University of Washington).

THE UNITED NATIONS INTERNATIONAL DRUG CONTROL PROGRAMME (UNDCP) is part of the United Nations Office on Drugs and Crime (UNODC), which was formerly called the United Nations Office for Drug Control & Crime Prevention (ODCCP). UNDCP cooperates with governmental and nongovernmental organizations as well as with the business community. Its experts help requesting states to become party to and give effect to the United Nations drug control conventions. UNDCP also performs laboratory services, provides training materials, and can refer those in need to the appropriate medical advice. In the area of demand reduction, a multiphase regional program designed to train professionals in the treatment of drug abuse has been successfully completed, created a core cadre of over 600 professionals and sustainable national training programs in training professionals in the treatment of drug abuse.

THE UNITED STATES DEPARTMENT OF STATE is the federal department in the United States that sets and maintains foreign policies.

ANJULI VERMA is the public education coordinator at the ACLU Drug Law Reform Project (DLRP), located in Santa Cruz, California. She creates and executes public education campaigns around the DLRP's litigation and is active in national ACLU campaigns to defend and disband regional narcotics task forces, expose drug laws' disproportionate impact on women and families, especially in communities of color, and educate the rave and other music communities about their rights.

GRAZYNA ZAJDOW is a senior lecturer at Deakin University. Dr. Zajdow's expertise is in sociology of alcohol and drug use, and women's experiences of alcoholic families.

LESLIE ZELLERS is an attorney who serves as the legal director of the Technical Assistance Legal Center. Her previous work includes conducting legal and policy work on tobacco prevention and childhood lead poisoning prevention for Contra Costa County. In addition, Ms. Zellers has been involved in drafting model ordinances/policies for communities seeking to regulate tobacco advertising, license tobacco retailers, and prohibit tobacco sponsorship at events such as rodeos and fairs. She is a Phi Beta Kappa graduate of the University of California at Berkeley, and a graduate of the UC Hastings College of the Law.